Exploring
Our Christian
Faith

Exploring Our Christian Faith

Revised Edition

Editor:
W. T. Purkiser

Writers:
Roy H. Cantrell ● J. Russell Gardner ●
W. M. Greathouse ● Wilbur H. Mullen ●
A. Elwood Sanner ● J. Ottis Sayes ●
Willard H. Taylor

BEACON HILL PRESS OF KANSAS CITY
KANSAS CITY, MISSOURI

Copyright, 1960, 1978
Beacon Hill Press of Kansas City

Library of Congress Catalog Card Number
Original (1960) Edition: 60-10576
Revised (1978) Edition: 78-59988

ISBN (revised edition): 0-8341-0552-7

Printed in the United States of America

Contents

Part V: Christian Living in Today's World

Preface to the Revised Edition

Exploring Our Christian Faith is a cooperative effort, prepared by a group of men who are or were classroom teachers. The desire of the writers is to put into the hands of colleagues and students materials which they have found useful in their own work. The book is therefore a textbook, and not an effort at original or creative writing.

The purpose of the volume is to provide an introduction to evangelical Wesleyan Christianity as understood in churches conventionally described as part of the holiness movement. For this reason it includes more than a survey of theology. Attention is given to the history of doctrine, to comparative religions, and to the ethics and practices of the Christian life.

First published 18 years ago, *Exploring Our Christian Faith* has proved its value by consistent use. This present revision has been undertaken for the purpose of updating the material to respond to new emphases and issues. The concluding chapters have been rearranged to complete the doctrinal study before turning to items related to living the Christian life in today's world. Suggestions were sought from classroom teachers using the textbook, and many have been incorporated in the revision. Particularly helpful were the suggestions of Drs. Rob Staples, Nazarene Theological Seminary, and John Allan Knight, Bethany Nazarene College. A new section on the Resurrection was contributed by Dr. C. S. Cowles, Northwest Nazarene College.

Special effort has been made in the opening chapters to combine biblical theology's assumption of a faith-commitment with the apologetic need to give reasons for the faith within (1 Pet. 3:15). It is not supposed that the faith is "proved"; it is hoped that it may be seen to be a reasonable faith. There is danger that the current reaction against reason may go too far.

Exploring Our Christian Faith has been a group project. The original panel of writers was convened for preliminary sessions in which the outline of the volume was hammered out. General specifications as to style, level of comprehension, and type of content were agreed upon. Assignments of chapters were made to each member of the panel. The initial writing of chapters 1—5, 9, 15, 17—18, and 23 was done by W. T. Purkiser, Ph.D., who also had overall responsibility for editing the whole. Chapters 6, 13, and 22 were written by A. E. Sanner, M.A., D.D.; chapters 7, 20, and 26 by W. H. Mullen, Ph.D.; chapters 8, 14, and 16 by W. M. Greathouse, M.A., D.D.; chapters 10 and 11 by R. H. Cantrell, D.R.E., D.D.; chapters 12, 27—28 by J. R. Gardner, Ph.D.; chapters 19, 24—25 by J. O. Sayes, D.R.E.; and chapter 21 by W. H. Taylor, Ph.D. Preliminary drafts were edited, duplicated, and circulated among the members of the panel for correction, comment, and suggestions. With the bulk of the manuscript thus prepared and shared, a second series of conferences was held in which many suggestions were discussed and incorporated into the manuscript.

An examination of the text will reveal that its authors have quoted from a wide range of sources representing almost every shade of theological opinion—fundamentalist, conservative, neoorthodox, and liberal. The citation of an author or volume is certainly not to be considered approval of the total theological viewpoint of the person or the work. The writers have used freely the terminology of present-day theological conversation without thereby adopting uncritically all of the insights suggested. It is felt that today's serious student should become acquainted with the language of contemporary discussion.

A special debt is acknowledged to Dr. H. Orton Wiley: teacher, colleague, and personal friend of the majority of the writing group. Dr. Wiley was a theologian par excellence, and is probably the author most frequently quoted herein.

While a cooperative volume has the strength of blending a large number of emphases and points of view, it has the weakness of variation in style and expression. No rigid conformity in these matters has been sought. Nor have all repetitions been eliminated. The same ideas are apt to come up and find expression in different contexts. It was felt that this problem is less serious in a textbook which would normally be used over the period of an academic year than it might be in a volume whose first use would be rapid, consecutive reading. Repetition may even serve a teaching purpose by reason of the greater emphasis it affords.

Keen eyes may note minor divergences of emphasis in the several chapters. These too have been tolerated for their possible educational value. It should go without saying that the volume in no way represents an "official" position on any of the points discussed. In the church in which all of the writers serve or have served, only the

General Assembly speaks for the church—and then, on doctrinal matters, only with the concurrence of two-thirds of the district assemblies.

The bibliography is not intended to be normative, but is included to summarize publication data for volumes cited in the text or in footnotes. As with reference to authors quoted or cited in the body of the text, the inclusion of a book in a footnote or the bibligraphy does not constitute an endorsement of the volume. All reading in the field of religion should be discriminating and thoughtful.

W. T. Purkiser, *Editor* Wilbur H. Mullen
Roy H. Cantrell A. Elwood Sanner
J. Russell Gardner, deceased J. Ottis Sayes
William M. Greathouse Willard H. Taylor

Original Work, 1959
Revised Edition, 1978

———◆—◆—◆———

Acknowledgments

Permission to quote from copyrighted materials has been received as follows:

Abingdon Press: Burtner and Chiles, *A Compend of Wesley's Theology;* William Cannon, *The Theology of John Wesley;* Frederick C. Grant, *Introduction to New Testament Thought;* Howard Grimes, *The Church Redemptive;* Paul E. Johnson, *Psychology of Religion;* Leslie Weatherhead, *The Will of God.*

George Allen and Unwin Ltd.: T. E. Jessop, ed., *The Christian Understanding of Man;* D. Elton Trueblood, *The Trustworthiness of Religious Experience.*

Association Press: Walter Rauschenbusch, *The Social Principles of Jesus.*

Baker Book House: article by Kenneth J. Foreman in *The Twentieth Century Encyclopedia of Religious Knowledge.*

Beacon Hill Press of Kansas City: Lewis T. Corlett, *Holiness in Practical Living* and *Holiness, the Harmonizing Experience;* Ralph Earle, article, "Holiness in the Greek Text," the *Preacher's Magazine;* William Greathouse, *The Fullness of the Spirit;* Howard Hamlin, *From Here to Maturity;* H. V. Miller, *When He Is Come;* T. Crichton Mitchell, *Mr. Wesley;* Orval J. Nease, *Heroes of Temptation;* Stephen S. White, *Essential Christian Beliefs;* H. Orton Wiley, *Christian Theology,* 3 vols.; H. Orton Wiley and Paul T. Culbertson, *Introduction to Christian Theology.*

Broadman Press: C. E. Matthews, *Every Christian's Job;* John T. Sisemore, *The Ministry of Visitation.*

Christianity Today: articles by G. W. Bromiley, Herman N. Ridderbos, William C. Robinson, Roger Nicole, and T. F. Torrance.

Century Company: Emory S. Bogardus, *Fundamentals of Social Psychology.*

Columbia University Press: John Baillie, *The Idea of Revelation in Recent Thought.*

Doubleday and Company, Inc.: Peter Berger, *A Rumor of Angels;* and Hans Kung, *On Being a Christian.*

E. P. Dutton Co.: R. A. Tsanoff, *The Moral Ideas of Our Civilization.*

William B. Eerdmans Publishing Company: G. C. Berkouwer, *Faith and Sanctification;* Carl F. H. Henry, *Christian Personal Ethics;* Paul King Jewett in *Inspiration and and Interpretation,* edited by John F. Walvoord; Leon Morris, *The Epistle of Paul to the Thessalonians;* Geerhardus Vos, *Biblical Theology;* H. M. Kuitert, *Do You Understand What You Read?* and George Elden Ladd, *I Believe in the Resurrection of Jesus.*

Epworth Press: C. Ryder Smith, *The Bible Doctrine of Man;* Vincent Taylor in *The Doctrine of the Holy Spirit;* Norman H. Snaith, *Distinctive Ideas of the Old Testament.*

Fortune: David Sarnoff, "The Fabulous Future."

Harper and Brothers: Gerald Kennedy, *God's Good News;* C. Edwin Lewis in *Harper's Bible Dictionary;* Charles Lowry, *The Trinity and Christian Devotion;* D. T. Niles, *The Preacher's Task and the Stone of Stumbling;* Radislov A. Tsanoff, *Ethics,* revised edition.

Light and Life Press: George Allen Turner, *The More Excellent Way.*

Littlefield, Adams and Co.: *Living Schools of Religion,* edited by Vergilius Ferm.

The Macmillan Co.: Gustaf Aulen, *Christus Victor;* Sir James Jeans, *This Mysterious Universe,* new and revised edition; Rufus M.

Jones, *The New Quest;* C. S. Lewis, *The Case for Christianity* and *The Great Divorce.*

Methuen and Co., Ltd.: J. K. S. Reid, *The Authority of Scripture.*

Muhlenberg Press: J. L. Neve, *A History of Christian Thought,* Vol. 1.

Thomas Nelson, Inc.: William G. Pollard, *Science and Faith: Twin Mysteries.*

Oxford University Press: article by H. Roux in *A Companion to the Bible.*

Pickering and Inglis, Ltd.: articles by Montague Goodman and G. C. D. Howley in *The Church: A Symposium,* edited by J. B. Watson.

Random House: Whittaker Chambers, *Witness.*

Fleming H. Revell: Hervin U. Roop, *Christian Ethics.*

Charles Scribner's Sons: Charles Gore, *The Holy Spirit and the Church;* Fritz Kunkel, *In Search of Maturity;* Paul Ramsey, *Basic Christian Ethics.*

SCM Press: Norman H. Snaith, *Hymns of the Temple.*

Twentieth Century Fund: Lewis L. Lorwin, *Postwar Plans of the United Nations.*

University of Chicago Press: George A. Barton, *The Religions of the World.*

The *Wesleyan Methodist:* article by Roy S. Nicholson.

Westminster Press: Emil Brunner, *The Scandal of Christianity;* Millar Burrows, *An Outline of Biblical Theology;* Floyd V. Filson, *One Lord, One Faith;* Frederick W. Schroeder, *Preaching the Word with Authority.*

Word Book, Publishers: Bernard Ramm, *The God Who Makes a Difference.*

Zondervan Publishing House: Paul S. Rees, *Stir Up the Gift;* and Victor Ray Edman, *They Found the Secret.*

PART I

Foundations of the Faith

CHAPTER 1

The Realm of Faith

The study of religion is one of the most challenging tasks any person can undertake. The field is vast, the varieties numerous, and the complexities great. One could well spend a lifetime and never come to the end.

Especially is this true of the Christian religion. The majesty of Christian truth lies in the fact that it is so simple a child can grasp it (Matt. 11:25), and yet so profound that the most mature mind must acknowledge its depth.

In its broadest definition, religion is the attempt to relate human life to what is conceived as being divine or worthy of man's highest devotion. As such, there are many religions among the races of men. Religion may be defined as man's search for God. It is a search which has proceeded along a multitude of paths and has ended in a great many blind alleys.

Christianity may be placed within this general definition of religion. However, Christianity is a religion which makes some unique claims. It is a religion which begins with a revelation and ends with redemption.

Religion is man's search for God.

Revelation is God's self-disclosure to man. *God reveals himself*

Redemption is the reconciliation of man to God through Jesus Christ, a reconciliation effected by the Holy Spirit.

Christianity, therefore, confronts us with its claim to be a revealed, redemptive religion. It holds, in essence, that neither man's quest for God nor God's approach to man is sufficient in itself. There must be a redemptive meeting of divine and human before man's need is met and God's purpose achieved. This is the faith we propose to consider in the pages which follow.

I. WHAT IS FAITH?

As is true of many terms used in religious discourse, "faith" has more than one meaning. The most frequent and most important use in the New Testament is to describe personal commitment in loyalty and trust to Jesus Christ, on the basis of which is experienced the redemptive power of God through the Holy Spirit. But "faith" is also used to describe the content or truth of the gospel, as when we read about "the faith" (Acts 24:24; Rom. 1:5; 1 Cor. 16:13; Gal. 1:23, *passim*). In this sense, we speak of "Foundations of Faith" and talk about "The Realm of Faith."

Closely connected with faith in both these senses is what we have called "revelation." Revelation is broadly defined as God's self-disclosure. It includes those acts and operations of God wherein He confronts man with His redeeming purpose.

In a later section we shall see that these acts and operations occur both in history and in the particular understanding of that history in an inspired record. Here it is important to note, as has been said, "every revelation of God is a demand," and "every revelation is a call and a commission."[1]

That is, revelation demands response. Faith is the name we give to this response when it is favorable; unbelief or doubt is what we call the human response when it is unfavorable. While we must not overlook the part the Holy Spirit plays in making possible a favorable response to revelation, we may simplify here and merely say that faith is man's affirmative response to God's revelation.

Such a response will be seen to be compounded of three elements. One is assent to what God says. Another is obedience to what God demands. The third is trust or reliance upon what God is. We shall consider the third element in a later chapter. At present it is important to note that assent to what God says is closely related to reason and intellect; and obedience to what God demands is allied to values and choices and directly involves the will.

---

1. William Temple, *Nature, Man, and God* (London: Macmillan, Ltd., first ed., 1934), p. 254; and Martin Buber, *Ich und Du*, p. 127, quoted by John Baillie, *The Idea of Revelation in Recent Thought* (New York: Columbia University Press, 1956), p. 84.

A. Faith and Reason

Faith as assent to truth-content or truth-claim is related to the use of reason. While we must keep in mind that faith in the religious sense includes more than mental assent, it is still of value to note the close connection of both faith and reason in the pursuit of truth. It is often supposed that reason and faith, knowledge and belief, are in some way contrary or opposed the one to the other. The endless controversies between science and religion, education and devotion, secular knowledge and religious belief, are all based on this mistaken idea.

1. *Historic Views*

Historically, there have been four positions held regarding the relation of faith and reason. First, there have been those who have claimed that faith and reason are equally valid, but entirely independent and unrelated. What faith indicates as true in the realm of religion, it is alleged, may be false to reason in the realm of nature. This led to the doctrine of the "twofold truth" in scholastic philosophy during the Middle Ages.

The net result is not a "twofold truth," but "two truths" bearing little or no relation each to the other. Religion and daily life are sundered, and an unsatisfactory theory of truth emerges. It is impossible to escape for long the native conviction of our minds that truth is all of one piece and cannot be split asunder.

Second, there is the view that reason is subordinate to faith. Its function is to accept what faith dictates, and to make it as palatable as possible to the minds of men. This is typified by Anselm (1033-1109) and is characteristic of mysticism.

Third, there is the position that faith is subordinate to reason. It is said that only those dictates of faith which reason finds satisfactory can be accepted. All else must be discarded. This is best known as rationalism, and is represented historically by Abelard (1079-1142) among others.

The fourth theory of the relation of faith and reason is that these two are not contradictory or opposed but are complementary, each necessarily supplementing the other in the quest for truth. Faith and reason, belief and understanding, are two halves of a complete whole. Together they make possible the acquisition of knowledge, not only in the realm of religion, but everywhere else as well. As Roger Hazelton writes, "There are four principles which, taken together, frame a perspective and determine a strategy for Christian thinking. They are: faith precedes understanding; faith needs understanding; faith pursues understanding; and faith achieves under-standing." For, "Faith is not the cancellation but the consecration of the intellect."

2. The Correlation of Faith and Reason

By reason here we understand the sum total of those conscious activities of our minds whereby evidence is assembled, weighed, compared, and inferences are drawn. By faith, we understand the capacity of the mind to accept as true that for which complete objective evidence is lacking.

Knowledge and belief, thus, are terms descriptive of the grounds upon which any truth-claim is held to be valid, and may be very difficult to distinguish in actual practice. Borden Parker Bowne, for example, defined knowledge as "what is self-evident in the nature of reason, and what is immediately given in experience, or cogently inferred therefrom." All else he describes as belief.[3]

The division is not easy to make. I may say, "I believe the sun will rise tomorrow," or, "I know the sun will rise tomorrow." I may say, "I believe John to be an honest man," or, "I know John is an honest man." If I use the more definite term *know,* I am claiming in effect that some objectively measurable evidence is available to guarantee the truth-claim. In either case, what distinguishes faith from knowledge is not the content of the judgment, but the ground of actual or possible evidence upon which it is held.

There is, obviously, faith in every inference, and inference in all faith. Inference means the drawing of conclusions based upon the accepted truth of other propositions (deductive) or the observation of a number of particular facts (inductive). For example, to observe that "all men are mortal" and that "Socrates is a man" leads to the inferred conclusion, "Socrates is mortal." Granting the truth of the premises, the conclusion must necessarily be conceded. Or, observing that all the crows I have seen are black in color, I may infer that all crows are black, even though I have seen but few of the kind in relation to the total number of crows which have existed, do exist, or will exist. Faith in the material truth of the premises with which one starts, in the uniformity of nature, or in the validity of inference

2. *Renewing the Mind* (New York: The Macmillan Co., 1949), pp. 73, 127. Those interested in thinking through the vital problem of the relation of faith and reason will find Mr. Hazelton's entire book helpful.

3. *Theory of Thought and Knowledge* (New York: American Book Co., 1897), Chapter V.

itself is necessary to the very life of reason. Not only the just, but the unjust also, live by faith.

Likewise, there is reason in all true faith. Too often faith has been defined as by the little boy, "Taking something for true when you know it ain't so." Faith and irrationalism are far from synonymous terms. The difference between faith and presumption lies in the fact that real faith is rationally defensible. Belief is not irrational prejudice. It is the mind reaching out into the yet unexplored.

There is nothing now known which was not initially a matter of faith. Faith has been compared with the air-borne column which leaps deep into enemy territory in time of war and holds the position until the hard-driving tanks and infantry of reason and verified experience can come up and consolidate the gains. Faith is the pioneer explorer; understanding is the homesteader and settler. Belief is the necessary early stage of knowledge. Knowledge is belief for which objective evidence has accumulated to sufficient degree to bring about general acceptance.

3. Faith and Certainty

Not all the ideas we have may properly be called beliefs. All of us, for example, have a variety of fancies, which we momentarily entertain, and which we recognize may or may not be true. In general, fancies concern matters which are not of any great practical importance. One may have fancies concerning the nature of angels, for example. They may be true or they may not be. In any case, the world stands and life goes on.

Then one finds that he has some ideas which may properly be called opinions. One is a little more sure of his opinions than he is of his fancies. Such, for example, might be the opinion one holds concerning the identity of Lucifer in Isaiah 14 or the character of the tongues spoken on the Day of Pentecost. One thinks his opinions are correct, and he is ready to argue for them; but no particular struggle is felt to surrender opinions which prove to be untrue.

Again, there are ideas which are beliefs. These are the ideas by which one lives, that make a difference in his adjustment to life. It is a jarring experience to lose a belief. To draw an example from the realm of human relations, one may be forced to change his opinion concerning the honesty of an acquaintance. But it is devastating to be driven to abandon belief in the integrity and honesty of a close friend. Beliefs have their roots in life. In turn, they guide and direct the course of life. "Faith without works is dead" (Jas. 2:20).

Finally, there are certitudes. These are beliefs which have not only become so clearly validated in life but so firmly embedded in the structure of reason and experience that their contradictories seem inconceivable. There are not many certitudes. A case in point is the certitude many have of the existence of God. Such a person finds himself incapable of rationally entertaining the idea that God does not exist. The conviction that God is has become a certitude for such believers. Nothing would make sense without it.

A confirming personal experience tends to establish a belief and deepen it into a certitude. One who has been "born again" does not hold his beliefs about Christ as hypotheses that are probably true but as certainties he knows to be true. "Logical probability here becomes personal certainty."[4]

Many confuse fancies and opinions with beliefs and certitudes. Some have gone through soul-shattering experiences because they could not distinguish between an opinion and a certitude. Of course, opinions may become beliefs, and beliefs may mature into certitudes. What is needed in every age is a people willing to change fancies and opinions as the need arises, while willing to live by beliefs and die for certitudes.

B. What Is Truth?

What has been said about faith in general terms holds when faith is considered as assent to the truth of what God makes known about himself. The nature and sources of this kind of truth we shall later investigate. Here it will be enough to note that the response of the human soul to divine revelation includes a rational assent, a "belief of the truth" (2 Thess. 2:13).

"Belief of the truth" suggests two important points. One is that belief is of value only when its content is "truth." We read in the same context (2 Thess. 2:11-12) of those who believe lies because they take pleasure in unrighteousness. For this reason, sincerity in belief is not a guarantee of either truth or safety. We hear often, "It doesn't matter what you believe, so long as you are sincere in that belief." Sincerity is necessary but not sufficient. Faith, to be sure, must be sincere; yet the most dangerous people in the world today are those who give every evidence of being utterly sincere, but utterly sincere in the belief of a colossal lie.

---

4. Thomas V. Morris, *Francis Schaeffer's Apologetics: A Critique* (Chicago: Moody Press, 1976), p. 104.

Again, truth is of value only when it is believed. Truth may be presented and rejected. We shall give further attention to this point in the next section. At the present moment our concern is to note that belief or faith has objective content. That is, believing is always believing something (or someone). Faith does not operate in a vacuum. Its goal or purpose is one with all man's intellectual quest, the grasp of significant truth.

1. *The Failure of Skepticism*

We cannot, then, avoid some consideration of Pilate's famous question, "What is truth?" (John 18:38). Asked with skeptical overtones, it is yet an important question. Many today join Pilate in the implication that there is no ultimate truth to be had by the human mind. When applied to truth in general, this attitude is known as skepticism. When applied to religious truth, it is called agnosticism.

Essentially, total skepticism is a self-refuting theory. If I assert, "There is no truth," I must be willing, if I am consistent, to recognize that my assertion itself is not true. It cannot truly be stated, "There is no truth," without excepting at least the assertion that there is no truth. Once this exception is made, there is no reason why others should not also be made. In *The Quest for Certainty*, for instance, John Dewey insists that there is no certainty, there are no absolutes, but all man's knowledge is instrumental and relative. One wonders how an author can be so certain of his uncertainty, so absolute in his assertion of relativity. Should not the complete doubter doubt his doubts also?

A popular religious writer has put the matter in strong terms:

> There has grown up among us a class of people whose religion consists for the most part in being open-minded about everything and convinced about nothing. . . . A generation that has tried to live within the framework of relativism is frightened to death of the idea that there may be absolute truths which can neither be dodged nor manipulated.[5]

2. *The Pragmatic Answer*

Modern pragmatism has popularized the view that truth consists in the desirable consequences of the idea in question. It is concluded that whatever works is true, and that truth has no other meaning than the desirable outcomes of the idea or doctrine under discussion. Thus belief in God may be accepted as true to the degree

---

5. Gerald Kennedy, *God's Good News* (New York: Harper and Brothers, 1955), p. 161.

that such belief causes people to behave better than unbelievers, or gives a desirable feeling of security.

There is a half-truth here, but only a half-truth. It is correct that true ideas have, in the long run, desirable consequences. Truth does work. It has cash value. It pays off in good results. But it is one thing to say that a doctrine or theory works because it is true, and something quite different to say that it is true because it works. Belief in God, when sincere, does lead to better behavior; it does have good consequences. But it is not true *because* it has such results. On the contrary, it has good results simply because it is first true. One may correctly say, "If this animal is a dog, it will have a tail." He cannot turn the proposition around and say, "If this animal has a tail, it is a dog." It could be a horse or a turtle. The quarrel of the idealist and the realist with pragmatism is not at the point of its major premise, "Whatever is true works." This is substantially correct. The quarrel with pragmatism is the quite illogical inference drawn from that premise, that "whatever works is true."

It does not help the cause of the pragmatist to add, as he usually does, "Whatever works in the long run is true." The explanation of Charles Peirce in the article which is usually cited as the source of modern pragmatism, "How to Make Our Ideas Clear," is of little help: "The opinion which is fated to be ultimately agreed to by all who investigate, is what we mean by truth, and the object represented in this opinion is the real."[6] Practically, it is difficult if not impossible to tell how long the "run" is, or what will ultimately be agreed to, if anything, by all who investigate. For a German citizen in 1939, Nazism was working beautifully in the Third Reich, and had been paying off for six years. True, it did not continue to work. The "long run" disqualified it. But who, in 1939, could tell how long the run would be? Behind the iron curtain today, materialistic communism seems to be working. At least it is working well enough to keep the rest of the world in continual uncertainty. The American pragmatist says, "Ah, but in the long run—" How long the run will be, and what will be left when the run is over, are questions for which pragmatism has no answer.

The point is, we must have a better definition of truth, and a bet-

---

6. In *Love, Chance and Logic*, pp. 56-57. This particular essay has been reprinted in the volume of Peirce's writings edited by Vincent Tomas entitled *Essays in the Philosophy of Science* ("The American Heritage Series": New York: The Liberal Arts Press, 1957).

ter criterion for discovering it, than is given by the simple dictum, "Whatever works is true," even if we add, "in the long run." For a liar, falsehood might work better than truth; and conceivably a clever liar might be able to cover his steps so as never to be discovered. But that does not make lying right or the lie a true statement. For a thief, the philosophy "Whatever I can steal undetected is mine" may work much more satisfactorily than the rigors of honesty. But that faulty philosophy is not true, and we need not wait for the developments of "the long run" to judge it false.

3. *The Nature of Truth*

Truth is, rather, the relationship of agreement or reference which holds between ideas in the mind *and* the existing state of affairs. Truth is that quality of a judgment or idea which adequately depicts, interprets, reveals, or represents an objective fact or state of affairs. "True" describes those concepts, ideas, and judgments which do thus correctly interpret reality. As Joseph A. Leighton has said, "Truth equals thought corresponding with existence,"[7] and, more fully, "Truth is the most adequate and consistent agreement of the meanings, distilled by reflexion from experimental fact, with fact and with one another."[8]

Truth, therefore, is polar in its nature. It stands for the subjective idea or belief in relation to the objective fact or state of affairs. Truth is not subjective alone (pragmatism), nor is it an eternal realm of subsistent ideas (idealism). Truth is a relationship between the idea and that to which it refers. Truth which relates to the unchanging is, by the same token, eternal and unchanging. Thus John Wesley could say with complete propriety, "In religion, whatever is true is not new; and whatever is new is not true." The statement, "The value of United Airlines stock on the New York Stock Exchange today is 48.7," may be true now and false tomorrow, because its objective pole is variable and changing. The statement, "If any man have not the Spirit of Christ, he is none of his," (Rom. 8:9) is eternally and unalterably true because it relates to the unchanging nature of One who is "the same yesterday, and to day, and for ever" (Heb. 13:8).

How specific truths are apprehended and verified is the task of epistemology or theory of knowledge to explain.

---

7. *Man and the Cosmos* (New York: D. Appleton and Co., 1922), p. 30.
8. *Ibid.,* p. 67.

4. *Religious Truth*

The importance of the nature of truth to the study of religion should be obvious. Religion purports to offer *true* ideas, beliefs, and certitudes; that is, those which correctly interpret, reveal, or represent that aspect of the universe which might in general terms be called "spiritual."

Bernard Ramm writes:

> Frequently religion is expressed as a matter of faith. This usually means that religion is a personal matter. It expresses one's feelings about the universe as a whole or the significance of human life or the worthiness of certain ethical convictions. In this context, religion presumes to be outside the territory of truth claims, for the very way faith is understood means that it is not concerned with testable materials.
>
> Such a view of religion is superficial. All human disciplines must come to terms with truth, and the magnitude of the claims of at least the great historical religions demands that religion too comes to terms with the problem of truth. A religion that does not conform to reality, however reality is defined at the moment, is a fiction.[9]

It is quickly seen that the objective facts or states of affairs to which religious truth refers are of a different order from those to which our scientific knowledge and everyday wisdom relate. We should not be surprised, therefore, to discover that the avenues by which religious truth is reached may also differ. The physical senses which serve us well in discriminating colors, sizes, shapes, and the tangible features of our environment do not give us much in the way of information about God, redemption, duty, and the life to come. The complaint that microscopes and telescopes fail to discover Deity is foolish indeed. One might as well try to listen to colors or see musical tones.

This should not seem strange to us. All areas of knowledge, all kinds of being, have their own peculiar conditions for the grasp of truth. An ax may split a log of wood but it cannot split an atom. There are realities open to what Paul Minear called "The Eyes of Faith"[10] which are closed to the physical sight.

It is here that rational faith, as the assent of the mind to the truth-content of God's revelation, becomes the major avenue to

---

9. *The God Who Makes a Difference: A Christian Appeal to Reason* (Waco, Tex.: Word Books, Publisher, 1972), p. 15.

10. *The Eyes of Faith* (Philadelphia: Westminster Press, 1946).

knowledge. We are concerned in this study with the structure of historic Christianity. Almost a summary of the Christian faith is the statement to the effect that "God was in Christ, reconciling the world unto himself" (2 Cor. 5:19). God made himself known through His mighty acts, particularly in the life and teachings, death and resurrection of Him whom Christians affirm to be the Incarnate Word; and secondly in the Book which is chiefly about that Word. The Christian faith, whatever more it may be, is at least the claim that God has made accessible to finite minds such truth about himself as is necessary for redemption. "We never know God wholly, yet we believe that we know Him truly."[11] That truth is embodied in the living Word, the Lord Jesus Christ, and mediated by and through the written Word, the Holy Bible. To this, we shall give more attention in a later chapter.

II. FAITH AND OBEDIENCE

When we first defined faith, we considered it as man's response to God's revelation. We noted that it means both assent to what God has said about His redemptive purposes for man and obedience to the demands stated. The first is faith as reasonable, and is concerned with truth—belief *that.* The second is faith as commitment, as concerned with obedience—belief *in.*

It will be noted that the Bible uses the term in both ways. It says, for example, "Without faith it is impossible to please him; for he that cometh to God must *believe that* he is, and *that* he is a rewarder of them that diligently seek him" (Heb. 11:6). Far more often, however, we read such statements as: "For God so loved the world, that he gave his only begotten Son, that whosoever *believeth in* him should not perish, but have everlasting life" (John 3:16); "He that *believeth on* the Son hath everlasting life: and he that *believeth not the Son* shall not see life; but the wrath of God abideth on him" (John 3:36); and, "*Believe on* the Lord Jesus Christ, and thou shalt be saved, and thy house" (Acts 16:31). Here faith has the sense of obedient trust, confidence in and reliance on a person.

The truth of God is not abstract theory. It is a gospel which has truth-content, to be sure, but which above all is a claim upon us. It is a call for trust, commitment, and obedience. In his commentary on

---

11. Hazelton, *Renewing the Mind,* p. 134.

Romans, C. H. Dodd states that, for the apostle Paul, "faith is that attitude in which, acknowledging our complete insufficiency for any of the high ends of life, we rely utterly on the sufficiency of God. . . . Nor does it mean belief in a proposition, though doubtless intellectual beliefs are involved when we come to think it out."[12]

Faith as assent and faith as obedience may be distinguished, but cannot be separated. In an earlier paragraph we noted that beliefs are what men live by, opinions are what they argue about. That to which one gives his allegiance is that which he really believes. Jesus said, "If any man will do his will, he shall know of the doctrine, whether it be of God, or whether I speak of myself" (John 7:17). Paul can identify obeying the gospel with believing the gospel (Rom. 10:16). St. Augustine is reported to have said, "The Word of God belongs to those who obey it"; and Martin Luther, "No one understands the Scriptures unless he be acquainted with the Cross."

SUMMARY

In this chapter we have considered religion as man's attempt to relate his life to what is conceived to be worthy of his highest devotion. In this sense Christianity is unique because it starts, not with man's quest for God, but with God's self-disclosure or revelation to man. We also considered the various ways in which the study of religion might be undertaken.

We then looked at faith as response to divine revelation. As such it means rational assent to what God makes known of himself, and this led to the consideration of reason in relation to faith, and of the nature of truth in general and religious truth in particular. Finally, we turned to faith as commitment, or obedience to the requirements of God's revelation.

In all this we have assumed both the existence of God and the fact of His self-disclosure. In our next two chapters we must examine these all-important stones in the foundation of our Christian faith.

---

12. *The Epistle of Paul to the Romans;* "Moffatt New Testament Commentary" (New York: Charles Scribner's Sons, 1932), pp. 15-16.

CHAPTER 2

Belief in God

We noted in the first chapter that religion in general may be thought of as man's search for a right relation to what is conceived as being divine and worthy of highest devotion. Christianity in particular is a religion based upon the claim that God has made himself known to man through a unique revelation in Christ, in whom He purposes to reconcile man to himself.

The core of all religious belief is confidence in the existence of a divine person (or persons), power, or agency to which it is important that the individual, family, tribe, or nation be rightly related. It is not too far wrong to say that the value of any religion depends upon the nature and particularly the moral qualities it attributes to its concept of the divine. As H. Orton Wiley says, "The existence of God is a fundamental concept in religion and therefore a determinative factor in theological thought. The nature ascribed to God gives color to the entire system. To fail here is to fail in the whole compass of truth."[1]

I. Leading Concepts of God

Among the races of men, there are many ideas of the divine. In some cultures, especially the more primitive, what is known as animism is the prevailing view. This is the belief in a multitude of divine powers, spirits, demons, and so forth, which are supposed to inhabit rocks, trees, houses, streams, rivers, mountains, and even on occasion hu-

---

1. *Christian Theology* (Kansas City: Beacon Hill Press of Kansas City, 1940), 1:217.

man beings. Witch doctors, voodoo, charms, sacrifices, and incantations are part of animism. Many of the tribal religions of Africa, as well as Taoism, the ancient religion of China, are animistic.

A. Polytheism Versus Monotheism

Polytheism is another concept of the realm of the divine. This is the belief in many gods, usually personifications of natural forces. Most familiar to us is the Graeco-Roman pantheon, with its many divinities often engaged in war among themselves, and in whose hands hapless humans were apt to find themselves as pawns. Abram came out of a polytheistic background in Ur of Chaldea, and his descendants faced it and often succumbed to it in their settlement in Palestine. Paul found polytheism in Athens so developed that an altar had been erected to "the unknown god," to prevent overlooking by accident any divinity which might wreak vengeance on the city.

Neither animism nor polytheism has ethical content. That is, the spirits or gods are not concerned with moral righteousness on the part of their devotees. Worship and religion consist in the making of such sacrifices and the participation in such incantations as are necessary to placate the divinities and persuade them to leave men to run their own affairs. The Greek philosopher Plato, more than half-serious, has one of his characters in *The Republic* argue that the unjust man has a better chance with the gods than the just man. This is because the unscrupulous may be expected to prosper more than the poor but honest person, and thus have more with which to buy sacrifices and build shrines and pay priests. The divinities of Greece and Rome were in many instances actually immoral. They differed from men only in the possession of immortality and greater power. Otherwise they lied, murdered, committed adultery and incest, and carried on a perpetual revelry. It is little wonder that moral conditions should prevail such as are described in the first chapter of Romans, when religion and the grossest forms of immorality were thought to be perfectly compatible.

Christianity is monotheistic. This is the belief in one supreme God and the denial of all other divinities. Judaism and Mohammedanism, among other world religions, are also monotheistic. Samuel M. Zwemer writes in connection with the Moslem faith: "The whole system of Mohammedan theology and philosophy and religious life is summed up in seven words: *La ilaha illa Allah, Mohammed rasul Allah.* 'There is no god but Allah and Mohammed is Allah's apostle'—on these two phrases hang all the laws and teaching and morals of Islam."[2]

In Deuteronomy, expressive of the faith of Judaism, we read: "Hear, O Israel: The Lord our God is one Lord: and thou shalt love the Lord thy God with all thine heart, and with all thy soul, and with all thy might" (6:4-5). Christianity, building on the foundation of monotheism laid in Judaism, is even more explicit. Paul says in 1 Tim. 2:5-6, "For there is one God, and one mediator between God and man, the man Christ Jesus; who gave himself a ransom for all to be testified in due time."

It has been suggested by some that monotheism is an evolutionary development, in which animism and polytheism were earlier stages. This was the position taken by August Comte in his so-called "Law of the Three Stages." The religious stage, he argued, has developed from an original primitive animism, through polytheism, to monotheism. This interpretation of the fact that there are levels of belief about the divine is purely supposition, with little of logical weight or anthropological evidence in its favor. In fact, some anthopologists[3] state that they find evidences in primitive cultures of an original and underlying monotheism. Animism and polytheism appear more to be degenerate forms of religious practice than an early stage in an evolutionary ascent.

Further, since the dawn of recorded history all three types of belief have been found existing at the same time, even as they are today. In the time of Abraham there were not only animism and polytheism, but a relatively clear-cut monotheism. Today, four thousand years later, there is not only a predominant monotheism, but also animism and polytheism persisting as they have for centuries.

Logically, the trend is in the opposite direction from that which Comte supposed to be the case. Once an incisive monotheism is forsaken, and the existence of a number of divinities subscribed to, the tendency is to multiply rather than diminish the number.[4] Early Christianity would never have come into conflict with Roman authority had Christians been willing to subscribe to the divinity of the

---

2. *The Moslem Doctrine of God* (New York: Young People's Missionary Movement, 1905), p. 15.

3. E.g., Zwemer and the "Vienna School." Cf. C. H. Dodd, *Epistle to the Romans,* pp. 25-26.

4. Cf. Paul Heinisch, *Theology of the Old Testament* (Collegeville, Minn.: The Liturgical Press, 1950), pp. 46-48.

Roman emperor. Roman polytheism could readily have accepted the divinity of Christ, for where there are many gods there is always room for one more. The early Christians, however, were uncompromising monotheists and would have nothing to do with "gods many, and lords many" (1 Cor. 8:5-6).

B. Forms of Monotheism

Monotheism, the belief in one supreme God, is itself found in three forms today, stemming from three possible relationships between God and the universe in which we live.

1. *Deism*

One of these is deism, the view that God created the universe, endowed it with natural powers and laws, and left it to run its own course with little or no control on His part. Deism typically denies the fact of a divine revelation and the necessity of any salvation for man apart from a rational morality. The "natural religion" movement of the eighteenth century, Thomas Paine, and the *Age of Reason* are examples of deistic thought. It is the practical creed of multitudes today who have no vital connection with the Christian Church, but who pay lip service to the existence of a Supreme Being.

In technical terms, deism emphasizes the *transcendence*—the separateness or apartness—of God. As Arthur Kenyon Rogers has observed, deism always manifests a state of "unequal equilibrium." It always tends to slip over into atheism (the denial of any divine existence whatsoever) on the one hand, or a more typical theism on the other.[5]

2. *Pantheism*

Another view of the relationship between God and the universe is pantheism, the theory that God and the universe are one and the same, that God is All and All is God. This stands at the opposite pole from deism. In earlier times it was exemplified by the Stoics, and by Plotinus and Neo-Platonism, the latter described as paganism's last stand against early Christianity. Pantheism today is best exemplified by such religious cults as Unity, New Thought, Christian Science, and the various theosophical societies.

Technically, pantheism stresses the *immanence* of God, His in-

---

5. *A Student's History of Philosophy,* 3rd ed. (New York: The Macmillan Co., 1932), p. 355.

wardness and omnipresence in the universe. It is an open question whether God can be identified with the universe without thereby being denied. To make everything God is in effect to make God nothing. Pantheism may well be but a pious form of atheism.

3. *Theism*

The third form of monotheism is known simply as theism. It is belief in a personal God who is the Creator, Sustainer, and Governor of the universe and all that therein is. It brings into balance both the transcendence and the immanence of God. It recognizes the essential truth in deism, that God is not to be identified with His universe. It embodies the essential truth in pantheism, that God cannot be separated or sundered from His universe.

Theism recognizes the dependence of the material order on the spiritual, but holds also to the fact that God is essentially more than that which He has brought into being. The universe is not God, nor is it independent of Him. God is related to the universe as a man is related to his walking, his speaking, his working (the idealistic form of theism); or God is related to the universe as an artist is related to the masterpiece he paints or an author to the book he writes (the realistic form of theism). God is IN the universe as a man is in all that he does, an artist or an author in every picture or book he creates. This is the divine immanence. But God is separate from and independent of His universe as a man is more than and separate from everything he does, an artist or author from every work he produces. This is the divine transcendence.

Christianity is completely committed to theism. Paul quotes with approval, "In him we live, and move, and have our being" (Acts 17:28): and says, "In him all things were created, in heaven and on earth, visible and invisible, whether thrones or dominions or principalities or authorities—all things were created through him and for him. He is before all things, and in him all things hold together" (Col. 1:16-17, RSV). The possibility of divine revelation, salvation, prayer, providence, and miracle—all depend upon the truth of theism. If the theistic faith in one God, Creator, Sustainer, and Governor of the universe be not true, redemption is impossible and Christianity is void.

It is important, then, that we give some consideration to the reasons for holding to theism as a rational faith. We must first look at the nature of proof as it is related to belief in God.

II. WHAT IS PROOF?

Since the days of Immanuel Kant (1724-1804) theologians have been reluctant to use the term proof in relation to reasons for faith in the existence of God. Kant took each of the prominent theistic arguments of his day, and contended that each of them, in some respect or other, falls short of complete logical certainty.[6] This, it must be admitted, was achieved by the same device the father used in breaking a bundle of sticks after his strong sons had failed—namely, by taking them apart and snapping them one by one. The student should consider the possibility that the theistic arguments may have a collective strength not possessed by any one of them individually.

More recently, Karl Barth has questioned the validity of attempts to establish rationally the existence of God.[7] While a total treatment of this question belongs to systematic theology, it would be sufficient here to note that the rational defense of the faith has been a concern of Christian thinkers since early Christians began to preach the gospel to a world conditioned by pagan philosophy.[8]

What is called "apologetics" includes an examination of reasons for accepting the claims made for the basic truths of revealed religion. It may readily be conceded that nobody can prove the truth of Christianity. No one can make the decision of faith for another. Yet the purpose of apologetics is to show that there are reasonable grounds—in fact, grounds of the highest probability—for believing.

What apologetics can do is remove hindrance to faith and serve as a *preparatio evangelica*, a "preparation for the gospel." This it may do by showing the inherent inconsistencies that lurk in unbelief. This it may also do by showing the inherent rationality of belief in the Supreme Being whom Christians claim has revealed himself in Scripture.[9]

---

6. *Critique of Pure Reason*, "Transcendental Doctrine of Elements," Part II, 2nd div., Bk. II, c. 3.

7. Cf. the brief treatment in Carl F. H. Henry, *God, Revelation and Authority*, Vol. 1, "God Who Speaks and Shows" (Waco, Tex.: Word Books, Publisher, 1976), 1:241-44.

8. Cf. Ramm, *God Who Makes a Difference*, p. 22.

9. Cf. F. R. Barry, *To Recover Confidence* (Naperville, Ill.: SCM Book Club, 1974), pp. 60-61; Harold J. Ockenga, *Faith in a Troubled World* (Wenham, Mass.: Gordon College Press, 1972), p. 26; and the brief history of apologetics in J. K. S. Reid, *Christian Apologetics* (Grand Rapids; Wm. B. Eerdmans Publishing Company, 1970). See particularly Reid's comment on Barth, p. 13. Barth's objection to "explicit apologetic" is directed toward the kind of theology which "for the sake of getting to grips with unbelief, loosens or even loses its hold upon essential Christianity."

A. The Two Meanings of Proof

If proof be considered as the presentation of such evidence as will compel the assent of all who follow it, in the same sense in which a theorem in geometry can be "proved," then proof of the existence of God cannot be achieved. However, teachers of mathematics will confess that even the demonstration of a theorem in geometry offers difficulties to some minds.

If, however, proof be understood as offering reasons for belief such as can be satisfactory to intelligent persons, then proof of the existence of God is both possible and necessary. Borden Parker Bowne indicated the limits of proof in both strict and accepted usage in the following passage:

> Proof, too, is limited by the nature of the knowing mind. It is only a stimulus to see, and a stupid mind cannot see. There is no such thing as an objective proof which proves in the absence of intelligence, something as a Buddhist prayermill prays in the absence of the suppliant. It is very common with the dull to mistake their own dullness for a lack of proof. But since proof is really only a stimulus to think in a certain way it is necessarily conditioned by the nature of the mind addressed. . . . What has been said thus far applies to proof in the strict sense of rational demonstration. But the word is often used with less stringency, and then proof consists in giving reasons which, while not compelling assent, produce conviction.[10]

B. Reasons for Unbelief

It should be noted that some who do not believe in God are unbelievers, not by reason of intellectual difficulties, but by reason of reluctance to accept the moral and ethical demands of such faith. Theirs is the mood of Friedrich Nietzsche (1844-1900), who said, *"Gott ist tot, alles ist erlaubt"*—"God is dead, everything is permitted." It is all but impossible to prove anything to one who, for personal reasons, does not wish to believe. Such will thrust aside as inconsequential the most convincing evidence. The tendency to "wishful thinking"— being easily convinced about what one wants to believe—is an ever-present frailty of the human mind.

Then, too, the student should recall what was said in the last chapter about the relation of faith and obedience. Faith as it relates to God is man's response to a self-disclosure which demands obedience. This introduces the element of commitment, and of choice.

---

10. *Theory of Thought and Knowledge,* pp. 184-85.

Belief in God is a rational faith, as we shall attempt to show in the balance of this chapter. But it is not in the first place achieved by a long process of logical induction, comparing and weighing evidence, formulating and testing hypotheses. It is born in the act wherein God confronts the individual human self with the claims of His gospel.

C. The Biblical Position

It has often been noted that the Judaic-Christian Scriptures contain no "proofs" of the existence of God. God is the "Given," the Starting Point with which all begins. In the Bible, the reality of God is taken for granted. His existence is assumed. What book would attempt to demonstrate the existence of its author? Gen. 1:1 introduces us to the central Figure of the Old Testament without effort to "prove" His being. In fact, such an idea would never have occurred to a Hebrew. The Hebrew term *yada,* "to know," in relation to God does not mean knowledge through reasoning, as for the Greeks. It means knowledge through experience of God, encountering His love or His anger in the concrete experiences of life. The fool who denies the existence of God (Ps. 14:1) is not a theoretical atheist but a practical atheist, for he makes his denial in his heart, not his head. Those who in Old Testament times "know not God" (Jer. 2:8) are judged, not for lack of intellectual knowledge, but in the moral sense of caring nothing for Him.

The same attitude prevails in the New Testament. God had acted in history in such decisive ways, and finally had so manifested himself in His only begotten Son, that to attempt any proofs of His reality would have been meaningless. Those who have heard, and seen, and looked upon, and handled (cf. 1 John 1:1) scarcely have need of logical proofs. The God of the New Testament was sublimely known as "God, even the Father of our Lord Jesus Christ" (2 Cor. 1:3 and elsewhere), and in this phrase the Old Testament concept is immeasurably enriched. As one scholar has well stated it, "The Old Testament tells us that God loves us; the New Testament shows us how much He loves us."

Floyd V. Filson writes, "In the minds of the New Testament writers, theism is interlocked with Christology. Statements concerning God contain a reference, expressed or implied, to the person and work of Jesus Christ."[11] Since, then, "God was in Christ, reconciling

---

11. *The New Testament Against Its Environment* (Chicago: Henry Regnery Co., 1950), p. 9.

the world unto himself" (2 Cor. 5:19), those who experienced such reconciliation for themselves had a certainty nothing else could equal.

Such considerations as these shift the emphasis once given to the so-called theistic "proofs." It is not now a matter of convincing the skeptic or compelling the assent of one who refuses obedience to God. Nor is it a question of inducing faith in one who chooses not to believe. It is rather to indicate that the faith to which man is called by the God of the Bible is not an arbitrary or unreasonable faith, but one which is in harmony with the deepest thought and instinct of those whom He has created in His own image.[12]

III. EVIDENCES FOR THEISM

The theistic arguments, as they are known, may better be considered, therefore, as converging lines of evidence rather than as the premises of a logical syllogism. As such, they carry weight and can offer conviction to the mind. These are some of the reasons intelligent persons may give for their belief in one God, the Creator, Sustainer, and Governor of the universe.

What we shall here consider is by no means a complete and exhaustive summary of the evidence.[13] Other lines of evidence may be added, and all may be enlarged. Enough is given to suggest the logical foundations upon which a reasonable theism rests.

A. The Cosmological Evidence

What is known as the cosmological argument is so called because it reasons from the existence of the universe (the cosmos) to the necessary existence of God as its First Cause.

Common sense testifies that nothing happens without a cause. Every event or happening must be accounted for in terms of an adequate cause. The whole structure of science rests upon the category of causality. Any other kind of universe would be unthinkable to us. Stephen S. White illustrates this as follows:

---

12. See Ramm, *God Who Makes a Difference*, pp. 30-32; and Reid, *Christian Apologetics*, p. 12.

13. Cf. L. Harold DeWolf, *A Theology of the Living Church* (New York: Harper Brothers, 1953), chapters 5 and 6. DeWolf adds "Evidence from the Objectivity of Abstract Truth," similar to the evidence from science below, as well as arguments based on rational and aesthetic experience.

If you should ask how a sapling in the front yard had been broken off, you would probably be satisfied if you were told that a ten-year-old boy had done it. You would reason that the cause which had been mentioned, a ten-year-old boy, was sufficient for the effect—broken-off sapling. On the other hand, if you should inquire as to how a large tree had suddenly been laid low, you would not accept the explanation that a ten-year-old boy had pushed it over. The cause in this case would not be adequate for the effect. But it would be very different if you learned that a tornado had swept that way the night before and had blown the large tree over. This explanation would not be doubted by you, because you would recognize at once that the cause was powerful enough to produce the effect.[14]

Since each event which occurs within the universe must be thought of as having a cause, the cosmos itself demands a cause adequate to account for its existence. The only alternative is to think of the universe as eternal and self-existent, an alternative which would seem closed to us if we take seriously the so-called "law of entropy" in thermodynamics. The significance of this is explained by Sir James Jeans, the noted Cambridge physicist, astronomer, and mathematician:

As we trace the stream of time backwards, we encounter many indications that, after a long enough journey, we must come to its source, a time before which the present universe did not exist. Nature frowns upon perpetual motion machines and it is *a priori* very unlikely that her universe will provide an example, on the grand scale, of the mechanism she abhors. And a detailed consideration of nature confirms this. The science of thermodynamics explains how everything in nature passes to its final state by a process which is designated the "increase of entropy." . . . The entropy of the universe must forever increase to its final maximum value. It has not yet reached this: we should not be thinking about it if it had. It is still increasing rapidly, and so must have had a beginning; *there must have been what we may describe as a "creation" at a time not infinitely remote.*[15]

The cosmological argument thus challenges us to reflect that this universe must have had a beginning, and by all the canons of common sense it must be caused by a Power sufficient for its rational explanation. Belief in God as the First Cause requires less credulity,

---

14. *Essential Christian Beliefs* (Kansas City: Beacon Hill Press of Kansas City, n.d.), pp. 5-6.

15. *This Mysterious Universe*, new and rev. ed. (New York: The Macmillan Co., 1937), pp. 179, 181.

certainly, than believing that the universe could be self-caused or eternal.

B. The Teleological Evidence

The next type of argument gets its name from the fact that it reasons from the evidences of purpose (Greek, *telos*) to be found in the universe to the necessary existence of a Purposer. Not only does this world exist, but it exists with every evidence of design in the multitude of adaptations which are apparent on every hand.

That living organisms, for example, should have eyes capable of sight requires as intricate adaptation of organ to function and to external conditions which could not conceivably have occurred other than by design. To suppose that chance could account for these adaptations is on a par with the degree of imagination exhibited by Thomas Huxley when he stated that if six monkeys were set to pounding on six typewriters, if only given enough time, they would eventually write all the books in the British Museum.[16]

The teleological argument may carry weight even with thinkers not trained in the philosophical disciplines. A best-seller of a few years back is the story of a newspaperman who had served the Communist underground in Washington. After his break with Communism, he wrote of his odyssey of thought:

> I do not know how far back my break with Communism began. Avalanches gather force and crash, unheard, in men as in the mountains. But I date my break from a very casual happening. I was sitting in our apartment on St. Paul Street in Baltimore. My daughter was in her high chair. I was watching her eat. She was the most miraculous thing that had ever happened in my life. I liked to watch her even when she smeared porridge on her face or dropped it meditatively on the floor. My eye came to rest on the delicate convolutions of her ear—those intricate, perfect ears. The thought passed through my mind: "No, those ears were not created by any chance coming together of atoms in nature (the Communist view). They could have been created only by immense design." The thought was involuntary and unwanted. I crowded it out of my mind. But I never wholly forgot it. I had to crowd it out of my mind. If I had completed it, I should have had to say: Design presupposes God. I did not then know that, at that moment, the finger of God was first laid upon my forehead.[17]

---

16. *Ibid.*, pp. 4-5.

17. Whittaker Chambers, *Witness* (New York: Random House, 1942), p. 16. Used by permission.

A particularly interesting adaptation of this argument is given by Sir James Jeans in the book referred to above. After exhibiting the mathematical structure of the universe, and noting how the purely deductive and a priori science of mathematics parallels the structure of the physical universe as revealed by telescope and microscope, he observes that "from the intrinsic evidence of his creation, the Great Architect of the Universe now begins to appear as a pure mathematician."[18] He further says:

> Thirty years ago, we thought, or assumed, that we were heading towards an ultimate reality of a mechanical kind. It seemed to consist of a fortuitous jumble of atoms, which was destined to perform meaningless dances for a time under the action of blind purposeless forces, and then fall back to form a dead world. Into this wholly mechanical world, through the play of the same blind forces, life had stumbled by accident. One tiny corner at least, and possibly several tiny corners, of this universe of atoms had chanced to become conscious for a time, but was destined in the end, still under the action of blind mechanical forces, to be frozen out and again leave a lifeless world.
>
> Today there is a wide measure of agreement, which on the physical side of science approaches almost to unanimity, that the stream of knowledge is heading towards a non-mechanical reality; the universe begins to look more like a great thought than like a great machine. Mind no longer appears as an accidental intruder into the realm of matter; we are beginning to suspect that we ought rather to hail it as the creator and governor of the realm of matter—not of course our individual minds, but the mind in which the atoms out of which our individual minds have grown exist as thoughts.[19]

The evidence from design has particular appeal to those best acquainted with the complexities of nature. A Cressy Morrison, in his 1944 volume *Man Does Not Stand Alone*,[20] reasons from the 10 billion to 1 probability against drawing 10 pennies numbered 1 through 10 from one's pocket in the precise sequence, 1, 2, 3, etc. The argument that follows is based on the fact that the universe is infinitely more complicated than 10 numbered pennies and the probability that all the conditions of life would emerge and develop by chance is so remote that it is quite unbelievable. The supposition that life would just happen calls for a greater miracle and greater faith than believing in God.

---

18. *Mysterious Universe,* p. 165.

19. *Ibid.,* 185-86.

20. (New York: Fleming H. Revell, 1944).

Arthur H. Compton, member of a noted American scientific family and Nobel Prize winner in physics, says, "For myself, faith begins with the realization that a supreme intelligence brought the universe into being and created man. It is not difficult for me to have this faith, for it is incontrovertible that where there is a plan there is intelligence—an orderly, unfolding universe testifies to the truth of the most majestic statement ever uttered—'In the beginning God.'"[21]

Dr. R. C. Wallace, a geologist and late principal of Queens University in Kingston, Ontario, Canada, wrote to his colleagues what he called his "valedictory" during the course of his last illness in January, 1955. He said:

> As a scientist, I have not been able to convince myself that the marvellous articulation and adaptation both of living things and of inanimate nature could have come itself or through the purely impersonal working of evolutionary laws alone. I feel that there is a mind beyond the visible processes, a fountainhead of all the love and beauty and goodness and truth which we as human beings so imperfectly reflect, a power that gives us freedom of choice, and an eternal hope. We call that power God. No one who truly loves nature can be satisfied that this life is all. For in the contemplation of the sunset or the storm, the minerals in the rock or the brilliance of the butterfly, the mind is caught up in a relationship that is beyond the world of passing things. We reach out into the eternal.[22]

In an article entitled "Nine Scientists Look at Religion," compiled by Kurt Singer and published in the *Reader's Digest,* Dr. Edwin Conklin, professor of biology at Princeton University, said, "The probability of life beginning from accident is compared to the probability of an unabridged dictionary resulting from an explosion in a printshop."[23]

Design, purpose, the adaptation of means to ends, in every case implies a Designer, a Purposer, One who foresees and guides the processes of adaptation so abundantly manifest in nature about us.

C. The Ontological Evidence

The ontological argument is named thus because it infers the being

---

21. Quoted by Barrett B. Baxter, *I Believe Because . . . : A Study of the Evidence Supporting Christian Faith* (Grand Rapids: Baker Book House, 1971), p. 64.

22. Quoted by Leonard Griffith, *Barriers to Christian Belief* (New York: Harper and Row, Publishers, 1962), pp. 41-42.

23. January, 1963, p. 16.

(Greek, *ontos*) of God from the idea of God. This much-debated argument was given its first and most persuasive statement by St. Anselm. Briefly, it runs as follows:

> God is that Being than whom no greater can be conceived;
> But a God existing in fact is greater than a God existing only in idea;
> Therefore, God *must* be thought of as existing in fact.

This, Anselm believed, was the argument to end all arguments. In this he was mistaken. It was almost immediately challenged by Gaunilon, a fellow monk, and has met with much debate ever since. Most objections miss one crucial point, however. Anselm never supposed that one could reason from the *idea* of perfect islands (as Gaunilon) or dollars (as Kant) to the *existence* of either islands or dollars. The idea of God is the only idea which *of necessity* permits the conception of nothing greater. Hence, that idea, and that alone, carries in it the conviction of objective existence.

Estimates of the value of the ontological argument vary from the shrug of Bishop Foster remarking that he could never see the point, to the contention of William Ernest Hocking that it is the greatest of all the theistic arguments.[24] The truth probably lies somewhere between these extremes. A modern statement is given by H. Orton Wiley as follows:

> The universality of the idea of God leads immediately to its acceptance as a necessary idea. By a necessary idea we mean any intuition which springs directly and immediately from the constitution of the human mind, and which under proper conditions must of necessity so spring. This only can account for the persistence of the idea of God, without which it could never have been perpetuated. "Neither a primitive revelation, nor the logical reason, nor both together could account for the persistence and universality of the idea of God without a moral and religious nature in man to which the idea is native" (Miley, *Systematic Theology,* I, 70). We may carry the argument one step farther, and insist that our intuitions give us objective truth. By a process of negative reason, we may argue that to deny this, is to deny the validity of all mental processes. To distrust its intuitions is to lead immediately to a distrust in the interpretation of sense-perceptions through which our knowledge of the external world is mediated. To hold otherwise is to land in agnosticism. But man's mental faculties are trustworthy. His rational intuitions are absolute

---

24. *The Meaning of God in Human Experience* (New Haven: Yale University Press, 1912), chapter 22. DeWolf, *Theology of the Living Church,* pp. 47-48, lists the ontological argument as one of three "fallacious arguments."

truth, and the intuition of God, universal and necessary in the experience of the race, finds its only sufficient explanation in the truth of His existence.[25]

D. The Moral Evidence

The moral argument derives its name from the inference it bases on the conscience and moral nature of man. This argument was first prominently presented by Immanuel Kant, who had rejected the cogency of the three previously discussed. It has been broadened by other thinkers to include other aspects of human experience such as reason and value experience, and the resulting thinking is sometimes known as the psychological argument. It bids us ponder the question how a supposedly nonmoral, irrational, and unfeeling universe could ever have given rise to creatures such as we are, with conscience, reason, and capacities to evaluate and enjoy. Dr. R. A. Millikan, noted American scientist, writes:

> But I would go a step further to answer the person who asks where the idea of God comes in. My own personal testimony is that I do not see how there can be a sense of duty or any reason for altruistic conduct that is entirely divorced from the conviction that what we call goodness is somehow worth while and that there is Something in the universe which gives significance and meaning to existence. Call it value if you will, but surely there can be no sense of value in mere lumps of dead matter interacting according to purely mechanical laws. To me, a purely materialistic philosophy is the height of unintelligence.
>
> Anaxagoras said in 460 B.C. that "All has been arranged by mind." The most influential of modern scientists—men like Einstein and Eddington and Jeans—have reechoed in our day those words of the Sage of Athens. In them there is, I think, significance for each of us as we seek today through our actions to do what we can to build a world in which disasters, such as we have gone through twice since 1914, cannot occur again.[26]

Kant himself was convinced that man's inescapable sense of ought, of conscience or obligation, requires us to accept as true (even in the absence of scientific proof) the freedom of the soul in moral choices, the immortality of the soul, and the existence of God. The fact of a moral law and the necessity of guaranteeing both the reward of virtue and the punishment of vice demand that we recognize (postulate, in Kant's term) the existence of God.[27]

---

25. *Christian Theology,* 1:229-30.
26. In the *Rotarian,* Vol. LXXXI, No. 1 (July, 1952), p. 11.
27. *The Critique of Practical Reason.*

It may well be contended that nothing could arise out of a purely material order which was not originally in it. Materialism, considered now in its denial of the existence of God, limps badly in its explanations of the origin of rational mind. As one has said, "Materialism may explain the material, but it cannot explain the materialist." Reason affirms that a universe without purposes and goals, a mere collection of material particles or forces, cannot give birth to an order of rational intelligences which are capable of purposes and goals, with the foresight necessary to attain such goals.

A thoughtful statement of this whole line of reasoning is given by Oxford scholar C. S. Lewis in *The Case for Christianity*.[28] Right and wrong, Lewis contends, are our best clue to the nature of the world in which we live. The moral law is the law of human nature, as the laws discovered in the sciences are the laws of nature. There is this significant difference, however: the laws of nature are laws only in the sense of being descriptions of the unvarying way in which things occur. The law of human nature is known by us to be a real *ought*, and independent of our obedience to it.

Lewis says, "It seems then, we are forced to believe in a real Right and Wrong. People may be sometimes mistaken about them, just as people sometimes get their sums wrong; but they are not a matter of mere taste and opinion any more than the multiplication table."[29]

The independent reality of right and wrong is witnessed even by the fact that the moral codes of one people may differ from the moral codes of others. The differences are not large. One can recognize the same law running through all moral codes, whereas conventions such as style of clothes and rules of the road differ completely. But some codes we recognize to be better than others. This is the significant fact. Lewis observes:

> In fact, of course, we all do believe that some moralities *are* better than others. We do believe that some of the people who tried to change the moral ideas of their own age were what we'd call Reformers or Pioneers—people who understood morality better than their neighbours did. Very well then. The moment you say that one set of moral ideas can be better than another, you are, in fact, measuring them both by a standard, saying that one of them conforms to that standard more nearly than the other. But the standard that measures two things is something different

---

28. (New York: The Macmillan Co., 1944).
29. *Ibid.*, p. 6.

from either. You are, in fact, comparing them both with some Real Morality, admitting that there is *really* such a thing as Right, independent of what people think, and that some people's ideas get nearer to the real Right than others.[30]

The existence of the moral law is, then, our best index as to the real nature of the universe. For moral law indicates that the Being behind the universe is a moral Being, and has produced an order in which good and evil are prime facts of human experience. Such a Being must at the very least be a supreme Personality, for only personality is capable of morality. Floyd E. Hamilton states, "It is unthinkable that all the splendid characteristics of mankind, such as justice, love and kindred characteristics, marred by sin though they are, should have been produced by a cause having none of these. A moral man must have a moral God as his Maker."[31]

E. The Evidence from Science

The modern scientific enterprise is often regarded as a major obstacle to religious faith. It has been easy to confuse "scientism" with science —scientism representing an illegitimate claim that truth is discovered only by the scientific method. Paradoxically, however, the success of the scientific method itself may be presented as an evidence for the existence of a Supreme Being.[32]

True science, as contrasted with scientism, is itself the expression of attitudes and a faith that are profoundly religious in nature. The aspiration for truth and understanding, faith that the world is a cosmos not a chaos and that it has intelligible laws which human reason can grasp, and scrupulous honesty in dealing with the data are all attitudes without which science would never come into existence, yet attitudes basically religious in nature.[33]

It is possible to argue reasonably that far from science being at odds with belief in God, it is itself one of the most persuasive arguments for His existence. There is an amazing kinship between the human mind and the universe as a whole. Nature, independent of

---

30. *Ibid.,* p. 11.

31. *The Basis of Christian Faith,* 3rd rev. ed. (New York: Harper and Brothers, 1946), p. 54.

32. Cf. "The Evidence of Scientific Experience" in D. Elton Trueblood, *Philosophy of Religion* (New York: Harper and Row, Publishers, 1957), pp. 90-105.

33. Cf. Vernon Sproxton, *Teilhard de Chardin* (Naperville, Ill.: SCM Book Club, 1971), p. 70; and Georgia Harkness, *Does God Care?* (Waco, Tex.: Word Books, Publisher, 1960), pp. 76, 95.

our minds, is yet amenable to their laws and understandable by our minds. There is a correlation between the mind and the order it apprehends. The human mind probes a nature it does not create and finds it an order in which it is not alien.

This is made clear in the fact that the most useful single tool in the investigation of the universe is mathematics—the one discipline that is not experimental, that depends on no observation, that is purely rational. Mathematics, the one rational human discipline, has proved to be the key to physics and astronomy to a degree almost beyond imagination.

William G. Pollard, director of the Associated Universities of Oakridge, Tennessee, and a pioneer in atomic research, points out that there have been a number of instances in the history of science in which a mathematical system developed originally as a pure product of the human mind without reference to the real world was later found to be applicable in every detail to an accurate description of nature.[34] He says:

> We have discovered that systems spun out by [the human] brain, for no other purpose than our sheer delight with their beauty, correspond precisely to the intricate design of the natural order which predated man and his brain. That surely has led to the discovery that man is amazingly like the designer of that natural order; how better to describe this discovery than to assert that man is indeed made in the image of God![35]
>
> Man has discovered that the workings of his own brain reflect in exact detail the structure of the mind which conceived and designed this universe, long before there were human brains at all.[36]

Twenty-five years before nuclear fission demonstrated its accuracy, mathematician Albert Einstein developed the formula $e = mc^2$ in which energy equals mass times the speed of light squared. It is little wonder that Einstein is quoted as having said, "I see at the beginning of the cosmic road—not eternal energy or matter, not inscrutable fate, not a fortuitous conflux of primordial elements, not the great Unknown—but the Lord God Almighty."[37]

34. *Science and Faith: Twin Mysteries* (New York: Thomas Nelson, Inc., 1970), p. 82.

35. *Ibid.,* p. 86.

36. *Ibid.,* p. 92.

37. Quoted, Baxter, *I Believe Because . . . ,* p. 55, from J. C. Monsma, *The Evidence for God in an Expanding Universe,* p. 68.

Another statement of this line of reasoning is given by Peter Berger, a sociologist, in *Rumor of Angels:*

> If there is any intellectual enterprise that appears to be a pure projection of the human consciousness it is mathematics. A mathematician can be totally isolated from any contact with nature and still go on about his business of constructing mathematical universes, which spring from his mind as pure creations of human intellect. Yet the most astounding result of modern natural science is the reiterated discovery (quite apart from this or that mathematical formulation of natural processes) that nature, too, is in its essence a fabric of mathematical relations. Put crudely, the mathematics that man projects out of his own consciousness somehow corresponds to a mathematical reality that is external to him, and which indeed his consciousness appears to reflect.[38]

Pollard also points out some startling changes in recent science-faith discussion. He says that formerly, the "mystery of the unknown" was the place where science and faith seemed to come together. Religion was defended against science by appealing to things science could not explain as indicating need for the hypothesis of God as the explanation. God became "the God of the gaps." As the gaps were filled in by continuing accumulation of scientific knowledge, there seemed to be less and less room for God.[39] "Now, however," says Dr. Pollard, "it is not in the unknown that we find God, but in the mysterious character of the known."[40]

> An important element of this mystery of the known is the way in which our knowledge of matter keeps beckoning us toward transcendent realities beyond space and time. The more deeply we probe into the secret of matter the more our knowledge seems to point us beyond space and time. The hints grow stronger that the underlying reality of things in nature is to be found beyond nature, in supernature.[41]

Science and religion, thus, are not two competing and mutually exclusive ways of understanding reality. They are, rather, "two ways of looking at the same reality, one enriching the other, but both leading you to the same mystery, a mystery common to the whole of reality. At the heart of the mystery is the one God who is the same

---

38. *Modern Society and the Rediscovery of the Supernatural* (Garden City, N.Y.: Doubleday & Company, Inc., 1969), pp. 58-59.

39. *Science and Faith*, pp. xiii-xiv, 27.

40. *Loc. cit.*

41. *Ibid.*, pp. 26-27.

for matter, space and time, life, and man as he is for Israel and Christ."[42]

In a statement of personal faith, Dr. Pollard adds, "If God is to be known at all, it must be at his initiative and to the extent he chooses to reveal himself to man and man responds to that revelation."[43] He says:

> It is my conviction that there is only one source for recovering an authentic religious perspective against the background of modern science. This is the drama of revelation and response which was enacted throughout the history of a single human culture, that of Israel, and which the Bible, the literature of this culture, records. This drama has a self-authenticating character. Its affirmations about God and man and the supernatural are entirely compatible with science as we know it today.[44]

A recent statement by Scottish theologian T. F. Torrance sets the entire matter in perspective:

> I do not believe that the Christian Church has anything to fear from the advance of science. In fact, the more truly scientific inquiry discloses the structures of the created world, the more at home we Christians ought to be in it, for this creation came into being through the Word of God, and in it that Word was made flesh in Jesus Christ our Lord. The more I engage in dialogue with scientists and understand the implications of their startling discoveries, the more I find that, far from contradicting our fundamental beliefs, they open the way for a deeper grasp of the Christian doctrines of creation, incarnation, reconciliation, resurrection, and, not least, the Holy Trinity. This is an age in which we are being emancipated from the tyranny of a narrow-minded scientism, an age in which true science and theology are thrown closely together in the service of God the Father Almighty.[45]

F. The Empirical Evidence

The empirical argument is known as such because it rests upon the experiences of God which come in conversion, sanctification, worship, and prayer. D. Elton Trueblood, the Quaker philosopher, has given one of the most complete statements of this line of reasoning in three books: *The Trustworthiness of Religious Experience,*[46] *The Logic of*

42. *Ibid.,* pp. xiii-xiv; cf. John Baillie, *et al., Science and Faith Today* (London: Lutterworth Press, 1953), p. 59.

43. *Science and Faith,* p. 93.

44. *Loc. cit.*

45. *Christianity Today,* Vol. XX, No. 25 (September 24, 1976), pp. 10-11

46. (London: George Allen and Unwin, Ltd., 1939).

Belief,[47] and more recently, *Philosophy of Religion.*[48] Space will permit only the barest outline here.

To one who has had a personal experience of the divine, all reasoning seems cold and inadequate. To meet God in a life-transforming conversion, in the fullness of sanctification, in prayer, and in worship leaves the soul with a certainty surpassing all power of logic to convey. But experience is essentially private. How can it be used as a line of evidence for one who has never had such an experience? Trueblood reminds us:

> The primary datum of religion may be stated as follows: *Millions of men and women, throughout several thousand years, representing various races and nations, and including all levels of education or cultural opportunity, have reported an experience of God as the spiritual companion of their souls.* In prayer and worship, whether at stated times or in the midst of everyday duties, they have been acutely conscious of Another who has sustained them in life's darkest as well as life's brightest moments.[49]

It is this direct experience of God which gives certainty to the individual. It claims, always, two things: first, that it is one of immediate relationship with the Divine—in William James's terms, "acquaintance with" rather than a secondhand "knowledge about"; and second, that it is an experience with objective reference, an experience of outer reality. This latter aspect of the claim of religious experience is a claim to knowledge, the knowledge of God. Such knowledge is just as real, and may be verified in the same fundamental ways, as our knowledge of the physical world about us. Rufus M. Jones has expressed it well:

> If God is Spirit and man is spirit it is not strange, absurd or improbable that there should be communion and correspondence between them. The odd thing is that we have correspondence with a world of matter, not that we have correspondence with a world of spiritual reality like our own inner nature. The thing that needs explanation is how we have commerce with rocks and hills and sky. It seems natural that we should have commerce with That which is most like ourselves.[50]

---

47. (New York: Harper and Brothers, 1942). Of the two, *Trustworthiness of Religious Experience* gives the more complete account.

48. Pages 143-58 give a recent summary in which adverse criticisms are considered.

49. *Trustworthiness of Religious Experience,* p. 12. The italics are in the original.

50. *The New Quest,* p. 146; quoted, *ibid.,* p. 28.

Trueblood points out that fundamentally all our knowledge rests upon the agreement of competent observers. This is true even in sense experience. Looking out of the classroom window, you see trees on the campus. How do you *know* they are there? Not only because you see them, but because all other sighted persons in the room also see them. It would be very disturbing if you alone saw the trees and your classmates affirmed that there were none there.

Is there agreement of testimony among those who have experienced God? There is. The saints can speak to each other with perfect understanding across centuries of time and around the world. And they are many in number. Trueblood says:

> The millions who have known what it is to pray or to be conscious, in worship, of the "real Presence," add to the stupendous fact. Many who would never think of writing down what they have experienced are able to tell it to their fellows as they have long done in the testimony meetings which stem from the Wesleyan revival. If we attend such an "experience meeting" and refuse to be bothered by the stereotyped expressions, we often get an overwhelming sense of the weight of the report. The testimony meeting corresponds to the gathering of data in a scientific enterprise. One after another, in perfect sincerity, arises to say, "Once I was blind, but now I see." "I sought the Lord and he heard me." "I know that my Redeemer liveth." Sometimes the sentences are not so felicitous, but what the simple believer is saying is, "I prayed to God and I came to know Him as a regenerating power. Now I walk with a new step."[51]

These multitudes are composed of persons from every walk of life, whose testimony would find credence in any court in the land. To explain away religion as being illusion demands that the testimony of these vast companies be discredited. But as Charles E. Raven has asked, "If these be mad, who is sane? If these be mad then madness is more beautiful, more reasonable, more beneficent, more effective than sanity."[52]

What about negative testimony—those who have not experienced the reality of God? Why are not all men aware of God? The answer, in Dr. Trueblood's words, is that "all knowing involves conditions, and the conditions vary with different objects of knowledge."[53] There are moral conditions imposed upon him who would

---

51. *Ibid.,* p. 37.

52. *Jesus and the Gospel of Love,* p. 73; quoted, *ibid.,* p. 39.

53. *Trustworthiness of Religious Experience,* p. 56.

know the Lord. The scorner, the braggart, the profane, and the super-cilious, together with those who manifest the attitude, Show me if you can, are not at all apt to meet God until by profound repentance they change their attitudes.

To one who would object that religious experience, the experience of God, is the product of wishful thinking, influenced by human desire, it should be pointed out that "religious experience has often been at complete variance with men's desires. It has been found in all generations that religion has made men uncomfortable, driving them to almost super-human sacrifice."[54] As George A. But-trick has said, "It is hard to understand why mankind should have created a fiction-God who demands sacrifice: it would have been so much easier in a heartless world to have taken painless poison."[55]

Rather, God has been known as One who judges, who demands, who appears when not desired and when least expected. Dr. True-blood states: "We help to restore balance when we remember men who, like St. Paul, have seen the living Christ, not when they expected it, and certainly not when they hoped for it, but in opposition to all their hopes and expectations."[56]

The empirical argument has always been the Christian logic par excellence, if argument it may be called. To doubting Nathanaels everywhere the invitation has been given throughout the Christian centuries, "Come and see." "We have found him," is the core of the message.[57]

Although exact mathematical proof of the existence of God may be beyond the human mind, there is an assurance of His love and grace which satisfies the heart. In a unique and sensitive statement of this, Norman Snaith writes:

> This is a type of certainty which I, for one, have about God. It is not contrary to reason, and given its own premises it is as logical as the rest. But it has its own premises, and they are the premises which have their basis in personal experience of a Person. Nobody ever argued me into it, and I am quite certain that nobody can argue me out of it. It never depended on that

---

54. *Ibid.*, p. 71.

55. *The Christian Fact and Modern Doubt;* quoted, *ibid.*, p. 72.

56. *Trustworthiness of Religious Experience*, p. 73.

57. Experience as a confirming evidence must not be confused with the philo-sophical pragmatism discussed in Chapter 1, which is a theory of the nature of truth rather than a method of its confirmation.

type of argument. If anyone should ask me how it is that I am sure of God, I could give no answer except that it is in the same kind of way in which I am sure of my wife. Just how it is that I am sure of that, I do not know. It has been strengthened by the intimacies and mutual trust of the years, but it began . . . ? The Christian is prepared to give reasons for the faith that is in him, but his faith does not depend upon such reasons.[58]

These, then, are some of the reasons which may be given for belief in God. They are adequate to satisfy the most rigorous mind, if it be not adversely conditioned by moral and personal considerations. Be it noted again that we have here converging lines of evidence. If any one of them, or even all of them taken individually, be judged insufficient to support the weight placed upon it, when woven together they comprise a cable of great strength.

Indeed, there are few items of important knowledge which rest upon one all-conclusive argument or piece of evidence. Even scientific laws and principles are verified, when they are, by similar converging lines of evidence, any one of which may be inconclusive, but all together quite convincing. Belief in God is a faith which becomes a certitude to one who has experienced Him. But at every stage it is a rational faith, for which sound and cogent reasons may be given.

SUMMARY

In this chapter we have considered some of the most important concepts of the divine, and the relation of God to the universe, of which He is the Source and Sustainer. The place of proof in relation to the existence of God was then examined, with a recognition of the fact that the most proof can offer is a degree of intellectual satisfaction as to the truth in question. The biblical certainty of God does not rest upon reason, but upon revelation, or the divine self-disclosure.

However, faith in God is eminently a rational faith. No other explanation of the universe in which we find ourselves, or of the sort of creatures we discover ourselves to be, is as adequate as the theistic faith in one God, the Creator, Sustainer, and Governor of the cosmos. Some of the major lines of evidence for this theistic faith were briefly surveyed.

We turn next to a study of a concept which has already assumed

---

58. *Hymns of the Temple* (London: SCM Press, Ltd., 1951), p. 82.

key importance in our discussion. It is the fact that God has revealed himself, or made himself known, to those whom He created in His own image. The nature and method of this divine self-disclosure is of utmost importance in the structure of our Christian faith.

CHAPTER 3

Divine Revelation and the Bible

In Chapter 1 we noted that religious faith may be defined as man's response to God's revelation. This faith has two major elements: an intellectual or rational side—assent to the truth God's revelation communicates; and a volitional side—obedience to the demands God's revelation makes. In Chapter 2 we gave major consideration to the existence of God as the Subject who discloses himself to man. In this chapter we must look further at that which is the actual starting point of biblical religion, namely, the fact that God has taken the initiative and has made himself and His purposes known.

In passing, it should be observed that a divine self-disclosure is implied in the theistic faith examined in the last chapter. If theism is true and God does exist, then it is to be expected that He would make His will known to His creatures. It is scarcely conceivable that God would have created man as he is now constituted and would have left him in ignorance of the purposes of his creation and of the will of his Creator. Yet such would be the case if there were no divine revelation.

We cannot rest in agnosticism, the position which holds that there may be a supreme First Cause but if there is we may know nothing about Him. That finite minds cannot comprehend in full the Infinite may readily be admitted. It is not necessary that we should know everything about God in order that we might know something about Him. It is poor logic which states that the Infinite so far transcends the finite that all which may be known of God is that He is unknowable.[1] An infinite God would certainly find ways of disclosing himself to finite minds.

Christianity rests squarely on the affirmation that God has in fact found ways (or a Way) to reveal himself to man. This self-disclosure is above and beyond what is sometimes called "general revelation," the knowledge of God which may be gained from a study of His handiwork in nature and by the use of the natural capacities of the mind. There have been philosophers, as for example Plato (428-348 B.C.) among the Greeks, who have come to important theological insights in this way. Theism may be the end product of philosophical speculation, and is a position shared by religions other than Christianity. What is distinctive about the Christian faith is derived from a totally unique and final "special" revelation.

Implied in what we have said about this special revelation is the fact that revelation is by its very nature personal. It is communication, through varying mediums, from Person to persons. It is God's disclosure of himself in His redemptive purposes, a disclosure to persons created in His own image. What is communicated is not in the first place abstract truths. As Pascal long ago observed, the God of the Bible is not the God of the philosophers, but the God of Abraham, Isaac, and Jacob, the God who makes himself known as the Savior and Companion on the long way man must go.[2]

As we shall see later in this chapter, revelation is not only personal, it is also propositional. That is, truth about God may be and is stated in words and concepts meaningful to the mind and of such kind as to be judged true in contrast with their contradictories which are false.

These two ideas have sometimes been regarded as mutually exclusive. They are in fact complementary. God not only shows himself, He also tells us about himself and our relationship with Him. "Telling" involves truth content expressed in "propositions" or affirmations.

When we look at the data, we find that God has revealed himself in three major ways, and these ways are actually one—just as God himself is affirmed by Christians to be Three in One. God has

---

1. Cf. the discussion of Herbert Spencer's agnosticism in Ralph Tyler Flewelling, *Personalism and the Problems of Philosophy* (New York: The Methodist Book Concern, 1915), pp. 61 ff.

2. Cf. Albert Gelin, *The Key Concepts of the Old Testament* (New York: Sheed and Ward, 1955), pp. 15-16.

Father
Son
Holy Spirit

revealed himself in history, a revelation by the Father; He has revealed himself in Christ, a revelation by the Son; and He has revealed himself in the Scriptures, a revelation by the Holy Spirit. The unity within this trinity of revelation is the supremacy of the revelation in Christ: for to Him the revelation in history points forward, and to Him the Spirit bears witness in the Scriptures (John 15:26).

I. GOD'S REVELATION IN HISTORY

God has first of all revealed himself by His mighty acts in history, primarily the history of the people descended from an emigrant from Ur of the Chaldees in the first part of the second millennium before Christ. This history has roots running back to creation, and would be meaningless apart from the record which interprets the unknown length of time before Abraham. But while Genesis gives 2 chapters to creation, it gives 14 to Abraham. While it gives 11 chapters to the ages before the "father of the faithful," it devotes 39 chapters to Abraham and three generations of his descendants in a period of a little over two centuries.

A. Historical Event as Revelation

The Bible itself, not improperly, has been called "The Book of the Acts of God,"[3] and its central theme is what God has done. Revelation is no timeless communication of ideas. It is a recital of what has happened. John Baillie has pointed out a remarkable breadth of agreement among recent writers on this point: "That God reveals Himself *in action*—in the gracious activity by which He invades the field of human experience and human history which is otherwise but a vain show, empty and drained of meaning." He continues:

> The Bible is essentially the story of the acts of God. As has often been pointed out, its most striking difference from the sacred books of all other religions lies in its historical character. Other sacred books are composed mainly of oracles which communicate what profess to be timeless truths about universal being or timeless prescriptions for life and worship. But the Bible is mainly a record of what God has done. Those parts of it which are not in a strict sense historiographic are nevertheless placed within a definite historical frame and setting which they presuppose

---

3. Suzanne de Dietrich, *Le Dessein de Dieu* (1948), p. 8. This is also the title of the 1957 publication by G. Ernest Wright and Reginald H. Fuller (New York: Doubleday and Company, Inc.).

at every point. The Mosaic law differs from other law books in that all its prescriptions presuppose the sealing of a covenant between Yahweh and Israel—a covenant which is conceived as being no part of a universal and timeless relation between God and man, but one which was sealed on Horeb-Sinai on a particular historical occasion.[4]

One writer names five historical events as of most importance in the framework of the Old Testament. These are (1) the call of and promise to the patriarchs; (2) the deliverance of the people of Israel from Egypt; (3) the covenant made at Mount Sinai; (4) the conquest of Canaan; and (5) the government of David. On each of these key events, archaeology and historical study have shed much light.[5] Two others should be added to make the list complete: (6) the judgment on idolatry in the Assyrian and Babylonian exiles; and (7) the restoration of the remnant from exile.

Of these, the deliverance from Egypt is clearly regarded by the Old Testament writers themselves as the central and climactic act of God in the pre-Christian centuries. In fact, at least one scholar finds in the deliverance of the people from bondage in Egypt the clue to the unity of the entire Bible, since the salvation thus wrought finds its universal fulfillment in Christ.[6] This deliverance was promised (Gen. 15:13-14; 46:4; 48:21; 50:24-25). By it God became known as the Savior (Exod. 15:2; Ps. 106:21); it was memorialized in the Passover, chief of the annual feasts, with the shedding of the blood of the paschal lamb. It was commemorated in the prayer of dedication offered with the firstfruits of the harvest at the feast of Pentecost: "The Lord brought us forth out of Egypt with a mighty hand, and with an outstretched arm, and with great terribleness, and with signs, and with wonders" (Deut. 26:8; cf. vv. 5-10). The appeal of psalmist and prophet alike was to the faithfulness and might of the God who saved His people from bondage (Ps. 8:8; Jer. 2:6; Dan. 9:15; Hos. 11:1).

B. Interpretation

Historical act becomes a revelation of God when interpreted through the eye of faith. The great prophets of the eighth century before

---

4. *Idea of Revelation in Recent Thought*, pp. 49-50.

5. Wright and Fuller, *Book of the Acts of God*, pp. 18-22.

6. Harold H. Rowley, *The Unity of the Bible* (Philadelphia: Westminster Press, 1953).

Christ watched the rise and fall of nations, and saw but too clearly the fate of their own little kingdom. But, one and all, they saw in the downfall of mighty empires the judgments of God, and in the misery and defeat of their own people the inevitable consequences of idolatry and rebellion against God. Syria and Assyria, Babylonia and Medo-Persia become instruments in the hands of God, who judges the nations. As G. Ernest Wright states, "The point is, then, that real historical events are here involved, but in themselves they do not make the biblical event. In the Bible, an important or signal happening is not an event unless it is also an event of revelation, that is, unless it is an event which has been interpreted so as to have meaning."[7]

But the salvation-history of the Old Testament is obviously an incomplete history. It is history with a forward look. In the loss of Israel's political independence, the prophets began more and more to look to the *eschaton,* the Day of the Lord, a Kingdom which was to come. History thus merges into prophecy. As Harold H. Rowley points out, prophecy is not fulfilled or completed in Judaism, but in the New Testament, and more particularly in Christ.[8] Floyd V. Filson has said: "Standing by itself, the Old Testament is an incomplete book, and its completion is to be found in Christ and the Christian gospel. It is an integral part of the Christian Scripture, and only in this context can it be rightly and fully understood."[9]

II. God's Revelation in Christ

Not only does revelation occur through God's acts in history, interpreted as such in faith; but the supreme self-disclosure is, in John Baillie's terms, "very God Himself incarnate in Jesus Christ our Lord."[10] The writer to the Hebrews states: "In many and various ways God spoke of old to our fathers by the prophets; but in these last days he has spoken to us by a Son, whom he appointed the heir of all things, through whom also he created the world. He reflects the glory of God and bears the very stamp of his nature, upholding the

---

7. *Book of the Acts of God,* p. 22.

8. *Unity of the Bible,* p. 94.

9. "The Unity of the Old and the New Testament," *Interpretation,* Vol. V, No. 2 (April, 1951), p. 151.

10. *Idea of Revelation in Recent Thought,* p. 28.

universe by his word of power" (Heb. 1:1-3*a*, RSV). In John 1:1, 14, 18 we read: "In the beginning was the Word, and the Word was with God, and the Word was God. . . . And the Word was made flesh, and dwelt among us, (and we beheld his glory, the glory as of the only begotten of the Father,) full of grace and truth. . . . No man hath seen God at any time; the only begotten Son, which is in the bosom of the Father, he hath declared him." H. Orton Wiley comments:

> In a stricter and deeper sense, Jesus Christ himself as the Personal and Eternal Word is the only true and adequate revelation of the Father. *No man hath seen God at any time; the only begotten Son, which is in the bosom of the Father, he hath declared him.* His testimony is the last word in objective revelation, and this testimony is perfected in the Christian Scriptures.[11]

In recent years this truth has received much-deserved emphasis in what is called "The Theology of the Word."[12] Here has been rediscovered what evangelical theologians have long recognized: that the event is always greater than the record of the event, and that the Living Word of God is ultimately the perfect revelation of the Father. There is a basic truth in Karl Barth's statement that "revelation in fact does not differ from the Person of Jesus Christ, and again does not differ from the reconciliation which took place in Him. To say revelation is to say, 'The Word became flesh.' . . . The equation, God's Word is God's Son, makes anything doctrinaire in regarding the Word of God radically impossible."[13]

It is hard to see how a divine Person could truly be made known to human persons other than through embodiment in human form. A personal God could not truly reveal himself other than through personality. The mightiest of all the acts of God are therefore to be found in the Incarnation, and in the birth, life, teachings, death, and resurrection of the Lord Jesus Christ.

III. God's Revelation in Scripture

To recognize that God has revealed himself in history and supremely in the person of His Son, Jesus Christ, our Lord, is to be led to a third

---

11. *Christian Theology*, 1:33.

12. Cf. the title of Karl Barth's *Die Kirchliche Dogmatik*, Vol. I, Part I, in the English translation: "The Doctrine of the Word of God." Also J. K. S. Reid, *The Authority of Scripture* (London: Methuen and Co., Ltd., 1957), Chapter VII, "The Theology of the Word," pp. 194-233.

13. "Doctrine of the Word of God," pp. 134, 156.

step. For the Bible is the Book which brings us knowledge of God's mighty acts and of the Incarnate Word. It is the Bible which makes possible the faith whereby men today enter into a redemptive relationship with God. In the preaching and writing of prophets and apostles, God has revealed himself and His truth.

A. The Bible as the Record of Revelation

The last 50 years in Christian thought has seen a remarkable revival of interest in the fact of divine revelation. Liberalism and modernism for decades had virtually abandoned the idea of a special revelation of God in time. What may be known of God was assumed to come through a generalized religious experience and through reason in the contemplation of nature. The Bible was regarded as just the record of religious experiences of remarkably sensitive men, and Jesus was thought of only as One who had come closest to a full understanding of the Divine. Human nature was regarded as inherently good, and religious education was esteemed to be the way of salvation. Combined with an evolutionary approach, history was interpreted as the scene of man's progressive victory over crime, vice, hatred, brutality, and evil.

Then came the holocaust of the First World War, and with it the death throes of humanistic optimism. Liberalism came to a pause. Some of its most enthusiastic partisans began to wonder if their answers were as good as they had at first been thought to be. The moral abandon of the 20s, the sobering insecurities of the 30s, and the terrifying spectacle of Hiroshima and Nagasaki in the 40s did something to the climate of human thought which made the survival of earlier liberalism as improbable as orchids in an ice age.

In theology and biblical studies a new attitude began to appear. It was seen that liberalism was religiously sterile, and that the analytical destructive criticism of the Bible had actually robbed it of spiritual significance and religious authority. Scholars began to lose confidence in the ability of philosophical theology to supply all the answers. From many sources, and among scholars of quite different backgrounds and schools of thought, a new trend back toward the positions of historic Christianity began to be evident.

The trend is too young and too broad to be fully defined at this time. In general, however, it is once again recognized that God *has* revealed himself in a special way: in His mighty acts in redemptive history, and more particularly in the life, death, and resurrection of Jesus Christ, the incarnate Word. This divine revelation is said to consist not so much in what are called "propositional truths" or statements *about* God as in the actual confronting of the individual soul by God through the Holy Spirit.

In this movement the Bible assumed a new importance because it is our best witness to the revelation God has wrought in history. The Scriptures are in that sense final, and can never be replaced in Christian thought. They, and they alone, carry us back to within a generation of the greatest of God's redemptive deeds, the "Christ-event," that is, the death and resurrection of the Lord Jesus. The unity of biblical religion is also reaffirmed, a unity which roots deep in the continuity of the historical process wherein divine revelation takes place.[14]

For much of this emphasis, conservative Christians may be grateful. The clear witness to the supernatural, the strong attack on humanistic liberalism, the insistence on the contemporaneity of the Word of God with its vital grip on our hearts, the recognition of the importance and unity of the Bible are all to the good. We can have enough confidence in the Word of God itself to believe that if it is diligently studied and faithfully preached it will finally prove its own authority. Our primary task is not to defend the Bible but to proclaim its truth to the world.

B. The Inspiration of the Scriptures

To many thoughtful conservatives the greatest weakness of these newer emphases lies in the lack of an adequate view of the inspiration of the Bible. Are the Scriptures to be thought of as merely the human witness to divine revelation, subject to error as other human productions, their record to be judged merely as other ancient writings are judged? Is the Bible the Word of God in itself, or only when and to the degree that God uses it to confront us by His Spirit in the reading or preaching of the Scriptures? Can we really have revelation without a Bible which is doctrinally inerrant and factually trustworthy?

1. *The Meaning of Inspiration*

It is at this point that the inspiration of the Scriptures becomes

---

14. The writings of Karl Barth and H. Emil Brunner are typical; to which may be added the names of C. H. Dodd, H. H. Rowley, William Temple, J. K. S. Reid, John Baillie, and G. Ernest Wright, to list but a few. It will be noted that to describe this trend as "neo-orthodox" is highly misleading, however influential neo-orthodoxy has been in stimulating it.

all-important. By inspiration is meant the process whereby God through the Holy Spirit has provided an accurate and true record and interpretation of His redemptive act in Christ, set down in documentary form by "holy men of God" who "spake as they were moved by the Holy Ghost" (2 Pet. 1:21). Christ, the living Word, is the perfect self-revelation of God. The Bible, the written Word, is the divinely inspired and completely adequate record of the redemptive ministry and work of Christ.

"To inspire" literally means "to breathe into." H. Orton Wiley states that inspiration is "the operation of the Holy Spirit upon the writers of the books of the Bible in such a manner that their productions become the expressions of God's will."[15] Dr. Wiley finds three factors in inspiration which make clear its possibility, should anyone doubt that an infinite God *could* find ways accurately to make known His will to human minds. The first is *superintendence,* whereby the Holy Spirit gives such guidance that the writings of chosen men are kept free from error. The second is *elevation,* in which enlargement of understanding and refinement of conception are given the human minds to whom the revelation is made. The third is *suggestion,* under which a direct communication of thoughts and even words is received from the divine Spirit.[16] "Revelation—that is to say, original revelation—is the truth emerging in the mind of someone for the first time. Inspiration is the impulse to write it down, to make it permanent, to hand it on."[17]

2. *The Christological Analogy*

It has frequently and rightly been said that the inspired Word partakes of the same twofold nature as the incarnate Word. This is known as "the Christological analogy." In Chapter VIII we shall see that the central Christian affirmation regarding Jesus is that in one personality He perfectly combines both the nature of God and the nature of man. In the words of the creed, Christ is "very God and very man." Deity and humanity are so related that the humanity does not obscure the deity, nor the deity cancel out the humanity.

Likewise, in Scripture we have the union of the divine and the human. It was holy *men* of God who spoke as they were moved by the

---

15. *Christian Theology,* 1:166.

16. *Ibid.,* 1:170.

17. Kenneth J. Foreman, "What Is the Bible?" *The Layman's Bible Commentary,* Balmer H. Kelly, editor (Richmond, Va.: John Knox Press, 1959), 1:21.

Holy Ghost (2 Pet. 1:21). Paul says, "For this cause also thank we God without ceasing, because, when ye received the word of God which ye heard of us, ye received it not as the word of men, but as it is in truth, the word of God, which effectually worketh also in you that believe" (1 Thess. 2:13). In Luke 10:16 we find the crucial words of Jesus, "He that heareth you heareth me; and he that despiseth you despiseth me; and he that despiseth me despiseth him that sent me." In these and many other verses we find the clear recognition of both divinity and humanity. The word received of the apostles is in truth the word of God, although the lips and pens of men communicated it. Christ's word is identified with the apostles' word, so that he who hears the apostolic witness hears Christ, and he who despises it despises Him who authorizes it.

It is vitally important that the divine and the human be held in proper balance. It does not honor Christ to deny His essential humanity (Docetism). It is fatal also to deny His deity (Arianism). Only One who is both God and man can be a Mediator, a Redeemer. In the same way, it does no honor to Scripture to deny its humanity, and it is damaging beyond repair to lose sight of its divinity. Only a Bible which is the Word of God in the words of man can have redemptive power.

a. The humanity of the Bible is in reality one of its chief sources of strength. If God would speak to men, He must needs speak *through* men, in language we can understand and using terms which grow up within our experience. The "holy men of God" who were the human agents in the preparation of Scripture came from every walk of life: shepherds, priests, prophets, kings, farmers, fishermen. Some were rich and some were poor; some were highly educated, some untrained in the schools. They wrote in varied style, literature of many types, and the words they used were words which came from their human environment. Thus the Bible speaks to us in language we cannot mistake. We find in its pages the kinds of persons we are: the quick and the slow, the impulsive and the deliberate; the intellectual, the man of action, and the person of deep feeling. All types of personality and temperament are reflected in both the writers themselves and those of whom they wrote.

b. But humanity is only half the picture. The other half is absolutely vital. There are many human books. There is only one Bible, only one divine Book. While it was holy *men* of God who wrote, they spoke and wrote as they were moved by (Greek, *carried along by*) the

Holy Spirit of God. That the earthly authors of Scripture were men as we are does not make the Bible any less the Word of God. It is the divine character of the Book which distinguishes it from all other religious literature, and which makes it the truly redemptive Word.

C. The Manner and Degree of Inspiration

Before turning to the nature of the authority of Scripture, two points remain to be considered. One of these is the *manner* of inspiration, the *way* in which the authority of the Bible is guaranteed. The other is the *degree* of inspiration, the extent to which the Bible may be said to be the Word of God. In each of these areas two opposing views will be considered.

1. *The Method of Inspiration*

Concerning the means God used to guarantee the trustworthiness of Scripture, there seem to be two major theories:

a. One is what might be called the dictation theory. It is sometimes known as "verbal" inspiration, although this latter designation is apt to be confusing in terms of the discussion going on today in theology wherein "verbal" is used in such a general way as to be virtually equivalent to "dynamic." Briefly, it is to the effect that the original writings of the Bible (the autographs, as they are called) were given word for word by the Holy Spirit, the writers acting much as stenographers taking dictation from their employers. Proof texts such as 1 Cor. 2:13 and Heb. 3:7 are cited.

It need not be denied that there are portions of the Bible which appear as actual verbal communications. Passages prefaced with "Thus saith the Lord" may be examples of this. However, to regard the whole of Scripture as thus dictated word for word is open to some extremely weighty objections. Bishop Charles Gore states that this view is not actually Christian at all, but has pagan origins:

> And we can notice at once that Philo's identification of inspiration, in the highest sense, with the annihilation or expulsion of the human faculties of thought and reason—so that the inspired man is the purely passive instrument of the Divine Spirit, which dictates through him—does not at all correspond to the facts about the higher prophets of Israel and was never the view entertained by the Christian Church. It was in fact derived from Greece and not from Israel.[18]

---

18. *The Holy Spirit and the Church* (New York: Charles Scribner's Sons, 1924), p. 255.

H. Orton Wiley lists three objections to this view.[19] First, mechanical dictation affirms the inspiration of the writings, but denies it to the writers. Contrariwise, the Scripture is "God-breathed" (2 Tim. 3:16) because of the inspiration of the *men* who wrote (2 Pet. 1:21).

Second, it is not in accord with the character of the writings themselves. For example, there are unquestioned differences in style among the 66 books, a fact not handily explained by the dictation theory. A business executive may use a number of different stenographers, but the style of his correspondence is always his own. Then, historical research (Luke 1:1-4) and acknowledged personal opinion (1 Cor. 7:12) are cited by the writers. The manner in which New Testament writers quote the Old Testament, not word for word, but freely, preserving the thought but not the wording; and the fact that the Gospel writers make little or no effort at verbal agreement (cf. Matt. 3:17 with Mark 1:11 and Luke 3:22) cannot readily be accounted for if the words of the Bible are stenographically reported.

Third, the dictation theory is out of accord with the known ways God works with His people, (taking account of and working through their unique personalities and perspectives.)

It might be added also that, if this theory be true, then only the autographs preserving the original Hebrew, Chaldean, and Greek words would be inspired. Translations into any other languages could not, by definition, partake of inspiration, for the words are different. If inspiration pertains only to the original wording, then no one who must gain his knowledge of the Bible through the use of translations would have access to the inspired Word. If, on the other hand, inspiration is a matter of the truth of the ideas presented, and not of the verbal symbols used to communicate those ideas, then a reasonably adequate translation may present inspired truth as well as the original wording. Any one of a number of verbal symbols may convey the same idea. The idea may abide although the symbols change.

b. As opposed to the dictation theory, there is what Dr. Wiley has called the "dynamical theory." This view seeks to place in proper balance both human and divine elements in the process of inspiration. If the dictation theory be likened to the relationship between an executive and his stenographer, then the dynamical theory may

---

19. *Christian Theology*, 1:173-75.

be compared to the relationship between an executive and his secretary, to whom he gives directions as to what to write, leaving the choice of diction to the secretary. In dictation, the personal characteristics and modes of expression of the stenographer never appear. In direction, the style is that of the secretary, and personal modes of expression are to be expected. The analogy may be carried a step farther, and the inclusion of a writing in the canon or list of authoritative books may be likened to the signing of the letter by the executive after it has been written at his direction.[20]

The dynamical theory regards the inspired writers as active agents in the communication of divine truth, rather than as passive instruments. It fits all the facts of Scripture, and gives complete authority to its truth.

2. The Degree of Inspiration

We come now to the question as to the degree of inspiration. Here, again, there are two opposing points of view:

a. One may be called partial inspiration, the theory that the Bible *contains* the Word of God and parts of it may and do *become* the Word of God as the Spirit of God speaks to the individual through the reading or preaching of the Scriptures.

However, to say that the Bible is not the Word of God but that it contains the Word of God is immediately to rob it of its authority over human life and thought. For who is to say what part is, and what part is not, the Word of God? That is, if we think only in terms of the Bible as containing God's revelation, immediately we put up our own reason, or instinct, or judgment, to decide how much is truly God's Word and what is merely the human shell in which the kernel is contained.

It is true that the Bible quotes Satan and wicked men. In these cases complete inspiration obviously means, not that the words spoken are true, but that they were truly spoken as reported. The Bible is to be taken in its organic unity as a valid record of the revelation of God in Christ. If one sets up subjective criteria as to what he will accept as the Word of God within the Bible, then his subjective criteria and not the Word become his real authority. In effect, one then says that the Word of God must conform to his judgment as to what it *should* be. But it is the Word of God which must judge our

---

20. Cf. the "endorsement theory" presented by Olin A. Curtis, *The Christian Faith* (Grand Rapids: Kregel Book Store, reprint, 1956), pp. 161-80.

thoughts and theories, not our thoughts and theories which judge the Word of God.

b. The other view is called plenary inspiration, the affirmation that in its organic wholeness the Bible *is* the Word of God. Plenary, in its simplest meaning, is *full or complete*. While personally disavowing it, John Baillie fairly defines "plenary inspiration" in the words:

> The only point in dispute among Christians has been whether such inspiration is to be regarded as having been "plenary," that is, whether the control exercised by the Holy Spirit was so complete and entire as to overrule all human fallibility, making the writers perfect mouthpieces of the infallible divine self-communication.[21]

A strong affirmation of plenary inspiration which both fixes and limits its meaning is given in the following Article of Faith:

> We believe in the plenary inspiration of the Holy Scriptures, by which we understand the sixty-six books of the Old and New Testaments, given by divine inspiration, inerrantly revealing the will of God concerning us in all things necessary to our salvation, so that whatever is not contained therein is not to be enjoined as an article of faith.[22]

It may clarify the issues to reflect that the full trustworthiness of the Bible, which is what plenary inspiration affirms, does not mean that Scripture can be judged independently of its declared purposes. While it contains nothing, properly understood, which is unscientific or unhistorical, yet the Bible is not a book of science or history. Its purpose is to make known the will of God, not to answer questions about nature or to satisfy our curiosity about general human history.

Nor does the plenary inspiration of the Bible imply that all parts of the sacred record are of equal importance. All are equally true, but all are not equally valuable. There is a vast range in meaning and worth between the genealogies of 1 Chronicles and the 53rd chapter of Isaiah; and between 1 Corinthians 7 and 1 Corinthians 13. It is the organic unity, the wholeness, of Scripture which conveys to us the knowledge of God. Martin Luther's insight is of value here: that our understanding of different portions of the Bible is to be governed by the manner in which they preach Christ.[23]

---

21. *Idea of Revelation in Recent Thought,* p. 111.
22. Article IV, "Articles of Faith," Constitution of the Church of the Nazarene.
23. Reid, *Authority of Scripture,* pp. 67-70.

It is only when limited and arbitrary standards of judgment are set up that the Bible may be charged with error. When considered in the light of its own purposes and by reasonable canons of value and truth, the Scriptures will be found to be without material error. Many problems vanish with a careful and sympathetic reading of the text itself. Other problems are found to disappear when we cease demanding that the statements of Scripture harmonize in mode of expression with 20th-century philosophy and science. It is perverse to insist that the Bible conform to modern attitudes and thought patterns. Instead, it is a Book for the ages. Had Scripture been written in the framework of present-day philosophical and scientific concepts, it would have been meaningless to the hundreds of generations which have lived before us.

An excellent statement apropos this whole subject is made by H. M. Kuitert:

> If we recognize that "infallibility" gets its meaning in association with "trustworthiness"—and that trustworthiness means that the Bible is as trustworthy as God Himself is—we will have made a good start towards dealing with this question. The trustworthiness of the Bible is closely related to the intention of the Bible. The crucial question, therefore, is whether the Bible is trustworthy as God's message of salvation.[24]

D. The Bible as Revelation in Itself

We conclude, then, that the Bible is more than a human record of or witness to a revelation which consists in the acts of God in history and in the person of the incarnate Christ. The inspiration of the Spirit has given us not only a trustworthy account of salvation-history and an accurate picture of the life, death, and resurrection of Christ as facts which occurred in past time; it has also given us an interpretation of those facts, which is part of the revelation itself.

1. *Revelation Through Interpretation*

We cannot limit the self-disclosing acts of God to the realm of objective history alone. God also acted by inspiring prophets and apostles correctly to interpret what was done historically. The fact without the interpretation is quite meaningless. Recording the facts of the crucifixion and resurrection of Christ is only part of the gospel.

---

24. *Do You Understand What You Read?* On Understanding and Interpreting the Bible. Translated by Lewis B. Smedes. Grand Rapids: Wm. B. Eerdmans Publishing Company, 1970), p. 103.

The rest lies in what those facts mean in redeeming men from sin. The witness to the redemptive deed is a necessary part of the deed itself.

Any limitation of the mighty acts of God to acts of one kind only is purely arbitrary. If God could act in history by delivering His people from Egypt, and by becoming flesh and dwelling among them, there is no very good reason to deny that He also acted by inspiring prophets and apostles to record accurately and interpret properly those great acts.

2. *The Bible Inspiring Because Inspired*

The inspiration of the Spirit cannot be limited to either the writers or the readers of Scripture. Modern biblical scholars tend to stress the inspiringness of Scripture at the expense of its inspiration. That is, they affirm that the Holy Spirit inspires the reader to grasp the truth God would have him find. But this is possible only because the Spirit first inspired the writers in what they wrote. 2 Tim. 3:16 states: "All scripture is given by inspiration of God, and is profitable for doctrine, for reproof, for correction, for instruction in righteousness." Commenting on this, John Wesley correctly recognized a two-fold inspiration:

> The Spirit of God, not only once inspired those who wrote it, but continually inspires, supernaturally assists those that read it with earnest prayer. Hence it is so profitable for doctrine, for instruction of the ignorant, for the reproof or conviction of them that are in error or sin; for the correction or amendment of whatever is amiss, and for instructing or training up the children of God in all righteousness.[25]

The importance of the inner testimony of the Spirit to the truth of Scripture should not be obscured. But it must be balanced by a recognition of the inherent authority of the Bible. The Book of God is like a bag of seed. On the shelf, it shows little sign of the life that is in it. Put in the soil, warmed by the sun, and watered by the rain, it brings forth fruit unto salvation. But the life is not in the soil, or in the sun, or in the rain, but in the seed. One might plant an equal amount of sawdust without so much as a single sprout for his pains. Geoffrey W. Bromiley writes:

> An inspired Bible is of little value unless it comes alive for the reader—just as Christ Himself must be perceived and known

---

25. *Explanatory Notes upon the New Testament* (London: The Epworth Press, reprint, 1950), p. 794.

as Christ if His gracious work is to avail for us. Yet the fact remains that as Christ was and is the Son of God and Saviour irrespective of our human response, so too the Bible was inspired by the Holy Spirit and is therefore God's Word even if hearing we do not hear. And in the Bible it is surely the case that inspiration is used primarily of the act of the Holy Spirit in and through the authors, not the readers. . . . [In the readers] it is a work of enlightenment or illumination rather than inspiration. We may be grateful to Barth that he has directed our attention again to this aspect. We may join in prayer that the Spirit will breathe upon the Word and thus "inspire" it to us and for us. But we have still to recognize, have we not, that there is a prior work to which this present work is correlative, that the Spirit breathes upon a word which He has already inbreathed through the prophetic and apostolic authors. Otherwise it may be doubted whether all the safeguards that Barth genuinely proposes will preserve us from a final, radical subjectivism.[26]

3. *Truth Through Propositions*

We must not be misled by the claim that revelation does not mean truth *about* God, but that it means only the self-disclosure *of* God. It is often said today that divine revelation does not consist in propositional truths, that is, statements *about* the will and purposes of God. As we have already noted, evangelical scholars have always insisted that ultimately Christ himself is the Truth, the living Word, a Truth which may and must be known in personal experience. What we must not forget is that this personal experience becomes real through the faith conveyed in the form of propositions, statements of fact and meaning embodied in words. Jesus said: "But when the Comforter is come, whom I will send unto you from the Father, even the Spirit of truth, which proceedeth from the Father, he shall testify of me: and ye also shall bear witness, because ye have been with me from the beginning. . . . Neither pray I for these alone, but for them also which shall believe on me through their word" (John 15:26-27; 17:20). John adds, "But these are written, that ye might believe that Jesus is the Christ, the Son of God; and that believing ye might have life through his name" (20:31). What the apostles said and wrote is in the form of "propositional truth." Experience is always more than words can convey, but it can never be described or its meaning con-

---

26. "Barth's Doctrine of the Bible," *Christianity Today*, Vol. I, No. 6 (Dec. 24, 1956), p. 16.

veyed to others apart from propositions, as inadequate as these may be felt to be.[27]

4. *The Divine Authority of Scripture*

Finally, we need to take seriously the Christological analogy, of which we spoke earlier. The value of this analogy has been widely recognized. Thus Karl Barth wrote: "Like Jesus Christ Himself, the Holy Scripture is , in its own way and its own degree, true God and true Man, i.e., witness of the revelation, which itself belongs to the revelation, *and* historical literary document of a definite human-ity."[28] In the same vein, H. Emil Brunner said, "The Church must develop its doctrine of the Scriptures on the same lines as the doc-trine of the two natures. The Bible shares in the glory of the divinity of Christ and in the lowliness of His humanity."[29]

Both divinity and humanity are facts in the incarnate Word and in the inspired Word. Both must be recognized. That there is mystery in the Incarnation we cannot but admit. Yet its truth we gladly affirm. There is also mystery in the relation of divine and human in the Bible. But as the deity of our Lord was so related to His humanity as to preserve Him from sin, in a similar way the divinity (the in-spiration of the Spirit) of the Bible is so related to its humanity (its human authorship) as to preserve it from error and make it the trustworthy vehicle and integral part of revelation.

Although expressing some ideas one might wish to state differ-ently, J. K. S. Reid closes his study of the authority of Scripture with the statement:

> This authority, its nature and its locus, is on the whole well expressed by the phrase which simply says that the Bible is the Word of God. This may be accepted, if only for the reason that any other expression is less satisfactory. That the Bible *contains* the Word of God is also true in a sense, but it conveys a wrong impression. As Flacius says, salvation is not in the Bible like provi-sions in a sack which one can sling on his shoulder and take home. Nor can the Bible be divided into parts, a Word of God and

---

27. This is not to deny that some truth may be communicated through non-verbal symbols, and in artistic expressions. It may fairly be claimed, however, that truth about God is conveyed through verbal symbols arranged as logical propositions. Such are the data of theology.

28. *Kirchliche Dogmatik*, I/2, p. 555; quoted by James Barr in the *Scottish Journal of Theology*, Vol. XI, No. 1 (March, 1958), p. 86. See also the clear and strong statement in Wiley, *Christian Theology*, 1:187.

29. *Revelation and Reason*, p. 276; quoted by Reid, *Authority of Scripture*, p. 68.

its container. Since all is witness, there is a unity in the Bible that defies such partition. In fact, God marches up and down through the Bible magisterially, making His Word come to life at any point throughout its length and breadth. So too it is rightly enough said that the Bible *becomes* the Word of God. Yet this does not happen by haphazard but by God's action. Hence underneath this expression must be understood the truth that the Bible *is* the Word of God. Otherwise it is forgotten that the Bible becomes the Word of God by stated and steady appointment. At the same time, the expression conveys the truth that the Word of God really means God speaking, and that the Bible is the Word of God, not in the sense that God's Word is petrified in a dead record, but that the Bible itself is vivified by His living presence to convey what He has to say. Bible and Word of God are not two separate things, though they are distinguishable. The Bible is rightly said to be the Word of God and so to enjoy divine authority.[30]

SUMMARY

The importance of the Bible in the Christian faith has made this a necessary study. Belief in God is shared by many non-Christians. What is unique and important in Christianity is derived from the Scriptures, not from a minimum faith in the existence of God. Belief in God is the foundation stone, the starting place. However, until the superstructure of confidence in a divine revelation is raised upon that foundation, theism is little more than a rational answer to some of life's intellectual puzzles.

We have therefore considered God's revelation as His self-disclosure, making known himself and His redemptive purposes for man. This we found to be threefold: in history, supremely and perfectly in Christ, and in the truths of an inspired Scripture. But the Christian interpretation of the Bible, from which the content of our faith is derived, has a long and important history behind it. It is necessary, then, to go next to a brief survey of some of the historic interpretations of our Christian faith.

---

30. *Authority of Scripture,* pp. 278-79. See also Purkiser, "The Doctrine of the Word of God," Parts One and Two, *Nazarene Preacher,* Vol. 42, Nos. 1 and 2 (January and February, 1967), pp. 15-16; 45-57.

CHAPTER 4

Historic Interpretations of the Faith

We have seen that Christianity is a theistic faith with unique content derived from the special revelation of God in history and in His own Son as recorded in the Judaic-Christian Scriptures. The most casual survey of Christendom today reveals an almost bewildering array of denominations, churches, sects, and cults. Obvisouly the data of Scripture have been interpreted in various ways across the 20 centuries which have passed since Bible times.

It should be clear that any understanding of the Bible and its meaning today will of necessity reflect something of the great traditions that have grown up in the Christian world. None of us can "pull ourselves up by the roots," so to speak, and start our study with blank and unconditioned minds. We all read the Word of God through spectacles, as one has put it: "Doubtless there is no interpretation of the gospel possible in this age without wearing one of several pairs of spectacles. One of these pairs is that of Augustine as modified by Calvin and Luther. Another is that of Arius as modified by Socinus. Some wear the spectacles of Darwin and Herbert Spencer. Others wear those of James Arminius as modified by John Wesley."[1]

Our purpose in this chapter is to survey briefly some of the major interpretations given the message and meaning of Jesus from New Testament times. In part, this review will be concerned with church history; in part, with the history of theology. Only the high

---

1. Charles Ewing Brown, *The Meaning of Salvation* (Anderson, Ind.: The Warner Press, 1944), pp. xiii-xiv.

points can be considered, and those who are particularly interested may pursue further studies in the history of the Christian Church and the history of Christian doctrine.

I. THE APOSTOLIC PERIOD

A survey of the central Book of the Christian faith will reveal that it is actually a library of 66 different writings, composed over a period of some 15 centuries, relating briefly the origins of earth and its humanity, and somewhat more in detail the story of one family and nation throughout some 3,000 years. It is divided into two parts, one called the "Old" Testament or covenant, shared by Christians and Jews; and the other called the "New" Testament or covenant, written by and for Christians and those to whom the Christian gospel was to be presented. Further, Old and New Testaments will be found to be intimately and internally related. The Old Testament is incomplete, ending abruptly on a minor note, and finds its fulfillment in the New Testament. The New Testament, on its part, manifestly builds upon the foundation laid in the Old Testament. While written in a different language (Greek instead of Hebrew) and therefore using different verbal concepts, its basic thought patterns and religious attitudes are those of the Old Testament.[2] The Old Testament was the Scripture of the New Testament, and its "canon" or recognized list of authoritative books was complete a century or more before Christ.

A. New Testament Preaching

The books of the New Testament were all written within a generation of the events they describe, though possibly none of them sooner than 15 or 20 years after the crucifixion and resurrection of Jesus. Recent scholarship has emphasized that there are two kinds of material in the New Testament. These are called by their Greek names: *kerygma*, or the proclamation of the gospel to the non-Christian

---

2. This is important for understanding the New Testament and is presented, for example, in C. H. Dodd, *According to the Scriptures* (New York: Charles Scribner's Sons, 1953); Filson, *New Testament Against Its Environment;* Frederick C. Grant, *Introduction to New Testament Thought* (New York: Abingdon-Cokesbury Press, 1950), p. 73; Ethelbert Stauffer, *New Testament Theology.* Translated from the German by John Marsh. New York: The Macmillan Co., 1955), p. 18; and R. V. G. Tasker, *The Old Testament in the New Testament* (Philadelphia: Westminster Press, 1947), p. 13 ff.

world; and the *didache*, or teaching addressed to those who were already Christians, instructing them in matters of doctrine and ethics.[3] These two vital strands are interwoven throughout the books of the New Testament in varying proportions. Two of the Gospels illustrate this point. John 20:31, after indicating (v. 30) how much more could have been written in the Gospel than is actually given, states: "But these are written, that ye might believe that Jesus is the Christ, the Son of God; and *that believing ye might have life* through his name." Luke 1:3-4 says: "It seemed good to me also, having had perfect understanding of all things from the very first, to write unto thee *in order*, most excellent Theophilus, *that thou mightest know the certainty* of those things, wherein thou hast been instructed."

The outline of the *kerygma*, the evangelistic message of the Church, is seen most clearly in the sermons recorded in condensed form in the Acts: Peter's, Acts 2:14-40; 3:12-26; 4:8-12; 10:34-43; and Paul's, Acts 13:16-41. There are different ways of summarizing the themes which run through these sermons and through the balance of the New Testament, but the major points are:

1. The days foretold by prophets of old have come at last. God's promises to His ancient people are now being fulfilled in the Messiah. What has happened has been according to the Scriptures and in fulfillment of prophecy (Acts 2:14-21; 3:13, 22-25; 10:34-36; 13:16-26).

2. The Promised One is none other than Jesus of Nazareth, who was crucified by wicked hands. His suffering and death was foretold in the sovereign plan of God (Acts 2:22-23; 3:13-18; 4:8-10; 10:37-39; 13:27-29).

3. Him hath God raised up from the dead, again as foretold in Scripture. The Resurrection is the seal of certainty on all Christ said and did, and His victory over the forces of evil (Acts 2:24-32; 3:36; 10:40-41; 13:30-37).

4. The risen Christ is now exalted at the right hand of God, and shares the sovereignty of God, for He is both Lord and Christ—Lord being the term used in the Greek translation of the Old Testament (the Septuagint) to identify God himself (Acts 2:33, 34-36; 4:11).

5. The exalted Christ has shed forth the promise of the Father,

---

3. Cf. Dodd, *According to the Scriptures*; A. M. Hunter, *The Message of the New Testament* (Philadelphia: Westminster Press, 1944) and *Introducing New Testament Theology* (Philadelphia: Westminster Press, 1957); and James S. Stewart, *A Faith to Proclaim* (New York: Charles Scribner's Sons, 1953).

the gift of the Holy Spirit, upon His Church—"this, which ye now see and hear" (Acts 2:33).

6. Christ will come again from heaven and will judge men and nations, in the times of the restoration of all things—"It is he which was ordained of God to be the Judge of quick and dead" (Acts 10:42; cf. 3:20-21).

7. *Therefore*, repent, be converted and baptized, that your sins may be blotted out, and then you too shall receive the gift of the Holy Spirit. For there is no other salvation in any other name. "To him give all the prophets witness, that through his name whosoever believeth in him shall receive remission of sins" (Acts 10:43; cf. 2:37-40; 3:19; 4:12; 13:38-41).

This was the gospel, empowered by the Holy Spirit, which "turned the world upside down" (Acts 17:6). Around this solid core of proclamation gathered the *didache*, the teaching—that is, the explanation, interpretation, and application to life and conduct which, with the connecting history, makes up the balance of the New Testament.

B. Early Growth

During the lifetime of the apostles the gospel was carried throughout the Roman world, and according to tradition far beyond its borders. A number of the apostles themselves, including Peter and Paul, lost their lives in the bitter persecution of the Church begun by the Roman emperor Nero—a persecution continued intermittently over 250 years. During much of this time it was a capital crime merely to profess the faith of Jesus. But as always, "The blood of martyrs is the seed of the Church." Persecution, like water on an oil fire, only spread the blaze the more.

Our survey of the development of the faith since apostolic New Testament times will cover six additional periods: (2) The Patristic Period; (3) Augustine and the Catholic Church; (4) The Reformation: Luther and Calvin; (5) Arminius and the Remonstrants; (6) Wesley and the Evangelical Revival; and (7) Post-Wesleyan Developments to the Present Time.

II. THE PATRISTIC PERIOD

During what is called the patristic period (from the "fathers," as the early Christian leaders came to be known), Christianity both underwent its most severe persecution and enjoyed its most rapid growth. Some very significant trends in doctrine also began to emerge, as the early Christians attempted to give intellectual framework to the faith they had received through the New Testament writings and the apostolic preaching. No attempt is made to assign technical limits to the period, but for convenience it may be assumed to extend from the death of the apostle John to Augustine, about 300 years.

The spread of the Christian faith during these centuries is the miracle of history. "The March of Twelve Men," as it has been called, carried the Church as far northwest as Ireland, as far east as Persia and perhaps India, and south into Arabia and Africa. It is necessary to say a word about four features of this period: (1) the relations of Church and state; (2) ecclesiastical developments and the order of worship; (3) apologetics; and (4) the formulation of Christology.

A. Church and State

The earliest opposition to Christianity came from the Jewish Sanhedrin, and from leaders of Judaism in Gentile centers outside of Palestine. This is clearly seen in the account of the persecutions recorded in Acts. For the first 35 years the Roman authorities were either indifferent to the new religion or helped it by guaranteeing some measure of religious liberty. Judaism had been granted tolerance, and the new faith was regarded as a Jewish sect.

However, even before the end of the apostolic age, persecution from the imperial government began—based less on religious than on political and personal grounds. Nero began the earliest Roman persecution in A.D. 64, according to the Roman historian Tacitus, as a "red herring" to blame the Christians with a great fire in Rome which had been set by his orders but which aroused a great deal of popular fury. Church historians list 10 periods of persecution by the Roman authorities. Until the effort of Decius in A.D. 250 to stamp out Christianity throughout the entire empire, most of the persecutions, bitter though they were, were local and intermittent. Some of the brightest annals of Christendom record the unconquerable heroism of martyrs such as Justin, Polycarp, Simeon, Ignatius, Speratus, and hundreds of others known now to God alone.

About A.D. 250 the Decian persecution began, a brutal attempt to stamp out Christianity from the length and breadth of the Roman Empire. The motives of Decius and Valerian, who followed him, seem to have been political as much as anything else. Christians were blamed for the decay of Rome's internal strength and accused of disrupting its unity. However the real issue, from Nero to Diocletian, was the stubborn refusal of the Christians to render to Caesar that which was God's—willing though they were to render to Caesar the things that were Caesar's. Had the martyrs been willing to compromise their supreme loyalty to Christ, Christianity might have become just another Oriental sect, adding one more divinity to the multitude of gods Rome already knew.

The conversion of Constantine (A.D. 312) and his later emergence as sole emperor (A.D. 324) made Christianity the state religion of the empire. As has often been pointed out, this was not an unmixed blessing. Thousands were brought into the Church for prudential and political reasons without much knowledge of or personal faith in Jesus Christ. Influences were started which finally led to the emergence of the papacy, with its historic alliance of religious and political power.

B. The Church and Its Worship

This period also saw the growth of church government and the beginnings of liturgy in worship. The New Testament mentions elders or bishops, and deacons, as officers of the church. Originally, elders governed the local group, providing for its worship and discipline. With the death of the apostles and those fathers who had been companions of the apostles, elders known particularly as bishops began to take greater responsibility and leadership. In part, this was a necessary step to give the Church an authoritative voice in meeting such heresies as early Gnosticism. The bishops of the larger centers gradually assumed authority over congregations in the rural areas around, and quite early the bishop of Rome was given greater respect than others.

From a very simple worship based on the synagogue service of the Jews and including prayer, praise, the reading of Scripture, and a sermon, a more formal liturgy developed. The Lord's Supper and baptism took larger place, and the instruction of converts and interested inquirers began. The canon of the New Testament was settled. Special church buildings were used and ritual became more elaborate. Spiritually, there were both light and dark. Along with vital piety there was much nominal religion, lax in morals and indifferent in doctrine. Yet withal distinctive Christian attitudes existed. Tertullian in his *Apology* late in the second century defends Christians against false charges, and indicates that they abstain from the immodesty and immoral life of the theater, the cruelties of the arena, and the drunkenness and wild festive parties of their pagan neighbors. They provide for the poor, the aged, and orphans with one mind and soul. He says, "We have everything in common except our wives."[4]

C. The Growth of Apologetics

The Apostolic Church was a preaching Church. It had a message of salvation to proclaim, a message which it did not argue but was content to set forth with prophetic zeal. It was not long, however, until Christianity came under attack from pagan philosophers. Early Christians began to think out the implications of their faith and to defend its truth against all comers. Philosophers who were themselves converted, as for example Justin Martyr, found in Christianity not only salvation for their souls but satisfaction for the questionings of their minds. These defenses of the faith were called "Apologies." The writings of Justin, Aristides, Tertullian, and later Augustine's *City of God* may be mentioned.

The apologists not only defended Christianity; they attacked paganism with great vigor. They made much of the contrast between Christian and pagan in life and morals, pointing out the immorality ascribed to the gods in Roman and Greek myths, and the sensuality and stupidity of polytheistic worship.[5]

D. The Establishment of Christology

Possibly the greatest achievement of this early period, apart from the propagation of the redemptive gospel itself, was the formulation of the doctrine of Christ, and with it the concept of the Trinity. The New Testament writers had provided the materials in their clear-cut affirmation of the oneness of God, the unqualified diety of Christ, and the personality and deity of the Holy Spirit. To put these truths together was the great theological achievement of the clear thinking

---

4. Cf. Cyril C. Richardson, *The Church Through the Centuries* (New York: Charles Scribner's Sons, 1938), pp. 16-17. See also the ideal held by Cyprian described on p. 41. See also the excellent survey of this period in Robert A. Baker, *A Summary of Christian History* (Nashville, Tenn.: Broadman Press, 1959), pp. 13-54; and the briefer account in Archibald G. Baker, editor, *A Short History of Christianity* (Chicago: The University Press, 1974), pp. 17-32.

5. Cf. the brief descriptions in Kenneth Scott Latourette, *A History of Christianity* (New York: Harper and Brothers, 1953), pp. 83-84; and Justo L. Gonzalez, *A History of Christian Thought* (Nashville: Abingdon Press, 1970), 1:98-122.

and vigorous debate which led up to the Council of Nicea (A.D. 325) and on to the Council of Chalcedon (A.D. 451).

The occasion for the Council of Nicea was the teaching of Arius of Alexandria, who held that, while Christ was the first and highest of creatures, He was not eternal and He was not of the nature of God. Contending with Arius was Athanasius, later bishop of Alexandria, but only about 25 years of age at the time of the Council. He saw clearly that the issue at stake was the distinctiveness of Christianity and the reality of the Incarnation. He recognized that to worship a Christ who is not quite God is to open the door to the return to polytheism.

The victory finally went to Athanasius, and the Council adopted a creed, part of which reads:

> We believe in one God, the Father Almighty, maker of all things visible and invisible, and in one Lord, Jesus Christ, the Son of God, the only-begotten of the Father, that is, of the substance of the Father, God from God, light from light, true God from true God, begotten, not made, of one substance with the Father. . . . who for us men and for our salvation came down and was made flesh, suffered, rose again on the third day, ascended into the heavens, and will come to judge the living and the dead.[6]

Arianism did not die. It struggled on, and periodically reappears in theology, as it has in recent modernism or liberalism. But the Nicene Creed established the standard for the normative Christian understanding of Christ throughout the ages.

While Nicea ruled on the deity of Jesus, the Council of Chalcedon, a little over a century later, struggled with the concept of the Incarnation or the union of the divine and human natures of Christ —His deity and His humanity. Chalcedon was called to resolve controversies that had existed from the earliest Christian centuries. Its *Definition of Faith* attempted to make precise what had been understood in general terms for 200 years. Christ is declared to be of "the same nature with the Father as to his Godhead, and the [same nature] with us as to his manhood."[7]

III. AUGUSTINE AND THE CATHOLIC CHURCH

It is impossible to do justice to a great philosopher-theologian and to

---

6. Latourette, *History of Christianity*, p. 155.

7. Translation by Sellers, quoted in Gonzales, *History of Christian Thought*, 1:390.

a thousand years of church history in so few pages. Only the briefest summary can be given.

A. Augustine (354-430)

Augustine of Hippo in north Africa achieved eminence in two fields, philosophy and theology. His spiritual pilgrimage led him through godless sensuality, Manicheism (a strange mixture of Parseeism, Buddhism, and Christianity), neo-Platonism, total skepticism, and finally through the preaching of Bishop Ambrose of Milan and the study of Paul's writings, to Christ and the faith of his godly mother, Monica. So many and varied were Augustine's writings that widely differing influences stem from his thought. We can name but three.

1. *Augustine and Pelagius*

In his controversy with a British monk by the name of Pelagius, Augustine contended for what has come to be known as the doctrine of original sin. While in the heat of debate each contestant may have been driven farther than he might otherwise have gone,[8] the fact remains that Augustine established deep in Christian thought the conviction that salvation is by grace alone, a grace given to creatures who have inherited a racial predisposition to sin, and who therefore could never in themselves please God.

2. *Predestination*

Augustine's doctrine of grace led him to another position which is much more debatable. It is that God has, of His own great mercy and by His own free choice, predestined some to salvation and others to damnation, and that the number of the elect is fixed and certain and cannot be changed. Those whom God has elected will be saved and persevere, and if they sin they will repent, although no one can know for sure that he is among the elect.[9]

It is hard to see how the determinism to which this view leads could be derived from Scripture, apart from reading back into such New Testament terms as *proorizo* and *ekloge* meanings which actually come from the pagan philosophies to which Augustine had been exposed before his conversion. It is true that other church fathers

---

8. Cf. the analysis by E. L. Cherbonnier, *Hardness of Heart* (Garden City, N.Y.: Doubleday and Co., Inc., 1955), pp. 85-145; and the briefer account in Gonzalez, *History of Christian Thought,* 2:27-32.

9. Cf. Latourette, *History of Christianity,* pp. 178-79; Gonzalez, *History of Christian Thought,* 2:42-47.

occasionally hinted at similar views, but the real source of these notions would seem to be pagan rather than Judaic or Christian. God's election and predestination. as we shall see in a later chapter, are His gracious provision for and purpose to save all who savingly believe on the Lord Jesus Christ, and not an arbitrary prelimitation.

3. The Concept of the Church

It will be noted that Augustine's doctrine of predestination was picked up and stressed by Calvin and some of the reformers. On the other hand, Augustine's understanding of the Church became the foundation upon which the papacy was raised, identifying the Church which is the channel through which grace comes to men with a particular institution, the Roman Catholic church.

For Augustine, the Catholic church was the only means of grace, and its sacraments were acts of God whereby men could alone be saved. Other contributions of his thought to Catholic dogma are the place of church tradition along with Scripture as a rule of faith; an emphasis on baptismal regeneration; and a doctrine of the sinlessness of the Virgin Mary which has contributed to Mariolatry, or the worship of Mary.[10]

B. The Growth of Roman Catholicism

We have already noted the growing importance of the episcopate, or bishops, in the great centers of the Christian community, and in particular the leadership of the bishop of Rome. As early as the end of the second century we find Irenaeus, bishop of Lyons, claiming that the bishop of Rome was in an unbroken line of bishops appointed by Peter and Paul. The actual claim of the bishop of Rome to jurisdiction over the whole Christian Church was first made at the Council of Sardica in A.D. 343. By A.D. 500, the title "papa" or pope, which all the Western bishops had held, was limited to the bishop of Rome and the papacy began a rapid growth.

Actually, papal power developed in the vacuum left by the fall of the imperial authority in Rome when the city fell before Alaric and the Goths in A.D. 410. Several early popes acquired great political and economic power, and began the close alliance of church and state so typical of the medieval period.

---

10. Henry Cowan, *Landmarks of Church History to the Reformation* (New edition, revised and enlarged; New York: Fleming H. Revell, n.d.), p. 46; R. Baker, *Summary of Christian History,* 55-143.

Several other developments may be noted briefly. One is the growth of monasticism, or the retreat from society into monasteries and convents, and the rise of the orders of monks which became chief sources of strength for the papacy. The Benedictine order (A.D. 529), the friars or mendicant orders such as the Franciscans, the Dominicans, the Carmelites, and the Augustinians, and later the Jesuits are all typical of this aspect of Catholicism. Papal power and some distinctive Roman Catholic dogmas received tremendous impetus under Pope Gregory the Great (540-604), who revised the ritual (Gregorian chants, for example), stated definitively the doctrine of purgatory with masses for the dead, paved the way for the doctrine of transubstantiation (the actual presence of the body and blood of the Lord in the Mass), and furthered the veneration of relics of the apostles and saints.

During the centuries that passed, the Roman church grew powerful and wealthy. By 1000 all of Europe, with minor exceptions, was nominally Christian. (The Eastern branch of the Church had maintained some degree of independence, and the division into Roman Catholic and Greek Orthodox became final about 1350.) Wealth and magnificence led to corruption and spiritual decay. Religion became almost entirely a matter of the sacraments and tended to have less and less influence over life. The abuses which finally led to the Reformation were deep-seated and real.

Yet the Lord did not leave himself without a witness. Vital piety could still be found in out-of-the-way places. Among those great souls known as the mystics (not to be confused with pantheistic mysticism) the cultivation of the presence of God was earnestly practiced, and not in vain. Some of the great names of this movement are Bernard of Clairvaux, Francis of Assisi, Bonaventura, Raymond Lull, Hildegarde, Hugo of St. Victor, John "Meister" Eckhart, and John Staupitz, the Augustinian vicar-general whose influence on Martin Luther was so great.

IV. The Reformation

The Reformation involved vast movements of the human spirit which penetrated every area of life, social, cultural, political, and philosophical, as well as religious. It is with the distinctively religious aspect of the 16th century that we are primarily concerned. Four major movements combine to form the Reformation.

A. Luther and Justification by Faith

Martin Luther was born in 1483 at Eisleben in Germany. At the age of 22, while he was a law student at the University of Erfurt, where he had already received the degree of master of arts, the sudden death of a friend and a frightening experience in a thunderstorm awakened his sense of sin and led him to the study of theology in an Augustinian monastery.

The path to peace was a rugged one, and Luther's inner struggles continued through his ordination as a priest in 1507, his assignment to the University of Wittenberg, where he became doctor of theology, and a visit to Rome in 1511, where the evident corruption of the papal court deeply disgusted him. At last a phrase from Rom. 1:17 brought him the confidence in which he was to live and preach through the years of peril and toil which lay ahead: "The just shall live by faith." Justification by faith alone became the keystone of the Reformation.

The foundation for the Reformation was laid in Luther's spiritual experience. The occasion for its launching was the appearance of the Dominican monk by the name of Tetzel, who was raising money allegedly to build the new St. Peter's Cathedral in Rome. Tetzel was selling "indulgences," a kind of prepaid ethical money order drawn on the treasury of the merit of the saints, and popularly supposed to bring forgiveness of sins without either penance or repentance. This was more than Luther could stand, and on October 31, 1517, he posted his famous 95 theses on the door of the castle church in Wittenberg vigorously attacking the whole idea of indulgences based on the accumulated surplus merits of the saints.

The story of Luther's part in the Reformation has been told often and well.[11] Here it is enough to note that Luther's writings consistently set forth the basic principles on which Protestantism has since stood. These include: justification by faith alone, the supremacy of Scripture as the sole source of faith and morals, the universal priesthood of believers, and the right and duty of each Christian to read and understand the Bible. One of Luther's most notable achievements was the translation of the Scriptures into the German of his day.

---

11. Cf., e.g., R. H. Bainton, *Here I Stand. A Life of Martin Luther* (New York: Abingdon-Cokesbury Press, 1950). The story of the counter reformation, or more properly "the Catholic Reformation," is best told in Gonzalez, *History of Christian Thought*, Vol. III (1975), 3:178-255.

B. Calvin and the Reformed Churches

Contemporaneous with the work of Luther in Germany was that of Huldreich Zwingli (1484-1531) in Switzerland, which resulted in the development of what are known as the Reformed churches as distinguished from the Lutheran. The basis of Zwingli's break with Romanism was much the same as Luther's. He opposed indulgences, the existence of purgatory, the sacrificial value of the Mass, clerical celibacy, salvation by good works, and the intercession of the saints.

The outstanding Reformed leader was John Calvin (1509-64), a young Frenchman who had come under Protestant influence in Paris and had been converted there, and who came to Basel in Switzerland in 1534 and later settled in Geneva where he ministered for a total of 25 years. He early published his *Institutes of the Christian Religion,* which was revised four times by its author before his death, and which has ever since been one of the most influential works in Christian theological literature.

Calvin had read deeply in the works of the Stoics before his conversion (his first book being a commentary on Seneca's *De Clementia*). He was impressed by and gave large place to Augustine's doctrine of predestination with its corollary of the perseverance of the elect. His system was rigidly coherent, which perhaps helps to account for its influence. It was based on the absolute sovereignty of God, who disposes of each man according to the inscrutable decrees of His eternal counsel. It represents an attempt to set the Stoic theological determinism in a Christian framework without the pantheism of the pagan philosophy. It is to be doubted whether such an attempt could succeed.

The Reformed churches gained great strength in Switzerland, in Holland, and in Scotland, where the Church of Scotland and Presbyterianism accepted Calvinism. What is known as "moderate" Calvinism enjoys a widespread following among evangelical Christians in England and the United States.

C. Anglicanism

A third Reformation movement occurred in England. Its roots go back to John Wycliffe (c. 1320-84) and his followers, the Lollards. Its immediate historical occasion was the desire of England's King Henry VIII to have his marriage to Catholic princess Catharine of Aragon annulled so he could legally marry Anne Boleyn. When the Pope staunchly refused, Henry secured an act of Parliament in 1534 separating the church in England from papal control and declaring Henry himself to be the supreme head of the Church of England.

The development of Protestant convictions in England was slow and often mixed with political motivations. Gradually a distinctive liturgy was formed, and a theological climate developed out of which came the significant developments of the evangelical revival in the 18th century. As an "established" or state church, the Church of England (as well as the Episcopalianism that developed from it in the new world) has always been hospitable to a broad range of theological and liturgical positions.

D. The Anabaptists and the "Radical" Reformation

The Anabaptists derived their name from their insistence on personal conversion and the rebaptism of converts who had been baptized as infants (Greek, *ana-*, again; *baptizein*, to baptize). A wide range of opinion and practice was included under this name, but in general the Anabaptists urged a return to primitive Christianity and rejected traditional institutions of the church.

In contrast to the national or established churches, such as Lutheran, Anglican, and (in certain areas) Reformed, the Anabaptists preached individual conversion and the voluntary association of believers in local churches. They were regarded as dangerous radicals and bitterly persecuted not only by the Roman church but by their Lutheran and Calvinistic compatriots and martyred by the hundreds.

Most of the Anabaptist leaders were sober and able men, but the movement had a "lunatic fringe" that stood for violent revolution and establishment of the "kingdom of God" by military might. Many believed themselves living in the last days and believed themselves chosen by God to set up His rule on earth by whatever means necessary. Others took the opposite view and became complete pacifists. The plus contribution of the Anabaptists to the development of Protestantism was to provide an alternative to the state or established church. These "free" churches flourished and multiplied thoughout Protestant realms.

V. ARMINIUS AND THE REMONSTRANTS

Both Luther and Calvin accepted the Augustinian idea of divine predestination and the unconditional sovereignty of God. Calvin had stated it clearly in his *Institutes of the Christian Religion:* "We call predestination God's eternal decree, by which He determined with Himself what He willed to become of each man. For all are not created in equal condition; rather, eternal life is foreordained for some, eternal damnation for others. Therefore, as any man has been created to one or the other of these ends we speak of him as predestined to life or to death."[12]

Reformed theologians immediately following Calvin placed more and more emphasis on this view of predestination. But reaction arose, particularly in Holland. Jacob (or James) Arminius (1560-1609) was a pastor in Amsterdam, later chosen professor of theology at the University of Leyden. He had come into conflict with the hyper-Calvinists first over his interpretation of the seventh chapter of Romans, which he took to be the picture of an awakened but as yet unregenerate person struggling against the power of sin in his life. He also questioned the Calvinistic concept of the sovereignty of God, the doctrines of election and predestination, a limited atonement (that Christ died only for the elect), and the perseverance of the saints.[13] These views, he held, questioned the justice of God, made Him the source of sin, and could not be harmonized with the gospel of universal grace.

After Arminius' untimely death, the cause was taken up by Simon Episcopius, successor to Arminius in the chair of theology at Leyden, and Hugo Grotius, a noted jurist. The movement thus begun became known as the Remonstrant cause (from a publication in 1610 titled the *Remonstrance*, advocating its positions). It was later called Arminianism.

In the debate between the Remonstrants and the strict Calvinists which raged for some years until the Synod of Dort in 1618, the famous "Five Points" emerged. The Calvinistic position advocated: (1) unconditional election—that God has chosen those He will save without respect to or foreknowledge of personal faith and obedience on their part; (2) a limited atonement; (3) total depravity—that man

---

12. 3.21.4; cf. the excerpt in Hans J. Hillerbrand, editor, *The Protestant Reformation* (New York: Harper and Row, Publishers, 1968), pp. 179-213.

13. Cf. the definitive treatment in Carl Bangs, *Arminius: A Study in the Dutch Reformation* (Nashville: Abingdon Press, 1971). Dr. Bangs, in an unpublished Ph.D. dissertation, shows that a widely held view that Arminius suddenly changed his position while attempting to refute the hyper-Calvinists is not based on reliable evidence. Rather, his views developed gradually from his very early student years. He represented a moderate alternative to the extreme positions of Beza and Gomarus that already had some considerable following in Holland.

is incapable of favorable response to the grace of God apart from a specific gift of faith; (4) irresistible grace—that those who are elect will be brought to faith by the sovereign action of God; and (5) the perseverance of the saints—that those who are elect and regenerated can never be lost. This is often referred to as the TULIP theology— each letter representing one of the five points: Total depravity; Unconditional election; Limited atonement; Irresistible grace; and Perseverance of the saints.[14]

The Arminian position was almost directly counter at each of these points: (1) election conditioned on personal faith, (2) a universal atonement, (3) the inability of men to exercise saving faith without the universal prevenient grace of God, (4) the sufficiency of grace, and (5) the possibility of a lapse from grace. The Synod, predominantly Calvinistic, condemned the Remonstrants, excluded them from the church, and exiled some from the country.[15]

This was not the end of Arminianism. It is significant that several of its "points" have been adopted by many of those who trace their theological ancestry back to John Calvin. In its full-robed form it became the theology of John Wesley and of Methodism, as well as of those evangelical denominations which have taken their inspiration from the Wesleyan revival.

VI. THE EVANGELICAL REVIVAL: JOHN WESLEY

John Wesley (1703-91) exemplifies what has been called "Arminianism on fire."[16] Wesley's background and training was that of the "high" Church of England, devoted to ritual, rigid in the observance of fasts and religious exercises, and methodical (whence, eventually, "Methodist") in personal piety. His spiritual odyssey is a thrilling story, illustrating again the inability of orthodoxy and ritual to bring peace to the soul. His conversion in the meeting of the little society in Aldersgate Street, May 24, 1738, was the beginning of his great contribution to what history knows as "The Evangelical Revival."[17]

---

14. In addition to Bangs, cf. the treatment in Gonzalez, *History of Christian Thought*, 2:254-62.

15. Andrew C. Zenos, *Compendium of Church History* (Philadelphia: Presbyterian Board of Publication, 1896), pp. 250-51.

16. Cf. George Park Fisher, *History of Christian Doctrine* (New York: Charles Scrib-

17. Cf. the vivid description of Wesley's life in T. Crichton Mitchell, *Mr. Wesley* (Kansas City: Beacon Hill Press of Kansas City, 1957), pp. 9-96.

While Aldersgate Street is a well-known experience, not quite so well known is the outstanding spiritual crisis in December, 1744, after five years of street and field preaching, seeking earnestly to be entirely devoted to God in every department of his being. T. Crichton Mitchell describes it:

His spirit is revealed in the hymn:

> *O Love divine, how sweet Thou art!*
> *When shall I find this longing heart*
> *All taken up by Thee?*

Seeking such entire devotement, Wesley came to a great spiritual crisis in December, 1744. For two days he had been strangely lifeless, but as he was reading prayers at Snowsfields on December 24, something happened. He describes it in language as clear as that for Aldersgate, although not so detailed or extended: "I found such light and strength as I never remembered to have had before. I saw every thought, as well as action or word, just as it was rising in my heart; and whether it was right before God, or tainted with pride or selfishness. I never knew before, (. . . not as at this time) what it was to be still before God.

"I waked, by the grace of God, in the same spirit; and about eight, being with two or three that believed in Jesus, I felt such an awe and tender sense of the presence of God as greatly confirmed me therein: so that God was before me all the day long. I sought and found him in every place; and could truly say, when I lay down at night, 'Now I have lived a day!'"

Now Wesley was most reticent on the publicizing of his inner experiences. He may have erred on that side for a number of reasons; but surely here, if anywhere, is a man witnessing to a new work of God in his heart and to the flooding of his soul by the love of God.[18]

As indicated, Wesley was Arminian in theology, although his friend and early colaborer, George Whitefield, was a Calvinist. The

---

18. *Ibid.,* pp. 58-59. Concerning this quotation from the *Journal,* Dr. Olin A. Curtis says: "To anyone familiar with John Wesley's careful, realistic manner of speech, it is evident that we have here the same sort of testimony to the experience of holiness that we have in his Journal, May 24, 1738, to the experience of conversion. If the one is not quite so near a full definition as the other, it surely is just as expressive of the fact. I find it almost impossible to read Wesley's words in the light of all his later utterance about the doctrine of Christian perfection, and not consider this date, December 24, 1744, as the probable time when he began to love God supremely" (*The Christian Faith* [New York: Methodist Book Concern, 1903], p. 376). The whole treatment, pp. 374-84, is worthy of careful study. Cf. also George Allen Turner, *The Vision Which Transforms: Is Christian Perfection Scriptural?* (Kansas City: Beacon Hill Press of Kansas City, 1964), pp. 214-19. A different and more cautious interpretation is given by John Peters, *Christian Perfection and American Methodism* (New York: Abingdon Press, 1956), pp. 201-15.

societies and later the churches which stemmed from Wesley's ministry were from the beginning predominantly Arminian. It is to be noted, however, that while Dutch Arminianism was soon modified by Socinianism (denial of the Trinity) and Pelagianism, Wesley held ruggedly to a Trinitarian theology and to salvation by grace alone. His contest with Calvinism was based upon his conviction that the love of God in saving grace is offered to all men freely. He staunchly rejected all predestinarian views. As Burtner and Chiles comment:

> God's love is poured out on all men who will be made whole by its power. Any conception that implicitly or explicitly denies this distorts Christianity. Salvation by grace through faith does not permit view of God's sovereignty and justice which are not consonant with His mercy and love. Thus Wesley attacks election most vehemently on the basis of a conception of God in which love is dominant and a despotic deity unthinkable.[19]

Charles Wesley expressed his brother's view as well as his own when he described in verse the implications of Calvinistic predestination:

> *The righteous God consigned*
> *Them over to their doom;*
> *Then sent the Saviour of mankind*
> *To damn them from the womb!*
>
> *To damn for falling short*
> *Of what they could not do!*
> *For not believing the report*
> *Of that which was not true!*
>
> . . . .
>
> *Good God! That any child of Thine*
> *So horribly should think of Thee!*
> *Lo, all my hopes I here resign*
> *If all may not find grace with me!*[20]

Within this Arminian framework, Wesley developed two vitally important and distinctive doctrines, both of which he found in the New Testament, and in what had been a neglected strand of Christian teaching through the centuries.

---

19. Robert W. Burtner and Robert E. Chiles, *A Compend of Wesley's Theology* (New York: Abingdon Press, 1954), p. 43.

20. Mitchell, *Mr. Wesley*, p. 70.

A. The Doctrine of Assurance

A striking feature of Wesley's own experience of conversion became one of the pillars of the Evangelical Revival. It was the sense of assurance of salvation conveyed in the expression "the witness of the Spirit." He defines this witness as "an inward impression on the soul, whereby the Spirit of God directly witnesses with my spirit that I am a child of God; that Jesus hath loved me and given Himself for me; that all my sins are blotted out and I, even I, am reconciled to God."[21] This was a new and thrilling note in an age in which the majority of Christians despaired of such confidence.

That assurance is the birthright of every believer, Wesley preached everywhere. He states, "If it were possible . . . to shake the traditional evidence of Christianity, still he that hath the internal evidence (and every true believer hath the witness or evidence in himself) would stand firm and unshaken." The same note appears in the Wesleyan hymns:

> *What we have felt and seen*
> *With confidence we tell!*
>
> *The Spirit answers to the Blood*
> *And tells me I am born of God.*
>
> *The pledge of future bliss*
> *He now to us imparts;*
> *His gracious Spirit is*
> *The earnest in our hearts.*[22]

B. Christian Perfection or Perfect Love

Even more fundamental in Wesley's ministry was the doctrine of Christian perfection, or the term which he preferred, perfect love. Sanctification had been a neglected theme in Protestant theology up to Wesley's time. When considered at all, it had been conceived as a gradual and never-ending process in which the believer was more and more freed from sin. Wesley insisted that entire sanctification by faith was both possible and imperative now. Just a year before his death he wrote of the centrality of holiness: "This doctrine is the

---

21. Sermon on "The Witness of the Spirit," *Sermons* (1852 ed.), 1:87.
22. Mitchell, *Mr. Wesley*, pp. 74-75.

grand depositum which God has lodged with the people called Methodists; and for the sake of propagating this chiefly He appears to have raised us up."[23]

The term perfection, then as now, has been a stumbling block, but Wesley clearly explained that he did not consider perfection as freedom from ignorance, error, infirmities, or temptation. It is perfection of love, bringing deliverance from inner sin. It is "that habitual disposition of soul which . . . is termed holiness; and which directly implies, the being cleansed from sin, 'from all filthiness both of flesh and spirit'; and by consequence, the being endued with those virtues which were also in Christ Jesus; the being so 'renewed in the spirit of our minds' as to be 'perfect as our Father in heaven is perfect.'"[24] As Dr. Mitchell summarizes:

> To think of Christian perfection as only freedom from sin is to do despite to Wesley's message. He meant much more than that. Always he is positive about its being a sacrifice of the spirit "continually offered up to God, through Christ, in flames of holy love." Learn his wise counsel: "Let your soul be filled with so entire a love of Him that you may love nothing but for His sake." This is the circumcision of the heart; this is Christian perfection. It is sin removed from the soul of man and the heart made perfect in love toward God and all men. This is "the second blessing properly so-called."
>
> In a letter to Mrs. Adam Clarke, Wesley wrote: ". . . as to the image of God, how soon you may be a partaker of sanctification! And not only by a slow and insensible growth in grace, but by the power of the Highest overshadowing you, in a moment, in the twinkling of an eye, so as to utterly abolish sin and to renew you in the whole image . . . why may you not receive it now?"
>
> Wesley saw this doctrine verified in scores of witnesses up and down the land. He interviewed many people who were simple and ordinary men and women claiming quietly but confidently that this priceless gift of God's grace was in them. He wrote to Charles, "I think I see a hundred witnesses." He urged his preachers to keep spreading this message. He devoted whole conferences to considering the implications of the message and how best to present it, and insisted that where it was not preached "the work languished." He kept his people singing the hymns about it, and ever kept the central tenet of his message before them.

23. *Ibid.,* p. 75. See the careful studies, both growing out of Ph.D. dissertations, by Turner, *Vision Which Transforms;* and Leo G. Cox, *John Wesley's Concept of Perfection* (Kansas City: Beacon Hill Press of Kansas City, 1964).

24. Quoted, *ibid.,* p. 76.

> Give me a new, a perfect heart,
>> From doubt and fear and sorrow free;
>> _ The mind which was in Christ impart,
>> And let my spirit cleave to Thee.

Or again:

> A heart in every thought renewed,
>> And full of love divine,
>> Perfect and right and pure and good,
>> A copy, Lord, of Thine!

And this:

> Thy blood makes us clean both without and within;
> It conquers the world, and the devil, and sin.[25]

VII. POST-WESLEYAN DEVELOPMENTS

To describe the development of Christianity during the 19th and 20th centuries is a task which would require volumes. The closer we live to any historical period, the more difficult it is to assess its major contributions and enduring values. Kenneth Scott Latourette, whose concept of church history is that it is a record of periodic advance and recession, has dubbed 1815 to 1914 "The Great Century," a time of abounding vitality and unprecedented expansion, offset only by a growing materialism and secularism.[26] Many new Protestant denominations arose, and the genesis of a number of significant trends and movements is found within that century. The holiness movement, of which the Church of the Nazarene is the most numerous organized denomination, became the chief legatee of Methodism's "depositum" of the New Testament doctrine of entire sanctification. Other holiness denominations include the Brethren in Christ, Churches of Christ in Christian Union, Evangelical Church of North America, Evangelical Friends Alliance, Evangelical Methodist Church, Free Methodist Church, Holiness Christian Church of the U.S.A., The Wesleyan Church, and the Salvation Army. The above are members of the Christian Holiness Association. Denominations cooperating with the CHA are the Church of God (Anderson), Congregational Methodist church, the Holiness Methodist church, the Methodist Protestant church, and the Primitive Methodist church.

From the standpoint of evangelical Protestantism, some of the

---

25. *Ibid.*, pp. 76-77.
26. *History of Christianity*, pp. 1063-1345.

trends since the First World War have seemed promising. We have earlier considered the changing climate in biblical studies and theology, which is a decided improvement over the older humanistic liberalism. Many smaller denominations have arisen and grown with amazing rapidity, moving into the spiritual vacuum which had been left by religiously sterile modernism. A new interest in evangelism, personal and mass, as the supreme task of the Church is being widely shown. Significant developments have occurred in evangelical circles including the emergence of a neoevangelical thrust and the rise of Pentecostalism and the charismastic movement.

The leaven of biblical religion is at work in the last quarter of the 20th century. Leaven, by bulk, may be small, but its power is great and its presence indispensable (Matt. 13:33). Whether He come soon or late in terms of our lifetime, when our Lord comes, He *will* find faith in the earth (Luke 18:8).

SUMMARY

We have given brief consideration to seven periods in the development of Christianity since New Testament times. Each has made its distinctive and lasting contribution to our understanding of theology. Each is important for our grasp of the Christian faith as we know it today.

However, there are "untold millions who are dying untold" about the gospel of Christ. Christianity has its rivals in the world. We shall next give consideration to the other world religions and their relation to our Christian faith.

CHAPTER 5

Christianity and the Religions of Mankind

Christian concern about other religions is based on two motives. The first is the evangelistic or missionary motive, which is central to the Christian faith itself. Essntially, Christianity is not a body of beliefs to be argued. It is a message to be proclaimed. It is the good news of what God has done and is doing in Christ to reconcile the world unto himself. As such it concerns not only those in the West who have "inherited" the Christian faith, but all men everywhere. The second is the demand of personal conviction that alternatives be considered. No one can be quite sure of his own positions until he has some knowledge of the major contenders in the field.

Both motives justify a chapter on the relationship between Christianity and other world religions. Christians are commanded to go into all the world, preaching the gospel to every creature, teaching all nations to observe what Christ commanded (Mark 16:14; Matt. 28:19-20). But the world is found immediately to be a religious world. Many of these religions will be seen to be local and without particular interest in spreading beyond the nationalities or races in which they had their origins. But at least two of them are "missionary religions," rivals of Christianity for global adherence. To fulfill the task implied in being a Christian and to strengthen conviction in the finality of the gospel, it is important to know something of other world religions.

We have defined religion in an earlier chapter as man's quest for a right relationship with what he conceives to be ultimate or the most worthwhile in life. Simply, it is man's search for God, however ignorantly worshiped or inadequately conceived. In this sense, there have been and are a multitude of religions. It is extremely doubtful if there is any tribe anywhere which does not have some sort of religious observance, some concept of the reality of the divine. The number and variety of religions which have and do exist testify eloquently to the native hunger of the human soul for God.

No attempt will be made to catalog completely the religions of the world. John Clark Archer listed 12 "living faiths," although the number could well be enlarged by breaking down some into distinct subspecies: Primitivism, Taoism, Confucianism, Shinto, Hinduism (including Brahmanism), Jainism, Buddhism, Parsiism (or Zoroastrianism), Sikhism, Judaism, Islam (Mohammedanism), and Christianity.[1] Six of this number each claim more than 100 million adherents. In order of decreasing size these are Christianity, Confucianism, Islam, Hinduism, Primitivism (the religious practices and beliefs of the undeveloped or "primitive" tribes), and Buddhism.[2] The unfinished task of the Christian Church is clearly seen in the fact that two-thirds of the earth's population still has not even a nominal relationship with the gospel of Christ.

Apart from size, probably the most significant of the "ethnic" or racial religions, as they are called, are Buddhism, Mohammedanism, Hinduism, Taoism, Confucianism, and Shintoism. Of this six, two—Buddhism and Mohammedanism—are the missionary religions: that is, religions with the avowed aim of making converts in other than the national or racial group with which they started.[3]

Liberals tend to view the Hebrew-Christian faith as one religion among others: better, and more refined, perhaps, but stemming from the same forces at work in human nature which have given rise to the other racial religions. According to this view, the alleged uniqueness of Christianity is discounted and the values of other religions emphasized in comparison. Evangelism loses its significance as a goal for missionary activity, if indeed there is to be any such activity, and humanitarian efforts at civilizing or Westernizing less privileged people becomes the chief objective.

In contrast, conservative Christianity stands for the belief that in man's search for God, Christ alone is the Way, and that all other

1. *Faiths Men Live By* (New York: Thomas Nelson and Sons, 1934), p. 1.

2. *Ibid.*, p. 2.

3. August Karl Reischauer in *The Great Religions of the Modern World,* ed. by Edward J. Jurji (Princeton, N.J.: Princeton University Press, 1946), p. 90.

paths must lead to futility. This does not necessarily mean the denial of all values in other religions. No system of belief which is entirely wrong would ever gain an appreciable following. It does mean that the Christian recognizes no continuity or equality between his faith and others. Other religions testify to the universality of human need, the hunger of the heart for God. Christianity proclaims Christ as the only Way to meet that need, the supreme revelation of God to man. As D. T. Niles puts it:

> The Christian message cannot be grafted upon other beliefs or added to them. There is only one way in which the Christian message can be accepted and that is by a radical conversion to it, so radical that the New Testament speaks of it as a new birth (John 3:3; I Pet. 1:3), the coming into being of a new creation (II Cor. 5:17), a dying and a living again (Rom. 6:5-8).[4]

We turn now to a brief survey of the most representative and important of the ethnic religions in order to understand both the distinctive message of the Christian gospel to the non-Christian world and the credentials of finality the Christian may show for his faith. It should be said that only the barest outlines can be given here. World religions exist in the same bewildering profusion of doctrine and emphasis as is found in Christianity itself.

I. THE NONMISSIONARY RELIGIONS

We shall consider first what may be called the nonmissionary religions, those confined to the national or racial cultures of their origin, which have made no effort to become universal. The self-assumed role of these religions is in a sense the disavowal of final truth. Any ultimate revelation from God to man would necessarily include all nations and races within its scope.

In preparation for the 1957 Lyman Beecher Lectures on Preaching at Yale University, the late Daniel Thambyrajah Niles, a Ceylonese Christian minister and evangelist, asked three non-Christian friends each to write him a letter stating the central affirmation of the Christian faith as he understood it which contradicted what was fundamental in his own religion and stood as the reason why he could not become a Christian. In reply Dr. Niles received letters from

---

4. *The Preacher's Task and the Stone of Stumbling* (New York: Harper and Brothers, 1958), p. 99. See the relevant essays in Gerald H. Anderson, ed., *The Theology of the Christian Mission* (Nashville: Abingdon Press, 1961).

a Hindu, a Buddhist, and a Muslim.[5] Reference will be made to other aspects of these replies, but a statement made by "Nadarajah," the Hindu, illustrates the position implied in the nonmissionary religions. Hinduism, he says:

> . . . accepts all religions as true and believes that individuals born in them will attain salvation if they honestly follow the spiritual path preached by them. The Vedas proclaim that "God is one though the sages call it variously." In Sivagnana Siddhyar, an important scripture of Saivite Hinduism, it is said: "Whatever God you worship, even as Him, Shiva will appear there." Or, as it is state in the Bhagavad Gita, one of the scriptures of the Vaishnavite Hinduism, "Howsoever men approach Me, even so do I accept them, for on all sides whatever path they choose is Mine."[6]

A. Hinduism

Hinduism is the religion of some 300 million in India, from whence its name is derived. It is the oldest of the ethnic religions, its origins lost in antiquity. It takes a variety of forms, but predominantly it is a social system and philosophy based on the caste system. Caste, although now without legal support, determines each individual's occupation and social status, and is entirely hereditary. The laws of caste assumed the sanctity of moral law, and were more rigidly enforced than any moral code itself could be. More recent developments are moving in the direction of a much more flexible class system based on wealth, position, education, and personal prestige.[7]

Swami Nikhilananda, writing in *Living Schools of Religion* ("Religion in the Twentieth Century"),[8] gives the cardinal principles of Hinduism as the divinity of the soul, the unity of existence, the oneness of the Godhead, and the harmony of religions.[9] Hinduism disclaims being a historical religion, but claims to be based upon timeless, eternal truths taught in the Vedas. The Absolute Reality, Brahman or Atman, is sometimes spoken of as "He" and sometimes as "It," but is unknown and unknowable. Hinduism has a multitude of popular gods, such as Brahma, Vishnu, Siva, Kali, and Durga, all

---

5. *Ibid.*, pp. 15-16.

6. *Ibid.*, p. 31.

7. Joseph M. Kitagawa, *Religions of the East*, enlarged edition (Philadelphia: Westminster Press, 1960), p. 135.

8. Edited by Vergilius Ferm (Ames, Ia.: Little field, Adams and Co., 1956).

9. *Ibid.*, pp. 8-9. Kitagawa, *Religions of the East*, points out that virtually every belief or practice considered essential by some Hindus has been rejected by others.

supposed to be manifestations of the impersonal Absolute. At crucial periods in Hindu history, Brahma is said to have become incarnate: in Rama, Krishna, Buddha, and others. Christ, also, may be accepted as such an incarnation.

The human soul is eternal, having no beginning and no end, and is subject to numerous reincarnations and to *karma*, the law of cause and effect. "Salvation" comes through knowledge and understanding of the soul's divinity by the processes of *yoga*.[10] George A. Barton summarizes the variety of faith and practice found within Hinduism:

> It has no rallying-point; it stands for no one great idea or ideal. Some of its ideas are beautiful; many of its ideals noble: but in general it lacks consistency and coherency. In most of its varied manifestations Hinduism suffers by the divorce of religion from life. Salvation is to be attained by intellectual absorption or by some ritual acts. That it should affect conduct most of the systems deny or ignore. The ideals of the Bhagavad-Gita are noble, but Krishna as he is worshiped in Bengal fosters prostitution in his temples, while the cult of Civa often degenerates to immoral orgies. For the most part Hinduism is ethically impotent and many of her holy men are gross.[11]

Dr. Niles finds "the stone of stumbling" for the Hindu to be the Christian conviction that redemption for man is not in timeless truths and eternal principles but in what God has done in Christ at a point in history. While the Hindu may be willing to accept Jesus as an incarnation of Brahma, he is brought up short by the Christian proclamation that the incarnation, crucifixion, and resurrection of Christ are acts of redemption as well as revelation. In Dr. Niles's words:

> In Jesus not only was there revealed the mind and purpose of the eternal God, but there was also done in him a deed which brought salvation to mankind. It has been said that we saw on Calvary what was always true of God. But this is only a partial statement. Something happened on Calvary for the first time. God's redemptive activity within history reached its culmination there. So that a new possibility has been opened for man in Jesus Christ. He is invited to participate in the movement of

---

10. *Ibid.*, 6-12.

11. *The Religions of the World,* 4th ed. (Chicago: University of Chicago Press, 1937), pp. 199-200. Cf. John A. Hutchison, *Paths of Faith,* second edition (New York: McGraw Hill Book Company, 1975), pp. 109-45; and Robert S. Ellwood, Jr., *Many Peoples, Many Faiths* (Englewood Cliffs, N.J.: Prentice-Hall, Inc., 1976), pp. 59-103 for more complete studies.

salvation of which Jesus is the beginning and the ending, the pioneer and the goal (Heb. 12:2).[12]

B. Taoism

Taoism (pronounced *dow*-ism) is one of China's major faiths, and was founded by Li or Lao-tsze ("Old Master" or "Old Philosopher"), an ethical philosopher of the sixth century before Christ, who developed a code of morals involving many excellent points. The name of the religious development is derived from its emphasis on withdrawal from the world and contemplation of Tao, "the Way," as the path to peace and contentment.

The Tao itself is the power that pervades the entire universe. Virtue consists in the quiet submission to the power of Tao. The actual world of things is made up of two principles, existing either alone or in combination: the *yang*—light, summer, benevolent spirits and gods, the male principle; and the *yin*—darkness, winter, evil spirits, the female principle. Practical Taosim becomes a system of divination and incantation to determine the relative proportions of *yang* and *yin* in the circumstances of any individual's life.[13]

Through the centuries following the death of Laotsze, Taoism developed rapidly by including within itself the animism and demon worship of the masses. Its chief characteristic then became the fear of evil spirits and the consequent employment of Taoist priests to appease the demons and dragons and secure prosperity for the devotee. As such it still flourishes in rural China and among the uneducated masses of the cities.[14]

William James Hail, a leading student of Oriental life, writes:

> Taoism has had the most chequered career of any of the three religions of China. Once it commanded respect among the mighty, but Confucianism ultimately replaced it as the guardian of the State Religions. Then for a time it appealed to the religious needs or hopes of the more religious folk who would cultivate their spiritual life, or even prolong this life, but Buddhism eventually replaced it there, and it had to take its stand among the ignorant and superstitious who invoked its magic working powers to avoid disease, death, or trouble from vengeful spirits in the other world.[15]

---

12. *Preacher's Task*, p. 32.

13. *Living Schools of Religion*, pp. 84-89. Cf. Ellwood, *Many Peoples*, pp. 164 ff.

14. *Ibid.*, p. 90. Cf. Hutchison, *Paths of Faith*, pp. 223-29.

15. *Ibid.*, p. 83.

Actually, Taoism is so mixed with Buddhism and Confucianism that it is difficult to distinguish its followers from those of the other religions. Indeed, many Buddhists and Confucianists seek the protection sold by the Taoist priests as an additional safeguard against the ever-threatening evil workings of the demons. Floyd E. Hamilton, who has served as a missionary in the Orient, and whose apologetic in *The Basis of Christian Faith* is based upon the evident human factors involved in the growth and continuance of the ethnic religions, states: "It is easy to see . . . that there is nothing remarkable about either the growth or the continuance of this religion. It was a religion founded on fear, spread through fear, and existing through fear. It has no appeal to morality or regeneration."[16]

C. Confucianism

China's second great religion was founded by Confucius (K'ung Fu-Tzu, or Master K'ung), who was born 551 B.C. in the province of Lu (now Shantung) and who died 479 B.C. The China of his day was a feudal culture which had endured for fifteen hundred years, but which was beginning to disintegrate in a universal breakdown of respect for all morals and customs. A teacher by the age of 22, Confucius attempted to stem the ethical drift of his day by an appeal to the wisdom of the past, gathering and teaching the classics to all who would listen.

State education and family discipline were the methods whereby the sage attempted to regenerate Chinese society. Remarkable temporary success rewarded his efforts in Chungtu and the state of Lu, but lack of support from the ruler caused Confucius to resign and spend 13 years wandering through China with his disciples, seeking a place where he might put his theories into practice. Recalled at last to Lu, he spent the closing 5 years of his life collecting and editing the Classics, and embodying his wisdom in the *Analects.*

Confucianism gained its vogue during the Han dynasty, and until the last half century has been a determining factor in Chinese education and culture. Neither Confucius nor his immediate followers claimed supernatural origin or religious value for their ethical reform. Some question whether Confucianism may properly be called a religion, since it has no priests, no congregations, no temples or

---

16. P. 110. See the appraisals of Kitagawa, *Religions of the East,* pp. 59-63; Ellwood, *Many Peoples,* pp. 164-73; and Hutchison, *Paths of Faith,* pp. 209-61.

churches, and its adherents at the same time may be Taoists or Buddhists. However, the religious character of Confucianism lies in the worship of Heaven which the master himself encouraged, the worship of both royal and family ancestors, and the worship of Confucius himself.

Confucius spoke of *T'ien* or Heaven in terms both personal and naturalistic. Among his sayings are the statements that the superior man lives "in awe of Heaven"; that "at fifty he knew the will of Heaven"; "If you have committed sin against Heaven, you have not got a god to pray to"; and, "Does Heaven speak? The four seasons pursue their courses and all things are continually being produced, but does Heaven say anything?"[17]

Likewise, Confucius and his followers strongly supported the ancestor worship of their day. Ancestor worship is based on the idea that "as the foundation of things is Heaven, so the foundation of man is the ancestors." About it have gathered elaborate systems of mourning and burial of the dead, the practice of visiting graves, the building of ancestral shrines and temples, and the offering of food and wine in connection with anniversaries. Confucius wrote, "When parents are alive, they should be served according to the rules of propriety *(li)*. When they are dead, they should be buried according to the rules of propriety. After they are dead, they should be sacrificed to according to rules of propriety."[18]

Followers of Confucius' teachings, centuries after his death, began to worship their teacher as they worshiped their ancestors. For centuries, Confucian worship was a state cult, virtually the established religion of China. It was undoubtedly political, and did not preclude other religious worship. Only the very ignorant regarded Confucius as a god in the sense in which Lao-Tsze and Buddha were so regarded. Nor was Confucius thought of as a savior. He was (and is) worshiped as a hero, an ancestor, a great teacher, but as thoroughly human.[19]

The religious scene in China has drastically changed since the Communist takeover in 1949. Marxism in China as in Russia and elsewhere is dogmatically and aggressively antireligious. Propaganda and persecution combine to persuade the multitudes to forsake

---

17. Dr. Chan Wing-tsit in *Living Schools of Religion,* pp. 100-01.

18. *Ibid.,* p. 104. Cf. Ellwood, *Many Peoples,* pp. 156-64; and Hutchison, *Paths of Faith,* pp. 217-39.

19. *Living Schools of Religion,* pp. 106-9; Kitagawa, *Religions of the East,* pp. 74-98.

ancient religions in favor of new teachers. Hutchison comments, "Therefore the foreseeable future is dark for all of China's traditional faiths. Yet students of history know that the intentions of even the most powerful rulers sometimes come to unexpected conclusions. Students of Chinese history also know that the Chinese anvil has outworn many hammers."[20]

D. Shinto

Shinto is a Sino-Japanese term derived from words meaning "The Way of the Gods." It is the nationalistic faith of Japan, devoted for the most part to the worship of indigenous Japanese gods, and until very recently of the Japanese emperor. Two major streams divide Shinto into State (or Shrine) Shinto and Sectarian Shinto.

The deities or *kami* honored in Shinto are of varied sorts: primitive nature forces, interpreted as "ancestors"; the spirits of certain of the emperors; the spirits of heroes who died in the service of the nation; and in the case of Sectarian Shinto the spirits of the respective sect founders.[21]

The emperor worship associated with Shinto served to build the power of the imperial regime in Japan. It was founded upon the claim that the royal line is descended from the sun-goddess. When the Emperor Hirohito disclaimed his divinity after the capitulation of Japan at the close of the second world war (December, 1945), State Shinto ceased to be the established religion of Japan, and genuine religious liberty came to the nation for the first time. However, missionaries report the continued strength of Shinto in subsequent years, with Shrine Shinto receiving the same voluntary adherence which had previously been given to the sectarian forms. Where there are many deities, the loss of one does not make much difference.

Japan is presently in a crisis of values, and new indigenous religions are arising in bewildering number.[22] Herein lies both the danger and opportunity for the Christian missionary enterprise.

---

20. *Paths of Faith*, p. 261.

21. Cf. the review by Daniel Clarence Holtom, long a resident of and teacher in Japan, in *Living Schools of Religion*, pp. 146-52; also Ellwood, *Many Peoples*, pp. 184-92; Hutchison, *Paths of Faith*, pp. 265-74, 302-3; and Kitagawa, *Religions of the East*, pp. 278-303.

22. Cf. Ellwood, *Many Peoples*, pp. 204-7; and Hutchison, *Paths of Faith*, pp. 299-303.

In none of these ethnic faiths is there any claim to finality as a revelation from the true God to all mankind. Each has grown up within a national culture, and has spread only by the migration of its adherents to other areas. Comparative religion may find values in these cultural religions, particularly in earlier and purer forms. In no sense, however, either by their own claims or by historical or logical evidence, may they be considered as rivals of Christianity. They are expressions of the religious nature of man in his search for a satisfactory relationship with the ultimate. They are part of the "world" which God loved and gave His only begotten Son to redeem. An outstanding liberal and editor of a liberal criticism of the missionary movement, William Ernest Hocking, is said to have asked Missionary C. F. Andrews, "How do you preach the gospel to a Hindu?" Mr. Andrews replied, "I don't. I preach the gospel to a man."[23]

II. THE MISSIONARY RELIGIONS

We turn now to the two religions besides Christianity which are missionary or convert-making religions. These are Buddhism and Mohammedanism or Islam. At least in the sense of profession and purpose, these world religions are rivals with Christianity for the loyalty of all men.

A. Buddhism

Buddhism originated in India some six centuries before Christ with Prince Siddhartha Gautama (c. 563-483 B.C.), and has been confined almost entirely to the Asiatic contient. While Christianity moved westward from the Near East through Europe, Buddhism moved northward and eastward and has become the predominant religion of the Far East, from Tibet and central Asia to Japan, and from Java to Manchuria. Buddhism in China has been subject to the same pressures as native Chinese religions by the prevailing Marxist government. Buddhism has undergone such changes that it may better now be described as a family of religions.[24]

Gautama had spent his early life in ease and luxury. His father,

---

23. Niles, *Preacher's Task,* p. 89.

24. See the discussions in Ellwood, *Many Peoples,* pp. 106-37; Hutchison, *Paths of Faith,* pp. 109-45; and Kitagawa, *Religoins of the East,* pp. 155-221.

rajah of a small principality near the border of India and Nepal, had made every effort to see that the prince experienced only the beautiful and the pleasant. He married his cousin, Yasodhara, at the age of 16, and 10 years later had a son whom he named Rahula. However, at the age of 29, Gautama decided to renounce his princely life and go forth as a hermit seeking an answer to the mystery of life. For 6 years he pursued the asceticism of the Hindu, reduced almost to a skeleton by his austerities. Finding it unavailing, he sat in meditation under a tree where he received his enlightenment (whence Buddha, "The Enlightened or Awakened One"). Not only did the Buddha there find the answer to his own questing, but he discovered a message for the world. A man of magnetic personality, he spent the next 45 years spreading the wisdom he had discovered, dying at the age of 80 years.

The Buddha wrote nothing himself, and almost a hundred years passed before his "sayings" were put down in writing by his disciples. One of these sayings is quoted by August Karl Reischauer:

> I have overcome all foes: I am all-wise; I am free from stains in every way; I have left everything; I have obtained emancipation by the destruction of desire. Having myself gained knowledge, whom should I call my master? I have no teacher; no one is equal to me; in the world of men and of gods, no being is like me. I am the holy One in the world, I am the highest teacher. I alone am the *Sambuddha* (Perfectly Enlightened); I have obtained coolness (by extinction of passions) and have obtained *Nirvana*. To found the Kingdom of Truth I go to the city of Kasis (Benares); I will beat the drum of the immortal in the darkness of this world.[25]

What was the fruit of the Buddha's meditation, so vividly climaxed under the Bo tree (tree of Wisdom, Enlightenment)? Although inadequately, we may summarize what appears to be the teaching of Buddha under three heads:

1. *The Four Noble Truths*

The first is the truth of suffering, or "ill," including both mental and physical suffering, as involved in the very nature of life and individual existence. The second is the truth that desire is the cause of suffering: desire for possessions, enjoyment, and even separate or individual existence. The third truth asserts that suffering ceases when desire ends and the lust for life has been renounced and destroyed. The fourth truth is the truth of "the Eightfold Path" which

---

25. In *Great Religions of the World*, p. 97.

leads to the cessation of suffering. This is the only way to escape the endless cycle of rebirth which Gautama took over from Hinduism.

2. The Eightfold Path

The path to deliverance, or the eight steps in this path,[26] include: (1) Right Views: acceptance of the four truths, and renunciation of such unworthy attitudes and acts as covetousness, gossiping, and lying. (2) Right Desires: freedom from lust, ill will, and cruelty. (3) Right Speech: gentle, plain, and truthful. (4) Right Conduct: sex morality (in the case of monks, celibacy), abstention from killing any living being, honesty, etc. (5) Right Mode of Livelihood: without luxury, and within one's abilities. (6) Right Effort, including the effort to overcome evil, and to develop and maintain desirable conditions. (7) Right Awareness, including awareness of the transitoriness and baseness of the body. (8) Right Meditation: mind development to the point that it may concentrate upon a single subject, without distraction—the ultimate goal being a state of full Enlightenment, transcending consciousness, the highest possible state of perfection.

3. Karma and Nirvana

In addition to the above, the Buddha stressed the place of karma, the absolute law of cause and effect, in human life. As Bentley-Taylor summarizes it, "What you sow you reap, and neither man, priest, nor deity can suspend the operation of that law or withhold the consequences of a deed."[27] The lot one endures in this life, however, may be the effect of deeds in a prior life, and the effects of what is done in this life will carry on in future rebirths. Another important, though difficult, concept is that of Anatta, the doctrine of the nonego. The Buddha did not seem to believe that the same self exists in continuous reincarnations, but that the karma of the self carries through and provides the continuity. Later Buddhists compared consciousness with a rope woven of hundreds of short strands of hemp. No strand of hemp carries from one end of the rope to the other, but altogether they make one rope.

Nirvana is another difficult concept. It is the goal of all Buddhist striving, the cessation of rebirth, the end of suffering, the termination of all desire, a supreme consciousness of peace and rest, a perfect and passionless happiness. Many have thought of this as the equivalent of

---

26. Cf. David Bentley-Taylor in J. N. D. Anderson, ed., The World's Religions (Chicago: The Inter-Varsity Christian Fellowship, 1950), pp. 121-22.

27. Ibid., p. 123.

annihilation, but Buddhists attempt to give it positive content. The Buddha himself is said to have defined it negatively: "There is, disciples, a condition, where there is neither earth nor water, neither air nor light, neither limitless space, nor limitless time, neither any kind of being, neither ideation or non-ideation, neither this world nor that world. There is neither arising nor passing-away, nor dying, neither cause nor effect, neither change nor standing-still."[28]

Buddhism has developed in two major branches: *Hinayana Buddhism*, widely accepted in Burma, Thailand, and Sri Lanka, representing Gautama as a simple teacher whose wisdom could easily be understood by all; and *Mahayana Buddhism*, the most successful branch, which has spread through central Asia, Tibet, Mongolia, Korea, China, Japan, Nepal, Java, Sumatra, and Vietnam. Buddhism in either branch is virtually extinct in the land of its birth, India.

Mahayana Buddhism made some significant additions to Gautama's teachings: a supreme Reality from which the universe has emanated; the deification of the Buddha himself; the introduction of *Bodhisattvas* as a lower order of Wisdom Beings than true Buddhas, but who are worshiped; salvation by faith in Buddha and the Bodhisattvas, including endless repetition of their names; and the introduction of images and polytheistic idolatry, including worship of the Goddess of Mercy, Hearer of the World's Prayers, who in many Buddhist lands occupies a place similar to that of the Virgin Mary in Catholicism. Mahayana Buddhism has developed a number of sects, of which the most important are the Zen, or Meditation Sect; the Pure Land Sect; and Lamaism, the national religion of Tibet and Mongolia.[29]

Buddhism as a whole is a religion of withdrawal, of renunciation of individual life, whose goal is Nirvana, a goal attainable only by those who devote themselves to the mendicant and celibate monkhood, devoting their years to yellow-robed meditation. For all others, an endless series of rebirths under the law of *karma* is the rule. At first Buddhism was a reformation of existing Hinduism, and as such was probably ethically superior to its parent religion. However, Buddhism glorifies a way of life in which the ideal is the idle, begging "holy" man. The Eightfold Path soon degenerated into the renunciation of all social responsibility. The "genius" of Buddhism, if

---

28. *Sacred Books of the Buddhists*, 2:54; quoted in *World's Religions*, p. 126.
29. *Ibid.*, pp. 130-32.

such it be, lies in its readiness to compromise with the religions of the lands into which it goes. In every section of Asia where Buddhism has penetrated with success, it has incorporated into itself the religions it has found. Thus the Buddhism of China is a mixture of Taoism, Confucianism, and the original Mahayana Buddhism of India; while in Japan, Buddhism has included within itself much of Shinto.[30] Buddhism is an almost perfect example of what we have defined as religion, that is, *man's* search for the divine. It expressly denies any divine forgiveness or redemption. Its whole way of "salvation" is a way of good works and human striving through renunciation of life and through mental discipline.

This is clearly shown in the reply Dr. Niles received from his Buddhist correspondent. "Somaratne" wrote:

> Buddhists are taught that all things are mind-made, that all good actions and bad actions arise from the mind, and that salvation—in the sense understood by any religion—must be sought by oneself through one's own endeavour. They are also told that they must accept nothing for granted, that they must think out for themselves the truth or falsity, reality or non-reality, the good and the bad of all things. It is the fundamental teaching of Buddhists that everything arises from a cause and that the law of cause and effect is universal. . . .
>
> In Christianity, one prays to God as the Saviour and the dispenser of all good things in life. In Buddhism, each one is expected, by his own efforts, to ennoble himself in accordance with the Noble Eightfold Path.[31]

Dr. Niles points out that this is the condition of man under the law, and is a complete negation of the principle of divine grace. The Christian gospel is not a gospel of salvation by good works, or by religious activity, however sincere. It is a gospel of salvation by grace through faith.

Hamilton suggests four reasons for the past and present prominence of Buddhism in Asia, where it is the religion of about one-third of the total human race. First, its most rapid spread has been at those times when it enjoyed political support and prestige. Second, it displays remarkable facility for adapting itself to the religions and superstitions of any country into which it goes. Third, it offers the converts a way whereby they may earn their salvation, something which appeals to the natural religious instincts of the human kind.

---

30. Cf. *Great Religions of the Modern World,* p. 139.
31. *Preacher's Task,* pp. 71-72.

And finally, by making laziness a virtue and begging the most respectable means of livelihood, Buddhism makes it possible for large numbers to live without working, a mode of existence with fatal fascination for too many. These factors are quite sufficient to explain the growth and spread of the religion of the Buddha.[32]

B. Islam or Mohammedanism

The youngest of the world religions was founded by Mohammed, prophet of Allah, six centuries after Christ. Cradled in the same portion of the earth as Christianity, and spreading through nominally Christian lands, Mohammedanism grew even much more rapidly in its beginnings than did early Christianity. Estimates of its present following range from 250 to 350 million adherents. Islam has in recent years shown renewed missionary vigor, particularly in Africa.[33]

Islam means "submission or surrender to the will of God," and Moslem (or Muslim) means "one who submits." The founder of Islam, Mohammed (or Muhammad) was born about A.D. 570 and died in 632. An orphan from early age, marriage to a wealthy widow 15 years his senior relieved him of economic need and enabled him to spend time in meditation. His "call" came to him in 610 in a cave outside Mecca. Mohammed combined political genius with his religious nature, and soon established important centers of influence at Medina and at Mecca.

Although born in a polytheistic Arab culture, Mohammed had contacts with both Judaism and Christianity. He thought of himself as the last of the great prophets of the Old Testament, among whom he included Jesus—denouncing Christ's deity and denying His death on the Cross. His new religion was uncompromisingly monotheistic; its confession of faith is, "There is no God but Allah; and Mohammed is His prophet"; and its unpardonable sin is the sin of *shirk*, worshiping any other god. Mohammed substituted Friday for the Jewish Saturday and the Christian Sunday as a weekly Sabbath, and Mecca for the Jerusalem of the Jews.

Salma Bishlawy, who is herself a professing Moslem, summarizes the tenets and religious duties of Islam in her contribution

---

32. *Basis of Christian Faith*, pp. 108-9.

33. See the careful and complete discussions in Ellwood, *Many Peoples*, pp. 312-33; Hutchison, *Paths of Faith*, pp. 453-93; Kitagawa, *Religions of the East*, pp. 222-77.

to the volume *Living Schools of Religion*.[34] Its creed includes belief in God, in His angels, His prophets (of whom Mohammed is the last), and in the judgment day. Its religious duties include the six "pillars": (1) Pronouncing the formula, "There is no God but Allah, and Mohammed is His prophet," which automatically makes one a member of the faith with no other ceremony involved. (2) *Salat*, or ritual prayer five times a day, bowing in the direction of Mecca. (3) *Zakat*, an alms-tax, or the giving of money for the building of mosques, for help to the poor, and originally for the support of the Moslem state. (4) Fasting from dawn to sunset during the month in which the Quran (or Koran) was first revealed. (5) *Hajj*, or the pilgrimage to Mecca which each Moslem must make at least once in his lifetime unless it is physically or economically impossible. (6) *Jihad*, or the duty of Holy War, which has lately found little support in the Moslem world.

The Koran (from Quran, "recitation") is the Bible of Islam. It is alleged to be the word of God transmitted to Mohammed through the angel Gabriel from an original preserved in heaven. It is eternal and uncreated, and considered a perfect model of Arabic. Many biblical characters are mentioned, and many others which are of Arabic origin.

The ethics of Islam has incorporated the Arab materialistic hedonism, the Prophet's many wives, and the Koran portrayal of sensuous bliss, along with virtues of chivalry, hospitality, magnanimity, patience, and resignation to one's lot.[35] Miss Bishlawy puts it euphemistically: "It has been pointed out by scholars of many faiths that Islam has found its success by its great realism as to human nature. Its ethical teachings are not transformed into rigid demands interfering with the biological needs of human existence."[36] Edward J. Jurji states: "The ultimate goal of the conscientious Moslem is so to live that the weight of sin may be offset on the Day of Reckoning by one's good works."[37]

· A major factor in the rapid early spread of Mohammedanism was military force, against which no effective power was available until Charles Martel checked it at the Battle of Tours in A.D. 732.

---

34. Pp. 161-63.
35. Jurji, *Great Religions of the Modern World*, p. 191.
36. *Living Schools of Religion*, p. 169.
37. *Great Religions of the Modern World*, p. 192.

The Moslems were fanatical soldiers, driven by the teaching of their Prophet and his Koran that "the sword is the key to heaven and hell; a drop of blood shed in the cause of Allah, a night spent in arms, is of more avail than two months of fasting and prayer: whoever falls in battle, his sins are forgiven and at the day of judgment his limbs shall be supplied by the wings of angels and cherubim."[38]

Muslim nationalism and the close identification of Arabic and Islamic concerns have increased the political tensions in the Near East between Arabs and Israelis in Palestine and Arabs and Christians in Lebanon.[39]

Christian missions among the Moslems have had meager success compared with missionary work among other religions. Part of this is due to the law of apostasy in Islam which decrees death for the one who forsakes the Prophet's way, and which even today may mean death by poison and certainly the loss of family, inheritance, and livelihood.[40] Theologically, the "stone of stumbling" for the Moslem is the unqualified Christian claim for the deity of Christ, and the preaching of the Cross, which is explicitly denied in the Koran (4:157). As D. T. Niles says:

> The Muslim refusal of the Christian faith assumes that it is enough for God to deal with men and for man to deal with God in the way recorded for us in the Old Testament. All that was necessary was a final prophet who would give clearer teaching about the way to live according to God's laws. God is merciful and sovereign, and man not only can but also ought to leave it at that. The Christian faith, on the other hand, arises from the fact that whatever man may think or be satisfied with, God has acted in Jesus Christ to open for man a new possibility apart from the law, whereby instead of the law being a gateway to God's grace it becomes the avenue by which man can render grateful thanks to God for what God has freely done. It is not that Jesus Christ enables us to obey the law but that he delivers us from it and thereby opens to us the possibility of making obedience to the law our offering to him.[41]

As far as the popular mind is concerned, Islam demands no moral regeneration. Its pictures of the hereafter are such as to appeal to the lower instincts. It makes no "impossible" demands of human

---

38. Quoted by Hamilton, *Basis of Christian Faith,* p. 104.

39. Cf. Kitagawa, *Religions of the East,* 270-77.

40. Anderson, *World's Religions,* p. 98.

41. *Preacher's Task,* p. 48.

nature. It takes man much as he is, and makes few requirements of him apart from abstinence from intoxicating liquor, and the ceremonial observances outlined above. It has veiled its women, and encouraged polygamy after the Prophet's own example. It is not too hard to see why multitudes should flock to the scimitar. Nothing supernatural would be needed to account for the spread of such a creed as this.

III. THE UNIQUENESS AND FINALITY OF CHRISTIANITY

A final quick comparison between the ethnic religions we have surveyed and the Christian faith we are studying is now in order. An objective comparison of Christianity with the religions considered here provides a most convincing argument for the supernatural origin of the Christian gospel. Where other world religions enjoyed natural advantages or had human forces at work in their behalf, the apostles and their intrepid followers faced only insuperable odds.[42]

Their Founder was condemned and executed as a common criminal. A member of a despised and subject nation, Jesus the Nazarene was rejected by His own people and executed as a rebel in a manner as despised as hanging in our day. He wrote nothing, founded no institutions, organized no societies, and by all available evidence never traveled more than 50 miles from Nazareth during His adult ministry.

The early Christians themselves were largely uneducated and inexperienced in public life. They were men of the poorer trades, and political refugees most of their lives. Large numbers of them were slaves. The doctrine they taught soon brought them into direct conflict with the greatest political power of the age. For many years the mere suspicion that one was a Christian was in effect a death warrant, and, as many understand Paul's words in 1 Cor. 15:29, to be baptized was to be baptized for death.

Not only that, but the ethical demands of the new faith ran directly counter to the sinful propensities of unregenerate human nature. The sexual license of the pagan cults of the day was condemned in no uncertain terms. Dishonesty, laziness, drunkenness, and immorality were banned. The highest possible standards of

---

42. Cf. the more complete treatment in Hamilton, *Basis of Christian Faith,* pp. 115-31.

ethical living were enjoined, and no compromise with sinful human "weakness" was permitted.

Again, Christianity refused compromise with existing religions. Jesus Christ alone is the Way to God. "Neither is there salvation in any other:" the Church proclaimed, "for there is none other name under heaven given among men, whereby we must be saved" (Acts 4:12). The gospel required the affirmation of a simple but clear-cut creed: "Jesus is Lord" (Rom. 10:9). In many ways the Christian faith was humbling to human wisdom (1 Cor. 1:22-27). Had it been only an ethical system, it might have appealed naturally to the ethically rigorous. Had it been only a system of doctrine, it might have drawn the philosophically astute. Had it been a system of ritual and ceremony, it could have attracted the religiously sensitive. It possessed none of these characteristics. Its ethical ideals were the highest possible, but they were possible only to those who through repentance and faith in a historical Person had experienced a moral rebirth. Its doctrine, while reasonable, was not the achievement of human reason, but the insight provided by divine revelation. Its meager ritual was but symbolic of a deliverance by grace through faith, as the unmerited gift of God through Jesus Christ. Everything about it was humbling to human pride and self-sufficiency.

The most natural and plausible explanation of the spread of early Christianity is given in the last verse of the Gospel of Mark: "They went forth, and preached every where, *the Lord working with them*, and confirming the word with signs following" (Mark 16:20).

A modern scholar states that to reduce the difference between Christianity and other religions to mere expressions of general religious truth, and to make Christianity only a higher species of human faith, would mean not only the end of Christian missions but of Christianity itself:

> Jesus Christ is either the only Saviour of the world, or He is not a Saviour at all, but only a religious genius. The essence of Christianity, according to the Bible, consists not in its incidental affinities with other religions, but in its distinctive elements. The Gospel is related to other faiths as either-or. "We cannot simultaneously affirm: there is salvation in none other; and the others, Buddha, *et al.*, represent the same thing as Jesus, only perhaps a bit less perfectly."[43]

---

43. H. Emil Brunner, quoted by Paul King Jewett, "Emil Brunner's Conception of Revelation," in John F. Walvoord, ed., *Inspiration and Interpretation* (Grand Rapids: Wm. B. Eerdmans Publishing Co., 1957), p. 110.

SUMMARY

In this chapter we have looked at the two great classes of world religions other than Christianity: the racial or national religions and the missionary or convert-making religions, Buddhism and Islam. In comparison, Christianity clearly shows the marks of its divine origin.

Having come to the end of our survey of "Foundations of the Faith," we are ready now to proceed directly to a study of the faith as it is set forth in the Bible. What follows is not a systematic theology, nor is it an attempt to cover completely all of the doctrines of Christianity. It is rather an attempt to expound those teachings which are most relevant to each of us personally in our desire to grasp the practical meaning of our Christian faith.

PART II

The Basis of Redemption

CHAPTER 6

The Christian Concept of God

In Chapter 2 we considered evidence for a theistic faith. There we saw that belief in God is a reasonable belief. However, theism can do little more than affirm the existence or personality of the Supreme Being. It falls far short of the biblical position. For the writers of the Bible, God is not a postulate of reason but a fact of experience. "The lion hath roared, who will not fear? the Lord God hath spoken, who can but prophesy?" (Amos 3:8) It was a simple fact of Hebrew religious experience that God had made himself known in great events, such as the Exodus, and through great personalities, such as the prophets. Who could doubt it? Only the fool (Ps. 14:1), and he was a practical rather than a theoretical atheist, who did not take God into account.

With the Hebrews the problem was not atheism but polytheism; not, Does God exist? but, What God exists? And so it is in our time. Because nearly everyone believes in God in some sense, the first question, logically, is not the existence of God but the character of God. The question for most people is not so much, Is there a God? but, Who is God? and, What is He like?

After offering some suggestions as to a definition of God we shall attempt to answer the question, What is God like? as this answer comes to us in the Christian revelation.

Just as the Bible nowhere attempts to establish the existence of God, so it proposes no definition. The Hebrews were prohibited from making any graven image of God, and they made no effort to restrict God to a definition. We do have a description of Him, however, in the conversation between Moses and the Lord at the scene of the burning bush in the Sinai desert. Moses inquired of the Lord, "Behold, when I come unto the children of Israel, and shall say unto them, The God of your fathers hath sent me unto you; and they shall say to me, What is his name? what shall I say unto them? And God said unto Moses, I AM THAT I AM: and he said, Thus shalt thou say unto the children of Israel, I AM hath sent me unto you" (Exod. 3:13-14).

The enigmatic quality of this description of God is evidence that a complete definition of God is fundamentally impossible. Just as a graven image of God cannot picture Him, so a definition of God cannot explain Him. After we have said all we can about God, there remains a great element of mystery. "For as the heavens are higher than the earth, so are my ways higher than your ways, and my thoughts than your thoughts" (Isa. 55:9).

Nonetheless, God has made a true disclosure of himself. He is not the great Unknown or the Inscrutable. God has revealed himself in such a way that we may know Him truly, even though we may not comprehend Him fully. This summary of the biblical description of God may serve provisionally:

> He is One, supreme, living, personal and spiritual, holy, righteous and merciful. His power and knowledge are all-sufficient, and He is not limited in time or place. . . . He is the God of all the earth, who is no respecter of persons or nations. Two new elements [in the New Testament] entered man's religious thought and gradually lifted its whole content to a new plane—Jesus Christ's experience and manifestation of the Divine Fatherhood, and the growing conviction of the Church that Christ Himself was God and the full and final revelation of God.[1]

In this chapter we shall try to set forth the principal aspects of the Christian understanding of God as seen in the Scriptures and in the consensus on the Christian faith.

I. A SOVEREIGN GOD

"We believe in one eternally existent, infinite God, Sovereign of the universe; that He only is God, creative and administrative . . ."[2]

---

1. T. Rees, "God," *The International Standard Bible Encyclopedia,* James Orr, ed. (Grand Rapids: Wm. B. Eerdmans Publishing Co., 1939), 2:1260.

2. Article I, "Articles of Faith," Constitution of the Church of the Nazarene, current *Manual, in loc.*

The biblical term *Lord,* used by the Jews in place of the unutterable name for God, YHWH,[3] implies particularly the sovereignty of God. As Frederick C. Grant has written: "It might even be said that the fundamental doctrine of the whole Bible . . . is the *sovereignty of God,* the idea of God as king, and of His kingship . . . over the nation and over the whole universe, material and spiritual."[4]

Morally and spiritually, this means that men must acknowledge God as the Lord, the supreme, sovereign Governor of their lives, indeed, of all existence. "And God spake all these words, saying, I am the Lord thy God, which have brought thee out of the land of Egypt, out of the house of bondage. Thou shalt have no other gods before me" (Exod. 20:1-3). "Then said Jesus unto him, Get thee hence, Satan: for it is written, Thou shalt worship the Lord thy God, and him only shalt thou serve" (Matt. 4:10).

A. God Is One

"Hear, O Israel: the Lord our God is *one* Lord" (Deut. 6:4). Monotheism, the doctrine that there is one God rather than many, is the clear teaching of Scripture and reason. The mind of man finds all truth to be of a piece and rebels at any idea of a basic disunity in the structure of the universe. Scholars have debated the question of how clearly the earliest Old Testament worthies sensed the fact that God is one, but be that as it may, the Bible in both Testaments urges an ethical monotheism upon all who read its pages. By this is meant that, if God is the Lord and has a sovereign claim upon the lives of all men, there must be, not many gods, but one. "Monotheism is neither a characteristically Christian view nor even a biblical one, save as an inference derived from the truth that God is the Lord."[5]

It may be questioned whether the unity of God is a vital issue in our day, except in areas of the earth where missionaries face primitive peoples. Yet *practically* it is a live issue as between faith and unbelief. Is there a cohesive, intelligent Power in the universe, who makes it a *universe,* or are we at the mercy of unreasoning powers fundamentally chaotic? The faith of the Bible is that God is one and that He has a moral claim upon the lives of all men. "Which is the

---

3. The Word *Jehovah* is a combination of the letters YHWH with the vowels of the Hebrew word for "Lord," *Adonai.*

4. *Introduction to New Testament Thought,* p. 117.

5. H. Emil Brunner, *The Christian Doctrine of God:* Dogmatics: Vol. I (Philadelphia: Westminster Press, 1950), 1:137.

first commandment of all?" a scribe wistfully inquired of Jesus. Our Lord replied, "The first of all the commandments is, Hear, O Israel; the Lord our God is one Lord: *and thou shalt love the Lord thy God with all thy heart, . . .*" (Cf. Mark 12:28-30.) "If there is but one God, then he must be the God of all men."[6]

B. God Is the Creator and Sustainer of All

Among the reasons why God is the Lord, the supreme Sovereign, is that He is the Creator and Sustainer of all. In the beautifully simple terms of the book *More Than Words,* "God is the personal being who made the universe and keeps it going."[7] Many problems of a philosophical nature could detain us here, but the Christian faith, as it is rooted in the Bible, is not extensively concerned with theoretical matters. The principal concern of the biblical writers is to set forth the nature and character of God in His relationship with man. It was the profound faith of these men that the world and all the material universe owe their existence and continuance to the power of an almighty God. "In the beginning God created the heaven and the earth" (Gen. 1:1). Speaking of the *Logos* as the Agent in creation, John writes, "All things were made by him; and without him was not any thing made that was made" (John 1:3). The writer of Hebrews echoes the same confidence: "God, . . . hath . . . spoken unto us by his Son, . . . by whom also he made the worlds" (Heb. 1:1-2).

If we ask *how* God created all things, we learn that it was by the word of His power (Ps. 33:6, 9). God spoke and it was done. The world is the result of the creative act of God and is not an extension of the divine substance nor an eternal entity independent of God. The world has real existence, but is dependent upon God and is adapted to Christian ends.[8]

If we ask how God *sustains* all things, we learn that by the eternal *Logos,* the rational principle or structure of the universe, "all things consist" or hold together (Col. 1:17), and that He upholds "all things by the word of his power . . ." (Heb. 1:3). Many philosophers who wrestle with the problem of that which is beyond physics are

6. H. H. Rowley, *The Faith of Israel* (Philadelphia: Westminster Press, 1953), p. 73.

7. Anonymous, *More than Words* (Greenwich, Conn.: The Seabury Press, 1955), p. 68.

8. Cf. William Adams Brown, *Christian Theology in Outline,* (New York: Charles Scribner's Sons, 1906), chapter 13.

finding answers to their questions that are fundamentally in agreement with the Christian faith. The study of reality makes sense. It yields its secrets to intelligence. If it requires a mind to understand nature, is it unreasonable to believe that it requires a Mind to produce and sustain nature?

C. God Is Transcendent and Immanent

The infinite God not only stands *above* the entire universe, but also dwells *within* it; God is both *transcendent* and *immanent*. This, we have seen in Chapter 2, is what distinguishes theism from deism and pantheism.

Solomon recognized the transcendence of God in his prayer at the dedication of the Temple: "Behold, the heaven and heaven of heavens cannot contain thee; how much less this house that I have builded?" (1 Kings 8:27). God has brought the universe into being and sustains it by His power, but He is not dependent upon it for His existence. Rather, He stands above or transcends it. The Christian view of God decisively rejects pantheism, whether in the form of some pagan religions or in the modern cults which claim to be Christian but still teach that "God is all, and all is God." God is *not* all. All is *not* God. He has made all that is, but He is separate and distinct from it in His transcendence.

But God is also immanent. He is nearer to all His creation than any spatial representation could possibly indicate. When the apostle Paul stood on Mars' Hill and addressed the men of Athens, he declared that it was God's purpose for men to "seek the Lord, if haply they mighty feel after him, and find him, though he be not far from every one of us: for in him we live, and move, and have our being" (Acts 17:27-28).

The prophet Isaiah described both the transcendence and the immanence of God when he said, "For thus saith the high and lofty One that inhabiteth eternity, whose name is Holy; I dwell in the high and holy place, with him also that is of a contrite and humble spirit, to revive the spirit of the humble, and to revive the heart of the contrite ones" (Isa. 57:15). The almighty God, who is the Maker of heaven and earth, not only looks down upon the nations and sees them "as a drop of a bucket" (Isa. 40:15), but also dwells among them, nearer than life and closer than breathing, the very *ground* of their existence.

II. AN ALL-SUFFICIENT GOD

Implicit in the Christian's understanding of God is the confidence that He is all-sufficient. This is the religious value of the rather formidable terms omnipotence, omnipresence, omniscience, and the like. As Edwin Lewis put it, "The Christian religion is interested in God mainly as to his purpose with human life, and believes that with respect to that purpose he is *utterly adequate.*"[9]

A. God Is Omnipotent

God is capable of doing all that His nature suggests. "Is any thing too hard for the Lord?" (Gen. 18:14). The doctrine of the omnipotence of God does not teach that He can do everything conceivable. For example, He *cannot* lie, He *cannot* be unfaithful, He *cannot* do something irrational. He is, however, capable of doing all things consistent with His own character and necessary to His government of the universe.

Some very earnest, capable thinkers have been unable to reconcile both the goodness and the unlimited power of God. As they have reflected upon the problem of evil, they have concluded that God either cannot fully control the world (in which case He would be limited) or will not (in which case He would not be good). Clinging to a belief in His goodness, they limit His power. However, it seems more reasonable and practical to posit *both* the goodness and the power of God. In the light of the biblical revelation, we *cannot* deny His goodness; and as One who is worthy of *absolute* trust and faith, we *dare* not deny His power. We shall give more consideration to this problem in the next chapter.

The discovery of the almost incredible extent of our universe, where distances are measured in light-years, has given us a new understanding of the omnipotence of God, as well as of His other attributes. As we remember, Sir James Jeans, the noted British astronomer, called it *This Mysterious Universe.* Yet it is one that, for all its magnitude and terrifying power, exhibits the marks of beauty, order, and design—evidence of intelligence. It is quite beyond us to grasp with the mind and heart the might and power of our God, but it is enough to confess, with the historic Christian Church, "I believe in God the Father *Almighty*, Maker of heaven and earth."[10]

---

9. *A Manual of Christian Beliefs* (New York: Charles Scribner's Sons, 1927), p. 22.
10. *The Apostles' Creed.*

B. God Is Omniscient

Except for such self-limitation as He may have imposed, the wisdom and knowledge of God are without limit. Theologians differ as to the extent of such self-limitation. A moot question concerns the foreknowledge of God and the freedom of man. Does God know what my choice in the future will be? Arminians generally make a distinction between predestination and foreknowledge, whereas Calvinists generally identify the two. That man is free, and, consequently, responsible is a biblical axiom. However one resolves the moot question, he should hold to the conviction that man, by grace, is able to choose or reject the way of salvation and must bear the consequences.

Except as noted, nothing stands outside the bounds of God's knowledge, and by His wisdom, the use of knowledge, He is absolutely capable of sustaining all things in such a manner as to accomplish His own wise and holy purposes. "Who hath directed the spirit of the Lord, or being his counsellor hath taught him? With whom took he counsel, and who instructed him, and taught him in the path of judgment, and taught him knowledge, and shewed to him the way of understanding?" (Isa. 40:13-14).

C. God Is Omnipresent

It is impossible for anything to exist apart from the presence of God. "Whither shall I go from thy spirit? or whither shall I flee from thy presence?" (Ps. 139:7). If God has brought all things into existence by His creative power and sustains the entire universe through His wisdom and might, it follows that wherever His creatures are, there God is also. "For in him we live, and move, and have our being" (Acts 17:28). No matter how far man may range in the universe, either outwardly in space or inwardly in the structure of matter and being, he will find the presence of God. Apart from the Logos, no existence would be possible.

III. A Living, Personal God

One of the dramatic biblical descriptions of God is that He is *living*. At least 28 times in the Bible God is said to be the *living* God. For example, one of the reasons why David was so aroused over Goliath was that this Philistine had defied "the armies of the living God" (1 Sam. 17:26, 36). In the Psalms we find great spiritual desire phrased in such words as, "My soul thirsteth for God, for the living God" (Ps. 42:2).[11] In numerous places throughout the New Testament the same truth is announced (see Matt. 16:16; Acts 14:15; Rom. 9:26; Heb. 3:12; Rev. 7:2).

This basic biblical revelation of the living God has great meaning for the vigorous contemporary debate over the nature of God. Is God a person? Not a few significant writers in current philosophy and theology stumble over the biblical teaching that the Ground of the universe is personal, the *living* God who spoke by the prophets and became incarnate in Jesus Christ. Alfred N. Whitehead in philosophy and Paul Tillich in theology are representative of those who teach that God has personal qualities but is not a person.

D. Elton Trueblood has shown convincingly that, for at least two reasons, this philosophy is inadequate.[12] Our world unquestionably has persons in it, one of the most astounding facts of existence. If God, the Creator and Sustainer of the universe, is not a person, the stream of life has risen higher than its source. Moreover, so much of man's genuine religious experience is described in personal terms. If God is a process, a "thrust" toward life and consciousness, or even if He is "being-itself," He is not "Thou," but "It." But this does not conform to the experience of the Old Testament prophets nor with the revelation of God in Jesus Christ.

God is a person who is a center of consciousness, who confronts His people in a living encounter, who has purposes and designs, who speaks, acts, and, most of all, who has given us the highest revelation of himself in Jesus Christ, a person. The sum of the matter is that if God is not actually a person—however superior to our imperfect experience of personality—He is not the final explanation of the most remarkable fact in a material universe: persons. In the words of William Temple, one of the great theologians of this century, ". . . the explanation of the world is to be sought in a Personal Reality, or to use the historic phrase, in a Living God."[13]

One of the reasons why religious naturalists have rejected the belief in God as a person is that *by definition* they hold such a being to

---

11. Cf. Ed. Jacob, "God: O.T.," in *A Companion to the Bible* (New York: The Oxford Press, 1958), p. 141, where "life" is described as a mysterious reality which can only be accepted and which no one dreams of disputing; hence the being of God is an indisputable datum.

12. Trueblood, *Philosophy of Religion*, pp. 264-71.

13. *Nature, Man, and God*, p. 265.

be limited and finite. But it is the teaching of the Bible that no such limitation follows. The relationship between man and God is an "I-Thou" relationship, not "I-It." God is a person, *and* He is eternally existent, infinite. "Before the mountains were brought forth, or ever thou hadst formed the earth and the world, even from everlasting to everlasting, *thou* art God" (Ps. 90:2). Thus the Psalmist both addresses God in personal terms, "Thou," and affirms His eternal existence and infinite power.

In the biblical faith no tension exists in the simple confidence that the God of all the earth, infinite, eternal, is also a loving, holy person. If we define a person as "a being with conscious intelligence, equally able to be conscious of self and of others, and also able both to entertain purposes and to appreciate values,"[14] we have said nothing that inherently rules out an infinite, eternally existent God. As Dr. Trueblood reminds us, "Conscious love is not a limitation, but the greatest emancipation we know or can imagine."[15]

Far inferior to the biblical idea is the doctrine that God is a great impersonal being, without consciousness or purposes. How does one address such a being, or pray to and commune with an "It"? It is the Christian faith, grounded in the Scriptures and reason, that God is the *Living God,* a person who is also eternally existent and infinite.

IV. A GOD WHO IS FATHER

"The fundamental and central idea about God in New Testament teaching is His Fatherhood, and it determines all that follows."[16] The principal contribution of the New Testament to our understanding of God is that He is "the God and Father of our Lord Jesus Christ" (Eph. 1:3 and elsewhere). However, this is not to say that the teaching of God as Father is found only in the New Testament; for not only did the ethnic religions and Greek philosophers occasionally speak of God as Father, but the Old Testament really provides the roots of the concept for the New Testament (see Ps. 103:13; Isa. 63:16; Jer. 3:19; Mal. 2:10). However, outside the New Testament the thought of God as Father is not central, but rather an attribute alongside others,

---

14. Trueblood, *Philosophy of Religion,* p. 264.
15. *Ibid.,* p. 269.
16. *International Standard Bible Encyclopedia,* 2:1261.

indicating that God is Creator or Originator rather than One with whom man could enjoy intimate, close fellowship.[17]

It is in the life and teachings of Jesus that we find God to be preeminently *Father.* No other name for God was so often upon His lips. It dominated His whole thought and experience of God, and became the basis of deduction concerning the nature of God, as when He said, "Behold the fowls of the air: for they sow not, neither do they reap, nor gather into barns; yet your heavenly Father feedeth them. . . . Therefore take no thought, saying, What shall we eat? or, What shall we drink? . . . for your heavenly Father knoweth that ye have need of all these things" (Matt. 6:26, 31-32).

The newness and distinctiveness of this revelation of God is seen in several characteristics set forth dramatically both in the parables and in the life of our Lord. For one thing, God the Father not only welcomes the repentant sinner as he returns, but actually goes out to seek him. "What man of you, having an hundred sheep, if he lose one of them, doth not leave the ninety and nine in the wilderness, and go after that which is lost, until he find it?" (Luke 15:4). Also, in Jesus we have not merely the announcement of this truth about God, but the living embodiment of it in His incarnation, vicarious death, and resurrection from the dead: "God was in Christ, reconciling the world unto himself" (2 Cor. 5:19).

Pagans had occasionally thought of God as Father in the sense that He had brought them into being; Israel had a partial revelation of God as Father, but thought of it chiefly in terms of Israel's blessings. Jesus, the final revelation of the Father, not only announced the fatherhood of God, but also manifested more fully the Father's outgoing love in coming to *seek* as well as to save the lost.

It follows that if God is truly our Heavenly Father, many other things may be said of Him and of us in this light. The facts and laws of life, even those that bring severities as well as joys, are such as a Father would allow. The experiences of life that often seem so difficult are such as the Father permits His children to have. It may be too optimistic to say with Robert Browning:

> *God's in His heaven—*
> *All's right with the world.*

---

17. Cf. John M. Shaw, *Christian Doctrine: A One-Volume Outline of Christian Belief* (New York: Philosophical Library, 1954), pp. 129-30.

All may not be right with the world, but God *is* in His heaven, and this is our *Father's* world.

If God is our Father we may be confident of His kindness and care; we may be sure that we are *able* and *intended* to be sons and brothers; we may know that God is personal, approachable, merciful; and we may, if we choose, enjoy intimate, personal fellowship with Him, through Jesus Christ.

V. A GOD OF HOLY LOVE

In the biblical concepts of *holiness* and *love* we have a rich disclosure of the nature of God. The holiness of God predominates in the Old Testament, while in the New Testament the *love* of God predominates. In theology, sometimes one of these qualities has been emphasized to the neglect of the other. In either case the Christian revelation of God has been impoverished, for their is an indissoluble connection between holiness and love in the being of God. When the New Testament affirms that "God is love" (1 John 4:16), it presupposes the Old Testament disclosure of "the Holy One of Israel" (Isa. 1:4). And when, by the mouth of Moses, the Lord commanded Israel, "Ye shall be holy: for I the Lord your God am holy" (Lev. 19:2), He intimated the essential outgoing quality of His nature in a love that has always sought the highest good for man. The God of the Christian revelation is One whose nature is *holy love*. The God who is Love has an innermost nature that is holy.

In order, however, to see the full meaning of these terms it will be necessary to discuss them separately.

A. The Holiness of God

A careful study of this term reveals a number of concepts implicit in its meaning. It implies the essential character of the being of God, perhaps synonymous with "divinity" or "deity." It speaks of *separation* or *apartness*, the supernal majesty of God that transcends His creatures and produces in them awesome reverence and godly fear. It witnesses to moral and ethical perfection, righteousness, truth, faithfulness, absolute integrity. George Allen Turner finds three basic meanings for the term holiness, especially in the Old Testament. These are *radiance, separation*, and *purity*.[18] These various concepts may

---

18. *Vision Which Transforms*, pp. 16-19.

be grouped under the subjects *the majestic otherness of God* and *the moral excellence of God*.

1. The Majestic Otherness of God

On the basis of the root meaning of the Hebrew word for *holiness* it can be shown that the holiness of God implies, in the first instance, the awesome transcendence of God, His otherness or separateness from creation. It is of the very nature of God, the Source and Ground of all that is, to transcend, or rise above, His handiwork in majesty and glory ineffable. Thus, when a man is allowed to enter the immediate presence of God, he is stricken with something akin to terror. At the burning bush Moses takes off his shoes, and, before God in the Temple, Isaiah cries out in awe. "The English expression that best expresses the idea of holiness in the sense of the Old Testament is divine exaltation or majesty."[19]

It may be urged, in a day of flippancy and irreverence even among Christian people, that a renewed understanding of the holiness of God in this sense would be wholesome. "Who is like unto thee, O Lord, among the gods? who is like thee, glorious in holiness, fearful in praises, doing wonders?" (Exod. 15:11). We may be grateful beyond words that God has made himself known to sinful man, but we may profitably remember that God has not revealed *all* that may be known about himself. At the end of his sufferings Job did not find answers to his questions, but instead a stronger faith in God, whom he now knew more intimately but yet not fully.

The holiness of God, to begin with, then, means a radiant, majestic otherness, characteristic of the One who dwells "in the light which no man can approach unto; whom no man hath seen, nor can see: to whom be honour and power everlasting. Amen" (1 Tim. 6:16).

2. The Moral Excellence of God

While the foregoing concept of the holiness of God is basic or primary in the sense of a first truth in the disclosure of God, all scholars agree that the moral aspect of God's holiness became increasingly prominent in the Old Testament and is the almost exclusive emphasis in the New Testament. Indeed, many of these scholars believe that the holiness of God in the Old Testament is not without moral meaning in the earliest instance. Inasmuch as sin and evil were the chief reason for the separation between God and man, the holiness

---

19. C. Peipenbring, *Theology of the Old Testament,* p. 108; quoted, *ibid.,* p. 26.

of God early meant separation from sin: negatively, as opposition to all unrighteousness and evil; and positively, as promoting and strengthening all righteousness, truth, and goodness.

In the Old Testament we see a growing struggle between the priests, who encouraged a ceremonial holiness, and the prophets, who stressed the ethical holiness of God and His moral demands upon men. It was not enough, according to the prophets, to bring the sacrifices to the Temple and tread the courts of the Lord on the holy days. The holiness of God was ethical and moral, calling for justice, goodness, and integrity in men (cf. Isa. 1:10-20).

Perhaps the most graphic example of the moral quality of God's holiness to be found in the Old Testament is in the experience of the prophet Isaiah, whose favorite description of God became "the Holy One of Israel." Overwhelmed by the glorious vision of God, the prophet became acutely aware of his own sinfulness, as well as the uncleanness of his people. In that blazing Presence either the prophet or his sin must perish. An angelic being touched his lips with a live coal and assured him that his iniquity had been taken away and his sin purged (Isa. 6:1-8). As H. H. Rowley writes: "The holiness of God is thus seen to be the antithesis of all moral stain, that quality in God which is not only a rebuke to all in man that is contrary to His will, but in whose presence sin cannot live."[20]

It is this ethical quality of holiness that we meet in the New Testament, especially in the teaching of Jesus. He called for righteousness that went deeper than a ceremonial conformity, deeper even than individual acts: a righteousness that searched and cleansed the motive life of men. The demand for such holiness was based upon the nature of God. "Be ye therefore perfect, even as your Father which is in heaven is perfect" (Matt. 5:48). The holiness of God means righteousness, truth, faithfulness, and absolute integrity. In the words of William N. Clarke, "Holiness is the glorious fulness of God's moral excellence held as the principle of his own action and the standard for his creatures."[21]

B. The Love of God

The holiness and love of God are not to be thought of as in contradic-

---

20. *The Faith of Israel,* p. 66.

21. *An Outline of Christian Theology* (New York: Charles Scribner's Sons, 1898), p. 89.

tion. In human experience this is often so, but not in the being of God. As Edwin Lewis comments, "God's holiness is his deep concern for what is *right*. His love is his deep concern for men's good."[22] The nature of sin and evil are such that they work to the destruction of man's best interests. God cannot tolerate sin, not only because He is holy, but also because His nature is love. He wishes and seeks our highest good and happiness *through* righteousness.

Even in the Old Testament the holiness of God is seen to be outgoing, seeking the redemption of men. The experience of Hosea is an example. In spite of his wife's infidelity, Hosea loved her and diligently sought her restoration to his home. Through this anguish God led Hosea to see the waywardness of His people and, withal, His love, wooing them back to faithfulness. It has been said that, even in the Old Testament, it was not a righteous God and *yet* a Savior, but a righteous God and *therefore* a Savior.

In order to see the love of God as the New Testament reveals it to us, it is necessary to distinguish between two kinds of love, *eros* and *agape*. The first, the classical word for love, has a self-regarding frame of reference and seeks some value for self-fulfillment. The second is quite the opposite. It is energetic good will seeking to promote the well-being of others, even at the price of sacrifice. It is this love, *agape*, that is predicated of God. And when one views the whole sweep of the biblical story, he sees that this is fundamental to our understanding of God. It is the grace of God that has been seeking the redemption of men from the very beginning. Only the love of God goes out to the unlovely, the hateful and degraded, and seeks, not to get, but to give. The apostle summarizes it thus: "Herein is love, not that we loved God, but that he loved us, and sent his Son to be the propitiation for our sins. . . . and not for ours only, but also for the sins of the whole world" (1 John 4:10; 2:2).[23]

A knowledge of this love could come to us only by revelation. It would have been nonsense to have ascribed this *agape* love to any of the gods of paganism or Greek philosophy. The god of Plato, for example, was the principle of good, needing nothing and so desiring and loving nothing. The biblical concept of God as *Agape* would not have been appropriate to his description of God. Only through the

---

22. Lewis, *Manual of Christian Beliefs*, p. 22.

23. Cf. Anders Nygren, *Agape and Eros*, Translated by Philip S. Watson (Philadelphia: Westminster Press, 1953).

Christian revelation could a knowledge of love come that could be described as William Blake has written:

> *Love seeketh not itself to please*
> *Nor for itself hath any care;*
> *But for another gives its ease*
> *And builds a heaven in hell's despair.*[24]

The God of the Christian religion is a God of holiness and love, qualities so intermingled as to be inseparable. He is a God of *holy love*. This holy love involves not only absolute separation from sin but also an immense concern for the sinner and a devotion to his salvation.

VI. A GOD WHO IS THREEFOLD IN BEING[25]

Our major consideration of the Christian concept of the triunity of God must wait until we have had opportunity to consider the doctrines of Christ and of the Holy Spirit. It is important here, however, to note that there are two major distinctions in the Christian view of God as contrasted with either the Judaic or philosophic views. The first of these is that God is "the God and Father of our Lord Jesus Christ." The other is that God is a Trinity in essential being, revealed as Father, Son, and Holy Spirit.

It cannot be said too often that this latter belief is not an abstract intellectual puzzle, designed as an intelligence test for the mind. It is the most practical aspect of the Christian doctrine of the Godhead. It is forged in the experience and life of the Church, and shaped in the most concrete expression of its experience of the Divine. For the Christian view of God has always encompassed the sublime mystery that God is One, and that Christ is God and the Spirit is God. The result is the conviction that God is Three in One. Theologically stated, this is the doctrine of the Trinity.

SUMMARY

In addition to the minimum assertion of the existence of God as found in theism, the Christian faith greatly enriches and deepens the

---

24. *Songs of Experience:* "The Clod and the Pebble," stanza 1.
25. Refer to chap. 9 for a more complete discussion of the Trinity.

knowledge of God. It discovers in the Bible strong declarations of the sovereignty, all-sufficiency, and living personality of God. God is known to be a Heavenly Father—especially the "God and Father of our Lord." He is further seen to be a God of holiness and love. A correct understanding of the nature and being of God is essential to the fullness of our Christian faith.

CHAPTER 7

God and the World

We must now examine that important phase of the biblical understanding of God which has to do with His creation and providential control of the cosmos. Cosmology is the term usually employed to describe the doctrines associated with the origin and structure of the universe. Stated this way, the doctrine is more a problem for science or philosophy than for religion. "Cosmology" sounds cold and forbidding, but it ceases to be an impersonal set of theories when it is brought under the purview of Christian theology. In a Christian perspective, cosmology becomes a consideration of God's relation to the world. The relation is personal and religious. In God's world—and that this is God's world is the basic assumption of Christian cosmology—there are actually no impersonal or nonreligious problems.

The purpose of this chapter is to consider some of the relationships of God with His world. Three aspects of the God-world relationship are of particular concern for theology: (1) the significance of creation; (2) the meaning of providence, or God's continued activity in the universe; and (3) the major problem arising from the doctrine of providence, or the problem of evil. A consideration of these three topics constitutes the material of the chapter. It is the deliberate aim throughout to explore in a quite general way the meaning of the biblical doctrine of creation rather than give a detailed analysis of particular texts.

I. THE SIGNIFICANCE OF CREATION

There never has been a satisfactory alternative to the first four words of Genesis. Some thinkers have obscured the personality of God by incoherent metaphysics; some have confused Him with the physical world; a few have made God and matter coeternal; a few have denied Him altogether. But take away a personal, creative God, and cosmology is impossible. Our sciences do an excellent job of describing the operations of nature; but it is impossible to give a strictly scientific account of beginnings, since the operation which produced the cosmos and continues to support it preceded the original creation. Ultimate causes are found, not *in*, but *behind*, the phenomenal, observable world.[1] "Things which are seen were not made of things which do appear" (Heb. 11:3).

The theist has an immediate advantage over the nontheist in that he begins with an adequate source. No sensible thinker pretends that God's relation to the world is thereby explained by a snap of the fingers. But granting the difficulty of understanding the God-world relationship, this task is less difficult than constructing a cosmological theory without God.

The author of Genesis made no effort to give a metaphysically precise account of the beginning and structure of the universe. It is unreasonable to expect that the creation record should be scientifically complete, since the purpose of the account is obviously religious. The attempt to force Genesis into a modern scientific structure grows out of a misguided apologetic that does injustice to both Genesis and science.

A. What the Creation Account Denies

The creation story is nontheless tremendously significant both for what it denies and for what it affirms. Materialism, pantheism, and dualism are clearly excluded by the Genesis record.

1. *Materialism*

This is the theory that matter, or nature and its laws, are sufficient for the explanation of all the facts. There is no going beyond nature. The theory may be summarized by the view of Thomas Hobbes that all that exists is matter and all that occurs is motion.

For the Hebrews, such a theory was ultimate absurdity. In fact they tended to go to the other extreme in attributing all effects to the immediate action of God (Psalm 29). There were no secondary causes.

---

1. The close relation of theology to metaphysics is apparent here and throughout. For a personalistic metaphysics see Borden Parker Bowne, *Metaphysics* (Boston: Boston University Press, revised edition, 1898; copyright, 1943); or Edgar Sheffield Brightman, *Person and Reality* (New York: Ronald Press Company, 1958).

God was the Source of all things: the light, darkness, good, evil, storm, sunshine, wind, rain, life, death. Materialism fails in its inability to account for origins, not only of the physical world, but of life and values, and above all, spirit or persons.

2. *Pantheism*

This, as we have seen, is the theory that God and the universe are identical or coextensive. There is no God *and* the universe. God *is* the universe. God is the totality of all things; or the totality of all things is God. Spinoza's metaphysics, for example, is a systematic pantheism.

This theory makes no room for the transcendence of God. It is very clear in Genesis that, no matter how much God involves himself in creative action, He is above His creation, superior to it, and not identical with it. Even allowing that God may have been creating universes from all eternity, He always precedes His creation as the Ground or Cause without which it would not exist.

3. *Dualism*

This theory has many forms, but the basic idea is that God and matter are eternally parallel existences, neither one being the cause of the other.

There is no room for such a theory in biblical cosmology. From the standpoint of biblical explanation, the physical universe is never pictured as a parallel or collateral existence. Such a view would violate the creative axiom that God is prior. Genesis is unambiguous in its view that creation is derived and not coeternal. "In the beginning God created the heaven and the earth" (Gen. 1:1). The Psalmist probably had this account in mind when he wrote: "Of old hast thou laid the foundation of the earth: and the heavens are the work of thy hands" (Ps. 102:25).

B. What the Creation Account Affirms

On the positive side, the following affirmations are grounded firmly in the scriptural insights into God's creative relation to the universe:

1. *An Adequate Account of Beginnings*

The basic weakness in most theories is usually not a matter of logic or grammar, but of adequacy. As noted in our survey of the cosmological argument, to attempt to account for this universe apart from God is to end up with more in the effect than is provided in the cause. Nontheistic views tend to violate the law of causal adequacy.

With such a God as revealed in the Scriptures there is no reason to doubt His ability to bring the universe into existence. "Lift up your eyes . . . ," says Isaiah, "and behold who hath created these things, that bringeth out their host by number: he calleth them all by names by the greatness of his might, for that he is strong in power; not one faileth" (Isa. 40:26). If it be argued that God is not adequate, then the way is open for the fallacy of an infinite regress of causes, a solution which solves nothing. But so far as creative power is concerned, there is no need to go beyond God. To go behind an adequate cause, such as God is, to ask for another cause, violates not only Scripture but reason itself. To ask for a cause of an adequate cause is but to submit one's reason to an endless regress. While the aseity or self-existence of God is not an easy concept, still the thought of God as the ultimate Creator does provide a resting place for the mind.

2. *Behind the Physical Is the Spiritual*

This is a positive way of denying that matter is the ultimate reality. "God is a spirit," and the energy which He exerts to maintain the universe is spiritual. The data of both physics and philosophy agree with the basic scriptural insights that "the things which are seen" are merely phenomenal, while "the things which are not seen" are truly real. He who would find his ultimate cause in matter logically eliminates the spiritual values of the universe. Through spirit or mind we can account for matter, but matter by itself is a contradiction. This does not mean that matter is unimportant or that it is not part of God's world. This paragraph seeks only to assert the priority of spiritual reality.

3. *God Is the Principle of Order in the Universe*

Whatever the reason for the original chaos of matter, it was the Spirit of God who brooded over it and reduced the chaos to cosmos, the disorder to order, the indefinite to the definite.

The above denials and affirmations are direct implications of the biblical doctrine of creation. However the Hymn of Creation is interpreted, in terms of solar, creative days or in terms of geological eras, the implications for Christian cosmology are the same: God was prior to the physical universe; God was the Originator of the universe; God is the Reason for the continuation of the universe.

II. The Meaning of Providence

Whereas the doctrine of creation deals with the relation of God to the beginning of the physical universe, providence is the term usually employed in theology to describe God's present relation to the world. Providence is the doctrine that deals with God's control, care, and continued preservation of the universe.

A. Assumptions of Belief in Providence

What are the assumptions of the doctrine? It is reasonable to suppose that if God created the universe He continues to maintain His relationship with it. What that relationship is in specific terms is the heart of the doctrine of providence. *Deus absconditus,* an absentee God, will not satisfy the factors in the equation as implied in the Scriptures and in the inherent rational and physical demands of the universe. Deism does not deny the creative agency of God in the beginning; but having created, the view says, God then withdrew from the world, allowing it to continue according to the inexorable laws of cause and effect. God, in this view, is the completely transcendent, austere, afar-off First Cause.[2]

There is no quarrel with the notion that God is the Ultimate Cause of all things, but when the "First" is emphasized, God is seen as the end factor in a long chain of causes and effects beginning with the present and extending backwards in time to the first in the series, that is, to God. Such a view does not do justice to the present, sustaining relationship which God maintains with the universe. Before an adequate doctrine of providence can be maintained three basic assumptions are necessary.

1. *Immanence*

In the doctrine of divine providence, as in the doctrine of God in general, the first basic assumption is that God is immanent in the world. This does not deny His transcendence or His priority to the cosmic process, but affirms God's actual presence and power in the ongoing of the universe. In this view there is no abstract "nature" nor are there "laws" which operate on their own. What is called nature is the continued energizing of God's will, and its laws are the consistent patterns of God's operations.

An abstraction is something seen out of its context or apart from the whole. Nature is an abstraction. Law is an abstraction. They

---

2. The 18th century was the "classic" period of deistic thought, but some see in modern neo-orthodoxy a theological modification of deism. It is reflected in the view that God is "wholly other."

become concrete, or properly related, only when seen as the functions of God. "Mother Nature" gets credit for many acts of care and wisdom which must surely be attributed to the Heavenly Father, who cares for the birds of the air and the lilies of the field (Matt. 6:26-30). Transcendence says that God is above His universe, or not identical with it. Immanence says that God is *in* His universe, but not coextensive with it. The extreme form of transcendence leads to deism. The extreme form of immanence leads to pantheism. But neither extreme is necessary. Just as an artist is "outside" his work and "in" it, God is both superior to His universe and involved in its processes. God is transcendent as Creator. He is immanent as Sustainer.

2. *Preservation*

The second basic assumption is that God's power is at every moment the reason for the preservation of both nature and its processes. He upholdeth all things "by the word of his power" (Heb. 1:3). Paul refers to the same concept when he says that "by him all things consist" (Col. 1:17). "Consist" means to cohere or to hold together. In a sense, God is continually creating the universe according to the laws of time and change. The doctrine of "continuous creation" does not destroy continuity, as some have strangely contended.[3] God's constant exertion of will to maintain the universe seems the only rational basis of continuity. Otherwise there is the paradox of self-sustaining, self-perpetuating nature. The Bible knows no such doctrine.

3. *Uniformity*

The third assumption is that God in nature is the basis of law and order. God's operations are consistent, rational, coherent. Without law, the whole of life as we know it would be impossible. Every grain of sand, every drop of water reveals precise formulas of composition, structure, and action. Nature's processes are basically uniform and for the most part predictable. Insofar as nature functions according to law, it is a blessing. The pilot takes his plane off the ground confidently because he knows he can depend on the laws of thermodynamics. The chemist nonchalantly handles explosive material with the conviction that it is safe when handled according to certain

---

3. For instance, A. M. Hills, *Fundamental Christian Theology* (Pasadena, Calif.: Pasadena College, 1931), 1:299.

rules. A publisher will spend thousands of dollars printing almanacs, calendars, charts, all of which depend upon the regularity of the motion of the earth, the moon, the tides. The farmer invests in fertilizer and machinery with the confidence that the tiny seeds he puts into the ground will yield 30- and 60- and 100-fold. The divine source of the regularity of nature is implied in God's beautiful promise to Noah: "While the earth remaineth, seedtime and harvest, and cold and heat, and summer and winter, and day and night shall not cease" (Gen. 8:22).

B. Providence and Miracles

Does the regularity of nature rule out the possibility of miracles? Many philosophers have thought so. Even some theologians have joined in the repudiation of the extraordinary. Such a point of view is based on too narrow a concept of nature. If nature is all there is, as materialists say, then of course there is no room for anything except what can be explained in terms of nature itself. But even if the latter be true—which it is not—to rule out a miracle because it violates the laws of nature is still to assume that there are no "natural" laws which provide for events which appear to be unique.

The definition of miracle depends on one's total point of view. Probably many who agree that turning water into wine in a moment is a genuine miracle would also content that the production of the sweet juice in a ripened grape is but a "natural" process and therefore no miracle.[4] But both are miracles from one point of view. In a theistic context, all is supernatural, i.e., all is the work of God, whether the action is instantaneous or a process. God is no less the Source of the ripened grape than He is the Source of the wine in the waterpots. But because of the familiarity and the regularity of the ripening grapes, the temptation is to say that the process is "natural," while the immediate production of grape juice is "supernatural." Miracle is therefore defined as any action which contravenes the laws or processes of nature.

On the other hand, if all of nature is miracle, i.e., God's action, there is no reason to assume that God's action is limited to the regular pattern of nature. Because God is rational and orderly, He usually acts in a consistent manner; but He is also free to "speed up the pro-

---

4. This turn of thought is suggested by C. S. Lewis, *Miracles* (New York: The Macmillan Co., 1947), p. 163.

cess" or to express His will in a manner so far unknown to us. There is an implicit fallacy in speaking of a miracle as a "violation" of the laws of nature. God does not violate His own laws. As ordinarily understood, a miracle is an event or action which deviates from the known laws of nature. From the total theistic perspective, a miracle is an action of God *in addition* to His regular mode of action. The concept of miracle in either case in no way contravenes the concept of providence. In fact, the willingness and ability of God to act in ways that are out of the ordinary pattern of nature add richness to the doctrine of providence, and reveal God more in the capacity of Heavenly Father than as an austere First Cause.

C. Providence and Prayer

How do prayer and providence relate? The doctrine of prayer has many rich and satisfying aspects. Certainly the exercise of prayer is not exhausted by asking for things. Prayer involves a total attitude of commitment and dependence upon God. It has its subjective effects in increased faith, changed perspective, and restored confidence. But it is also the power of possibility. "With God all things are possible" (Mark 10:27). Prayer is a channel of power. It is an open door. It is spiritual adventure. It is working together with God. Seen as such, it in no way contradicts the doctrine of providence.

In fact, the possibility of answered prayer attests the scriptural validity of providence itself. Prayer is the evidence on the personal level of God's immediate concern with His creation. It may be that prayer is the key to miracles and many of God's extranatural actions. Prayer undoubtedly is a condition for the release of power, both as an agency of change on the human level and in nature.

The Scriptures abound in their testimony to the power and possibility of prayer. Certainly no spiritual exercise is more frequently commended or more abundantly illustrated. In terms of experience, 10 million Christians would gladly add to the testimony of the Scriptures their own witness to the power of prayer. For the Christian familiar with the ways of God, prayer and providence are never incompatible. They are the closest possible adjuncts. In fact, it might well be asked how one could know of God's providence by personal experience without prayer.

The Bible knows nothing of a "closed universe." Miracle and prayer both amply demonstrate the presence of God in His own system. There is certainly no *a priori* reason why God should be bound by fixed, inexorable laws. Evidence both from the sciences and from personal experience indicates that the "laws of nature" are not absolute. God created at the beginning, but He continues to operate within the framework of nature, and constantly invades the regular pattern in ways that show His freedom from the merely natural. Revelation, the spiritual awakening and renewal of man, the impulse to divine service, all indicate continued dynamic interaction between God and His own world.

III. The Problem of Evil

Any discussion of God's relation to the universe is incomplete unless some consideration is given to the problem of evil. "Evil" here refers to those experiences suffered by nature and the human body which are not the result of moral choice. Man does not causally will a hurricane or cancer. Sin, on the other hand, involves moral decision.

Paradoxically, the more one insists on the doctrine of providence, the more difficult it is to explain the presence of evil. The immediate reaction of some thinkers to this dilemma is either to separate God from any sustaining relationship with the universe or to invent a level of creative relationship which is entirely impersonal, and hence beyond God's personal and moral responsibility. Either alternative sacrifices too much from the Christian point of view. No view is adequate which leads to the inherent contradiction of either a self-sustaining or an impersonal universe. A solution at the expense of God's personal presence in the universe is no solution. While the philosophical solution to the problem of evil is complicated by the doctrine of divine causality, God is himself the only practical answer to the problem in human life.

What is the problem of evil? The problem has been variously stated since Epicurus first propounded the dilemma between God's power and His goodness. The problem arises when one tries to give a coherent account of the meaning of reality. Experience is very contradictory in presenting both good and evil, plenty and poverty, pleasure and pain, creativity and discreativity, joy and sorrow. Life is full of faith, hope, love, heroism, willing sacrifice, health; but it is also full of distrust, despair, hate, cowardice, selfishness, suffering. The earth has both Mount Zion and Vesuvius; there are both the quiet of a New England twilight and the vicious destructiveness of a coastal hurricane. The fact is that these contradictions occur in the same world— God's world. That is the problem.

A. Attempted Solutions

What are some attempted solutions? The history of philosophy and religion reveals many attempts to "solve" the problem of evil.[5] The following are the most familiar.

1. *Evil Is Illusion*

This view is as old as Buddhism and as modern as Christian Science. What is usually called evil, it is said, is only appearance. It has no ultimate reality. Even agreeing that evil is not ultimately real, it still is very real in experience. Cancer, imbecility, tornadoes are agonizingly real in terms of pain, sorrow, and destruction, whatever their metaphysical status.

2. *Evil Is Actually Good*

Because of limited understanding, we are told, we cannot see the place that evil has in the total structure of experience. However, this theory is basically an appeal to ignorance. To say we cannot understand may be completely true, but it is not a solution. Furthermore, if what appears to be evil is actually good, then all distinctions between values disappear. Certainly one should not kill germs. Probably the chief objection lies in its impossible demand on personal faith. Can one have faith that polio is good?

3. *Evil Is the Natural Result of Human Freedom and Sin*

If men had not sinned, says this view, then there would be no evil. It is certainly true that much evil is caused by sin, but not all evil is caused by sin. If all evil is the effect of sin, then it should be possible to establish connection between cause and effect. But both the scriptural insights on this point and practical experience show that in many cases there is no such connection. "Who did sin, this man, or his parent, that he was born blind?" asked the disciples of Jesus. The answer of Jesus was, "Neither hath this man sinned, nor his parents" (John 9:2-3). In present-day experience it would be most difficult to show that the tornado which sweeps through Kansas is the result of anybody's sin. Of course, it might be argued that a tornado is not evil—at least by one not living in its path.

4. *Evil Is Sent by God Along with the Good*

God is the impartial Source of both. There can be no other origi-

---

5. For comparative lists of "solutions" see Trueblood, *Philosophy of Religion*, p. 355 ff.; or Edgar Sheffield Brightman, *A Philosophy of Religion* (New York: Prentice-Hall, Inc., 1940), p. 259 ff.

native power in the world except God, it is argued; therefore both good and evil are part of God's creative process. This view suffers from the same weaknesses as the second point above, with the further and more compelling objection that God is made the efficient cause of evil. Of course, if evil is part of the divine teleology, then it could be argued that what God wills must be good. But again all value distinctions would be illusions. Suffering in such a case should be as pleasant as good health, tragedy as acceptable as happiness, death as good as life. It is most difficult to think of God as sending the accident that causes the death of a child.

5. *Evil Is God's Punishment for Sin*

Evil is "penally ordained," as some put it.[6] This view breaks down on the grounds that it is not just the persons who sin who feel the effect of "punishment," but many innocent people become the victims of the same evil circumstances. This view not only violates the biblical insight that "each man shall bear his own sin," but it places God in the grossly unfair situation of punishing the good along with the evil. According to Jesus, Pilate's murder of the Galileans and the tragedy of the tower of Siloam in Jerusalem had no connection with the sins or innocence of the people who suffered (Luke 13:1-5). Finally, it seems that the punishment is often bigger and more destructive than the sin itself.

6. *Evil Is Due to a Finite Element in the Nature of God*

Evil is said to be the direct "result" of limitations in the nature of God, so that whenever He acts, the finite as well as the infinite elements appear in His creation.[7] God is infinitely good, but His will is said to be restricted by nonrational elements which appear as evils in His creation. This view is better than the one which says that God wills evil, but it too readily ascribes to the nature of God what had better be excluded. This "solution" not only pushes the problem back into eternity without adding clarification, but it immediately becomes subject to the weaknesses inherent in any theory of dualism.[8] Admittedly, the view does not rob God of His good will, but it puts a

---

6. For instance, Gustav Oehler, *Theology of the Old Testament* (Grand Rapids: Zondervan Publishing House, reprint, 1950), p. 122.

7. This is the view of E. S. Brightman, and in the form he presents it, is one of the better-known recent attempts to deal with the problem. See Brightman, *Philosophy of Religion,* p. 313 ff.

8. In fairness to Brightman, he frequently denied that his view led to dualism.

"foreign element" within the very essence of God, which provides grounds for a dualistic cosmology.

B. Understanding the Problem

In rejecting the above views on the problem of evil, can one find a clear-cut biblical solution? In the sense of an argued, speculative theory, no. But the Bible does provide much material as a basis for meaningful interpretation of the problem. Based on positive assertion or strong implication in the Book of Genesis, the following points emerge as helpful:

1. *Evil Was Present Prior to Adam's Sin*

Some scholars find it as early as the chaos in 1:1. Others see a hint of evil in the command to "subdue" the earth in 1:28. The original word for subdue is *kabash,* which means to "bring into subjection." A similar suggestion occurs in 2:15, where part of the work of man is to "keep" the garden. In the context, the "keep" implies the Hebrew meaning "to take heed" or guard. It is the same word as used of the flaming sword "which turned every way to keep the tree of life" (3:24). The word "evil" itself occurs as early as 2:9, where it already appears as a clear-cut alternative to the good. In 3:1 the presence of evil is brought into sharp focus by the serpent. The data surely suggest that evil in some form preceded the seduction of Adam and Eve. Therefore, as said earlier, it is wrong to infer that all evil is the result of human freedom.

2. *Evil Is Present as an Alternative to Good in a Realm Outside of, and Possibly Prior to, the Physical Creation*

It seems that intelligent creatures of the heavenly realm were subject to the presence of evil. Jude 6 speaks of "the angels which kept not their first estate." Jesus refers to the devil as one who "abode not in the truth" (John 8:44). The implication is that the evil one departed from the realm of truth for its opposite.

3. *Wherever There Is Something Created, There Exists the Possibility of Discreativity* [9]

This appears to be true whether of heavenly beings, the human race, or physical nature. On the other hand, there is no biblical sug-

---

9. This point of view is ably expounded by Edwin Lewis, *The Creator and the Adversary* (New York: Abingdon-Cokesbury Press, 1948).

gestion that evil, or even the possibility of evil, existed prior to anything created. Dualism is not a Bible doctrine. God is always prior to evil. Concomitant with creation, however, the way was made possible for destructiveness, suffering, sin. It is clear that there can be no discreativity until there has been creativity. Some thinkers, in seeking justification for evil, argue for its necessity as a contrast to the good. In this case, good seems to lose its logical priority. Good surely exists without evil, but evil cannot exist without good. Good is therefore prior, and ultimate dualism is impossible.

This is another way of saying that God himself has made the possibility of evil in the very act of creation. But God has fully accepted the risk and responsibility of creation, considering it of greater value to create than not to create. The coordinate to creation is redemption. Any attempt to justify the ways of God to man in regard to creation must be seen in the light of His redeeming activity. Evil as a possibility had to be defeated in the realm of actuality. This is the glory of redemption, and herein lies the practical answer to evil, which is considered next.

C. Toward a Biblical Answer

If there is any effective answer to the problem of evil it must be a concrete, specific, practical answer, because the problem is concrete and specific. Evil enters every phase of human experience, and until there is a new heaven and a new earth, it must be contended with in the present life. A philosophical hypothesis as to the source of evil, while good and worthwhile, will never meet the need on the experiential level. The problem is therefore not objective, but subjective: not how or whence evil comes, but, How shall I meet it? On this level, the Scriptures offer a full and satisfying solution to the problem of evil. Three aspects of the problem present themselves for consideration: (1) the answer to moral evil within, (2) the answer to evils that come from without, and (3) the answer to the problem as it affects the hope of the Christian for the future.

1. Moral Evil Within

The solution to the problem of moral evil, or personal sin, is found in the forgiveness of God and the sanctifying grace of the Holy Spirit. Forgiveness is the divine answer to the agonizing sense of personal failure and guilt. It not only changes the present but reorganizes the past. A man becomes truly free from his old sins. Sanctification is the cleansing of the inner person from selfishness and waywardness, concomitant with the positive enduement of love and moral power. Salvation is a matter of total adjustment of the self to God. The relationship between the human and the divine is dynamic and creative. The willing, surrendered attitude of the soul is answered by the plenitude of God's love and power. No longer is evil a discreative, disruptive agency in the soul. "Greater is he that is in you, than he that is in the world" (1 John 4:4). The fuller implications of the doctrine of personal salvation are discussed in the section on God's redemptive purpose.

2. Natural Evils from Without

The Scriptures set forth abundant help on the way to meet the evils that present themselves from without. As stated above, the prime prerequisite is, of course, the presence of the Holy Spirit as the inner, redeeming Agency at the very heart of one's life. A man is only as strong without as he is within. Evils do come. Once again, the problem is not whether a man has to face suffering, tragedy, ignorance, darkness. He will. The problem is, How? There are several ways of meeting evil and solving the problem thereby:

a. First is to accept the evil, although not sent by God, as an educative opportunity.[10] There is much to be learned from suffering: patience, sympathy, faith, trust. Paul says that "we rejoice in our suffering, knowing that suffering produces endurance, and endurance produces character" (Rom. 5:3-4, RSV). The writer of Hebrews, speaking of the suffering of Christ, said that, "though he were a Son, yet learned he obedience by the things which he suffered" (5:8). By accepting evil as a learning opportunity, it is no longer a "dead end." It is caught up into a larger meaning and transformed into a tool for the development of character and perspective. Probably there is no evil in any form but what can be an instrument of instruction.

b. A second way is to meet the evils of life with the faith which emerges from a vision of the superior goodness of God. That God is good is the theistic minimum in personal faith. Whatever the attributes applied to God, whatever God is, whether more or less, the absolute minimum is that He must be good. It is tragic that theology, which should always be an instrument of faith, has become to many anguished souls the instrument for belief in divinely caused tragedy.

---

10. Suffering as part of the divine pedagogy is essentially the view of Nels Ferré. For a brief summary of his position see his *The Christian Understanding of God* (New York: Harper and Brothers, 1951), pp. 118 ff.

There rings in the ears of the writer the bitter cry of the mother by the side of her daughter's hospital bed, "God shouldn't have done this to me!"

The vision that God is good shows up evil for what it is. It is deficient, not self-dependent; it is subject to control, transmutation. It is not a dead end; it is never willed by God. The triumph of Job lay in his unshakable faith that God was not the cause of his sufferings. True, he searched desperately for some reason for his suffering, but he never did find any philosophical solution. His answer came in his vision of God. The vision was the solution. He had seen God and that was enough.

So it was with the Psalmist. His problem was the apparent triumph of evildoers. "When I thought to know this," he said, "it was too painful for me; until I went into the sanctuary of God; then understood I their end" (Ps. 73:16-17). The vision of God not only clarifies the problem, but it shows that God is working to transmute the evil into an agent for good. "The patriarchs, moved with envy, sold Joseph into Egypt: but God was with him" (Acts 7:9).

Herein is the role of faith in the midst of evil: That "in everything God works for good with those who love him" (Rom. 8:28, RSV). God does not send evil but He works through it. He is infinitely resourceful in His ability to turn every evil to His own purposes. "Surely the wrath of man shall praise thee: the remainder of wrath shalt thou restrain" (Ps. 76:10).

On the human level, such faith in God is the instrument of victory. "This is the victory that overcometh the world, even our faith," says John (1 John 5:4). Paul says: "Be not overcome of evil, but overcome evil with good" (Rom. 12:21). Faith and love are more basic than evil. For the theist, it is written into the very structure of the universe that the good, the beautiful, the true are superior to their opposites. It is the faith of the Christian that they shall never fail.

3. *Ultimate Redemption*

The third biblical answer to evil is oriented toward the future and the cosmic aspects of evil. What is the basis for the hope that God's blessings will flow "far as the curse is found"? The hope is found in the total redeeming work of Christ.

As Logos, without whom "was not any thing made that was made" (John 1:3), Christ is active in His own realm as the Guarantor that evil shall be destroyed. He is, with reference to the past, the Creator; in the present, the Sustainer; in the future, the Fulfiller, or

Redeemer of all creation. "For of him, and through him, and to him are all things" (Rom. 11:36). His task is complete when He accomplishes the purpose for which He was manifested: "That he might destroy the works of the devil" (1 John 3:8).

At present "we see not yet all things put under him," as the writer of Hebrews declares, but the implication is clear that by anticipation God has "put all things in subjection under his feet. For in that he put all in subjection under him, he left nothing that is not put under him" (Heb. 2:8). The agency of Christ is to redeem creation at whatever point evil has invaded. "For the earnest expectation of the creation waiteth for the revealing of the sons of God. For the creation was subjected to vanity, not of its own will, but by reason of him who subjected it, in hope that the creation itself also shall be delivered from the bondage of corruption into the liberty of the glory of the children of God. For we know that the whole creation groaneth and travaileth in pain together until now" (Rom. 8:19-22, ARV).

The total redemptive plan of God is beautifully expressed in Paul's letter to the Ephesians. The key to the Epistle is found in the statement of what God "hath purposed in himself: that in the dispensation of the fulness of times he might gather together in one all things in Christ, both which are in heaven, and which are on earth" (Eph. 1:9-10). The Revelator sees the final redemption in terms of a "new heaven and a new earth" (Rev. 21:1). Here is the end of creation, and the redemptive ultimate. Creation and redemption, which from the first invasion of evil have been in dynamic relationship but not at one, become identical in the vision of the seer. The New Jerusalem is synonymous with redeemed creation. "There shall be no more death . . . there shall be no more curse" (Rev. 21:4; 22:3).

Redemption is the divine correlate to creation. "Creation was subjected to vanity" (Rom. 8:20, ARV), or to the law of decay and death, but creation is justified by the saving work of Christ in nature and personality. God's specific answer to the physical effects of evil is the new heavens and the new earth; the answer to the dissolution of the human body is the resurrection; the answer to personal sin is deliverance from sin, both in the temporal and in the eternal order. The answer to all evil, in whatever form, is Christ.

Cosmology begins in the work of the Logos, who created the universe. The doctrine finds its ultimate purpose in Him who is both the "beginning and the end." Christ is the Creator, the Sustainer, the Fulfiller of all things.

SUMMARY

In this chapter we have considered three aspects of God's relationship with the cosmos: His creation, His providence in relation to prayer and miracle, and the ever-perplexing problem of evil in a universe subject to the government of a good God. At each of these points the biblical faith speaks with clarity and strength. The answers it gives are an important part of the structure of our Christian faith.

CHAPTER 8

Biblical Christology

What think ye of Christ? whose son is he? (Matt. 22:42)

Christology is that area of doctrine which deals with the person of Jesus Christ as Redeemer. As such it is the living heart of Christianity.

Biblical Christology is confessional. It is an expression of the faith of committed men. "With the heart man believeth unto righteousness; and with the mouth confession is made unto salvation" (Rom. 10:10). "Whosoever believeth that Jesus is the Christ is born of God" (1 John 5:1). "Whosoever shall confess that Jesus is the Son of God, God dwelleth in him, and he in God" (1 John 4:15).

The meaning of these scriptures becomes clear when we consider the implications of Simon Peter's confession of Christ at Caesarea Philippi (Matt. 16:15-18). Jesus declared Peter's confession to be the product, not of human reason, but of divine revelation: "Flesh and blood hath not revealed it unto thee, but my Father which is in heaven." This man had committed himself to Christ in personal surrender and therefore *knew* by the Spirit of God that Jesus was the Son of God. Only one who has made such a commitment is in a position to pronounce on Christ (John 7:17).

St. Paul puts it quite simply, "No one can say 'Jesus is Lord' except by the Holy Spirit" (1 Cor. 12:3, RSV). The truth of Christ is of such a nature that it can be neither proved nor disproved by human reason alone.

We acknowledge therefore our particular dependence upon the Spirit for the illumination of our understanding. It is heartening to recall that we have a specific promise upon which we may rely. Speaking of the Holy Spirit, Jesus said, "He shall glorify me: for he shall receive of mine, and shall shew it unto you" (John 16:14).

Although Christology is a matter primarily of scriptural teaching, we cannot understand it apart from its development within the life and thought of the Church. In attempting to sketch the broad lines of biblical Christology, therefore, we shall draw upon the history of Christian thought.

I. THE CHRIST EVENT

We have no strictly objective account of Jesus Christ, nor could there be such a thing. All we know of Him has been recorded and interpreted by those who had found Him to be the Son of God, the Savior of the world. The Gospel narratives are not so much biographical accounts as confessions of faith. They all breathe the spirit of the apostle John, who wrote, "That which was from the beginning, which we have heard, which we have seen with our eyes, which we have looked upon, and our hands have handled, of the Word of life; that which we have seen and heard declare we unto you, that ye may have fellowship with us: and truly our fellowship is with the Father, and with his Son Jesus Christ" (1 John 1:1-3).

Notice that John combines history and confession. The glory of Christianity is its historicity. Our Lord and Savior was no mythical personage but a flesh-and-blood Man who lived 19 centuries ago. But Christianity is not mere history. Like all the history of the Bible, it is *interpreted* history. The Evangelists believed it was their divine commission to proclaim to the world that "God was in Christ, reconciling the world unto himself" (2 Cor. 5:19). This is to say that for the Evangelists and apostles the Jesus of history had become the Christ of experience. "Though we have known Christ after the flesh, yet now henceforth know we him no more" (2 Cor. 5:16).

We do not hesitate, therefore, to employ the New Testament method of interpreting certain aspects of the Christ event which appear to have special doctrinal significance. These are: The Virgin Birth, The Circumcision, Jesus' Normal Development, The Baptism, The Temptation, Jesus' Passion and Death, Jesus' Burial and Resurrection, The Ascension.

A. The Virgin Birth

The account of Jesus' virgin birth is given in Matthew (1:18-25) and in Luke (1:26-56). Matthew sees this miracle as a fulfillment of Isaiah's prophecy (7:14), while Luke views it as a fundamental historical fact in the work of redemption.

The Virgin Birth was sheer miracle. It is entirely beside the point to try to explain the event scientifically. However, there is nothing unscientific about the matter; it is rather beyond science, in the realm of God's free activity.

This doctrine safeguards two vital truths concerning Christ, His deity and His sinlessness.

1. *The Virgin Birth and Christ's Deity*

The preexistence of Christ implies the Virgin Birth. In Jesus the eternal Word was made flesh. "The meaning of the Virgin Birth is ultimately dogmatic: it is one of the many ways in which the New Testament asserts that the Son of God came into history; he did not come out of it."[1]

2. *The Virgin Birth and Christ's Sinlessness*

The angel announced to Mary: "The Holy Ghost shall come upon thee, . . . therefore also *that holy thing* which shall be born of thee shall be called the Son of God" (Luke 1:35). Because He was conceived of the Holy Spirit, Jesus was free from original sin. All other men are "born of the flesh" (i.e., depraved); therefore they must be "born again, . . . of the Spirit" (John 3:3-7). This was unnecessary in Jesus' case because from His mother's womb He was "born of the Spirit." In Him as the Last Adam the gift of the Spirit was restored and the race renewed in the image of God.

B. The Circumcision

In conformity with the Levitical law, Jesus was circumcised the eighth day (Luke 2:21). In effect this rite was an *imputation of sin* to Jesus. By His birth He was presented to us "in the likeness of sinful flesh" (Rom. 8:3); by His circumcision He was ritually "made to be sin for us" (2 Cor. 5:21). By His birth He was "made of a woman . . ."; by His circumcision He was "made under the law" (Gal. 4:4).

The full significance of this imputation is seen when we consider that circumcision symbolized the putting off of the carnal nature (Deut. 30:6; Col. 2:11).

C. Normal Development

Jesus is presented to us in the Gospels as a normal child who devel-

---

1. J. S. Whale, *Christian Doctrine* (New York: The Macmillan Co., 1945), p. 109. See the extensive Christology in W. T. Purkiser, Richard S. Taylor, and Willard H. Taylor, *God, Man, and Salvation:* A Biblical Theology (Kansas City: Beacon Hill Press of Kansas City, 1977), pp. 303-65.

oped intellectually, physically, spiritually, and socially (Luke 2:52). The Temple incident when He was 12 would suggest His unique awareness of the Father, but the canonical Gospels avoid all apocryphal stories which would destroy the picture of a normal childhood. His was "the unfolding of a pure and normal human nature apart from sin."[2]

Because His life was lived under the direction of the Holy Spirit, Jesus grew up as a God-centered Person. He sanctified every stage of human life. As Irenaeus wrote:

> He came to save all through means of himself, infants, and children, and boys, and youth, and old men. . . . At last He came to death itself, that He might be "the firstborn from the dead, that in all things he might have the pre-eminence," the Prince of life, existing before all and going before all.

D. The Baptism

Jesus' baptism was the inauguration of His Messianic ministry. The voice from heaven is probably to be understood as the sealing of Jesus' Messianic consciousness, while the descent of the Spirit upon Him like a dove was a revelation to John that Jesus was the Anointed of the Lord (John 1:32-34).

Moreover, by His baptism Jesus was "numbered with the transgressors" (Isa. 53:12). So evident was this to John that he protested to Jesus, "I have need to be baptized of thee." But Jesus countered, "Suffer it to be so now: for thus it becometh us to fulfil all righteousness" (Matt. 3:14-15). Some scholars, without spiritual insight, still stumble over Jesus' baptism; to them the incident suggests that Jesus was conscious of guilt. Rather He was making himself sin for us. It was, in the language of Chrysostom, as though He had said, "As I was circumcised that I might fulfil the Law, I am baptized that I may ratify grace. If I fulfil a part and omit a part, I leave the Incarnation maimed. I must fulfil all things that hereafter Paul may write: 'Christ is the fulfilment of the Law unto righteousness for every one that believeth.'"[3]

E. The Temptation

Immediately upon being baptized Jesus was driven by the Spirit into

---

2. Wiley, *Christian Theology,* 2:151.

3. Quoted by David Smith, *The Days of His Flesh* (New York: George H. Doran Co., n.d.), p. 32.

the wilderness to be tempted by the devil (Mark 1:12). Historically, our Lord's temptations were satanic suggestions that He follow the pattern of popular Messiahship. Theologically, we are to understand them as a genuine encounter with Satan. Jesus was truly tempted, actually enticed to sin. Thus He is in a position to understand from the inside *our* encounter with temptation (Heb. 2:18).

Jesus' victory was complete. Throughout His earthly life He maintained an unbroken communion with the Father. This we understand as a necessary precondition of His atoning sacrifice. In the words of P. T. Forsyth, "The holiness of Christ was the one thing damnatory to the Satanic power."[4] By His positive righteousness the incarnate Son of God "condemned sin in the flesh," in order that He might become the Prince of our salvation and mediate to us His own victory over sin (Rom. 8:1-4).

F. Passion and Death

The Cross is the central point of New Testament faith. Historical studies of the Gospels indicate that the Passion narrative was the magnet which attracted all the other gospel materials about itself. An examination of apostolic preaching leads to the conclusion that the earliest gospel was the vivid portrayal of the Crucifixion (1 Cor. 2:1-2; Gal. 3:1).

The heart of the New Testament evangel is that "Christ died for our sins" (1 Cor. 15:13). His sufferings were "on our behalf" and "in our stead."

The New Testament declares that Jesus' death was a threefold accomplishment. It effected a *propitiation* of the divine holiness and justice (Rom. 3:21-26), *redemption* from the thralldom of Satan and sin (John 12:31-33; Heb. 2:14; Mark 10:45), and *reconciliation* between God and man (Col. 1:21-22; 2 Cor. 5:18-21).

The Cross is, furthermore, the focal point of divine revelation. "Hereby perceive we the love of God, because he laid down his life for us" (1 John 3:16). In the Cross, "mercy and truth are met together; righteousness and peace have kissed each other" (Ps. 85:10).

> *All the light of sacred story*
> *Gathers round its head sublime.*

The stress of the New Testament, however, is not upon revela-

---

4. Quoted by Stewart, *Faith to Proclaim,* p. 95.

tion but upon redemption. Supremely the apostles saw in Christ's sufferings and death the fulfillment of the Suffering Servant passage in Isaiah 53, where the prophet says, "But he was wounded for our transgressions, he was bruised for our iniquities: the chastisement of our peace was upon him; and with his stripes we are healed" (v. 5).

G. Burial and Resurrection

Summarizing the New Testament *kerygma,* St. Paul wrote: "I delivered to you as of first importance what I also received, that Christ *died* for our sins in accordance with the scriptures, that he was *buried,* that he was *raised* on the third day in accordance with the scriptures" (1 Cor. 15:3-4, RSV). The death, burial, and resurrection of Jesus are three links in an unbreakable chain of gospel tradition. To put it differently, they are but three phases of one event.

Jesus' burial is associated also with His descent into Hades. In his Pentecostal sermon St. Peter quoted the 16th psalm: "Thou wilt not leave my soul in hell, neither wilt thou suffer thine Holy One to see corruption" (Acts 2:27). While our Lord's body was being preserved from corruption He himself was invading the realm of the dead. "He that ascended, . . . descended first into the lower parts of the earth" (Eph. 4:9). What the precise ministry of Christ was in Hades we are not told in the New Testament (1 Pet. 3:18-20), but we must understand the descent into Hades as the first stage of His exaltation. For He emerged with the triumphant declaration, "Fear not; I am the first and the last: I am he that liveth, and was dead; and, behold, I am alive for evermore, Amen; and have the keys of hell and of death" (Rev. 1:17-18).

The New Testament evangel is meaningless apart from the Resurrection. "The third day he rose again from the dead." This victory over death was attested by "many infallible proofs" (Acts 1:3), chief among these being the empty tomb, on the one hand, and the transformed disciples, on the other. By His resurrection the sheep who were scattered by His death were gathered again into the fold. As one scholar puts it, the revival of the disciples is the strongest argument for the resurrection of Jesus.

Jesus' resurrection was not simply a resuscitation of His flesh-and-blood body, for "flesh and blood cannot inherit the kingdom of God" (1 Cor. 15:50). It was rather a transformation of His earthly into a heavenly, His natural into a spiritual body. Thus it is the pattern of our resurrection (Phil. 3:20-21).

Theologically, the Resurrection was God's stamp of approval

upon Jesus as His Son (Rom. 1:4; Acts 3:13-15), the ratification of the gospel (1 Cor. 15:13-20), and the prophecy of *our* resurrection (1 Cor. 15:20-23).[5]

H. The Ascension

The Ascension marks the close of the earthly life of our Lord. He was "taken up . . . into heaven" (Acts 1:11). Wiley and Culbertson state:

> This transference from earth to heaven must not be understood to mean merely a removal from one part of the physical universe to another, but a local withdrawal into what is known as "the presence of God." The ascension was a passing into a new sphere of mediatorial action, the taking possession of the presence of God for us, and is, therefore, immediately associated with His High Priestly intercession. He appears "in the presence of God for us" (Heb. 9:24).[6]

The Ascension means that we now have "boldness to enter into the holiest by the blood of Jesus" (Heb. 10:19-20). It signifies the exaltation of Christ to the headship of the Church and to the place of supremacy in the universe (Eph. 1:21-23). Lastly, the Ascension signifies the withdrawal of Christ in the flesh in order to establish the conditions by which the Holy Spirit could be given to the Church (John 7:39; Acts 2:33).

How better can we summarize the Christ event than in the words of the Apostles' Creed? "I believe in God the Father Almighty . . . And in Jesus Christ, His only Son, our Lord, who was conceived by the Holy Ghost, born of the Virgin Mary, suffered under Pontius Pilate; was crucified, dead, and buried; He descended into hell; the third day He rose again from the dead; He ascended into heaven, and sitteth on the right hand of God the Father Almighty; from thence He shall come to judge the quick and the dead."

II. Christological Controversy

From the earliest days the Church has sought a satisfying answer to the question, "What think ye of Christ? whose son is he?" In addressing itself to the problem of Christ's person, the Church discovered

---

5. Cf. the emphasis on the importance of the Resurrection in Chapter 12 *infra*.
6. *Introduction to Christian Theology* (Kansas City: Beacon Hill Press, 1946), p. 212.

that there are dangerous pitfalls which must be avoided if we are to have an adequate, scriptural Christology.

The student of Christian doctrine must understand these errors in order to avoid them himself. There are only a certain number of possible answers which can be given, and many which seem to be new and appealing are found upon examination to be but some old heresy stated in current terminology.

At the risk of oversimplification we shall divide the question into three main sections: Errors with Respect to Jesus' Humanity; Errors with Respect to Jesus' Deity; Errors with Respect to the Unity of Jesus' Person.

A. Errors with Respect to Jesus' Humanity

Christologies which fail to do full justice to our Lord's humanity are classified generally as Docetic (from the Greek verb *dokeo,* meaning "to seem"). According to this viewpoint Christ's humanity was not genuine. He appeared to be human, but close analysis proves this to be an illusion. Thus Jesus was a *quasi* human, not genuinely "bone of our bone, flesh of our flesh." The Church was as quick and decisive in its condemnation of Docetism as of those heresies which deny our Lord's deity.

The earliest Docetic views grew out of the type of thought known as Gnosticism. Before the second century Gnostic thought began to penetrate Christian theology. One of the basic assumptions of Gnosticism is the evil of matter. A flesh-and-blood man would necessarily be sinful by reason of his materiality.

Accordingly, Gnosticism denied the Incarnation. Christ simply *seemed* to be human. His alleged "body" was but an appearance to the senses, an extended theophany of the same nature as His appearance in the fiery furnace with the three Hebrew youths.

Another early denial of the humanity of Jesus is found in a third century Trinitarian heresy known as Sabellianism. Sabellius held that God has manifested himself in three personal modes. "God as Father is Creator; and manifested through the Incarnation the same God is known as the Son and fulfills the office of Redeemer; and lastly, as the Holy Spirit, God carries on His spiritual ministry in the Church."[7] This is to deny the personal distinction between the Father and the Son. Such a view does violence to the plain teachings of the

---

7. Wiley, *Christian Theology,* 1:411.

New Testament where Jesus is represented as praying to the Father and as coming to do the Father's will. The Church rightly condemned this position as heretical.

B. Errors with Respect to Jesus' Deity

1. Gnosticism

We have seen that the Gnostics denied the humanity of Christ; they also rejected His true deity. They maintained that the heavenly Christ who appeared among men was but an *emanation* from the one true God. In Colosse these teachers placed Christ among the hierarchy of angels, thus denying His true headship (Col. 2:18-19). The entire number of intermediary beings emanating from God and linking Him to this world the Gnostics called the *pleroma*. St. Paul's answer to this heresy was that *Christ* is "the Pleroma of the Godhead," who suffered in the flesh to reconcile us to the Father (Col. 1:19-22; 2:9 ff.).

Near the close of the first century Cerinthus taught at Ephesus that the heavenly Christ descended upon the human Jesus at His baptism, remained upon Him during His ministry, and ascended back to the spiritual world at Jesus' death. In effect, Jesus and Christ were two different persons. St. John was addressing himself against this heresy when he wrote, "Who is a liar but he that denieth that Jesus is the Christ? He is antichrist, that denieth the Father and the Son" (1 John 2:22).

2. Ebionism

The Ebionites were a Jewish sect contemporary with the Gnostics. Fervently loyal to the Old Testament, these "poor folk" (so their name implies) held to such a rigid view of monotheism that they could find no place for Jesus within the Godhead. They taught that He was the natural son of Joseph and Mary, who so completely fulfilled the Jewish law that God chose Him to be Messiah, and that He is destined to return and set up a Jewish kingdom.

3. Arianism

This heresy is also a Trinitarian error, but it affects Christology deeply. Arius, a presbyter of Alexandria in the fourth century, explained that he and his followers were persecuted because they taught that "the Son has a beginning and God is without a beginning." They maintained that the Father was not always the Father, for there was a time when the Son was not yet created and hence God was not yet Father of His Son. He did not become Father, they said, until the creation of His Son. This Son proceeds, not from the *being*, but from the *will* of the Father. The Son is the first and highest of creatures, but He is not God except in an accommodated sense as a created divinity. He was preexistent but not eternal.

If Arianism is true, Christians worship "the creature more than the Creator, who is blessed for ever" (Rom. 1:25). Thus Christianity is reduced to the level of pagan idolatry. The Council of Nicea in A.D. 325 condemned Arianism as heresy.

4. *Unitarianism*

Unitarianism is a revival of Ebionism, with certain modifications. In general it is the view that Jesus was simply a good man, a religious genius of exceptional insight. Sometimes these thinkers speak of the divinity of Jesus or refer to Him as the Son of God. His divinity, however, is only a higher degree of the goodness which is inherent in every man, and He is the Son of God in the same sense in which we all are the sons of God.

C. Errors with Respect to the Unity of Jesus' Person

1. *Apollinarianism*

Apollinaris of Laodicea was the first Christian teacher to err with respect to the very difficult problem of the relation of the divine and human natures in the person of Jesus. He could not understand how a divine Person (the Logos) could be united with a human personality, and he sought a solution by advocating an incomplete humanity in Jesus. As G. C. Berkouwer explains, "Had the Logos assumed a complete human nature, he would have adopted also human variability and human sin. . . . A genuine union is possible only when the Logos, as the principle of self-consciousness and self-determination, *takes the place of,* instead of assuming, the human spirit."[8] The Logos, according to Apollinaris, was substituted in Christ for a human spirit. Christ's humanity was thus *incomplete* and *passive.* The human nature of Christ was not the same, therefore, as that of other men. All that was of any account in Christ was divine, and the human was no more than a passive instrument. "At bottom there is but one nature and hence Apollinaris did not shrink from saying that Christ was not a complete man."[9] The Council of Constantinople, in A.D. 381, con-

---

8. G. C. Berkouwer, *The Person of Christ* (Grand Rapids: Wm. B. Eerdmans Publishing Company, 1954), p. 64.

9. *Ibid.,* p. 65.

demned Apollinarianism and affirmed the completeness of Christ's humanity.

2. Nestorianism

Nestorius, fourth century bishop of Constantinople, was accused of separating the two natures of Christ into two persons. Following what became known as the Antiochan school of Christology, Nestorius seemed to understand the union of the Logos and man in Christ to be simply a *moral* union on the analogy of God's indwelling in the Christian. Jesus was simply a human person bound to the Logos in a moral union of friendship.[10] This view was condemned in A.D. 431 at Ephesus, and again at Chalcedon in A.D. 451.

3. Eutychianism

Incipient in Apollinarianism was a view which later Eutyches developed into a full theory. His thesis was that upon a union of the two natures there could be only one nature, Christ's humanity being absorbed by His deity. Hence this view is sometimes known as *absorptionism.* It is also called *monophysitism* (from *mono,* "one"; *physis,* "nature"). Before the Incarnation there were two natures, the divine Logos and the human ovum in the womb of the Virgin Mary; but in the union of these natures the human element was divinized. Christ thus had only one nature, the divine. His humanity was only an appearance.

4. Monotheletism

Monotheletism was "a veiled re-edition of the monophysite error."[11] It declared that in Christ the two natures were united without mixture, but that there was only one will (*mono,* "one"; *thelema,* "will"), one mode of operation. This is a subtle point, but monotheletism must be judged erroneous by denying the reality of Jesus' human will. This view gives us an incomplete humanity in Jesus, and an inadequate account of the relationship of divine and human natures in one person.

5. Adoptianism

Adoptianism arose in Spain in the latter part of the eighth century. It was in reality a revival of Nestorianism. It taught that Christ was the Son of God naturally, only in respect to His deity; but that in

---

10. *Ibid.,* p. 67.
11. M. Schamus, *Katholishe Dogmatik,* 2:656; quoted, *ibid.,* p. 69.

respect to His humanity, He was merely a man like other men, who was made Son by adoption. "According to His divine nature, He was the Only Begotten; according to His human nature, He was the First Begotten."[12] His humanity was adopted into His divinity by a gradual process perfected by the Resurrection.

D. Ecumenical Christology

In combating these various errors with respect to Jesus, the Church has forged a Christology which may be termed ecumenical or catholic. Whether we examine the Augsburg Confession, the Helvetic Confession, the Westminster Confession, The Thirty-nine Articles of the Church of England, the Twenty-five Articles of Methodism, or the Articles of Faith of the Church of the Nazarene, we find essentially the same position:[13]

> We believe in Jesus Christ, the Second Person of the Triune Godhead; that He was eternally one with the Father; that He became incarnate by the Holy Spirit and was born of the Virgin Mary, so that two whole and perfect natures, that is to say the Godhead and manhood, are thus united in one person very God and very man, the God-man.
> We believe that Jesus Christ died for our sins, and that He truly arose from the dead and took again His body, together with all things appertaining to the perfection of man's nature, wherewith He ascended into heaven and is there engaged in intercession for us.[14]

III. THE PERSON OF CHRIST

Christ is presented to us in the New Testament as the Word made flesh, God manifest in human personality. In Jesus Christ man did not become God, but God became man. The New Testament presents Jesus to us as man: "There is one God, and one mediator between God and men, the *man* Christ Jesus" (1 Tim. 2:5). But in this genuinely human life God was personally and redemptively present: *"God was in Christ, reconciling the world unto himself"* (2 Cor. 5:19). Paradoxical as this may sound, it is the New Testament witness, confirmed by nearly 2,000 years of Christian experience.

---

12. Wiley, *Christian Theology,* 2:164.
13. *Ibid.,* pp. 166-68.
14. *Manual,* Church of the Nazarene, Article II.

A. The Humanity of Christ

First of all, *Jesus Christ was a man,* in the full psychological sense, sharing truly and fully in the conditions of our empirical humanity, sin only excepted. The perfect life was at the same time a true human life. He was no archangel or demigod, playing a human role to edify us; "For verily he took not on him the nature of angels; but . . . the seed of Abraham" (Heb. 2:16). In the words of Carlyle concerning Richard I, Jesus was "a man living upon victuals."[15]

He ate and drank; He knew hunger, thirst, and weariness; He was tempted as we are tempted; His heart knew the bitterness of grief and disappointment. "His was the highest, holiest Manhood which this world has seen or can see, and at the last . . . He was nailed to a gallows to die with criminals, the innocent victim of fear, bigotry, jealous hatred, political opportunism and legalized murder. He was crucified, dead and buried."[16]

The New Testament speaks with one voice, "Behold the man!" The essential truth is that "it behoved him to be made like unto his brethren" (Heb. 2:17). He needed no one to "testify of man: for he knew what was in man" (John 2:25). "The face on which uncounted generations have seen the light of the knowledge of the glory of God was a face like all men's faces."[17]

B. The Deity of Christ

The second fact with which we are confronted in the New Testament is this: *In Jesus of Nazareth we meet the living God.* In repudiating all mere humanistic interpretations of Jesus, the Church has been held by a great conviction. As Charles Lowry states it:

> This conviction is that in Jesus Christ, in his life and sacrificial death, in his whole human historical existence, we have to do, not with a man among men, not with an angel of mercy and peace, not with a great demi-god, one among many mighty powers of the universe, but with God, the Almighty God, the only God there is. To express this and to leave us in no doubt as to this meaning, the Creed says "Very (or true) God"; "Begotten, not made" (as we, finite creatures, are made); "Being of one substance with the Father" (an awkward translation of the words which mean: "Of the same identical being or reality as the Father");

---

15. Quoted by Whale, *Christian Doctrine,* p. 89.
16. *Ibid.,* p. 100.
17. *Loc. cit.*

"Who for us men and for our salvation came down from heaven."[18]

1. *The Synoptic Gospels*

The Gospel accounts which underscore the utter humanness of Jesus also bear witness to the fact that Jesus was conscious that He was more than a mere prophet. Writes J. S. Whale:

> The most cautiously scientific criticism of the Gospels confirms their historical testimony that Jesus' language about himself has at least a four-fold meaning: it implies a unique oneness with God, a unique moral authority over men, a unique ministry of salvation towards them, and a unique mastery over the powers of evil.[19]

Jesus speaks with the authority of God, deliberately and cautiously. He pits His authority over against that of the Old Testament (Matt. 5:21-48). He claims the power to forgive sins (Mark 2:5-12; Luke 7:47-50). He claims to know the Father in a unique way (Matt. 11:27). On this basis He invites men to come to Him for rest of soul (Matt. 11:28-30). He evokes from Peter the confession that He is the Christ, the Son of God (Matt. 16:16-17). He accepts the homage of worship (Matt. 14:33). He claims the right of pronouncing final judgment upon men (Matt. 7:21-23; 10:32-33). When asked by Caiaphas, "Art thou the Christ, the Son of the Blessed?" He breaks His silence and answers, "I am" (Mark 14:61-62). Commenting on these claims, R. W. Dale declares, "These are not words that we ever heard before, or have ever heard since, from teacher or prophet. Who is he? That question cannot be silence when words like these have once been spoken."[20]

2. *Pauline Epistles*

St. Paul writes of Jesus as the Son of God (Rom. 1:3-4), whom the Father sent into the world (Rom. 8:3; Gal. 4:4). This clearly implies the apostle's conviction of our Lord's preexistence.

Two passages are worthy of particular notice. In Colossians (1:15-22) Jesus is said to be the Image of the invisible God, the Creator of all things visible and invisible, the Sustainer of the universe, the Head of the Church, and the Pleroma of God in human flesh, through whose death we are reconciled to the Father. In Philippians

---

18. Charles W. Lowry, *The Trinity and Christian Devotion* (New York: Harper and Brothers, 1946), p. 61.

19. *Christian Doctrine*, p. 102.

20. Quoted by Whale, *ibid.*, p. 103.

(2:5-8) Paul declares the Son to be preexistent *en morphe theou.* This Greek phrase means that the Son shared fully in the life of God, that He was the manifestation of the divine majesty. The Son, however, did not selfishly prize this heavenly glory He shared with the Father; rather, "he emptied himself" of His glory, taking upon himself "the form of a slave" in order to redeem mankind. "And being found in fashion as a man, he humbled himself, and became obedient unto death, even the death of the cross" (v. 8). What glorious condescension! St. Paul expresses this same precious truth elsewhere in one sentence: "For ye know the grace of our Lord Jesus Christ, that, though he was rich, yet for your sakes he became poor, that ye through his poverty might be rich" (2 Cor. 8:9). The Son of God became the Son of Man that the sons of men might become sons of God.

3. *The Fourth Gospel*

The Fourth Gospel contains the most exalted Christological passage in the New Testament (1:1-18). These verses place Christ in the Godhead. God has eternally spoken His Word. Through Him He created all things. That Word became flesh in Jesus Christ. The invisible God has now become manifest in Jesus of Nazareth, so much so that He can say, "He that hath seen me hath seen the Father" (14:9).

The apex of New Testament Christology is the climactic utterance of the Fourth Gospel, "My Lord and my God" (20:28).

C. The God-Man

"The experience of Christian men," says J. S. Whale, "confirms the classic experience of the first age of Christendom, that the Man Christ Jesus has the decisive place in man's ageless relationship with God. He is what God means by 'Man.' He is what man means by 'God.'"[21]

Here admittedly is paradox. Jesus is man; Jesus is God. To soften this paradox is to denude the gospel and to cut the ground from under Christian experience. No mere creedal point is at stake, but the Christian Church stands or falls with the conviction which originated it, namely, that "God was in Christ, reconciling the world unto himself." "Hereby know ye the Spirit of God: . . . every spirit that confesseth not that Jesus Christ is come in the flesh is not of God: and this is that spirit of antichrist" (1 John 4:2-3).

---

21. *Ibid.,* p. 104.

In William Hazlitt's famous essay, *Of Persons One Would Like to Have Seen*, there is described a long and brilliant conversation between poets and critics about the great figures of the past. It concludes with an observation by Charles Lamb: "If Shakespeare were to come into the room we should all rise to meet him. But if that Person were to come into it, we should all fall down and try to kiss the hem of his garment." Although he was no theologian, Lamb put his finger on the essential mystery of Christ's person.

We have traced the numerous attempts men have made to explain the mystery of His person. Such attempts lead almost inevitably either to a loss of His complete humanity or a reduction of His essential deity. He transcends the power of logic to synthesize His qualities. He is inexplicable because He cannot be put into a "class." The great merit of the creeds and confessions of the Church is that they left the paradox as such: "very God and very man."

It is much wiser to follow the intuitions of our hearts and confess with Thomas, "My Lord and my God," than to become timid and hesitant because we cannot explain the mystery of Christ. The only language about Christ which is adequate for Christian experience is the language of amazement and praise which fills the New Testament. "A deep instinct has always told the Church that our safest eloquence concerning the mystery of Christ is in our praise. A living Church is a worshipping, singing Church; not a school of people holding all the correct doctrines."[22]

This is not to say that thought is sinful. The Incarnation is not irrational. The Incarnation was possible because man in the essential structure of his being was created in the image of God. God is personal; man is personal. Thus personality is a kind of "least common denominator" between God and man. God could not have expressed His personal righteousness and love in a rock, a tree, or even a chimpanzee! But because man was in His image He could dwell in a human personality. Perhaps we could say with William Temple, "The *form* of [Jesus'] consciousness is human, its *content* divine. The whole content of His Being—His thought, feeling, and purpose, is also that of God. That is the only 'substance' of a spiritual Being, for it is all there is of Him at all."[23]

The New Testament does not get lost in rational explanations. It

---

22. *Ibid.*, p. 104.

23. William Temple, *Foundations* (London: Macmillan and Co., Ltd., 1912), p. 248.

simply proclaims the wondrous fact: "The Word was made flesh, and dwelt among us, (and we beheld his glory, the glory as of the only begotten of the Father,) full of grace and truth. . . . And of his fulness have all we received, and grace for grace. . . . No man hath seen God at any time; the only begotten Son, which is in the bosom of the Father, he hath declared him" (John 1:14-18).

SUMMARY

New Testament Christology is confessional: "No man can say 'Jesus is Lord' except by the Holy Spirit." The Gospel accounts are not so much biographies as confessions of faith. From them we may draw the salient historical events in Christ's life which have theological significance. In order to understand the limits of our thought concerning Christ we must be acquainted with the history of the Church's thinking concerning the person of Christ. The errors into which men have fallen may serve to warn us against pitfalls for our theology. But after we have traced the development of Christology we must return to the New Testament itself for our own position. We discover that the New Testament presents Jesus Christ to us as a flesh-and-blood Man in whom the living God is redemptively and personally present.

The biblical teaching concerning the Holy Spirit is the next theme to which we go in exploring our Christian faith.

CHAPTER 9

The Holy Spirit

We have already learned that the Christian view of the Godhead embraces both unity and triunity. So great was the peril of polytheism in Old Testament times that the major emphasis in the Old Testament is on the unity of the Godhead. In the New Testament it becomes clear that the Father is God, Christ is God, and the Holy Spirit is God. It is to the doctrine of the Holy Spirit that we now turn.

There is much less in the Bible about the Spirit than there is about God the Father or God the Son. This "divine reticence" has been explained by Bishop H. C. G. Moule as due to the fact that the Holy Spirit "is the true Author of the written Word; and His authorship there is occupied with the main and absorbing theme not of Himself but of another Person, the Son of God."[1]

However, our understanding of the nature and ministry of the Spirit is of first importance. He has been called "The Conservator of Orthodoxy,"[2] and beliefs about the Holy Spirit have been correctly indicated as a major test of vital biblical theology. John Owen, the 17th-century English divine whose book entitled *Pneumatologia* (1674 —the title means "Doctrine of the Spirit") is one of the earliest classics on the subject, holds that before the coming of Christ the great testing truth was the oneness of God's nature and His universal sovereignty, the person of the Father. At the coming of Christ the great question was whether the Church, orthodox on the first point,

---

1. *Veni Creator* (London: Hodder and Stoughton, 1895), p. 11. See also Purkiser, Taylor, and Taylor, *God, Man, and Salvation*, pp. 239-50.

2. By Daniel Steele, *The Gospel of the Comforter* (Chicago: The Christian Witness Co., 1917), p. 325 ff.

would now receive the incarnate Son. In the age of the Spirit the testing point becomes the recognition of the person and work of the Holy Spirit. "The sin of despising His Person and rejecting His work now is of the same nature with idolatry of old, and with the Jews' rejection of the Person of the Son."[3]

We turn first to the biblical teaching concerning the Spirit; and then to the theological position wherein the Church has put together its belief in the unity of the Godhead on the one hand and its conviction of the deity of Christ and the personality and the deity of the Holy Spirit on the other hand.[4]

I. The Spirit in the Old Testament

There are 86 references to the Spirit of God or the Spirit of the Lord in the Old Testament. The first of these is in the second verse of the Bible. The Pentateuch gives us 14, as do Judges and I and II Samuel. Ezekiel and Isaiah between them have 28, the Psalms 6, and the remainder are scattered throughout the other books. The Hebrew term for spirit is *ruach,* and it is used also to speak of breath or wind, and the spirit of man. While no hard-and-fast rule can be made, in general the designation "Spirit of God" refers to the power, might, and majesty of the Creator God; while the "Spirit of the Lord" points to the love, favor, and help of the Redeemer God.[5]

William M. Greathouse divides the Old Testament references to the Spirit into three groups: Those which relate to the Spirit's activity in the world in general; those which speak of God acting redemptively in and through His people; and those referring to the coming of the Messiah and the age of the Spirit.[6]

---

3. Cf. *ibid.,* pp. 2-3.

4. A note is in order regarding usage in speaking of the Holy Spirit. The King James Version of the New Testament translates *hagion pneuma* in the majority of cases by the phrase "Holy Ghost," using "Holy Spirit" only four time. *Pneuma* without the adjective Holy when it refers to the Third Person of the Trinity, the KJV uniformly translates "Spirit." The KJV was published in 1611, and in the last three and a half centuries the word ghost has taken on an entirely different meaning from what it had originally. When quoting the King James Version, it is important to quote it accurately, and at such times the term "the Holy Ghost" should be used. At other times it is more accurate and meaningful to speak of "the Holy Spirit."

5. Cf. A. B. Davidson, *The Theology of the Old Testament* (Edinburgh: T. and T. Clark, 1904), p. 125. Cf. Purkiser, Taylor, and Taylor, *God, Man, and Salvation,* pp. 166-70.

6. *The Fullness of the Spirit* (Kansas City: Beacon Hill Press of Kansas City, 1958), pp. 41-46.

A. The Spirit and the Cosmos

We have already mentioned the reference to the Spirit of God in Gen. 1:2, where He is said to have "moved upon the face of the waters" in creation. Similarly, the Psalmist says, "By the word of the Lord were the heavens made; and all the host of them by the breath [*ruach* or spirit] of his mouth" (33:6). The Spirit is mentioned in relation to human life: "The spirit of God is in my nostrils" (Job 27:3); and in relation to animal life: "Thou sendest forth thy spirit, they are created: and thou renewest the face of the earth" (Ps. 104:30).

The Spirit of God strives with or abides in man (Gen. 6:3); He bestows supernatural knowledge and wisdom (Gen. 41:38); He gives special artistic ability (Exod. 35:30) and wisdom to govern (Judg. 3:10). He is omnipresent in the created order: "Whither shall I go from thy spirit? or whither shall I flee from thy presence? If I ascend up into heaven, thou art there: if I make my bed in hell, behold, thou art there. If I take the wings of the morning, and dwell in the uttermost parts of the sea; even there shall thy hand lead me, and thy right hand shall hold me" (Ps. 139:7-10). As Dr. Greathouse notes: "He is personal Spirit, permeating yet distinct from His creation. He is present, moreover, not only as the sustaining power of the world, but also as a disturbing moral influence in the lives of sinful men. The Spirit of God *is* the Holy Spirit."[7]

B. The Spirit of God in Redemption

A second class of Old Testament passages speak of the Spirit in relation to God's redemptive activity among His people. This has to do not only with what we should think of as spiritual redemption, but often in relation to deliverance from oppression and danger. Thus in Judges and 1 Samuel there is frequent mention of the Spirit of the Lord "coming upon" or "coming mightily upon" judges and leaders as a supernatural Power taking hold of them and enabling them to do exploits beyond the ordinary. Othniel, Gideon, Jephthah, Samson, Saul, and David are mentioned in connection with such enduements.

A somewhat similar manifestation of the Spirit is connected with prophecy in the Old Testament. In Num. 11:25-26, the Spirit came upon the 70 elders chosen to assist Moses and they prophesied. In 1 Sam. 19:20, the Spirit of God fell on Saul's messengers, so that they also prophesied. Ezekiel makes special reference to the Spirit in

---

7. *Ibid.,* p. 42.

relation to his prophetic visions, speaking of the Spirit entering into him (2:1-3), lifting him up and taking him away (3:13-14), lifting him up between heaven and earth (8:3), and bringing him to the east gate of the Lord's house (11:1).

The term "holy Spirit" is used three times in the Old Testament in contexts which seem to imply a definitely moral and spiritual meaning akin to that of the New Testament. One is in Ps. 51:11 in connection with David's penitent prayer for restoration and cleansing: "Cast me not away from thy presence; and take not thy *holy spirit* from me." The other two are in Isa. 63:10-11, a passage which speaks of the mighty acts of God in deliverance of His people, and their senseless rebellion against Him: "But they rebelled, and vexed his holy Spirit: therefore he was turned to be their enemy, and he fought against them. Then he remembered the days of old, Moses, and his people, saying, Where is he that brought them up out of the sea with the shepherd of his flock? where is he that put his holy Spirit within him?"

It is not to be thought that these passages teach in the full Christian sense a regenerating or sanctifying work of the Holy Spirit during the Old Testament period. The Old Testament, as we shall next see, speaks of the age of the Spirit yet to come; and John comments concerning Jesus' promise of the Spirit that "the Holy Ghost was not yet given; because that Jesus was not yet glorified" (John 7:39). The Old Testament Scriptures rather testify to the fact that the redemptive workings of God in behalf of His own and the impulses and responses of the soul in worship are the province of the Spirit's ministry in all ages, before Pentecost as well as afterward.

C. The Spirit and Messianic Prophecies

A third class of Old Testament references to the Spirit relate to the coming Deliverer. Isaiah, in particular, speaks of the Spirit anointing the Branch (11:2), the Servant of the Lord (42:1); and states the commission which Jesus accepted as His own (Luke 4:18): "The spirit of the Lord God is upon me; because the Lord hath anointed me to preach good tidings unto the meek; he hath sent me to bind up the brokenhearted, to proclaim liberty to the captives, and the opening of the prison to them that are bound; to proclaim the acceptable year of the Lord, and the day of vengeance of our God" (61:1-2).

The Messianic age is to be particularly the age of the Spirit. This is "the promise of the Father" (Acts 1:4) of which Jesus spoke, a promise fulfilled at Pentecost. Here we read again from Isaiah: "Because the palaces shall be forsaken; the multitude of the city shall be left; the forts and towers shall be dens for ever, a joy of wild asses, a pasture of flocks; *until the spirit be poured upon us from on high,* and the wilderness be a fruitful field, and the fruitful field be counted for a forest" (32:14-15); "For I will pour water upon him that is thirsty, and floods upon the dry ground: I will pour my spirit upon thy seed, and my blessing upon thine offspring" (44:3); "So shall they fear the name of the Lord from the west, and his glory from the rising of the sun. When the enemy shall come in like a flood, the Spirit of the Lord shall lift up a standard against him" (59:19).

Ezekiel says: "Then will I sprinkle clean water upon you, and ye shall be clean: from all your filthiness, and from all your idols, will I cleanse you. A new heart also will I give you, and a new spirit will I put within you: and I will take away the stony heart out of your flesh, and I will give you an heart of flesh. And I will put my spirit within you, and cause you to walk in my statues, and ye shall keep my judgments, and do them" (36:25-27).

Zech. 12:10 promises, "I will pour upon the house of David, and upon the inhabitants of Jerusalem, the spirit of grace and of supplications."

The prophecy in Joel 2:28-29 is quoted by Peter at Pentecost: "And it shall come to pass afterward, that I will pour out my spirit upon all flesh; and your sons and your daughters shall prophesy, your old men shall dream dreams, your young men shall see visions: and also upon the servants and upon the handmaids in those days will I pour out my spirit."

Greathouse shows the relevance of these promises to the New Testament when he writes:

> An understanding of these prophecies is absolutely essential to our grasping the significance of the Messiah and His ministry. The Messianic age was to be marked by a *universal* and *sanctifying* outpouring of the Spirit—first on Israel and then on all flesh. God was going to put his Holy Spirit *within* the hearts of His people, enabling them to do His holy and righteous will. This came to be the clear hope of the Jews in the period preceding the New Testament. They believed that, because of the sins of the nation, the Spirit had ascended to heaven about the time of Malachi, but that He would return at the time of the Messiah to be diffused upon all people, both Jews and gentiles. The prophecies we have just quoted provided the basis for this hope—*that in the day of the Messiah there would be an unprecedented gift of the Holy Spirit, not only removing their guilt but also sanctifying their inner nature.* Among the rabbis Sim-

eon b. Johai gave this typical paraphrase of Ezek. 36:26: "And God said, 'In this age, because the evil impulse exists in you, ye have sinned against me; but in the age to come I will *eradicate* it from you.' "[8]

D. The Spirit and the Scriptures

In connection with the Old Testament teaching about the Spirit of the Lord, it is well to note what the New Testament says concerning the work of the Spirit in the formation of the Old Testament Scriptures. It was because the Holy Spirit moved them that holy men of God spoke and wrote (2 Pet. 1:21). David "said by the Holy Ghost, The Lord said to my Lord, Sit thou on my right hand, till I make thine enemies thy footstool" (Mark 12:36). God spoke by the mouth of David (Acts 4:25), and the Holy Spirit spoke by Isaiah (Acts 28:25). The Holy Spirit spoke, signified, and witnessed by what was written in the Old Testament in the songs of Psalmists, the types of Leviticus, and the messages of the prophets (Heb. 3:7; 9:8; 10:15).

II. The Holy Spirit in the New Testament

The entire biblical concept of the Spirit receives its clarification in the New Testament, when the age of the Spirit dawned at last. Here we find the personality of the Holy Spirit clearly shown, and the scope of His ministry in the Church and in the world set forth.

A. The Personality of the Spirit

It has long been argued by unitarian liberalism that the Spirit of God in both Old and New Testaments is simply the power, influence, or activity of God the Father in the world. Some popular modern cults such as Jehovah's Witnesses and Christian Science join in the denial of the personality and deity of the Spirit.

It is never proper to refer to the Holy Spirit as "It." Care should always be taken to use the personal pronouns "He," "His," or "Him" in speaking of the Spirit. It is true that the King James Version uses "it" in such passages as Rom. 8:16, 26. The reason is that the Greek *pneuma*, or "spirit," is a neuter noun, and the pronoun is translated literally to agree. Later versions have corrected this excessive literalism.

It will, of course, be kept in mind that the personality of the

---

8. *Ibid.*, pp. 45-46. Cf. Turner, *Vision Which Transforms*, pp. 61-72.

Holy Spirit implies nothing material or physical. Just as God the Father, the supreme Personality, is Spirit and without physical form or material body, so the Third Person of the Trinity is a divine Person who is incorporeal. That human persons have bodies does not indicate that body is essential to personality, for animals also have bodies, and inanimate objects are material in substance. The essential marks of personality are thinking, feeling, acting, and the capacity to make moral choices.

A true and vital Christian experience derives much from a clear sense of the personality of the Spirit. To fail at this point, and to think of the Spirit of God as simply a divine influence or power, is to come very close to the superstitious paganism which seeks to possess and manipulate the *mana* or supernatural power which will glorify the self. When the Holy Spirit is seen as a Person, then the concern will properly be, How may He possess and use more of me? Recognition of the personality of the Spirit keeps God central in human life.

To fail of full recognition of the Spirit's personality is to limit the worship which is due Him. To sing with the hymn writer:

> *I worship Thee, O Holy Ghost;*
> *I love to worship Thee,*

can be meaningful only when the Spirit is known as a Person. How important this is to personal religious experience we shall note when we study the place of the Spirit in renewing and sanctifying the believer's heart.

As we turn to the New Testament, we find a wealth of evidence for the personality of the Spirit in the abundant references to Him and His work. In the Synoptic Gospels (Matthew, Mark, Luke) and the Acts there are 88 references to the Holy Spirit. In the Epistles of Paul there are 120 such references. The General Epistles add 14 more; Revelation contains 17; while the Gospel of John, one of the most significant books of the New Testament in terms of its teaching about the Holy Spirit, has a total of 16. Virtually all of these citations testify to the fact that the Spirit is a divine Person.

1. *Personal Acts*

Throughout the New Testament many personal acts are attributed to the Spirit of God.[9]

---

9. Because of its consistent use of "Spirit" in translating *pneuma*, most of the references in the balance of this chapter are from the *New American Standard Bible* (NASB).

a. He *teaches:* "The Holy Spirit will teach you in that very hour what you ought to say" (Luke 12:12, NASB); "But the Helper, the Holy Spirit, whom the Father will send in My name, He will teach you all things, and bring to your remembrance all that I said unto you" (John 14:26, NASB; cf. also Luke 2:26).

b. He *speaks:* "It is not you who speak, but the Spirit of your Father who speaks in you" (Matt. 10:20, NASB; also Mark 13:11); "And the Spirit said to Philip, 'Go up and join this chariot'" (Acts 8:29, NASB); "And while Peter was reflecting on the vision, the Spirit said to him, 'Behold, three men are looking for you'" (Acts 10:19, NASB); "He that hath an ear, let him hear what the Spirit saith to the churches" (Rev. 2:7, 11, 17, 29; 3:6, 13, 22; see also Acts 13:2; 20:23; 21:11; 28:25; Rev. 14:13; 22:17).

c. The Spirit also *leads:* "Then was Jesus led up of the spirit into the wilderness to be tempted of the devil" (Matt. 4:1; Luke 4:1); "And they passed through the Phrygian and Galatian region, having been forbidden by the Holy Spirit to speak the word in Asia; and when they had come to Mysia, they were trying to go into Bithynia, and the Spirit of Jesus did not permit them" (Acts 16:6-7, NASB); "For all who are being led by the Spirit of God, these are sons of God" (Rom. 8:14, NASB); "But when He, the Spirit of truth, comes, He will guide you into all the truth" (John 16:13, NASB).

d. He *witnesses:* "We are witnesses of these things; and so is the Holy Spirit, whom God has given to those who obey Him" (Acts 5:32, NASB); "The Spirit Himself bears witness with our spirit that we are children of God" (Rom. 8:16, NASB); "And the Holy Spirit also bears witness to us" (Heb. 10:15, NASB; cf. also John 15:26; 1 Pet. 1:11; and 1 John 5:7).

e. The Holy Spirit *makes intercession* or prays for God's people: "In the same way the Spirit also helps our weakness; for we do not know how to pray as we should, but the Spirit Himself intercedes for us with groanings too deep for words; and He who searches the hearts knows what the mind of the Spirit is, because He intercedes for the saints according to the will of God" (Rom. 8:26-27, NASB).

In addition, it may be noted that the Spirit *sends* (Acts 13:4); He *seals* (Eph. 1:13; 4:30); He *moves men* by inspiration (2 Pet. 1:21); He *convicts* of sin, and in respect to righteousness and judgment (John 16:7-8); He *glorifies* Christ (John 16:14-15); and He *anoints* (1 John 2:20, 27).

None of these ways of speaking would be proper in relation to an influence, a power, or even a mode of the divine operation. They clearly testify to the strong sense of the personality of the Holy Spirit on the part of the New Testament writers.

2. *Qualities of Thought and Purpose*

All of the personal acts described above are such as require qualities of intelligence and purpose. Some of the latter are definitely ascribed to the Spirit.

a. For example, the Holy Spirit *esteems some courses of action better than others:* "For it seemed good to the Holy Spirit and to us to lay upon you no greater burden than these essentials" (Acts 15:28, NASB).

b. He *knows the mind of God:* "For what man knoweth the things of a man, save the spirit of man which is in him? even so the things of God knoweth no man, but the Spirit of God. For who hath known the mind of the Lord, that he may instruct him?" (1 Cor. 2:11, 16).

c. He *selects leaders for the Church:* "Be on guard for yourselves and for all the flock, among which the Holy Spirit has made you overseers, to shepherd the church of God which He purchased with His own blood" (Acts 20:28, NASB).

d. He *loves:* "Now I urge you, brethren, by our Lord Jesus Christ and by the love of the Spirit to strive together with me in your prayers to God for me" (Rom. 15:30, NASB).

e. He *wills:* "But one and the same Spirit works all these things, distributing to each one individually just as He wills" (1 Cor. 12:11, NASB).

As in the personal acts, so in choosing, knowing, loving, and willing we have terms which can properly be used only of persons.

3. *The Spirit Is Treated as a Person*

Attitudes and acts toward the Holy Spirit are described which are correctly directed only toward persons.

a. Just as God the Father and Jesus Christ, so the Holy Spirit may be blasphemed: "Therefore I say to you, any sin and blasphemy shall be forgiven men, but blasphemy against the Spirit shall not be forgiven" (Matt. 12:31, NASB; cf. also Mark 3:29; Luke 12:10).

b. He may be lied to: "But Peter said, 'Ananias, why has Satan filled your heart to lie to the Holy Spirit, and to keep back some of the price of the land?'" (Acts 5:3, NASB).

c. He may be resisted: "You men who are stiffnecked and uncircumcised in heart and ears are always resisting the Holy Spirit; you are doing just as your fathers did" (Acts 7:51, NASB).

d. He may be insulted or treated despitefully: "How much severer punishment do you think he will deserve who has trampled under foot the Son of God, and has regarded as unclean the blood of the covenant by which he was sanctified, and has insulted the Spirit of grace?" (Heb. 10:29, NASB).

e. He may be grieved: "And do not grieve the Holy Spirit of God, by whom you were sealed for the day of redemption" (Eph. 4:30, NASB).

4. *The Testimony of John*

In the Gospel of John there is testimony to the personality of the Spirit of a very unique and unmistakable kind. It is found in the five great key passages on the Spirit in the Last Supper discourse: John 14:16-17; 14:26; 15:26; 16:7-8; and 16:13-15. We have noted that the Greek term for Spirit, *pneuma,* is a neuter noun, and the normal rules of grammar call for the use of a neuter pronoun, "it" or "its." Deliberately disregarding the laws of Greek grammar, Jesus throughout consciously uses the personal pronouns "he," "his," and "him." Vincent Taylor states of the doctrine of the Spirit in the Gospel of John:

> The Fourth Gospel is the crown of the biblical revelation concerning the Spirit because, while it begins with history and the events of time, it soars into the heavenly realms of faith and experience, revealing to us what the history and the events mean. Perhaps the best description of its nature is still that of Clement of Alexandria: "Last of all, John, perceiving that the *bodily* facts had been set forth in the Gospels, being urged by his friends and inspired by the Spirit, composed a *spiritual* Gospel."[10]

Bishop H. C. G. Moule, in a very eloquent passage, relates the teaching of the Gospel of John to the rest of the scripture revelation concerning the Holy Spirit:

> In this central and decisive passage then we have the Holy Ghost revealed to us in so many words as HIM, not only as It; as the living and conscious Exerciser of true personal will and love, as truly and fully as the First "Paraclete," the Lord Jesus Christ Himself. And now this central passage radiates out its glory upon the whole system and circle of Scripture truth about the Spirit. From Gen. 1:2 to Rev. 22:17 it sheds the warmth of divine per-

---

10. "The Spirit in the New Testament," in Headingly Lectures, *The Doctrine of the Holy Spirit* (London: The Epworth Press, 1937), p. 66.

sonal life into every mention of the blessed Power. With the
Paschal Discourse in our heart and mind, we know that it was
He, not It, who "brooded" over the primeval deep. He, not It,
"strove with man," or "ruled in man" of old. He, not It, was in
Joseph in Egypt, and upon Moses in the wilderness of wandering,
and upon judges and kings of after-days. He, not It, "spake by the
prophets," "moving" those holy men of God. He, not It, drew the
plan of the ancient Tabernacle and of the first Temple. He, not It,
lifted Ezekiel to his feet in the hour of vision. He, not It, came
upon the Virgin, and anointed her Son at Jordan and led Him to
the desert of temptation, and gave utterance to the saints at Pentecost, and caught Philip away from the road to Gaza, and guided
Paul through Asia Minor to the nearest port for Europe. He, not It,
effects the new birth of regenerate man, and is the Breath of his
new life, and the Earnest of his coming glory. By Him, not by It,
the believer walks, and mortifies the deeds of the body, filled not
with It, but Him. He, not It, is the Spirit of faith, by whom it is
"given unto us to believe on Christ." He, not It, speaks to the
Churches. He, not It, says from heaven that they who die in the
Lord are blessed, and calls in this life upon the wandering soul of
man to come to the living water.[11]

B. The Deity of the Holy Spirit

Closely related to the evidence for the personality of the Spirit is the
evidence for His deity. A quick review of the verses cited above will
reveal how many of them give strong presumptive evidence to the
fact that the Holy Spirit is God. In addition, we may call to mind the
number of times in which Father, Son, and Holy Spirit are named
together in a coordinated way. For example, the baptismal formula
found in the Great Commission employs "the name of the Father and
the Son and the Holy Spirit" (Matt. 28:19). In 1 Cor. 6:11 we read,
"And such were some of you; but you were washed, but you were
sanctified, but you were justified in the name of the Lord Jesus
Christ, and in the Spirit of our God" (NASB). Similarly, the benedic-
tion of 2 Cor. 13:14, "The grace of the Lord Jesus Christ, and the love
of God, and the fellowship of the Holy Spirit, be with you all"
(NASB). Peter's greeting, likewise, joins the three names in different
order: "According to the foreknowledge of God the Father, through
sanctification of the Spirit, unto obedience and sprinkling of the
blood of Jesus Christ" (1 Pet. 1:2).

In the Acts of the Apostles, Peter charges Ananias with the sin
of lying to the Holy Spirit, and then says, "Thou hast not lied unto

11. *Veni Creator*, pp. 8-11.

men, but unto God" (Acts 5:4). Resisting God in the Old Testament is said by Stephen actually to be resisting the Holy Spirit (Acts 7:51). Paul, in 1 Cor. 3:16-17 and 6:19, equates the Holy Spirit with God as abiding in the temple of human personality. Moule says, in reference to the deity of the Spirit:

> Meanwhile, the scriptural basis for this belief is strong, and capable of simple statement. In Scripture the Spirit is as freely called "the Spirit of the Son," "the Spirit of Christ," as "the Spirit of God," "the Spirit of the Father." And he is as freely said to be "sent" by the Son as by the Father. But we gather from Scripture, with abundant fulness, and in many directions, that the works of the blessed Three Persons in redemption bear always a deep and steadfast reference to their eternal inner relations.[12]

C. The Holy Spirit and the Church

In our study of God's redemptive purpose to which we shall turn in the next major section of this book, we shall discover again and again the vital part taken by the Holy Spirit in our salvation. Both individually and collectively, Christianity is the creation of the Spirit of God confronting man with God in Christ. From the Day of Pentecost to the final *parousia* or appearing of Christ in His second coming, the Church has its being in the work of the Spirit. As Vincent Taylor has notably summarized:

> It is not too much to say that the New Testament Church is the community of the Spirit. The Spirit enters into the most intimate relationships with believers, indwelling, teaching, revealing, sealing, guiding, inspiring, uniting, constraining, interceding, empowering. He is the life and light of God in the mind and soul of man, both in the individual and in the Church. There is scarcely an aspect of Christian belief and practice which is not in some way or other associated with His presence and power. Man's capacities are enlarged, new gifts are added, fresh aspirations are imparted, higher planes of life and conduct are made possible, as men are led, guided, and inspired by the power of the Spirit of God. It is especially notable that the fruits of the Spirit are ethical. . . . The broad stream of New Testament teaching concerning men "filled with the Spirit" is related to conduct, duties, service, insight, and saintliness. The Spirit is "Holy," and His power is directed to the sanctification and enrichment of life.[13]

---

12. *Ibid.*, pp. 29-30.
13. *Doctrine of the Holy Spirit*, pp. 49-50.

III. THE SPIRIT AND THE HUMANITY OF JESUS

An important element in New Testament teaching about the Holy Spirit is that which is concerned with His relation to the manhood of our Lord. This is seen in three areas: the birth of Jesus, His baptism, and His life and ministry.

A. The Birth Narratives

Both Luke and Matthew lay special emphasis on the birth of Jesus, and both make clear the place of the Spirit in those wonderful events which produced the manhood of our Lord. Luke, in particular, stresses the work of the Holy Spirit in relation to the ministry of John the Baptist, whose parents were both said to have been filled with the Spirit (1:41-45, 68-69). John himself was "filled with the Holy Ghost, even from his mother's womb" (Luke 1:15). The vital ministry of the forerunner, preparing the way of the Lord, was directed from the very first by the Holy Spirit.

The Incarnation itself was the direct act of the divine Spirit. Both Luke and Matthew bear testimony to the fact that the conception of Jesus by the Virgin Mary was by the power of the Spirit of God. While it might be conceded that the Incarnation involves a fundamental mystery, it is clear that the Word was made flesh to dwell among us by the supernatural agency of the Third Person of the Trinity. The angel said to Mary, "The Holy Ghost shall come upon thee, and the power of the Highest shall overshadow thee: therefore also that holy thing which shall be born of thee shall be called the Son of God" (Luke 1:35). To Joseph, the angel said, "Joseph, thou son of David, fear not to take unto thee Mary thy wife: for that which is conceived in her is of the Holy Ghost. And she shall bring forth a son, and thou shalt call his name Jesus: for he shall save his people from their sins" (Matt. 1:20-21).

In this striking manner, God chose to bear witness to the sinlessness of His only begotten Son. It is useless to speculate on what other means could have been used. No other would so testify to the uniqueness of Christ's nature and to the union of the divine and human natures in a single personality. The inception of the manhood of Jesus and the generation of the God-Man was therefore due to the direct agency of the Holy Spirit.

B. The Baptism

Special significance is also attributed to the manifestation of the

Spirit at the baptism of Jesus by John at the river Jordan. All four Gospels relate the descent of the Spirit upon the Lord at that time, and the testimony from heaven which was then given. The Synoptics (Matthew, Mark, and Luke) describe the coming of the Spirit as a dove, resting upon Jesus as He came up out of the water, together with the voice from heaven saying, "This is my beloved Son, in whom I am well pleased," (Matt. 3:16-17) or, "Thou art my beloved Son, in whom I am well pleased" (Mark 1:10-11; Luke 3:21-22). John records this as the Messianic sign which had been given to him as an indication of the One who should come: "And John bare record, saying, I saw the Spirit descending from heaven like a dove, and it abode upon him. And I knew him not: but he that sent me to baptize with water, the same said unto me, Upon whom thou shalt see the Spirit descending, and remaining on him, the same is he which baptizeth with the Holy Ghost" (John 1:32-33).

Some scholars have felt that the baptism was the moment when Jesus became the Messiah (or Anointed One), or at least when He became conscious of His Messianic destiny. It seems much better to say rather that "the Spirit did not descend upon Jesus at that precise moment, not having been upon him before; but it was then revealed that Jesus was the permanent Bearer of the Holy Spirit. Jesus, that is, did not *become* the Messiah at His baptism. The descending dove and the voice from heaven simply *identified* Him as the Anointed of the Lord."[14]

At this moment also Jesus was identified as the One who should baptize with the Holy Spirit. John's preaching had been, "I indeed baptize you with water unto repentance: but he that cometh after me is mightier than I, whose shoes I am not worthy to bear: he shall baptize you with the Holy Ghost, and with fire" (Matt. 3:11; also Mark 1:8; Luke 3:16). Thus the Spirit identified Jesus both as the Bearer of the Messianic Spirit and as the One who would fulfill the promises of the outpouring of the Messianic age. In this twofold fulfillment was the basis for the thrilling announcement, "The kingdom of heaven is at hand."

C. The Life and Ministry of Jesus

Not only the birth and baptism, but the entire life and ministry of our Lord, are intimately related to the work of the Holy Spirit. It is the

---

14. Greathouse, *Fullness of the Spirit,* p. 48.

teaching of the New Testament, in Moule's words, that the manhood of Jesus was "begun and maintained in its perfect holiness and power by the Holy Spirit as the immediate personal divine Worker. It is accordingly by the Holy Spirit that the Lord Jesus Christ is the Second Man."[15]

A few points may be called to mind. It was by the Spirit that Jesus was led (driven, Mark 1:12) into the wilderness for the Temptation (Matt. 4:1-11; Luke 4:1-13). He "returned in the power of the Spirit into Galilee," where in the synagogue at Nazareth He publicly read from the prophecy of Isaiah, "The Spirit of the Lord is upon me, because he hath anointed me to preach the gospel to the poor; he hath sent me to heal the brokenhearted, to preach deliverance to the captives, and recovering of sight to the blind, to set at liberty them that are bruised, to preach the acceptable year of the Lord" (Luke 4:14, 18-19).

The very solemn warning about the peril of blasphemy against the Holy Spirit was directly connected with the Spirit's power in the healing ministry of the Lord. It was the bitter charge that Christ was casting out demons by the power of Beelzebub, the prince of demons, that brought the caution expressed in Matt. 12:24-32 and Mark 3:22-30. Reckless attributing of the works of Christ to Satan when they were actually wrought by the power of the Spirit brought those guilty perilously close to the sin which kills man's capacity to respond to God's call.

As Greathouse summarizes the place of the Spirit in Jesus' life and ministry: "His whole life in fact was a manifestation of the Holy Spirit. 'The fruits of the Spirit are the virtues of Christ.' *He was the perfect Pattern of the Spirit-filled life.* No speaker in tongues was He, or super-righteous bigot! So possessed of God, and yet so sane! So holy, and yet so humble! The Spirit whispers to us, 'Let this mind be in you, which was also in Christ Jesus.'"[16]

IV. THE DOCTRINE OF THE TRINITY

We are now in a position to consider the way in which the Church has put together the data drawn from its life and experience when confronted by God in Jesus Christ through the Holy Spirit. It may

---

15. *Veni Creator,* p. 34.
16. *Fullness of the Spirit,* p. 49.

rightly be said that the doctrine of the Trinity is at once the deepest truth of the Christian faith, the root of all else, and the most difficult to explain.

It is sometimes supposed that theologians and philosophers, in a mood of detachment, have foisted this teaching upon Christians, who otherwise would have a very simple, easy faith. But this does not conform with the facts. It is true that theologians and churchmen have tried to understand and explain this doctrine, and their attempts have not always been helpful. However, not until it is understood that the roots of the doctrine of the Trinity are fundamentally biblical and religious will this truth be seen in its true perspective. If there is a problem in this doctrine, it is one that has been posed by the facts of revelation and Christian experience. Men who had a knowledge of God, the Creator and Father of all, came into a personal knowledge of God through His Son, and discovered profound inner illumination and power through the Holy Spirit. The Christian cannot truly speak of God without recourse to the doctrine of the Trinity. God is one, but He has made himself known to men in three "Persons," Father, Son, and Holy Spirit. "For through him [i.e., Christ] we both have access by one Spirit unto the Father" (Eph. 2:18). As Frederick C. Grant has stated it:

> The doctrine of the Trinity, which attributed to the Holy Spirit the most explicit personal existence, was the result, as we have seen, of the church's attempt to combine all these data of revelation without infringing upon the doctrine of the unity or "oneness" of God. It was no example of "metaphysics," or of philosophy in general, invading the realm of faith, but of a vigorous effort to safeguard the truth of revelation.[17]

The conclusion of the Church in general has been phrased in words that go back to Tertullian, a Latin church father of the early third century: God is *una substantia,* one in being or nature, *et tres in personae,* and three in persons. The Church early defended its Trinitarian faith in creeds aimed against Arianism, the teaching that Jesus Christ and the Holy Spirit were not really of the same substance, or nature, with the Father. Through the centuries the finest minds of the Christian Church have been gripped by the truth of this doctrine, and, although at times it has been rejected as of secondary value, it has always returned with new power and meaning. In our own day we have seen a resurgence of belief in the importance and

---

17. *Introduction to New Testament Thought,* p. 112.

necessity of Trinitarian Christianity. Karl Barth, perhaps the most influential theologian of the 20th century, has made it foundational to his whole massive system of doctrine, discussing it exhaustively in more than 200 pages of his *Prolegomena to Church Dogmatics*.[18] It is doubtful if the Christian Church as a whole has ever been more convinced of the truth of this doctrine than now.

Despite this great unanimity, however, it must be confessed that a final and fully satisfying statement on the Trinity seems impossible. A part of the reason for this lies in the mystery of God's being. As we have said before, our revelation of God is true, but to comprehend the being of God fully is quite beyond the capacity of finiteness. An element of mystery remains here as in many other areas of life, not all of them religious. We are not content, however, to leave the matter there; for "all men by nature desire to know," and we are better satisfied when we can drive some of our mysteries into a corner.

Current discussion moves in two directions. One group of Christian thinkers places emphasis upon the unity of God and seeks to explain the triunity of God in that light. These tend to use the analogy of the individual person as an explanation of God's oneness-in-threeness. An example would be the content of human consciousness: the one self thinks, feels, and wills simultaneously. The person is present and active in each function, yet distinguishes among them. This group of writers moves in the direction of *modalism,* the view that God is one in nature and person, showing different faces at different times. It is at pains, however, to disavow Sabellianism, an extreme modalism.

Another group places its emphasis upon the *triunity* of God and seeks to explain the unity of God in that light. These scholars insist that each of the "Persons" of the Trinity should be thought of as something like separate, distinct personalities, but whose intensive unity exceeds anything in human experience. These thinkers move in the direction of tritheism, or three Gods. However, just as the first group seeks to avoid the error of modalism, so this group wants to escape the charge of *tritheism.* The first uses the personal analogy, the second the social analogy. Neither, however, is held exclusively of the other and it is recognized by all that an analogy can only reflect imperfectly the being of God. Basically, all such writers and thinkers are

18. *The Doctrine of the Word of God, Prolegomena to Church Dogmatics.* Vol. I, Part I. Trans. G. T. Thompson (New York: Charles Scribner's Sons, 1936), pp. 339-560.

trying, against odds, to express the fullness and complexity of the nature of God as revealed in Jesus Christ.

It is helpful to remember that the higher one ascends in the scale of existence, the more complex he discovers unity to be. A mathematical point is absolute, undivided unity. A cell, however, is more complex in its unity, and a human self is complex beyond description, yet capable of a high degree of integration and unity. In the Trinity we have one God who has three "modes of existence" or "ways of being." Each is fully, unqualifiedly God in nature, distinguishable but inseparable.

It should be said, by way of concluding this topic, that the best statements stress the basic elements in the Christian doctrine of the Trinity, and try to keep the matter simple. This is what each of us should do in his own thinking and religious life. God is one; we address Him as "Thou," but He has revealed himself as the *Father*, our Creator; the *Son*, our Redeemer; and the *Holy Spirit*, our Sanctifier.

> We have not to see the three Persons alongside each other on the divine throne, but we have to see the love of the Father revealed and given through the Son by the Holy Spirit, so to say one behind the other in the order of their relation to us. We have the Father, through the Son, by the Holy Spirit.[19]

SUMMARY

A great deal more might be said concerning the doctrine of the Holy Spirit, but we must be content with the main outlines of the scriptural teaching. To the foundation laid in the Old Testament we find that the New Testament adds a clear sense of both the personality and deity of the Spirit. This results in the Christian concept of the triune God.

We turn next to the biblical concept of man in our survey of our Christian faith.

---

19. Emil Brunner, *The Scandal of Christianity* (Philadelphia: Westminster Press, 1951), p. 50. The extensive and full treatment of the doctrine of the Trinity properly belongs to the sphere of systematic theology. Many excellent works are available, to which the serious student may turn. An excellent starting place for further study in this area is Wiley, *Christian Theology*, 1:394-440. For the development of the doctrine in the history of theology, see Gonzalez, *History of Christian Thought*, 1:123-392.

CHAPTER 10

What Is Man?

It is often said that there are four major themes in Christian doctrine: God, man, sin, and salvation. It is in order for us to consider next the creature who is the object of God's infinite love. The biblical view of man is directly opposed to the materialistic and naturalistic views so widespread today in communistic and totalitarian regimes. Walt Whitman, with great penetration, observed:

> As I stand aloof and look there is to me
> something profoundly affecting in large
> masses of men following the lead
> of those who do not believe in man.[1]

In opposition to this, the Christian believes in man, the infinite worth of the human individual, and the priceless potential to be realized through the redeeming grace of God.

It is our purpose in this chapter to survey the major doctrines of biblical anthropology. This latter term has both a scientific and a theological meaning. Scientific anthropology deals with questions relating to primitive man, the distinctions among the races, and the factors which enter man's development and progress. Theological anthropology deals with the facts of man's moral and religious constitution and history as related to Christian doctrine. While there is

---

1. From "Thought," by Walt Whitman. On the subject of this chapter, cf. G. C. Berkouwer, *Man: The Image of God* (Grand Rapids: Wm. B. Eerdmans Publishing Co., 1962; Purkiser, Taylor, and Taylor, *God, Man, and Salvation,* pp. 67-78 and 251-67; and Mildred Bangs Wynkoop, *A Theology of Love* (Kansas City: Beacon Hill Press of Kansas City, 1972), pp. 102-24.

much of vital interest to the theologian in scientific anthropology, our concern here must of necessity be limited to the ethical and religious aspects of human existence.

I. Outline of the Biblical View

It may be well to sketch briefly the biblical attitude toward man. One of its most striking features is the sense of contrast we find. There is, for example, the amazement and awe of the Psalmist:

> When I consider Thy heavens, the work of Thy fingers,
> The moon and the stars, which Thou hast ordained;
> What is man, that Thou dost take thought of him?
> And the son of man, that Thou dost care for him?
> Yet Thou hast made him a little lower than God,
> And dost crown him with glory and majesty! (Ps. 8:3-5, NASB).

Here it is worthy of note that man is but a little lower than *Elohim* (the Hebrew may mean either God or angels). He is not a little higher than the animals. His evaluation is from above, not from below. He is radically distinguished from the brute creation.

Set over against this appraisal of the dignity and worth of man is the biblical view of his utter weakness apart from God, and his estrangement from the fellowship of his Creator. "Lord, what is man, that thou takest knowledge of him! or the son of man, that thou makest account of him! Man is like to vanity: his days are as a shadow that passeth away" (Ps. 144:3-4). "Thou carriest them away as with a flood; they are as a sleep: in the morning they are like grass which groweth up. In the morning it flourisheth, and groweth up; in the evening it is cut down, and withereth" (Ps. 90:5-6). "All flesh is grass, and all the goodliness thereof is as the flower of the field: the grass withereth, the flower fadeth: because the spirit of the Lord bloweth upon it: surely the people is grass" (Isa. 40:6-7).

It is this clear-eyed vision of both the potential and the peril of humanity which makes the biblical view so thoroughly realistic. In words attributed to Pascal, "Man is the glory and scum of the universe." The great objection to all secular theories of man is that they are either too optimistic or too pessimistic. On the contrary, the biblical position is amazing in its realism. As Frederick W. Schroeder put it:

> The Bible emphasizes at one and the same time man's kinship to God and his alienation from God. He is seen as being but

little lower than the angels, but it is also recognized that he is conceived in sin. The authentic answers which theology gives to questions concerning man's nature and destiny, his freedom, his responsibility, the Christian hope, the ultimate fulfillment of history can all be traced back to Biblical sources. Theology frequently borrows its conceptual formulations from philosophy, but when it strays too far from the Bible and takes its lead primarily from philosophy, it usually ends up with theories contradicted by the facts of human experience. The assumption of man's perfectability, based on the theory of evolution, is a good case in point.[2]

II. The Origin of Man

The simplest, most profound, and most satisfactory explanation of human origins ever offered is found in Genesis, in the great "Poem of the Dawn," of chapter 1, and in the following chapter.[3] In Gen. 1:26-28 we read:

And God said,
> *Let us make man in our image, after our likeness,*
> *And let them have dominion over the fish of the sea,*
> *And over the fowl of the air,*
> *And over all the land*
> *And over every creeping thing that creepeth upon the land.*

And God created man in his own image,
In the image of God created he them.
Male and female created he them.

And God blessed them.

And God said unto them,
> *Be fruitful, and multiply, and replenish the earth, and subdue it,*
> *And have dominion over the fish of the sea,*
> *And over the fowl of the air,*
> *And over every living thing that moveth upon the earth.*[4]

In Genesis 2, a parallel account is given: "And the Lord God formed man of the dust of the ground, and breathed into his nostrils the breath of life; and man became a living soul" (Gen. 2:7).

---

2. *Preaching the Word with Authority* (Philadelphia: Westminster Press, 1954), pp. 89-90.

3. Cf. Wiley, *Christian Theology,* 1:450.

4. Version and arrangement from *ibid.,* p. 454.

A. Science and the Bible

Reams have been written on the alleged contradictions between science and the early chapters of Genesis, and this voluminous literature cannot be reviewed here. In considering the biblical account of man's origin, today's student will need to keep in mind a simple but profound distinction. This is the distinction between science, properly so called, and philosophical and religious explanations of the universe.

Science is that human endeavor which seeks to find the unifying principles (or laws) that underlie the phenomenal world (the world of things and events). It is, properly speaking, analytical and descriptive, concerned with the orderly processes of nature. Philosophy is the attempt to "see life steadily, and see it whole," to seek for the ultimate purposes behind the whole of existence, the "whence? whither? and why?" of our being. It is synthetic and normative, concerned with the realm of values.

When these distinctions are firmly grasped, it will be seen that science as such has nothing to say about ultimate causes and purposes, or about that which lies outside the realm of observable phenomena and their explanation. This does not mean that scientific men may not theorize about the beginnings of life or the origins of man, for the philosophic instinct is very strong in the human mind. But when they do so theorize, they are not working as scientists but as philosophers or, if their thought embraces the idea of God, as theologians. It goes almost without saying that the philosophic opinions of the scientific are of little more value than the scientific opinions of philosophers. It also goes without saying that a top-flight scientist may be a second-rate amateur philosopher, and an even worse theologian. As T. E. Jessop has written:

> By the scientific account of man is in fact meant sometimes the knowledge of man that is found *within* the sciences (knowledge scientifically evidenced), sometimes a speculative extension of this knowledge. The two must be sharply distinguished. The latter is a form of philosophy, but it is popularly accepted as scientific because it is based on science, is put forth in the name of science, and comes to us sometimes—by no means always—through scientists.[5]

It may readily be conceded that it is absolutely impossible to

---

5. "The Scientific Account of Man," in *The Christian Understanding of Man,* T. E. Jessop, *et al.* (London: George Allen and Unwin, Ltd., 1938), p. 4.

reconcile naturalistic evolution with the biblical view of origins. But let it clearly be seen that naturalistic evolution is a philosophical theory, not a scientific finding, however much some of its proponents may seek to build upon the legitimate prestige of the natural sciences.

When each discipline remains within the bounds it sets up for itself, there can be no conflict between science and true theology. This is not to ignore the multitude of conflicts which have been generated across the ages by one or the other or both stepping outside their areas of concern and competence.

We must remember that basically there are two ways of accounting for almost any event that happens. We may seek in the realm of anterior conditions, efficient causes; or we may seek in the area of purposes, ends, values, final causes. If we observe a man running to catch a bus, we may account for his running on the basis of the physiological structure of his body—nerves, tissues, muscles, and bones coordinating in the release of energy derived from the cereal he ate for breakfast. Or we may account for the running on the basis of the man's purpose to reach his job on time, or to be on time for a date with his girl friend. The two accounts are very different, but are not therefore contradictory.

David Sarnoff published a memorable statement at this point:

> In its early stages, modern science seemed at odds with religion; but this was merely a token of its immaturity. The more familiar story, in our time, is that of scientists who become increasingly aware of the mystery of the universe and come to religion through knowledge of the limitations of science. Indeed, how can those who play with the building blocks of the universe, its atoms and electrons and genes, fail to be touched by awe? Every victory of science reveals more clearly a divine design in nature, a remarkable conformity in all things, from the infinitesimal to the infinite.[6]

B. The Creation of Man

One of the most significant aspects in the biblical account of human origins is its insistence upon man's creatureliness. Man is not presented as a "fallen god," as in some of the ancient mythologies; nor is he seen as the product of an eternal Nature. He is viewed as the crown of a series of creative acts. He stands confronted by God as a

---

6. "The Fabulous Future, "*Fortune*, Vol. 51, No. 1 (January, 1955), p. 116. (Used by permission of *Fortune Magazine* and General Sarnoff.)

creature by his Creator. Man alone of all God's handiwork is addressed as "thou."

The creation of man was the result of a voluntary act of the divine will. No longer do we have the word "Let there be," which involves the immediacy of the creative fiat in conjunction with secondary causes; but "Let us make man in our image, after our likeness"—an expression which asserts the power of the creative word in conjunction with deliberate choice. This is the culmination of all former creative acts.

Mention has been made of parallel accounts of creation, as given in the first and second chapters of Genesis. There is neither clash nor contradiction in these two accounts. In the latter, man is seen as related to the material universe, with body formed of the dust of the ground; and in the former, the major emphasis is upon his moral responsibility.

C. The Dual Nature of Man

Implied in what has been said is the biblical view of the duality of man's nature as both material and immaterial or spiritual. Through his body, man is related to the earth. He is described as flesh. There is no thought in scripture that matter is inherently evil, as the Gnostics and many of the Greek philosophers would have it. The Christian view involves the entire man and therefore of necessity includes that which is physical.[7]

On the other hand, man is immaterial. Through his higher nature he is related to another world. Two views have been held concerning the immaterial side of the human species. One is that man's nature is dichotomous; that is, twofold, with body and soul as its constituent elements. This view would regard soul and spirit as one and the same entity, but viewed in different relations. In relation to God, as coming from God, adapted to communion with God, and capable of being indwelt by God, it is spirit. Viewed as related to the body which it inhabits, and the world about, it is soul. In both Old and New Testaments there may be found an interchangeable use of the terms "soul" and "spirit."

The other view of human nature is trichotomous. This theory holds that man consists of three component parts—body, soul, and spirit—and that the soul and spirit are almost as distinct from each

---

7. Cf. Rom. 6:12; 8:23; 12:1; 1 Cor. 6:19; 1 Thess. 5:23.

other as soul and body. The spirit is declared to be the organ of divine life and of communion with God, the seat of the divine indwelling. The soul is seen as the seat of the natural life, where the natural faculties of the conscious being dwell. It is the intermediary between the body and the spirit, the seat of the personality. Some scriptural references may be noted which lend support to this theory.

It is well to remember that body, soul, and spirit are so united as to form one integrated personality. What may prove of value in logical analysis need not be enlarged into psychological division.

The manner in which the soul or spirit of man is propagated has been discussed by theologians through the Christian centuries. The most common views have been labeled (1) Preexistence, (2) Creationism, (3) Traducianism. The preexistence theory of the origin of the soul is that the human self has a history prior to its embodied life in this world, as well as a subsequent history. While some have thought thereby to explain the depravity of the soul, the problem is only transferred from the present to the past. Creationism holds that each ego is an immediate creation of God, while the body is propagated through the parents. One of the prime objections to this idea is that it requires an immediate creation by God of a self with sinful tendencies.

Traducianism, on the other hand, would seem open to fewer objections than either preexistence or creationism. It is the view that the soul originates in connection with the origin of the body, as a psychophysical unity. Wiley and Culbertson explain:

> This holds that the souls of men as well as their bodies are derived from their parents. It is asserted that new souls develop from Adam's soul like the shoots of a vine or a tree. The theory has been widely held in the Protestant churches. It implies that the race was immediately created in Adam, both in respect to body and soul, and both are propagated by natural generation. Thus, the expression, *Adam begat a son in his own likeness*, is interpreted to mean that it is the whole man who begets and is begotten. This theory seems to provide the best explanation for the transmission of original sin or depravity.[8]

D. The Unity of the Race

Scientific and biblical anthropology are in substantial agreement as to the unity of the human race. The species is one, springing from a

---

8. *Introduction to Christian Theology*, p. 156.

common ancestry, belonging to a common stock. All the races among men have a oneness in physical characteristics and genetic chromosome structure. The body is one in anatomical structure, one in chemical elements, one in physiological constitution, and one in pathological susceptibilities. No matter what the color of skin or peculiarities of features, there is an unmistakable identity in bones, teeth, temperature, pulse frequency, and liability to disease, while the blood of human beings everywhere is said to be readily distinguishable from that of animals.

Not only physiological, but psychological, resemblances testify to the unity of the race. The mental differences in mankind are the results of many factors, but basically all races possess a oneness of psychological endowment. There are the same intellectual faculties which constitute the rationality of mind, the same sensibilities with their marvelous adjustment to the manifold relations of life.

The study of the world's languages points to a common origin. Affinities among the languages of widely separated peoples have been discovered, which testify to a primary language unity. Great similarities in traditions are also apparent, and the universal appeal of philosophy and religion points to an underlying unity of the human family.

All of this agrees with the testimony of scripture. "God created man, in the likeness of God made he him; male and female created he them; and blessed them, and called their name Adam, in the day when they were created" (Gen. 5:1-2). All human beings came from one source, and all partake of one common nature because all are derived from one parentage.

However diversified men may now be from climate and other external circumstances, from depravity or idolatry, or from civilization and restoration by the gospel, all are of one nature and possess properties in common. Paul assures us that God, who made the worlds and all things therein, "hath made of one blood all nations of men for to dwell on all the face of the earth, and hath determined the times before appointed, and the bounds of their habitation" (Acts 17:26). It is therefore a clear teaching of the Bible that the whole human race upon "all the face of the earth" came originally from one parentage, and all are of "one blood, of one nature" (Acts 17:26).

III. THE IMAGE OF GOD

It is the nature of the human race as responsible and moral which finds the greatest stress in the Scriptures. We have already noted the pregnant statement of Gen. 1:26-27 which distinguishes man as made in the "image of God." The nature of that divine image has been described in a number of ways. It has been considered to be the power of understanding truth, of creating the beautiful, and of doing what is right, which man shares with God.[9] It has been considered as residing in the fact that God speaks to men, who answers Him as a being who is responsible.[10] A somewhat similar concept is that the image of God in man consists in the capacity of the human to respond gratefully to God's seeking love.[11] Edmond Jacob finds the image of God to be man's representative function, in that man is appointed to have dominion over nature, in dependence upon Him whose representative he is.[12] H. Orton Wiley summarizes the image of God in man as twofold: a natural or essential image, and a moral image.[13] It is not, certainly, an image of form or figure, but of the spiritual nature of man.

A. The Natural Image

The natural image of God in man refers to the elements of personality or selfhood—what Walther Eichrodt called "the Creator's greatest gift to man, that of the personal I."[14] All that distinguishes the personal life of a human being from the life of an animal is part of the natural image of God. Intellect, conscience, the capacity for moral self-direction, the intimation of immortality, the rational powers of abstract intelligence are all part of the likeness of God, the finite reflection of what in the Creator is infinite truth, beauty, and goodness.

Reflection on the vast chasm which separates the conscious life of man from that of the brutes will increase our wonder at the natural image of the divine in the human. Here is creation of the first

9. Alan Richardson, "Adam, Man," in Alan Richardson, ed., *Theological Word Book of the Bible* (London: SCM Press, 1950), p. 14.

10. Emil Brunner, "The Christian Understanding of Man," in Jessop, *Christian Understanding of Man*, pp. 153-57.

11. Walter Marshall Horton in *ibid.*, p. 233.

12. *Theology of the Old Testament* (New York: Harper and Brothers, 1958), pp. 169-71.

13. *Christian Theology*, 2:29-50. Much of the following discussion is indebted to Dr. Wiley's treatment.

14. *Man in the Old Testament* (Chicago: Henry Regnery Co., 1951), p. 30.

order. All the vast potential of civilization, art, culture, and science was wrapped up in the word of God's ancient penman: "In the image of God made he man" (Gen. 9:6).

B. The Moral Image

Without trespassing on the theme of the next chapter, we may note that, while the natural image which God stamped upon man is summed up in "personality," the moral image is expressed in the term "holiness" or ethical character. The second term has to do primarily with the use made of the powers God has placed in the creature of His love. Having the power of self-determination, man is responsible for the use of his freedom. Having affections reaching out to the objects of his choice, he is responsible for the quality of those affections. Having intellectual power, he is responsible for the content of his thought and the uses to which he puts his accumulated store of knowledge.

The moral image of God in man refers to the dispositions and tendencies within him. It is part of the character or quality of personality, the rightness or wrongness of the use of the powers with which he is endowed. It gives man his moral nature and makes possible a holy character.

It is axiomatic in biblical thought that man was created holy. Wiley defines created holiness as "a spontaneous inclination or tendency toward the good—a subjective disposition which always answers to the right. It is more than innocence. Man was created not only negatively innocent but positively holy, with an enlightened understanding of God and spiritual things, and a will wholly inclined to them."[15]

Some of the implications of this conception are spelled out in Wiley and Culbertson.[16] Primitive holiness was not a mere possibility of holiness, a nature free from either virtue or sin. It was a positive attitude of the soul, characterized by a spontaneous tendency to obey the right and reject the wrong. On the other hand, it was not ethical holiness. Adam's holiness was not the result of his moral choices. It was a holiness of nature rather than a holiness of personal agency, for as John Wesley observed, "A man may be righteous before he does what is right, holy in heart before he is holy in life."

---

15. *Christian Theology,* 2:44.
16. *Introduction to Christian Theology,* pp. 158-59.

The presence of the Holy Spirit was for Adam (as for any human being) the source of holiness. He walked and talked with God in a blessed and intimate communion of the Spirit. The presence of the Holy Spirit was thus an original and abiding element in the holiness of man. As John Miley pointed out, only thus can the true nature of human depravity be realized. The fall of man was not only a loss of the subjective state of holiness, but it involved also the corruption of man's nature as a result of the operation of influences which came by the withdrawal of the Holy Spirit.

IV. BIBLICAL PSYCHOLOGY

We have now to look in more detail at the biblical portrayal of human nature. There is something of an anachronism in speaking of biblical "psychology," inasmuch as psychology is usually identified with the modern discipline of comparatively recent development. Further, the Scriptures are more concerned with what we should call ethics, and particularly religious ethics, than they are with what we should properly describe as psychology. There is no attempt at technical use of terms. The words used to describe human nature are drawn from everyday speech, and are popular and religious in use rather than precise and scientific. For all of this, the Bible, as psychologist Henry C. Link has told us, is still "the greatest and most authentic textbook on personality," and discoveries of the present day tend to confirm rather than to contradict what is found there.[17]

A. The Physical Nature

Mention has earlier been made of a dualistic view of man which distinguishes between what may in general be called the body on the one side and the mental and spiritual nature on the other. That this dualism is functional rather than final is seen in the fact that the biblical view of the eternal state involves a resurrection of the body (cf. Chapter 23). Four major biblical terms are used to describe the physical substratum of personality, two from the Old Testament (*aphar* or "dust," *basar* or "flesh") and two from the New Testament (*soma* or "body," and *sarx* or "flesh").

In Gen. 2:7 we read that "the Lord God formed man of the dust of the ground, and breathed into his nostrils the breath of life; and

---

17. *The Return to Religion* (New York: The Macmillan Co., 1937), p. 103.

man became a living soul." Here the material elements in the human body are spoken of as dust *(aphar)*. Dust united with breath or spirit becomes flesh *(basar)*, living or ensouled matter.[18] When breath or spirit leaves the body, it then returns to the dust (Gen. 3:19; Job 34:14-15).

The Hebrew has no term for body as such. Flesh *(basar)* is used instead. "Man is flesh *(basar)*, made from the dust of the earth, and animated by *ruach* (spirit), so that he is a *nephesh* (living being)."[19] Flesh and spirit are often used in contrast, flesh standing for weakness and spirit for power (cf. Isa. 31:3). However, it cannot be insisted too strongly that flesh is never thought to be evil. It is God's creation, and He looked upon it and called it good (Gen. 1:31). The fact that flesh was used for sacrifice upon God's altar is sure evidence that the flesh is of itself neither unholy nor unclean.

In the New Testament, *soma* is the word most often used for the individual body. When used of a human body, there is never a suggestion that it is intrinsically evil. For example, Paul speaks of glorifying God in the body (1 Cor. 6:20), of magnifying Christ in his body (Phil. 1:20), and the believer's consecration is to present his body a living sacrifice "holy and acceptable unto God" (Rom. 12:1). The resurrection of Christ concerned His body, as the resurrection of the believer will involve his mortal body. The person as a whole may be denoted by the term body, as is seen in Rom. 12:1. Body, however, may also be used in the New Testament in the sense of a spiritual unity or organism, as "the body of Christ" (Rom. 12:5) or contrastingly "the body of sin" (Rom. 6:6), much as we would speak of a student body or "the body politic."

The New Testament term for flesh *(sarx)* is used in two rather sharply distinguished ways, which the uninstructed are apt to confuse. First, it is used in the Old Testament sense of physical organic being, structure of skin, muscle, nerve, fat, and bone, and of man's physical or human nature in general. In this sense it has no moral overtones, and is not in any way evil. For example, the Lord Jesus Christ is spoken of as the Word made flesh *(sarx)*, dwelling among us (John 1:14). Flesh is here no more than humanity. Again, Christ was of the seed of David according to the *sarx* (Rom. 1:3). Paul said, "The

---

18. Cf. Davidson, *Theology of the Old Testament*, p. 203.

19. Norman H. Snaith, *The Distinctive Ideas of the Old Testament* (Philadelphia Westminster Press, 1946), p. 193.

life which I now live in the flesh [*sarx*] I live by the faith of the Son of God" (Gal. 2:20).

Against this must be set the frequent New Testament (especially Pauline) use of the term flesh for that within human nature which is inherently evil, or what in the next chapter we shall call original sin, carnality, or depravity. Peter speaks of putting away the filth of the flesh (1 Pet. 3:21), and Jude of the garment spotted by the flesh (Jude 23). Paul, particularly, sets the flesh and the Spirit of God in sharpest contrast. His old life under the bondage of the law he regards as being "in the flesh" (Rom. 7:5). A total of 16 times in his writings Paul contrasts flesh and Spirit in such a way as to denote moral conflict. Prime examples will be found in Rom. 8:3-9 and Gal. 5:16-21, 24.

That this use of the term flesh cannot possibly mean the physical being of man is seen in such expressions as, "So then they that are in the flesh cannot please God. But ye are not in the flesh, but in the Spirit, if so be that the Spirit of God dwell in you" (Rom. 8:8-9); and, "They that are Christ's have crucified the flesh" (Gal. 5:24). It is also noteworthy that of the 15 works of the flesh listed in Gal. 5:19-21, only 5 have any possible connection with the body. The rest are sins of the spirit.

The importance of this for Christian thought lies in the fact that many present-day religious thinkers identify sin with the physical or human nature of man, and hence come up with the argument that no one can be free from sin as long as he lives in the physical body. This argument loses all its surface plausibility when it is seen that neither the Old nor the New Testament lends any support to the suggestion that matter or the human body or human nature per se is to be identified with sinfulness. Any Bible support for such a view is gained only by totally misunderstanding the ethical significance attached to *sarx* in the New Testament.

B. The Mental and Spiritual Nature

The other member in the psychophysical partnership is described in scripture by a wide number of terms. Adequately to treat all of these would require a volume in itself. However, several of the leading terms may profitably be considered.

1. *Spirit* (Hebrew, *ruach*; Greek, *pneuma*)

Both Hebrew and Greek terms for spirit are the words also used for wind or breath, and since man breathes as long as he lives, by a very natural process of extension of meaning these words came to stand for the vital principle in man. The term is also used of God, and it is significant that in man spirit is thought of as the gift of God, and as that aspect of the person through which he may be related to God.

2. *Soul* (Hebrew, *nephesh*; Greek, *psyche*)

Both Hebrew and Greek words for soul are also frequently translated "life" in the English Bible. Soul is used both of the vital principle of biological life and also of the entire conscious life of the individual. It is the self and all that the self embraces; the personal center of feelings, desires, inclinations, with greater emphasis on feeling and desire.

It should be noted that, while man shares spirit with God, he shares soul with the animals (Gen. 1:21, 24, where "creature" translates *nephesh;* and Rev. 16:3). Generally speaking, soul is attributed to man and to animals, not to God. On the other hand, spirit is attributed to God and to man, not to animals.

In the New Testament the important question about the soul is not its present but its future. It is to be gained or lost (Mark 8:36; Luke 21:19). Paul describes God's judgment on every soul of man (Rom. 2:9); the writer to the Hebrews speaks of an anchor of the soul within the veil (6:19); James notes that the Word is able to save the soul when received with meekness (1:21); and Peter points to the salvation of the soul as being the end of faith (1 Pet. 1:9).[20]

3. *Heart* (Hebrew, *leb;* Greek, *kardia*)

In the Bible, the heart comes closest to standing for what we generally mean by the term person. It may be used to describe the inner man, taken as a whole, with all of its capacities, but stressing particularly choice and intellect.[21] It is the seat of knowledge and memory (Jer. 51:50; Luke 2:19); it devises plans (2 Sam. 7:3; 1 Cor. 4:5); it receives wisdom (2 Chron. 9:23; Matt. 12:35); the thoughts of the heart are frequently mentioned (Deut. 15:9; Ps. 19:14; 139:23; Matt. 9:4); the heart may be hardened (Exod. 8:15; Mark 3:5); it is

---

20. Cf. C. Ryder Smith, *The Bible Doctrine of Man* (London: Epworth Press, 1951), p. 139.

21. Readers will notice that our present usage almost reverses the biblical usage with regard to soul and heart. Whereas we tend to identify soul with intellect and heart with feelings, the Bible places the emphasis the other way around. Heart is more nearly related to thought and will, and soul more closely associated with feeling and desire.

deceitful and desperately wicked (Jer. 17:9; Rom. 1:21); and should be kept with all diligence, since from it are the issues of life (Prov. 4:23; Heb. 10:22).

4. *Mind* (Greek, *nous*)

Mind is primarily a New Testament term, and not used with great frequency (24 times). Its use is rather broad, and it stands for the inward self as the subject of persuasion or willing. The stress is upon action rather than abstract thought, as when Paul speaks of serving the law of God with the mind (Rom. 7:25), and pleads for the renewing of the mind in order that the believer may prove what is the good, acceptable, and perfect will of God (Rom. 12:2).

5. *Conscience* (Greek, *syneidesis*)

Conscience is also a New Testament word, although C. Ryder Smith believes that when the Old Testament speaks of God searching the "reins" (Hebrew, *kelayoth*) there is at least an indirect reference to what we call the conscience.[22] A much more complete study of conscience in the Christian life will be made in Chapter 27. With C. Ryder Smith we may briefly summarize the New Testament teaching as: *(a)* "Every man has a conscience" (2 Cor. 4:2; Rom. 2:15); *(b)* To obey conscience is to do so because an act is known to be right, not to escape the consequences of failing to obey (Rom. 13:5); *(c)* One who does what he believes right has the approval of a good or pure conscience; otherwise, the disapproval of an evil conscience (Acts 23:1; 1 Tim. 1:5; Heb. 10:22); *(d)* Persistent sin sears the conscience (1 Tim. 4:2); *(e)* Conscience is authoritative for the individual, but not infallible (1 Cor. 8:7; cf. 10:23-33); *(f)* Liberty of conscience ought to be exercised only in harmony with what is best for others as well as for oneself (2 Cor. 5:11; Acts 24:16).[23]

V. WHAT MAN OUGHT TO BE

What man *is* under the curse of sin is far removed from what he *ought to be*. Alongside the realism of the biblical picture of man is its high idealism. God made man to find fulfillment in obedience to the divine will. "Ye shall walk in all the ways which the Lord your God hath commanded you, that ye may live, and that it may be well with

---

22. *Bible Doctrine of Man*, p. 23.
23. *Ibid.*, pp. 169 ff.

you, and that ye may prolong your days in the land which ye shall possess" (Deut. 5:33). "He hath shewed thee, O man, what is good; and what doth the Lord require of thee, but to do justly, and to love mercy, and to walk humbly with thy God?" (Mic. 6:8)

God's plan for the human family finds its ideal expression in Jesus Christ, who shows us both what God is and what He expects to make of us. When Pilate introduced Jesus to the bloodthirsty mob, he spoke better than he knew: "Behold *the* man!" (John 19:5). God's purpose in redemption is that His people may be "conformed to the image of his Son" (Rom. 8:29); and, "We all, with open face beholding as in a glass the glory of the Lord, are changed into the same image from glory to glory, even as by the Spirit of the Lord" (2 Cor. 3:18).

The Bible is unmistakably clear that only divine grace can make of man what he ought to be. It does not on that account view man as a helpless puppet in the hands of irresistible forces. Scripture at once affirms the sovereignty of God and the freedom of man, nor is there felt to be any contradiction between these two terms. Only when divine sovereignty is interpreted in such an arbitrary and unreal way as to make of God a cosmic puppeteer pulling the strings of human action, or pushing pawns around on a board, or manipulating robots, does the sovereignty of God banish the freedom of man. Actually, it could be questioned whether such "sovereignty" is sovereignty at all. For a sovereign who governs rebellious subjects and wins their loyalty by grace and love without coercing their wills, illustrates the only kind of relationship to which the term sovereignty may rightly be given.

Man's freedom is also seen to be within limits which are established by the nature of the universe in which he lives, and by the will of the moral Creator to whom he is subject. Character, with all that is suggested by that term, also sets the limits to human freedom. The most galling chains men wear are those they forge on the anvils of their own evil choices. "Can the Ethiopian change his skin, or the leopard his spots? then may ye also do good, that are accustomed to do evil" (Jer. 13:23).

SUMMARY

Great and wonderful is man, "fearfully and wonderfully made" (Ps. 139:14), the summit and crown of all creation. Marred by sin, but still a creature of infinite possibilities through redeeming grace, man is a creature of two worlds, torn between the competing pulls of heaven and of earth.

We have noted the major features of biblical anthropology, the nature of the divine image in man, some of the more common terms used to describe human nature, and the scriptural ideal for man. We move on now to a closer look at the strange predicament of humanity, the universal disease of the moral nature known as sin, in our continued task of exploring our Christian faith.

CHAPTER 11

The Human
Predicament

One of the highest tributes ever paid to man is found in Shakespeare's *Hamlet* where in the opening scene we read:

> What a piece of work is man! how noble in reason! how infinite in faculty! in form and moving how express and admirable! in action how like an angel! in apprehension how like a god! [1]

Yet from this lofty ideal the plot descends to show the hero involved in intrigue, immorality, and murder, with the consequent guilt, shame, and tragedy.

This is man's predicament: With godlike qualities and unlimited potential, he finds himself living far below his possibilities. No serious thinker will deny the presence of sin (or something equivalent to it) in the human race. All the great dramatists have recognized the existence of sin in their portrayal of remorse, disillusionment, penalty, forgiveness, and reconciliation. Historians describe the reality of sin in depicting the struggles of mankind. Government, with its stress on the necessity of law and protection, is an acknowledgment of the presence of evil. Philosophers have wrestled with the problem of evil in man's existence. Contemporary psychology bears impressive testimony to the power of wrong attitudes and subtle motivations as destructive elements in human life. All religious worship and all theological thinking attempt to offer a solution to man's predicament.

The human predicament, then, is the reality of sin. This is foun-

---

1. *Hamlet*, 2:2.

dational in Christian theology. Among the four great focal themes of the Bible and of revealed religion—God, man, sin, and redemption—sin is seen as the ugly intruder. H. Orton Wiley states that these truths are so related that the basic views held concerning any one of them profoundly influence the others; and that any tendency to minimize the seriousness of sin has its consequences in a less exalted view of the person and work of the Redeemer.[2]

An adequate understanding of the concept of sin involves two basic areas of discussion. The first centers around the origin of sin. The second deals with the nature and definition of sin. These form the major divisions of this chapter.

I. The Origin of Sin

Various theories have been advanced to explain the origin and thus to some extent the nature of sin or moral evil in the human race. These theories may be divided into non-biblical and biblical views.

A. Non-biblical Theories

To a great extent non-biblical theories have attempted to account for the origin of evil from a rationalistic point of view. Rejecting the biblical explanation as mythology or allegory, these views attempt to account for moral evil from within the framework of a humanistic or naturalistic philosophy. The following discussion presents seven such explanations, and considers the objections to them as stated by conservative theology.

1. *Sin as Originating in an Eternal Principle of Evil*

One of the oldest theories of the origin of sin is the assumption that it has its source in a principle of evil which has existed eternally in the universe. Born in the Zoroastrianism of ancient Persia, this theory was revived in the Gnostic sects of early Christianity, in Manichaeism, and in some extremist groups in the medieval church.

According to this view, two principles have existed eternally, the principle of good and the principle of evil. These principles were symbolized by two independent personal spirits, each ruling absolutely in its own domain. The two principles are in perpetual conflict with each other, and all created beings are called upon to make a choice between them. The evil principle manifested itself in the crea-

---

2. Wiley and Culbertson, *Introduction to Christian Theology*, p. 160.

tion of a material universe, the substance of which is evil. Man's spirit is drawn to the spiritual kingdom, but his body is attracted to the material kingdom. Human sin is the defilement contracted by the spirit as a result of its alliance with matter, while redemption is deliverance from the connection with the material.

Although the teaching that sin originates in an eternally evil principle is contrary to biblical revelation, it has frequently appeared within the church. In the 1st century this view was espoused by the Gnostics. Manes, in the 3rd century, revived it. It appeared again in the Paulician heresy of the 12th century. Traces may still be found in the 19th and 20th centuries.[3]

The belief that sin arises from the existence of an eternal principle of evil is inconsistent with theism, for God ceases to be an infinite Being and an absolute Sovereign. He is everywhere and always limited by a coeternal power which He cannot control. This theory also destroys the nature of sin as a moral and spiritual evil, in that it makes sin virtually identical with the material body. Human responsibility is also lost, and sin becomes inevitable and inescapable.

2. Sin as the Limitation of Finite Being

The second non-biblical theory of the origin of sin ascribes it to man's finiteness. Sin is a mere negation, or limitation of being. Being, substance, is good. God as the absolute Being, or substance, is the supreme good. Absolute evil would be not-being. Thus the less of being, the less of good; and all negation, or limitation of being, is evil and sin. Because all men are finite, or limited, sin is the inevitable result. But sin is only negative. It has no positive existence or force, and needs no cause for its origination.

The theory which identifies sin with finiteness or limitation has several objectionable features. First, it is founded upon a pantheistic view of reality, and confuses the moral and spiritual with the physical and intellectual. Moreover, this theory makes it impossible to eliminate sin from the universe. For if sin is a necessary result of finiteness, and creatures can never be infinite, it follows that sin must be everlasting, not only in the individual person, but in the universe.

Further, the theory of sin as finiteness contradicts the essential concept of the moral character of sin. Not all sins are negative sins of

---

3. William B. Pope, *A Compendium of Christian Theology,* 3 vols. (New York: Phillips and Hunt, 1881), 2:21.

ignorance and infirmity. There are acts of positive depravity, of conscious transgression, and of willful and defiant choice of evil. Finally, this theory contradicts both conscience and Scripture by denying human responsibility, and in essence transfers the responsibility for sin from the creature to the Creator.

3. *Sin as a Necessary Opposite to Good*

A third non-biblical attempt to explain the origin of sin is the theory which accounts for sin by a so-called law of necessary opposition, or antagonism. All life, it is said, implies action and reaction. Such a law, it is claimed, governs the material world. The heavenly bodies are held in their orbits by the balance of centrifugal and centripetal forces. There is polarity, or the attraction of opposites, in light, in magnetism, and in electricity. All chemical changes are produced by a law of action and reaction. In the biological realm, it is said that there is no strength without obstacles to be overcome, no rest without fatigue, no life without death. In addition, it is held that the mind is developed by continual grappling with the problems of existence.

The same law, it is claimed, must prevail in the moral world. There can be no good without evil. Good is the resistance to, or the overcoming of, evil. In the area of human activity it is maintained that individual personality is developed by antagonism, by the action of contrary forces or opposite principles. Thus a moral world without sin is an impossibility. Sin is the necessary condition for the existence of virtue, it is alleged.

This theory, as the preceding, eliminates all personal responsibility, making sin an impersonal law of being. As such it is devoid of moral significance, with no implications for conscience. There is no ground for this view in the Bible, and in effect it is a negation of the essence of the gospel, making evil a necessity to the good.

4. *Sin as Arising from Man's Sensuous Nature*

A fourth non-biblical theory of the origin of sin locates it in the sensuous nature of man. Man is regarded as a dualism of body and soul, and between these two aspects of his nature there is continual warfare. The flesh is the means of interaction with the external world, while the soul is open to communication with God. Because of the flesh man has wants, appetites, and affections which find their objects in the material world. He also has other instincts, affections, and powers which are directed toward the spiritual world.

The spiritual aspirations of man, because they are higher, ought to be dominant in man's life. However, experience reveals that the reverse is true, and that the lower affections prevail over the higher aspirations. Man appears to be governed by the sensuous nature to an extent that is degrading and sinful. He prefers the visible and temporal to the unseen and eternal. He seeks the gratification which is to be found in material objects rather than the blessedness which is to be found in the things of the Spirit. Herein, according to this theory, are the source and the essence of sin.

The fallacy of the view that sin arises from the sensuous nature is readily apparent. The creatures presented in Scripture as most sinful are fallen spirits, who have no bodies and no sensual appetites. Again, the most vicious sins are not necessarily associated with the body or the flesh at all. Pride, malice, envy, ambition, and above all, unbelief and enmity to God are the truly deadly sins.

This theory also tends to make moral evil, as it was for the Greeks, mere weakness, the submission of the weak powers of the spirit to the stronger forces of the flesh. Further, if this theory is true, then the old, with less clamorous fleshly passions, would automatically be more pious than the youth or the person in the prime of life.

5. *The Socratic-Deweyan Theory.*

Many scholars, from Socrates in ancient Athens to the renowned John Dewey in the 20th century, have ascribed the origin of sin to ignorance. Socrates, and after him Plato, taught that the good life is ethical and moral. The good life could be achieved by inner, rational self-development.

Two doctrines contain the essence of the Socratic view. First, the primary task of the individual is self-knowledge, summed up in the phrase, "Know thyself." Second, knowledge equals virtue, for "he who knows will be good; he who is habitually good knows." From these two doctrines it can be deduced that no man errs or sins except through ignorance. Ignorance is thus the essence of sin, while knowledge is the essence of virtue.

Man is responsible for his actions because virtue, as knowledge, can be learned. Knowledge is insight into reality, which exists in the form of absolute ideas of truth, beauty, and goodness. Truth, beauty, and goodness are learned through a dialectical process of reason in which confusion is eliminated and a priori principles of thought judge the actual stuff of experience. It would follow naturally that the philosopher is the most virtuous, because he brings the force of reason to bear upon the lower impulses. On the other hand, the slave must be the greatest sinner because he does not possess sufficient knowledge to direct his life to proper ends.

John Dewey, in his profoundly influential philosophy of education, revived many of the ideas of Socrates in the 20th century. However, Dewey made experience, not logical reasoning, the source of all knowledge. Dewey insisted that knowledge gained in the experiences of life, by trying and testing in problematic situations, finds direct issue in conduct. A person learns to sit on a chair instead of on a hot stove by experience. Transferring the concept of knowledge finding expression in life to the area of the moral, Dewey writes: "There is every reason to suppose that the same sort of knowledge of good has a like expression in life."[4] In other words, man acts in ways which he believes will bring him pleasure and satisfaction. To Dewey, as to Socrates, sin is actually ignorance, the lack of knowledge, a deficiency of insight regarding the final results of an act.

There are serious difficulties in the Socratic-Deweyan concept of the origin and nature of sin. The first is the assumption that an intellectual apprehension of an objective truth or idea changes the moral character. A second weakness is the belief that understanding, or experience, may bring about mastery of the self. It is contrary to the facts of human experience to claim that those who possess the greatest amounts of knowledge, or those having the widest range of experience, are also those who consistently illustrate the highest type of morality. There are too many lawyers and Ph.D's in the penitentiary for such a simple solution as that. Finally, Christian thinkers reject the Socratic-Deweyan view because it is admittedly humanistic, ascribing to man inherent powers of personal redemption. In direct contrast to this view, biblical religion posits man's redemption directly on the grace of God.

6. *The Evolutionary-Lag Theory*

Many who accept the evolutionary account of man's origin state that what is called sin is actually a carry-over of animal qualities from lower stages of existence. This theory regards man as the consummation of the development of physical nature. However, the process of man's evolvement is not symmetrical, with every aspect of personality advancing evenly. Rather, the pattern of ascent is jerky and irregular, with gaps existing at certain periods.

Thus man has developed to a greater extent in physical and

---

4. *Democracy and Education* (New York: The Macmillan Co., 1939), p. 412.

mental abilities than he has in moral and spiritual capacities, with a resulting "gap" or "lag." Man is thought to be an organism in which the human has not yet escaped from the animal, and sin is the brute inheritance which every man carries with him. One writer describes this view of sin as "a relic of the animal not yet outgrown, a resultant of the mechanism of appetite and impulse and reflex action for which the proper inhibitions are not yet developed. Only slowly does it grow into a consciousness of itself as evil."[5]

The evolutionary-lag theory finds little support in Christian theology. To regard sin as the inevitable remnant of animal propensities is not only to deny that it is truly sin, but also to deny that man is truly man. Sin must be related to freedom or it is not sin. To explain sin as the natural result of overpowering lower impulses is to make the animal nature, and not the will, the cause of transgression.

Further, the theory denies the logic of evolution itself. For all other species live normally, each apparently perfectly adapted to its mode of living. No remnant of the reptile hinders the bird. The bird is a true bird. Only man is a misfit. And if man is a misfit, the theory of evolution is shattered at the very point on which it professes to be the strongest. Finally, biblical revelation points to man as a creature springing from the hand of the Creator, not an animal emerging from the lap of nature.

7. Social Theories of Sin

A persistent view in the history of ideas is that the origin of sin is to be found in society. This theory is aptly illustrated by the writings of Rousseau and Marx. Rousseau, the French philosopher, stated that "God makes all things good, but man meddles with them, and they become evil."[6] He further states that the progress of the arts and sciences has added nothing to man's happiness, but has actually corrupted morals.[7] To Rousseau, man's primitive state is the nearest to perfection possible, and he could speak reverently of the "noble savage." But as man gradually submitted to customs and traditions he lost his initial natural freedom and goodness. Instead he became enmeshed in chains forged by civilization. Culture and civilization furnish the background in which sin is inevitable.

To Karl Marx, sin is in reality nothing more than inequality, or

---

5. Borden Parker Bowne, *The Atonement* (Boston: Houghton Mifflin Co., 1909), p. 69.

6. *Emile*, Book I, p. 5.

7. *The Social Contract* (New York: E. P. Dutton and Co., n.d.), p. 152.

injustice, as revealed in society. To the founders of communism, sin originated when men first produced a surplus beyond their immediate needs, so that part of their labor was no longer expended merely on gaining a living, but was used to accumulate goods. Marx declares: "In political economy this primary accumulation plays much the same part that is played by original sin in theology."[8]

The attempt to account for the origin of sin from a social, or cultural, point of view fails to explain why there is something in the individual which succumbs to and cooperates with the evils that are labeled "social maladjustment" or "social exploitation." It fails to explain how individuals and societies arrived at a sinful state in the first place, and it fails to give an adequate account of why people remain in a degraded state. In brief, how can social evils become established in society and maintain themselves in life unless there is something in individuals, from one generation to the next, which provides fertile soil for the seeds of sin?

From the seven theories of the origin of sin presented thus far, it is evident that mankind *is* faced with a major predicament. While there is agreement that something exists in human life contrary to happiness and well-being, there are divergent views regarding its source. We may now turn to the Scriptures, with a view to discovering their solution to the problem of the origin of moral evil.

B. Biblical Teachings on the Origin of Sin

From the biblical point of view sin originated in an abuse of the freedom of the created will. Freedom of the will is the very essence of rational personality, and includes conscious freedom in the origination of activity as well as the choice of the end of action. The divine principle operative in the creation of intelligent moral beings implies freedom on the part of man voluntarily to select his destiny. Moral action and freedom to choose further demand a law by which character is determined. Otherwise there would be no moral quality, and neither punishment nor reward could result from either obedience or disobedience. The account of the abuse of the freedom of the will, and of the origin of sin, is found in the scriptural record of the fall of man.

Man was tempted by a supernatural being, described in the Bible as the serpent. This indicates that moral evil had an existence

---

8. Quoted by Mary F. Thelen, *Man as Sinner* (New York: King's Crown Press, 1946), p. 35.

prior to its first appearance in the human race and external to it. The Bible implies that in the purely spiritual realm there were angels who had revolted and lost their first estate (2 Pet. 2:4; Jude 6). Thus there was a fall in the angelic order before there was a fall in the human race. There was a tempter among the angels, who led them astray. It is with this tempter that the Christian view of evil reaches its first cause. This supernatural yet created spirit, Satan, was originally good, but fell from a high and holy estate and became the enemy of God. Sin is therefore personal in its origin. As has been said, beyond this reason cannot go, and revelation is silent.

The account of the probation and fall of man in Gen. 3:1-24 is an accurate record of fact, although it also contains rich and significant symbolism. All attempts to show that the Genesis account consists of a series of myths or that it is a spiritual allegory are contradictory to the claim of the writer that it is an integral part of a continual factual narrative. The account is assumed to be historical throughout both the Old and New Testaments. Christ himself referred to the Fall only indirectly (Matt. 19:4-5; John 8:44), but He apparently accepted the entire Old Testament writings as inspired (Luke 24:27; Matt. 19:4-5). Paul clearly accepted the Genesis record as factual (2 Cor. 11:3; 1 Tim. 2:13-15). There are also undeniable allusions to the Fall in later parts of the Old Testament (Job 31:33; Hos. 6:7).

That the description of the Fall contains highly important symbolism and is the source of key theological insights must not be forgotten. As Wiley notes, "Such facts as the inclosed garden, the sacramental tree of life, the mystical tree of knowledge, the one positive command representing the whole law, the serpent form of the tempter, the flaming defenses of forfeited Eden—all were emblems possessing deep spiritual significance as well as facts. In defending the historical character of the Mosaic account of the fall, we must not fail to do justice to its rich symbolism."[9]

The biblical account reveals that, while man was created in innocency and holiness, there existed in him the possibility of sin. Samuel Wakefield in his *Systematic Theology* states that our first parents, in their primitive state of trial, were evidently subject to temptation from intellectual pride, from sense, and from passion.[10] Olin A. Curtis in *The Christian Faith* lists four elements in the fall:

9. *Christian Theology,* 2:162.

10. (New York: Nelson and Phillips, 1859), p. 284.

First, there was physical craving, for "the woman saw that the tree was good for food, and that it was a delight to the eyes." This would indicate that the senses were involved, that the physical appetites were instrumental in the temptation.

Second, there was intellectual desire, or "cosmic curiosity" as he calls it, for "the tree was to be desired to make one wise." This curiosity was not necessarily the pursuit of truth which is motivated by and permeated with a moral quality. It was rather the impatient desire to examine the experiences of life with the irresponsible and uncontrolled techniques of the irrational child.

Third, the temptation included the individual drive to self-expression, for it included the challenge, "Yea, hath God said ye shall not eat of any tree of the garden?" Now the temptation had reached a climax, for here was the suggestion that man should refuse to occupy a subordinate position to any higher authority.

Finally, there was the element of social influence, for after Eve had transgressed "she gave also unto her husband with her, and he did eat."[11]

The immediate consequences of man's sin were alienation from God and an enslavement to Satan, together with the loss of divine grace, by which loss man became subject to physical and moral corruption. From the scriptural account of the origin of sin it is evident that God in no sense is the author of evil. The two basic factors which account for the origin of sin in the human race are the prior existence of Satan, who tempted man to sin, combined with man's freedom of choice in the presence of moral alternatives. In the final analysis it is clear that biblical teaching traces the origin of sin in man to the abuse of freedom in intelligent, responsible creatures.

Clearly implied in the temptation and sin of Adam and Eve are theological insights of key importance. It is seen here that sin is no part of essential human nature. It is an intrusion in human experience. Adam and Eve did not become human when they disobeyed God; if anything, they became less than they were created to be. Jesus Christ was perfectly human in everything humanity was meant to be —yet He was "holy, harmless, unstained, separated from sinners" (Heb. 7:26, RSV), free from the taint of sin. Sin is not to be found in man's physical nature, nor in the finiteness of his psyche. It is a foreign element, a condition subject to cure by divine grace.

---

11. Pp. 195-96.

It is evident, also, that temptation may come to those in whose natures there is no prior sinfulness. It is sometimes argued that temptability implies a sinful nature inwardly to which temptation can appeal. But temptation may come through desires and needs that may in themselves be quite neutral morally. Jesus was tempted without consenting to the suggestions of the Tempter and suffered no stain of evil. James indicates that sin occurs only if desire "conceives"—is impregnated by the consent of the will to an action contrary to God's law (James 1:14-15). Here is the answer to the objection sometimes heard against the possibility of a pure heart— that such a person would not be subject to temptation. Temptation may come to a sanctified person through desires that are human and natural and in no sense in themselves sinful.

Here, also, is a clue to the nature of those acts described in Scripture as acts of sin. They are not the result of human infirmities, limitations, shortcomings, or errors of judgment. They are acts of rebellion in view of a clear and explicit knowledge of God's will. Not unavoidable failure but disobedience is the essential nature of those acts or choices condemned in Scripture as sins.

Finally, Adam's and Eve's sin brought estrangement and alienation from God, expulsion from the Garden, and the loss of that initial holiness and innocence in which they had been created. The effect upon their children and descendants is suggested in Gen. 5:3, Adam "became the father of a son in his own likeness" (RSV). Adam was created in "the image of God" (Gen. 1:26-27). That image was not totally lost (Gen. 9:6), but it was defaced. Deprived of the relationship with God for which he and his descendants had been created, the condition of Adam and his descendants became one of depravity. This is "original sin . . . that corruption of the nature of all the offspring of Adam by reason of which every one is very far gone from original righteousness."[12]

II. The Nature of Sin

Because all definitions of sin are necessarily descriptive, no one encompasses its complete significance. Positively, sin involves the substitution of self for God as the ultimate end of life. Negatively, sin is

---

12. Article IV, "Articles of Faith," Constitution of the Church of the Nazarene, current *Manual, in loc.*

transgressing a law of God. In discussing the nature of sin, several suggested definitions are first presented, followed by a discussion of sin as described in the Bible. To complete the study of the nature of sin, the concept of original sin is considered.

A. Definitions of Sin

Sin has been defined as selfishness.[13] This definition is partially correct, but selfishness is too indefinite a term to do justice to certain aspects, such as moral weakness, which necessarily are involved in the concept of sin.

Another definition, widely held, is that "sin is the want of conformity to the divine law or standard of excellence."[14] However, sin is of necessity an act rather than a deficiency. Certainly the biblical injunctions and warnings against sin are meaningless if the volitional element is eliminated.

A third definition of sin is given by Reinhold Niebuhr: "The biblical definition of basic sin as pride is an admirable summary of the whole Biblical doctrine of sin."[15] But this definition describes a symptom instead of the essence of sin, and is based more on overt behavior than on subjective power of choice. Another noted scholar has written that "man's predicament is estrangement, but his estrangement is sin."[16] The objection here is that again a partial definition is given. Moreover, the element of guilt is reduced or eliminated, for estrangement may result from factors external to an individual.

As a provisional definition of sin as act or deed, we may state John Wesley's useful and scriptural formulation: "Sin is a voluntary transgression of a known law." By legitimate extension, sin also includes those attitudes, dispositions, and propensities which lead to such voluntary transgression, and which we shall later discuss as original sin. This definition involves freedom of personality, and makes meaningful the biblical warnings and commands regarding sin.

---

13. A. H. Strong, *Systematic Theology* (Philadelphia: Griffin and Rowland Press, 1907), 2:567.

14. Charles Hodge, *Systematic Theology*, 3 vols. (New York: Charles Scribner's Sons, 1893), 2:187.

15. *The Nature and Destiny of Man*, 2 vols. (New York: Charles Scribner's Sons, 1943), 1:186.

16. Paul Tillich, *Systematic Theology*, 2 vols. (Chicago: University of Chicago Press, 1957), 2:46.

B. Sin in the Old Testament

In the Old and New Testaments alike sin is regarded chiefly as a breach or rupture of relations between the individual and the personal God, an estrangement due to disobedience. In the account of the Fall, sin is seen as direct disobedience to God's command. In Gen. 6:5 it is stated that "God saw that the wickedness of man was great in the earth, and that every imagination of the thoughts of his heart was only evil continually." In the Levitical code sin is regarded as a breach of covenant between the people and their God. David recognized his grievous sin as an offense against a holy God, and cried, "Against thee, thee only have I sinned, and done this evil in thy sight" (Ps. 51:4). The prophets saw sin as stark rebellion against a loving and holy God.

The Old Testament is rich in its ethical terms, and diverse in its definitions and descriptions of sin. Indicating the many-sidedness of the Old Testament in characterizing sin, A. B. Davidson writes:

> In the sphere of religion, sin is idolatry; in the sphere of speech, truth is righteousness and sin *falsehood;* in the sphere of moral life, justice is righteousness, and sin is injustice; in the sphere of the mind of man sin is the *want of sincerity,* either toward God or man, *guile; purity,* the opposite of this, being purity of heart, simplicity, openness, genuineness.[17]

C. Sin in the New Testament

The importance of the problem of sin in the New Testament writings is shown by the fact that its vocabulary includes at least 28 synonyms for sin, with a total of 386 occurrences. There are 8 different roots from which these 28 synonyms are derivations. By far the most frequently occurring root is *hamart,* which appears some 214 times out of the total of 386, and carries the basic meaning of missing the mark.[18]

In the Synoptic Gospels, Jesus portrayed the ideal human life as a life of fellowship with God the Father. Sin is the lack of this fellowship. Jesus also traced sin to the inner motives of man, equating the sinful purpose with the outward act. In the Fourth Gospel sin is represented in various ways. It is darkness as opposed to light (John

---

17. *Theology of the Old Testament,* p. 231.
18. Turner, *Vision Which Transforms,* pp. 98-106.

9:41). It is bondage as opposed to freedom (John 8:34). Sin is also regarded as unbelief (John 16:9). Christ also contrasted the flesh and the spirit and taught that spiritual birth from above is necessary to all men (John 3:3, 5-8). The world as the sphere of the operation of sin and Satan is regarded as sinful and corrupt (John 18:36).

The apostle Paul's teaching about the nature of sin is profound and incisive. While Paul carefully refrains from labeling the flesh as a thing of material substance as sinful in itself, he does point out that the mind of the flesh is in antagonism to God (Rom. 8:6-9). Paul also represents men as dead in trespasses and sins, and exposed to the wrath of God (Eph. 2:1-3). With Paul, the locus of sin is the will. It entered the world by man's choice. Sin itself is a perversion of the will and is therefore alien to man's true nature. However, man is responsible for his sin and guilty in consequence of it. It brings him under the holy wrath of God (Rom. 1:18). While the degree of spiritual light which men enjoy varies, all have light enough to render them inexcusable for their sin (Rom. 1:20).

Perhaps the strongest New Testament treatment of sin occurs in the letters of John. A direct and penetrating definition of sin is found in the statement: "Whosoever committeth sin transgresseth also the law: for sin is the transgression of the law" (1 John 3:4). The essence of sin is a deliberate "lack of conformity to law." Sin is lawlessness. Sin is an active state of rebellion against God. But sin is more than an act; it is a state, for St. John writes that "all unrighteousness is sin" (1 John 5:17). Thus sin to John consisted not only of perverted acts, but also of a state of unrighteousness or disorder of the moral nature lying behind such acts.

The consequences of sin are guilt and penalty. Guilt is personal condemnation, a feeling of alienation and lack of worth which follows the act of sin. It includes the double idea of personal responsibility for the act and a liability to punishment because of it. The chief result of sin is the racial consequence of death. Individually the primary penalty is spiritual separation from God, which culminates in the catalogue of miseries that afflict, to some degree, each member of the race.

D. Original Sin

An important part of the biblical understanding of sin has to do with its racial character. That there is a profound and permanent perversity in the heart of man is the fundamental, uncompromising assertion of Christianity about human nature.[19] To this perversity Christian theology has given the name "original sin." The doctrine of original sin is not a mere appendage to Christian thought, but is one of the foundation stones of the structure. Only in the light of man's enslavement to sin does the plan of redemption become intelligible. If man can solve his problems without divine assistance, then the incarnation of God in Christ is largely meaningless.

1. The Nature of Original Sin

The doctrine of original sin claims that fallen man is subject to a condition of radical evil which is enslaving. In John Wesley's words: "Original sin is the corruption of the nature of every man, whereby man is in his own nature inclined to evil, so that the flesh lusteth contrary to the Spirit."[20]

This concept is denied by Pelagius and the Socinians, who hold that while Adam by his transgression exposed himself to divine displeasure, yet neither he nor his posterity sustained any moral injury by his disobedience. The only penalty incurred by Adam was expulsion from the garden of Eden and the assignment of hard labor. Adam's posterity, like Adam himself, is placed in a state of trial, possessed of innate goodness, and the individual members of the race may maintain their innocence and purity by daily improving their moral stature amid multiplied temptations.

On the contrary, the effect of the Fall upon the human race is described in the Scriptures as the universal reality of death, together with a positive bias of human nature towards evil.

Paul teaches that through one man sin entered into the world (Rom. 5:12-18), bringing with it the twin disasters of universal sin and the condemnation of universal death. Death as a consequence of sin passed upon all men through racial propagation. Thus original sin and inherited depravity are identical.

From a scriptural point of view, every member of the human race is subject to a moral corruption (Eph. 4:22-24; 2 Pet. 1:4), which is a source of actual sin, and is itself sinful. In the Bible the sinful acts and dispositions of men are referred to and explained by a corrupt nature. That there is an inborn corrupt state, from which sinful acts and dispositions flow, is evident from David's confession: "Be-

---

19. D. R. Davies, *Secular Illusion or Christian Realism?* (London: Latimer House, 1942), p. 42.

20. *Works,* 5:144.

hold, I was shapen in iniquity, and in sin did my mother conceive me" (Ps. 51:5). This passage is not to be interpreted as meaning that the act of conception, or procreation, is an act of sin. Neither does it indicate that the process of birth is impure. It does recognize that the Psalmist and his parents are part of the human race, and as such they carry the taint or stain of sin in the race.

Further, all men are declared to be by nature children of wrath (Eph. 2:3). Here "nature" signifies a condition inborn and original, as distinguished from that which is subsequently acquired. While depravity is primarily a biblical doctrine, it is not exclusively such. For history reflects the influence of depravity, literature portrays its agonies, and contemporary depth-psychology sets forth views strangely akin to the biblical idea of depravity.

2. *The Transmission of Depravity*

The manner of the transmission of depravity is admittedly a difficult point. Probably the most acceptable theory is simply an application of the law of heredity to man's total being. It is the law of organic life that everything produces its own kind. The law of like producing like does not refer exclusively to the biological features of man's existence, but also embraces psychological qualities. The law of genetic transmission determines the likeness of offspring to parents. That we should resemble our parents and the whole human family psychologically and morally is no more mysterious than that we should resemble them physically.

That there are difficulties involved in precise descriptions of the processes connected with the transmission of depravity cannot be denied. It must be stressed that original sin is not physical. On the other hand, it is a depravation which results originally from deprivation, a corruption of nature coming from the loss of original righteousness. The parents of the race could not transmit to their offspring a quality of holiness which they did not possess. They could only pass on what was an inherent part of their own natures. As a branch cut off from the vine withers and becomes corrupt, humanity deprived of original righteousness is depraved and morally corrupt (John 15:1-2, 6; Eph. 4:22; 2 Pet. 1:4).

SUMMARY

This chapter has presented the tragic plight, the predicament, of man. Destined to be a noble, godlike creature, he has become an ignoble and animal-like being. The failure of man to achieve his potential is known theologically as sin.

Many attempts to provide an explanation for the origin of sin are humanistic and rationalistic. Each of these views has objectionable features from the standpoint of biblical theology, which explains the origin of sin in the fall of man.

After a discussion of the nature of sin as acts or deeds, we examined the scriptural view of sin as a condition or state of corruption, or what is known to theology as original sin or inherited depravity.

However, the last word on sin is spoken, not by man, but by God, in the redemptive grace He has provided as the remedy for the human predicament. This is the subject of the chapters which follow in exploring our Christian faith.

CHAPTER 12

Atonement: The Death and Resurrection of Christ

Atonement has to do with God's way of dealing with man's sin and His provision for reconciling human beings to himself. Its full scope includes both the death and the resurrection of Jesus Christ.

As one views the doctrine of the Atonement he is conscious that he is approaching the holy of holies of the Word of God. Moving in silent wonder toward the "secret place of the Most High," he sees beyond the curtains of that inner sanctuary the meeting place of God with man, the trysting place of mercy and judgment and the rendezvous of life with death. Sacred in its intent and meaning for the human heart, the Atonement is one of the most profound subjects that divine revelation has ever proposed for the contemplation of the human mind.

The doctrine of the Atonement has always been central in the teaching of the evangelical churches. For them it has constituted the "very marrow of theology," as Louis Berkhof puts it, and provided the key which either unlocks or interlocks with all the other great doctrines of the Bible. Called by some "the anchor of faith," by others "the refuge of hope," it has by all conservative thinkers been considered as "the heart of the gospel," and "the keystone of the Christian religion."[1]

---

1. *Vicarious Atonement Through Christ* (Grand Rapids: Wm. B. Eerdmans Publishing Co., 1936), p. 11.

Highlighting its preeminence is the emphasis which the Bible itself puts upon it or its essential factors or elements. Remove from the Scriptures the types, the symbols, the prophecies, the annunciations, and the exhortations which center in this subject, and both the Old and New Testaments will fall apart from lack of any principle of integration. And the same could be said of all the great systems of Christian theology. Small wonder is it, therefore, that a subject so mysterious in its nature, so involved in its relations, and so crucial in its importance should receive the most varied treatment of any doctrine in the whole field of theological thought.

I. BIBLICAL TERMS RELATING TO THE ATONEMENT

To avoid excessive speculation, one must pay careful attention to biblical terms relating to the Atonement. This rather exacting "inductive method" is the only sure protection against "every wind of doctrine" (Eph. 4:14) which would impede the progress of truly Christian thought.

A. The Hebrew Words

It is generally agreed by Old Testament scholars that the most important original word used is the verb *kaphar*, translated generally "to make atonement." This verb, which is used over 100 times in the Old Testament, conveys the primary idea "to cover." The derivative noun, *kopher*, signifies a "covering" or means of concealment or protection. Suggesting the latter idea is its use in Gen. 6:14, where Noah was commissioned to cover *(kaphar)* the ark with pitch. In the sense of "covering" human sin from the sight of God, its use in Leviticus 16 is the outstanding reference.

The act of covering in Scripture, however, cannot be separated from the substance of the covering. Attention is therefore repeatedly centered on the "blood" of the sacrificial animal as providing that covering (cf. Leviticus 16). This, in the New Testament, is fulfilled in the precious blood of Christ, as of a lamb unspotted and undefiled (1 Pet. 1:19), "by whom we have now received the atonement" (Rom. 5:11).

In addition to this primary or explicit meaning of the word *kaphar*, there are also a number of secondary or implicit meanings. These, as translated in our English Bible, include the verbs "purged," "cleansed," "forgiven" (Isa. 6:7); "annulled," "disannulled," "abolished" (Isa. 28:18); "pacified" or "appeased" (Ezek. 16:63; Gen.

32:20); "keep off," "put off" (Isa. 47:11); and "make reconciliation" (Ezek. 45:15). Added to these are the substantives "sum of money," "price" (Exod. 21:30), "ransom" (Exod. 30:12), and "satisfaction" (Num. 35:31-32), which are correlatives of the noun *kopher.* In these root meanings one can see the germinal truths which later developed into the varied theories of the Atonement.

B. The Greek Terms

The first Greek equivalent for the Old Testament *kaphar* is the New Testament word *katallasso,* meaning to "reconcile" or to recover favor with another. Hence as used in Rom. 5:10 it means the sinner's recovery of God's favor through the death of His Son, through whom "we have now received the atonement" (Rom. 5:11). It is interesting to note, however, that the Greek noun translated "atonement" in the KJV is rendered "reconciliation" more correctly in more recent translations. Since this is the only instance in the New Testament where "atonement" is used while the word "reconciliation" is rarely used in the Old, it is clear that the idea of a mere "covering" for sin is as much an understatement for the former as a full "reconciliation" was an overstatement for the latter. In other words, the New Testament puts a redemptive content into the term which marks a distinct advance in Christian thought. As "reconciliation" is not an Old Testament word, so "covering" is not the New Testament meaning of atonement.

A second Greek term associated closely with the Atonement is the verb *hilaskomai,* which means to propitiate, expiate, or render merciful. (Cf. Luke 18:13, "God be merciful to me a sinner.") As correlative of this verb is the noun *hilastarion,* which is used as the Greek substitute for the Hebrew *kapporeth,* or mercy seat (Heb. 9:5). A second close relative is the noun *hilasmos,* which signifies the substance or content of the propitiation. It thus stands in the same relation to the verb "propitiate" as "covering" does to the verb "cover," or "atonement" to the verb "atone."

The third important Greek verb is *lutroo,* to liberate on receipt of a ransom (1 Pet. 1:18). Since the prominent idea is "to buy back" from a state of captivity, its derivative noun, *lutrosis,* connotes the total work of "redemption," or "deliverance" effected through Christ (Luke 1:68; 2:38). This concept of redemption required two new features to complete the picture. One was the more-than-human nature of the *lutrotas,* the Redeemer, or the One who paid the price. For "ye were not redeemed with corruptible things, as silver and gold, . . . but with the precious blood of Christ, as of a lamb without blemish and without spot" (1 Pet. 1:18-19). The other was the more-than-human power of the delivering Spirit (Rom. 8:2).

C. The English Equivalents

1. *Atonement*

According to the *Oxford University Dictionary* this word as taken in theology to indicate "the restoration of friendly relations between God and sinners" was first used in 1526.[2] This indicates a time span of nearly fifteen hundred years before "reconciliation," in the New Testament sense, was subsumed under the word "atonement." With the passing of nearly another hundred years, the additional concepts of "propitiation" and "expiation" were added, so that by 1611 theologians were speaking of atonement as "the propitiation of God by the expiation of sin."[3] Hence by the time the King James translators were completing their work, the word "atonement" was variously used by theologians in the sense of "reconciliation," "propitiation" and "expiation," thus providing them their warrant for translating "reconciliation" in Rom. 5:11 as "atonement." But since this substitution is not made in any ancient version of the New Testament, the revised rendering "reconciliation" is more accurate in this instance.

The implications of the word, however, are in full accord with the original, for the underlying idea of at-one-ment clearly suggests the restoration of harmony between estranged persons which reconciliation always includes.

2. *Reconciliation*

The ideas involved in this term have both personal and judicial implications. The personal have already been indicated as canceling out the estranged relationship which exists between God and man on account of sin. But our record as lawbreakers is still against us, even though our attitude be presently adjusted. Hence God, as righteous Judge, must do something about that record. This He graciously does in absorbing the demerit of the account against us through the person of His Son. The aspect of the truth involved here is well expressed by H. Orton Wiley in these words:

> But reconciliation means more than merely laying aside our enmity to God. The relation is a judicial one, and it is this judicial

---

2. *Ad loc.*
3. *Ibid.*

variance between God and man that is referred to in the idea of reconciliation. Moreover, the reconciliation is effected, not by the laying aside of our enmity, but by the nonimputation of our trespasses to us. This previous reconciliation of the world to Himself by the death of His Son [Rom. 5:10], is to be distinguished also from "the word of reconciliation" [2 Cor. 5:18-19] which is to be proclaimed to the guilty, and by which they are entreated to be reconciled unto God.[4]

3. Propitiation and Expiation

In "propitiation" we have the introduction of a Latin expression, *propitiare*, "to render favorable," interposed between itself and its Greek and Hebrew antecedents. As is often the case when words from a different context are adopted, a certain amount of theological "infiltration" takes place. This is indicated by William Carver when he states: "The word is Latin and brings into its English use the atmosphere of heathen rites for winning the favor, or averting the anger of the gods."[5]

But the Christian conception is far removed from the heathen idea of "buying God off" for unmerited favors, or of appeasing the wrath of a vengeful Deity. This is indicated by the fact that in every New Testament use of the word it refers either to the act of showing mercy or to the place where mercy is shown, namely the mercy seat (Rom. 3:25; 1 John 2:2; 4:10). And as if to banish any remaining vestige of doubt about God's willingness to show favors, Paul states that, "while we were yet sinners, Christ died for us" (Rom. 5:8), thus taking the initiative in setting forth His Son to be our Propitiation (Rom. 3:24-25).

But the love of God for the sinner in no wise lessens the hatred of God for man's sin. The culmination of that hatred, as seen in the sufferings of His Son on Calvary, is nothing less than the recoil of holy character against sin. In Christ, then, as the meeting place of holy wrath against sin and holy love for sin's victims, is to be found true "propitiation for our sins: and not for ours only, but also for the sins of the whole world" (1 John 2:2).

As propitiation looks to the demands of the divine nature, so expiation looks to the requirements of the divine law. As violating that law and thus incurring guilt and meriting penalty, sin must have its consequences endured and its guilt expunged from the record.

---

4. *Christian Theology*, 2:231-32.
5. *International Standard Bible Encyclopedia*, 4:2467.

Where this is done, the claims of the Lawgiver himself are met. Hence theologians early in the 17th century began to speak of "propitiation through expiation," and both as accomplished through the atoning work of Christ.

4. Redemption

The Atonement as viewed from the manward side includes not only the idea of reconciliation but also the idea of redemption. For man is not only estranged from God in sin; he is in bondage to a foreign power by sin, since "whosoever committeth sin is the servant of sin" (John 8:34). Sin thus does worse for a man than he imagines; it makes him an enemy of the One who loves him, and it also makes him a captive of the one who hates him. As reconciliation removes the enmity on the one hand, so redemption abolishes the captivity on the other.

The etymology of "redemption" is the Latin *redemptio,* which comes from the verb *redimere,* which signifies to "repurchase," to "buy back," or to "recover by purchase."

Preceding the Latin is the Greek noun *apolutrosis,* composed of a preposition meaning "out of" and a verb meaning to "release" or "set free." Together they indicate deliverance, or emancipation out of a state of bondage or servitude. This emancipation is effected by a threefold redemptive activity indicated by three distinctive Greek verbs.

The first is *agorazo* which means "to purchase in the market." The market indicated is the slave market, so well known in New Testament times, where slaves were exposed to public auction. The subjects of this divine redemption are seen as "sold under sin" (Rom. 7:14), living in sin (John 8:34), and subject to the curse of death as prescribed by the law (Gal. 3:10). The Redeemer assumes their place under the law, becomes a "curse" in their stead (Gal. 3:13), sheds His blood for a "ransom" (Matt. 20:28; 1 Tim. 2:6), and sets them free from the guilt of sin, the penalty of the law, and the fear of death (Heb. 2:14-15).

The second verb is *exagorazo* which means "to purchase out of the market." W. E. Vine points out that this term was used especially to describe the purchase of a slave with a view to giving him his freedom.[6] Paul uses this beautiful term four times (Gal. 3:13; 4:5;

6. Cf. *Expository Dictionary of New Testament Words,* 4 vols. (London: Oliphants, Ltd., 1939-41), 3:263.

Eph. 5:16; Col. 4:5—the last two times with reference to the believer's use of time). *lutreo – to loosy*

The third word, *lutroo*, which means "to loose," "set free by paying a price," indicates that the Redeemer gives the "slave" thus purchased the status of a perfectly free man. Christ is no more a slave-owner, or a "slave driver," than He is a slave trader. On the contrary, "If the Son therefore shall make you free, ye shall be free indeed" (John 8:36). As invested with full citizenship, the onetime slave is now accorded the full protection of his government, the inheritance of property, and participation in the affairs of state. Redemption then takes a slave condemned to die from the slavepen, sets him free as a son, and makes him an heir of God and a joint heir with his great Emancipator, Jesus Christ (Rom. 8:17).

Leon Morris, after a penetrating study of redemption in the New Testament, states that whenever the redemptive category is employed one or more of three aspects of the Atonement are especially in mind: *(a)* The state or condition out of which man is to be redeemed; namely, slavery or captivity to sin, in which man finds himself unable to liberate himself without the help of Another. *(b)* The price or cost to the Redeemer. This must always be considered, and redemption cannot be made a simple equivalent of deliverance. *(c)* The resultant state of the believer, brought into the liberty of the sons of God, a liberty which may paradoxically be called slavery to God. "The whole point of this redemption is that sin no longer has dominion; the redeemed are those saved to do the will of their Master."[7]

II. REPRESENTATIVE THEORIES OF ATONEMENT

Bible writers did not attempt to formulate any complete system of theology. Two observations will make the reason clear. First, the books of the several writers were composed at different times and in widely separated places. As a result no one writer had available all the others had written on the same subjects when he composed his particular epistle. Hence his teaching could not be "sytematic" in the sense of a "scientific and connected presentation of Christian doctrine."

In the second place, the New Testament authors wrote primarily

---

7. *The Apostolic Preaching of the Cross* (London: Tyndale Press, 1955), pp. 57-59.

from the outthrust of the original evangelistic impulse of the Church. Theirs was neither "dogmatic" nor even "systematic" thought, but what Emil Brunner has appropriately styled "missionary theology." This apostolic type, as distinguished from the later "dogmatic" type of the Church councils, was "inductive" rather than "deductive" in its logic, conversational in form, and evangelistic in purpose.[8]

But once the Scriptures were completed, the canon determined, and different centers of Christianity established, it became necessary to coordinate and harmonize the teaching of different leaders and schools. Hence arose the formulation of those embryonic theologies known as the "Confessions and Creeds," including the Apostles', the Nicene, and the Athanasian creeds.

Meanwhile certain systematic theories of atonement were being worked out. These centered their attention upon some particular purpose, plan, or method as providing the explanatory principle in the divine transaction. In this introductory exploration we shall present views of the early, medieval, and modern church periods.

It should be definitely stated, however, that while theologians differ in their interpretations of the Atonement, there is little disagreement about the *fact* of the Atonement. *How* the death of Christ saves us is a subject which has been argued throughout the history of Christian thought; *that* the death of Christ saves us is beyond argument for those who accept the record of the Scriptures. Probably no single theory can do justice to all the facets of the fact. There is "no theory of the atonement which is quite as satisfying as the simple statements of the vicarious death of Christ in the gospels."[9] James S. Stewart has observed:

> We may take it for certain that any formula or system which claims to gather up into itself the whole meaning of God's righteousness, or of Christ's redeeming work, is *ipso facto* wrong. The only right way to see the cross of Jesus is on your knees. The apostle [Paul] himself reminds us of that, when he declares, immediately after one of his greatest accounts of his Lord's atoning death, "Before the name of Jesus every knee should bow." (Phil. 2:10). In this world, men kneel to what they love. And love has a way of breaking through every carefully articulated system: it sees so much more than the system-makers.[10]

---

8. Cf. *Christian Doctrine of God*, pp. 101-3.

9. Reinhold Niebuhr, *Beyond Tragedy* (New York: Charles Scribner's Sons, 1948), p. 17.

10. *A Man in Christ* (New York: Harper and Brothers, n.d.), p. 3.

A. Early Christian Views of Atonement

By the early part of the third century three well-defined theological centers had been established. These were (1) in Asia Minor with Irenaeus at its head, (2) at Alexandria with Origen as its principal, and (3) in North Africa with Tertullian as its leading representative. Each of these leaders made his own contribution to the doctrine in question, but the view of the first two are most distinctive.

1. *The "Recapitulation" Theory of Irenaeus*

Irenaeus (A.D. 125-200) has been called "the first writer of the Post-Apostolic Age who deserves the name of a theologian." He was fundamentally biblical in his theological approach to every Christian doctrine, and was distinctly opposed to philosophical speculation in matters of religion. His thinking was therefore Christocentric rather than Logos-centric.

He views Christ as the Second Adam, who "sums up" in himself all that the first Adam should have embodied. Using the expression in Eph. 1:10, ARV, "to sum up all things in Christ," as his key, he taught that "God in Christ joined again to Himself those men who had been divided from Him in sin." "He has therefore in His work of recapitulation summed up all things, both waging war against our enemy, and crushing him who at the beginning had led us away captive in Adam—in order that, as our species went down to death through a vanquished man, so may we ascend to life again through a victorious one."[11]

2. *The "Ransom" Theory of Origen*

To Origen (A.D. 185-254) has gone the honor of being the greatest among the representatives of the Alexandrian School. A disciple of the far-famed Clement of Alexandria, he became "celebrated as a philosopher, philologist, and polemicist."[12]

Famous also for his allegorical method of interpreting Scripture, he became known in a somewhat less enviable sense as the father of the "ransom-to-Satan" theory of atonement. J. L. Neve gives a good summary of this theory as follows:

> Through sin the souls of men had come under the sovereignty of the devil. So Jesus offered his soul unto death as an

---

11. John Lawson, *The Biblical Theology of Saint Irenaeus* (London: Epworth Press, 1948), pp. 141, 144.

12. J. L. Neve, *A History of Christian Thought*, 2 vols. (Philadelphia: Muhlenberg Press, 1946), 1:83.

exchange or ransom in order that they might be redeemed from the devil. But the devil was not aware that he was unable to endure the presence of a sinless soul. He was deceived into accepting the ransom, because he did not possess the touchstone whereby possession of the ransom might be retained. For he reigned over us until the soul of Jesus had been given to him as a ransom —to him who deceived himself, thinking that he could be master over it, not realizing that it did not suffer the agony which he applied to hold it down.[13]

With all the weaknesses of this view, both by way of "omission and commission," it does include the necessity of a propitiation before God, and our consequent reconciliation with Him in virtue of Christ's bearing the penalty which fully belonged to us.[14]

B. Significant Medieval Theories

Though affecting the thinking of many, the systems proposed by Irenaeus and Origen never received the exclusive sanction of the Catholic church. Certain insights, however, were retained, while other aspects were worked over into more acceptable forms. For example the "debt-to-Satan" theory was altered by Athanasius (323-73) into a "debt-to-God" idea, which in turn was endorsed by Augustine (354-430). But no new revolutionary views troubled the theological waters until the days of Anselm (1033-1109) and Abelard (1079-1142).

1. The "Satisfaction" Theory of Anselm

St. Anselm, archbishop of Canterbury and first of the great scholastic theologians, is known both for his "ontological argument" for the existence of God and his unique "satisfaction" view of the Atonement. As truly philosophical as he was deeply pious, he felt that both reason and faith must be employed in the task of understanding the mysteries of redemption. Hence in his first great works, *Monologion* and *Proslogion,* he uses reason to establish the existence of God; and in his final treatise, *Cur Deus Homo? (Why Was God Man?),* he uses both reason and revelation to consider the nature of atonement. States J. L. Neve:

> The key to the understanding of Anselm's range of ideas is the fundamental idea of the Kingdom of God. God is the Lord and King of the World. In the beginning He created the angels to inhabit His Kingdom. After their fall, God created man as a substi-

---

13. *Ibid.,* p. 89.

14. *Ibid.*

tute for the loss which He had suffered. But through a wilful disobedience Adam also sinned and refused God's purpose. Sin, therefore, is embedded in the will and consists of the lack of righteousness which man owes God. God's honor is thus offended. For His honor consists in this that His will and plan should come to completion and every creature should subject itself to Him. Since Adam and mankind constitute a unity, in him and with him all men have sinned.[15]

His argument from this point is that, since God is universally dishonored and disgraced by man in sin, He will have to act either in punishment or in satisfaction to His own honor. He cannot good-naturedly pass sin by, for that "would bring disorder into His kingdom." And if He punishes man with eternal condemnation as his sin deserves, He will still have defeated His "own eternal plan of man's salvation in His kingdom." There remains, therefore, only the alternative of "satisfaction." Neve continues further:

> It was this that made necessary the incarnation of the Son of God. Only as God-Man (Deus-Homo) could Christ take our place and render that satisfaction. The significance of a real satisfaction lay exclusively in the giving up of His life. Such a voluntary self-sacrificing death of a sinless one God had to reward. But for himself the God-Man was in need of no reward. Therefore He gives His reward, the fruit of His work, to those for whose salvation He became man, namely to His brethren who are burdened with debt.[16]

2. The "Moral Influence" Theory of Abelard

In the writings of Abelard a distinctively new variation is added to the Atonement theme. In his view the Atonement does not so much meet the requirements of either the divine law or the divine nature as it does the psychological nature of man. In identifying this position more clearly, H. Orton Wiley states:

> He maintained that it was the rebellion of man that needed subduing, and not the wrath of God that needed propitiating. In place of a satisfaction to divine justice, he held that the atonement should be regarded as a winning exhibition of divine love. . . . Christ died for the twofold purpose of subduing the opposition of sinners and removing their guilty fears, through a transcendent exhibition of divine love.[17]

---

15. *Ibid.,* p. 195.
16. *Ibid.*
17. *Christian Theology,* 2:237.

In overlooking both the legal and judicial implications of sin, this view obscured the true meaning of the Cross, as well as the nature of God as holy love. It did, however, do much to offset the motive of fear with the motive of love as the true basis of devotion to God. Abelard's views were later adopted and eagerly promulgated by Socinian, Unitarian, and Bushnellian theology.

C. Dominant Theories of the Modern Age

Theology, as a function of the Church, takes shape from the state and condition of the Church. Its biblical threads of truth are the same, but the number and color of threads used in the completed fabric are not the same. Hence the doctrinal garments of the "new man" of the Protestant Reformation were in colorful contrast with those worn by the "old man" of medieval Catholicism. In fashioning the new patterns, the masterminds involved were those of Luther, Calvin, and James Arminius. From them, or their doctrinal descendants, arose a number of important new theories of the Atonement. Five of these will be mentioned.

1. The "Penal Satisfaction" Theory of John Calvin

Standing at the headwaters of the stream of Reformed theology is the towering figure of the great French theologian and reformer, John Calvin (1509-64). Neither so creative nor so dynamic as Luther, he was Luther's superior in keenness of logical analysis and ability to systematize the new conception of Christianity which had been brought to light through the Protestant Reformation. Author of the immortal *Institutes of the Christian Religion,* he was also father to the equally famous "penal satisfaction theory" of the Atonement.

This theory is so named because of the unique role it assigns to the punishment inflicted on sin in the scheme of redemption. The bearing of this punishment was the primary purpose for which Christ, as man's Substitute, came into the world. As Wiley well puts it, "The Satisfaction theory maintains that the immediate and chief end of Christ's work was to satisfy that essential principle of the divine nature which demands the punishment of sin."[18]

This punishment of sin, however, is neither an arbitrary act on the part of God nor a diplomatic gesture to indicate that He will uphold His moral government. Its necessity arises from three other considerations. First, sin, as intrinsically evil, merits punishment in

---

18. *Ibid.,* p. 242.

its own right. Second, God, as essentially and eternally holy, demands punishment in His own right. Third, law, which is immutably just and good, demands punishment for its violation in its own right. In keeping with these considerations, "the true view is," as A. A. Hodge explains it, "that God is determined, by the immutable holiness of his nature, to punish all sin because of its intrinsic guilt or demerit, the effect produced on the moral universe being incidental as an end, and dependent as a consequence, upon the essential character of punishment, as that which expiates guilt and vindicates righteousness."[19]

Limiting the Atonement, however, to "the elect,"[20] Hodge states that the motive back of the redemptive process was "the amazing love of God to his own people, determining him, in perfect consistency with his truth and justice, to assume himself, in the person of his Son, the responsibility of bearing the penalty and satisfying justice."[21] The Arminian position at this point would extend the motive of "amazing love" to all the world, for which Christ died (John 3:16).

As to its nature, Dr. Hodge states that Christ "assumed the lawplace of his people," "obeyed and suffered as our Substitute," "cancelled the claims of penal justice," and "merited the rewards of the original covenant of life."[22] And as to its effect, "it expiated the guilt of sin," "fulfilled the demands of the law," "propitiated justice," and "reconciled us to God."[23] The Wesleyan position here would make these benefits available, not only to God's actual family, but to His potential fold as well, consisting, not of whosoever has been chosen, but of "whosoever will" (Rev. 22:17).

The Arminian theology would further put the central emphasis upon the mercy instead of the justice of God, thinking of the divine nature as holy love. This in turn provides the strongest possible appeal to man (1 John 3:16), upholds in full the principles of moral government, and harmoniously relates the biblical facts of propitiation, expiation, reconciliation, and redemption, already discussed, to the entire character and claims of the divine majesty.

---

19. *The Atonement* (Grand Rapids: Wm. B. Eerdmans Publishing Co., 1953), p. 53.
20. *Ibid.*, p. 412.
21. *Ibid.*, p. 29.
22. *Ibid.*, pp. 29-30.
23. *Ibid.*, p. 31.

2. The "Governmental" Theory of Hugo Grotius

One of the most eminent theologians and jurists that Holland has produced, Hugo Grotius (1583-1645), has become celebrated both for his foundational treatise on international law, *De Jure Belli et Pacis,* and his "governmental theory of the atonement." The central idea of this view is that God is not to be regarded as an offended or "dishonored" party, but as the Moral Governor of the universe. As such it is His supreme business, not to secure any personal "satisfaction" so much as to "uphold the authority of His government in the interests of the general good." "Consequently," as Wiley further explains, "the sufferings of our Lord are to be regarded, not as the exact equivalent of our punishment, but only in the sense that the dignity of the divine government was as effectively upheld and vindicated, as it would have been if we had received the punishment we deserved."[24]

As amended by Richard Watson, the early Methodist theologian, this theory was made to include the satisfaction of God's moral nature as essential, along with the support of His government. Later John Miley, also widely known in Methodist circles, worked the theory over until it included these features: *(a)* the principle of substitution, *(b)* the principle of conditional salvation, *(c)* the vindication of public justice, and *(d)* the real remission of the penalties for sin. The satisfaction to public justice which it provided, however, was not to be construed either as "penal satisfaction" or as satisfaction of God's honor. Hence the views of Anselm as well as Calvin are excluded from its orbit.

3. The "Ethical" Theory of A. H. Strong

In the writings of Augustus Strong, the scholarly Baptist theologian, we find another significant shift in the center of attention. This time the spotlight moves away from man, whether in the individual or in the group, and focuses upon the character of God himself. If we were to think of Strong's "ethical theory" as constituting a theological ellipse we could indicate its two foci as *(a)* the holiness of God and *(b)* the humanity of Christ.

As related to the first, the Atonement must meet an ethical demand of the divine nature "that cannot be evaded, since the holiness from which it springs is unchanging." Strong states in part:

> The Ethical theory holds that the necessity of the atonement
> is grounded in the holiness of God, of which conscience in man is

---

24. *Christian Theology,* 2:253.

a finite reflection. There is an ethical principle in the divine nature which demands that sin shall be punished. Aside from its results, sin is essentially ill-deserving. As there is an ethical demand in our natures that not only others' wickedness, but our own wickedness be visited with punishment, and a keen conscience cannot rest till it has made satisfaction to justice for its misdeeds, so there is an ethical demand in God's nature that penalty follow sin.[25]

This satisfaction is accomplished by the Atonement, "by the substitution of Christ's penal sufferings for the punishment of the guilty." Such substitution, however, as he proceeds to explain, "is unknown to mere law, and above and beyond the powers of law. It is an operation of grace." But this grace neither "violates nor suspends law, but takes it up into itself and fulfills it." Consequently "the righteousness of the law is maintained, in that the source of all law, the judge and the punisher, himself voluntarily submits to bear the penalty, and bears it in the human nature that has sinned."[26]

In reference to the second focus, the humanity of Christ, Strong states:

> The Ethical theory of the atonement holds that Christ stands in such relation to humanity that what God's holiness demands, Christ is under obligation to pay, and inevitably does pay, and pays so fully in virtue of his twofold nature, that every claim of justice is satisfied, and the sinner who accepts what Christ has done in his behalf is saved.[27]

But if God can justly make such demands upon Christ for humanity it is evident that He must be identified with humanity. Hence, as Strong further affirms:

> The solution of the problem lies in Christ's union with humanity. Christ's sharing of man's life justly and inevitably subjected him to man's exposures and liabilities, and especially to God's condemnation on account of sin.[28]

The best summarization of this view—as well as its ablest defense—is given by Strong himself. Its many good points, with its occasional weaknesses, must be passed by in this brief treatment, but its essential principles may briefly be stated in the author's own words:

---

25. *Systematic Theology*, 2:751.
26. *Ibid.*, p. 752.
27. *Ibid.*, p. 754.
28. *Ibid.*, p. 755.

The Atonement, then, on the part of God has its ground (1) in the holiness of God, which must visit sin with condemnation, even though this condemnation bring death to his Son; and (2) in the love of God, which itself provides the sacrifice, by suffering in and with his Son for the sins of men, but through that suffering opening a way and means of salvation.

The Atonement, on the part of man is accomplished through (1) the solidarity of the race; of which (2) Christ is the life, and so its representative and surety; (3) justly yet voluntarily bearing its guilt and shame and condemnation as his own.[29]

4. The "Racial" Theory of Olin A. Curtis

Moving forward to a wider perspective than that offered by "government," "penal satisfaction," or "moral influence," this significant interpretation focuses attention upon a new humanity as the ultimate objective of the Atonement. Coming to its distinguished Methodist author in a series of totally new insights, it finds its fullest embodiment in his book, *The Christian Faith.* In this volume he states: "Our Lord's death was a racial event through and through. He suffered, as the Race-Man, for the whole race. He carried the race in his consciousness."[30]

Curtis identifies Christ with humanity in all its physical, intellectual, moral, social, and spiritual needs and aspirations. Emphatically he affirms:

> Jesus Christ, as the representative Race-Man endured in his death the precise racial penalty for human sin: and by the total event and experience under that penalty so expressed God's hatred of sin as to render possible the immediate foundation and gradual formation of a new race of men which shall at last perfectly manifest the moral love of God. The atonement is exactly in the death of Christ, if regarded in this comprehensive manner.[31]

Significantly this new race not only has its redemptive ground through the death of Christ, but also its "dynamic center" in the indwelling life of Christ. He is, for the redeemed, not only a historical fact, but equally important, a contemporary force. "The center of the new race," Curtis explains, "is the Son of God himself with a racial experience complete by suffering."[32] Related at once to the areas of self-fulfillment for the individual and full social realization for the

---

29. *Ibid.,* p. 761.
30. P. 321.
31. *Ibid.,* p. 329.
32. *Ibid.,* p. 334.

race, Christ is seen as the indispensable source of all human completion. "Men are made absolutely complete only through each other and in Christ. The finishing dynamic help comes only from the racial center, and that center is our Lord."[33]

Organically conceived, redemption for Curtis is progressively attained. The Atonement therefore is neither an isolated event nor an end in itself. It is rather the indispensable means to an end, and that end is "the expression of the moral love of God, or the expression of the fulness of the divine holiness in a race of redeemed men."[34] In the vast sweep of divine activity through history by which this end is realized, five interrelated stages occur:

> First, there is an ethical start in racial death. Second, there is an effective ethical movement in the death of Christ, and third, there is a racial start in the resurrection and ascension and session of our Lord. Fourth, there is an effective racial movement in the actual formation of the new race by the conversion of moral persons. Fifth, the holy racial goal is reached when the redeemed race, expressing the moral love of God, is completed in the organism at the final resurrection of the body.[35]

Related to the Adamic race, penally, by the death of Christ, and entered only on the most rigid moral terms, this new race moves through history as the one thoroughly reliable servant of the moral concern of God.

> Offering to every moral person the possibility of a holy completion in himself, in his brethren, and in his Redeemer, and of coming to a perfect service, a perfect rest, and a perfect joy, this new race will, at last, be the victorious realization of God's original design in creation.[36]

5. The "Classic" Motif of Gustaf Aulén

As the outstanding representative of contemporary Swedish or Lundensian theology, Gustaf Aulén presents what he calls the "classic" view of the Atonement in his brief but stimulating book entitled *Christus Victor.* Constituting a historical examination of the three main types of atonement theory—the "ransom," the "satisfaction," and the "moral influence" ideas—this work aims at the recovery of the full biblical ideas of the doctrine as represented in the original apostolic

---

33. *Ibid.,* p. 318.
34. *Ibid.,* pp. 326-27.
35. *Ibid.,* pp. 327-28.
36. *Ibid.,* p. 334.

teaching, summarized particularly by Irenaeus (A.D. 135-202), and rediscovered for Protestantism by Martin Luther.

In this view the Atonement is invested with a new dimension, that of cosmic conflict between the forces of righteousness and the powers of darkness and evil. It consequently involves the supreme concerns of God, man, and the devil—issues which must be fought out victoriously, at whatever the cost to the Almighty himself. Hence the author states:

> This type of view may be described provisionally as the dramatic. Its central theme is the idea of the atonement as a Divine conflict and victory: Christ—Christus Victor—fights against and triumphs over the evil powers of the world, the "tyrants" under which mankind is in bondage and suffering; and in Him God reconciles the world to Himself.[37]

This concept, as Aulén maintains, was not only "the dominant idea in the New Testament," but "has in reality held a place in the history of Christian doctrine whose importance it would not be easy to exaggerate."[38] Rooted deeply in the "drama of redemption in the Pauline Epistles" (e.g., 1 Cor. 15:24, 56; Gal. 1:4; Col. 2:15), it was "the ruling idea of the Atonement for the first thousand years of Christian history." Gradually replaced by the Latin or Anselmic view of the Roman church, it was later "more vigorously and profoundly expressed than ever before, in Martin Luther, and has therefore every right to claim the title of the classic Christian view of the Atonement."[39]

But the pivotal point of the theory is not so much the idea of conflict as the fact that God himself is the One who suffers most in the conflict, yet emerges victorious. In the crucible of the Cross, torn by the hatred of men from without and by His love for men from within, He assumed the full consequence of man's sin in himself, thus enabling His love to meet all the demands of His holiness, all the requirements of His justice, and all the claims of His law. "He is recconciled by the very act in which He reconciles the world to Himself."[40]

Thus, "God through Christ saves mankind from His own judgment and His own law, establishing a new relation which transcends

---

37. Translated by A. G. Hebert (New York: The Macmillan Co., 1931), p. 20.
38. *Ibid.*, p. 22.
39. *Ibid.*, pp. 22-23.
40. *Ibid.*, p. 21.

the order of merit and of justice."[41] Since "the Divine Love cannot be imprisoned in the categories of merit and of justice," the law can no longer say the last word with regard to the relation between God and the world since "Christ brings the law to an end."[42] Showing at once the inadequacy of any view centering around "influence" or "penal satisfaction," the classic view, according to Aulén, "defies rational systematization; its essential double-sidedness, according to which God is at once the Reconciler and the Reconciled, constitutes an antinomy which cannot be resolved by a rational statement."[43] It shows a continuity in the divine action and a discontinuity in the order of justice; while the Latin, or "satisfaction" type, shows "a legal consistency, but a discontinuity in Divine operation."[44]

D. Principles of Evaluation

Having briefly reviewed some of the most important theories of the Atonement, we shall conclude our survey with some criteria for their evaluation. Reserving detailed analysis and criticism for the more advanced studies in systematic theology, we may at any rate lay down a few general principles by which the adequacy or inadequacy of any theory may be judged. These principles may be summarized in four basic propositions:

1. The Atonement is the sole method revealed in Scripture for dealing with the many-sided problem of sin. It is God's way of meeting the emergency caused by the fall of the human race, and the only way.

2. Conceived in infinite wisdom, motivated by infinite love, and invested with infinite power, the Atonement provides exhaustless resources for the solution of every facet of the problem of sin. "But where sin abounded," as Paul exultantly puts it, "grace did much more abound" (Rom. 5:20).

3. The Atonement must ever be viewed as a twofold revelation of the character and nature of God—His character as holy, and His nature as love. In the Cross, God says two things: first, that He hates sin; second, that He loves the sinner (John 3:16).

4. Any view of the Atonement, to be adequate, must grasp the

---

41. *Ibid.,* p. 88.
42. *Ibid.,* p. 84.
43. *Ibid.,* p. 107.
44. *Loc. cit.*

full nature of the problem, disclose the completeness of the solution, and envision in it all the loving purpose of a holy Redeemer.

It is in respect to the last two principles that the various theories of the Atonement show their particular strengths or weaknesses. With regard to the first two there is little difference. All the systems mentioned agree that "there is none other name under heaven given among men, whereby we must be saved" (Acts 4:12) except the name of Jesus only.

But when we come to the third and fourth propositions, wide divergencies between the theories begin to appear. Each must be evaluated in the degree to which it meets the requirements of both God's holiness and His love, and in the degree to which it grasps the full significance of sin's problem and the adequacy of its divine solution. Here it may well be found that no single explanation contains all the truth; nor is any lacking in some contribution it may make to our limited and necessarily human understanding of the divine Cross "on which the Prince of Glory died."

III. The Resurrection of Christ[45]

Any theology true to the New Testament cannot leave out consideration of Christ's redemptive work at the Cross. Equally important is the fact and meaning of the empty tomb. It is not particularly good news to hear that someone has died. It is, however, very good news to hear that Someone has been raised from the dead.

That is precisely the message delivered first to the women who had gone to anoint the body of Jesus: "'I know that you are looking for Jesus who has been crucified,'" announced the angel. "'He is not here, for *He has risen,* just as He said. Come, see the place where He *was* lying'" (Matt. 28:5-6, italics added). The disciples were incredulous when they heard this. The women's words "appeared to them as nonsense, and they would not believe them" (Luke 24:11).

The doubts of the Eleven were soon dispelled. Jesus appeared to His own in many different ways over a 40-day period of time (Acts 1:3). He was seen by over 500 believers before his ascension (1 Cor. 15:3-7). The impact of the Resurrection turned despairing disciples

45. Material for the following section (III) was prepared by Dr. C. S. Cowles, Northwest Nazarene College. All scripture references are taken from the *New American Standard Bible* (NASB) unless otherwise noted.

into courageous apostles "giving witness to the resurrection of the Lord Jesus" (Acts 4:33). Their proclamation sent a shock wave reverberating around the world and down across the centuries. Their radiant confidence created the Christian Church, inspired the New Testament, and gave rise to a new day of worship. Today Jesus is confessed as Lord by the largest group of worshipers in the world.

A. Resurrection Celebration in the New Testament

In a central way, the New Testament embodies the revelation that God has exalted Jesus as Lord and Christ by raising Him from the dead. "The entire New Testament," states Floyd Filson, "was written in the light of the resurrection fact. To all of its writers, Jesus is the central figure of history, and they understand and interpret his career in the light of his Resurrection."[46] Everything moves toward and proceeds from that center-point event.

1. *The Gospels*

Mark states his confession of faith at the outset: "The beginning of the gospel of Jesus Christ, the Son of God" (1:1). The story he is about to tell centers in the man Jesus whom God has vindicated as the promised Messiah (Christ). Jesus is, in a special sense, the "Son of God." This, in Mark's judgment, is "gospel," *good news!*

Throughout the four Gospels are numerous predictions of Jesus' suffering, death, and resurrection. "He began to teach them that the Son of Man must suffer many things and be rejected by the elders and the chief priests and the scribes, and be killed, and after three days rise again" (Mark 8:31). Within the shadow of the Cross Jesus warns His disciples that "'you will all fall away, because it is written, "I WILL STRIKE DOWN THE SHEPHERD, AND THE SHEEP SHALL BE SCATTERED."'" Then He goes on to promise, "'After I have been raised, I will go before you to Galilee'" (Mark 14:27-28).

The Gospels rise to their pinnacle point in the empty tomb and the repeated appearances of Jesus to His own. In differing ways each documents the Master's victory over death and His ongoing presence within the community of believers. As C. Milo Connick observes, "A remarkable aspect of the story of Jesus is that it has no end. . . . He was not a mere memory. He was a continuing presence."[47]

---

46. *Jesus Christ the Risen Lord* (Nashville: Abingdon Press, 1941), p. 31.

47. *Jesus: The Man, the Mission, and the Message* (Englewood Cliffs, N.J.: Prentice-Hall, Inc., 1974), p. 414.

2. Apostolic Preaching

Fifty days after the Resurrection, the promised Holy Spirit loosed the tongues of the disciples to communicate the greatest story ever told. Peter's historic sermon on the day of Pentecost is typical:

"Men of Israel, listen to these words: Jesus the Nazarene, a man attested to you by God with miracles and wonders and signs which God performed through Him in your midst, just as you yourselves know—this Man, delivered up by the predetermined plan and foreknowledge of God, you nailed to a cross by the hands of godless men and put Him to death.

"And *God raised Him up again,* putting an end to the agony of death, since it was impossible for Him to be held in its power. . . .

"This Jesus *God raised up again,* to which we are all witnesses. . . . Therefore let all the house of Israel know for certain that God has made Him both Lord and Christ—this Jesus whom you crucified" (Acts 2:22-36, italics added).

From that day forward, apostolic proclamation centered in the gospel of Jesus crucified and raised by God: "With great power the apostles were given witness to the *resurrection of the Lord Jesus,* and abundant grace was upon them all" (Acts 4:33, italics added). In every sermon recorded in the Book of Acts, the predominant message is that "'the God of our Fathers *raised up Jesus,* whom you had put to death by hanging Him on a cross'" (5:30, italics added).

3. The Apostle Paul

What turned Saul of Tarsus around on the Damascus road was not a vision of Christ crucified, but of Christ alive! "I am Jesus whom you are persecuting" (Acts 9:5). The death of Jesus on a cross conclusively demonstrated to his Jewish mind that Jesus was *not* the promised Messiah, but a fraudulent pretender. Nothing short of a personal revelation of Jesus risen could have sent him out, in the power of the Spirit, proclaiming, "'He is the Son of God'" (9:20). The central position of the Resurrection in Paul's preaching can be seen in his first recorded sermon:

"When they had carried out all that was written concerning Him, they took Him down from the cross and laid Him in a tomb. But *God raised Him from the dead;* and for many days He appeared to those who came up with Him from Galilee to Jerusalem, the very ones who are now His witnesses to the people. And we preach to you the good news of the promise made to the fathers, that God has fulfilled this promise to our children in that *He raised up Jesus. . . . He whom God raised* did not undergo decay. Therefore let it be known to you, brethren, that through Him forgiveness of sins is proclaimed to you, and through Him everyone who believes is freed from all things, from which you could not be freed through the Law of Moses" (Acts 13:29-39, italics added).

In his first letter to the Corinthians, Paul sets forward what is to him "of first importance," namely, "that Christ died for our sins according to the Scriptures, and that He was buried, and that *He was raised on the third day* according to the Scriptures" (1 Cor. 15:3-4, italics added). After citing the appearances of the risen Lord to many witnesses, including himself (vv. 5-8), Paul establishes the absolute centrality of the Resurrection-event for the Christian's life and faith: "If Christ has not been raised, then our preaching is vain, your faith also is vain. . . . And if Christ has not been raised, your faith is worthless; you are still in your sins (15:14, 17). "This all-embracing signifance of the resurrection of Christ," in Herman Ridderbos's judgment, "is in Paul . . . not only the fruit of his profound theological reflection, but above all of divine revelation."[48]

B. The Historicity of the Resurrection-Event

When Paul preached Christ crucified and risen to the Athenians, they were quite sceptical: "Now when they heard of the resurrection of the dead, some began to sneer" (Acts 17:32). These philosophers were neither the first nor the last to question this startling claim regarding Jesus of Nazareth. The first Easter day was still young when befuddled soldiers, assigned to guard Jesus' tomb, went empty-handed to the chief priests. They were bribed and counseled to spread the first lie in regard to the Resurrection: "'You are to say, "His disciples came by night and stole Him away while we were asleep"'" (Matt. 28:13).

From that disclaimer onward, there have been no lack of critics rejecting the bodily resurrection of Jesus—both without and within the church. Rudolf Bultmann says, "The resurrection cannot . . . be demonstrated or made plausible as an objectively ascertainable fact on the basis of which one could believe."[49] He puts it even more sharply when he protests: "A historical fact which involves a resurrection from the dead is utterly inconceivable."[50] It must be said in his defense that he does hold to the resurrection of Jesus when it is

---

48. *Paul: An Outline of His Theology,* John Richard DeWitt, trans. (Grand Rapids: Wm. B. Eerdmans Publishing Co., 1975), p. 55.

49. *Theology of the New Testament,* 2 vols. (New York: Charles Scribner's Sons, 1951, 1955), 1:305.

50. *Kerygma and Myth,* ed. by H. W. Bartsch (London: S.P.C.K., 1953), p. 39.

understood that He rose again in the faith and proclamation of the disciples.[51]

In view of the fact that the bodily resurrection of Jesus is straightforwardly affirmed by the New Testament and assumes the central role in the development of Christian theology, it is imperative to examine the attacks upon the veracity of this cardinal doctrine.

The Jews have historically accepted the explanation of the soldiers that the body of Jesus was stolen by His disciples while they slept. In the second century A.D., some Gnostic teachers suggested that it was not Jesus who was crucified, but Simon of Cyrene by mistake. Some have postulated that the women arrived at the wrong tomb on Easter morning, and that they originated the story of His resurrection. Many have proposed the theory that Jesus never died, but slipped into a coma on the Cross, from which He revived in the coolness of the sepulchre.

Such speculations do not merit serious consideration. Of more significance are those objections based upon the New Testament records themselves. Let us examine the most prominent of these difficulties.

1. *Nobody Witnessed Jesus Rising from the Dead*

There were no eyewitnesses to the actual Resurrection itself. The Gospels are silent as to precisely when or how Jesus did arise.

This objection fades away when we consider the large number who testified that He was raised, and that He had appeared unto them (Acts 1:3; 1 Cor. 15:3-8). Nobody has seen electricity. But few who have seen and felt its effects would doubt that it exists. Hans Kung makes a helpful observation:

> The very reserve of the New Testament Gospels and letters in regard to the resurrection creates trust. The resurrection is neither depicted nor described. The interest in exaggeration and the craving for demonstration, which are characteristic of the Apocrypha, make the latter incredible. The New Testament Easter documents are not meant to be testimonies for the resurrection but testimonies to the raised and risen Jesus.[52]

2. *The Gospels Were Written Decades After the Events*

Most scholars admit that at least a full generation (30 years)

---

51. *Theology of the New Testament,* 1:305 ff.

52. *On Being a Christian,* Edward Quinn, trans. (Garden City, N.Y.: Doubleday & Co., Inc., 1976), p. 347.

passed before Mark—the first Gospel to be written—appeared. The Gospel writers collected and edited the tradition about Jesus that had been passed on through the church by means of preaching, teaching, songs, and the sacraments for several decades. None of the Gospels are written in the first-person form of eyewitnesses, but rather in the third-person recording the testimony of eyewitnesses. It is this generally accepted fact about the transmission of the gospel until it was organized in written form by the evangelists which underlies much of the modern-day scepticism concerning the historicity of the events they record. Since the gospel was passed on by word of mouth for so many years, it suffered inevitable distortion and invention—so the critics claim.

In answer to this, we can confidently assert that this very distance between the Gospel documents and the events they record *strengthens their credibility.* The evangelists were in a position to sift through many strands of both oral and written traditions (Luke 1:1-4) in bringing together a composite portrait of Jesus evidencing a great deal of objectivity. Historians contend that it takes at least 30 years before a true perspective regarding any historical phenomenon can be gained. It is inconceivable that the four Gospels—once they were written—could have been so immediately and universally accepted by the Church as authoritative if they were filled with falsehoods and inaccurate claims. One of the reasons why these four Gospels were adopted, and not some others such as the Gospel of Peter, was precisely because the story they related agreed substantially with the recollection of a great many eyewitnesses who were still alive at the time of their first circulation. The test of time only served to deepen the Evangelists' conviction that "in the life, death, and resurrection of the man Jesus, God entered into the life of man in a decisive fashion."[53]

3. *There Are Many Discrepancies Between the Various Resurrection Accounts*

When the early tradition cited by Paul in 1 Cor. 15:3-8 is placed alongside of the Gospels, it is clear that we have five distinct and sometimes conflicting records of what happened. How many women went to the tomb? At what time did they arrive? How many angels did they see? Where were the angels when they spoke to the wom-

---

53. William Hordern, *A Layman's Guide to Protestant Theology* (New York: The Macmillan Co., 1955), p. 20.

en? To whom did Jesus first appear? Where and when did the appearances actually occur?

The differences in detail between the various sources is itself an evidence of authenticity of the New Testament documents and the veracity of the story they tell about the resurrection of Jesus. If five exact signatures can be produced, any banker will testify that four of them are bound to be forgeries. C. Milo Connick states, "Nothing shouts invention so loudly as witnesses who recite in harmony."[54] Five witnesses to an accident are sure to render five differing and conflicting accounts of what they saw. But there will be no doubt in their minds—or in the minds of those who read their reports—as to the fact that an accident occurred. Neither need a Christian doubt the bodily resurrection of Jesus because the reports of the first witnesses differ in detail. One fact was indelibly burned into each of their minds: "*'God raised Him up on the third day,* and granted that *He should become visible,* not to all the people, but to witnesses who were chosen beforehand by God, that is, to us, who ate and drank with Him *after He arose from the dead'*" (Acts 10:40-41, italics added).

4. Jesus' Appearances Were Subjective "Faith-occurrences"

This idea, popularized by Bultmann, is supported by the fact that there is a marked difference between the Risen Lord and Jesus as the disciples had previously known Him. He is not the same as before. They have difficulty recognizing Him. He is no longer limited by time or space. He appears and vanishes unannounced. He meets His disciples without opening locked doors. There is an element of mystery, awe, and reticence in their response toward him: "When they saw Him, they worshiped Him; but some were doubtful" (Matt. 28:17).

It is this very ethereal character of the risen Lord's appearances which lends credence to Bultmann's claim that what is important in Christianity is not the resuscitation of a corpse, but that there arose in the hearts and consciousness of Jesus' disciples the conviction that He had indeed conquered death and was alive forevermore.

William Barclay admits that the idea that Peter and the disciples "thought themselves and loved themselves into seeing a vision of Jesus" has its appeal.[55] But he goes on to say that "the line between it and downright hallucination is precariously thin. . . . An hallucina-

---

54. *Jesus: Man, Mission, Message,* p. 410.

55. *The Mind of Jesus* (New York: Harper and Brothers, 1961), p. 297.

tion remains an hallucination, even when it produces the very effect that one wishes to be true."[56]

In addition we could say that the disciples were the least likely candidates for such delusions following the Crucifixion. The accounts are unanimous in painting a portrayal of men who were utterly disillusioned and who had abandoned all hope. This is not the kind of mentality that fosters invention on the scale of a resurrection from the dead!

That the faith of the disciples was grounded upon a mighty act of God within human history when He raised Jesus is supported by at least three compelling data:

a. The existence of the Church. There is no satisfactory explanation for the dramatic transformation of the disciples from disheartened, demoralized, and discouraged followers to dynamic witnesses in less than 50 days apart from an occurrence as totally unimaginable as a resurrection from the dead. As Hans Kung puts it, "This *Passion* story with its disastrous outcome—why should it ever have entered into the memory of mankind?—was transmitted only because there was also an *Easter* story."[57]

b. The existence of the New Testament. Who could have conceived of writing 27 books with the historic impact of the New Testament if its subject matter had to do with a crucified criminal, and nothing more? "The resurrection of Jesus . . . formed the climax and interpreting center of the account of what God had done for men through Jesus," according to Floyd Filson. "It was the key fact."[58]

c. The observance of Sunday as the Christians' day of worship. Jesus was a Jew. So were His disciples. Though He ignored some of the traditions of the elders in regard to Sabbath observance, Luke records that He "went to the synagogue, as his custom was, on the sabbath day" (4:16). There is no hint that He ever suggested a change in the day of worship for His followrs. What, then, could have incited the earliest Christians—most of whom were devout Jews—to break a sacred tradition traced back to creation itself (Gen. 2:1-3)? What explanation can be given for such a radical—and to orthodox Jews, blasphemous—departure from the plainly stated command of God (Exodus 20:8-11) other than a historic occurrence on the order of

---

56. *Ibid.*
57. *On Being a Christian,* p. 345.
58. *Jesus Christ, Risen Lord,* p. 48.

creation itself? Surprisingly, there is no record in the New Testament of controversy regarding this gradual but permanent shift from observing the Jewish Sabbath as the day of worship to the "Lord's Day," the first day of the week—the day of Jesus' resurrection, and the day on which He made repeated appearances to His own. Early Christians debated many things, but Sunday worship was not one of them.

The historicity of Jesus' resurrection cannot be presented as a full-proof sign compelling belief: in that case, faith would be unnecessary. But neither is Resurrection-faith devoid of objective historical content. Biblical faith is historically based, and never more so than in the bodily resurrection of Jesus from the dead. Again, Paul's word is decisive: "If Christ has not been raised, then . . . your faith also is vain" (1 Cor. 15:14). Or as George Elden Ladd states the issue:

> The bodily resurrection of Christ is the only adequate expla-
> nation to account for the resurrection faith and the admitted
> "historical" facts. . . . for one who believes in the God who has
> revealed himself in Christ, the resurrection is entirely rational and
> utterly consistent with the evidences.[59]

C. The Centrality of the Resurrection

The resurrection of Jesus was God's mighty saving deed accomplished on the plane of human history which intersects our existence at the center, determines our destiny, and speaks to that which is of ultimate concern to us—death and life.

Since Christian theology has to do with that which concerns us ultimately, it is important to see the central position which the doctrine of the Resurrection occupies in the understanding of biblical faith. It is Floyd Filson's contention that "Biblical theology finds its clearest starting point and interpreting clue in the resurrection of Jesus Christ."[60] Jesus raised by God is not one pearl of gospel truth among many on the golden chain of revelation: it is the chain itself! Break it, and all of the other equally marvelous claims regarding Jesus lose their credence. The Resurrection is the "axial-point" in the whole scheme of divinely revealed truth. Let us examine several of the larger concerns of theology in this light.

---

59. *I Believe in the Resurrection of Jesus* (Grand Rapids: Wm. B. Eerdmans Publishing Co., 1975), p. 27.

60. *Jesus Christ, Risen Lord*, p. 25.

1. *The Doctrine of God*

God's self-revelation is fully and finally completed in the resurrection of Jesus. Until that moment, man's understanding of God was partial and limited. The bottom line of this partial understanding is succinctly stated by Job: "The Lord gave and the Lord has taken away" (Job 1:21). God is the Author of life: but He is the Executor of death as well. He is the one who "takes" people out of the land of the living. Thus, in every culture and among all peoples, all thinking about God has been tinged with terror and overlaid with fear.

With the resurrection of Jesus, a radically new revelation about God emerges. He is *not* the Author of death. Nor is He a daemonic divinity who delights in tormenting mankind with disease, disaster, and hardship. Rather, the God and Father of our Lord Jesus Christ *is a God who raises the dead!* Death never was God's original intention for mankind. Death is the natural consequence of man's revolt against God, and against the gracious laws by which the world is ordered. "For the *wages of sin is death,* but the free gift of God is eternal life in Christ Jesus our Lord" (Rom. 6:23, italics added). The apostle Paul lays the responsibility for sin and death where it should be: "Through one man sin entered into the world, and death through sin, and so death spread to all men, because all sinned" (Rom. 5:12). God is "not wishing for any to perish but for all to come to repentance" (2 Pet. 3:9). Jesus clarified the nature of God when He said, "'He is not the God of the dead, but of the living'" (Mark 12:27).

We need cringe no longer under the tyranny of death. Now we are set free to rejoice in the revelation of God as the One who "raised Christ Jesus from the dead" (Rom. 8:11). The glory of the Father is finally, fully, and perfectly revealed in His great saving work accomplished in Jesus' atoning death and victorious resurrection. Now we can celebrate "the love of God, which is in Christ Jesus our Lord" (Rom. 8:39).

2. *The Doctrine of the Son*

The Resurrection is our key to understanding Jesus. Paul puts the issue clearly when he states that Jesus was "declared with power to be the Son of God *by the resurrection from the dead,* according to the Spirit of holiness, Jesus Christ our Lord" (Rom. 1:4, italics added). God vindicated the crucified Messiah as "My beloved Son, in whom I am well pleased" (Matt. 3:17) when He raised Him from the dead. Hans Kung affirms, "Jesus' cause—which his disciples had given up as lost—was decided at Easter by God himself. Jesus' cause makes sense and continues, because he himself did not remain—a failure—in death, but lives on completely justified by God."[61]

Looking backward through the empty tomb, we see the Cross no longer as the tragic insanity of man's evil nature, but *as the triumphant demonstration of God's suffering love.* Apart from the Resurrection there is little to distinguish Jesus' death from that of many other religious luminaries. If God had not raised Jesus, we would never have heard about the Cross—least of all, from the disciples. But because God raised Jesus, we can look upon the Cross for an eternity and not exhaust its redemptive riches.

The life and ministry of Jesus appear in an entirely different light in the perspective of the Resurrection. Miracle workers abound both within and beyond the Scriptures. But because of the *supreme miracle* accomplished when God raised Him, His miracles become signs attesting to the irruption of the kingdom of God among men. "If I cast out demons by the Spirit of God," says Jesus to His detractors, "then the kingdom of God has come upon you" (Matt. 12:28). Most of what Jesus taught has Old Testament or Rabbinical precedent. But His words become *the Word* in the light of the empty tomb: "The words that I have spoken to you are spirit and are life" (John 6:63).

It is difficult to imagine how someone could stumble over the doctrine of the Virgin Birth or of the preexistence of the Son if, in deed and in fact, God raised Jesus from the dead.

Looking through the empty tomb forward, the Ascension, the outpouring of the Holy Spirit, the emergence of the Church, the *parousia* (Second Coming), and the final judgment become entirely logical movements in God's exaltation of the Son. Because Jesus is "the first-born from the dead" (Col. 1:18), the apostle Paul can make these sweeping claims concerning Him:

> He is the image of the invisible God, the first-born of all creation. For in Him all things were created, both in the heavens and on earth . . . all things have been created through Him and for Him. And He is before all things, and in Him all things hold together (Col. 1:15-17).

John the Revelator has an encounter with the Living Christ in which Jesus says, "'Fear not, I am the first and the last, and the living one; I died, and behold *I am alive for evermore,* and I have the keys of Death and Hades'" (Rev. 1:17-18, RSV, italics added). The man Jesus

---

61. *On Being a Christian,* p. 352.

is also the eternal Son of God. He was present and active with the Father from before the creation, sustains the universe by the power of His might, and stands beyond the end of time as the One toward whom everything is moving to its final consumation (Eph. 1:10). These kinds of "cosmic claims" would be utterly preposterous apart from the fact that *He is alive forevermore!*

3. *The Doctrine of the Holy Spirit*

Jesus promised His disciples, "'It is to your advantage that I go away, for if I do not go away, the Counselor will not come to you; but if I go, I will send him to you'" (John 16:7, RSV). The gift of the Holy Spirit was keyed to the Resurrection-event. Not until He had been crucified, raised, and exalted to the right hand of the Father would the promised Spirit be given to the disciples.

When the Holy Spirit was poured out in great glory and with mighty power on the Day of Pentecost, of what did those Spirit-filled disciples speak? Of the ecstasy of the Spirit? Of *glossalalia?* Of gifts? Of exalted experiences? No! They spoke of Jesus crucified and *raised!* The sign *par excellence* of the Spirit's baptism, throughout the New Testament, is that of tongues loosed to magnify Jesus as Lord and Christ (Acts 2:32, 36). The superlative gift of the Spirit is not one of confusion, but of communication: "No one can say, 'Jesus is Lord,' except by the Holy Spirit" (1 Cor. 12:3, NASB). As Jesus had taught: "'He will not speak on His own initiative, but whatever He hears, He will speak . . . He shall glorify Me; for He shall take of Mine, and shall disclose it to you'" (John 16:13-14).

The outpouring of the Holy Spirit is preceded by the Resurrection-event and followed by Resurrection-proclamation. It constitutes the *second movement* in God's exaltation of the Son. The *first movement* was the Resurrection. And the *final movement* will be the revelation of Jesus in clouds of glory signalling the end of this present age. The Holy Spirit is God's gracious Gift to His Church between the times of Jesus' first coming and His coming again, making real the person of Jesus to all who exercise the obedience of faith.

To understand this inherent unity between the Son and the Spirit helps us check excessive claims in regard to the person and work of the Holy Spirit. In zeal toward encouraging believers to be "filled with the Spirit," a false dichotomy is often created between believing in Jesus for the forgiveness of sins and receiving the Holy Spirit in all of His fulness. The inevitable implication of such emphasis is that the Spirit is greater than the Son, and he who has been filled with the Spirit is superior to the one who has "only" saving faith in Jesus.

There are not two classes of Christians: sons and super-sons. To be filled with the Spirit is to be filled with Jesus and with all the fullness of God (Eph. 3:16-19). The Spirit reveals the Son, the Son exalts the Father, and the Father sends the Spirit. There is no competition in the Godhead. The Wesleyan doctrine of two works of grace does not proceed from some inherent division within the Trinity, but from the nature of man—or, more specifically, the dual nature of sin. The question is not whether *we have* the Spirit when we believe in Jesus, but whether the Spirit *has us* under the control of the lordship of Christ. This is the proper distinction to be made between *initial* and *entire* sanctification.

4. *The Doctrine of Salvation*

Knowing and confessing that God has raised Jesus is the key to personal salvation in the New Testament Church: "If you confess with your lips that Jesus is Lord and believe in your heart that God raised Him from the dead, you will be saved" (Rom. 10:9). Such New Testament emphasis is at variance with the evangelistic message widespread in evangelical Protestantism today. Most gospel appeals center upon the atoning sacrifice of Christ on the Cross and minimize —or ignore altogether—the good news of the Resurrection.

In the Book of Acts the gospel of the Resurrection always comes first. Then the hearers cry out, "'Brethren, what shall we do?'" (Acts 2:37). The apostolic response is: "'Repent, and let each of you be baptized in the name of Jesus Christ for the forgiveness of your sins; and you shall receive the gift of the Holy Spirit'" (Acts 2:38). The order of the apostolic *kerygma,* proclamation, is important: first the "good news" of God who has exalted Jesus as Lord and Christ by raising Him from the dead, then the offer of an already accomplished reconciliation to the Father through the shed blood of Jesus (Rom. 5:8, 10; 2 Cor. 5:18-21; Col. 1:18-23). It is the "gospel" of the Resurrection that "is the power of God for salvation to every one who believes" (Rom. 1:16).

5. *The Doctrine of Christian Hope*

Christianity looks ahead to the final consummation of all things in the *parousia*—revealing—of Jesus in great power and glory at His second coming. This hope is more than wistful longing: it is a settled confidence based upon the already accomplished resurrection of Jesus from the dead. Paul makes this clear when he says,

For if we believe that Jesus died and rose again, even so God will bring with Him those who have fallen asleep in Jesus. . . . For the Lord Himself will descend from heaven with a shout . . . then we who are alive and remain shall be caught up together with them in the clouds to meet the Lord in the air, and thus we shall always be with the Lord (1 Thess. 4:14-17).

How do I know that Jesus is coming again? He has already come. And in His first coming He defeated death never to die again. He who was raised is now present and active in my heart and life by the Holy Spirit. Jesus *has* come. He is *now* manifested as Living Lord. And He *will* come again just as He promised. The Second Coming is not tangentially affixed to the main body of Christian truth: it is centered at the heart of Christianity as the logical and necessary completion of the victory already won when God raised Jesus. Christian hope is grounded in history—the history of Jesus raised by the power of God.

D. The Resurrection as Power for Freedom from Sin and Life in the Spirit

Jesus crucified and raised is more than an astounding event of past history. It is more than the explanation of how the Church came into existence. It is more than a certain way of understanding Christian theology.

The resurrection of Jesus is that mighty deed of God which announces that Satan has been dethroned, the power of sin has been broken, and the terror of death has been tamed. It is the incredible proclamation that spiritual prison doors have been thrown open and captives set free. It is God's great "emancipation proclamation." It signals the infusion of new life whereby we are made "partakers of the divine nature" (2 Pet. 1:4). The apostle Paul spells out the "good news" of Christian freedom in this graphic passage:

Therefore we have been buried with Him through baptism into death, in order that *as Christ was raised* from the dead through the glory of the Father, *so we too might walk in the newness of life.* . . . knowing this, that our old self was crucified with Him, that our body of sin might be done away with, that we should no longer be slaves to sin; for he who has died is freed from sin. Now if we have died with Christ, we believe that we shall also live with Him, knowing that Christ, having been *raised from the dead,* is never to die again; death no longer is master over Him. . . .

Even so consider yourselves to be dead to sin, but alive to God in Christ Jesus. . . . But now having been *freed from sin* and enslaved to God, you derive your benefit, resulting in sanctification, and the outcome eternal life (Rom. 6:4-11, 22, italics added).

Freedom in Christ gathers around three great ideas.

1. *We Are Not Only Forgiven Sins, but Released from the Power of Sinning*

Forgiveness is a partial but inadequate understanding of the scope of God's great saving deed. Forgiveness focuses upon sinful deeds, but cannot deal with the sinful nature from which such acts originate. Thus forgiveness implies a negative stance toward sin: it presumes that the sinner—because he is still under the power of the nature of sin—will keep on sinning, and will need forgiveness continaully.

The apostle Paul faces up to this pessimistic view of sin and salvation when he asks the question, "Are we to continue in sin that grace might increase?" (Rom. 6:1). His answer is decisive: "God forbid!" (6:2). There is a better way for those who are in Christ: that is to be set free from the nature—and hence liberated from the power—of sin! As Rudolf Bultmann points out: " 'Forgiveness of sins' is insofar ambiguous as it seems to declare only release from the guilt contracted by 'former sins,' whereas the important thing for Paul is release from *sinning*, release from the power of sin."[62]

2. *Through the Death and Resurrection of Jesus, the Power of Sin Was Broken*

All that constituted our situation under the tyranny of sin was laid upon the sinless shoulders of the Son of God. There, upon the Cross, all of the aroused fury of sin's demonic power hurled itself against the defenseless Jesus, and He died.

But here is the astonishing occurrence: *when sin destroyed Jesus, it destroyed itself!* It expended all of its force. It exhausted all of its terror. It emptied itself of all of its power. For, having slain Jesus, there was nothing more that it could do. Death can no longer be a threatening power to a dead man. "He who has died," says Paul, "is freed from sin" (Rom. 6:7).

That is not the end of the drama, however. On the third day God raised up Jesus on the other side of the death-event, alive forevermore. As such Jesus lives totally free from the oppressive power of sin: "The death that He died, He died to sin, once for all; but the life that He lives, He lives to God" (Rom. 6:10). To live in the freedom of Christ's victory is to exist beyond the boundary of sin's irresistible control.

---

62. *Theology of the New Testament,* 1:286.

By faith we too can be "buried with Him through baptism into death" (Rom. 6:4). The old self-centered self can be "crucified with Him" in order that our "body of sin"—that is, the old nature which was falsely oriented toward God—"might be done away with, that we should no longer be slaves to sin" (6:6). When we are united with Christ in His death through a total surrender of ourselves to His lordship, all that constituted our previous existence as those separated from the life of God dies. It ceases to exist. And we make the great personal discovery that sin has no power over dead men.

Alexander Solzhenitsyn relates an encounter between an insignificant political prisoner and Abakumov, the third most powerful man in Stalin's Russia. The prisoner is behaving with impudent independence in the presence of this czar of the Soviet slave-labor camp system—a tyrant who has been responsible for the untimely deaths of millions. The prisoner refuses to wilt under Abakumov's threats, and responds in this classic passage:

> Just understand one thing and pass it along to anyone at the top who still doesn't know that you are strong only as long as you don't deprive people of *everything*. For a person you've taken *everything* from is no longer in your power. *He's free all over again.*[63]

And he who has *surrendered everything* to the lordship of Jesus—died out to *everything*—is free all over again.

This death we die to sin does not mean that the presence of sin is suddenly banished from the world of our existence and that we are henceforth exempt from all temptation. Paul hurries on in this same chapter to admonish us, "Do not let sin reign in your mortal body that you should obey its lusts" (6:12). The potentiality for sin always lies close at hand. We continue to be free moral agents, having the capacity to choose good or evil. We are not set free from the *possibility* of sin, but from the *compulsion* to sin.

3. We Are Set Free from Sin in Order to Live a New Life

We are not only "buried with Him through baptism into death," but we are "raised from the dead through the glory of the Father" and are "alive to God" (Rom. 6:4, 11). Or as Paul puts it in another passage, "Therefore if any man is in Christ, he is a new creature; the old things passed away; behold, new things have come" (2 Cor. 5:17). What dies when the old passes away is not self, but the sinful corruption which impregnated, perverted, and distorted the God-created

---

63. *The First Circle*, Thomas P. Witney, trans. (New York: Harper and Row, Pub., 1968), p. 83.

self. Liberated from the power of sin, the true self can now emerge in all of the purity, wholeness, and beauty which characterizes its creation in the image of God. Notice the metaphors that Paul uses to describe our new life in Christ.

a. "Walk in newness of life" (6:4). In our old life under the bondage of sin, every step we took—whether patently evil or perfectly righteous—led us increasingly away from God. But now that we have become "obedient from the heart to that form of teaching to which [we] were committed" (6:17), every step we take leads us closer to heaven and home. Even when, through the infirmity of the flesh, we stumble and fall, we discover that we have fallen closer to the Master. And the "helping" Spirit is there to pick us up and get us going again (Rom. 8:26).

We are driven no longer to works of righteousness by the promise and punishment of the law, but we are impelled by a mighty new affection to a life of holiness and brotherly love, "for the love of Christ controls us" (2 Cor. 5:14). We no longer labor to *impress* God, but to *express* Him, "for we are His workmanship, created in Christ Jesus for good works" (Eph. 2:10).

b. "United with Him" (6:5). What does it mean to be filled with the Spirit, entirely sanctified? It simply means to be "united with Him." It is to be at home in the presence of Jesus. St. Anselm put it succinctly: "What is life but to love God and enjoy His presence forever?" Paul gave classic expression to this vital relationship with Jesus when he said, "There is therefore now no condemnation for those who are in Christ Jesus. For the law of the Spirit of life in Christ Jesus has set you free from the law of sin and death" (Rom. 8:1-2). To be "united with Him" means a life that is free from the oppressive tyranny of sin—a life in which there is no condemnation, no guilt, no disobedience, no separation, no alienation, no estrangement, no uneasiness. It is, as one has said, to be "comfortable in the presence of the Son of God."

c. "Crucified with Him" (6:6). Our human life in Christ is lived on this side of the final boundary separating time from eternity. We still exist in a sin-cursed world dominated by "the powers . . . the world forces of this darkness . . . the spiritual forces of wickedness in the heavenly places" (Eph. 6:12). Jesus warned His disciples that "in the world you have tribulation, but take courage; I have overcome the world" (John 16:33).

As long as we are in the world we will experience repeated

crucifixions with Christ. We will be crucified upon crosses of rejection, ridicule, persecution, nonacceptance, failure, weakness, bodily suffering, heartbreak, and finally—physical death. But here is good news: we never have to walk alone! When we are subjected to fresh experiences of death, we are crucified *with Him!* No wonder the apostle can glory in "the fellowship of His sufferings, being conformed to His death" (Phil. 3:10).

   d. "Alive to God in Christ Jesus" (6:11). The death that we die under the power of sin always leads to decay, disintegration, and destruction. The death that we died with Christ however, sets us free for a richer and more authentic life. To be crucified with Christ—whether initially in the experience of full surrender or in the course of faithful discipleship—does not destroy us, but liberates us. The wonderful paradox of the death-resurrection event in the life of the believer is that we die only to those things which are always already passing away, and we are becoming increasingly alive to those spiritual realities which will live on forever. He is no fool who surrenders what he cannot keep to gain what he cannot lose!

   Those who have died with Christ in order that they shall also live with Him (6:8) enjoy the "benefit, resulting in *sanctification,* and the outcome, *eternal life*" (6:22, italics added).

IV. The Extent of the Atonement

Before leaving our study of the atonement, it will be well to consider the question of its extent. We have seen in Chapter 4 and will observe again in the next chapter sharp differences of opinion at this point between Calvinists and Arminians. Calvinistic theology originally stood for a limited as versus a universal atonement. The penal satisfaction theory of John Calvin logically demands the conclusion that Christ died only for the elect. Francis Turretin wrote: "The mission and death of Christ are restricted to a limited number—to His people, His sheep, His friends, His Church, His body; and nowhere extended to all men severally and collectively."[64] It should be said that many who call themselves Calvinists do not now accept this particular doctrine.

   On the contrary, Arminian theologians have uniformly argued

---

64. *The Atonement* (New York: Board of Publication of the Reformed Protestant Dutch Church, 1859), pp. 125-26.

for belief in the universal extent of the Atonement. Christ's death was for all alike, and secures for all a measure of prevenient grace which makes possible a personal faith when the gospel is preached. That not all are saved is not due to a limitation placed by God either in the value of the Cross or, as we shall see when we consider predestination in Chapter 13, in the call He extends by His Spirit.

There is a wealth of New Testament scripture to support this conviction. In passing, though, it should be said that passages which speak of Christ dying for the Church, for His people, or for those who have in fact been converted,[65] do not give basis for the claim that He died *only* for these. That others are not mentioned does not prove that they are excluded. All theories which limit the death of Christ to the elect alone must be judged in the light of four great classes of scripture reference:

a. *Those passages which speak of the death of Christ in behalf of all persons, or the world, the ungodly, without limitation.* Such, for example, are statements like: "In due time Christ died for the ungodly" (Rom. 5:6); "One [that is, Christ] died for all" (2 Cor. 5:14); "Who gave himself a ransom for all" (1 Tim. 2:6); "That he by the grace of God should taste death for every man" (Heb. 2:9); and, "He is the propitiation for our sins; and not for ours only, but also for the sins of the whole world" (1 John 2:2; cf. also John 1:29; 2 Cor. 5:18; and Gal. 4:4).

Closely related are those verses which describe the Atonement in such terms as could only mean the inclusion of all persons within its scope: "God sent not his Son into the world to condemn the world; but that the world through him might be saved" (John 3:17); "I came not to judge the world, but to save the world" (John 12:47); "So then as through one transgression there resulted condemnation to all men, even so through one act of righteousness there resulted justification of life to all men" (Rom. 5:18, NASB); and, "We have seen and do testify that the Father sent the Son to be the Saviour of the world" (1 John 4:14).

b. *Those references which represent God's will as including the salvation of all men.* It is inconceivable that God should love and desire the salvation of all and not make such possible through the Atonement. Jesus is spoken of as "The Saviour of the world" (John 4:42) and "of all men, specially of those that believe" (1 Tim. 4:10). Jesus himself

---

65. Cf. Rom. 6:8; 1 Cor. 15:3; Gal. 1:4; Eph. 5:25-27; Heb. 13:12.

said, "The bread that I will give is my flesh, . . . for the life of the world" (John 6:51). Paul records, "For this is good and acceptable in the sight of God our Saviour; who will have all men to be saved, and to come unto the knowledge of the truth" (1 Tim. 2:3-4). Peter affirms, "The Lord is not slack concerning his promise, as some men count slackness; but is longsuffering to us-ward, not willing that any should perish, but that all should come to repentance" (2 Pet. 3:9).

  c. *Those statements which speak of the universal proclamation of the gospel to all men in good faith.* Is it conceivable that God should extend His invitation through preaching to all men if many (perhaps the majority) are excluded from the benefits of the Atonement, and therefore could not under any circumstances be saved? Christ's own preaching was addressed to all: "Come unto me, all ye that labour and are heavy laden, and I will give you rest" (Matt. 11:28); "Jesus stood and cried, saying, If any man thirst, let him come unto me, and drink" (John 7:37). Peter, at Pentecost, quoted Joel 2:32, "And it shall come to pass, that whosoever shall call on the name of the Lord shall be saved" (Acts 2:21), a verse which Paul also quoted in Rom. 10:13. Almost the last words of Revelation are a universal invitation: "And the Spirit and the bride say, Come. And let him that heareth say, Come. And let him that is athirst come. And whosoever will, let him take the water of life freely" (Rev. 22:17; cf. also Luke 2:10; Mark 16:15-16; John 1:7-12; 3:36; Acts 17:30; 1 Cor. 1:21; Col. 1:28; Titus 2:11).

  d. Finally, there are *verses which distinctly affirm that Christ died for some who, despite the provision made for them, may be lost.* An irresponsible attitude by professing Christians in matters of personal liberty results in the danger of which Paul warns in Rom. 14:15: "Destroy not him with thy meat, for whom Christ died" (cf. also 1 Cor. 8:11). The writer to the Hebrews embodies this idea in a most solemn warning: "Of how much sorer punishment, suppose ye, shall he be thought worthy, who hath trodden under foot the Son of God, and hath counted the blood of the covenant, wherewith he was sanctified, an unholy thing, and hath done despite unto the Spirit of grace?" (10:29). Peter also states that some whom the Master bought will be destroyed: "But false prophets also arose among the people, just as there will also be false teachers among you, who will secretly introduce destructive heresies, even denying the Master who bought them, bringing swift destruction upon themselves" (2 Pet. 2:1, NASB).

Put together inductively, these verses result in the almost inescapable conviction that the value of Christ's atoning death is the same for all mankind. The fact that some are saved and some are not is never to be explained on the basis of any limitation at the Cross or in the selective will of God.

SUMMARY

The biblical basis for the fact of the Atonement is so firmly laid that no one need miss the glorious and mysterious truth: "Christ died for our sins" (1 Cor. 15:3). He was "put to death for our trespasses and raised for our justification" (Rom. 4:25, RSV). The greatest minds of the Church have sought to explain *how* eternal life issues from Calvary. In the end, one must admit that the *how* may never be as clear as the *that*, or the theory as deeply satisfying as the fact. Faith accepts the reality while it seeks to understand its mystery.

The next topic is closely related to the doctrine of atonement, building upon it as superstructure upon foundation. For atonement issues in redemption, the first stage of which is reconciliation to God. The basis upon which we come to God is clearly stated in our Christian faith.

PART III

God's Redemptive Purpose

CHAPTER 13

The Conditions of Reconciliation

Two missionaries, busy proclaiming the gospel and bringing healing to bodies and minds, had been arrested, beaten, and locked in a dungeon. With irrepressible spirits, they prayed and sang praises to God, in the presence of the other prisoners. Suddenly and unexpectedly, an earthquake rocked the jail and broke the inmates loose from their shackles. The jailer, who guarded the prisoners with his life, was on the point of committing suicide, when one of the missionaries cried out the assurance that no one had escaped.

His own life spared, the jailer "called for a light, and sprang in, and came trembling before Paul and Silas" (the missionaries) "and said, Sirs, what must I do to be saved?" (Acts 16:29-30). The jailer in the city of Philippi had given expression to a universal and haunting conviction: man needs salvation and looks for a Savior.

The principal concern of the Bible is the redemption of men, their reconciliation to God. For this reason, God chose a people, Israel, *to* whom He could speak by His prophets, and *through* whom He could prepare a Savior. What Jesus Christ wrought *for* us in His life, death, and resurrection, the Holy Spirit seeks to make real and actual *in* us.

Despite very real and substantial differences among Christians at this point, most are agreed that man is in need of salvation, not from his frailties, but from a profound moral problem—sin. They are also agreed that this salvation is by the grace of God, through faith, rather than through man's self-improvement. Salvation, it is further agreed, results in certain radical changes in man's status before God and in his actual moral and spiritual condition.

The chief differences in this area of theology are, first, between Roman Catholics and Protestants generally, who hold quite different views on the relation of the church to salvation; and secondly, between two large groups of Protestant Christians: in general, those of the Calvinists or Reformed tradition and those of the Arminian-Wesleyan persuasion. In addition to this, many theologians of a more liberal stamp seem not to give much attention to the order of salvation *(ordo salutis)* at all, passing at once from the doctrine of the Incarnation to that of the Church and the sacraments.[1]

The concern of this chapter will be to describe *the first steps* in the process whereby a sinner, rebellious and without spiritual life, becomes a child of God, reconciled and forgiven, a new creature in Christ Jesus.

I. THE DIVINE INITIATIVE

In our own time we have seen a renewed emphasis upon the doctrine that God has taken the initiative in the redemption of men. Some years ago in Los angeles, Lynn Harold Hough, of Drew University, was lecturing to a large group of ministers on current leaders of Christian thought. In discussing the contribution of Karl Barth he likened this theologian's message to the story of a dramatic rescue. A group of men, at work in a coal mine, were trapped deep in the earth because of the cave-in of a shaft. Their only hope lay in rescue from the outside. This, Dr. Hough said, is what the great continental theologian is trying to say. Man is entombed under the thralldom of sin, and God, by His grace, is seeking his rescue. The initiative is God's.

While such an analogy may be distorted, it is fair to say that our time has brought a fresh emphasis upon the needed divine initiative. If man is ever to be saved, it must be through the grace and power of God.

A. Salvation Through Grace

Grace has been defined as "the unmerited favor of God." It has also been described as "God's personal attitude toward man, His action and influence upon him."[2] The grace of God is the fountain of all our

---

1. Cf. John B. Harrington, *Essentials in Christian Faith* (New York: Harper and Brothers, 1958), where one searches the index in vain for such terms as salvation, repentance, justification, regeneration, sanctification, etc.

2. A. T. Mollegen, "Grace," *A Handbook of Christian Theology,* Marvin Halverson and Arthur A. Cohen, editors (New York: Meridian Books, Inc., 1958), p. 154.

blessings, but particularly do we relate the grace of God to the salvation of man. "For by grace are ye saved through faith; and that not of yourselves: it is the gift of God" (Eph. 2:8).

If the Holy Spirit may be described as "God dynamically present with us," we may say that the Holy Spirit communicates the grace of God to us. It is by the Spirit that God calls men unto salvation; it is by the Spirit that He convicts them of sin and awakens them to their need. It is by the power of the Holy Spirit that men turn unto God in repentance and faith, and it is by the Spirit that men are born again and renewed in the image of God.

We are concerned here, however, with what has been termed prevenient grace (the grace that *goes before* salvation). John Wesley said that prevenient grace includes:

> . . . the first wish to please God, the first dawn of light concerning his will, and the first transient conviction of having sinned against him. All these imply some tendency toward life; some degree of salvation; the beginning of a deliverance from a blind, unfeeling heart, quite insensible of God and the things of God.[3]

Prevenient grace is ". . . mercy towards the guilty and help for the impotent soul."[4]

For those who take seriously the biblical doctrine of original sin and total depravity, a significant problem exists at this point. If man is indeed "dead in trespasses and sins" (Eph. 2:1), so that ". . . he cannot now turn and prepare himself by his own natural strength and works to faith and calling upon God,"[5] how *can* he be saved?

As noted above, real differences arise at this point, particularly between those who follow the conclusions of Arminius and Wesley and those who accept the teachings of John Calvin. Both of these groups look back to the Reformation with great appreciation, hold the Bible to be the Word of God, and are in the forefront of present-day conservative Christianity. Nonetheless, a very real difference of conviction between them does exist on this issue and should be faced forthrightly.

Those of the Reformed or Calvinist tradition believe that because a sinner is dead in trespasses and sins he cannot possibly desire to be saved, or repent and believe on Jesus Christ, until he has been regenerated, or made alive to spiritual realities. Consequently, in this

---

3. Burtner and Chiles, *Compend of Wesley's Theology,* pp. 139-40.
4. Pope, *Compendium of Christian Theology,* 2:359.
5. *Manual,* Church of the Nazarene, current issue, *ad loc.*

view, the first step in reconciliation is regeneration or the awakening of the elect, those whom God has chosen. The next step is effectual calling (which cannot be resisted), followed by repentance, or conversion, faith, justification, sanctification, and perseverance (eternal security).

Those of the Arminian-Wesleyan persuasion, believing just as firmly in original sin and man's inability in spiritual things, hold the order of salvation to be quite different. Salvation is by the grace of God, but it is not restricted to a group arbitrarily limited by an unconditional election. It is for all men. Through the free gift of God's grace in Jesus Christ *all men, not merely the elect, are given a gracious* (as opposed to *natural*) ability to hear and heed the gospel call. Thus the first step in reconciliation is not an irresistible regeneration of certain ones arbitrarily chosen, but a universal bestowment of the grace of God upon *all* men, ". . . enabling all who will to turn from sin to righteousness, believe on Jesus Christ for pardon and cleansing from sin, and follow good works pleasing and acceptable in His sight."[6] Prevenient grace, then, enables the sinner, otherwise dead in trespasses and sins, to hear the gospel call, repent, and believe on the Lord Jesus Christ, and be saved. "Then as one man's trespass led to condemnation for all men, so one man's act of righteousness leads to acquittal and life for all men. For as by one man's disobedience many were made sinners, so by one man's obedience many will be made righteous" (Rom. 5:19-20).[7]

B. The Gospel Call

It is doubtful if the call of God to salvation has ever been uttered in more beautiful words than these words of Jesus: "Come unto me, all ye that labour and are heavy laden, and I will give you rest. Take my yoke upon you, and learn of me; for I am meek and lowly in heart: and ye shall find rest unto your souls. For my yoke is easy, and my burden is light" (Matt. 11:28-30).

1. *Definitions and Implications*

The gospel call is just what the words imply: a summons to an individual to accept the gospel. As H. Orton Wiley says, "The first

---

6. *Ibid.*

7. The entire context, especially Rom. 5:12-21, should be studied carefully for an understanding of Paul's teaching on the *free gift*, or *prevenient grace*. The RSV, from which this quotation is taken, is recommended for this reference.

step toward salvation in the experience of the soul, begins with vocation or the gracious call of God which is both direct through the Spirit and immediate through the Word."[8] God's call is to His kingdom and glory (1 Thess. 2:12), to salvation (2 Thess. 2:13-14), to life eternal (1 Tim. 6:12), to His marvelous light (1 Pet. 2:9).

There is a universal call to all men by means of agencies other than the Word in the Scriptures (see Rom. 1:18-20), and a particular or direct call through the preaching of the gospel. The former is inadequate without the latter, however, so the Church is required to teach all nations its message. "How then shall they call on him in whom they have not believed? and how shall they believe in him of whom they have not heard? and how shall they hear without a preacher?" (Rom. 10:14) It is by the grace of God and through the preaching of the gospel that the call comes to men (see Gal. 1:15 and 2 Thess. 2:14).

The gospel call may be seriously offered to all men, for it is universally intended, and, by the prevenient grace of God, is sufficient and efficacious. The Calvinistic notion that God offers an external call to the nonelect and an internal, effective call to the elect only is repugnant to the whole tenor of the Bible and to what we know about the God of John 3:16, who is no respecter of persons (Acts 10:34).

Two observations should be made before passing on to further implications of the gospel call. If it is the intention of God that all men should hear the gospel, then it is the obligation of the Church to be earnest and diligent in obeying the Great Commission (Matt. 28:19-20). God has made us our brothers' keepers in this as in other concerns; if all men are to hear the gospel call, the Church *must* "make disciples of all nations" (Matt. 28:19, RSV).

The other observation is that, although the gospel call is genuine and efficacious, it is not compulsive. The call to salvation is an invitation, not an irresistible demand. The grace of God, we must solemnly remember, *may* be resisted. God *is* almighty and man's freedom *is* limited, but God has chosen to limit himself by giving one of His creatures real, though limited, freedom. If this be not true, then man is not responsible for moral choices and God is the only real Person in the universe. When Jesus wept over the city of Jerusalem, knowing what her final end would be, He certainly seemed to

---

8. *Christian Theology,* 2:340.

recognize this dreadful power in man: "O Jerusalem, Jerusalem, . . . how often would I have gathered thy children together, . . . and ye would not!" (Matt. 23:37). This matter will be discussed later in the section on "The Human Response," but let it be said here that a great many scriptures are rendered meaningless unless it be granted that man *may* resist the grace of God—to his own ruin.

2. *The Meaning of Predestination and Election*

In the New Testament there is a close relationship between the gospel call and predestination or election. One author has cited several instances of such a relationship (see Rom. 8:28-30; 9:11, 23 f.; 2 Thess. 2:13 f.; 2 Tim. 1:9; 2 Pet. 1:10).[9] It may be well, then, at this point to discuss the meaning of predestination and election.[10]

A study of the foregoing references will reveal a clear connection between "calling" and "election." Rom. 8:28, for example, speaks of those "who are the called according to his purpose." The following verses go on to describe a process wherein, *apparently,* God calls only those who are foreordained and predestinated, and guarantees their justification and glorification. Even more difficult is Rom. 9:11, where Paul has been alleged to argue that both election and calling are arbitrary and unconditional, independent of any attitude or conduct upon the part of men. The other reference *may* be interpreted in the same way. It is important to note, moreover, that such passages as Rom. 9:10-13 refer to the election of *nations* rather than individuals, as Gen. 25:22-23 and Mal. 1:2-4 make clear.[11]

Thus far, however, we have urged that the gospel call is an earnest, honest invitation to all men, that it is efficacious to all who receive it, but that it may be resisted. In the light of the scripture references just cited, can the Arminian-Wesleyan interpretations be defended? What is the meaning of predestination or election, and how is the gospel call related?

---

9. Millar Burrows, *An Outline of Biblical Theology* (Philadelphia: Westminster Press, 1946), p. 232, n. 2.

10. A distinction is sometimes made between predestination and election. H. Orton Wiley makes such a distinction: "The church is both predestinated and elected, the former referring to the plan of redemption as manifested in the universal call; the latter to the elect or chosen ones who have closed in with the offers of mercy." See his *Christian Theology,* 2:337-38. This difference, however, is not often made, writers usually holding the terms to be interchangeable. *Webster's New International Dictionary of the English Language,* second edition, unabridged, uses each term as a synonym of the other. The terms are used interchangeabley in this chapter.

11. Cf. *Beacon Bible Commentary,* 8:203.

In the words of H. Orton Wiley, "Predestination is the gracious purpose of God to save mankind from utter ruin. It is not an arbitrary, indiscriminate act of God intended to secure the salvation of so many and no more. It includes provisionally all men in its scope, and is conditioned solely on faith in Jesus Christ."[12] This view is what has been called single predestination.

The next thing that must be said, however, is that biblical predestination is imponderable and indefensible unless each reference is seen in its immediate context and in the context of the entire Bible. That God has arbitrarily predestined some to salvation and others to perdition is the doctrine of double predestination and, in the Arminian view, is foreign to the tenor of Scripture.

The biblical references quoted above can be and have been interpreted to teach absolute, unconditional predestination. John Calvin, of course, has made this view famous, though he was not the first to advocate it:

> Predestination we call the eternal decree of God, by which he has determined in himself, what he would have to become of every individual of mankind. For they are not all created with a similar destiny; but eternal life is foreordained for some, and eternal damnation for others. Every man, therefore, being created for one or the other of these ends, is, we say predestined either to life or to death.[13]

Anyone is free to accept this interpretation if he chooses, but even the professed followers of Calvin have modified his views considerably, some adopting a *sublapsarian* view (that election occurs *after* the Fall; hence, in this view, all are guilty anyway), others adopting flat contradictions (that God has absolutely predestined all; *even so, men are free and responsible*) or leaving the whole matter in the realm of mystery. If one decides that Calvin's view is essentially correct, he must then be prepared to accept the implications: man is not free nor responsible. Unconditional predestination is determinism pure and simple. Who is willing to defend such a position?

With respect to the references in Romans, however, the context makes it clear that Paul intended no such teaching as rigid predestinarians have drawn from them. In Romans 8, Paul is encouraging the Christians to believe that in their sufferings God will not forsake

---

12. *Christian Theology*, 2:337.

13. John Calvin, *Institutes of the Christian Religion*, translated by Henry Beveridge, 2 vols. (Grand Rapids: Wm. B. Eerdmans Publishing Co., 1953), III, xxi, 5.

them, but has promised to save them to the uttermost by His great power (see Rom. 8:31-39). The key expression in this instance is "called according to his purpose." Note, however, that the purpose of God is the redemption of "all things in Christ" (Eph. 1:10). Accordingly, Paul felt himself a debtor to preach the gospel to *all* men, ". . . both to the Greeks, and to the Barbarians; both to the wise, and to the unwise. . . . for it is the power of God unto salvation to every one that believeth" (Rom. 1:14, 16). Nowhere does Rom. 8:28-30 indicate that the "calling" is limited. In fact, Paul gives the lie to such a view in his own earnest labors, ". . . warning *every* man, and teaching *every* man in all wisdom; that we may present *every* man perfect in Christ Jesus" (Col. 1:28, italics added).

Moreover, as John Wesley said:

> St. Paul does not affirm, either here or in any other part of his writings, that precisely that same number of men are called, justified, and glorified. He does not deny that a believer may fall away and be cut off between his special calling and his glorification (Rom. xi. 22). Neither does he deny that many are called who are never justified. He only affirms that this is the method whereby God leads us step by step toward heaven.[14]

With respect to the references in Romans 9, it must be remembered that in the three chapters, Romans 9—11, Paul is setting forth his reasons why the Jews have not accepted Christ. His conclusion is that, in the providence of God, the Jews, like olive branches, have been broken off from the trunk, whereas the Gentiles, like wild olive branches, have been grafted in. The first were broken off because of unbelief, and the second were grafted in by faith. The former may yet be returned to the tree, if they believe, whereas the latter could be broken off also, unless they ". . . continue in his goodness . . ." (Rom. 11:17-24). There is certainly no unconditional election here. As Edwin Lewis reminds us:

> What Paul says about foreknowledge, predestination, election, and reprobation must not be so understood as to take all meaning out of what he says about human freedom and responsibility, the universality of God's grace, and the reason why Christ came into the world.[15]

The biblical teaching on predestination or election means, first, that God is sovereign, free to do whatever He chooses to do, and sec-

---

14. *Explanatory Notes upon the New Testament*, p. 551.

15. "Predestination," *Harper's Bible Dictionary*, M. S. Miller and J. L. Miller, editors (New York: Harper and Brothers, 1952), p. 577.

ondly, that salvation is by His grace and power alone. Believers are saved by the power of God through faith. God has foreordained that believers will be saved and unbelievers lost. Man's true destiny is to be conformed "to the image of His Son," but only those who respond in faith to the gospel call are among the elect. The elect, so defined, are predestined to be saved, and not by their own efforts, but by the power of God. This is the religious value of biblical predestination.

Someone has told the story of a man who in the dead of winter was crossing a frozen river. Fearful lest the ice should break, he gingerly made his way on hands and knees, testing the ice before him. He was amazed, however, soon to hear the clatter made by another man driving a team and wagon across the river at the same point. Some believers live the Christian life with as little faith as the man crossing the river in fear. The biblical doctrine of predestination should teach us to have faith in the power of God not only to begin but also to consummate our salvation.

James Arminius wrote of predestination:

> It is an eternal and gracious decree of God in Christ, by which he determines to justify and adopt believers, and to endow them with life eternal, but to condemn unbelievers and impenitent persons . . .[16]

The words of John Wesley on the subject are very similar:

> I believe election means . . . a divine appointment of some men to eternal happiness. But I believe this election to be conditional, as well as the reprobation opposite thereto. I believe the eternal decree concerning both is expressed in those words: "He that believeth shall be saved; he that believeth not shall be damned." And this decree, without doubt, God will not change, and man cannot resist.[17]

3. *The Relationship Between the Gospel Call and Election.*

The God who loves all the world calls upon His Church to take the gospel invitation to all men, for God "will have all men to be saved, and to come unto the knowledge of the truth" (1 Tim. 2:4). For this cause Christ Jesus "gave himself a ransom for all" (1 Tim. 2:6).

It is true, as Jesus said, that "many are called, but few are chosen" (Matt. 22:14). But it is evident from the total context of the Bible that God is calling *all* men, and that men are elected or chosen be-

---

16. *The Writings of Arminius*, James Nichols and W. R. Bagnall, editors (Grand Rapids: Baker Book House, reprint, 1956), 2:470.

17. Burtner and Chiles, *Compend of Wesley's Theology*, p. 54.

cause they believe; they do not believe because they have been elected. "Wherefore the rather, brethren, give diligence to make your
calling and election sure: for if ye do these things, ye shall never fall"
(2 Pet. 1:10).

II. THE HUMAN RESPONSE

Both the Scriptures and Christian theologians of all persuasions
teach that after the Spirit has made the offer of salvation to a sinner
he must respond of his own choice. Even those steeped in Augustin-
ian-Calvinism believe, with magnificent inconsistency, that *after* the
elect have been irresistibly regenerated, they will in freedom repent
and believe unto salvation. Thus St. Augustine himself is credited
with the assertion, "He that made us without ourselves, will not save
us without ourselves."

Indeed a good deal of the controversy between Calvinism and
Arminianism, at this juncture, is a striving about words. Both sides,
as noted above, believe in the total inability of the natural man apart
from grace, and both believe that only the "whosoever will" (Rev.
22:17) can be saved. The following, for example, is from John Wesley, a strong Arminian:

> It was impossible for Lazarus to come forth, till the Lord had
> given him life. And it is equally impossible for us to come out of
> our sins, yea, or to make the least motion toward it, till He who
> hath all power in heaven and earth calls our dead souls into
> life.[18]

The above may be compared with a quotation from Kenneth J.
Foreman, a contemporary Calvinist, and will show how much agreement actually does exist between these two viewpoints:

> No Christian thinker denies these New Testament promises
> (John 6:37; Rev. 22:17), which in simplest language possible
> declare that any one who seriously desires to be saved can be and
> will be saved.... But in either case it is agreed that the readiness
> of God antedates the readiness of man; that without the readiness
> of God, without his saving power, the willingness of man would
> be frustrated.[19]

A clear biblical example of the balance between the divine initiative and the human response is found in Phil. 2:12-13: "Wherefore,

---

18. *Ibid.*, p. 148.

19. "Soteriology," *Twentieth Century Encyclopedia of Religious Knowledge*, Lefferts A.
Loetscher, editor (Grand Rapids: Baker Book House, 1955), p. 1050.

my beloved, . . . work out your own salvation with fear and trembling. For it is God which worketh in you both to will and to do of his good pleasure." As John Wesley once urged in a sermon,[20] God works in us; therefore we *can* work; it would not be possible otherwise. God works in us; therefore we *must* work. The human response to the divine initiative is mandatory: "Behold, I stand at the door, and knock: if any man hear my voice, and open the door, I will come in to him, and will sup with him, and he with me" (Rev. 3:20).

A. Repentance

The gospel call becomes effective to the unregenerate when the Holy Spirit draws him, by means of the Word of truth, to an awareness of his spiritual need (see John 6:44; 1 Cor. 2:4; 1 Thess. 2:13). It is the work of the Holy Spirit to bring awakening and conviction to the unredeemed, and this occurs as He comes to the Church (John 16:8), through it bringing awakening and conviction to the world. Wiley and Culbertson state:

> Awakening is a term used in theology to denote that operation of the Holy Spirit by which men's minds are quickened to a consciousness of their lost estate . . . Conviction is that operation of the Spirit which produces within men a sense of guilt and condemnation because of sin. To the idea of awakening there is added that of personal blame.[21]

The hearts of men are pierced and opened by the Spirit through a demonstration of the truth (see Acts 2:37; 16:14).

The first step in the human response, repentance, occurs at this point. Awakened to his condition, convicted of personal guilt, the seeking sinner is called upon to *repent*.

What does it mean to repent? Repentance has been defined as ". . . a sincere and thorough change of mind in regard to sin . . ."[22] Repentance is required of all who by act or intention have become sinners. This, of course, would include all men. God now commands "all men every where to repent" (Acts 17:30); "For all have sinned, and come short of the glory of God" (Rom. 3:23).

Repentance in the Old Testament was expressed by the words "turn" and "return" and carried with it the thought of rebellious subjects returning to their rightful king, or a faithless spouse return-

---

20. Burtner and Chiles, *Compend of Wesley's Theology,* pp. 148-49.
21. *Introduction to Christian Theology,* p. 260.
22. *Manual,* Church of the Nazarene, current issue, *ad loc.*

ing to his or her mate. It is thus clear that to repent meant more than merely a change of mind or a reversal of judgment. Some examples of the morally neutral use of the word may be found in the Old Testament, particularly where it is said that God had repented of a certain course of action. However, to repent in the sense of turning back to God from idols and false gods involved a more profound decision. It called for a reorientation of the entire person. What the Lord required was not sacrifice, but a clean heart.

Likewise, in the New Testament, repentance calls for a radical change of the personality. To repent is to turn from sin with real regret and to turn to God in confession, submission, and amendment of life. Just as in the Old Testament, Christian repentance means a basic reorientation of the whole person: his mind, his feelings, his will. It is easy to limit repentance to regret and willingness to make amends; this led to the Roman Catholic idea of penance. It is also easy to restrict repentance to the emotional reaction of remorse and sorrow, but this too is inadequate.

Repentance means a radical break with sin and an earnest turning to God. It is for this reason that some theologians consider this moment to be, in its narrower sense, conversion. In common usage, conversion often refers to the entire process of repentance, faith, and salvation, but in a narrow sense it may also designate "the process by which the soul turns, or is turned from sin to God, in order to its acceptance through faith in Christ."[23] It is thus closely related to, though not identical with, repentance in the aspect of turning away from sin; and also to faith, in the turning to God.

It may also be noted that in the New Testament, with a growing revelation of the nature of God, a better understanding of sin and repentance also came. Sin is to be seen, not only in acts that are wrong, but also in the quality of spirit, the intention, or motive life. Thus David did well to repent of his adultery and murder, but these were also crimes. Jesus taught that such sins are first matters of the heart and disposition and call for repentance at the center of the person. Edwin Lewis writes: "Men are called upon to repent not merely for the evil things they do, but for their evil thoughts and purposes and for that in themselves that leads them to evil."[24]

Repentance, then, is a *sine qua non* of entrance into the kingdom

---

23. Pope, *Compendium of Christian Theology,* 2:367.
24. "Repentance," *Harper's Bible Dictionary,* p. 609.

of God. When Jesus began His ministry in Galilee, it is recorded that He preached the gospel of the kingdom of God, saying, "Repent ye, and believe the gospel" (Mark 1:15). The necessity of repentance arises from the nature of sin as rebellion against God. Sin is destructive to happiness and holiness alike. Unless one turns from sin in complete renunciation he cannot find either fulfillment or goodness. "I tell you, Nay: but, except ye repent, ye shall all likewise perish" (Luke 13:3).

The question may be raised, If this be such a significant step, is it an act of God or of man? It is both. It is the gift of God, as the Bible plainly states (see Acts 5:31; 11:18, Rom. 2:4; 2 Tim. 2:25), but it is a gift of capacity. Just as God *assists* man in his thinking and feeling, without setting them aside, so He assists man in his choices and decisions, including his purpose to repent. Repentance is an act of man, but the possibility is offered to man in the prevenient grace of God.

In summary, it may be said that repentance implies conviction for sin, godly sorrow for such wrongdoing, admission of guilt in confession, and reformation of life. Where it is possible and feasible, restitution may be made as an evidence of amendment. Such restitution should be thought of as an expression of purpose to reform one's way of living and not as an act of penance calculated to purchase divine favor. In returning to God, man does in the truest sense return to himself and to his neighbor; thus through acts of restoration one may "bear fruits that befit repentance" (Luke 3:8, RSV).

It is often said that, although Protestants do not believe in the sacrament of *penance,* they do believe that an attitude of penitence is appropriate to anyone who has been redeemed from sin. One remembers in gratitude his deliverance and looks upon present limitations and faults with regret, praying both to be forgiven any possible trespass and to be given grace to become a finer, better child of God.

Before leaving the discussion of repentance and turning to faith, the next condition of reconciliation, we should pause to note the inherent relation between them. What God hath joined together none of us should rend asunder! Repentance presupposes a prior faith: "How then shall they call on him in whom they have not believed?" (Rom. 10:14), and faith implies a prior repentance. Paul testified that his own preaching called for "repentance toward God, and faith toward our Lord Jesus Christ" (Acts 20:21). Salvation is indeed by faith alone, but faith springs out of and follows repentance. Jesus indicated the connection between the two when He began His public preaching ministry with the declaration that men should repent and believe the gospel (Mark 1:15). Repentance is in order to saving faith. Faith without preexisting repentance is presumption, but repentance divorced from faith leaves one in the outer court, still under the law. Both repentance and faith are gifts of God, and wherever Jesus met men in personal encounter He brought both. Zacchaeus, for example, truly repented, giving evidence of it in generous restitution. But he evidently also believed, for Jesus testified of him, "This day is salvation come to this house" (Luke 19:9).

B. Faith

The term *faith,* as we have seen, has several shades of meaning. In some instances it stands for a tenet or article of belief. A book on theology, for example, may bear the title *The Christian Faith.* Belief or assent is one usage of the word faith. Faith also may imply dependability or reliability. This is the meaning of faith in Paul's list of the fruit of the Spirit in Gal. 5:22-23. Faith, in this case, means fidelity or faithfulness. In addition to these meanings, faith carries another commonly used in everyday life. This is *trust.* We have faith in the grocer when we buy the food he sells; we exercise faith when we deposit money in the bank, or ride in an automobile, or buy a prescription from the druggist. It is our present concern, however, to think of faith as a condition of salvation, or as a part of the human response to the divine initiative. An understanding of the shades of meaning just discussed will help us as we seek to learn the meaning of saving faith.

What is this faith that is a condition of reconciliation? What does it mean when the Scriptures say, "Believe on the Lord Jesus Christ, and thou shalt be saved" (Acts 16:31)? The consensus of biblical scholars is that both in the Old Testament and in the New the primary element in faith is trust. The Hebrew word translated "faith" carries with it in almost every case the thought of reliance upon God. The same idea may be seen in the best-known verse of the Bible: "For God so loved the world, that he gave his only begotten Son, that whosoever believeth *in* him should not perish . . ." (John 3:16). Here also is the thought of a firm reliance upon, a confident trust in, the Son of God. If the primary element in faith is trust, then ". . . saving faith is a personal trust in the Person of the Saviour."[25]

Faith includes an assent of the mind to elements of truth, for

25. Wiley, *Christian Theology,* 2:367.

salvation is difficult if not impossible without some knowledge of the gospel. But faith is more than assent. Orthodox belief alone does not guarantee salvation. Faith also includes a willingness to follow the Savior in obedience. This is evident from the nature of repentance as, in part, a reformation of life. But faith is more than consent to moral obligation. Saving faith is an act of the entire being; assenting to such truth as may be known, consenting to the plea for obedience in careful discipleship, the repentant believer stakes his all upon the Redeemer. This is stated by John Wesley:

> The true, living, Christian faith, which whosoever hath that is born of God, is not only an assent, an act of the understanding; but a disposition, which God hath wrought in the heart; "a sure trust and confidence in God, that, through the merits of Christ, his sins are forgiven, and he is reconciled to the favour of God."[26]

It may be appropriate here to raise the question in what sense faith is the sole condition of salvation. The Protestant Reformation resurrected the important Christian doctrine of justification by faith alone. In describing faith as *one* of the conditions of reconciliation, have we nullified a basic tenet of Protestantism? No one has ever stated more emphatically that faith is the *only necessary* condition of salvation than John Wesley; yet he also preached with equal vigor the necessity of repentance as a prerequisite of faith, and good works as a necessary consequent of faith. A certain knowledge of the way of salvation, for example, is necessary to saving faith. And surely both Scripture and experience make it plain that no man can really have faith unto salvation who has not turned from his sins in a radical change of mind and heart.

An attempt has already been made, in the previous section, to indicate the essential unity of repentance and faith. Implicit in the very act of believing on the Lord Jesus Christ is the turning away from other masters. The basic change of mind defined as repentance is actually a vital element in saving faith. Paul implied that when he wrote the infant church in Thessalonica, ". . . ye turned to God from idols to serve the living and true God" (1 Thess. 1:9). Nonetheless, it is essential to realize that salvation is by faith, rather than works, for it is the gift of God's grace.

> *In my hand no price I bring;*
> *Simply to Thy cross I cling.*

---

26. Burtner and Chiles, *Compend of Wesley's Theology*, p. 160.

No price, not even repentance, restitution, good works, or the act of faith itself, can purchase redemption. Salvation is by grace through faith; it is a gift of God.

SUMMARY

The purpose of the chapter has been to set forth those conditions that are necessary to reconciliation. We have said that God has taken the initiative in the redemption of man. God has called us by His grace, shown us our true destiny, yet has left the final decision with us. Through the free gift of prevenient grace, procured by the death of His Son, God has granted to all men a *gracious* ability to hear and heed the gospel invitation. This calls for a free response on the part of man; otherwise he is not a person. When the Church does its work, in the power of the Spirit, sinners are awakened and convicted of their sins. And when these, whose hearts have been opened, turn from their sins to believe on the Lord Jesus Christ, they will be saved. "For whosoever shall call upon the name of the Lord shall be saved. . . . as it is written, How beautiful are the feet of them that preach the gospel of peace, and bring glad tidings of good things!" (Rom. 10:13, 15).

We move on now to a study of the nature of the new life in Christ which is the end and purpose of our Christian faith.

CHAPTER 14

The New Life

One of the classic declarations of the New Testament is that of St. Paul: "Therefore if any man be in Christ, he is a new creature: old things are passed away; behold, all things are become new" (2 Cor. 5:17). Men made new by the power of God are the credentials of the Christian gospel.

Our purpose in this chapter is to examine the nature of the gracious act of God by which men enter newness of life in Christ. Actually it is a three-sided miracle. Known commonly as conversion, this personal crisis to be understood must be viewed from different scriptural perspectives. Seen from one vantage point this change is *justification;* from another it is *regeneration;* from yet another, *adoption.* A treatment of this subject would be incomplete, moreover, without a delineation of the doctrine of the *witness of the Spirit.*

In popular religious speech the initial crisis of grace is called *conversion.* There are some advantages to this term. It is a term easily understood, meaning literally *a turning.* This is true in both the original languages of the Bible and in English. Furthermore, the term has the advantage of being comprehensive; it embraces the entire crisis of initial salvation. Properly speaking, justification and adoption describe the objective phases of this crisis, while regeneration and the witness of the Spirit treat its subjective aspects. To refer to the initial crisis of personal salvation as justification alone, as we often do, is either to stress only one side of the experience or use the term in a wider sense than it technically applies. To refer to it as regeneration or the new birth is to stress the subjective phase of the experience and the moral and spiritual changes which it accomplishes. But to refer to the first work of grace as conversion is to speak broadly and comprehensively.

While conversion has the advantage in popular religious terminology, in the Bible the term is generally used in a narrower sense to describe the human side of a person's turning from sin to salvation. Once in the Old Testament conversion is placed before repentance: "After that I was turned, I repented" (Jer. 31:19). Usually, however, it is connected with repentance as the human act of turning from sin, as in Isaiah, as quoted by our Lord: "Lest at any time they should see with their eyes, and hear with their ears, and should understand with their heart, and should be converted, and I should heal them" (Matt. 13:15). We remember Jesus' categorical statement: "Except ye be converted, and become as little children, ye shall not enter into the kingdom of heaven" (Matt. 18:3). St. Peter also used the term in his second recorded sermon: "Repent ye therefore, and be converted, that your sins may be blotted out" (Acts 3:19).[1] The various passages employing the term seem to substantiate the position of Dr. Wiley: "Through grace, preveniently bestowed, man turns to God and is then regenerated. Thus conversion in its truest scriptural meaning is the pivotal point, wherein through grace, the soul turns from sin, and to Christ, in order to regeneration."[2]

I. Justification

Justification by faith is one of the cardinal principles of the New Testament. Martin Luther spoke of it as the article upon which the Church stands or falls. If we lose the doctrine of justification by faith, the whole structure of evangelical religion will collapse. Give up this doctrine, says Bishop Merrill, and the name of Jesus loses its charm, the Blood is robbed of its efficacy, and the Spirit is reduced to a mere idea devoid of power to quicken the soul into the life of righteousness. Along with the dethronement of Christ will come the undue exaltation of human virtue and a loss of the sense of the exceeding sinfulness of sin. John Wesley put the matter simply and positively when he exclaimed, "Pardoning love is the root of it all."

A. Justification Defined

Justification may be defined as "that gracious and judicial act of God,

---

1. Wiley, *Christian Theology,* 2:376-77. For a treatment of these topics from the point of view of biblical theology, see Purkiser, Taylor, and Taylor, *God, Man, and Salvation,* pp. 439-62.

2. *Ibid.,* p. 378.

by which He grants full pardon of all guilt and complete release from the penalty of sins committed, and acceptance as righteous, to all who believingly receive Jesus Christ as Lord and Saviour."[3] Mr. Wesley observes, "The plain, scriptural notion of justification is pardon, the forgiveness of sins. It is that act of God the Father whereby, for the sake of the propitiation made by the blood of his Son, he showeth forth his righteousness [or mercy] by the remission of sins that are past."[4]

To be justified, therefore, is (1) to be pardoned from sin, (2) to stand acquitted before the bar of divine justice, (3) to be accepted into the favor of God, not on the basis of any meritorious works of our own but solely on the condition of our faith in Christ's propitiatory sufferings.

B. The Ground and Conditions of Justification

The human condition of our acceptance before God is *sola fides,* faith alone. After arraigning the entire human race before the judgment bar of God and pronouncing them guilty, St. Paul wrote:

> But now *the righteousness of God* without the law is manifested, being witnessed by the law and the prophets; even the righteousness of God which is by faith of Jesus Christ unto all and upon all them that believe: for there is no difference: for all have sinned, and come short of the glory of God;
> Being justified freely by his grace through the redemption that is in Christ Jesus: whom God hath set forth to be a propitiation through faith in his blood, to declare his righteousness for the remission of sins that are past, through the forbearance of God; to declare, I say, at this time his righteousness: that he might be just, and the justifier of him that believeth in Jesus. . . . *Therefore we conclude that a man is justified by faith without the deeds of the law* (Rom. 3:21-26, 28, italics added).

This passage is the *locus classicus* of the doctrine of justification by faith. (1) Man's righteousness has utterly failed. (2) In the gospel God's righteousness is disclosed. Since God has provided Christ as a propitiatory Offering for the sins of the world, the way is now open for the Father to pardon the penitent believer in Jesus without sacrificing His own perfect justice. (3) On these grounds a man is justified by faith without the deeds of the law.

---

3. *Manual,* Church of the Nazarene, current issue, *ad loc.*

4. Quoted by Wilbur F. Tillett, *Personal Salvation* (Nashville: Cokesbury Press, 1930), p. 214.

C. The Nature of Justification

1. *Justification and Righteousness.*

In defending his doctrine of justification by faith alone St. Paul cites the Old Testament example of Abraham. It must have come as quite a shock to the Jews to be shown from the Scriptures that Father Abraham was justified, not by works, but by faith. Paul's proof is drawn from Gen. 15:6, "For what saith the scripture? Abraham believed God, and it was counted to him for righteousness" (Rom. 4:3). Applying this principle to us Paul declares, "To him that worketh not, but believeth on him that justifieth the ungodly, *his faith is counted for righteousness*" (4:5, italics added).

Neither here nor anywhere else do we find set forth the idea that Christ's personal, active obedience to God is substituted for the believer's disobedience. Such a mechanical view of imputation is repugnant to the conscience and foreign to the Word of God. Safeguarding the true doctrine of imputation from this perversion, Mr. Wesley cautioned:

> Least of all does justification imply, that God is deceived in those whom He justifies; that He thinks them to be what, in fact, they are not; that He accounts them to be otherwise than they . are. It does by no means imply, that God judges concerning us contrary to the real nature of things; that He esteems us better than we really are, or believes us righteous when we are unrighteous. Surely no. The judgment of the all-wise God is always according to truth. *Neither can it ever consist with His unerring wisdom, to think that I am innocent, to judge that I am righteous or holy, because another is so. He can no more, in this manner, confound me with Christ, than with David or Abraham.*[5]

We do believe, however, that the New Testament teaches that on the grounds of Chirst's active righteousness (His sinlessness) and His passive righteousness (His sufferings) the just and holy God does pardon any individual who penitently receives Jesus Christ as his personal Savior. All who come to Him through Christ, God receives as righteous, no longer imputing their sins to them, but freely justifying them in spite of all their past misdeeds.

2. *Justification Is Pardon for Our Sins*

This is evident from the following scriptures (italics added): "Be it known unto you therefore, men and brethren, that through this

---

5. *Sermons:* "Justification by Faith"; quoted by Burtner and Chiles, *Compend of Wesley's Theology,* p. 163.

man is preached unto you *the forgiveness of sins:* and by him all that believe are *justified* from all things, from which ye could not be justified by the law of Moses" (Acts 13:38-39). "Whom God hath set forth to be a propitiation through faith in his blood, to declare his righteousness *for the remission of sins* that are past, through the forbearance of God; to declare, I say, at this time, his righteousness: that he might be just, and *the justifier* of him which believeth in Jesus" (Rom. 3:25-26). "But to him that worketh not, but believeth on him that *justifieth the ungodly,* his faith is counted for righteousness. Even as David also describeth the blessedness of the man, unto whom God *imputeth righteousness* without works, saying, Blessed are they whose *iniquities are forgiven,* and whose *sins are covered.* Blessed is the man to whom the Lord *will not impute sin"* (Rom. 4:5-8, italics added).

In these scriptures "justification," "the forgiveness of sins," "the remission of sins," "imputeth righteousness," and "not imputing their sins" are used interchangeably. We conclude, therefore, that they are practically synonymous.

3. Justification Is More than Pardon

If justification means only pardon, why do the Bible and theology insist on the more difficult term justification in preference to the simpler term? The answer is important. As far as the immediate salvation of the sinner is concerned, the important idea *is* pardon; but if the sinner's salvation is viewed from the higher perspective of the redemptive scheme, justification is a far more expressive and appropriate term. For this reason, in the words of A. A. Hodge:

> Justification is more than pardon. To *pardon* is, in the exercise of sovereign prerogative, to waive the execution of the penal sanctions of the law; to *justify* is to declare that the demands of the law are satisfied, not waived. Pardon is a sovereign act; justification is a judicial act.[6]

II. REGENERATION

Justification must never be considered alone but always as in vital relationship with regeneration. Justification and regeneration are like two sides of one coin. While expressing entirely different ideas, the two truths must always be kept close together. They are inseparably joined in experience; they must be linked in Christian thought also.

---

6. Quoted by Tillett, *Personal Salvation,* pp. 218-19.

"The necessity for justification lies in the fact of guilt and penalty, while that of regeneration is due to the moral depravity of human nature after the fall. The former cancels guilt and removes penalty; the latter renews the moral nature and re-establishes the privileges of sonship."[7] The two are concomitant in personal experience, although logically justification precedes regeneration.

Justification is what God does *for* us through Christ; regeneration is what God does *in* us through the Holy Spirit. Justification is objective, a change in relationship; regeneration is subjective, a change of nature. Justification means the imputation of righteousness; regeneration means the impartation of holiness.

Regeneration is thus the beginning of our personal sanctification. By the birth of the Spirit the renewal of our fallen natures in the image of Christ is begun. The new life principle imparted in regeneration is a principle of holy love. The new birth effects initial sanctification.

A. Regeneration Defined

"Regeneration, or the new birth, is that gracious work of God whereby the moral nature of the repentant believer is spiritually quickened and given a distinctively spiritual life, capable of faith, love, and obedience."[8]

The term *regeneration* is derived from the Greek word meaning literally "to be again" or "to become again." The *word* occurs only twice in the Bible, both times in the New Testament. One of these references is not generally regarded as applying to personal salvation (Matt. 19:28). In the other reference the word is used as we now use it. "Not by works of righteousness which we have done, but according to his mercy he saved us, by the washing of regeneration, and renewing of the Holy Ghost" (Titus 3:5).

The *idea* of regeneration is found throughout the New Testament expressed by many terms. These include "born of God" (John 1:13; 1 John 3:9; 4:7; 5:1, 18); "born again" (John 3:3, 5, 7; 1 Pet. 1:23); "born of the Spirit" (John 3:5-6); "quickened" (Eph. 2:1, 5; Col. 2:13); and "passed from death unto life" (John 5:24; 1 John 3:14).

In his "Sermon on the New Birth," John Wesley defines regeneration as "that great change which God works in the soul when He

---

7. Wiley, *Christian Theology,* 2:402.

8. *Manual,* Church of the Nazarene, current issue, *ad loc.*

brings it into life; when He raises it from the death of sin to the life of righteousness. It is the change wrought in the whole soul by the Almighty Spirit of God, when it is created anew in Christ Jesus; when it is renewed after the image of God in righteousness and true holiness." In a word, "Regeneration is the communication of life by the Spirit, to a soul dead in trespasses and sins."

B. The Nature of Regeneration

There is an element of mystery in the new birth. Speaking of this miracle Jesus said, "The wind bloweth where it listeth, and thou hearest the sound thereof, but canst not tell whence it cometh, and whither it goeth: so is every one that is born of the Spirit" (John 3:8). Regeneration is truth that transcends but does not contradict human reason. We know *that* it is; we cannot comprehend *how* it is.

1. *The Scriptural Method of Presenting Regeneration*

The Bible views this initial crisis of redemption in three ways:

a. It is represented as a divine generation. "Of his own will begat he us with the word of truth, that we should be a kind of firstfruits of his creatures" (Jas. 1:18). "Whosoever believeth that Jesus is the Christ is born of God: and every one that loveth him that begat loveth him also that is begotten of him" (1 John 5:1).

b. It is represented as a divine creation. "For we are his workmanship, created in Christ Jesus unto good works" (Eph. 2:10). "If any man be in Christ, he is a new creature: old things are passed away; behold, all things are become new" (2 Cor. 5:17). "For God, who commanded the light to shine out of darkness, hath shined in our hearts, to give the light of the knowledge of the glory of God in the face of Jesus Christ" (2 Cor. 4:6).

c. It is represented as a divine resurrection. "And you hath he quickened, who were dead in trespasses and sins" (Eph. 2:1). "And you, being dead in your sins and the uncircumcision of your flesh, hath he quickened together with him, having forgiven you all trespasses" (Col. 2:13).

2. *The Analogy of Creation*

Although the new birth cannot be described philosophically, it can be pictured analogically. St. Paul has given us an analogy which suggests something of the splendor of the new life into which he was introduced on the Damascus road. In 2 Cor. 4:6 he says: "For God, who commanded the light to shine out of darkness, hath shined in our hearts, to give the light of the knowledge of the glory of God in the face of Jesus Christ." James S. Stewart writes of this:

> Something had happened comparable only to the great *Fiat Lux* of creation's dawn. That the sublime passage in the Genesis prologue was actually in the apostle's mind seems beyond doubt. "The earth was without form and void"—had not his own soul known that chaos? "And darkness was upon the face of the deep" —was not that a very picture of his experience before Christ came? "But the Spirit of God was hovering over the waters"— and looking back, Paul could see how true it was that from his very birth . . . the Spirit of God had been brooding over him and guiding his destiny. "And God said, 'Let there be light': and there was light." To me, it was the birth of light and order and purpose and beauty, the ending of chaos and ancient night. And to me, as at that first creation, the morning stars sang together, and all the sons of God shouted for joy. God who said, "Let there be light," has shone within my heart; He has scorched me with His splendor, and remade me by His strength; and I now walk for ever in a marvelous light—the light of the knowledge of the glory of God in the face of Jesus Christ.[9]

3. *The Analogy of Birth*

John Wesley sees in the miracle of the new birth a very close analogy to the natural birth. A child in his mother's womb has eyes, but cannot see; he has ears, but cannot hear. The use of his other senses is very imperfectly developed, and he has no knowledge of any of the things of the world and no natural understanding whatever. The existence of the child in the womb is not usually called life. It is only when he is born into the world that we say he really begins to live.

"How exactly doth the parallel hold in all these instances!" Wesley exclaims. "While a man is in a mere natural state, before he is born of God, he has, in a spiritual sense, eyes and sees not; a thick impenetrable veil lies upon them: he has ears, but hears not; he is utterly deaf to what he is mot of all concerned to hear. His other spiritual senses are all locked up: he is in the same condition as if he had them not. Hence he has no knowledge of God. . . .

"But as soon as he is born of God," Wesley continues, "there is a total change in all these particulars." The "eyes of his understanding are opened" and he beholds "the glory of God in the face of Jesus Christ." His ears are opened and he hears the inward voice of God saying, "Be of good cheer; thy sins are forgiven thee. Go and sin no

---

9. *Man in Christ*, p. 82.

more." Moreover, he "feels within his heart the mighty working of the Spirit of God"—"the peace which passeth all understanding," "joy unspeakable and full of glory," "the love of God shed abroad in his heart by the Holy Ghost which is given unto him." "All his spiritual senses are then exercised to discern spiritual good and evil. By the use of these, he is daily increasing in the knowledge of God, of Jesus Christ whom He hath sent, and of all the things pertaining to His inward kingdom. And now he may be properly said to live: God having quickened him by His Spirit, he is alive to God through Jesus Christ. . . . God is continually breathing, as it were, upon the soul; and his soul is breathing unto God. . . . By a kind of spiritual respiration, the life of God is sustained; and the child grows up, till he comes to the 'full measure of the stature of Christ.'"[10]

"In this passage, more than anywhere else in the whole Wesleyan literature," William Cannon observes, "we find the clearest expression of the nature of the new birth and catch the brightest reflection of the moral and spiritual aspects of justification shining in human life. If justification, says Wesley, implies only a relative change, one in which our outward relationship to God is altered 'so that instead of enemies we become children,' then the new birth implies a *real* change, not external but internal, 'so that instead of sinners we become saints' and start on the road to perfection."[11]

C. Regeneration and Sanctification

We see, therefore, the close relationship between regeneration and sanctification. In New Testament language every Christian believer is a "saint." Negatively, he is sanctified in the sense that he has been washed from the acquired depravity of his sinning (Titus 3:5; 1 Cor. 6:11). Positively, he is sanctified in the sense that he is a new creature with new habit patterns: by the grace of God he lives "soberly, righteously, and godly, in this present world" (Titus 2:12).

But the new birth is not identical with sanctification. The new birth is the "launching pad" for sanctification; man's renewal in the divine image actually begins at the instant of regeneration. The new birth, however, is an instantaneous act; sanctification has a progressive aspect, initiated by regeneration, carried forward by the Spirit

---

10. Burtner and Chiles, *Compend of Wesley's Theology*, pp. 168-70.

11. *The Theology of John Wesley* (New York: Abingdon-Cokesbury Press, 1946), p. 125.

until the second crisis of heart cleansing, and continued until glorification as a process of spiritual maturation.

Regeneration is a complete act, but it does not effect man's entire sanctification. Scripture, reason, and experience indicate that a "residue of recalcitrancy" remains. This deeper cleansing is effected by the baptism with the Spirit.

III. ADOPTION

Viewed from yet another angle the initial crisis of personal salvation is spoken of in the Bible as adoption. While concomitant with justification and regeneration in experience, in the order of thought adoption logically follows them. Justification removes our guilt, regeneration changes our hearts, and adoption receives us into the family of God.

Like the term *regeneration,* adoption has a wider application in the New Testament than to the restoration of the individual. (1) St. Paul speaks of Israel's election to service in the redemptive economy of God as "the adoption" (Rom. 9:4). (2) The term is also applied to "the redemption of our body" at the Second Coming (Rom. 8:23). This last reference bears a close relation to Matt. 19:28, where Christ speaks of the regeneration of all things.

A. Adoption Defined

H. Orton Wiley defines adoption as "the declaratory act of God, by which upon being justified by faith in Jesus Christ, we are received into the family of God and reinstated in the privileges of sonship."[12]

B. The Nature of Adoption

The necessity of adoption arises from the fact of our natural alienation from God because of sin. By nature we are all "without Christ, being aliens from the commonwealth of Israel, and strangers from the covenants of promise, having no hope, and without God in the world" (Eph. 2:12). Adoption is the deliverance from this condition of alienation.

If regeneration gives us moral likeness to God, adoption reinstates us in the Father's household as sons and daughters of God.

---

12. *Christian Theology,* 2:428.

1. *Adoption Restores the Privileges of Sonship*

By faith in Jesus Christ we are *now* the sons of God (1 John 3:2; Gal. 3:26). Since we are children of God, we are heirs; heirs of God and joint heirs with Christ, the Son (Rom. 8:17). If the Hebrews under the old covenant were the slaves of God, we who are Christians under the new covenant are the sons of God (Gal. 4:7).

2. *Adoption Effects Deliverance from All Servile Fear*

"For ye have not received the spirit of bondage again to fear; but ye have received the Spirit of adoption, whereby we cry, Abba, Father" (Rom. 8:15).

3. *By Adoption We Enjoy the Right and Title to Heaven*

As children of God we have an inheritance reserved in heaven for us (1 Pet. 1:4). This inheritance is variously described as a Kingdom (Luke 12:32; Heb. 12:28), a better country (Heb. 11:16), a crown of life (Jas. 1:12), a crown of righteousness (2 Tim. 4:8), and an eternal weight of glory (2 Cor. 4:17).

4. *Our Adoption Will Be Universally Proclaimed*

This will be when we are "manifested" as the children of God at the second coming of Christ (Rom. 8:18-23). Meanwhile we have the assurance of our adoption by the testimony of the Spirit within our hearts (Gal. 4:6).

IV. The Witness of the Spirit

"We believe that justification, regeneration, and adoption are simultaneous in the experience of seekers after God and are obtained upon the condition of faith, preceded by repentance; and to this work and state of grace the Holy Spirit bears witness."[13]

The witness of the Spirit was one of the distinctive notes of the Evangelical Revival under the Wesleys and has remained as one of the characteristic emphases of the Wesleyan tradition. John Wesley wrote of this doctrine: "None who believe the Scriptures to be the word of God can doubt the importance of such a truth as this; a truth revealed therein, not only once, not obscurely, not incidentally; but frequently, and that in express terms; but solemnly and of set purpose, as denoting one of the peculiar privileges of the children of God."[14] We will have occasion to return to this topic briefly in Chap-

---

13. *Manual,* Church of the Nazarene, current issue, *ad loc.*
14. *Sermons,* 1:93.

ter 18 in relation to entire sanctification. Here let us examine this precious truth under three heads: (1) The Witness of God's Word; (2) The Witness of the Holy Spirit; (3) The Witness of the Human Spirit.

A. The Witness of God's Word

In order to safeguard the doctrine of assurance from the vagaries of subjectivism and mysticism we must first establish the objective witness of the Scriptures to the facts of personal salvation. The Scriptures we believe to be our sole and sufficient Rule of Faith. What testimony do they bear to our salvation?

1. *The Assurance of Pardon*

"Let the wicked forsake his way, and the unrighteous man his thoughts: and let him return unto the Lord, and he will have mercy upon him; and to our God, for he will abundantly pardon" (Isa. 55:7). "He that covereth his sins shall not prosper: but whoso confesseth and forsaketh them shall have mercy" (Prov. 28:13). "If we confess our sins, he is faithful and just to forgive us our sins, and to cleanse us from all unrighteousness" (1 John 1:9).

2. *The Assurance of Acceptance*

"Come unto me, all ye that labour and are heavy laden, and I will give you rest" (Matt. 11:28). "Him that cometh to me I will in no wise cast out" (John 6:37). "There is therefore now no condemnation to them which are in Christ Jesus" (Rom. 8:1).

3. *The Assurance of Salvation*

"If thou shalt confess with thy mouth the Lord Jesus, and shalt believe in thine heart that God hath raised him from the dead, thou shalt be saved. For with the heart man believeth unto righteousness; and with the mouth confession is made unto salvation. For the scripture saith, Whosoever believeth on him shall not be ashamed. For whosoever shall call upon the name of the Lord shall be saved" (Rom. 10:9-11, 13).

4. *The Assurance of Sonship*

"But as many as received him, to them gave he power to become the sons of God, even to them that believe on his name: which were born, not of blood, nor of the will of the flesh, nor of the will of man, but of God" (John 1:12-13).

5. *The Assurance of Eternal Life*

"Verily, verily, I say unto you, He that heareth my word, and believeth on him that sent me, hath everlasting life, and shall not come into condemnation; but is passed from death unto life" (John 5:24).[15] "If we receive the witness of men, the witness of God is greater: for this the witness of God which he hath testified of his Son. He that believeth on the Son of God hath the witness in himself: he that believeth not God hath made him a liar; because he believeth not the record that God gave of his Son. And this is the record, that God hath given to us eternal life, and this life is in his Son. He that hath the Son hath life; and he that hath not the Son of God hath not life. These things have I written unto you that believe on the name of the Son of God; *that ye may know that ye have eternal life*" (1 John 5:9-13, italics added).

6. *The Assurance of God's Continued Favor*

"If we walk in the light, as he is in the light, we have fellowship one with another, and the blood of Jesus Christ his Son cleanseth us from all sin" (1 John 1:7). "And you, that were sometime alienated and enemies in your mind by wicked works, yet now hath he reconciled in the body of his flesh through death, to present you holy and unblameable and unreproveable in his sight: *if* ye continue in the faith grounded and settled, and be not moved away from the hope of the gospel . . . As ye have therefore received Christ Jesus the Lord, so walk ye in him' (Col. 1:21-23; 2:6).

> *For feelings come, and feelings go,*
> *And feelings are deceiving.*
> *My warrant is the Word of God;*
> *Naught else is worth believing.*
>
> *Though all my heart should feel condemned*
> *For want of some sweet token,*
> *I know One greater than my heart,*
> *Whose word cannot be broken!*

> —MARTIN LUTHER

B. The Witness of the Holy Spirit

In addition to the objective witness of God's Word there is the subjective witness of the Spirit of God. 'And hereby we know that he

---

15. In this verse the verb "believeth" is in the present tense. It would read literally, "He that . . . believes, and keeps on believing, hath everlasting life. . . ." Eternal life is "the life of God abiding in the soul of man," and is conditional upon our continued faith, love, and obedience. Cf. 1 John 3:15.

abideth in us, by the Spirit which he hath given us" (1 John 3:24). "Hereby know we that we dwell in him, and he in us, because he hath given us of his Spirit" (1 John 4:13). Such statements as these cannot be applied to the objective witness of the Bible; they refer to an internal assurance deep within the human consciousness. There are three figures employed in the New Testament to set forth this inner testimony of the Spirit of God.

1. *The Seal of the Spirit*

We read in 2 Corinthians that God "hath also sealed us, and given the earnest of the Spirit in our hearts" (1:22). In New Testament times letters, contracts, and all kinds of official documents were sealed with wax. A warm blob of wax was placed upon the paper where it was folded together; the sender or signer then pressed his signet into the wax, authenticating what was thereby sealed. The Holy Spirit in the believer's life is the divine seal upon that life. "The foundation of God standeth sure, having this seal, The Lord knoweth them that are his. And, Let every one that nameth the name of Christ depart from iniquity" (2 Tim. 2:19). If the submissive heart is the wax, the Holy Spirit is the Sealer; and the image of Christ is the visible mark of identification. The seal is at once an assurance to the believer and a sign to the world.

2. *The Earnest of the Spirit*

In a commercial agreement the earnest is a partial payment which binds the bargain and obliges both buyer and seller to complete the transaction. The Holy Spirit is the first installment, as it were, of the infinite treasure God plans to bestow upon us in heaven. So long as we walk in the Spirit we have the *guarantee*, plus the *foretaste*, of heaven. Eternal life is not merely future; it is a present experience which reaches into eternity. Heaven will be the fulfillment of the love, joy, and peace of the Holy Spirit—lifted to infinity! "This is life eternal, that they might know thee the only true God, and Jesus Christ, whom thou hast sent" (John 17:3).

3. *The Testimony of the Spirit*

The passages are here crucial. "And because ye are sons, God hath sent forth the Spirit of his Son into your hearts, crying, Abba, Father" (Gal. 4:6). "The Spirit itself beareth witness with our spirit, that we are the children of God" (Rom. 8:16). By this witness John Wesley understands St. Paul to mean "an inward impression on the soul, whereby the Spirit of God immediately and directly witnesses to my spirit, that I am a child of God, that Jesus Christ hath loved me, and given Himself for me; that all my sins are blotted out, and *I*, even *I*, am reconciled to God."[16]

By the Spirit of adoption the pardoned sinner is enabled to look up to God and say, "Father!" Beyond this it is almost impossible to go into psychologizing the witness of the Spirit. Bernard of Clairvaux put it poetically, "The love of Jesus, what it is, none but His loved ones know."

C. The Witness of the Human Spirit

To the direct witness of the Holy Spirit there is added the indirect witness of our own spirits. The Spirit of God bears witness *along with* our spirits. There is a joint witness of His Spirit and mine that I have passed from condemnation to acceptance and sonship. This indirect witness confirms the direct, assuring me that I am not presuming upon God. Within my own consciousness I perceive that I am a new creature, that old things have passed away and all things have become new. This I *know* if I am born of the Spirit.

To the man born blind the Pharisees put questions he could not answer. But he could not be silenced. "One thing I know," he said, "that, whereas I was blind, now I see" (John 9:25). A born-again Christian has the same kind of indisputable evidence. St. Paul could say, "But I am not ashamed, for I know whom I have believed and I am sure that he is able to guard until that Day what has been entrusted to me" (2 Tim. 1:12, RSV). And St. John wrote, "Hereby we do know that we know him, if we keep his commandments" (1 John 2:3). Again, "We know that we have passed from death unto life, because we love the brethren" (1 John 3:14). And yet again, "My little children, let us not love in word, neither in tongue; but in deed and in truth. And hereby we know that we are of the truth, and shall assure our hearts before him" (1 John 3:18-19).

"But how shall I know that my spiritual senses are rightly disposed?" John Wesley answers: "Even by the testimony of your own spirit: by 'the answer of a good conscience toward God.' By the fruits which He hath wrought in your spirit, ye shall know the testimony of the Spirit of God. Hereby you shall know that you are in no delusion, that you have not deceived your own soul. The immediate fruits of the Spirit, ruling in the heart, are 'love, joy, peace, bowels of mercies, humbleness of mind, meekness, gentleness, long-suffering. And

---

16. Burtner and Chiles, *Compend of Wesley's Theology*, p. 95.

the outward fruits are, the doing good to all men; the doing no evil
to any; and the walking in the light—a zealous, uniform obedience to
all the commandments of God."[17]

SUMMARY

The purpose of this chapter has been to set forth the wonder and
glory of the many-sided miracle commonly called conversion. The
instant we exercise saving faith in Christ we are *justified*—pardoned
from our sins, released from the penalty of death, and accepted into
the favor of God; *regenerated*—re-created by the power of the Holy
Spirit in the image of God and given a distinctively spiritual life,
capable of faith, love, and obedience; *adopted*—received back into the
family of God with all the privileges and blessings pertaining thereto.
To this miracle the Spirit of God witnesses—objectively, in the Scriptures; subjectively, within the believer's heart. The change, finally, is
no fictional thing; the believer discerns in his own inner consciousness and in his entire outlook on life a supernatural change. "If any
man be in Christ, he is a new creature: old things are passed away;
behold, all things are become new."

We turn now to a survey of the results of the new life in Christ
in delivering the believer from a life of sinning, an important theme
in exploring our Christian faith.

17. *Ibid.*, p. 97.

CHAPTER 15

Deliverance from Sin

This chapter deals with one of the most pressing problems of Christian experience, if one is to judge by the amount of concern it receives. It has to do with the nature and extent of the changes which occur in regeneration, particularly in relation to the believer's moral life. Numerous and vocal segments of Christianity in today's world think and speak of Christian experience in such ways as to permit constant sinning in the life of the child of God. Justification is viewed as constant forgiveness for constant sinning. Contrary to this, it is the conviction of Christians of Arminian and Wesleyan persuasion that the new birth provides a measure of grace sufficient to keep the believer from willful sin.

I. The Problem

The question we are here considering has two facets, each of which must receive consideration before we turn to the Scriptures for their teaching. One has to do with the nature of sin itself; the other with the very nature of Christian experience.

A. The Nature of Sin

Thinkers of Calvinistic background generally consider sin to be any "want of conformity unto, or transgression of, the law of God."[1] No distinction is made between those acts or omissions which are known and voluntary and those which are the result of ignorance or in matters beyond our control. All deviations from an objective stan-

---

1. *The Shorter Catechism.*

291

dard of perfect righteousness are classed as "sins." Indeed, some go so far as to make sinning virtually equivalent with being human and finite.

It is quite apparent that in such a broad sense no human being living in this world could be saved from daily sinning. Salvation would have to dehumanize in order to deliver from sinning and sinfulness if such be the legitimate definition of sin. It must be admitted that current discussions on the subject are greatly confused by the ambiguity of the term "sin" as it is thus loosely used. When sin is identified with humanity, and made to include all manner of unconscious and involuntary lapses from absolute perfection of behavior, no person can expect to be freed from it in the course of life on this earth.

However, such a broad use of the term "sin," whatever basis it may find in some types of theology, is far from the ordinary biblical usage. It is true that there is in the Old Testament the rare mention of "sins of ignorance," particularly in Leviticus and Numbers. It should be noted that here the context is the ceremonial law, with its many requirements which might unconsciously be transgressed or omitted. But even in the Old Testament the prevailing usage is that which regards sin as rebellion against God. Even where terms are used which employ such metaphors as "going astray," "missing the right way," the common meaning is a moral one; man misses the right way because he chooses to follow the wrong one.[2] As C. Ryder Smith has said, "The ultimate definition of 'sin' in the Old Testament is *ethical,* and . . . this definition obtains throughout the New."[3]

In the New Testament particularly, whenever sin is used to describe human conduct, it is almost always ethical—that is, it implies conscious choice. John Wesley's memorable definition, "A voluntary transgression of a known law,"[4] has never been bettered as a concise statement of what the New Testament almost always means when it uses the term sin to speak of what people do. There are a few passages in the New Testament where sinning can possibly be defined as including mistakes, involuntary shortcomings, and unconscious lapses; but *none* where it *must* be so defined. On the other

2. C. Ryder Smith, *The Bible Doctrine of Sin* (London: Epworth Press, 1953), p. 17 and throughout.

3. *Ibid.,* p. 2.

4. *A Plain Account of Christian Perfection* (Boston: The Christian Witness Co., n.d.), pp. 42-43.

hand, there are many verses which use the term sin in such a way that the broad or legal definition *cannot possibly* be considered what the writer had in mind. In the last analysis, usage determines meaning. For this reason, a concordance may be a better tool for word studies in the Bible than a lexicon or dictionary.

In respect to the meaning of sinful acts, a single reference may make this clear: "Whosoever is born of God doth not commit sin," (1 John 3:9) is quite meaningless if sin is broadened to include every deviation from absolute perfection, whether known or unknown, voluntary or involuntary. On the other hand, it does have an important meaning for Christians when the term sin is properly interpreted as conveying the idea of ethical or motivated action.[5]

The issue here is more than an empty debate over terminology. It comes close to the heart of Christian ethics, and is vital for an understanding of the Christian life. Four important points must be noted here:

1. In the words of Dr. H. Orton Wiley, "Calling that sin which is not sin, opens the door also to actual sinning."[6] That is, *if we accept the broad or legal definition of sin, we are forced to admit that virtually everything human beings do is sin* because ideally it could be better, and thus falls short of an absolute standard of perfection. But to make everything sin is, in effect, to make nothing sin. It is impossible to grade sins. If forgotten promises, faulty judgment, and human limitations and infirmities are sins, then there is no qualitative distinction possible between such so-called sins on the one hand and lying, theft, or immorality on the other. The door then is left open wide to sin of all sorts.

2. The Christian consciousness and conscience recognize that *there is a significant qualitative difference between mistakes, errors, and lapses on one side and voluntary transgressions of divine law on the other.* When judged by the law of objective right, there is no difference between a forgotten promise and a broken promise. When judged by the law of objective right, there is no difference between a misstatement of fact made in ignorance and a lie. In each case, something promised has not been performed and an untruth has been stated.

But there is a tremendous difference in these two types of situa-

5. Cf. W. T. Purkiser, *Conflicting Concepts of Holiness* (Kansas City: Beacon Hill Press of Kansas City, 1953), pp. 45-56. See also John 8:34-36; Rom. 6:1, 15, 18, 22; Heb. 9:26.

6. *Christian Theology,* 2:508.

tions subjectively and ethically. In the case of both forgotten promise and ignorant misstatement, there is regret—but not the condemnation of guilt. There is sorrow but not sin. Lapses of memory and ignorance are always deplorable and should be avoided as far as possible. But the Christian consciousness does not find in these infirmities anything which would interrupt its fellowship with God or bring to it condemnation and a sense of guilt.

Conscience always finds the essence of sin to lie in the realm of intent and of motive. This is not in any sense to minimize the material or objective side of the moral law. It does not give license for well-meaning blundering. It does not afford encouragement to carelessness or sentimentalism in shrugging off actual delinquency with the remark, "I meant to do right." It does, however, recognize that sin is fundamentally a matter of choice, of intention, and of purpose.

3. This distinction is vital because it is scriptural. *The Bible throughout recognizes the fact of faults and infirmities, and it distinguishes them sharply from sin.* For example, Christ saves us from our sins (Matt. 1:21) and cleanses from carnal sin (1 John 1:7); but He sympathizes with and is touched with the feeling of our infirmities (Heb. 4:15). This represents a crucial difference in attitude toward sin on the one hand, both outer and inner, and human frailties on the other. Similarly, the Holy Spirit convicts of sins (John 16:8), frees us from the law of sin and death (Rom. 8:2), but He helps us with our infirmities (Rom. 8:26). Forgiveness and cleansing are the experiences of a moment. Infirmities and human limitations cannot be dealt with in a crisis experience, either regeneration or entire sanctification. They must be met on the battlefield of life day by day and overcome or sublimated by the Spirit's help.

4. Finally, *the divine law itself is of such nature that it can be kept only by those whose love and motives are pure, and not by outward conformity alone,* however detailed such might be. This is the great truth of the first division of the Sermon on the Mount, where Jesus states that the primary realm of observance of God's law is in the heart, and says, "Except your righteousness shall exceed the righteousness of the scribes and Pharisees, ye shall in no case enter into the kingdom of heaven" (Matt. 5:20; cf. vv. 21-48). The same truth is also given the scribe in Matt. 22:37-40: "Jesus said unto him, Thou shalt love the Lord thy God with all thy heart, and with all thy soul, and with all thy mind. This is the first and great commandment. And the second is like unto it, Thou shalt love thy neighbour as thyself. *On these two commandments hang all the law and the prophets*" (italics added).

Such is clearly the import of Paul's statement in Rom. 13:8-10: "Owe no man any thing, but to love one another: for he that loveth another hath fulfilled the law. For this, Thou shalt not commit adultery, Thou shalt not kill, Thou shalt not steal, Thou shalt not bear false witness, Thou shalt not covet; and if there be any other commandment, it is briefly comprehended in this saying, namely, Thou shalt love thy neighbour as thyself. Love worketh no ill to his neighbour: therefore love is the fulfilling of the law." And again in Gal. 5:14, we find: "For all the law is fulfilled in one word, even in this; Thou shalt love thy neighbour as thyself." In James S. Stewart's eloquent words:

> Sin according to Jesus is something more than the Shorter Catechism has put into its definition, "any want of conformity unto, or transgression of, the law of God." It is something more than a blundering running of our heads against the inexorable laws of the universe. It is another nail hammered into love's cross, a clenched fist thrust up into the face of God. It is a blow struck at a loving heart.[7]

B. Justification and Continued Sinning

Quite apart from the ambiguity of the term sin as it is often used is the contention that Christian experience is primarily justification, or forgiveness, and as such does not mean an end to actual sinning. We have seen in an earlier chapter that justification is always accompanied by regeneration, or the renewal of the heart. But there are those who use the term regeneration to describe the imparting of a divine nature in such a way as to leave the old sinful human nature virtually unmodified.[8]

There is a very instructive paragraph in *Protestant Thought Before Kant*, by A. C. McGiffert, which outlines the source of this widely held notion. McGiffert points out that Paul taught that salvation is possible in this life by a transformation of moral character effected by the regenerating and sanctifying presence of the Holy Spirit in human life. Catholic theologians concurred that salvation must bring about deliverance from sin. Failing to find such deliverance in the

---

7. *The Life and Teaching of Jesus Christ* (New York: Abingdon Press, n.d.), p. 82.

8. This is sometimes called the "two natures" theory. It not only ignores the dynamic unity of the normal human psyche, but virtually denies the scriptural doctrine of the new birth. It is the human being which is born again, not the addition of an abstract spiritual entity to an otherwise unchanged soul. 2 Cor. 5:17 is a sufficient refutation to this idea: "Therefore if any man be in Christ, he is a new creature: old things are passed away; behold, all things are become new."

worldliness and carnal corruption of the church, they taught that this life is a preparation on earth for salvation from sin in the life to come. Luther and the reformers in general reacted against Catholicism at this point. They returned salvation to the course of this life, but based it upon divine forgiveness and not upon a transformation of ethical character.[9] While McGiffert was concerned with pre-Kantian Christian thought, it might be added that the Wesleyan theology completes the return to the Pauline New Testament basis by recognizing that salvation is both *for* this life and *from* the power of sin in this life.

Floyd V. Filson has correctly sensed the purpose of the gospel for man when he says:

> Accurate interpretation of the New Testament has long been hindered by a tendency to let forgiveness stop at negative results. The guilt of sin is cared for. The individual will not be damned or punished. But this does not leave the individual where the Gospel seeks to bring him, in grateful living fellowship with the Father. Repentance and forgiveness involve the turning of the sinner from his evil ways, with sorrow and with the deep desire to be forgiven, restored to fellowship with God, and renewed in right purpose. A forgiveness that does not give a strong sense of moral obligation and issue in a faithful response to the will of God lacks reality.[10]

One widely known New Testament scholar points out that Paul consistently avoided the use of the term "forgiveness of sins." This he thinks was probably due to the fact that the phrase is ambiguous to the extent that it might seem to some to speak only of release from the guilt of past sins. Paul's important concern was rather for "release from *sinning,* release from the power of sin."[11]

Far from the true Christian attitude toward sin is the complacency implied in the phrase, "to sin every day in word, thought, and deed." To quote James S. Stewart again:

> To know oneself forgiven, and forgiven at so great a cost, is always a moral dynamic of the first order. It is a mainspring of the dedicated life. It creates character. It works righteousness. It brings honor to the throne. It makes the forgiven sinner Christ's man, body and soul, forever.[12]

For to be united to Christ means to be *identified with Christ's*

---

9. P. 25.

10. *One Lord, One Faith* (Philadelphia: Westminster Press, 1943), p. 198.

11. Bultmann, *Theology of the New Testament,* 1:287.

12. *Life and Teaching of Jesus,* p. 88.

attitude to sin. It means seeing sin with Jesus' eyes, and opposing it
with something of the same passion with which Jesus at Calvary
opposed it. It means an assent of the whole man to the divine
judgment proclaimed upon sin at the cross. It means, as the writer
to the Hebrews saw, "resistance unto blood" (Heb. 12:4). It means,
as Paul put it tersely, death. In face of all this, to find antinomianism in Paul is simply to caricature his Gospel.[13]

II. THE NEW TESTAMENT ON DELIVERANCE FROM SIN

We are ready now to examine the teachings of the New Testament
itself with regard to this problem. Does regeneration result in actual
deliverance from the power of sin in this life? Or is it a "covering" of
sins which still hold dominion, the "imputation" of a righteousness
which does not exist? Should our major stress rest upon justification
or forgiveness, understood not only to include the sins of the past but
those of the present and future also? Or should our major emphasis
be on regeneration and the power of grace to remake the human
spirit?

That this is no academic question, but one of vital importance
to the practical Christian life, is clearly evident. If one expects no
more in Christian experience than continual "sinning and repenting," "confessing each night the sins of the day," he is certain to have
a different attitude toward the resources of divine grace than if he
recognizes that sinning has no place in the Christian life. To expect
defeat is to insure it.

It must be clearly understood that no real Christian for a moment attributes victory over sin in the life to his own strength or
stability. He recognizes that it is not only the grace of God which
has forgiven the sins of the past, but it is the grace of God through
the presence of the Spirit which keeps him from sin in the present.
To suppose that sin is necessary in the Christian life in order to "keep
the believer humble" is quite absurd, for all sin is an expression of
pride and self-sufficiency. As John Fletcher long ago remarked, if sin
makes one humble, then Satan should be the most humble being in
the universe, whereas he is the embodiment of all pride. On the other
hand, any realistic appraisal of the Christian's liability to mistakes,
infirmities, and human shortcomings is quite sufficient to keep him
humble.

Apart from isolated apparent exceptions which we shall exam-

13. *Man in Christ,* p. 196.

ine later, the whole tenor of the New Testament supports the thesis that regeneration means an end to sinning, in the sense of the willful and conscious violation of divine law. Salvation in the New Testament sense is not only deliverance from the consequences and penalty of sin; it is also deliverance from the dominion and power of sin.

We shall study some representative passages which will serve to set the scriptural teaching before us, and then turn to verses which have been alleged to teach the necessity of daily sin in the believer's life. The "pro" passages will be grouped into: the position of the Gospels; the teaching of Paul; and the claim of the General Epistles.

A. The Gospels

Matthew and Luke each have an important statement about the nature and effect of Christ's gospel at this point, before we turn to what Jesus himself taught.

Matthew preserves the statement of the angel to Joseph before the birth of our Lord: "And she will bear a Son; and you shall call His name Jesus, for it is He who will save His people from their sins" (1:21, NASB). As one commentator has said, "This is a great foundation statement of the gospel standing at the outset of the New Testament."[14] It is a statement which not only explains the name which is above every name, but sets forth the purpose of the Incarnation.

The preposition *"from"* is particularly noteworthy. In the Greek, it is *apo*, which means "forth from, away from; *hence it variously signifies* departure; distance of time or place; avoidance; riddance; derivation from a quarter, source, or material; origination from agency or instrumentality."[15] This is a far cry from saving His people "in their sins," as would be the case if salvation left the person subject to the dominion and power of sin. "The very name of our Lord, given by Divine command, lays a firm foundation for the trust of the guilty; and opens the most glorious hope to man, even that of salvation from the guilt and penalty, from the power and pollution, of sin in this life, and beyond it a resurrection from the dead, immortality, and eternal felicity."[16]

---

14. Francis Davidson, editor, *The New Bible Commentary* (Grand Rapids: Wm. B. Eerdmans Publishing Co., 1956), *ad loc.*

15. *A Greek-English Lexicon of the New Testament*, revised by Thomas Sheldon Green (New York: The Macmillan Co., 1890), p. 17.

16. *One-Volume New Testament Commentary* (Grand Rapids: Baker Book House, 1957), *ad loc.*

Luke also in a pre-Nativity passage cites the hymn of Zacharias, father of John the Baptist, which sets forth the meaning of the new age which had dawned:

> *The oath which He swore to Abraham our Father,*
> *To grant us that we, being delivered from the hand of our enemies,*
> *Might serve Him without fear,*
> *In holiness and righteousness before Him all our days.*
>
> (1:73-75, NASB).

It is of course true that this great promise goes beyond the initial work of redemption in human hearts and includes what Paul later called "the fulness of the blessing of the gospel of Christ" (Rom. 15:29). It does, however, give the lie to the claim that the maximum in Christian living in this world is a continual "sinning and repenting." John Wesley states: "Here is the substance of the great promise, that we should be always holy, always happy; and being delivered from Satan and sin, from every uneasy and unholy temper, we shall joyfully love and serve God, in every thought, word, and work."[17]

In the actual teachings of Jesus we find the same uncompromising challenge with regard to sin. In the Sermon on the Mount, Christ early set forth the principle that the test of eternal life is not profession but obedience to the will of God. "Ye shall know them by their fruits," He said (Matt. 7:16, 20). "'Not everyone who says to me, "Lord, Lord," will enter the kingdom of heaven, but only he who does the will of my Father who is in heaven. Many will say to me on that day, "Lord, Lord, did we not prophesy in your name, and in your name drive out demons and perform many miracles?" Then I will tell them plainly, "I never knew you. Away from me, you evildoers!"'" (vv. 21-23, NIV). Commenting on this, Basil F. C. Atkinson says, "A life of service and holiness is the only ultimate test of true regeneration."[18] It is doing the will of God and refraining from iniquity (Greek, *anomia,* lawlessness, violation of law, iniquity, sin) which distinguishes false profession from genuine possession.

John cites the words of Jesus addressed to the crippled man who was healed by the pool of Bethesda, "Behold, thou art made whole: sin no more, lest a worse thing come unto thee" (5:14). It may be argued that this categorical command had particular reference to

---

17. *Notes upon the New Testament, ad loc.*
18. *New Bible Commentary, ad loc.*

some sin which had as its penalty or consequence the disease which made its victim a cripple. It is far more reasonable to suppose that Jesus is pointing up the spiritual significance of physical healing, and lays the injunction, "Sin no more," upon the soul as the ideal by which all His disciples can and should live. A. J. MacLeod says, "He [Jesus] meets the restored men later in the temple, and emphasizes the moral significance of the act of healing. The miracles of Jesus had an ethical and spiritual intention: inasmuch as a principle of righteousness was involved in the act of healing, there must be no lapse into sin."[19]

Another key statement in the Fourth Gospel is found in John 8:34-36. In controversy with the Pharisees, Jesus said, "'I tell you the truth, everyone who sins is a slave to sin. Now a slave has no permanent place in the family, but a son belongs to it forever. So if the Son sets you free, you will be free indeed'" (NIV). The freedom is clearly freedom from any necessity to commit sin, the freedom hailed by Paul in Rom. 6:18, 22.

B. The Pauline Writings

In the doctrinal and ethical epistles of Paul, Romans and Corinthians, we find a strong emphasis upon the empirical results of divine grace in delivering from the dominion of sin. Paul's strong sense of the transformation which comes to the man who is "in Christ" (cf. 2 Cor. 5:17) is clearly seen.

In treatment of the doctrine of justification by faith (Romans 1—5), we find an incidental reference which bears on our present topic. It is the apostle's statement that, "while we were yet sinners, Christ died for us" (5:8). The relevance lies in the use of the term "yet" or "still" sinners. Here the implication is unmistakable that those who accept the grace of God in Christ through faith are no longer sinners. A change of status has been accompanied by a change in nature.

It is in the great sanctification passage in Romans (cc. 6—8) that Paul's strongest emphasis appears. In the first division of this epistle, chapters 1—5, Paul has dealt with the question, How can the guilty, those who have committed sins, be justified by a holy God? In the second major division he deals with the question, How can those who are sinful by nature be made righteous? The answer lies in the

19. *Ibid.*

actual experiencing by the believer of what was wrought for him on the Cross by Christ, an experiencing made real by the regenerating and sanctifying power of the Holy Spirit.

The sanctification passage opens with a possible objection raised against the doctrine of justification by free grace: "What shall we say then? Shall we continue in sin, that grace may abound?" (6:1). To this, the apostle returns a ringing answer, "God forbid"—"impossible, a horrible thought!"[20] "We died to sin; how can we live in it any longer?" (v. 2, NIV). Even baptism itself, which pictures not only the washing away of sins committed but a deeper death to the sin nature (v. 6), teaches us that it is impossible for a true believer to continue in sin.

Paul then turns to the metaphor of slavery: "Let not sin therefore reign in your mortal body, that ye should obey it in the lusts thereof. . . . For sin shall not have dominion over you: for ye are not under law, but under grace. What then? shall we sin, because we are not under the law, but under grace? God forbid" (vv. 12, 14-15). As Frederick L. Godet points out, "The question of verse 15 is not a repetition of that in verse 1. The discussion has advanced. The principle of holiness inherent in salvation by grace has been demonstrated. The apostle only asks himself whether it will have the power necessary to rule man without the assistance of a law."[21]

The answer to this new statement of the question is given by Sanday and Headlam as: "St. Paul's reply in effect is that Christian freedom consists not in freedom to sin but in freedom from sin."[22] He who commits sin is the slave of sin, and the end is eternal death. He who obeys God has become the servant of righteousness, and bears "fruit unto holiness, and the end everlasting life" (v. 22). Here is definite statement of the fact that to be under grace and the servant of God is to be delivered from the dominion and power of sin.

The latter part of Romans 7 (vv. 14-23) is often cited as evidence for the fact that the Christian cannot live without sin in the course of this life.[23] Here, however, we have the apostle's résumé of the struggles of an awakened soul to keep the law of God in his own strength.

---

20. William Sanday and Arthur C. Headlam, *A Critical and Exegetical Commentary on the Epistle to the Romans* (New York: Charles Scribner's Sons, 1896), *ad loc.*

21. *Commentary on the Epistle to the Romans,* trans. by A. Cusin, rev. by T. W. Chambers (Grand Rapids: Zondervan Publishing House, 1956 reprint), *ad loc.*

22. *Critical and Exegetical Commentary on Romans, ad loc.*

23. As by Hodge, *Systematic Theology,* 3:213 ff.

"The apostle is speaking here neither *of the natural man* in his state of voluntary ignorance and sin, nor *of the child of God,* born anew, set free by grace, and animated by the Spirit of Christ; but of the man whose conscience, awakened by the law, has entered sincerely, with fear and trembling, but still *in his own strength,* into the desperate struggle against evil."[24]

That 7:14-23 is not the norm for Christian experience is clearly seen in the victorious statement of Rom. 8:1-4: "There is therefore now no condemnation to them which are in Christ Jesus, who walk not after the flesh, but after the Spirit. For the law of the Spirit of life in Christ Jesus hath made me free from the law of sin and death. For what the law could not do, in that it was weak through the flesh, God sending his own Son in the likeness of sinful flesh, and for sin, condemned [not condoned] sin in the flesh: that the righteousness of the law might be fulfilled in us, who walk not after the flesh, but after the Spirit." Here the Spirit of life, God's Holy Spirit, makes real the deliverance of grace, a deliverance which provides freedom from sin. That the apostle's great treatment of sanctification deals with the total work of the Spirit in renewing human nature, and not with its beginning only in the new birth, we shall see in our next two chapters. The point to note here is the clear-cut and undeniable teaching that sin in the Christian life is an anomaly and out of place. G. T. Thomson and Francis Davidson write of these verses:

> Sin is foreign to human life. It is an intrusion. By sending His Son *in the likeness of sinful flesh* God dealt with sin. . . . Flesh was the realm of sin; but in the case of believers God put that sphere of influence out of court, the death of the Son annulling the power of sin over saints completely and permanently. Man in Christ is free for ever from the law of sin and death. The just requirement of the law, a righteous life, is accomplished not through the law (for it has failed) but through grace.[25]

In his Corinthian correspondence, letters which deal with some of the doctrinal and practical issues which had arisen in the church, Paul also addresses this problem. One great verse flatly denies that any temptation is overwhelming, or any sin in Christian life inevitable: "No temptation has overtaken you but such as is common to man; and God is faithful, who will not allow you to be tempted beyond what you are able, but with the temptation will provide the

24. M. Bonnet, *Commentary,* p. 85; quoted by Godet, *Commentary on Romans,* p. 294.
25. *New Bible Commentary, ad loc.*

way of escape also, that you may be able to endure it" (1 Cor. 10:13, NASB).

In his great resurrection passage in 1 Corinthians 15, Paul interjects a strong appeal to righteous living. False teachers had denied the Resurrection, and shallow minds had reasoned that, since death ends all, "let us eat and drink; for to morrow we die" (v. 32). Paul strongly reacts against the evil consequences of this false teaching. "Awake to righteousness, *and sin not;* for some have not the knowledge of God: I speak this to your shame" (v. 34). Three facts may be noted here: (1) righteousness precludes sin; (2) any other view is not in line with the knowledge of God; and (3) to condone sin is a matter of deep shame and condemnation to the Christian.

In Galatians, the apostle indicates again that true justification in Christ does away with a life of sin. "But if, while we seek to be justified by Christ, we ourselves also are found sinners, is therefore Christ the minister of sin? God forbid. For if I build again the things which I destroyed, I make myself a transgressor" (2:17-18). John Wesley comments:

> "*For if I build again*—by my sinful practice—*the things which I destroyed*—by my preaching, *I* only *make myself*—or show myself, not Christ, to be *a transgressor;* the whole blame lies on me, not Him or His gospel. As if he had said, The objection were just, if the gospel promised justification to men continuing in sin. But it does not. Therefore, if any who profess the gospel do not live according to it, they are sinners, it is certain, but not justified, and so the gospel is clear."[26]

C. The General Epistles

The teaching of the General Epistles is not less clear than that of the Gospels and the Pauline writings. The entire argument of the Book of Hebrews, for example, is the superiority of the gospel over the Jewish law. One of the most persuasive arguments for this superiority is that Christ provides a real deliverance from sin to those who accept His high priestly mediation and sacrifice (chapters 9 and 10). The climax of this argument is reached in 9:26: "But now once at the consummation He has been manifested to put away sin by the sacrifice of Himself" (NASB). The term translated "to put away" is a strong verb meaning "to displace, set aside; to abrogate, annul, violate, swerve from; reject, condemn."[27] He who bore away the sin of the world

---

26. *Notes upon the New Testament, ad loc.*
27. Green, *Lexicon,* p. 3.

(John 1:29) is certainly concerned, not only with the condemnation and guilt of a broken law, but with the dominion and power of sin in the lives of His brethren.

In 2 Peter 2 we find a vivid description of false teachers and false professors who had allied themselves with the Christian Church, even taking part in the Communion love feasts (v. 13). Among the characteristics of these pseudo-Christians we find the statement, "that cannot cease from sin." It is thought-provoking, to say the least, to find the inability to live above sin listed as one of the marks of a hypocritical and false profession of Christianity.

It is in the First Epistle of John that we find some of the strongest and clearest statements. John's whole purpose in writing is "that ye sin not" (2:1). Even his statement of the unfailing remedy for the tragic intrusion of sin into a believer's experience is prefaced with a conditional statement which makes it clear that such sin is not necessary: "And if any man sin, we have an advocate with the Father, Jesus Christ the righteous" (2:1). In 2:4, he states, "He that saith, I know him, and keepeth not his commandments, is a liar, and the truth is not in him."

1 John 3:6, 8-9 contrasts the results in the moral life of the two great life principles by which men may live: "No one who abides in him sins; no one who sins has either seen him or known him; . . . He who commits sin is of the devil, for the devil has sinned from the beginning. The reason the Son of God appeared was to destroy the works of the devil. No one born of God commits sin; for God's nature abides in him, and he cannot sin because he is born of God" (RSV).

These words are so clear and vigorous that almost any comment would weaken their force. It may be noted, however, that the expression, "He cannot sin, because he is begotten of God," in verse 9 does not teach that the Christian *is not able to sin,* but that *he is able not to sin.* The impossibility expressed here is a logical impossibility, not a psychological impossibility. This may be made plain by a paraphrase of the verse: "Whosoever is an honest man doth not steal; for his honesty remaineth in him: and he cannot steal, because he is an honest man"; or, "Whosoever is a truthful man doth not lie; for his truthfulness remaineth in him: and he cannot lie, because he is a truthful man." Both paraphrases make perfect sense; but they do not mean that the honest or truthful person is unable to steal or lie, but simply, should such a person begin to steal or lie he would no longer be honest or truthful. The regenerating seed of God is so utterly contrary to the principle of sinful conduct that they cannot coexist in the same person at the same time.

A similar declaration is found in 1 John 5:18, "We know that whosoever is born of God sinneth not; but he that is begotten of God keepeth himself, and that wicked one toucheth him not." Textual scholars point out that the last clause may well be translated, "He that was begotten of God keepeth him, and that wicked one toucheth him not." This is a very probable rendering, and shows that "John was thinking of the way Jesus Christ looks after His own and protects them from the assaults of the devil."[28] The victorious life of the believer is not a matter of credit to himself, but is of and through the grace of Christ. But the first clause of the verse stands even more certain: "We know that whosoever is born of God sinneth not."

D. Actual as Well as Ideal

That verses such as have been given above cannot be waved away with the assertion, "This is the ideal, but not the actual life of the Christian," is seen in such references as the following:

"And they were both righteous before God, walking in all the commandments and ordinances of the Lord blameless" (Luke 1:6).

"But we have renounced the hidden things of dishonesty, not walking in craftiness, nor handling the word of God deceitfully; but by manifestation of the truth commending ourselves to every man's conscience in the sight of God" (2 Cor. 4:2).

"Ye are witnesses, and God also, how holily and justly and unblameably we behaved ourselves among you that believe" (1 Thess. 2:10).

III. Some Problem Passages

We may not leave this topic without a brief consideration of some passages in the New Testament which would seem to support the view that the new birth does not provide deliverance from the necessity of sin. Old Testament passages are sometimes listed, but are not considered here since the Old Testament does not give a complete view of redemption as provided in Jesus Christ. It will be seen that most passages cited in defense of "sinning sainthood" are found to be in harmony with the whole tenor of Scripture when they are understood in their contexts.

---

28. R. J. Drummond and Leon Morris in *New Bible Commentary, ad loc.*

The phrase in the Lord's Prayer, "Forgive us our sins" (Luke 11:4) or "Forgive us our debts," (Matt. 6:12) is sometimes given to prove the fact of daily sin in the believer's life. It may be possible to explain this phrase by pointing out that the Lord's Prayer is first of all a social prayer, to be prayed by a group, and therefore may include those who have actually committed sins. This is the suggestion made by Charles Ewing Brown in *The Meaning of Salvation.*[29] However, the fact that Jesus immediately coupled with this phrase the condition that we forgive those who are indebted to us (Matt. 6:14) leads one to think that our continued forgiveness for past sins is conditioned on our spirit of forgiveness toward those who sin against us. Such is certainly the teaching of the parable of the two debtors in Matt. 18:23-35.

The last part of Romans 7 is also frequently quoted as showing the necessity for sin in the Christian life. This, as we saw earlier in the chapter, can be maintained only by ignoring the context of chapters 6 and 8 with their unmistakable testimony to freedom from the binding law of sin and death.

Rom. 14:23, "For whatsoever is not of faith is sin," is sometimes given to prove that any passing doubt or question in the mind is sinful. Even a most casual reading of the context will show that Paul is, in fact, arguing the ethical character of sin. It is going contrary to one's own convictions that makes an act or practice sinful.

Jas. 4:17, "Therefore to him that knoweth to do good, and doeth it not, to him it is sin," is supposed to indicate that falling short in any regard from the highest good known, regardless of the reason, is of the nature of sin. There is a wholesome warning here against sins of omission. Refusing to do what God commands is as much sin as doing what God forbids. However, the "therefore" prefacing the statement points to its relation to a context. That context warns us that we must acknowledge the will of God in all our plans. To fail to do so is sin.

A frequent proof text for the doctrine of sinning sainthood is 1 John 1:10. This is read as if it said, "If we say we are not sinning, we make him a liar, and his word is not in us." What it actually says is something quite different: "If we say that we have not sinned, we make him a liar, and his word is not in us." "All have sinned, and come short of the glory of God" (Rom. 3:23), and no devout Christian denies that he is a sinner saved by grace. We have all sinned. When

---

29. P. 157.

we came to Christ it was without exception with sins to be forgiven and unrighteousness from which to be cleansed. But neither this verse nor any other gives a scrap of evidence to show that he who is forgiven and cleansed must continue in sin.

Summary

We have been concerned in this chapter with a limited but very widespread interpretation of the Christian life which would deny its complete victory over sin by the grace of God in Christ. Sin we have defined as willful and voluntary transgressions of divine law, and not infirmities, limitations, errors, and shortcomings arising from purely human limitations. We have surveyed the drift of the New Testament scriptures, and examined some of the negative passages. We may state the outcome in the words of an ancient wise man: "Let us hear the conclusion of the whole matter: Fear God, and keep his commandments: for this is the whole duty of man" (Eccles. 12:13). It is to this end that Christ suffered, died, and rose again, and commissioned the preaching of our Christian faith in all the world.

CHAPTER 16

The Nature of
Sanctification

The purpose of this chapter is to examine and set forth the nature of scriptural sanctification. If the scope of the chapter is broad, the aim is quite definite: to put the idea of sanctification in its biblical context. Subsequent chapters will deal in a more detailed way with questions here raised. Such matters as the relation of crisis to process in sanctification and the effects of entire sanctification in Christian experience call for further and fuller treatment. Before proceeding to these considerations we must study the essential idea of sanctification.

I. THE IDEA OF THE HOLY

No modern treatment of holiness should ignore the work of Rudolf Otto. The thesis of his volume, *The Idea of the Holy,* offers a starting point for a discussion of the biblical teaching of sanctification.

"Holiness," Otto avers, "is a category of interpretation and valuation peculiar to the sphere of religion."[1] In common use today, holiness means moral purity. The term is almost exclusively ethical. Otto's concern is to point out another element in the idea of holiness.

---

1. *The Idea of the Holy,* J. W. Harvey, translator (London: Oxford University Press, 1957), p. 5. On the theme of chapters 16-18, see Cox, *John Wesley's Concept of Perfection;* Richard E. Howard, *Newness of Life* (Kansas City: Beacon Hill Press of Kansas City, 1975); Purkiser, Taylor, and Taylor, *God, Man, and salvation,* pp. 462-507; and Wynkoop, *Theology of Love.*

For this element he coins the word "numinous," from the Latin *numen*. The numinous he speaks of as a "moment," an awareness which defies rational analysis. An analogy he finds in the category of the beautiful. A sunset cannot be put into a syllogism.[2] But while the numinous cannot be strictly defined, we can hint at its meaning by looking closely at the feelings it evokes. Anyone who has a true experience of God's gracious presence may discover, by examining the heart of his awareness, what Otto calls *mysterium tremendum*. This is the sense of awe, wonder, and adoration which invades the being mightily in Christian worship with the words, "Holy, Holy, Holy, Lord God Almighty!" In Charles Wesley's words it is

> *The speechless awe that dares not move*
> *And all the silent heaven of love.*

Otto finds at least three elements in the adjective *tremendum*: awefulness, overpoweringness, and energy. The holy evokes awe; it overwhelms the soul with a sense of majesty; it pulsates with supernatural power. Examining the noun *mysterium* he quotes Tersteegen, "A God comprehended is no God." God is the "Wholly Other," quite beyond the sphere of the usual, the intelligible, and the familiar, filling the mind with wonder and astonishment.[3] That is, God is not to be "scaled down" to the measure of human reason. He discloses himself to the true worshiper's heart, yet remains hidden. He is apprehended but not comprehended.

God not only daunts; He also fascinates. In a "strange harmony of contrasts" the soul is filled with awe and transported to the heights of bliss as it encounters the Holy One. To illustrate, Otto quotes from William James's *Varieties of Religious Experience,* where one writes:

> For the moment nothing but an ineffable joy and exaltation remained. It is impossible fully to describe the experience. It was

---

2. W. E. Sangster, *The Pure in Heart:* A Study in Christian Sanctity (New York: Abingdon Press, 1954), p. 4.

3. Otto, *Idea of the Holy,* p. 26. Commenting on the phrase, John W. Harvey says: "But Otto, who was, I think, the first to make this religious use of the phrase, is not open to the criticism of exaggerating and isolating the divine transcendent Otherness. God for him is not, so to speak, *wholly* 'wholly other.' That aspect of Deity, the mysterious overplus surpassing all that can be clearly understood and appraised, is asserted emphatically against any excessive anthropocentric tendency to scale down the Sacred and Holy to the measure of our human reason. But it is an aspect only, one note that has to be preserved in (to use another favourite phrase) the 'harmony of contrasts.'" —Translator's Preface, xviii.

like the effect of some great orchestra, when all the separate notes have melted into one swelling harmony, that leaves the listener conscious of nothing save that his soul is being wafted upwards and almost bursting with its emotion.[4]

He cites Jonathan Edwards:

The concepts which the saints have of the loveliness of God and that kind of delight which they experience in it are quite peculiar and entirely different from anything which a natural man can possess or of which he can form any proper notion.[5]

Awe and adoration, tremor and bliss—this is what Otto means by the numinous. This element he finds in the Hebrew *qadosh*, the Greek *hagios*, and the Latin *sacer*. Although these words carry in them the idea of moral purity or ethical excellence, if the numinous element were removed from them, something precious would perish. They would pass from the realm of the spiritual to become terms of interest only to moralists.

This raises a question of paramount importance. How has "holiness" become a moral idea? Did the religious become the moral? Did the ethical gradually evolve out of the numinous? Such an evolutionary explanation Otto vigorously rejects on the grounds that the religious and the moral are qualitatively different. Although they are related like the warp and woof of fabric, they are distinct the one from the other. "The idea 'ought' is only 'evolvable' out of the spirit of man itself, and then in the sense of being 'arousable,' because it is already potentially implanted in him. Were it not so, no 'evolution' could effect an introduction for it."[6] As God encounters the soul, the numinous *excites* the ethical (by "the law of the association of feelings"). The numinous charges the ethical and gives commanding support to the conscience. Only in the presence of God does transgression become "sin." *Holiness is therefore a complex in which the religious and the ethical interpenetrate.* Commenting on Otto's conclusion W. E. Sangster writes: "The numinous and the ethical combine like oxygen and hydrogen in water and become indistinguishable in experience. So there emerges the unitary but 'complex category of "holy" itself, richly charged and complete and in its fullest meaning.'"[7]

The fusion of these two elements is seen in Abram's encounter with God. "And when Abram was ninety years old and nine, the

---

4. P. 66; from *Idea of the Holy*, p. 37.

5. *Ibid.*, p. 38.

6. *Ibid.*, p. 43.

7. Sangster, *Pure in Heart*, p. 9; quotation from Otto, *Idea of the Holy*, p. 45.

Lord appeared to Abram, and said unto him, *I am the Almighty God; walk before me, and be thou perfect"* (Gen. 17:1, italics added). But it is Isaiah's Temple experience which gives us the classic illustration of holiness as the blending of the numinous and the ethical. The prophet glimpsed Jehovah high and lifted up and heard the seraphim cry, "Holy, holy, holy, is the Lord of hosts." At this cry the doorposts of the Temple began to move and the house was filled with smoke. Smitten by this disclosure of Jehovah's glory, Isaiah cried out, "I am a man of unclean lips." Immediately a seraph flew to him with a burning coal and touched his lips, declaring, "Lo, this hath touched thy lips; and thine iniquity is taken away, and thy sin purged" (Isa. 6:1-7).

Geerhardus Vos sees in this passage an "intermarriage between majesty and purity." He comments:

> The reaction upon the revelation of Jehovah's holiness is a consciousness of sin. But this consciousness of sin carries in itself a profound realization of the majesty of God. It contemplates the holiness not as "purity" simply. It is better to define it "majestic purity" or "ethical sublimity." It is associated with exaltation no less than the other branch.[8]

We conclude, therefore, that the numinous and the ethical are the two essential elements in the idea of the holy. Only as we hold these two elements together in thought and experience can we hope to understand the biblical teaching of sanctification.

II. SANCTIFICATION IN THE OLD TESTAMENT

We turn now to a more careful analysis of the Hebrew terms employed by the Old Testament to express the idea of sanctification. We shall find it profitable further to consider the application of these terms. Finally we shall give attention to the expansion and development of these concepts in the Old Testament.

A. The Meaning of Holiness

One of the largest families of words in the Old Testament is the word *qodesh* and its cognates. Usually translated "holiness," the word carries three main meanings. According to its usage it means glory, or separation, or purity.[9]

---

8. *Biblical Theology* (Grand Rapids: Wm. B. Eerdmans Publishing Co., 1954), pp. 267-68.

9. George Allen Turner, *The More Excellent Way* (Winona Lake, Ind.: Light and Life Press, 1952), pp. 21-24; Turner, *Vision Which Transforms*, pp. 16-19; Vos, *Biblical Theology*, pp. 264-76; Snaith, *Distinctive Ideas of the Old Testament*, pp. 21-42.

1. Holiness as Glory

In many instances *qodesh* carries the idea of "breaking forth with splendor." Numerous passages speak of the glory of Jehovah. God's holiness was manifest in the burning bush, the pillar of fire, and on flaming Sinai (Exod. 3:1-5; 14:24; 19:18). The Lord said, "The tabernacle shall be sanctified by my glory" (Exod. 29:43). And again, "I will be sanctified in them that come nigh me, and before all the people I will be glorified" (Lev. 10:3). Upon the dedication of Solomon's Temple, "the glory of the Lord had filled the house of the Lord" (1 Kings 8:11). Thus the Shekinah came to mark the presence of Jehovah among His people.

2. Holiness as Separation

The verb form "to make holy" includes among its meanings to "cut off," "separate," or "elevate." God is the Wholly Other, standing apart and in opposition to other, imaginary gods. "Who is like unto thee, . . . among the gods? who is like thee, glorious in holiness?" (Exod. 15:11). "There is none holy as the Lord: for there is none beside thee" (1 Sam. 2:2). When applied to things, holiness "always signifies *separated for deity,* or belonging to the sphere of deity."[10] It was basically in this sense that Israel was a "holy nation" (Deut. 7:6).

3. Holiness as Purity

A third meaning of the root *qodesh* is purity. Some scholars think it came from two roots, one of which means "new," "fresh," "pure."[11] Holiness means purity, whether ceremonial or moral. For the ancient Hebrew our distinction between ritual and ethics would have been difficult to grasp. In his approach to God the two were merged. From the beginning *qodesh* contained both ethical and ceremonial imperatives. The blending of these two elements is seen most clearly in the Holiness Code of Leviticus.[12] There both physical and moral cleanness are the condition of worship. Cleanness and holiness are virtually synonymous.

These three meanings are not contradictory or mutually exclusive; they are rather complementary and inclusive. In some passages all three meanings are apparent.

10. Davidson, *Theology of the Old Testament,* p. 152; Snaith, *Distinctive Ideas of the Old Testament,* p. 30.

11. Turner, *More Excellent Way,* p. 23; *Vision Which Transforms,* pp. 18-19; Vos, *Biblical Theology,* p. 265.

12. Chapter 19 ff.

B. The Holiness of God

It is quite evident from the scriptures we have considered that only God is holy *per se*. Holiness is the unique and exclusive quality of Deity. Snaith observes truly:

> When the prophet says in Amos 4:2 that Jehovah "hath sworn by his holiness," he means that Jehovah has sworn by His Deity, by Himself as God, and the meaning is therefore exactly the same as in Amos 6:8, where Amos says that "the Lord God hath sworn by Himself."[13]

No less than 30 times Isaiah uses the term in this sense when he speaks of "the Holy One of Israel."[14] Holiness is not so much one of His attributes as the entirety of the divine character. It is the "godness" of God.[15]

As God, He shines forth with a *glory* peculiar to himself. "Holy, holy, holy, is the Lord of hosts: the whole earth is full of his glory" (Isa. 6:3).[16] As God He stands *separate* and apart, exalted above all that is not himself (Isa. 40:9-31). "God is separate and distinct because He is God."[17] As God He is *absolute purity.* "Thou art of purer eyes than to behold evil, and canst not look on iniquity" (Hab. 1:13). Holiness is thus the goodness of God. This moral goodness is dynamic and not static, as we learn from Isaiah's Temple experience.

Snaith insists that "the God of the Hebrews was essentially active in the world which He has made." Thus, "Transcendence does not mean remoteness. It means otherness." "Jehovah is always active, always dynamically here, in this world. The Hebrew does not say that Jehovah *is,* or that Jehovah *exists,* but that He *does.*"[18]

The Jewish scholar K. Kohler emphasizes the same truth. Holiness, he says:

> . . . indicates spiritual loftiness transcending everything sensual, which works as a purging power of indignation at evil, rebuking injustice, impurity and falsehood, and punishing transgression

---

13. Snaith, *Distinctive Ideas of the Old Testament,* p. 43; cf. also p. 21.

14. Isa. 1:4; 5:19, 24; 10:17, 20; 12:6; 17:7; 29:19; 30:15; 31:1; etc. See Otto J. Baab, *Theology of the Old Testament* (New York: Abingdon-Cokesbury Press, 1949), pp. 35-36.

15. Baab, *Theology of the Old Testament,* p. 34.

16. Snaith says, "To such an extent is *qodesh* an essential characteristic of Jehovah that there are many instances where it is synonymous with *kabod,* in the sense of the burning Splendour of the Presence of the Lord" (*Distinctive Ideas of the Old Testament,* p. 30).

17. *Ibid.,* p. 30.

18. *Ibid.,* p. 47.

until it is removed from the sight of God, which, having purged the soul of wrong, wins it for the right, and which endows man with the power of perfecting himself.[19]

While God is the "Wholly Other," He is not, therefore, "*wholly* 'wholly other.'"[20] His burning holiness is a dynamic sanctifying energy, His purity, love, and goodness communicating themselves to the creature who has been conditioned to receive. The holy God is the sanctifying God.

C. The Holiness of Things

Places and things have a derivative holiness by virtue of their relationship to God. Vos observes, "'Holiness,' when predicated to a thing, would be equivalent to 'the property of God.'"[21] Only God is inherently holy: only God is God. A thing is holy which has passed over into the category of the Separate.[22]

The ground near the burning bush was "holy" in this sense (Exod. 3:5). God commanded Moses to "sanctify" Mount Horeb by setting bounds around it (Exod. 19:23). The Tabernacle (and later the Temple) was *the* holy place, for there God chose to dwell in a unique sense.

Among the things described as holy were the vessels of the Tabernacle (Num. 3:31), the oil (Exod. 30:25, 32), the incense (Exod. 30:35-37), the shewbread (1 Sam. 2:5), and the priests' clothing (Exod. 28:2, 4).

Moreover, certain seasons and days were set aside as holy because they belonged in a special way to God. The Sabbath was preeminently holy because God had himself cut it off from the other days of the week as a period of rest for man and beast (Gen. 2:3; Exod. 20:8-11).

The English equivalent of "holy" in all these cases would be *hallowed* or *sacred*.

D. The Holiness of Persons

In the ceremonial or cultic sense persons are holy in the Old Testament in the same way as things. In rare cases personal holiness was purely cultic; for example, soldiers engaged in a religious war were

---

19. Quoted by Turner, *More Excellent Way*, pp. 26-27.
20. J. W. Harvey, preface to Otto, *Idea of the Holy*, xviii.
21. *Biblical Theology*, p. 269.
22. Snaith, *Distinctive Ideas of the Old Testament*, pp. 31, 47.

said to be "holy" (1 Sam. 21:5-6). In most cases, however, the cere-monial was blended with the moral, at least by implication. The holiness code opens with the solemn word, "Ye shall be holy: for I the Lord your God am holy" (Lev. 19:2). There follow many instruc-tions which are cultic; yet interwoven are many ethical injunctions which find their way into the loftiest passages of the New Testament.

Priests came highest in the scale of holiness. "The priest is *qodesh*, not because . . . he is a person connected with a holy place, but be-cause he belongs to Jehovah."[23] At first every male that opened the womb of an Israelite woman belonged to the Lord (Exod. 13:2). Later Jehovah instructed Moses, "I have taken the Levites for all the first-born of the children of Israel." Thereafter the firstborn son was "redeemed" from the priesthood (Num. 8:18). The sons of Aaron and the Levites by special rites and ceremonies were "hallowed" (Exod. 29:1), or "sanctified" (Lev. 8:12), for their sacred ministry.

Prophets were also spoken of as "holy" (2 Kings 4:9). Jeremiah was "sanctified" before his birth to be "a prophet unto the nations" (Jer. 1:5). Frequently the nation was described as "holy" (Deut. 7:6; Exod. 19:5-6). Snaith points out:

> We have two reasons given why Israel is holy to Jehovah. One is because Jehovah delivered Israel from Egypt and chose him to be a peculiar people to Himself, Deut. 14:2. The other is, in the words of Jeremiah 2:3, "Israel was *qodesh* unto Jehovah, the firstfruits of his increase," though even here a reference to the Wanderings is found in the previous verse.[24]

Practically all Old Testament scholars point out that the ethical aspects of holiness became increasingly prominent under the in-fluence of the great prophets. Sangster makes the point, however, that the prophets did not introduce anything new into the idea of holiness. Moses anticipated the greatest prophets centuries before the prophets appeared.[25] To the extent that God was revealed as a Being of moral purity and holy love, it can be argued that holiness was never a purely cultic term.[26] From the dawn of revelation holiness implied likeness to God. Separation involved separation *to* God; in itself this implied separation *from* sin. Positively, holiness meant, "Thou shalt love thy neighbour as thyself" (Lev. 19:15-18).

---

23. *Ibid.*, p. 44.
24. *Ibid.*, footnote on p. 43.
25. Sangster, *Pure in Heart*, pp. 14-20.
26. Baab, *Theology of the Old Testament*, p. 38.

This is not to overlook the fact, however, that under the influence of the eighth-century prophets holiness came to mean preeminently *justice* and *righteousness*. By their time ritual had become virtually separated from righteousness. Sickened by the empty ceremonialism which went hand in hand with immorality and injustice, Amos cries out in behalf of God, "I hate, I despise your feast days, . . . But let judgment run down as waters, and righteousness as a mighty stream" (5:21, 24). In the same vein the Lord speaks through Hosea: "For I desired mercy, and not sacrifice; and the knowledge of God more than burnt offerings" (6:6). In Isaiah the demand meets us on nearly every page. It is this prophet who sums up the matter in one succinct sentence: "God that is holy shall be sanctified in righteousness" (Isa. 5:16).

The statement of P. T. Forsyth is typical:

> The very history of the word holiness in the Old Testament displays the gradual transcendence of the idea of separation by that of sanctity. It traverses a path in which the quantitative idea of *tabu* changes to the qualitative idea of active and absolute purity. The religious grows ethical, that it may become not only more religious but the one religion for the conscience and for the world. The one God can only be the holy God.[27]

E. Sanctification

While holiness refers to the state or condition of godlikeness, sanctification describes the act or process by which persons or things are made to partake of this quality.

> The verb *hiqdish* (hallow, sanctify) is used of ceremonial dedications and purifications by way of signifying to all concerned that such and such was actually Jehovah's, or to make it clear that it (he) had now come to be Jehovah's.[28]

The work of sanctification includes both the human act of consecration and the divine act of cleansing and hallowing. Although the ceremonial idea dominates the Mosaic writings, the prophetic idea of sanctification stresses the thought of moral purification. Isaiah, as we have seen, sees righteousness as the distinguishing mark of sanctification (5:16). In Ezekiel ceremonial and moral elements are blended in the description of this great work (36:25-27). "The puri-

---

27. *Positive Preaching and the Modern Mind* (New York: George H. Doran, 1907), p. 310. Forsyth does betray an "evolutionary" view of this development when he says the quantitative "changes to" the qualitative.

28. Snaith, *Distinctive Ideas of the Old Testament*, p. 45.

fication from all defilement and the renewing of the heart through the Spirit of God is the essence of the sanctifying activity of God."[29] It is this prophetic view of sanctification which becomes the controlling New Testament teaching.

III. PERFECTION IN THE OLD TESTAMENT

In addition to the idea of holiness there is in the Old Testament another realm of ideas suggested by the word "perfection." Turner points out that the former is primarily a priestly term, while the latter has an affinity with prophetic circles. He quotes Kittel as saying:

> While the terms associated with "holiness" stress the contrast between Jehovah and man, which can only be bridged by an act of cleansing, those associated with "perfection" point to man's kinship with God and the possibility of fellowship.[30]

We read of certain persons who are "pleasing" to the Lord, and they are described as "sincere," "just," "upright," and "perfect" in their generations. The notables in this category are Enoch (Gen. 5:22-24), Noah (Gen. 6:8-9), and Job (Job 1:1, 8), but the list is much longer.

An examination of the adjectives used to describe Noah will help us to understand the idea of perfection. He is said to be "just" and "perfect." The adjective *tsaddiq* ("just") occurs about 500 times, and means "hard," "even," "straight."[31] Once it is used to describe a *correct* weight (Deut. 25:15). Applied to Noah it means that he was "right" with God and his fellows. The second adjective is *tamim*. Of this word Turner says:

> This form occurs about 85 times, of which 44 instances refer to animals for sacrifice translated "without blemish" (39 times) or "without spot" (A.V. 5 times). . . . It is used to describe man's character 23 times and is translated (A.V.) "perfect" (7 times), "upright" (12 times), "sincere" (3 times). . . . It is used of Jehovah's character and conduct about the same number of times as of man's, suggesting the possibility of man resembling God.[32]

Various forms of the root from which *tamim* comes are found

29. Kittel, "Holiness," *Schaff-Herzog Encyclopedia of Religious Knowledge,* 5:217; quoted by Turner, *Vision Which Transforms,* p. 35.

30. Turner, *More Excellent Way,* p. 31.

31. *Ibid.,* p. 32; *Vision Which Transforms,* pp. 44-45.

32. *More Excellent Way,* p. 33; *Vision Which Transforms,* pp. 42-44.

hundreds of times in the Old Testament. They all suggest the importance of "integrity" or wholeness, the necessity of single-mindedness
in our devotion to God.

Another adjective in 14 passages is translated "perfect." This
word is *shalem* and usually refers to a man's "heart." Hezekiah used
shalem when he prayed: "O Lord, . . . I have walked before thee . . .
with a perfect heart" (2 Kings 20:3; Isa. 38:3).[33] The thought here is
blamelessness of motive before God.

It is the Shema, the Hebrew affirmation of faith, which states
the divine demand for perfection: "Hear, O Israel: The Lord our God
is one Lord: and thou shalt love the Lord thy God with all thine
heart, and with all thy soul, and with all thy might" (Deut. 6:4-5). In
the following chapter we read that it was love which moved Jehovah
to choose Israel to be His special people and that love, coupled with
obedience, is the proper response to God's electing mercy (7:6-11).
And it was Deut. 30:6 which gave John Wesley the text for his famous sermon on Christian perfection: "And the Lord thy God will
circumcise thine heart, and the heart of thy seed, to love the Lord
thy God with all thine heart, and with all thy soul, that thou mayest
live." Turner sees here provision for "the excision of an evil tendency
and an integration of motive in terms of loyalty, love, obedience, and
therefore—'life.'"[34]

IV. THE PROMISE OF PENTECOST

Could men be holy before Christ? Isaiah's Temple experience is a
glowing affirmative answer (Isaiah 6). Perfection was possible.[35] But
it was only the spiritually elite who were able to climb the mount of
spiritual transfiguration; those locked up in the law remained in the
valley of repeated failure (Heb. 10:1-4). Before all could know freedom from sin there must be a spiritual outpouring upon the people
of God. It was this effusion of the Spirit of God to which the prophets
looked forward with yearning anticipation.

Jeremiah quotes the Lord as saying concerning that day: "I will
put my law in their inward parts, and write it in their hearts; and
will be their God, and they shall be my people. And they shall teach

---

33. See also Deut. 25:15; 1 Kings 8:16; 11:4; 15:3, 14; 1 Chron. 12:38; 28:9; 29:19;
2 Chron. 15:17; 16:9; 25:2.

34. Turner, *More Excellent Way,* p. 35; *Vision Which Transforms,* p. 47.

35. Gen. 17:1; Deut. 18:13; Ps. 101:2, 6.

no more every man his neighbour, and every man his brother, saying, Know the Lord: for they shall all know me, from the least of them unto the greatest" (Jer. 31:33-34).

Ezekiel also is the mouthpiece of the Lord when he prophesies: "Then will I sprinkle clean water upon you, and ye shall be clean:... A new heart also will I give you, and a new spirit will I put within you:... And I will put my spirit within you, and cause you to walk in my statutes" (Ezek. 36:25-27).

In the mouth of Joel the Lord says concerning that day: "I will pour out my spirit upon all flesh,..." (Joel 2:28-29). It is significant that the Jewish rabbis interpreted these and similar promises as descriptive of a future sanctifying activity of the Spirit of God which would characterize the Messianic age. Typical of rabbinic literature is the paraphrase of Ezekiel by Simeon b. Johai: "And God said, 'In this age, because the evil impulse exists in you, ye have sinned against me; but in the age to come I will eradicate it [sic] from you.'"[36]

V. New Testament Sanctification

The key New Testament holiness text is the declaration of the apostle Peter on the Day of Pentecost, "But this is that which was spoken by the prophet Joel; ..." (Acts 2:16 ff.). The long-expected outpouring of the Spirit had come. The Spirit era which Ezekiel foresaw was here. Jeremiah's prophecy had become history; as the writer to the Hebrews says, "For by one offering he hath perfected for ever them that are sanctified. Whereof the Holy Ghost also is a witness to us: for after that he had said before, this is the covenant that I will make with them after those days, saith the Lord, I will put my laws into their hearts, and in their minds will I write them" (10:14-16).

The importance of this truth can hardly be overemphasized. Rather than being on the periphery, sanctification is at the very heart of the new covenant. Heralding the Messiah's coming, John the Baptist said, "I indeed baptize you with water unto repentance:... he shall baptize you with the Holy Ghost, and with fire" (Matt. 3:11). Commenting upon this promise H. V. Miller declares:

> This, then, is the constant emphasis of the New Testament— the work, the presence, the purity, the power of the Holy Spirit. Dispensationally all was to climax in Him. His coming to the

---

36. Turner, *More Excellent Way,* p. 57; cf. Greathouse, *Fullness of the Spirit,* pp. 46-48.

individual heart of the believer in purifying, empowering presence was the final fruition of all the ages past.[37]

A. The Meaning of Sanctification

The New Testament doctrine of sanctification is built solidly upon the foundation of Old Testament teaching. A careful survey of the New Testament references to the subject indicates that while the prophetic-ethical teaching is dominant, the cultic-religious meaning is retained. There is a merging, a sublimation of Old Testament ideas.

1. *Ceremonial Sanctification*

Several references are distinctly Old Testament in their point of view. For example, reference is frequently made in the New Testament to holy places.[38] Paul refers to "holy things" (1 Cor. 9:13). We read of "holy prophets" (Acts 3:21) and "holy apostles" (Eph. 3:5). Jesus instructs us to hallow, or recognize as holy, the name of God (Matt. 6:9). In his First Epistle, Peter echoes this petition of the Lord's Prayer (3:15). Jesus also speaks of positional sanctification when He cites the Old Testament verse which declares that the altar sanctifies the gift (Matt. 23:17, 19). Paul explains that the unbelieving husband or wife is sanctified by the believing partner and that the children of such a union are "holy" (1 Cor. 7:14).

In the Fourth Gospel we read that the Father sanctified the Son and sent Him into the world (John 10:36) and that the Son sanctified himself (John 17:19).

The Christian Church is said to be a "holy temple" (1 Cor. 3:17; Eph. 2:21). From another point of view it is the new people of God, a "holy nation," in which all the people constitute a "holy priesthood" (1 Pet. 2:5-10). For this reason all Christian believers are described in the New Testament as saints, or "holy ones" *(hagioi).* This title is found 61 times in the New Testament.[39] The Church is the *ecclesia* of God, the body of the called-out ones. By virtue of their calling, God's people are separated from the world to become His special possession. Thus Paul's salutation to the Corinthian church is "to them that are sanctified in Christ Jesus" (1 Cor. 1:2).

---

37. *When He Is Come* (Kansas City: Nazarene Publishing House, 1947), p. 10.

38. Matt. 24:15; 27:53; Acts 6:13; 7:33, et al.

39. In Matthew, Acts, Romans, 1 Corinthians, 2 Corinthians, Ephesians, Philippians, Colossians, 1 Thessalonians, 2 Thessalonians, 1 Timothy, Philemon, Hebrews, Jude, and Revelation. Cf. Acts 9:13, 32, 41; 26:10; Rom. 1:7; 8:27; 12:13; 1 Cor. 1:2; 6:1-2; Eph. 1:1, 15, 18, et al.

That separation and devotement to God do not exhaust the meaning of the term "saint" is certain from the fact that the "saints" are called to "holiness." Implicit within separation is moral sanctity: "But as he who called you is holy, be holy yourselves in all your conduct" (1 Pet. 1:15, RSV). Implicit sanctification must become explicit by an all-pervasive hallowing of life. Nevertheless, the Church is holy in the *religious* sense as the separated people of God.

2. *Ethical Sanctification*

The central idea of Christianity is the purification of the heart from sin and its renewal in the moral image of God. We do not lose sight of the numinous element in sanctification when we speak of it as ethical, for we are sanctified by the supernatural operation of the Spirit of God. As the numinous and ethical were merged in Isaiah's Temple experience (Isaiah 6), these two elements were merged in the outpouring of the Spirit upon the infant Church at Pentecost (Acts 2:1 ff.). The numinous was there—the sound as of the mighty wind, the cloven tongues of fire, the gift of language. God's glory was manifest and the disciples were invaded and possessed of the Holy Spirit. However, the far-reaching effects of this divine invasion were moral —their hearts were purified from sin (Acts 15:8-9).

Negatively, sanctification means *purification.* Under *hagiazo* Thayer lists two kinds of purification in Christian experience: (1) "to purify by expiation, free from guilt of sin"; (2) "to purify internally by reformation of soul." This corresponds to the two epochs we call justification (or regeneration) and entire sanctification.

In the new birth there is "purification by expiation of the guilt of sin" (1 Cor. 6:11; Jas. 4:8a). Wiley refers to this as the cleansing from acquired depravity.[40] By "the washing of regeneration" (Titus 3:5) the pollution acquired by our sinning is removed and we are "clean" (John 15:3). For this reason we say that sanctification begins in regeneration.

In entire sanctification the heart is purified from the root or inbeing of sin, effecting single-mindedness of devotion to God (John 17:17, 19; Eph. 5:26; 1 Thess. 5:23; Jas. 4:8b). Entire sanctification is not so much a state as a condition preserved moment by moment as we walk in the light (1 John 1:7).

Positively, sanctification means *the restoration of the moral image of God.* It is the putting on of the new man, "created after the likeness of God

---

40. *Christian Theology,* 2:480; cf. Wynkoop, *Theology of Love,* pp. 249-67.

in true righteousness and holiness" (Eph. 4:24, RSV). This positive sanctification includes a progressive work. It is initiated in regeneration, accelerated by the infilling of the Holy Spirit, and consummated by glorification. The process is described by Paul in these words: "We all, with unveiled face, beholding the glory of the Lord, *are being changed* into his likeness from one degree of glory to another" (2 Cor. 3:18, RSV, italics added). The consummation is envisioned by John: "When he shall appear, we shall be like him; for we shall see him as he is" (1 John 3:2).

B. Sanctification as Total Process

The word *hagiasmos* occurs 10 times in the New Testament and is rendered "sanctification" by the American Revised Version in each instance.[41] The Greek word "connotes state and that not as native to its subject but as an outcome of action or progress."[42] In several passages where the word is used the writer appears to be viewing the subjective aspect of salvation as a total process.[43] Both Paul and Peter speak of the "sanctification of the Spirit" in this way (2 Thess. 2:13; 1 Pet. 1:2).

Viewed morally, salvation *is* sanctification. Salvation is subjectively the hallowing of our lives by the Holy Spirit. From beginning to end our personal salvation is His gracious work. This sanctification is all of a piece, a "continuity of grace" carried forward through the personal activity of the sanctifying Spirit. "The Holy Spirit," says John Wesley, "is not only holy in himself, but the immediate cause of all holiness in us." Everything He does in human experience is a work of sanctification. Sanctification, says Wiley, is "in a broad sense . . . the whole work wrought *in* us by the Holy Spirit."[44]

C. Initial Sanctification

Sanctification begins in regeneration. The new life principle imparted by the Holy Spirit is the principle of holiness. "The love of God is shed abroad in our hearts by the Holy Ghost which is given unto us" (Rom. 5:5). Writing to the Corinthian church Paul said, "Know ye not that the unrighteous shall not inherit the kingdom of God? Be

---

41. Rom. 6:19, 22; 1 Cor. 1:30; 1 Thess. 4:3-4, 7; 2 Thess. 2:13; 1 Tim. 2:15; Heb. 12:14; 1 Pet. 1:2. -

42. Turner, *More Excellent Way*, p. 83; *Vision Which Transforms*, p. 116.

43. 1 Cor. 1:30; 2 Thess. 2:13; 1 Pet. 1:2, and possibly Heb. 12:14.

44. Wiley and Culbertson, *Introduction to Christian Theology*, p. 313.

not deceived: neither fornicators, nor idolaters, nor adulterers, . . . shall inherit the kingdom of God. And such were some of you: but ye are *washed,* but ye are *sanctified,* but ye are *justified* in the name of the Lord Jesus, and by the Spirit of our God" (1 Cor. 6:9-11, italics added). In his sermon on "Sin in Believers," John Wesley has an illuminating comment on this passage:

> "Ye are washed," says the apostle, "ye are sanctified;" name-ly, cleansed from "fornication, idolatry, drunkenness," and all other *outward* sin; and yet, at the same time, in another sense of the word, they were unsanctified; they were not washed, not *inwardly* cleansed from envy, evil surmising, partiality.[45]

We therefore speak of initial sanctification as partial rather than entire. This term, says Wiley, "is not an indefinite one, referring to the cleansing away of more or less of the sinner's defilement. It is a definite term, and is limited strictly to that guilt and acquired depravity attaching to actual sins, for which the sinner is himself responsible."[46]

Initial or partial sanctification is also implied by Paul's exhortation in 2 Cor. 7:1, where he urges his readers, "Having therefore these promises, dearly beloved, let us cleanse ourselves from all filthiness of the flesh and spirit, *perfecting holiness* in the fear of God" (italics added). This verse argues for both initial and entire sanctification. The Corinthians were to bring to completion the holiness which was only partial.

D. Entire Sanctification

Both general and initial sanctification, as thus analyzed, are concepts so widely accepted among Protestants that they do not need further elaboration. The crucial question concerns the possibility of *entire* sanctification. It is in this area that Wesley's doctrine is distinctive. It is the conviction of those who follow Wesley that "the blood of Jesus Christ . . . cleanseth from all sin" (1 John 1:7).[47]

Although implied by many New Testament passages, the doctrine of entire sanctification seems to be demanded by others, i.e., John 17:17, 19; 2 Cor. 7:1; Eph. 1:4; 5:26; 1 Thess. 5:23; and perhaps Heb. 13:12.

In His high priestly prayer for the disciples Jesus makes it abun-

45. *Works,* 5:150.
46. Wiley, *Christian Theology,* 2:480.
47. Literally, "cleanses and keeps on cleasning" (Greek present tense).

dantly clear He is not praying for the world. "I pray not for the world, but for them which thou hast given me; . . . They are not of the world, even as I am not of the world. Sanctify them through thy truth: thy word is truth" (John 17:9, 16-17). Sanctification must mean purification rather than separation because the disciples are already said to be separated. Furthermore, it must mean a purification for *believers,* for they are declared to be such, and set apart from the world (vv. 8-9, 16). This prayer was answered on the Day of Pentecost by the baptism with the Holy Spirit. The spokesman for the apostles, Simon Peter, who was there, declared that "God . . . [gave] them the Holy Ghost, . . . *purifying their hearts* by faith" (Acts 15:8-9, italics added). John 17:20 makes it clear that Jesus' prayer is for believers of all ages.

Paul's exhortation to the Corinthians in 2 Cor. 7:1 is cited by Turner as decisive. It is addressed to those who are already sanctified in the lower sense, i.e., they are "saints" (1 Cor. 1:2; 2 Cor. 1:1); but they are not cleansed from all defilement. "This complete cleansing is an imperative for the present, and not merely a distant goal, as the use of the present tense implies."[48] Positively, the command is to "perfect"—to bring to completion—the holiness which has been initiated by the new birth. For this reason it is appropriate to style this "entire sanctification."

In Eph. 1:4 *hagios* ("holy") is joined with *amomos* (literally, "without blemish"). "He hath chosen us in him before the foundation of the world, that we should be holy and without blemish before him in love." *Amomos* suggests an unblemished sacrificial victim (Lev. 22:21). It describes Christ twice (Heb. 9:14; 1 Pet. 1:19), and Christians six times.[49] God's eternal purpose for His people in Christ is a holiness which means blamelessness of love.

Eph. 5:25-27 moves in the same vein. The critical nature of *entire* sanctification as the means of effecting blameless love is obscured by the King James Version but is made clear by most of the revised versions including the Revised Standard Version: "Christ loved the church and gave himself up for her, that he might sanctify her, *having cleansed her* by the washing of water with the word, that the church might be presented before him in splendor, without spot or wrinkle or any such thing, that she might be holy and without blemish" (ital-

---

48. Turner, *More Excellent Way,* p. 89; *Vision Which Transforms,* p. 122.
49. Eph. 1:4; 5:27; Col. 1:22; Phil. 2:15; Jude 24; Rev. 14:5.

ics added). This accurate translation makes clear the truth that Christ gave himself up to sanctify the Church, *which has already had the bath of regeneration.* Verse 27 informs us that this entire sanctification accomplishes the blamelessness set forth in 1:4.

In 1 Thessalonians, Paul rejoices that his converts received the gospel "in power, and in the Holy Ghost, and in much assurance" (1:5), but his prayer is that their faith might be perfected (3:10), "to the end he may stablish your hearts unblameable in holiness before God, even our Father, at the coming of our Lord Jesus Christ with all his saints" (3:13). The apostle goes on to remind the Thessalonians that this sanctification is God's will and call to those to whom He had given His Holy Spirit (4:3-8). The climax of his appeal is 5:14-24. Turner sees here a remarkable similarity of sequence to that of Matt. 5:33-48. The burden of the entire letter finds expression in verses 23-24: "And the very God of peace sanctify you wholly; and I pray God your whole spirit and soul and body be preserved blameless unto the coming of our Lord Jesus Christ. Faithful is he that calleth you, who also will do it." The term here translated "wholly" is the strongest word Paul could employ. It is a compound word, *holoteleis*, meaning literally "wholly" and "perfectly." Commenting upon this prayer Morris writes:

> The prayer is that God may *sanctify you wholly.* There is a manward aspect of sanctification in that we are called upon to yield up our wills for the doing of God's will. But the power manifest in the sanctified life is not human, but divine, and Paul's prayer is phrased in the light of this. In the deepest sense our sanctification is the work of God within us. This work may be ascribed to the Son (Eph. v. 26) or to the Spirit (Rom. xv. 16), but in any case it is divine. The word *wholly* is an unusual one (holoteleis), being found only here in the New Testament. It is a combination of the ideas of wholeness and completion, and Lightfoot suggests that the meaning may be given here as "may He sanctify you so that ye may be entire."[50]

The second part of the petition shows that Paul is uttering a fervent prayer that *the entire man,* "intact in all its parts," may be preserved holy and blameless until the Parousia. This hallowing of the entire moral and physical being is appropriate in the light of Paul's teaching that the body is the temple of the Holy Spirit (1 Cor. 6:19). "The

---

50. Leon Morris, *The Epistles of Paul to the Thessalonians;* "Tyndale New Testament Commentaries" (Grand Rapids: Wm. B. Eerdmans Publishing Co., 1957), p. 107.

faithfulness of God," Morris notes, "is the ground for certainty that the prayer offered will be answered."[51]

The above passages by no means exhaust the New Testament evidence for entire sanctification, but they are sufficient to establish the possibility of entire sanctification in this life.

E. Christian Perfection

The passages we have examined in the preceding section afford instructive examples of the merging and sublimation of the priestly and prophetic ideals of the Old Testament. The two streams flow together and become one. Christian perfection and entire sanctification are two terms to describe the same experience. Perfection in love before God *is* Christian holiness.

The verb *teleio* occurs 25 times in the New Testament. It means to fulfill, to bring to an end, to attain to a certain norm or standard. Paul uses the adjective *teleios* 7 times. In several instances the meaning is clearly "mature" in the moral sense (1 Cor. 14:20: Eph. 4:13-14). In 1 Cor. 2:6, 15, however, the "perfect" are equated with the "spiritual" (also 1 Cor. 3:1). A study of this latter passage indicates that the "perfect" are the fully sanctified. J. Weiss concludes that while perfection is usually future in Paul (Phil. 3:12), yet sometimes (1 Cor. 2:6; Phil. 3:15) it is already present.[52] He holds that Paul's use of *teleios* in Col. 1:28 and 4:12 designates moral and spiritual perfection.

The evidence, therefore, points to the double meaning of perfection. A Christian may be both perfect and imperfect, depending upon the sense in which the words are used.

1. *Perfection in love*

One of the most important sections on perfection is Matt. 5:43-48, climaxing with the Master's command: "You, therefore, must be perfect, as your heavenly Father is perfect" (RSV). "Therefore" is the key to this verse. Jesus is saying, according to the context, "As your Father is perfect in love, sending His blessings upon friend and enemy alike, you must be perfect in your love toward all men." It is evident that this is the love of *agape*—spontaneous, uncaused goodwill, flowing from the inner nature. This love is not conditioned

---

51. *Ibid.,* p. 108.

52. *Der Erste Korintherbrief* (1910), p. 74; quoted by Turner, *More Excellent Way,* p. 95; *Vision Which Transforms,* p. 132.

by its objects but is created by the Holy Spirit (Rom. 5:6, 8; 1 John 4:13-21).

This love is the fulfillment of the Law (Matt. 22:35-40; Rom. 13:8-10). As Paul puts it, "Love worketh no ill to his neighbour: therefore love is the fulfilling of the law" (Rom. 13:10). Perfect love implies the elimination of all resentment and ill will. Negatively, its *quality* is pure; nothing contrary to love remains in the heart of the sanctified man. Positively, the *quantity* of love is capable of infinite enlargement.

Wesley has given us an 11-point summary of his doctrine of Christian perfection, in the following short propositions:

1. There is such a thing as perfection; for it is again and again mentioned in Scripture.

2. It is not so early as justification; for justified persons are to "go on unto perfection" (Heb. vi. 1).

3. It is not so late as death; for St. Paul speaks of living men that were perfect (Phil. iii. 15).

4. It is not absolute. Absolute perfection belongs not to man, nor to angels, but to God alone.

5. It does not make a man infallible: None is infallible, while he remains in the body.

6. Is it sinless? It is not worth while to contend for a term. It is "salvation from sin."

7. It is "perfect love" (I John iv. 18). This is the essence of it; its properties, or inseparable fruits, are, rejoicing evermore, praying without ceasing, and in everything giving thanks (I Thess. v. 16 & c).

8. It is improvable. It is so far from lying in an indivisible point, from being incapable of increase, that one perfected in love may grow in grace far swifter than he did before.

9. It is amissible, capable of being lost; of which we have numerous instances. . . .

10. It is constantly both preceded and followed by a gradual work.

11. But is it in itself instantaneous or not? . . . It is often difficult to perceive the instance when a man dies; yet there is an instant in which life ceases. And if ever sin ceases, there must be a last moment of its existence, and a first moment of our deliverance from it.[53]

2. *Perfection in Christlikeness*

The perfection of maturity, "the measure of the stature of the fulness of Christ," is the final goal of Christian development. When

---

53. *Works,* XI, 441-42.

one views this consummation, he confesses with self-abasement, "Not as though I had already attained, either were already perfect: but I follow after, if that I may apprehend that for which also I am apprehended of Christ Jesus" (Phil. 3:12). "But . . . we await a Savior, the Lord Jesus Christ, who will change our lowly body to be like his glorious body, by the power which enables him even to subject all things to himself" (Phil. 3:20-21, RSV).

F. The Fullness of the Spirit

One final word should be added. Entire sanctification or perfect love is by the baptism with the Holy Spirit (Acts 1:4-5; 15:8-9). The living heart of this precious experience is the personal indwelling of the Spirit (John 14:15-17). As the key to the New Testament doctrine of sanctification is Peter's declaration that Joel's prophecy had been fulfilled, the key to spiritual victory in the Christian's life is found in Paul's exhortation to the Ephesians, "Be filled with the Spirit" (5:18).

SUMMARY

The purpose of this chapter has been to examine and set forth the biblical doctrine of sanctification. As a starting point we considered Rudolf Otto's thesis that holiness is a complex, a "strange harmony of contrasts." In addition to the "rational" ethical element Otto discovers a "non-rational" element for which he coins the term "numinous." To save holiness from becoming simply the interest of ethicists we must recognize this numinous element. The numinous and the ethical must be kept together as the warp and woof of true holiness.

A survey of Old Testament holiness teaching substantiates in the main Otto's contention. *Qodesh* and its cognates keep these elements together. *Qodesh* is a gem of three facets, suggesting glory, separation, and purity. God only is holy per se. His holiness is no static quality; it is a dynamic, sanctifying energy imparting itself. Places and things have a derivative holiness by virtue of their relationship to God. When so predicated holiness means "the property of God." This cultic meaning of holiness is also ascribed to people, but from the dawn of divine revelation holiness in men meant godlikeness. It was the prophets, however, who brought this truth out in bold relief. Isaiah's statement is definitive: "God that is holy shall be sanctified in righteousness" (5:16). Sanctification describes the impartation of holiness from Deity to things or persons. The idea of sanctification likewise became more ethical under prophetic influence.

In addition to the idea of holiness there is in the Old Testament a second realm of ideas associated with the word "perfection." While holiness is a priestly concept, perfection is a distinctly prophetic concept. It suggests man's likeness to God, the possibility of man's "pleasing" God. The Shema states the Lord's demand for perfection and defines it as perfect love. Deut. 30:6 is a promise that the Lord will work such perfection in the hearts of His people. This leads us into the prophetic longing for holiness. The great spiritual leaders of Israel discovered this treasure, and some came to possess it by faith, but the multitudes were left to traverse the treadmill of victory and defeat. The great prophets, however, foresaw the Christian dispensation and recognized as its distinguishing feature a universal sanctifying outpouring of the Spirit of God.

The New Testament recognizes that the day of fulfillment had come. At Pentecost the prophets' visions became reality. Tracing the idea of sanctification through the New Testament, we find that the doctrine is a consummation of Old Testament thought in which priestly and prophetic streams merge in glorious fullness. New Testament sanctification synthesizes the numinous and the ethical. The fullness of the Spirit means both power and purity, the mystical indwelling of the Holy Spirit and the ethical fruit of the Spirit. Through the personal agency of the Holy Spirit we may be purified from both the guilt and the inbeing of sin, made perfect in love, and finally restored to complete Christlikeness. It is every believer's privilege, therefore, to be perfect as his Father in heaven is perfect and to be filled with the Holy Spirit.

CHAPTER 17

Crisis and Process
in Sanctification

Notice has been taken of the general agreement as to the bare meaning of the term sanctification: God's provision for renewing human nature in deliverance from sin. G. C. Berkouwer introduces his book on the Reformed or Calvinistic concept of sanctification with a noteworthy paragraph:

> In any discussion about sanctification it is evident that we are concerned, not with a maze of theoretical abstractions, but with the bread-and-butter problems of this life. One can even say that a discussion about sanctification is the more relevant because also the unbeliever evinces interest in what the church professes in the matter. For he detects in this teaching a presumptuous note, the pretension, namely, of being saintly, of being different. And, of course, this pretension seems to the accuser entirely unwarranted.[1]

The question which will concern us in this chapter is the central issue of the Wesleyan position: that sanctification—"the redemptive touch of our faith on all of life"[2]—may be completed in this world by the act of God in relation to the believer's faith. The major alternative to this position is that sanctification is a process of unending growth in which full deliverance from sinning and sinfulness is never

---

1. *Faith and Sanctification:* Studies in Dogmatics (Grand Rapids: Wm. B. Eerdmans Publishing Co., 1952), p. 9. Berkouwer is professor of systematic theology, Free University of Amsterdam, and one of the outstanding exponents of Reformed (Calvinistic) theology in our day.

2. *Ibid.,* p. 12.

attained and that entire sanctification occurs at or "in the hour and article of death."

The term "crisis" as used in our chapter heading is meant to indicate an act of God at a given point in the believer's life. It expresses the conviction that sanctification is not a long-drawn-out and never-completed process, but that it reaches a focal point of divine action at a given time and place. The term "process" on the other hand is intended to point up the fact that entire sanctification is not a static and changeless condition which admits of no progress or growth, but is the beginning point in purity from which a lifetime of maturity may develop.

John Wesley himself gives warrant for the terminology used here. He states it clearly in a sermon which represents his settled and final conviction:

> By justification we are saved from the guilt of sin, and restored to the favor of God; by sanctification we are saved from the power and root of sin, and restored to the image of God. All experience, as well as Scripture, shows this salvation (from the power and root of sin) to be both instantaneous and gradual. It begins the moment we are justified, in the holy, humble, gentle, patient love of God and man. It gradually increases from that moment, as 'a grain of mustard-seed, which, at first is the least of all seeds,' but afterwards puts forth large branches, and becomes a great tree; till, in another instant, the heart is cleansed from all sin, and filled with pure love of God and man.[3]

The question here is deep and fundamental. It is closely tied in with issues as to the source of sanctification and its meaning for an actual change in the quality of the spiritual life. We shall therefore turn first to the evidence from Scripture for the critical or instantaneous character of God's work of sanctification; and then to the nature and meaning of process in sanctification, the gradual aspect of which Wesley spoke.

I. Crisis in Entire Sanctification

We are here discussing the time element in sanctification. Does the actual sanctification of human nature result from growth and self-discipline, or may it be traced to an act of God's grace completed in a moment of time?

---

3. *Sermons,* 2:236.

It might be pointed out that some present-day theologians who follow John Calvin state that it is both, but with such an interpretation as to make it in effect neither. A case in point is Lewis Sperry Chafer in Vol. VI of his eight-volume *Systematic Theology*. Chafer contrasts what he calls "positional sanctification," which is instantaneous and which occurs at the moment of conversion, and "experimental sanctification," which is progressive and never completed in the course of this life.[4]

Closer examination makes it clear that neither "positional" nor "experimental" sanctification is sanctification at all. The former is an imputed "holiness" which makes no actual change in the moral state of the believer. The latter is specifically said to have no relationship at all to yieldedness to God or victory over sin. "Its meaning is that the knowledge of truth, devotion, and Christian experience are naturally subject to development,"[5] a concept which in no way conforms to the biblical meaning of sanctification.

Charles Hodge gives a statement of the growth theory of sanctification which is far more true to the meaning of the term as such, although he staunchly defends the Calvinistic position that it is never entire or complete in this life. At the foundation of all scriptural presentation of sanctification, Hodge says, is the truth

> that regeneration, the quickening, of which believers are the subject, while it involves the implanting, or communication of a new principle or form of life, does not effect the immediate and entire deliverance of the soul from all sin. . . . According to the Scriptures, the universal experience of Christians, and the undeniable evidence of history, regeneration does not remove all sin.[6]

No more eloquent statement of the need for sanctification in believers will be found than that which follows. Hodge then states his understanding of sanctification:

> Sanctification, therefore, consists in two things: first, the removing more and more the principles of evil still infecting our nature, and destroying their power; and secondly, the growth of the principle of spiritual life until it controls the thoughts, feelings, and acts, and brings the soul into the image of Christ.[7]

---

4. (Dallas, Tex.: Dallas Seminary Press, 1947), 6:284-85. Cf. Purkiser, *Conflicting Concepts of Holiness*, pp. 15-44, where these views are examined at length.

5. *Ibid.*, p. 285.

6. *Systematic Theology*, 3:220.

7. *Ibid.*, 3:221.

This process, it should be said, is claimed never to be complete so long as we live in this world.

In Hodge's statement we have some important points of agreement with the Wesleyan position. Sanctification is recognized as not identical with nor effected at the time of justification or regeneration. There is a corruption remaining in believers, which results in the need for sanctification. The goal of sanctification is seen to be the removing of the principle of evil still infecting our nature, and the control of thoughts, feelings, and acts in such a way as to bring the soul into the image of Christ.

A major issue therefore lies in the temporal element. When, and under what circumstances, is sanctification completed? It is our conviction that both the New Testament and the experience of God's people through the ages will confirm the possibility and importance of complete sanctification wrought by the Holy Spirit within in an instant of time. In his Jones Lectures on Evangelism, published under the title *Stir Up the Gift,* Paul S. Rees writes:

> What is needed today is a humble and realistic facing of two towering facts: (1) the New Testament offers and (2) the collective Christian experience of the centuries confirms a release of the Spirit of God in the lives of Christians sufficiently distinct from the initial coming of the Spirit in conversion to make a crucial difference between defeated living and victorious living, between discipleship that is inwardly divided and discipleship that is inwardly unified, between service that is relatively barren and often dull, and service that is joyous, potent and fruitful.[8]

The alternatives, then, are not *either* progressive sanctification *or* crisic sanctification. It is not either/or but both/and. The question is whether in the progress of the Christian walk there is a critical step that in a real way corresponds to New Testament affirmations about purity of heart, freedom from sin, cleansing, perfection or completeness in love, and the fullness of the Spirit. Wesleyans affirm that there is such a step subsequent to regeneration. Non-Wesleyans generally deny such a crisis, and are left, as a result, with the need for explaining the New Testament statments that affirm it.

We should be reminded here that the single term sanctification by no means exhausts the full New Testament teaching concerning the deliverance of believers from inner sin. There are also such related concepts as the baptism with the Holy Spirit, heart purity, crucifixion or death of the old man, perfect love, the rest of faith, the

---

8. (Grand Rapids: Zondervan Publishing House, 1952), p. 148.

fullness of the blessing of Christ, and others. "This experience [that is, entire sanctification] is also known by various terms representing its different phases, such as 'Christian Perfection,' 'Perfect Love,' 'Heart Purity,' 'The Baptism with the Holy Spirit,' 'The Fullness of the Blessing,' and 'Christian Holiness.'"[9]

Biblical evidence that entire sanctification is an instantaneous act of God's grace wrought in response to the believer's faith may be grouped into three classes: the use of the terminology of crisis; the stipulation of the means or agency of sanctification; and the significance of the Greek aorist tense. We shall examine these in order, and add a fourth, the testimony of experience.

A. The Terminology of Crisis

An important point as we look at the New Testament description of the deeper Christian life is the fact that the terminology used to describe it is so often the terminology of crisis. Words are used, many of them by analogy of course, which refer to acts that are properly the events of a moment rather than to processes which may not be brought to completion in this life.

Even the verb "to sanctify" carries with it the overtones of an action which is most naturally thought of as occurring at a particular point in time. As we have seen, it carries a twofold definition, "to set apart" and "to make holy." It may be granted that it is possible to conceive a gradual "setting apart" or "making holy." But the action described is much more naturally thought of as momentary and immediate. Particularly is this so when we reflect that "to sanctify" in its most typical New Testament sense refers to an act of God.

Among other New Testament descriptions of the means whereby the sanctification of the believer is accomplished is the familiar designation, the baptism with the Spirit. Jesus said to His disciples, "John truly baptized with water; but ye shall be baptized with the Holy Ghost not many days hence" (Acts 1:5). All of the Gospels contrast the baptism of John with water unto repentance and the remission of sins with the baptism of Christ with the Holy Spirit as fire unto thorough purging and preservation of character and life (Matt. 3:11-12; Mark 1:8; Luke 3:16-17; John 1:33). Baptism is a term which always implies action at a given time, and never that which is drawn

---

9. Article X, "Articles of Faith," *Manual,* Church of the Nazarene, current edition, *ad loc.*

out over a long period of time, and perhaps never completed until death. The gradual baptism with the Spirit is as absurd as gradual baptism with water.

Again, the terms crucifixion and death are used as descriptive of sanctification. Rom. 6:6, "Knowing this, that our old self was crucified with Him, that our body of sin might be done away with, that we should no longer be slaves to sin" (NASB). Rom. 6:11, "Even so consider yourselves to be dead to sin, but alive to God in Christ Jesus" (NASB). Gal. 2:20, "I have been crucified with Christ; and it is no longer I who live, but Christ lives in me; and the life which I now live in the flesh I live by faith in the Son of God, who loved me, and delivered Himself up for me" (NASB). "But may it never be that I should boast, except in the cross of our Lord Jesus Christ, through which the world has been crucified to me, and I to the world" (NASB). "Therefore consider the members of your earthly body as dead" (Col. 3:5, NASB).

All of these references contain a common thought: there is a death, in sanctification, of a sin principle, a carnal condition of the ego. Crucifixion as a mode of execution was sometimes swift, sometimes slow, but always certain. Dying may be long, but death is instantaneous. In the framework of New Testament thought, death would be conceived as happening at a given moment. Gradual death would be but a figure of speech for a mortal illness. Death itself would be instantaneous.

Sanctification has already been defined as involving cleansing, purifying. The New Testament contains frequent references in which the term *katharizein,* "to purify," is used of believers (e.g., Acts 15:9; 2 Cor. 7:1; Eph. 5:26; Titus 2:14; John 15:2).[10] Cleansing and purification *may* be continuous processes, but the natural meaning of these words indicates that there is always an initial moment when the cleansing or purification takes place. Purity may be and is a condition to be maintained, as in 1 John 1:7. But the condition cannot be maintained until it is created, and this suggests an act.

The Spirit's fullness is referred to as a gift, to be received. "The gift of the Holy Spirit" is frequently mentioned through the New Testament, often as "the promise of the Father" (e.g., Acts 2:38-39). Jesus, in Luke 11:13, said, "If ye then, being evil, know how to give good gifts unto your children: how much more shall your heavenly

---

10. Cf. Turner, *More Excellent Way,* p. 85, n.; *Vision Which Transforms,* p. 118.

Father give the Holy Spirit to them that ask him?" "And they of the circumcision which believed were astonished, as many as came with Peter, because that on the Gentiles also was poured out the gift of the Holy Ghost" (Acts 10:45). As C. Ryder Smith says in speaking of the giving of the Spirit:

> To thrust the gift upon men would be a contradiction in terms, but the whole purpose of the Gospel is to make men holy. Here, as elsewhere, the doctrines of the Holy Spirit and of the derivative holiness of men are correlative. In the Holy Spirit God offers to share his holiness with every man. It is the incoercive aggression of a Father's heart. While no man can be holy against his will, any man, if he will, may begin to be holy . . . Similarly the "holiness" of the Christian is, in turn, aggressive. While the Jews have always tended to keep to themselves, real Christians never do.[11]

Just as the gift of the Spirit implies the "incoercive aggression of a Father's heart," offering but not forcing, so it implies that which passes into the possession of its receiver at some given moment. Not only would forcing a gift upon a person be a contradiction in terms, but so would be the "gradual" giving of a gift.

One of the great New Testament analogies of entire sanctification is the crossing of the Jordan into Canaan by the covenant people of the Old Testament (cf. Heb. 4:1-11; Jude 5; 1 Cor. 10:1-11). Just as their deliverance from Egypt represents the first crisis in redemption, their inheritance of the Promised Land represents the second crisis. It is true that "crossing the Jordan has often been thought of as symbolical of death, but it is much more helpful, and truer to the facts, to think of it as the entrance into the life of fullness of blessing to which the Captain of the Lord's host brings us. 'Let us therefore fear, lest, a promise being left us of entering into his rest, any of you should seem to come short of it' (Heb. iv. 1)"[12] Crossing the Jordan was clearly an event, not a process, and as much the act of a given point of time as the crossing of the Red Sea 40 years earlier. So entrance into the believer's "rest of faith" is an epochal event, not an endless effort.

Other terms might be added. Entire sanctification is variously described as putting off the old man and putting on the new man created after God in righteousness and true holiness (Eph. 4:20-24). It is the destroying of the body of sin (Rom. 6:6). It is being made free

11. *Bible Doctrine of Man,* p. 194.

12. Hugh J. Blair, *New Bible Commentary,* p. 226. Blair is a minister of the Reformed Presbyterian Church of Ireland.

from the law of sin and death by the law of the Spirit of life in Christ Jesus (Rom. 8:2). It is being filled with the Spirit (Eph. 5:18). It is a circumcision of heart (Deut. 30:6; Col. 2:11). It is being made perfect in love (1 John 4:17-18).

When now we summarize all these verbs, we gain an almost irresistible impression of climax, epoch, or crisis: "to set apart," "to make holy," "to baptize with the Spirit," "to crucify," "to put to death," "to mortify," "to cleanse," "to purify," "to give and receive as a gift," "to cross into the promised land," "to enter the rest of faith," "to put off the old man and put on the new," "to destroy the body of sin," "to be made free from the law of sin and death," "to be filled with the Spirit," "to be circumcised in heart," "to be made perfect in love." All of these terms describe actions which most naturally take place at a definite time and place, and which do not admit of degrees. They all testify to the fact that complete sanctification is a crisis experience, and not a long-drawn-out and never-completed process of growth.

B. The Means or Agency of Sanctification

Another important line of evidence for the crisis nature of the work of entire sanctification is found in Bible descriptions of the means or agency whereby we are to be sanctified. It is significant that growth or death are nowhere mentioned as having any part to play in the sanctification of believers. Instead, it is the Word of God, the blood of Christ, the Holy Spirit, and faith which are indicated as the factors concerned with sanctification.

1. *The Blood of Christ*

Sanctification is effected through the offering of the body and blood of Jesus Christ once for all: "By the which will we are sanctified through the offering of the body of Jesus Christ once for all" (Heb. 10:10); "Wherefore Jesus also, that he might sanctify the people with his own blood, suffered without the gate. . . . Now the God of peace, that brought again from the dead our Lord Jesus, that great shepherd of the sheep, through the blood of the everlasting covenant, make you perfect in every good work to do his will, working in you that which is well pleasing in his sight, through Jesus Christ, to whom be glory for ever and ever. Amen" (Heb. 13:12, 20-21).

2. *The Holy Spirit*

The divine agency which sanctifies is that of the Holy Spirit: "And God, who knows the heart, bore witness to them, giving them the Holy Spirit, just as He also did to us; and He made no distinction between us and them, cleansing their hearts by faith" (Acts 15:8-9, NASB); "But I have written very boldly to you on some points, so as to remind you again, because of the grace that was given me from God, to be a minister of Christ Jesus to the Gentiles, ministering as a priest the gospel of God, that my offering of the Gentiles might become acceptable, sanctified by the Holy Spirit" (Rom. 15:15-16, NASB); "But we should always give thanks to God for you, brethren beloved by the Lord, because God has chosen you from the beginning for salvation through sanctification by the Spirit and faith in the truth" (2 Thess. 2:13, NASB); "Peter, an apostle of Jesus Christ, to those who reside as aliens, scattered throughout Pontus, Galatia, Cappadocia, Asia, and Bithynia, who are chosen according to the foreknowledge of God the Father, by the sanctifying work of the Spirit, that you may obey Jesus Christ and be sprinkled with His blood" (1 Pet. 1:1-2, NASB); and, "Seeing ye have purified your souls in obeying the truth through the Spirit unto unfeigned love of the brethren, see that ye love one another with a pure heart fervently" (1 Pet. 1:22). God himself is invoked to sanctify completely the Thessalonian believers: "And the very God of peace sanctify you wholly; and I pray God your whole spirit and soul and body be preserved blameless unto the coming of our Lord Jesus Christ" (1 Thess. 5:23).

3. *The Scriptures*

The Word of God, functioning in the believer's heart as truth and light, is the formal cause of sanctification: "Sanctify them through thy truth: thy word is truth. . . . Neither pray I for these alone, but for them also which shall believe on me through their word" (John 17:17, 20). "But if we walk in the light, as he is in the light, we have fellowship one with another, and the blood of Jesus Christ his Son cleanseth us from all sin" (1 John 1:7).

4. *Faith*

Faith, not works or human striving, is the sufficient condition for entire sanctification on the part of the believer. This is seen in the references already quoted from Acts 15:8-9; 26:18; Rom. 6:11; Gal. 3:14; and 2 Thess. 2:12. Charles Ewing Brown argues that the growth theory of sanctification easily slips over into a concept of sanctification by human effort or works.[13] Biblical sanctification is by faith.

---

13. *The Meaning of Sanctification* (Anderson, Ind.: The Warner Press, 1945), pp. 33-34.

Whatever is attained by human effort must of necessity be gradual; what is obtained by faith as the gift of God may be instantaneous. This is the import of Wesley's statement:

> Sanctification, too, is not of works, lest any man should boast. 'It is the gift of God', and is to be received by *plain, simple faith.* Suppose you are now laboring to 'abstain from all appearance of evil,' 'zealous of good works,' and walking diligently and carefully in all the ordinances of God; there is then only one point remaining; the voice of God to your soul is, 'Believe, and be saved.' First, believe that God has *promised* to save you from all sin, and to fill you with all holiness; secondly, believe that He is *able* thus 'to save to the uttermost all that come unto God through Him;' thirdly, believe that He is *willing,* as well as able, to save *you* to the uttermost; to purify you from all sin, and fill up all your heart with love. Believe, fourthly, that He is not only able, but willing to do it *now.* Not when you come to die; not at any distant time; not tomorrow, but *today.* He will then enable you to believe, *it is done,* according to His Word: and then 'patience shall have its perfect work, that ye may be perfect and entire, wanting nothing.'[14]

C. The Testimony of the Tenses

A third line of evidence which is most significant to those who have some knowledge of the Greek of the New Testament is found in the use of a form of the Greek verb known as the aorist tense. There is nothing exactly corresponding to the aorist in the English language. It was consistently used to describe an action thought of as a single, completed event. The study of the use of the aorist in passages relating to sanctification was pioneered by Dr. Daniel Steele, professor of New Testament Greek in the School of Theology at Boston University from 1884 to 1893. Dr. Steele's study was entitled "The Tense Readings of the Greek New Testament," and was published as Chapter V of *Milestone Papers.*[15] This work was followed up by an intensive investigation by Olive M. Winchester and Ross E. Price, the results of which are published under the title *Crisis Experiences in the Greek New Testament.*[16]

These studies show that the New Testament writers were very sensitive to the implications of various tense forms of the verbs they used. For actions thought of as continuing processes over a period of

---

14. *Sermons,* 2:224.

15. Pp. 53 ff. This chapter has been preserved in print as an appendix in Brown's *Meaning of Sanctification,* pp. 202-26.

16. (Kansas City: Beacon Hill Press of Kansas City, 1953), especially pp. 85-103.

time, they consistently used one of the "linear" verb forms, the imperfect or the present. For actions thought of as unitary events, even those which might have taken some time in their actual performance, the New Testament writers consistently used the aorist (from *aoristos,* "unlimited" as to time), the so-called "punctiliar" tense.[17] It would probably be too much to argue that the consistent use of the aorist in reference to sanctification, cleansing, and purifying proves that these works are instantaneous. It must certainly be conceded that the fact that many of the New Testament references to the sanctification or cleansing of believers are made in the aorist tense makes highly improbable the progressive and incomplete concept of sanctification that denies the possibility of instantaneous cleansing.

E. F. Walker, whose background and early training were within the tradition of gradual sanctification, has written:

> At some point of time between the moment of conversion and the moment of glorification, the souls of the elect are purified from sin and perfected in love.
>
> Even if sanctification were a gradual process, there would be a moment of its completion. Logically, all theories of sanctification are bound to its instantaneousness. If it belongs to the resurrection, even, it is instantly completed at the moment when the body is glorified. If at death, there is a moment when death takes place. If by growth, there is a minute when full growth is attained. No theory of sanctification gets rid of its instantaneousness.
>
> The word "sanctify" in the Greek text of John 17:17 is in the aorist tense and the imperative mood. This fact is conclusive that the work of sanctifying here prayed for cannot be gradual, but must be instant and complete. The office of the Greek aorist is to express a point in the expanse of time—past, present, or future. Crosby's Greek Grammar says: "The action is represented by the aorist as momentary or transient, as a single act." Winer's learned New Testament Greek Grammar declares: "The action represented by this tense is to be viewed as momentary." The imperative mood with the aorist tense means to do or be at once and completely. The word "sanctify" is in this mood and tense, and signifies "instantly and completely sanctify."
>
> Jesus did not pray the Father to sanctify His disciples by a gradual process, but by an instantaneous act. If ever that prayer

---

17. Cf. Ralph Earle, "Holiness in the Greek Text," the *Preacher's Magazine,* Vol. 22, No. 3 (May-June, 1946), pp. 9-10. This able scholar says: "The consistent use of the aorist in speaking of the destruction of sin and the death of self certainly favors an act rather than a process. That is, we can affirm that the regular practice of using the aorist rather than the imperfect throws the balance on the side of instantaneousness" (p. 10).

was answered—and we believe it was answered on the day of Pentecost—those disciples were at once made holy. Grow in grace, before and after their sanctification, they certainly could, and no doubt did. But "suddenly," in the upper room, the sanctifying Spirit accomplished in them this work prayed for. And this is still the law of the Spirit of life in Christ Jesus; growth in holiness, but instant sanctification. Whenever this prayer of Jesus is answered for any one who has believed in Him, in that moment he can truthfully sing—

> 'Tis done! Thou dost this moment save,
> With full salvation bless:
> Redemption through Thy blood I have,
> And spotless love and peace.

It is reasonable to assume and Scriptural to believe that sanctification will be effected just as soon as all the conditions of it are met.[18]

D. The Testimony of Experience

Of next importance to the witness of the Word of God is the testimony of the Christian consciousness. A great volume of testimony from both Calvinistic and Wesleyan sources witnesses to the *need* for sanctification as felt in the experiences of those who are born again. There is also an impressive array of Christian testimony humbly confessing to the cleansing from inner sin by the sanctifying baptism with the Holy Spirit.

Wesley himself supplemented his biblical approach to entire sanctification with careful and searching empirical examination. He records interviews with hundreds of members of the early Methodist societies who professed the experience of entire sanctification. In each case he inquired as to the manner in which the experience was obtained. After years of such inquiry, he made the statement: "... and every one of these (after the most careful inquiry, I have not found one exception either in Great Britain or Ireland) has declared that his deliverance from sin was instantaneous: that the change was wrought in a moment."[19]

Not to be ignored is the significant testimony to a second religious crisis coming from outside what is known as the typical holiness churches. A great many believers have testified to a second crisis experience who have not recognized in that work what Wesleyans

---

18. *Sanctify Them,* pp. 54-55; quoted, Winchester and Price, *Crisis Experiences in the Greek New Testament,* pp. 102-3.

19. *Sermons,* 2:223.

would call entire sanctification. It is variously called "the baptism with the Spirit," "the surrendered life," "the fullness of the Spirit," or by some other term.

A significant study was made in 1951-52 by J. Robertson Mc-Quilkin, then a member of the faculty of Columbia Bible College in Columbia, South Carolina, and published in *Christian Life* for March, 1954. The study was made by questionnaire distributed to 5,000 students enrolling in Bob Jones University, The Bible Institute of Los Angeles, Columbia Bible College, Prairie Bible Institute, Providence Bible Institute, and Wheaton College in Illinois. All of these schools will be recognized as representing an evangelical tradition which is non-Wesleyan in its orientation.

The students were asked to check responses to questions concerning the occasion of their conversion, the major factor leading to conversion, the major subjective element in their conversion, as well as questions concerning a call to Christian service, and the type of urban or rural background in which their early lives had been spent. Included were two questions concerning a second crisis experience:

> If you are a Christian, but do not remember any specific time of conversion, has there been a crisis experience, such as surrender, etc.? Yes ( ) No ( )
>
> If you do remember the occasion of your conversion has there been a subsequent crisis experience as surrender, etc.? Yes ( ) No ( )

Among the 75 percent of the young people who had come from Christian homes, one out of seven reported that he did not know just when he had been converted, but was sure that he had become a child of God. The most significant figures for our purposes here, however, are found in the fact that out of the total number, 90 percent stated that they had received a second crisis experience, which they variously called "surrender," a life of "victory," "the second work of grace," "the second blessing," or "the baptism with the Spirit." Furthermore there was no difference in this 90 percent figure among those who knew the time and place of their conversion and those who did not.[20]

Many thousands of witnesses will be found in more distinctly holiness circles to add to the weight of testimony. The positive testi-

---

20. *Christian Life* (March, 1954), p. 87; and correspondence, April 16, 1954, J. Robertson McQuilkin to W. T. Purkiser; and February 8, 1957, Paul G. Culley, M.D., dean of the Graduate School, Columbia Bible College, to W. T. Purkiser. See also Harold John Ockenga, *Power Through Pentecost* (Eerdmans, 1959).

mony of these thousands may not easily be set aside. Not all are wise or learned, nor do all occupy positions of large influence in the church world. But they manifest a quality of consecration and a humble devotion to the highest ideals which immeasurably strengthen the word of their testimony.[21]

A particularly helpful summary of experience outside typical Wesleyan circles is given in *They Found the Secret,* written by the late Victor Raymond Edman, for many years president of Wheaton College in Illinois. The volume consists of detailed accounts of the higher Christian experience of 20 outstanding personalities of the present and recent past. Edman says,

> From a multitude of witnesses throughout the centuries I have chosen just a few by way of illustration. The pattern of their experiences is much the same. They had believed on the Saviour, yet they were burdened and bewildered, unfaithful and unfruitful, always yearning for a better way and never achieving by their efforts a better life. Then they came to a crisis of utter heart surrender to the Saviour, a meeting with him in the innermost depths of their spirit; and they found the Holy Spirit to be an unfailing fountain of life and refreshment. Thereafter life was never again the same . . .[22]

II. PROCESS IN SANCTIFICATION

Much that is meant by the processes of sanctification will be taken up in detail in the next chapter, and in Part IV on "The Christian Life." Here it is important to note that crisis and process are not mutually exclusive terms. Wesleyan theologians have never thought of the crisis of entire sanctification in such terms as to make it a static and unimprovable state or condition. It has never been thought of as an end or a terminus, but as a starting point.[23]

In summary fashion, it may be said that process in sanctification

---

21. Nor may this witness fairly be offset by the negative testimony of such works as H. A. Ironside's *Holiness: The False and the True.* A defense attorney would be thrown out of court who would offer to counter the testimony of 2 men who saw his client commit a crime with the testimony of 20 men who did not see the deed! Ironside is ably answered by Henry E. Brockett in *Scriptural Freedom from Sin.* (Kansas City: Beacon Hill Press of Kansas City, 1941).

22. (Grand Rapids: Zondervan Publishing House, 1960). See also E. Stanley Jones, *Victory Through Surrender* (New York: Abingdon Press, 1966).

23. Cf. J. A. Wood's classic *Purity and Maturity* (Chicago: S. K. J. Chesbro, 1903) for the typical Wesleyan position. Cf. also Donald S. Metz, *Studies in Biblical Holiness* (Kansas City: Beacon Hill Press of Kansas City, 1971).

includes three major elements: the unfolding implications of consecration; the developing and maturing of the gifts, graces, and fruits
of the Spirit; and the sublimation and control of human instincts and
tendencies.

A. The Unfolding Implications of Consecration

A full-orbed view of sanctification has been shown to include both
human and divine elements, both consecration and cleansing. Christian consecration, "setting apart, dedication to divine purposes,"
(Rom. 12:1-2) is by nature and definition complete, entire, and without reservations. However, an important and perhaps the most significant part of that consecration is what has been called descriptive-
ly "the unknown bundle." The believer not only presents to God as a
living sacrifice all that he is and knows, but all that he will be and
will know in the future. Like marriage, consecration is "for better,
for worse; for richer, for poorer; in sickness and in health; forsaking
all others," to cleave totally unto God.

This is to say that, while consecration is complete as a single act,
the working out of its implications is the process of a lifetime. Many
future decisions will have to be made in the light of that initial self-
devotement to God. It is very misleading and completely wrong to
call these future decisions "reconsecration" or "progressive consecration." They rather involve the recognition of what was implied in
the initial consecration which made possible faith for entire sanctification.

B. The Developing and Maturing of Christian Graces

The gifts and graces of the Spirit are subject to almost limitless development within the scope of the sanctified life. Not until carnal im-
purities are cleansed from the moral nature can the believer develop
as he should the "fruit of the Spirit" (Gal. 5:22-23). The only maximum to the maturing of Christian character in the sanctified is "the
measure of the stature of the fullness of Christ" (Eph. 4:13), a goal
which is not to be reached this side of eternity.

Developing spirituality has sometimes been identified with
sternness and critical rigidity in imposing the ideals of Christian
living on others. Far from this, it is actually growth in love, in joy, in
peace, in goodness, in faithfulness, in gentleness or kindness, in long-
suffering or patience, in meekness ("adaptability," as J. B. Phillips[24]),

---

24. *Letters to Young Churches, ad loc.*

and in self-control. These graces fall as bands on the spectrum from the pure white light of Christ's character. They are the ideal of every sanctified believer.

C. The Control of Human Instincts and Tendencies

An important part of the processes of sanctification is found in progressive and increasing control and sublimation of human tendencies and needs in the interests of the spiritual life. In this area, as Dr. H. V. Miller pointed out, sanctified Christians must practice suppression.[25] Paul clearly stated this imperative in a great passage in 1 Corinthians: "And every man that striveth for the mastery is temperate in all things. Now they do it to obtain a corruptible crown; but we an incorruptible. I therefore so run, not as uncertainly; so fight I, not as one that beateth the air: but I keep under my body, and bring it into subjection: lest that by any means, when I have preached to others, I myself should be a castaway" (9:25-27).

SUMMARY

In this chapter we have given consideration to the temporal aspect of sanctification. We have noted both process and crisis in entire sanctification, and have surveyed the evidence leading us to the conviction

> . . . that entire sanctification is that act of God, subsequent to regeneration, by which believers are made free from original sin, or depravity, and brought into a state of entire devotement to God, and the holy obedience of love made perfect.
>
> It is wrought by the baptism with the Holy Spirit, and comprehends in one experience the cleansing of the heart from sin and the abiding indwelling presence of the Holy Spirit, empowering the believer for life and service.
>
> Entire sanctification is provided by the blood of Jesus, is wrought instantaneously by faith, preceded by entire consecration; and to this work and state of grace the Holy Spirit bears witness.
>
> This experience is also known by various terms representing its different phases, such as "Christian perfection," "perfect love," "heart purity," "the baptism with the Holy Spirit," "the fullness of the blessing," and "Christian holiness."
>
> . . . that there is a marked distinction between a pure heart and a mature character. The former is obtained in an instant,

---

25. *The Sin Problem* (Kansas City: Nazarene Publishing House, 1947), chapters on "Scriptural Suppression" and "Scriptural Counteraction."

the result of entire sanctification; the latter is the result of growth in grace.

. . . that the grace of entire sanctification includes the impulse to grow in grace. However, this impulse must be consciously nurtured, and careful attention given to the requisites and processes of spiritual development and improvement in Christlikeness of character and personality. Without such purposeful endeavor one's witness may be impaired and the grace itself frustrated and ultimately lost.[26]

We proceed now to an examination of the results of entire sanctification as we continue to explore our Christian faith.

26. Article X, "Articles of Faith," *Manual,* Church of the Nazarene, current edition, *ad loc.*

CHAPTER 18

The Effects of
Entire Sanctification

This chapter brings to a close the section on "God's Redemptive Purpose." It is concerned with some of the practical effects of the experience of entire sanctification. Others of these will be dealt with in the following section on "The Christian Life," but of concern here are some of the more immediate personal consequences of entire sanctification in the life of the individual believer.

It is well at this point to consider Charles Ewing Brown's insight[1] that entire sanctification does not result in a dead uniformity of results in different individuals. Individual differences are a feature of the spiritual life as well as of other areas of personal activity. The grace of God is the same, but human response varies. It is wrong to expect the baptism with the Holy Spirit to endow all believers with apostolic effectiveness. In fact, of the 120 who received the fullness of the Spirit on the Day of Pentecost, only a handful took places of prominent leadership. The majority remained anonymous, although vitally important, followers.

With this in mind, we may examine some of the effects of the sanctifying lordship of the Holy Spirit in individual lives. Four subtopics will be considered: (1) the implications of cleansing; (2) the assurance of entire sanctification; (3) enduement with spiritual power; and (4) the life of holiness.

---

1. Cf. *Meaning of Sanctification*, pp. 135 ff.; also Richard S. Taylor, *Life In the Spirit* (Kansas City: Beacon Hill Press of Kansas City, 1966), pp. 109-217.

I. THE IMPLICATIONS OF CLEANSING

We have noted that at the core of the Wesleyan concept of entire sanctification is the conviction that the "second blessing" or the baptism with the Holy Spirit results in the cleansing of the heart from all remaining inherited sin, making the believer "holy in all manner of living" (1 Pet. 1:15, ARV). That this is the New Testament standard for all believers is borne out by the most critical examination of the entire drift of Scripture.[2]

A. Direct Effects of Cleansing

Such a cleansing would have the immediate effect of delivering the believer from his prior unending struggle with the carnal nature, or inner sin. This means that the negative or privative effects of the "flesh nature" are canceled. Paul speaks of the struggle of the flesh and Spirit as a limitation in the believer's life: "For the flesh lusteth against the Spirit, and the Spirit against the flesh: and these are contrary the one to the other: so that ye cannot do the things that ye would" (Gal. 5:17).[3] This struggle continues until the flesh is crucified with its "affections and lusts" (v. 24). In his sanctification appeal to the Thessalonians, Paul speaks of perfecting that which was lacking in their faith (1 Thess. 3:10), and he traces the lack of stability, unity, and mutual confidence in the Corinthian church to the fact that these believers were carnal, and not spiritual (1 Cor. 3:1-3).

Unsanctified Christians are apt to be vacillating when they should be steadfast, cowardly when they should be courageous, lacking in the fruit of the Spirit, and imperfect in faith and love. A comparison of the recorded lives of the apostles before Pentecost and after indicates many of the areas in which the removal of carnality provides release and victory in the Christian life.

Cleansing would also mean that the positive or dynamic effects of the sin nature in believers are removed. "Evil concupiscence" (Col. 3:5; 1 Thess. 4:5)—used in the sense of desire for that which is inherently evil, or wrong in itself—is purged away. Dispositional evils such as pride, self-will, carnal temper, envy, malice, animosity, bitterness of spirit, selfish ambition, and un-Christlikeness in attitude are

---

2. Cf. Turner, *More Excellent Way,* chapter 5; and *Vision Which Transforms,* pp. 13-160.

3. Some scholars prefer to understand the limitation here as imposed by the Spirit, restraining sinful acts. The interpretation adopted seems more in harmony with Paul's high view of the regenerate life.

cleansed away. On its active side, carnality in believers is a propensity or drift toward actual sinful conduct, a proneness to worldliness, a nature "corrupt according to the deceitful lusts" (Eph. 4:22). From such dynamic propensities, entire sanctification provides a *catharsis* or cleansing (2 Cor. 7:1).

B. Holiness Is Not Dehumanizing

Cleansing in entire sanctification is often misunderstood. Some have understood it as a sort of dehumanizing, and have stigmatized those who teach it with promoting something akin to ascetic sainthood. Nothing could be farther from the truth. Sanctification rather returns human nature to normality by taking out the foreign and intrusive element of sin.

It will be found on close examination that much of the opposition to entire sanctification is based on nonbiblical views of sin which make it actually identical with humanity.[4] In biblical theology, rather, sin is found to be an intruder. It is not intrinsic to human nature. Its presence is an abnormality.

This means that all legitimate and natural features of our humanity remain after entire sanctification. The eradication of sin does not change the need for the suppression and control of impulses, desires, and tendencies which are perfectly natural, and yet which may lead into actual sin. Two wrong notions may arise in this regard: (1) when impulses are felt which are seen to lead to evil, the individual may conclude that he is not sanctified, although those impulses on examination may prove to be perfectly legitimate and natural in and of themselves; (2) or, because the Christian knows he is sanctified, he may conclude that all his impulses are right, and adopt uncritically the dictum of Augustine to "love the Lord, and do as you please."

Holiness, then, means the *destruction* of carnality and the *direction* of humanity. E. P. Ellyson wrote:

Sanctification does not destroy a single natural soul faculty. All of the natural appetites, senses and capacities are left. In the

---

4. This is the ghost of the ancient Gnostic heresy and came into Christian theology via Augustine and Calvin. It has become very vocal in our day through the influence of neo-orthodox and existential theologians, who, as Paul Scherer is reported to have said, reverse the Pauline dictum and assert that "where grace abounded, sin doth much more abound." Its best refutation is that it destroys the possibility of a real Incarnation, for Christ was made flesh and dwelt among us, yet without sin in either conduct or character. See Taylor, *Life in the Spirit,* pp. 149-68.

work of cleansing, God does not destroy man's eyesight to keep him from looking at obscene pictures, his passion to keep him from lust, or his temper to keep him from getting angry. He simply takes sin out of these soul capacities and places righteousness therein, leaving him free, under the Spirit's indwelling, to constantly choose and will the will of the Master.[5]

The native instinctive equipment of the sanctified person is not modified. The dynamics of personality are vital to human life, and while purged of sin are left intact. These urges, impulses, drives, and powers are neither good nor bad in themselves. They are like the engine in the automobile which supplies its motion but does not determine its direction. The same engine will drive the automobile to the pool hall and bar, or to the church and on errands of mercy. The same instinctive urges which destroy the soul if misdirected may build its greatest usefulness when guided aright.

No complete listing of the dynamic features of human personality will be attempted here. Some of these major drives which must be kept under control are (1) self-preservation, including food, "flight, and fight"; (2) sex, or race preservation; (3) play, the need for motor activity; (4) herd or sociability tendencies; (5) self-assertion; (6) curiosity, the desire to learn and know; and (7) acquisitiveness. None of these is sinful in itself. Any may become the occasion for sin if not brought into subjection to the ideals of the Christ-life.

Different persons at different ages will need to apply controls at different points. The emergence of many of these basic drives is a matter of maturation. The young may find sex, play, and herd tendencies most clamorous. Older people may need to guard at the point of food, self-assertion, and acquisitiveness. What proves a battleground at one stage in development may not be a problem at another.

One writer has listed some purely psychological drives of the human being as points at which disciplines must be applied: (1) A natural gravitation to "ease, idleness, luxury, comfort, self-liberty, and making of ample provision for bodily comforts and enjoyments." (2) A tendency to be warm and enthusiastic toward certain virtues and graces, particularly those with which we are naturally well endowed, while utterly sluggish and indifferent to other virtues and graces. (3) "The human spirit is instinctively and universally in love with itself, and without being educated to it, will intuitively look out

---

5. *Ye Must* (Marshalltown, Ia.: Christian Messenger Publishing Co., 1904), p. 149.

for itself, and mix up the principle of self-love in everything it does." (4) Excessive levity and foolishness: "A soul filled with God . . . is cheerful but not volatile." (5) Unevenness, fluctuation of mood, and a corresponding tendency to act spasmodically.[6]

C. Holiness and Temptation

It is a truism to state that sanctification does not mean freedom from either temptation to sin or the possibility of sin. "Sinless perfection" is the name customarily given to the view that entire sanctification renders relapse into sin an impossibility. This notion has never been taught by responsible holiness theologians. That persons without carnal dispositions and tendencies may be subject to solicitation to evil is seen in the records of the temptation of Adam and Eve (Gen. 3:1-6) and of Jesus (Matt. 4:1-11; Luke 4:1-3; Heb. 4:15). The advantage of the sanctified in temptation has to do with the nature of the desire which is its occasion and in the measure of grace available to offset the strength of the desire.

Any understanding of temptation must start with the clear recognition that temptation in itself is not sin, although it involves a desire for that which under the circumstances would be sinful. J. A. Wood writes: "No temptation or evil suggestion to the mind becomes sin till it is cherished or tolerated. Sin consists in yielding to temptation. So long as the soul maintains its integrity so that temptation finds no sympathy within, no sin is committed and the soul remains unharmed, no matter how protracted or severe the fiery trial may prove."[7]

That temptation involves desire is the clear teaching of Jas. 1:14, "But each person is tempted when he is lured and enticed by his own desire" (RSV). In the case of the sanctified, such desires concern needs and urges which are legitimate and natural. Unsanctified persons have all these desires, of course, and in addition perverted or corrupted desires for that which is inherently evil. It should be said again that, while entire sanctification destroys desires which are inherently sinful, it does not take away appetites or desires which are capable of satisfaction without violation of divine law.

---

6. George D. Watson, *Spiritual Feasts* (Cincinnati, Ohio: Revivalist Office, 1904), pp. 49 ff.

7. *Perfect Love* (Chicago: Christian Witness Co., 1905), p. 63. Cf. also R. T. Williams, *Temptation: A Neglected Theme* (Kansas City: Nazarene Publishing House, 1920); and Taylor, *Life in the Spirit,* chapter 12.

It is this latter point which Paul makes the distinction between the carnal and the human in Rom. 8:7. The carnal is that which is not subject to the law of God, neither indeed can be. Those desires, impulses, tendencies, and urges which have no legitimate expression in harmony with divine law are declared carnal, of "the flesh." On the other hand, those desires, impulses, tendencies, and urges which do have a legitimate expression in harmony with divine law are human. Such human desires become occasions for temptation when under the circumstances yielding would involve sin. The hunger of Jesus in the wilderness is an instance which illustrates this. To desire food after a 40-day fast involved an appetite that was purely human. To satisfy that desire by yielding to the suggestion of Satan to prostitute divine powers for such a purpose would have involved sin.

In many cases the Pauline test in Rom. 8:7 yields unquestionable results. There is no legitimate expression for envy, covetousness, animosity, malice, carnal temper, or selfish ambition. Under no circumstances may desires arising from these dispositions be satisfied in harmony with the law of God. On the other hand, desires originating in the urges and needs listed in the last section *do* find constructive outlets in harmony with the will of God for human life.

It must be admitted that there are borderline cases which are difficult if not impossible to test. Of these, Thomas Cook writes:

> Some precious souls are in constant bondage because they have never been taught to discriminate between evil thoughts and thoughts about evil. They must discern between the things that differ. So long as we are in the world, and so long as we have five senses coming in contact with a world abounding with evil, Satan will be sure to use these as avenues of temptation. . . . It may seem difficult to some to ascertain whether certain states of mind are the result of temptation or the uprisings of evil in their own nature. But when suggestions of evil . . . are opposed to our usual inclinations and desires, and cause pain, we may safely conclude that they are from without and not from within, and no self-reproach need ensue.[8]

On the positive side, the sanctified have the added advantage in temptation through the enthronement within of the Holy Spirit with the grace He gives. Much may be learned from a study of the temptation of Jesus, and the sources of His victory (Matt. 4:1-11; Luke 4:1-13). It will be noted that three factors were important here: (1) Jesus made His final appeal to the Word of God, "Thus saith the

---

8. *New Testament Holiness* (London: Epworth Press, 13th printing, 1952), p. 17.

Lord." (2) In each temptation, the Lord made an immediate refusal. (3) The temptation followed His anointing with the Holy Spirit; He was spiritually prepared for the conflict.

D. Holiness and Infirmities

Mention was made in Chapter 15 of the fact that the New Testament concept is such as to exclude from sinfulness what are sometimes called "infirmities," those weaknesses and shortcomings which are part of our human and biological inheritance. It must now be indicated that the cleansing of entire sanctification does not directly affect this aspect of our humanity.

H. Orton Wiley speaks of infirmities as "involuntary transgressions of the divine law, known or unknown, which are consequent on the ignorance and weakness of fallen man. . . . Infirmities bring humiliation and regret, but not guilt and condemnation. These latter attach to sin only. Both, however, need the blood of sprinkling."[9] This closely follows the statement of John Wesley:

> The best of men still need Christ in His priestly office, to atone for their omissions, their shortcomings (as some improperly speak), their mistakes in judgment and practice, and their defects of various kinds. For these are all deviations from the perfect law, and consequently need an atonement. Yet that they are not properly sins, we apprehend may appear from the words of St. Paul, He that loveth, hath fulfilled the law; for love is the fulfilling of the law (see Rom. 13:10). Now mistakes, and whatever infirmities necessarily flow from the corruptible state of the body, are no way contrary to love; nor, therefore, in the Scripture sense, sin. . . . Not only sin, properly so-called, that is, a voluntary transgression of a divine law; but sin, improperly so-called, that is, involuntary transgression of a divine law, known or unknown, needs the atoning blood. I believe there is no such perfection in this life as excludes these involuntary transgressions, which I apprehend to be naturally consequent on the mistakes and ignorances inseparable from mortality. Therefore, sinless perfection is a phrase I never use, lest I should seem to contradict myself. I believe a person filled with the love of God is still liable to involuntary transgressions.[10]

Infirmities may arise from physical, intellectual, or social causes. Wesley mentions as "mental infirmities" the inability to understand the divine mysteries taught in God's Word, the divine providences occurring in life, and the purposes of God involved in much that

---

9. *Christian Theology,* 2:507.
10. *Plain Account of Christian Perfection,* pp. 42-43. See Heb. 9:7.

transpires about one. He includes lack of ability to discern and comprehend, forgetfulness, wandering thoughts in prayer, difficulty in reaching decisions, inability to reason correctly because of personal prejudices. These, he says, "are found in the best of men, in a larger or smaller proportion. And from these none can hope to be perfectly freed till the spirit returns to God that gave it."[11]

Roy S. Nicholson wrote:

There are "physical," "emotional," and "spiritual" infirmities over which Satan accuses one. These may appear in connection with bodily appetites and desires, hunger, sleep, bad dreams, sickness and affliction, nervousness, excitability, and physical exhaustion; fear of danger, inability to perfectly control moods under all circumstances; measuring one's reaction to the truth by another's visible demonstration to the same truth, inability to accomplish the things desired, dejection over being misunderstood by those in whose behalf some good thing was undertaken which missed the intended aim; and a definite feeling of inferiority which deters one from doing the little he could lest it be misunderstood by those who are able to do more than he feels he can do.[12]

In the loving discipline of the Father God (Heb. 12:5-11); in the faithful intercession of Christ, our great High Priest (Heb. 4:15-16); and in the help of the indwelling Holy Spirit (Rom. 8:26) the sanctified believer finds increasing ability to meet and handle the problem of his infirmities. It should be remembered only that involuntary transgression may become willful sin if, when reproved or brought to mind by the Spirit, it is not confessed and renounced. To excuse or condone what might be improved or corrected is to become guilty of actual transgression.

E. Holiness and Moods

A final topic in this area is the relationship between faith and feelings in the sanctified life. It is probable that more sincere young Christians have been perplexed by fluctuating feelings than by any other aspect of their personal lives. Because the experiences of reconciliation and entire sanctification are often attended by joy and high emotion, some have tended to identify the experience with the emotion. Then when the emotion subsided, they have plunged into darkness and doubt.

---

11. Cf. *Works,* 6:2-5; and 12:375-76.
12. In the *Wesleyan Methodist,* 109:52 (Dec. 24, 1952), p. 819.

On the face of it, there is grave error in identifying feelings with the grace of God. There is by no means a correlation between high emotions and spiritual status. "Too many bad people feel good, and too many good people feel bad" for such to be true. Jesus is described as a "man of sorrows, and acquainted with grief" (Isa. 53:3), who wept when confronted with the bereavement of His friends (John 11:35-36). Paul confessed his continual heaviness and sorrow of heart for his own nation (Rom. 9:1-2), and found occasion to need encouragement from Christian friends (Acts 28:15).

Our emotions are affected by physical, social, psychological, and circumstantial factors which have no relationship whatsoever to the spiritual and moral state. John Wesley wrote concerning moods:

> As long as we dwell in a house of clay, it is liable to affect the mind; sometimes by dulling or darkening the understanding, and sometimes more directly by damping and depressing the soul, and sinking it into distress and heaviness. In this state, doubt or fear, of one kind or another, will naturally arise. And the prince of this world, who well knows whereof we are made, will not fail to improve the occasion, in order to disturb, though he cannot pollute, the heart which God hath cleansed from all unrighteousness.[13]

> A will steadily and uniformly devoted to God is essential to a state of sanctification; but not a uniformity of joy, or peace, or happy communion with God. These may rise and fall in various degrees; nay, and may be affected either by the body or by diabolical agency, in a manner which all our wisdom can neither understand nor prevent.[14]

While the fluctuation of feelings is normal, the emotions are subject to control. Writing from the viewpoint of one highly trained in psychology, Leslie Ray Marston lists seven rules which are of prime value in managing moods:

1. "Assume the bodily posture of the desired emotion or mood and thereby aid in dispelling the undesirable and establishing the desired emotion or mood." This is the technique of "whistling in the dark," and is based on the obvious relationship between bodily changes and sensations, and the mental side of emotion.

2. "Preserve bodily health to insure emotional health." Recognition that sickness, fatigue, and hunger have profound effect upon the emotional tonus will show the importance of sound physical health in promoting a sense of well-being.

---

13. *Works,* 6:776.
14. *Works,* 8:58.

3. "Avoid excessive and long-continued emotional stimulation." Emotion taps reserves of energy which may be restored with difficulty, and which when depleted seriously endanger physical health.

4. "Expend the energy of emotion in action." The function of emotion is to prepare for action. If such action or some vigorous release is lacking, the energies pent up within the system may result in nervous disorders.

5. "Intelligently direct the energy of emotion to harmless and if possible beneficial ends if its natural or instinctive direction would prove harmful or socially undesirable." This is the process of sublimation, and is generally more wholesome and beneficial than repression.

6. "Develop healthy and varied interests." The overdevelopment of a single interest may cause one to become erratic, eccentric, or unbalanced. Varied interests provide resources for satisfaction of psychological needs.

7. "Organize the interests of life into a unity." This is the function of religion, which provides a master interest large enough to integrate every other legitimate need and interest.[15]

II. The Assurance of Entire Sanctification

The New Testament has less to say about assurance of entire sanctification than it does about justification and regeneration. John Wesley referred to 1 Cor. 2:12 in this connection: "Now we have received not the spirit of the world, but the Spirit which is from God, that we might understand the gifts bestowed on us by God" (RSV). In relation to the Holy Spirit and our Christian assurance, John says: "And hereby we know that he abideth in us, by the Spirit which he hath given us" (1 John 3:24); "Hereby know we that we dwell in him, and he in us, because he hath given us of his Spirit" (4:13); and, "It is the Spirit that beareth witness, because the Spirit is truth. He that believeth on the Son of God hath the witness in himself" (5:6, 10).

The assurance of sanctification has been questioned by W. E. Sangster.[16] The ground of Sangster's objection is that no one can

15. *From Chaos to Character* (Winona Lake, Ind.: Light and Life Press, 1944), pp. 80-89.

16. Specifically in his widely read book *The Path to Perfection* (New York: Abingdon-Cokesbury Press, 1943).

know what possible sin lurks in the depths of his subconscious self. On this basis he discredits all testimony to holiness. However, Wesleyan theologians have never alleged that we know our hearts to be clean on the basis of introspective self-knowledge alone. It is rather on the direct testimony of the Spirit, who searcheth all things and who knows what is in man. Actually, Sangster's argument would be just as valid, or invalid, if applied to the knowledge of sins forgiven. We cannot know by searching our hearts that our sins have been remitted. We can only know on the basis of the Spirit's witness. Commenting on Sangster's argument, George Allen Turner writes:

> But, is it necessary to know all about one's self to be assured of entire sanctification? If there is any such thing as the immanence of the Divine Spirit and the "witness of the Spirit" why may it not include the assurance of purity that is a result of divine activity rather than of human achievement? If holiness of heart is a matter of self-effort, the assurance and assertion of cleansing is presumptuous and boastful; if it is a gift effected by the Spirit of God, why cannot one, without pride, declare what he believes God has wrought? If God can cleanse one's heart, why can He not also give the subject assurance of that fact? If such a purging from the sinful quality of acts and thoughts is impossible it amounts to an admission that Christianity does not have a complete answer to the sin problem except in some eschatological sense. On this basis much of the unqualified language of the New Testament must be set at naught. In short, the objections to a claim of cleansing from all conscious sin seem less formidable than their alternative.[17]

In *A Plain Account of Christian Perfection,* the question is asked, "When may a person judge himself to have attained this [state of Christian perfection]?" Wesley's answer is:

> When, after having been convinced of inbred sin, by a far deeper and clearer conviction than that he experienced before justification, and after having experienced a gradual mortification of it, he experiences a total death to sin, and an entire renewal in the love and image of God, so as to rejoice evermore, to pray without ceasing, and in everything to give thanks. Not that "to feel all love and no sin" is a sufficient proof. Several have experienced this for a time before their souls were fully renewed. None, therefore, ought to believe that the work is done till there is added the testimony of the Spirit, witnessing to his entire sanctification as clearly as his justification.[18]

This, however, is not all of the matter. There is another element,

---

17. *The More Excellent Way,* pp. 253-54.
18. Pp. 50-51.

the fruit of the Spirit, which must be considered. Here, again, in the *Plain Account,* the question is asked: "But how do you know that you are sanctified—saved from your inbred corruption?" This time, the answer is enlarged:

> I can know it no otherwise than I know that I am justified. "Hereby know we that we are of God (in either sense), by the Spirit that he hath given us." We know it by the witness and by the fruit of the Spirit. And, first, by the witness, as, when we were justified the Spirit bore witness with our spirit that our sins were forgiven, so when we were sanctified he bore witness that they were taken away.[19]

Three additional words should be said before leaving this subject.

a. The first is that the witness of the Spirit to entire sanctification is not a substitute for faith. Nor can it, in the nature of the case, be prior to faith. We are sanctified, as we are justified, on condition of faith alone. There is no other way. The order is faith first, with which the cleansing is simultaneous; and then the witness, either immediately, or in some cases after a delay. Should the witness precede faith, then faith would not be grounded in the word and faithfulness of God, but in a subjective impression. Further, the witness of the Spirit is God's testimony to what has actually been wrought. Since sanctification is by faith, the Spirit could not testify to its completion until the subject had believed.

b. The second word is that the witness of the Spirit is not an emotion or feeling, any more than it is a rational inference from the fact of conditions met. The witness of the Spirit is an inner persuasion, a conviction of the mind, an insight of the soul. It comes with the suddenness and certainty of the mind's grasp of a geometrical or logical demonstration: *I see that!* High emotional exhilaration may follow such an inner certitude, but the emotion is the by-product of the witness and not the witness itself.

c. The third word is that the witness is not a physical manifestation, such as prostration, shouting, or speaking in unknown tongues. Some have argued, from a misreading of Acts 2 and 1 Corinthians 12 and 14, that the only New Testament evidence of the fullness of the Spirit is speaking in unknown tongues. There is absolutely no evidence that the manifestation of Pentecost involved unknown

---

19. P. 75.

tongues, for the apostolic preaching was understood by men of many lingual backgrounds. The Corinthian manifestation obviously had nothing whatsoever to do with entire sanctification or the baptism with the Spirit, because the Corinthian church was the least spiritual and most carnal of all the New Testament churches (1 Cor. 3:1-3). The witness of the Spirit is an inner certainty so complete that one needs no secondary and easily counterfeited "signs" to corroborate it. As C. W. Ruth used to say, "You need not go outside and light a candle to see if the sun has risen."[20]

III. ENDUEMENT WITH POWER

Two extremes must be avoided in regard to entire sanctification by the baptism with the Holy Spirit. One is that the sole purpose of the baptism with the Spirit, or the fullness of the Spirit received after conversion, is to empower the individual for service. This is the position of Reuben A. Torrey, first president of the Moody Bible Institute:

> It is evident that the baptism with the Holy Spirit is an operation of the Holy Spirit distinct and additional to His regenerating work. . . . A man may be regenerated by the Holy Spirit and still not be baptized with the Holy Spirit. In regeneration, there is the impartation of life by the Spirit's power, and the one who receives it is saved: in the baptism with the Holy Spirit, there is the impartation of power, and the one who receives it is fitted for service.[21]

The other extreme is to emphasize the subjective cleansing wrought by the Spirit to the exclusion of the empowerment of the Spirit. Coordinate with cleansing is commission, and the divinely given anointing necessary thereto.

This is clearly the teaching of the New Testament. Each of the references of Jesus to the coming of the Holy Spirit before Pentecost speaks of the outreach of the Christian life in the power of the Spirit:

---

20. The current bibliography on glossolalia (speaking in unknown tongues) is too extensive to be reviewed here. Some helpful titles are Harvey J. S. Blaney, *Speaking in Unknown Tongues: The Pauline Position* (Kansas City: Beacon Hill Press of Kansas City, 1973); Charles D. Isbell, "Glossolalia and Propheteialalia: A Study of 1 Corinthians 14," *Wesleyan Theological Journal,* Vol. 10 (spring, 1975); John P. Kildahl, *The Psychology of Speaking in Tongues* (New York: Harper and Row, 1972); W. T. Purkiser, *The Gifts of the Spirit* (Kansas City: Beacon Hill Press of Kansas City, 1975); William J. Samarin, *Tongues of Men and Angels. The Religious Language of Pentecostalism* (New York: The Macmillan Co., 1972); and Vinson Synan, *The Holiness-Pentecostal Movement in the United States* (Grand Rapids: Wm. B. Eerdmans Publishing Co., 1971).

21. *The Person and Work of the Holy Spirit* (New York: Fleming H. Revell, 1910), pp. 174, 176.

"And, behold, I send the promise of my Father upon you: but tarry ye in the city of Jerusalem, until ye be endued with power from on high" (Luke 24:49); "Nevertheless I tell you the truth; It is expedient for you that I go away: for if I go not away, the Comforter will not come unto you; but if I depart, I will send him unto you. And when he is come, he will reprove the world of sin, and of righteousness, and of judgment" (John 16:7-8); and, "Ye shall receive power, after that the Holy Ghost is come upon you: and ye shall be witnesses unto me both in Jerusalem, and in all Judaea, and in Samaria, and unto the uttermost part of the earth" (Acts 1:8).

Paul also speaks of the power of the Spirit, predominantly in the inner man, but also in relation to Christian service: "Now the God of hope fill you with all joy and peace in believing, that ye may abound in hope, through the power of the Holy Ghost" (Rom. 15:13). Power for service is indicated in vv. 18-19, "For I will not dare to speak of any of those things which Christ hath not wrought by me, to make the Gentiles obedient, by word and deed, through mighty signs and wonders, by the power of the Spirit of God; so that from Jerusalem, and round about unto Illyricum, I have fully preached the gospel of Christ."

Paul emphasized the inner strength imparted by the Spirit in another verse: "That he would grant you, according to the riches of his glory, to be strengthened with might by his Spirit in the inner man" (Eph. 3:16). The sanctified life in relation to service is also seen in 2 Tim. 2:21, "If a man therefore purge himself from these, he shall be a vessel unto honour, sanctified, and meet for the master's use, and prepared unto every good work."

There are various manifestations of the power of the Spirit in Christian living, as was indicated in the verses above. The Spirit's power is varied according to the area of its need and appropriation. Some of these may be summarized as follows:

1. Power for Personal Living

Col. 1:10-12 lists as factors in the Christian's power: a walk worthy of God, fruitfulness in good works, increasing knowledge of God, patience and long-suffering with joyfulness, and thankfulness.

2. Power for Positive Witness

The effectiveness of testimony is directly related to the assurance of experience: "We speak that we do know, and testify that we have seen" (John 3:11). The Spirit anoints testimony to Christ, making it effective (John 15:26-27).

3. *Power in Prayer*

There is an intimate relationship between the Spirit and power in prayer (Rom. 8:26). It may properly be said that the measure of true prayer in the individual life is the measure of the Spirit's fullness.

4. *Power of Singlehearted Devotion or Dedication to Christ*

A consecration sealed by the Spirit is made effective in daily life. There is real power in the concentration of singleness of purpose as an aspect of consecrated living.

5. *Power for Christian Service*

The anointing of the Spirit is essential to effectiveness in service. All spiritual power is resident in the Holy Spirit, and its measure is the measure to which He is allowed to work.

Certainly the power of the Holy Spirit is not hysterical excitement and the loss of rational control. The power of Pentecost is the power of love and of a sound mind (cf. 2 Tim. 1:7). It is power to overcome hatred, discouragement, bitterness, melancholy, and gloom. It is power to witness and to live the clean life that is necessary for effectiveness in witnessing. It warms the heart, strengthens the mind, quickens the intellect, and elevates and intensifies each capacity.[22]

IV. THE LIFE OF HOLINESS

Some of the broader implications of the holy life will be considered in Part IV, "The Christian Life." It is appropriate here, however, to stress the fact that one of the major effects of entire sanctification is a heightened quality of spiritual life. The outer life is the natural expression of the inner experience. Heart and life, motive and act, subjective experience and objective expression are truly inseparable.

To emphasize unduly either the subjective or the objective aspects of Christian living leads to dangerous extremes. To emphasize the subjective or inner aspects of religion at the expense of the objective or outer aspects leads to what is known as antinomianism. This is a disregard for the demands of right conduct. It is the attitude that a right belief or a good motive is all that is important. The Calvinist may drift into antinomianism when he emphasizes "Christ for us"

---

22. Brown, *Meaning of Sanctification,* pp. 133-37.

more than "Christ in us." The Arminian may also drift into antinomianism when he adopts the sentimental attitude to "love the Lord, and do as you please."

To emphasize the objective or outer aspects of Christianity at the expense of the subjective or inner side is to fall into the snare of legalism or Phariseeism. This is the attitude which strives to make clean the "outside of the cup" while lust, envy, pride, malice, and all manner of uncleanness lurk within. Outward righteousness is essential, but unless it is the expression of inward righteousness, it rests upon an insecure foundation and falls short of the Christian gospel.

SUMMARY

This chapter has been devoted to a survey of some of the effects of entire sanctification, particularly in the life of the individual believer. We noted the results of cleansing in relation to both carnal and human nature, and the place of self-discipline, temptation, infirmities, and moods in the sanctified experience. We then studied the witness of the Spirit as seen both in the general doctrine of Christian assurance and in connection with entire sanctification. The power of the Spirit and the life of holiness completed our review of this topic.

We leave now the doctrinal and somewhat subjective and personal aspects of redemption and turn to the great themes related to the Christian life, in this task of exploring our Christian faith.

CHAPTER 19

The Nature of
the Church

*Thou art the Christ, the Son of the living God. . . . upon this rock I will build my
church* (Matt. 16:16, 18).

> *The Church's one Foundation is Jesus Christ, her Lord.*
> *She is His new creation by water and the Word.*
> *From heav'n He came and sought her to be His holy bride;*
> *With His own blood He bought her, and for her life He died.*
>
> —SAMUEL J. STONE

"I believe in the holy catholic church."—Apostles' Creed.

Thus we read, sing, and confess the uniqueness of the Church of
Jesus Christ. It is His unique creation purchased with His own blood.
It is unique in that it is an institution that includes a belief in itself
among the items of its creed. It is unique in the metaphors which are
used to describe it: a body, a bride, and a building. It is unique in the
way it is sustained and preserved by the perpetual indwelling presence of the Holy Spirit. It is unique in that it represents a new order
of spiritual life on earth.

The purpose of this chapter is to sketch the outlines of the doctrine of the Church in the Christian faith. This theme has proved of
great interest in recent years, and deservedly so. It is through the
Church and its ministry across the ages that we individually receive
the gospel, and it is in the Church that we find spiritual nurture and
fulfillment. We shall consider the origin, characteristics, duality,
organization, and purpose of the Church, and its relation to the kingdom of God.

I. THE ORIGIN OF THE CHURCH

Although Jesus Christ is the Founder of the Church, the idea finds root in the Old Testament. Jesus related His work to what had gone before in His repeated reference to the fact that "the kingdom of God" or "the kingdom of heaven" was at hand. Stephen spoke of the "church in the wilderness" (Acts 7:38).

The word church is used to translate a Greek word *ecclesia,* which means "the called-out ones." However, this same Greek word was used in the Septuagint Greek version of the Old Testament to describe the assembly or congregation of Israel. In a real sense, the Old Testament church was "a community of the Spirit," based on God's covenant with His chosen people, and preparing the way for the coming of the Savior of the world. H. Orton Wiley summarizes the contribution of the Old Testament period under two heads: "*First,* in that it cultivated and matured the religion which should finally issue in the kingdom of God; *secondly,* and chiefly, because it was the community that gave Christ to the world."[1]

A. The Intermediate Group

No doctrine of the Church would be complete which did not recognize the place of the intermediate group of disciples who followed Jesus during His earthly ministry. The Lord referred to His little flock in terms which show the disciples to be an intermediate link between "the church in the wilderness" and the Church of the Day of Pentecost. While Jesus used the word church but twice, and both times in ways which implied that it was yet to come (Matt. 16:13-20; 18:17), His followers formed the initial group which was its nucleus.

B. The Foundation of the Church

The New Testament makes it clear that Christ himself is the Foundation of the Church. Jesus indicated this in response to Peter's great confession: "Thou art the Christ, the Son of the living God" (Matt. 16:16). "And Jesus answered and said unto him, Blessed art thou, Simon Bar-jona: for flesh and blood hath not revealed it unto thee, but my Father which is in heaven. And I say also unto thee, That thou art Peter, and upon this rock I will build my church; and the gates of hell shall not prevail against it" (vv. 17-18).

---

1. *Christian Theology,* 3:105.

There are those who interpret these words in such a way as to make Peter the rock upon which the Church is built. But neither the grammar of the passage nor the New Testament as a whole will support this interpretation. While Peter took the lead on the Day of Pentecost, James appears as the head of the Church in Acts 12:17; 15:13; 21:18. Indeed the Book of Acts lays a great deal more emphasis upon Paul's work than upon Peter's. Certainly if Christ has meant that Peter was to be the foundation of the Church, early Christians would have recognized this fact.

Paul emphasizes that the true Cornerstone of the foundation is Jesus Christ himself: "Now therefore ye are no more strangers and foreigners, but fellowcitizens with the saints, and of the household of God; and are built upon the foundation of the apostles and prophets, Jesus Christ himself being the chief corner stone; in whom all the building fitly framed together groweth unto an holy temple in the Lord: in whom ye also are builded together for an habitation of God through the Spirit" (Eph. 2:19-22).

C. Born of the Spirit at Pentecost

The Day of Pentecost has been considered the birthday of the Church. One hundred and twenty "charter members" were present when the Holy Spirit descended in accordance with the promise of Jesus. This company then became the new temple of God. From that hour to the present, people gathered in the community of the Spirit in the name of Jesus Christ have been the Church of God.

II. Characteristics of the Church

The distinguishing characteristics of the Church may be summarized by considering its definition, its membership, and the metaphors used in the New Testament to describe it.

A. Definition

The Church may be defined as the body of people who have confessed Jesus as the Son of God and have believed and trusted Him as their Savior, uniting under His leadership to carry out His purposes in the world. "The Church of God is composed of all spiritually regenerate persons, whose names are written in heaven."[2]

---

2. Hills, *Fundamental Christian Theology*, p. 506.

B. Membership

Membership in the Church in New Testament times, as today, depended upon a confession that Jesus is Lord. Only those who believed this and who lived in obedience to the command of Christ were in the Upper Room when the Spirit came. Such a confession before men is necessary in order to be accepted in the sight of God. "Whosoever therefore shall confess me before men, him will I confess also before my Father which is in heaven. But whosoever shall deny me before men, him will I also deny before my Father which is in heaven" (Matt. 10:32-33). Church organizations may make lesser requirements, but we are reminded by the writer of the Book of Acts that membership in the universal Church is a divine action: "And the Lord added to their number day by day those who were being saved" (Acts 2:47, RSV).

C. Metaphors Used to Describe the Church

As the new temple of the triune God, the Church has been variously designated as the people of God, the body or bride of Christ, and the community of the Holy Spirit. However, most of the metaphors in the New Testament relate the Church to Christ.

The Church is described as the body of Christ with our Lord himself as the Head. In Eph. 1:22-23 we read: God "hath put all things under his feet, and gave him to be the head over all things to the church, which is his body, the fulness of him that filleth all in all." In Col. 1:18, 24 we find: "He is the head of the body, the church . . . Now I rejoice in my sufferings for your sake, and in my flesh I complete what is lacking in Christ's afflictions for the sake of his body, that is, the church" (RSV). As a body, the Church possesses vitality, unity, and the means to express the Spirit.

The Church is often referred to as the bride of Christ. Jesus called himself the Bridegroom (Matt. 9:14-15), and the disciples or believers who wait for the Bridegroom are the bride, as in the parable of the 10 virgins (Matt. 25:1-13). John mentions the great marriage supper when the Lamb will take to himself His bride: "Let us be glad and rejoice, and give honour to him: for the marriage of the Lamb is come, and his wife hath made herself ready" (Rev. 19:7). Paul expressed his desire that the Corinthian church should be chaste and holy when presented to Christ: "For I am jealous over you with godly jealousy: for I have espoused you to one husband, that I may present you as a chaste virgin to Christ" (2 Cor. 11:2).

The Church is spoken of as the household of God, a building of which Jesus Christ is the Chief Cornerstone (Eph. 2:19-20).

The metaphor of the flock and the sheepfold has been used in connection with the Church. Jesus referred to himself as being the Shepherd of the flock. "I am the good shepherd, and know my sheep, and am known of mine" (John 10:14). Paul uses the same metaphor in his speech to the elders at Ephesus and refers to them as the "overseers of the flock" (Acts 20:28).

III. THE DUAL NATURE OF THE CHURCH

In considering the Church, one must keep in mind its dual nature. It is both divine and human, spiritual and material, invisible and visible, catholic and local, triumphant and militant, possessing continuity and vitality. In this respect, the Church is like its Founder, both of the nature of God and of the nature of man.

A. Divine and Human

The Church is a divine institution, perfect in plan and order, brought into being by the sacrifice of Jesus. The gates of hell shall not overthrow it. Yet the Church is a human institution composed of fallible human beings subject to the limitations of the flesh and of this world. The Church is in the world but not of the world. It must accept some of the stress and strain of this world, but it need not be defeated or discouraged by it.

B. Invisible and Visible

The Church is also invisible and visible. The invisible Church is composed of all people who have believed in Christ, who have named Him as Lord and Savior, regardless of membership in any group. The visible Church is composed of those who have joined some local group which confesses Jesus Christ as the Son of God.[3]

C. Catholic and Local

The Church is also catholic and local. The term catholic actually

---

3. The concept of an "invisible Church" has been questioned. It rests chiefly on Heb. 12:22-24 in which a unity of the Church on earth and in heaven is assumed, and is used as a synonym for "universal" or "catholic." The concept must not be pressed too far, as it may lead to a view of salvation that is unscripturally individualistic and disassociated from the fellowship of believers on earth.

means "universal," and cannot rightly be monopolized by any one organization. All who have confessed Jesus as Lord and Savior belong to the invisible catholic or universal Church. In contrast, the church is local and particular. The New Testament speaks of the church of God at Corinth, the church of God at Thessalonica, and in many other localities. It also speaks of the churches scattered abroad (Rom. 16:5; 2 Cor. 11:28). However, the local character of the church is always incidental,[4] for the local churches were bound up in a larger unity under the leadership of the apostolic group. It should be noted also that there is New Testament authority for church organization.

D. Triumphant and Militant

The Church is both militant and triumphant. The Church militant is the Church in action, waging its battle against sin and unrighteousness in this present world. It is composed of those who are actively participating in its mission here on earth. The Church triumphant is the Church at rest, composed of those who have fought the good fight and have crossed the sea of death into the presence of Christ. They have finished their work and wear the crown of eternal life (2 Tim. 4:7-8).

E. Continuous and Vital

The Church possesses continuity and vitality. All of us have derived our knowledge of the faith from the Church. It is Christ's instrument to proclaim the faith. Therefore the Church has continuity in one or more areas of its life. Some emphasize continuity in theology, others in worship, still others in the ministry. Traditionalists tend to emphasize continuity to the detriment of the vitality of the Church. But the Church must also possess the power of the Spirit. It must not only respect the past, but accept the challenge and opportunity of the present and future.

The continuity and vitality of the Church are closely related to its unity and variety. We may speak of "the church and the churches."[5] There is one true Church, invisible and universal, the divine Church of Jesus Christ. But there are many and various visible churches: Eastern Orthodox, Roman Catholic, and the many branch-

---

4. Cf. Robert Rendall, "The Church: What It Is," *The Church,* edited by J. B. Watson (London: Pickering and Inglis, Ltd., 1949), p. 26.

5. W. Burnet Easton, Jr., *Basic Christian Beliefs* (Philadelphia: Westminster Press, 1957), pp. 136-57.

es of Protestantism. Variety in the visible Church is one aspect of its humanness.

F. A Field and a Force

The Church has also been described as a field and a force,[6] or a life and a work.[7] There are those who emphasize the idea that the Church is a field to be worked and have therefore sought to bring unconverted persons into full membership. Others view the Church as a force for righteousness, and believe therefore that church membership should mean something in terms of personal religious experience. Again, some emphasize the Church as a life in fellowship and personal growth; others stress the idea of vocation in the Church's striving to possess the world for Christ. But none of these ideas need be exclusive. The Church indeed must be a force, but it must also cultivate a field in which its message may be fruitful. Likewise, the Church must be both a life and a work.

G. Sect or Church?

Recent students of the Church have tended to make a sharp distinction between sect and church in the religious world. Religious bodies are classified as "sects" or "churches" in accordance with certain criteria set up to distinguish types of emphasis. In general, the sect tends to be more exclusive in its membership and requirements; the church tends to be more inclusive and cosmopolitan. In following the literature on the subject the student will need to be aware of the fact that "sect" does not necessarily mean "sectarian," but is used as a sociological term to describe a religious group which emphasizes the distinctiveness of its place and mission in the family of churches.[8]

6.. O. L. Shelton, *The Church Functioning Effectively* (St. Louis: Christian Board of Publication, 1946), p. 37.

7. Frank M. McKibben, *Christian Education Through the Church* (New York: Abingdon-Cokesbury Press, 1947), p. 16.

8. Cf. Elmer T. Clark, *The Small Sects in America* (New York: Abingdon-Cokesbury Press, 1949); Horton Davies and Charles S. Braden, "Centrifugal Christian Sects," *Religion in Life*, 25:3 (summer, 1956), pp. 323-46. For evaluations of the Church of the Nazarene in relation to "sect" and "church" types, see Walter G. Muelder, "From Sect to Church," *Christendom*, 10:4 (autumn, 1945), pp. 450-62; George Hedley, *The Christian Heritage in America* (New York: The Macmillan Co., 1946), pp. 143-47; Willard L. Sperry, *Religion in America* (New York: The Macmillan Co., 1947), p. 226. These evaluations, and that of Clark, *Small Sects in America*, are discussed by R. V. DeLong, "The Church of the Nazarene and Its Need of a Seminary," the (Nazarene Theological) *Seminary Tower*, 2:1 (winter, 1946), pp. 1-4, 13-16.

IV. The Organization of the Church

The matter of church organization has long been argued among Christians. Some have taken the extreme view that the Bible gives no warrant for any kind of organization, but the Church must always be an "organism," without any highly developed human organization. An examination of the New Testament, on the other hand, reveals clear evidence of the beginnings of church organization.

A. Early Church Organization

The vacancy in the Twelve made by the suicide of Judas resulted in the choice of Matthais to replace the betrayer, even before the coming of the Spirit on the Day of Pentecost. The momentum of the new experience at Pentecost carried the Church forward without much attention to the need for organization. But as activities and numbers increased, it was soon realized that some provision must be made for "secular" concerns of the group. The apostles did not feel it was wise for them to take time from the preaching of the Word, so they suggested that the Church elect deacons to "serve tables" and to take care of the widows who were being neglected (Acts 6:1-8). This was the beginning of offices in the Church. Paul continued the idea of different functions being assigned to various persons according to the talents and gifts given by God. Romans 12 and 1 Corinthians 12 are good places to study the variety of offices and gifts in the Church in relation to the unity of the body of Christ and the responsibilities of all believers.

In interpreting the New Testament in regard to church government (or polity, as it is more commonly known) two extremes must be avoided. One has already been mentioned: the view that the New Testament sanctions no organization whatever, or at least one of the most meager sort. The other extreme is the view that the New Testament sets forth a formal plan of organization which must be followed out in all details in every age of the Church. A far more reasonable position than either of the extremes is one which recognizes that the New Testament lays down no formal plan of organization, but rather offers some general principles or guidelines within which each church may perfect its organization as seems best.

In the Primitive Church the disciples were informally bound together as learners and followers. Their activities were varied and appealed to the whole personality. A spirit of anticipation was marked, and each day brought new discoveries. The group was held together mainly by the dynamic of Christ's presence, continued in the presence of the Holy Spirit. There was little reason for concern with organization. But continued growth soon increased the responsibilities of the apostles until delegation of authority and responsibility became the obligation of the entire group. It is simply because the apostles attempted to project an organization for no age but their own that the principles they acted upon have enabled the Church to adapt its organization to the needs of every age.

B. Early Church Officers

We have already seen that the rapid growth of the Church soon led to the filling of offices. Early Church officers mentioned in the New Testament are elders, bishops, deacons, and deaconesses. Elders were recognized in the earliest days (Acts 11:30) and were ordained in every church (Acts 14:23). Paul directed Titus to ordain elders in every city who were blameless, husbands of one wife, and with faithful children (Titus 1:5-6).

The terms bishop and elder seem to have been used interchangeably in the New Testament. Paul, addressing the elders from Ephesus, called them "overseers" *(episcopous)* of the flock (Acts 20:28), the same term being translated "bishop" in Phil. 1:1; 1 Tim. 3:1; and Titus 1:7. The officials of the church at Philippi were "bishops and deacons" (1:1).

These overseers or bishops were to be men of mature judgment. Paul describes the requirements of the office in great detail in 1 Tim. 3:1-7 and Titus 1:7-9. The deacons also were to be men of the highest type. Their work included "serving tables" (Acts 6:2-3); yet like Stephen (Acts 6:7) and Philip (Acts 8:5-40) they would on occasion witness and preach. Paul lists the qualifications of the deacons in 1 Tim. 3:8-13, very similar to those given for bishops.

Christian women were also active in the work of the Church, and some of them soon came to be known as deaconesses. Phoebe of Cenchrea would probably be considered one of these (Rom. 16:1), and Paul speaks of ministering widows and describes their activities in 1 Tim. 5:5-10.

C. Present-day Organization

We have noted that the New Testament does not lay down specific forms of government or detailed descriptions of church offices. Across the centuries Christians have developed a variety of church organizations and differing concepts of the offices of the Church. In some circles, bishops have a higher standing than elders. In others, elders and deacons are not ministers, but laymen ordained by the local church to carry on the affairs of the laity. The Church of the Nazarene recognizes only one office in the ministry, and that is the office of elder. Ordination as an elder is permanent as long as the minister's character is unimpeached. All other officials are elected periodically, and are amenable to the church for its effective functioning.

At present there are three major types of church government known as (1) the episcopal; (2) the congregational; and (3) the presbyterian. In the episcopal type of government, authority is vested in the ministry. Pastors of the local congregations are chosen by the bishops, and the ministers are accountable to the next highest authority. Chief examples of this type are the Roman Catholic church, the Church of England, the Episcopal church, and the United Methodist church.

In the congregational type of government, authority is vested in the local church. Each church is autonomous, and is related to a denominational organization only through its own voluntary, cooperative spirit. The pastors of the churches are elected by the congregations. Examples of this form of church polity are the Congregational-Christian churches and the various Baptist groups.

In the presbyterian form of government, authority is vested in both the ministry and the laity. Usually the churches have the privilege of choosing their own pastors, but subject to the nomination or approval of some higher church official. Local congregations also have a large degree of autonomy within the limits established by the general organizational pattern of the parent denomination.

The Church of the Nazarene has a form of government similar to the presbyterian type described above in that it combines both episcopal and congregational features. The basic plan of organization is a representative type of government similar to that of the United States. The executive and legislative branches have delegated powers. Each local church owns its own property and is allowed freedom to carry on its own affairs, but is united in larger denominational projects with other churches of the district and with the general church.

On each level the polity of the Church of the Nazarene calls for a balance of power and responsibility between the clergy and the laity. In the local church the pastor is the chairman of the church board and president of the local congregation; but he is amenable to the congregation which elects him and to the lay church board, which sets his salary and hears his report. On the district level there is a district superintendent, who is an elder and is in charge of the work in his geographical area; but his power is balanced by a district advisory board composed of two to four ministers and two to four laymen, and he is amenable to a district assembly, which sets his salary, elects him to office, and hears his annual report. Similarly, the general superintendents care for the affairs of the general church, functioning with the General Board, composed of an equal number of laymen and ministers elected by the General Assembly. The latter body is the highest authority in the church, and it also is composed of an equal number of ministers and laymen.

V. The Purpose of the Church

Ultimately the purpose of the Church is to be found in the purpose of its Founder and Head. Jesus said that He had come "to seek and to save that which was lost" (Luke 19:10); and, "I am come that they might have life, and that they might have it more abundantly" (John 10:10). Similarly, He said, "As my Father hath sent me, even so send I you" (John 20:21).

A. In the Early Church

These purposes of Christ are made more specific in the Great Commission: "All power is given unto me in heaven and in earth. Go ye therefore, and teach all nations, baptizing them in the name of the Father, and of the Son, and of the Holy Ghost: teaching them to observe all things whatsoever I have commanded you: and, lo, I am with you always, even unto the end of the world. Amen" (Matt. 28:18-20). From this command we derive several functions of the Church: (1) a recognition of divine sovereignty, or worship: "All power is given unto me in heaven and in earth"; (2) evangelism and missions: "Go ye therefore, and teach all nations, baptizing them . . ."; (3) education: "teaching them to observe all things whatsoever I have commanded you"; (4) fellowship and communion: "Lo, I am with you alway."

These directions and purposes were followed by the disciples in the life and activities of the Early Church. After Pentecost the disciples continued their worship, communion, and fellowship together, and as they witnessed concerning the risen Lord, many were added to the Church daily. "And they continued stedfastly in the apostles' doctrine and fellowship, and in breaking of bread, and in prayers. . . .

And they, continuing daily with one accord in the temple, and breaking bread from house to house, did eat their meat with gladness and singleness of heart, praising God, and having favour with all the people. And the Lord added to the church daily such as should be saved" (Acts 2:42, 46-47). "And with great power gave the apostles witness of the resurrection of the Lord Jesus: and great grace was upon them all" (Acts 4:33). After an initial experiment with a form of property sharing, the Early Church abandoned the common holding of goods and launched into the more spiritual activities and functions generally associated with the Church.

The functions of the Church may also be read in the various gifts of the Spirit given to the Church: "Having then gifts differing according to the grace that is given to us, whether prophecy, let us prophesy according to the proportion of faith; or ministry, let us wait on our ministering: or he that teacheth, on teaching; or he that exhorteth, on exhortation: he that giveth, let him do it with simplicity; he that ruleth, with diligence; he that sheweth mercy, with cheerfulness" (Rom. 12:6-8). An indication of functional offices in the Church is found in Eph. 4:11-12: "And he gave some, apostles; and some, prophets; and some, evangelists; and some, pastors and teachers; for the perfecting of the saints, for the work of the ministry, for the edifying of the body of Christ."

B. Present-day Statements

The major functions of the Church are suggested in the chapter titles of Part II of a book by Albert W. Beaven which has been widely read: Securing Commitment and Enlistment of Individuals; Building Them into the Fellowship; Making Them God-conscious Through Group and Private Worship and Inspiration; Enlarging Their Insights Through Education; Expanding Their Powers Through Stewardship; Increasing Their Effectiveness Through Organization; Securing the Tools for Their Work; Moulding Them into a Community Force for Righteousness; Broadening Their Horizon to Include the World Task; and Developing Their Co-operative Relations with Fellow Christians.[9]

Frank M. McKibben offers another list of functions of the Church and its specific purposes:

    1. To interpret religion.

---

9. *The Local Church* (New York: Abingdon-Cokesbury Press, 1937).

2. To provide worship and training in the devotional life.

3. To promote and enrich the fellowship of Christians.

4. To extend the fellowship to include an everincreasing number of people.

5. To provide incentive, training, and opportunity for individuals to participate in efforts to improve society.

6. To aid individuals.

7. To enlist and train workers for the local church, community and world.

8. To maintain a wholesome and effective institutional life.[10]

In summary, we may define the functions or purposes of the Church as five in number: (1) to provide and maintain worship in order to fulfill the requirements of the first four of the Ten Commandments; (2) to go into the highways and hedges and to the uttermost parts of the earth making disciples of all men, turning them from darkness to light and from the power of Satan unto God, that they may receive forgiveness of sins and inheritance among them that are sanctified by faith that is in Christ (cf. Acts 26:18); (3) to teach them to observe all Christ has commanded; (4) to build them into a harmonious fellowship of the saints; (5) to love and serve all men, thereby helping to relieve suffering and sorrow and to establish the rule of Christ in society. Growing out of these functions we may speak of the worship, evangelistic, educational, stewardship, fellowship, and social service activities of the church.

VI. THE CHURCH AND THE KINGDOM

A later chapter will be given to the consideration of the kingdom of God and of His Christ. It may here be said that the Church represents the Kingdom inaugurated, in relation to the consummation of the Kingdom at the *parousia* or return of Christ. The task of the Church is to call men to bow before the sovereignty of Christ, to acknowledge Him as Lord and King, and to pray and work that His kingdom may come and His will be done in earth as in heaven (Matt. 6:10).

The Kingdom inaugurated is the guarantee that the Kingdom shall be consummated, that every knee shall bow, and every tongue shall "confess that Jesus is Lord, to the glory of God the Father" (Phil. 2:10-11). In the language of Oscar Cullmann, borrowed from the closing weeks of World War II, D-day has passed, and we fight and look for V-day, which is soon to come. While the battle may be bitter,

---

10. *Christian Education Through the Church*, pp. 17-18.

and the labor hard, D-day is the guarantee that V-day shall dawn, and that the very gates of hell shall not prevail against the Church of the Lord Jesus Christ (Matt. 16:18).

SUMMARY

In this chapter we have considered the nature of the Christian Church. Although based upon Old Testament developments, it is unique in that it was purchased by the death of Jesus Christ. Its membership is a group of called-out ones whose corporate and individual task is to fulfill the purpose of Christ on earth. It is called the people of God, the Body of Christ, the fellowship of the Spirit. It is a divine-human organization, possessing spiritual and material qualities, invisible and visible, triumphant and militant, vital and continuous. It is a producing field and a vital force, and is striving to make all men Christ's disciples. It is organized for worship, evangelism, education, stewardship, service, and fellowship.

To carry out its purposes the Church requires the power of the Holy Spirit, and it harnesses the power within human lives through organization and the leadership of church officers. While government and institutional patterns may vary, all are designed to fulfill the will of God. Looking forward to the consummation of its work in the consummation of the Kingdom at the appearing of Jesus Christ, the Church lives and works to bring to all men everywhere the gospel implicit in our Christian faith.

CHAPTER 20

The Means of Grace

The "means of grace" refers to those special exercises associated with the Christian faith which serve as a vehicle for the blessing of God and the impartation of spiritual power.

Primary among the means of grace are the two sacraments of the Church, baptism and the Lord's Supper. Because the sacraments have unique significance of their own in their symbolic and historical connection with the Church, their meaning is not exhausted in treating them as means of grace.

Historically, the sacraments have been considered the outward signs of inner and spiritual graces.[1] But whatever else they are in theological import, the sacraments provide deep and abiding spiritual values in Christian growth and understanding; hence they are classified with other important functions of Christian development: viz., worship, prayer, meditation, and devotional reading. All these are channels for the inflow of spiritual life; or, to change the figure, they are the great common meeting places of the soul with God. They, individually and together, are the elements which provide the energy of Christian experience. Without them, the Christian faith is a matter of observation and objective pronouncements. The means of grace are open doors to active, personal participation in the dynamic of the spiritual life. It is they that keep both the individual soul and the Church alive and healthy.

---

1. O. A. Curtis says very beautifully that "each sacrament *is a symbol of an event in grace.*" *The Christian Faith,* p. 425.

I. BAPTISM

Baptism is one of the two sacraments recognized in the Protestant tradition. The term comes from the Greek *baptizo,* to wash, consecrate. In practice it refers to the rite in which water is used as a symbol of a person's faith in Christ and his connection with the Church.

Both the theological significance and the mode of baptism vary greatly in different branches of the Christian church. Doctrinally speaking, the extremes extend from belief in baptismal regeneration in infancy, as held by the Episcopalians, to adult believers' baptism only, as practiced by the Baptists. Some groups deny that baptism is the occasion of regeneration but hold that it is valid for either children or adults. In mode, the basic difference is whether water should be applied to the candidate or the candidate immersed in the water.

It is not the purpose here to discuss in further detail the various beliefs and practices. Almost any standard religious encyclopedia will treat the origin and history of baptism and its usages in the Church.[2] The chief purpose here is to consider its value as a means of grace.

The value of any rite or ecclesiastical object lies in the richness of its religious connotation and the depth of its symbolic significance. Baptism did not originate with the New Testament, but it has been associated with New Testament religion from the very first. For John the Baptist, it was the sign of repentance and the public testimony of the person's candidacy for the Kingdom of heaven. Jesus endorsed John's use of baptism by His own submission to the rite and His public avowal of the practice, "though Jesus himself baptized not, but his disciples" (John 4:2). It qualifies as a sacrament by Jesus' approval of the rite and His command to His disciples to "teach all nations, baptizing them in the name of the Father, and of the Son, and of the Holy Ghost" (Matt. 28:19).

In Acts, baptism always signified the identification of the individual or family with Christ. For the individual it marked the separation between the old life and the new. On a wider scale, it soon became the unique, distinguishing characteristic which divided the Christian world from the pagan. Still today the discriminating missionary will not administer the ordinance of baptism to a convert until the break with his old religion is final and complete.

---

2. For an excellent survey of the N.T. meaning and practice of baptism, see Alfred Plummer's article in Hastings' *Dictionary of the Bible,* 1:238-45.

Something of this unique significance of baptism is lost in the Christian country where the ordinance is often nothing more than a perfunctory rite or is treated with indifference. But when seen in its full sense as a symbol of one's identification with Christ and the new life implied thereby, the ordinance of baptism for an adult is emotionally and spiritually satisfying. When the infant who has been baptized comes to the age of understanding, the knowledge that from his infancy he has been under the fostering protection of the Church and the promise of his parents to bring him up in the "nurture and admonition of the Lord" (Eph. 6:4) may be in itself a discovery with deep sacramental meaning.[3]

Further spiritual import is derived from the sacrament in the thought that one is following the example of our Lord himself, who, when presenting himself for baptism, said that "it becometh us to fulfil all righteousness" (Matt. 3:15). Jesus did not need baptism with water in any actual spiritual sense; but it was a public acknowledgment of His identity with transgressors (Isa. 53:12), and it was fitting or becoming that He should be an Example for His followers. For the Christian today, baptism is not, in itself, a saving ordinance, and some groups (for example, the Salvation Army and the Quakers) dispense with it altogether as a requirement of membership. But as an ordinance blessed by Christ himself, and as a historically rich symbol of the regenerating Spirit, the rite of baptism may be the occasion for profound spiritual illumination. It also awakens in the believer the deeply satisfying awareness that he has joined the great throng of baptized Christians, living and dead, who make up the Church of Jesus Christ.

II. THE LORD'S SUPPER

The Lord's Supper is the second of the two sacraments in the Protestant tradition. Of the two, it is the more fruitful as a means of grace. The reasons for this lie in the greater symbolic depth of the Communion service and the simple fact that the Communion is a repeated observance while baptism, except in rare cases, is a once-for-all ordinance.

The Christian sacrament of the Lord's Supper was instituted by Christ himself on the occasion of His last meal with His disciples

---

3. See the sympathetic treatment of infant baptism in Donald M. Baillie, *The Theology of the Sacraments* (New York: Charles Scribner's Sons, 1957), pp. 80 ff.

before His apprehension and trial. In each of the three Gospel accounts (Matt. 26:26-28; Mark 14:22-25; Luke 22:17-20), Jesus attaches special significance to the breaking of the bread and the drinking of the wine. Scholars are not agreed on how the Passover meal and Jesus' last supper with His disciples relate to each other, but it appears that the Last Supper grew out of the Jewish feast. In any case, the special breaking of the bread and the giving of thanks indicate that Jesus was going beyond the Jewish ceremony in establishing the sacramental significance of the elements.

In the Gospel accounts the bread is His body, the wine His blood, the blood of the new covenant shed for the remission of sins. Paul's rendering of the scene (1 Cor. 11:23-26) makes it clear that both the partaking of the broken bread and the drinking of the wine are for a remembrance. But not only a remembrance—they "do shew the Lord's death till he come." The sacramental meal of bread and wine becomes a continuing symbol of the blood and body of Christ. It looks two ways—to the past in remembrance, to the future in anticipation. Someone has referred to it as a suspension bridge between the two comings of Christ.

What significance does the Lord's Supper have as a continuing ordinance in the Church?

First, it is a visible symbol of the presence of Christ. The meaningfulness and richness of the symbol are not lessened despite the tendency of evangelical thought to deny the more sacramental or "high church" notions of the communion service. The presence of Christ is a matter of faith, not of consecrated elements. Christ is always in the midst where there are people gathered in His name, whether or not the sacramental emblems are present. The bread and wine are meaningful because of Christ, not vice versa. But where Christ is already present in spirit, the sacrament of the Lord's Supper is deeply effective as a visible token of His spiritual presence.

Second, the sacramental elements not only symbolize the blood and body of Christ, but *they are constant reminders that the only source of spiritual sustenance is in Christ.* John alone of the Gospels does not give the account of the Last Supper, but Jesus undoubtedly intended that there should be sacramental significance in His feeding of the multitude and His subsequent teaching about the bread which came down from heaven (John 6:33 ff.). When His listeners asked for this bread, Jesus said, "I am the bread of life." As usual, the Jews understood on a physical level what Jesus meant on a spiritual level. They "therefore strove among themselves saying, How can this man give us his flesh to eat?" Jesus then spoke the most sacramentally meaningful words He ever uttered: "Verily, verily, I say unto you, Except ye eat the flesh of the Son of man, and drink his blood, ye have no life in you. Whoso eateth my flesh, and drinketh my blood, hath eternal life; and I will raise him up at the last day. For my flesh is meat indeed, and my blood is drink indeed. He that eateth my flesh, and drinketh my blood, dwelleth in me, and I in him" (John 6:53-56). No other scriptural statement points up so dramatically the mysterious unity which exists between Christ and His followers. It is the profoundly spiritual doctrine of mutual immanence, the Johannine equivalent of the Pauline concept of "in Christ."[4]

Third, it is a symbol of unity in the Church. It is the center of many radii. The universal acknowledgment that Christ is the sole Life of the Church brings all parties to the common Communion table. The sacramental bread is the visible sign which says that there is no bread but Christ. Creeds and polity may differ, but all churches must eat His flesh and drink His blood.

Fourth, the sacrament of the Lord's Supper is a symbol of fellowship. Here Communion goes beyond its symbolic import. It not only is a symbol of fellowship of souls who, because they love Christ, love one another. Acknowledgment of the common need breaks down all racial, cultural, and social barriers. "There is neither Jew nor Greek, there is neither bond nor free, there is neither male nor female: for ye are all one in Christ Jesus" (Gal. 3:28). It is the communion of the saints through a common Lord and a common symbol.

Who may participate in the sacramental meal? In the evangelical wing of the Church, the Lord's Supper has been considered a ministry rather than a mystery. It is a service which "belongs to the people," rather than an ecclesiastical treasure subject to the control and distribution of the Church. It was a big day in the progress of the Reformation when Zwingli abolished the Mass from Zurich. On April 13, 1525, the first truly evangelical Communion service since the days of the early Christians was held in the Great Minster, Zwingli's church. The people received the Communion in "both kinds," the bread and the wine. To hold back the cup was no longer the prerogative of the priest. The sacrament was liberated from its

---

4. Curtis says that it is this aspect of the sacrament which "furnishes to the communicant the possibility of an experience which is properly called mystical." *Christian Faith*, p. 431.

clerical control. While it has been generally considered that an ordained minister should administer the sacrament, some churches look with favor on the view that any regular leader of a congregation may with propriety conduct the ceremonial meal. Too often the sacrament is regarded as a tool of ecclesiastical power and the right of exclusion rather than a means of grace to the seeking soul. The only test of qualification for participation in the sacrament in the Early Church was one that was self-imposed: "Let a man examine himself" (1 Cor. 11:28). To eat unworthily was to show a lack of discernment of the meaning of the meal. That was a sin.

The sacramental invitation which goes forth in most Protestant churches today is some variant of the beautiful words of the *Book of Common Prayer:* "Ye who do truly and earnestly repent you of your sins, and are in love and charity with your neighbors, and intend to lead a new life, following the commandments of God, and walking henceforth in his holy ways, draw near with faith, and take this holy Sacrament to your comfort; and make your humble confession to Almighty God, devoutly kneeling."[5]

The basic qualifying test is true repentance. Its immediate purpose is renewal, commitment, and spiritual comfort. It is for all those who love our Lord Jesus Christ. The concept of "closed Communion," a practice which admits only the enrolled members of the particular group, is foreign to both the spirit and practice of the mainstream of the Christian Church. John Wesley thought the Lord's Supper might well be a "converting ordinance."[6] Summarizing a sermon which he preached the next day he said, among other criteria, "that no fitness is required at the time of communicating, but a sense of our state of our utter sinfulness and helplessness." Wesley certainly made richer use of this sacrament than many of his followers would allow.

As a means of grace within the Church itself, the sacrament of the Lord's Supper is preeminent. It was instituted by Christ himself, perpetuated by the apostles, practiced in some form in the Christian Church down to the present, and is hallowed by the tenderest associations of Christian fellowship and love. It is amazing that any Christian church could be indifferent to this sacred institution. To

---

5. Note also the invitation form in the *Discipline of the United Methodist Church,* where it is seen that Wesley, and subsequent Methodism, adopted the Anglican form almost word for word.

6. *Journal,* June 27, 1740.

enjoy the richness of the symbol and to cherish it as a means of grace is not a compromise with so-called sacramentalism. There is danger if the sacrament is considered inherently virtuous, *ex opera operato*. But so long as it remains an outer sign of an inner faith, its value is inestimable as a means of grace to the individual worshiper and as a symbol of the corporate unity and faith of the Church.

III. Worship

Worship is the formal expression of praise and devotion to God. In the final sense, all worship is private, even in a crowded sanctuary, for worship is an individual attitude which springs from the inner man. Nevertheless, corporate worship adds to one's devotion a quality and a dimension which may be gained in no other manner. The joining together in sweet accord of heart and voice in common adoration provides one of the richest channels of grace to the soul. The devotional contribution of the Church is seen in the following three major functions:

A. Personal Values

Public worship brings the person under the direct impact of the symbolic and spiritual treasures of the Church. *First, through the place of worship.* The physical aspects of worship, including the church building, are themselves tremendously significant components in the total experience of worship. Both extremes, either complete barrenness of religious symbol or ecclesiastical ornamentation, are to be deplored. Both may inhibit the act of worship. On the other hand, window and spire, altar and pew, pulpit and aisle, may unite in a dignity which helps to bring rest to the eyes and quiet to the mind. The physical place of worship presents a great opportunity for the church to incorporate some of the profound symbolism of the Christian faith. The sanctuary itself may thus become a channel of spiritual meaning and a ministration of grace to the soul. Certainly a theology of worship and architecture have something to say to each other.

Second, through the order and discipline of the service. The literal bringing of oneself under the voluntary restraint of formal worship has a salutary effect on both the body and the spirit. "Let all things be done decently and in order," (1 Cor. 14:40) is not only an admonition of respect for public worship, but a principle of spiritual self-discipline. The cluttered mind, the restless spirit, will find clarity and poise in the submission to the silences and other directed acts of worship. The discipline of the church service is a means of grace for the child as well as the adult, although the value may not be apparent to him until more mature years.

Third, through congregational singing. In its hymnology, the Church has one of its richest treasures. Here are combined the choicest words and music of devotion. Almost any standard hymnal will have in it the great hymn combinations of Bernard of Clairvaux and Dykes, Grant and Haydn, Wesley and Marsh, besides the words and music of more recent composition, with its experiential emphasis. Congregational singing "breaks up the fountains of the deep," freeing the spirit to overflow into the joyous words and melody of the song. The massive effect of singing in unison seems to intensify the spirit of praise and to stimulate a legitimate spiritual exhilaration.

Fourth, through the reading of the Scriptures. The public reading of scripture, if done with literary understanding and vocal clarity, adds an element of authority that is not usually present in private and silent reading. The words come in an atmosphere already solemnized by the invocation of divine blessing. The worshiper lifts his eyes to the front and opens his heart with expectancy. The Holy Spirit "attaches" himself to the words and they come laden with conviction, inspiration, or instruction; words sharper than any two-edged sword, entering into the very joints and marrow of the soul (Heb. 4:12). There has always been great spiritual power associated with the public reading of the Scriptures. The sweeping reformation during the reign of Josiah, king of Judah, came as a result of the reading of all "the words of the book of the covenant which was found in the house of the Lord" (1 Kings 23:2). A similar revival of religious enthusiasm occurred among the newly returned Jewish exiles under the leadership of Nehemiah. When Ezra stood up to read, first asking the divine blessing on the reading, "the people answered, Amen, Amen, with lifting up their hands: and they bowed their heads, and worshipped the Lord with their faces to the ground" (Neh. 8:6).

Fifth, through public prayer. The offering of prayer is that part of worship where the minds and hearts of the worshipers are directed specially to God in acknowledgment of human dependence upon Him and to invoke His blessing upon the assembled congregation. Many forms of public prayer are possible: the congregation in unison, in chorus, individual prayers in succession, or a single prayer which seeks to gather up all the possible petitions of the group and offer them to God. In any case, prayer as a part of worship should be entered into, either vocally or silently, by the whole congregation. Both extempore and written prayers have their particular values. The former are more common in the holiness churches and reflect the spontaneity of the Spirit. John Wesley used both kinds. The Prayer Book is rich in the cumulative insight of the great saints of all time. In either case, prayers which are not perfunctory, but which are in the spirit and in the understanding also (1 Cor. 14:15), constitute a very vital adjunct to worship as a means of grace to the soul.

Sixth, through the use of the creeds. The use of the Apostles' or Nicene Creed adds an element of strength to the public service. The creed not only serves as a reminder of the great and cherished doctrines of the Christian faith, but it provides a sense of continuity with the historic Church of Christ. The ecumenical creeds were born out of great tribulation. Too often the nonliturgical church of today accepts lightly, indifferently, and quite thoughtlessly a great heritage which has been bequeathed at the cost of blood. "The blood of Christians is seed," said Tertullian.[7]

Seventh, through hearing the preaching of Scripture. Preaching is central in the Protestant concept of worship—the exegesis, exposition, and proclamation of the Word. "Faith," said Paul, "comes from hearing, and hearing by the word of Christ" (Rom. 10:17, NASB). The command to preach is always balanced by the command to the people to hear (Deut. 6:4; Matt. 11:15; 15:10).

Preaching as part of worship has the values attributed to prophecy: speaking to people "for edification and exhortation and consolation" (1 Cor. 14:3, NASB). Through preaching, those who worship are enabled "to quicken the conscience by the holiness of God, to feed the mind with the truth of God, to purge the imagination by the beauty of God, to open the heart to the love of God, to devote the will to the purpose of God."[8] "Christian worship," says John Huxtable, "is a dialogue between God and his people, a family conversation in which God discloses himself through the reading of Scripture and the preaching of the Word, in which the Spirit makes God's activity in an ancient day contemporary with his people in every generation."[9]

---

7. *Apology, L, The Ante-Nicene Fathers,* Vol. VIII.

8. Quoted from William Temple by R. E. O. White, *A Guide to Preaching* (Grand Rapids: Wm. B. Eerdmans Publishing Co., 1973), p. 10.

9. *The Bible Says* (Naperville, Ill.: SCM Book Club, 1962), p. 109.

B. Fellowship Values

Public worship brings us into the fellowship of others. Christian worship grew out of Christian brotherhood. The Church as an organization was originally a fellowship, based on a common need, a shared faith in the resurrected Lord, and the public outpouring of the Holy Spirit. There is something very wholesome and exciting about the original fellowship as revealed in the description of Luke: "And they continued stedfastly in the apostles' teaching and fellowship, in the breaking of bread and the prayers. . . . And day by day, continuing stedfastly with one accord in the temple, and breaking bread at home, they took their food with gladness and singleness of heart, praising God, and having favor with all the people. And the Lord added to them day by day those that were saved" (Acts 2:42, 46-47, ARV).

For the Jews, individual worship was an anomaly. Worship in the Old Testament was always a corporate enterprise. The Jewish custom of worshiping together was carried over to the Christian Church. During the transition period between Judaism and Christianity, the Christians even continued to worship in the Temple. Luke says that the disciples "were continually in the temple, praising and blessing God" (Luke 24:53). It is likely that the Holy Spirit came upon the assembled group in a Temple room. Later the Christians met in private homes, wherever they could find a common meeting place. The fellowship *was* the Church; the Church was the fellowship. It was the true *koinonia* (fellowship, participation, communion), a concept which has claimed the attention of so many recent religious thinkers.

The practice of solitary worship was largely a phenomenon of the Middle Ages, when mysticism flourished. While there are proper Christian exercises that are individual, e.g., meditation, private prayer, worship most nearly reaches its ideal when Christians as a group, in unison of spirit and devotion, lift their hearts unto God. John Wesley said: "Christianity is essentially a social religion . . . To turn it into a solitary religion, is indeed to destroy it."[10] Solitary worship certainly is not the recommended norm of the New Testament. The command is to "let us consider one another to provoke unto love and good works; not forsaking our own assembling together, as the custom of some is" (Heb. 10:24-25, ARV).

---

10. "Sermon on the Mount," Discourse IV.

Christians united in their worship and common commitment, not only in formal services, but in all the activities associated with a community of Christians, provides the most wholesome milieu possible in this world for the spiritual growth and development of the individual Christian. Just as the individual person needs society in order to become a true individual, the Christian needs his community in order to be a mature member of the Church of Christ.

In the common fellowship, Christians provide mutual help and inspiration. Many a flagging faith has been revived within the warmth and brotherly concern of the group. There is a mysterious spiritual alchemy which takes place when Christians come together for worship. The individual spirits and minds flow together into a new whole which is different from, and greater than, the sum of the parts. It is what is often referred to as the "spirit of the meeting." When it is present, power and conviction and blessing are the concomitants. From such meetings flows the dynamic of the Church. Action is born here. The individual goes forth with a sense of his own spiritual responsibility, but he sees himself as part of a larger whole, an organic unity made up of many parts (1 Corinthians 12; Ephesians 3), but the whole constituting the Church, against which the gates of hell cannot prevail (Matt. 16:18). The present fellowship of the saints is both a type of, and a prelude to, the Kingdom of heaven.

C. Enlarged Vision

The third factor in worship which makes it a rich means of grace has already been implied, viz., its continued call to personal purity and creative response. The meaning of God's grace is forever hampered by the lack of vision. What God's grace can do for the seeking soul and for society is vitally dependent upon the vista of possibilities envisioned for it. In true worship, God and the individual come face-to-face; the worshiper sees himself in the light of God's demand. The meeting is both a judgment and a revelation. In the full illumination of the encounter with God, the worshiper is aware of his own shortcomings, and he stands condemned. "Woe is me!" cries Isaiah when he sees God "high and lifted up" (Isa. 6:5 ff.). But he also envisions what he can become by the grace of God. His judgment is his opportunity. A seraph touches his lips and he hears the words, "Thine iniquity is taken away." Paul caught the meaning of the experience when he said, "Where sin abounded, grace did much more abound" (Rom. 5:20). Worship prepares the heart for creative response.

The creative response to vision is action. "What wilt thou have me to do?" is always the question which springs spontaneously to the lips of one who has seen God. For with the vision of God comes also the awareness of the world's need and the immensity of the gap between what is and what should be. True worship opens the eyes to the possibilities of progress and to the great adventure of working with God in the building of His kingdom (1 Cor. 3:9). The vistas are as exciting as they are infinite. There is no excuse for inactivity.

IV. Prayer

Prayer is a means of grace which enriches and permeates all other means.[11] It is at once the simplest and the most profound of all spiritual exercises. For the child, prayer may be very real but confined to simple requests for God's care through the night and the supplying of his needs. For the saint, prayer is an exciting adventure of communion and the opening of the floodgates of possibility. "All things are possible to him that believeth" (Mark 9:23). Prayer is both "Give us this day our daily bread" and "the power, and the glory" (Matt. 6:11, 13).

The concept of prayer as used in the Bible is very rich in its varied meanings. Among other things, "to pray" as a verb means to petition, judge oneself, bow down, want, call for. As a noun, prayer means a whisper, meditation, intercession, a pouring out, and at least 70 times it means a song of praise.[12] These meanings are not only very suggestive, but they show the poverty of prayer conceived solely as a petition or as a duty to be performed. Prayer is interaction with God.

Why pray? There are many reasons. The following reflect both the fact of human need and the exciting possibilities of prayer:

First, prayer is an acknowledgment of dependence upon God. Such acknowledgment is axiomatic in the life of the Christian. It is the exact opposite of the attitude of the Sophist Protagoras, who proclaimed that "man is the measure of all things." The man who truly prays recognizes the prior claims of God. God is the measure of all things.

---

11. Still one of the best books on prayer is the one with that title in the "Great Christian Doctrine" series, edited by James Hastings (New York: Charles Scribner's Sons, 1915). The book is also a mine of bibliographical material on prayer.

12. See the exhaustive concordances of either Strong or Young for these and other meanings.

Second, in prayer we see God. Prayer clears away the clouds of doubt and self-seeking which obscure the vision of God. The man who truly prays is one with the Psalmist who cried, "When thou saidst, Seek ye my face; my heart said unto thee, Thy face, Lord, will I seek" (Ps. 27:8). True prayer is a divine-human encounter.

Third, in prayer we see ourselves. Prayer is an invitation for the divine inspection. "Search me, O God, and know my heart: try me, and know my thoughts" (Ps. 139:23). With inspection comes revelation. Laid bare are our fears, resentments, smallness, pride. But with the revelation of need comes the gracious awareness of God's presence to cleanse and heal. "He restoreth my soul" (Ps. 23:3).

Fourth, prayer is a spiritual channel for the release of God's power. Real prayer opens up the depths of human personality, where vocal, articulate speech is replaced by the inarticulate groanings of the Spirit (Rom. 8:26). This kind of prayer is an open door to the tremendous spiritual potential which is available for actualization in the life and experience of the pray-er.

Fifth, prayer is the medium of intercession for the souls of others. Not to many is given the ministry of true intercession, for it involves a special kind of commitment. It is accompanied by an agony and burden of spirit which was evident among the great Bible intercessors—Abraham, Moses, Job, Stephen, Paul. In intercession a person is indeed a co-worker with God in the salvation of souls.

Sixth, prayer is fellowship. This is prayer at its highest. The concern is not petition, whether for self or others. It is communion with God for its own intrinsic worth.

Prayer as a means of grace opens up the channels of one's own soul and taps the resources of God. Prayer is the soul's vital breath. As the very essence of spiritual life, it is the opposite of fainting. "Men ought always to pray, and not to faint" (Luke 18:1). Genuine prayer is probably the highest form of spiritual consciousness.

V. MEDITATION

It has been said that there is a tribe of South American Indians who believe that the soul does not move as fast as the body; hence, when the Indians are traveling on the trail, they pause periodically to let the soul catch up with the body. That tradition carries a profound lesson for this age: We need to let the soul catch up. The obsession for material security, the desire for continuous activity, the superficiality of many of the entertainment mediums, have crowded out the time and concern for the cultivation of the soul through meditation.

Meditation as a spiritual exercise has enriched the Christian faith with the insights born out of the contemplation of great truths about God and existence. Here is where we owe a great debt to the mystics. Spiritual truths are rooted deep in the ultimate moral structure of the universe. They are not to be discovered except in the inner dimensions of the soul, which needs relaxation from tension and a positive inward turning of the mind. Without meditation the soul becomes too easily satisfied with the changing surface water of human ideas and ideals, instead of the hidden springs of living water which flow into the soul with qualities of eternal reality.

Meditation and quiet are essential for perspective. In the Bible, some of the men who occupied the most strategic positions in the working out of God's revelation were men who spent time in isolation before or during their public ministry. Moses had 40 years in the wilderness of Midian to discover and to contemplate the relationship of God to his people, Israel. It was while Elijah was alone on the side of rugged and barren Mount Horeb that he heard God speak in a "still small voice" (1 Kings 19:12). The Lord took Amos as he "followed the flock" on the edge of the wilderness of Tekoa (Amos 7:15). John the Baptist was "in the deserts till the day of his shewing unto Israel" (Luke 1:80). Jesus spent 40 days in contemplation and self-examination in the wilderness after His baptism and the public declaration by God of the divine sonship (Mark 1:13). Immediately after his conversion Paul went into Arabia (Gal. 1:17), probably to the region of Sinai or Horeb, where Moses and Elijah had already found a clear perspective of their divine mission.

Not every person can spend 40 years, or even 40 days, in the wilderness, but every Christian needs some time for relaxation of spirit and contemplation of the real meaning of his calling and place in God's plans. Isolation is no substitute for the fellowship of Christian people; this was the error of the hermits and many of the monastics. But, as in the case of all the biblical men mentioned above, the person who spends time alone with God will surely come back to his task with a new sense of mission and a transfigured perspective. Behind the Christian task must be a divine vision. Vision, depth, clarity, insight, balance, proportion are born in spiritual contemplation. He who would explore the true dimensions of his faith and know the "breadth, and length, and depth, and height" of the love of God must spend time in meditation.

VI. Devotional Reading

This topic is treated last in this chapter, not because it is necessarily the most important, but because the literature of devotion is probably the richest unexplored supply of spiritual resources available to the searching soul.[13]

The inner life is a creation and a growth. The capacity for introspection is a divine endowment, but the growth and development are functions of the participative practices of the soul. Not only is the soul what it lives on, but the outer life is a reflection of the inner. The wise man in Proverbs said, "Keep thy heart with all diligence; for out of it are the issues of life" (Prov. 4:23). Jesus said, "A good man out of the good treasure of the heart bringeth forth good things: and an evil man out of the evil treasure bringeth forth evil things" (Matt. 12:35). In terms of the specific topic, one could paraphrase these words and say: A man who readeth good literature will bring forth riches from the abundance of his heart; but a man who readeth not hath nothing to bring forth; for not only is he lacking something with which to draw, but the well is dry.

The rich soul is invariably the reader of great devotional literature. He is known and can be recognized by his awareness of the universal truths which characterize the spiritual language of the saints. The truths which move men are universal. The language of the soul is the only language understood at once by all spiritual men of every age and of every clime. To whom does St. Augustine belong? Is he a Roman Catholic bishop? Yes, of course, but how can he be restricted to the confines of his title? Is he not rather a great Christian, yea, a great saint, not because an ecclesiastical council has conferred sainthood upon him, but simply because he lived deeply and intensely, tapping the very springs of spiritual power and insight? To whom does Thomas a Kempis belong, or Francis of Assisi, or Fenelon, or Jacob Bohme, Lancelot Andrewes, William Law, Friedrich von Hugel, or Kierkegaard? They are restricted to no age, no geographical limits, no group. They belong to the world.

If one would explore the boundaries of the spiritual life, one must saturate himself with the best that these men have said and thought. The shelves of our public and religious libraries are laden with the very richest of soul food waiting to be taken down and

---

13. The best available anthology of devotional literature is Thomas S. Kepler (ed.), *The Fellowship of the Saints* (New York: Abingdon-Cokesbury Press, 1948).

digested. In the religious classics, the great souls of the past have recorded their spiritual adventures. What a tragedy that these books should be left unexplored! The words of these men after many centuries speak to the heart with great spiritual force. Hear Augustine say: "Oh! that thou wouldst enter into my heart and inebriate it, that I may forget my ills, and embrace Thee, my sole good . . . Let me die— lest I die—Only let me see thy face."[14] Or Bonaventura: "Piety enlightens the mind to know what is best . . . It inflames the soul with a desire for what is good."[15] St. Francis speaks to us about humility: "No man can attain to any knowledge or understanding of God, save by the virtue of holy humility: for the straight way upward is the straight way downward."[16] Thomas a Kempis says: "It is vanity to desire to live long, and not to care to live well." Again, a Kempis: "I had rather feel compunction than know the definition thereof."[17] It was from a Kempis that John Wesley learned "simplicity of intention, and purity of affection." To him, they were "'the wings of the soul' without which she can never ascend to the mount of God."[18]

Many other reasons may be given for reading the great devotional classics. Three reasons are paramount. *First, one should read for his own soul's sake.* It is essential to healthy growth. The soul cannot thrive on the superficial and ephemeral material which usually parades under the guise of devotional literature. The great insights of the saints become the material for introspection. The Psalmist spoke about communing with his own soul on his bed. How rich is that meditation when the mind is furnished with the great thoughts of the holiest men!

Second, one must read if he, in turn, would give spiritual food to others. This is especially important for preachers and religious leaders throughout the total structure of the Church. The average pastor appears before his people 150 times a year. He is continually giving from his own spiritual resources, but he cannot feed others unless he is first fed. The richness of his ministry is almost invariably related to the devotional resources of his library.

Third, it is out of the fullness of the inner life that doctrine emerges. Deep

14. Kepler, *Fellowship of the Saints*, p. 76.

15. *Ibid.*, 138.

16. *Ibid.*, 127.

17. *Ibid.*, 233.

18. *Plain Account of Christian Perfection.*

devotion is the mother of great theology. Theology is not something mechanically produced to buttress a preconceived doctrine. True theology is born out of the soul, and it remains great doctrine only so long as it continues to be touched by the Spirit of God. "The letter killeth, but the spirit giveth life" (2 Cor. 3:6). But the soul must be first nourished by great ideas, meditation, prayer. The literature of devotion helps to keep the heart and mind in a state of creative ferment. "Out of the abundance of the heart the mouth speaketh" (Matt. 12:34).

SUMMARY

The chapter might be summarized by the simple observation that the total function of the Church and its related activities is to serve as a meeting place between the seeking soul and the grace of God. The dispensation of God's grace is by no means limited to the Church, but the Church as the special creation of Christ contains the richest deposit of devotional resources of any institution upon earth. The Christian today is the beneficiary of a spiritual heritage stretching from the Hymn of Creation to the treasures of the last Sunday morning worship service. "Thy testimonies have I taken as an heritage for ever: for they are the rejoicing of my heart" (Ps. 119:111).

PART IV

The Final Consummation

CHAPTER 21

The Kingdom of God

When Jesus began His ministry in Galilee, He went about the countryside preaching "the gospel of the kingdom." He proclaimed, "The time is fulfilled, and the kingdom of God is at hand: repent ye, and believe the gospel" (Mark 1:15; Matt. 4:17). The kingdom of God was the core of His message. The term "kingdom" He employed numerous times; in fact, we have every reason to believe that the Gospel writers have recorded but a partial list of the references. The four Evangelists included, however, more than 60 different instances where the word "kingdom" appears. In the Book of Acts "kingdom of God" is found 6 times. Paul the apostle refers to "the kingdom of God" 9 times. Thus the idea of the Kingdom merits some consideration in any definition of the Christian faith.

I. THE USAGE OF "KINGDOM OF HEAVEN"

Matthew has preferred to use the term "kingdom of heaven" in place of "kingdom of God." Only 4 times (6:33; 12:28; 21:31, 43) does he employ the latter phrase, whereas he makes use of the former 32 times. It has been customary to explain Matthew's preference by saying that "heaven" indicates the heavenly character of the Kingdom, that is to say, it comes down from above and is the gift of God and not the creation of man. Support for this interpretation is found in the reference in the Lord's Prayer, where a unique plea is made: "Thy kingdom come. Thy will be done in earth, as it is in heaven" (Matt. 6:9-10). In this connection "kingdom" means the will of the Father in heaven which will be realized on earth. Plausible as this explanation seems, practically all modern scholarship asserts a different reason for this preference of Matthew.[1]

The native tongue of the Jews in Jesus' day was Aramaic, a Semitic language closely akin to Hebrew. No doubt our Lord used this language in all of His preaching and teaching. His sayings as found in the Gospels were translated from this vernacular language to the Greek, which was the literary language of the day. The reverence of the Jewish people for the name of God caused them to avoid the vocalizing of it. They feared any profane reference; therefore they sought substitutes for the name. "Heaven" was one of the most common substitutes. In all likelihood Jesus himself used "kingdom of heaven" more than "kingdom of God," having been brought up in the Jewish community and therefore possessing appreciation for its spiritual sensitivities. Intentionally directing his Gospel to the Jews, the writer Matthew simply translated the phrase as Jesus used it on most occasions. He was attempting "to be all things to all men," thereby giving the message the best advantage possible with his own people.

Mark, Luke, and John, on the other hand, prefer the phrase "the kingdom of God" because it would have more meaning for the Gentile world. "Kingdom of heaven" would sound to the Gentile ear something like "kingdom of the skies" or "kingdom of the clouds."[2] The sum of the whole matter is simply that the Gospels indicate that the two terms are interchangeable, and "the difference between them is one of linguistic idiom and not of meaning."[3]

II. THE MEANING OF "BASILEIA"

The Greek word for kingdom is *basileia,* a noun derived from the verb *basileuein,* which means "to be king, to reign, to rule." The noun *basileia* cannot be defined in simple terms because its meaning has both a concrete and an abstract dimension. In its concrete expression, *basileia* means "realm," "territory," "domain," or "people over whom a king rules."[4] In its abstract expression, it denotes "sovereignty, royal

1. George L. Ladd, *Crucial Questions About the Kingdom of God* (Grand Rapids: Wm. B. Eerdmans Publishing Co., 1952), p. 122.

2. *Ibid.,* pp. 123-24.

3. *Ibid.,* p. 130. Cf. also J. W. Hodges, *Christ's Kingdom and Coming* (Grand Rapids: Wm. B. Eerdmans Publishing Co., 1957), p. 121.

4. Matt. 4:8; 12:25-26; 24:7; Mark 3:24; 6:23; Luke 4:5; Heb. 11:33.

power or dominion."[5] Thus, whenever we encounter *basileia* while reading the New Testament we must determine whether the reference is to the realm of a king or to his sovereign power or to both. When employed with verbs of motion, as when it is said "to be at hand" or "to come," *basileia* obviously could not be referring primarily to a realm, but to the approach of a reign or rulership. "To preach the kingdom" must mean "to proclaim a reign, not a realm."[6]

Any discussion therefore of the meaning of the phrase "the kingdom of God" must take into account this essential difference between the concrete usage and the abstract usage of the word *basileia*. In concrete terms the phrase designates the new order, material and social, which will be established through Christ; but in abstract terms it denotes "the kingly rule of God" in the hearts of men made possible through the life, death, and resurrection of Christ. Indeed, this latter sense is the correct point of departure for any interpretation of the kingdom of God. However, the interpretation, to be complete, should note the dimension of the Kingdom as a realm or domain over which the King rules.

III. THE KINGDOM OF GOD IN THE OLD TESTAMENT

The phrase "the kingdom of God" does not appear in the Old Testament. However, although the specific phrase is missing, the idea is abundantly evident, as the following references indicate: "Thou art the God, even thou alone, of all the kingdoms of the earth" (2 Kings 19:15); "The Lord shall reign for ever and ever" (Exod. 15:18); "Your Holy One, the creator of Israel, your King" (Isa. 43:15); "As I live, saith the King, whose name is the Lord" (Jer. 46:18); "His kingdom ruleth over all" (Ps. 103:19); "The Lord sitteth King for ever" (Ps. 29:10). The idea comes to its fullest expression in Ps. 145:11-13, where the Psalmist declares: "They shall speak of the glory of thy kingdom, and talk of thy power; to make known to the sons of men his mighty acts, and the glorious majesty of his kingdom. Thy kingdom is an everlasting kingdom, and thy dominion endureth throughout all generations."

A double thrust of meaning is evident in the Old Testament

---

5. Matt. 16:28; Luke 1:33; 19:12, 15; 22:29; John 18:36; Acts 1:6; Heb. 1:8; 1 Cor. 15:24; Rev. 12:10; 17:12.

6. Cf. G. Abbott-Smith, *A Manual Greek Lexicon of the New Testament.* (3rd ed., Edinburgh: T. and T. Clark, 1937).

understanding of the Kingdom.[7] (1) God is already King; He is reigning now over all the earth and above all the world's tumult. He brought the world into existence and therefore is its Governor. Nations are subject to Him and even at times become instruments of His will. God's unquestionable sovereignty is the very cornerstone of the Old Testament faith.[8] (2) According to the Old Testament the fulfillment of the kingdom of God lies in the future. God rules over His people, Israel, and in a sense they are the poeple of the Kingdom. But outside the people are the nations which are not subject to Him. God appoints Israel as His priestly ruler in relation to all the other nations, not in order that Israel should dominate them, but as a servant to them to bring them unto Him (Exod. 19:4-6).

The tragedy is that Israel fails to fulfill the responsibility to which the prophets call her again and again. The impotence and defeat of Israel lead to a new understanding among the prophets. They look forward to a new age when the reign of God will truly take place. The true Israel will be exalted, justice will be established, and all men will worship the Lord.[9] Here we see the futuristic element developing. Nature will be restored to the glory of Paradise; the wildness of the animal world will be vanquished so that the wolf will lie down with the lamb, the cattle will feed in abundant pastures, and the light of the moon will be as the light of the sun (Isa. 11:1 ff., 30:23 ff.).

According to this futuristic understanding of the Kingdom, the exaltation of Israel is a vital element. The Kingdom, which is described in terms of earthly perfection and felicity, will be inaugurated by a King who comes from the house of David. Jerusalem will be its central location and will bring about peace, honor, and pure worship among all nations.[10]

The coming Kingdom is also Messianic in character. With the disintegration of the Hebrew monarchy because of the waywardness of the people there came the promise of a Deliverer or Redeemer, God himself, who would set up the eternal Kingdom.[11] The Messiah

---

7. E. F. Scott, *The Kingdom of God in the New Testament* (New York: The Macmillan Co., 1931), pp. 19 ff.

8. Cf. John Bright, *The Kingdom of God* (New York: Abingdon-Cokesbury Press, 1953): "For the concept of the Kingdom of God involves, in a real sense, the total message of the Bible," p. 7.

9.. Cf. *ibid.*, pp. 71-97, in which he discusses the Remnant concept.

10. Isa. 11; Jer. 33:15-17; Joel 3:18-21.

11. Isa. 7:14; 9:2 ff.; Zech. 9:9.

is the King who brings the Kingdom. Zech. 9:9 contains those memorable words which gather up the Old Testament's teaching concerning the nature of the King who is coming: "Rejoice greatly, O daughter of Zion; shout, O daughter of Jerusalem: behold, thy King cometh unto thee: he is just, and having salvation; lowly, and riding upon an ass, and upon a colt the foal of an ass." This outlook becomes the very backbone of the New Testament teaching concerning the Kingdom.

The central problem of the Jewish understanding of the kingship of God was simply that, since He by right was King over the whole earth, why did He not set himself up as King in fact? Apparently the wickedness of God's people delayed the active taking up of His reign upon the earth. At the time of the coming of Christ, the futuristic concept of the establishment of the Kingdom prevailed. The Jewish writers known as apocalyptists, despairing completely of a deliverance from within history, looked forward to the end of this age and maintained a strong expectation that God would establish His reign amidst spectacular demonstrations of divine power, bringing salvation to His own people and judgment to His enemies.

The Zealots thought that God's kingdom would come more quickly if they precipitated its coming by political action. The Pharisees took a more religious approach to the problem by accepting the notion that the day of the Lord would dawn at the moment the law was perfectly obeyed by God's chosen people. All of this thought set the stage for the precursor of Christ, John the Baptist, who came out of the wilderness to declare that the day of the Lord had dawned and "the kingdom of heaven is at hand" (Matt. 3:1-6).

IV. THE HISTORY OF INTERPRETATION[12]

Throughout the history of the Christian Church two general interpretations of the Kingdom have prevailed. One has emphasized its futuristic or eschatological nature. The other has put primary stress upon its present nature. In the Early Church the futuristic concept held sway. The early fathers viewed the Kingdom as a future realm of blessedness which would be consummated after the second advent of Christ. Some of the fathers maintained that the coming Kingdom would be an earthly domain, while others made no clear statements

---

12. For concise, yet adequate, surveys, see Ladd, *Crucial Questions About the Kingdom,* pp. 22 ff.; Louis Berkhof, *The Kingdom of God* (Grand Rapids: Wm. B. Eerdmans Co., 1951), pp. 21 ff.

as to place. The only Early Church writer who did not accept the eschatological interpretation was Origen, whose rejection of the literalistic approach to the Bible permitted him to accept only a "spiritual" definition of the Kingdom.

The influence of Augustine in the development of the Church's consciousness of the meaning of the Kingdom cannot be fully determined. Augustine's conception of the kingdom of God is found primarily in his great work *De Civitate Dei.* He contrasts the *civitas terrena* (the city of the world), which is composed of all evil persons and forces and finds its historical expression in the heathen state, with the *civitas Dei* (the city of God), which is composed of all saints and the angels, and has its historical manifestation in the Church. The *civitas Dei* equals the Kingdom, which is thus to be identified with the Church. Louis Berkhof is quick to say that it is debatable whether Augustine was thinking of the visible ecclesiastical organization when he spoke of the Church. However, he does admit that it is most certain that he was instrumental in paving the way for the hierarchical conception of the Middle Ages.[13]

In reality, when Augustine identified the Church and the Kingdom he was in effect saying that the millennium Kingdom had been inaugurated with the first advent of Christ and would therefore not have any future fulfillment in the usual sense of the term. The resurrection of a believing soul from spiritual death was the sign of admission into the eternal Kingdom. The reformers took hold of the "spiritual" emphasis of Augustine and made it basic in their teachings. The facts of the case are, they did not formulate a doctrine of the Kingdom as clear-cut and elaborate as the theologians of the Middle Ages. Identifying the Kingdom with the invisible Church, they made the religious concept, the reign of God in the hearts of believers, the central emphasis. Contrary to groups such as the Anabaptists, who sought to set up in the world an external kingdom of God, the reformers expected the external, visible form of the kingdom of God to appear only with the second advent of Christ.

In what is known as the modern period of church history a diversity of thinking developed along the general lines suggested above. Johannes Weiss and Albert Schweitzer, in the face of a strong liberalism which attempted to eliminate the eschatological character of Jesus' teaching, maintained that the eschatological thrust of Jesus' preaching is the very heart of it. According to these two scholars the

---

13. *Kingdom of God,* p. 23.

Kingdom, for Jesus, was entirely a future, apocalyptic reality which would come into existence at the end of human history by a supernatural action of God. In fact, they claimed, Jesus expected the Kingdom to come during His own lifetime. The end was at hand and men must be prepared for it by living the strict ethical life which He propounded and exemplified. This ethic of Jesus was an "interim ethic," a temporary mode of living which must prevail between the time of its initial pronouncement and the advent of the Kingdom.

Weiss and Schweitzer insisted that the idea of the present reality of the Kingdom was an invention of the Gospel writers and therefore must not be considered authentic. Their interpretation of the nature of the Kingdom has become known as "consistent eschatology." Obviously this position does not take seriously the many sayings of our Lord which speak of the "present" character of the Kingdom.[14]

Since the day of Albert Ritschl, who practically divorced the concept of the Kingdom from the basic New Testament teaching by making it "the association of men for reciprocal and common action from the motive of love," there have been scholars who have played down the futuristic dimension and emphasized the present aspect. Harnack viewed the kingdom of God as the rule of the holy God in the hearts of men. The Kingdom is the power that works within the life. Dobschütz, Muirhead, Wellhausen, Sharman have likewise insisted that the eschatological dimension was either a nonessential element in Jesus' message of the Kingdom or frankly an addition of His disciples or the Primitive Church. The Kingdom as a present spiritual reality was the heart of the message of Jesus.

F. C. Grant also set aside the futuristic element and asserted that the Kingdom was to be understood purely in terms of social redemption. The divine sovereignty would eventually be realized here on earth through processes of growth. Two evangelical scholars, A. B. Bruce and James Orr, both relegated the futuristic element to the realm of the symbolic and interpreted Jesus' teaching of the Kingdom in terms of the rule of God in the hearts of men, which would bring about a transformation of society. When all the areas of human life and thought have been penetrated and regenerated by the power of the Kingdom, then the Kingdom will have come. This position, however, does not mean that there will be no second coming of

---

14. *Infra,* Section V; cf. E. F. Scott, *The Kingdom and the Messiah* (Edinburgh: T. and T. Clark, 1911).

Christ. The return of the Lord will transpire at the conclusion of this development brought about by the present action of the Kingdom.

The most discussed contemporary interpretation of the Kingdom is that which was set forth by the eminent British scholar, C. H. Dodd. "Realized eschatology" was first propounded by Dodd in his book entitled *The Parables of the Kingdom.*[15] Dodd's study of the parables of Jesus and the related sayings led him to believe that for Jesus the Kingdom had already come. The future had come into the experiences of men. The Absolute had entered the arena of history; the Eternal had come into time.

Jesus himself figures prominently in this theory because He is the fulfillment of the eschatological hope and therefore the advent of the kingdom of God. The Kingdom is not to be thought of as something yet to come; it is already here. The future is being realized in Jesus Christ and in the life of the Church. While many scholars feel that this interpretation is the most reasonable solution to the problem of the nature of the Kingdom, it fails to do justice to the teachings of Jesus which clearly speak of the future coming of the Kingdom. Furthermore, it tends to relegate the Kingdom to the realm of myth or symbol.

Other students of the theme of the Kingdom have attempted to hold the two dimensions in proper balance. Rudolf Otto, in his book *The Kingdom of God and The Son of Man,* sees the kingdom as basically future, yet already manifested in the person and mission of Jesus. W. G. Kümmel likewise understands the Kingdom as future and present. Emil Brunner maintains that the ultimate, absolute end, that is, the kingdom of God, has begun in the Church but its completion is still in the future. R. N. Flew has expressed the relationship of the future and present aspects as follows: "The kingdom has come in the person of Jesus. Its blessing can be enjoyed now through faith. But it is not fully come. The final consummation is delayed."[16]

Before leaving this survey of historical interpretations of the concept of the kingdom of God, attention needs to be given to a special emphasis which conservative scholarship has made with respect to the futuristic dimension. In fact the tendency of this wing of the Church has been to confine itself to the spelling out of the eschatological aspect almost to the neglect of the other or present aspect. Ladd

---

15. Dodd has found strong supporters for his interpretation in William Manson and John Knox.

16. *Jesus and His Church* (London: The Epworth Press, 1943), p. 32.

contends that the concern for the prophetic teachings of the Bible, plus the distressing condition of the world in recent decades, has created an intense interest in eschatology among conservatives.[17]

The point of departure in discussions of the theme of the Kingdom is the Parousia or the coming of the Lord, to be considered more at length in our next chapter. Conservatives divide into groups according to the understanding of the "when" of the Lord's coming and the relationship of the Kingdom to the advent. There are three groups, namely:

1. The postmillennialists, who assert that the Parousia will take place after a millennium in which the kingdom of God as a supernatural power working in the hearts of men and permeating like leaven all human relationships will bring about a transformation of the world of men until all men do the will of God, thus creating a "golden age" on earth (B. B. Warfield and James Orr were leading exponents of this position).

2. The premillennialists, who understand the Scriptures to say that the Parousia will take place before the millennium, and following it the kingdom of God will be realized in its glory (Zahn, Godet, Alford, *et al.* fostered this view).

3. The amillennialists, who repudiate the notion that the kingdom of God will involve a reign of Christ on the earth for 1,000 years. The tendency of this group is to think of the Kingdom in terms of a present spiritual reality. The millennial reign of Christ may refer to the rulership of Christ in the world through the Church. It has also been suggested that the millennium has reference to the reign of martyred Christians with the Lord in heaven. Louis Berkhof and Geerhardus Vos are two influential supporters of this interpretation.[18]

V. The Kingdom as Present and Future

Much of the debate as to whether the Kingdom is present or future has been irrelevant because both aspects are basic to the meaning of the Kingdom, especially as the New Testament views it. We are fully justified in asserting that the kingdom of God has a "here and now" and "there and then" character.

---

17. *Crucial Questions About the Kingdom*, p. 46.

18. Berkhof, *Kingdom of God*; Geerhardus Vos, *The Teaching of Jesus Concerning the Kingdom of God and the Church* (New York: American Tract Society, 1903).

The "here and now" characteristic is found abundantly in Christ's teachings. In Mark 4:3 ff. the kingdom of God is likened to a seed sown in the hearts of men in this life. In Mark 12:34 we read that Jesus told an interested scribe that he was "not far from the kingdom of God." Obviously Jesus was not referring to the man's death or to the establishment of the Church at Pentecost. Neither did He have a future cataclysmic event in mind. He was commenting on the spiritual relationship of the scribe to himself.

In the Gospels the presence and activity of Jesus are presented as a proof of the presence of the Kingdom. Following a miraculous deliverance of a blind and dumb demoniac, the Lord was drawn into a conversation with the Pharisees, who insisted that Jesus was able to do such deeds only because of His relationship to Beelzebub, the prince of demons. Jesus swiftly answers His critics and then comments, "But if it is by the Spirit of God that I cast out demons, then the kingdom of God has come upon you" (Matt. 12:22 ff., RSV). In Matt. 13:44-46 the Master describes the Kingdom as a treasure hidden in the earth, which men can discover now. Also the Kingdom is a pearl of great value which men of good judgment will give all to purchase. Another famous word of the Lord is found in Luke 17: 20-21: "Being asked by the Pharisees when the kingdom of God was coming, he answered, 'The kingdom of God is not coming with signs to be observed; nor will they say, "Lo, here it is!" or "There!" for behold, the kingdom of God is in the midst of you'" (RSV).[19]

While we have these precise references to the Kingdom as a reality which men may know now, there are numerous others which speak just as definitely of the futuristic dimension of the Kingdom. First of all, it is noteworthy that six of the Beatitudes are based upon rewards which are to be enjoyed in the future (Matt. 5:4-9). In Matt. 7:2-23 Jesus specifies who will and will not qualify for entrance into the future Kingdom. By parable and precept Jesus teaches the eschatological nature of the Kingdom. At the Last Supper, Jesus tells His disciples that He anticipates the day when He will drink the fruit of the vine new with His disciples in His Father's kingdom (Matt. 26:29).

Turning to the apostle Paul we discover that he does not often

---

19. Scholars who accept the position of "realized eschatology" find this verse along with Matt. 12:22 to be strong evidence for their interpretation. For a thorough criticism of their exegesis of these verses, see R. H. Fuller, *The Mission and Achievement of Jesus* (London: SCM Press, 1953).

use the word kingdom. However, his limited references suggest both the present and future characteristics. In Rom. 14:17 Paul describes the Kingdom as follows: "For the kingdom of God is not meat and drink; but righteousness, and peace, and joy in the Holy Ghost." In Col. 1:13 he speaks of Christian experience as a deliverance out of "the power of darkness" and a translation into "the kingdom of his dear Son." Both of these references obviously depict the reality of the power of the Kingdom in the heart of the Christian. But Paul does not overlook the futuristic aspect, for in 1 Cor. 6:9; 15:50; Gal. 5:21; Eph. 5:5; and 2 Tim. 4:1, 18 he has in mind an established realm.

The question might be asked, But how is it possible for the kingdom of God to be both present and future at the same time? Two observations are helpful at this point. First, if the meaning of the word kingdom is restricted to the idea of realm or domain, then duality of reference is impossible. The basic meaning, however, is that of "rulership, reign or kingly power."[20] Admittedly, there cannot be a rulership without a realm or domain, except in a temporary sense; that is to say, the king is ruling but his kingdom is not fully manifest. The kingdom of God is a present reality in that the sovereignty of God is realized in the world now, but His realm in which that sovereignty is exercised with consummate reality has not been created.

Second, the kingdom of God has come in the person and activity of Christ. As has already been suggested, the Kingdom's coming is uniquely related to the first coming of the Son of God as well as to the Second Coming. Although there are several important passages which set forth this fact, the most meaningful one is Luke 17:21, where Jesus declares, "The kingdom of God is within you," or "among you." Scholars have looked upon this verse as a *crux interpretum*.

The meaning of the Greek words *hentos humon* (within or among you) cannot be easily decided; it may be given either of the two translations. However, the issue at stake in this verse has to do with the signs of the advent of the Kingdom. Jesus seeks to turn the attention of the inquisitors away from future dimension of the Kingdom and to bring them to see His relationship to the Kingdom. The signs in this instance are those which are manifest in His lowly mission and refer to the response in the hearts of men to His ministry, whether the proclaimed word or the healings.

---

20. Cf. Jesus' parable in Luke 19:11-27. Note that the RSV translates *basileia* in v. 12, "kingly power."

Jesus himself, in His role as the Bearer of the announcement of the dawning Kingdom, is the sign that the Kingdom is at hand. Thus the Kingdom is a present reality in that it is dawning in the presence and work of Jesus. Another way of stating this truth is to say that the Kingdom is proleptically operative among men; it is casting its power ahead of itself, though its full dawning awaits a future time. The powers of the future, eschatological Kingdom have actually entered history in the person of Jesus Christ, but the Kingdom as a realm in which God's will is perfectly done is yet to come.[21]

It must be forcefully reiterated that the future dimension of Kingdom figures largely in the teachings of the Bible and most assuredly in the message of Jesus. By miracle and parable, Jesus insisted that the kingdom of God is not yet present, but is at hand. The imminent event is affecting the present order. The future has not come into the present in a "realized" eschatological sense, but the powers of the future event are at work already. As Fuller has commented, ". . . our Lord's earthly ministry is keyed up to a future event . . ."[22] It must always be kept in mind that if the decisive event had taken place in the ministry of Jesus there would have been no need of the Cross. The Cross and the Resurrection guarantee the fulfillment, for in these mighty acts the kingdom of the enemy has suffered a deadly blow from which it will never recover. On the other hand, the kingdom of God is assured of victory.

VI. THE KINGDOM AND THE CHURCH

The relationship of the Church to the kingdom of God constitutes a difficult problem. Are the Kingdom and the Church to be identified? Or is the Church a separate concept in the Christian understanding?

On the basis of the biblical materials the problem is not easily solved. For example, Jesus himself has little to say about the Church but He constantly speaks of the Kingdom. Indeed, the concept of the Kingdom rules His thought, but He mentions the Church only twice (Matt. 16:18; 18:17). These two verses where the word "church" appears are two of the most difficult verses with which interpreters are confronted. Outside the Gospels, the word "kingdom" is found only 32 times in comparison to the 120 times in the Gospels; but, on

21. Fuller, *Mission and Achievement of Jesus,* pp. 28-29; Ladd, *Crucial Questions About the Kingdom,* p. 89.

22. Fuller, *Mission and Achievement of Jesus,* p. 49.

the other hand, the word "church" appears 110 times in comparison to just twice in the Gospels.

Some scholars have looked at this statistical notation and have concluded that Jesus had no intention of starting a Church. Jesus appeared with His glorious ideal of the kingdom of God which was shortly to be fulfilled by supernatural means. Many people were inspired to follow Him. However, the failure of the Kingdom to be consummated led to the crystallization of the ideal into a society, which became known as the Church. E. F. Scott once wrote, "Jesus had proclaimed the kingdom, and instead of it there arose the church."[23]

The above reaction to the sparse reference to the Church by Jesus hardly treats all the factors related to the issue. While Jesus was proclaiming the gospel of the Kingdom, He was at the same time laying the groundwork for the creation of a social order to work for it. He was calling a new people to whom the Kingdom was given. The company of the Twelve was the nucleus of a larger body of followers who joined with Him during His lifetime. This was the embryonic Church.

In this same connection it needs also to be noted that, even if He did not intend to call a Church into existence, He nevertheless made it necessary by the very nature of His message, which brought men together in love and fellowship. The Early Church was certainly persuaded that she was fulfilling the intention of Jesus when she described herself as the *ecclesia*, the assembly or "the called out."

The communal life of the Early Church with its common financing and daily eating of bread witnesses to the Church's sense of divine existence. Furthermore, the rulership of God in the Old Testament was intimately related to a community of people who were God's people. It seems quite evident that Jesus regarded some outward form of association and organization as essential to the most effective promotion of the Kingdom.

Specifically, what is the relationship of the Kingdom to the Church? Throughout the history of the Church, Christians have insisted that the Kingdom and the Church are intimately related. But they have differed among themselves as to the extent and character of the relationship. Since the time of Augustine there has been a tendency among Christians, especially, in the Catholic tradition, to move toward an absolute identity. Roman Catholicism asserts that

---

23. *Kingdom of God in the New Testament,* p. 170.

the Kingdom is now being realized in the hierarchal church, which has been entrusted with supernatural power to the extent that, as it extends its influence more and more over the world, it fosters the establishment of the Kingdom.

Protestantism, on the other hand, has been careful to define what it means by the Church, so as not to be embarrassed should the activities of the Church, as seen by men, be far from what one would expect the kingdom of God to be. Thus it has been willing to identify the Invisible Church with the Kingdom.

"Invisible" in this instance means that group of individuals over whose lives God rules fully. This group is the ideal Church. "Visible," on the other hand, refers to the Church in its actual, historical character, as observed by men. Some people within the Visible Church could not qualify as members of the kingdom of God because God does not rule in their lives. As H. C. Sheldon has remarked, "These terms are only a convenient means of expressing the truth that the actual and the ideal—the ecclesiastical area as it appears to the eyes of men, and the Church as it exists for God's thought—are not commensurate."[24] It is not to be assumed that there are two distinct churches, but that there are different boundaries of the Church as it is seen from the human and the divine points of view. Thus, insofar as the Church is truly under the reign of God, it is the kingdom of God. However, the ideal order is never achieved in this human, finite order; thus Christians wait for the consummation. They look forward to the time when God himself will bring to perfection a spiritual brotherhood in which there exists a peculiar union of men whose lives are fully yielded to Him. Then the kingdom of God will have come.

VII. THE NATURE OF THE FUTURE KINGDOM

No other area of the theme under discussion tests the interpreter's powers of discernment more than this one. The principal reason is the lack of information in the Bible. A mystery exists at this point. It can be asserted without equivocation that the Bible teaches the coming of the Kingdom in perfection, but it offers little information as to whether a temporary earthly Kingdom is to be expected, to be followed by a heavenly Kingdom, or a final act in which both heaven

---

24. *System of Christian Doctrine*, Revised Edition (New York: Methodist Book Concern, 1903), p. 483.

and earth will be renovated is the divine plan. The Old Testament generally conceives the establishment to take place upon the earth, yet in some places a heavenly Kingdom is implied. In Isa. 65:17 and 66:22 the prophet speaks of the creation of new heavens and a new earth. No extensive and consistent statements of the character of the Kingdom prevail in the Jewish literature which was written in the period between the two Testaments. The teaching is threefold: (1) the Kingdom brings about a transformation of the heavens and the earth; (2) the Kingdom will be an eternal Kingdom on the earth; (3) the Kingdom is a temporal earthly order to be followed by an everlasting heavenly Kingdom.[25]

Several New Testament passages suggest an earthly realm. For example, Jesus said, "Blessed are the meek: for they shall inherit the earth" (Matt. 5:5). He also taught His disciples to pray, "Thy kingdom come. Thy will be done in earth, as it is in heaven" (Matt. 6:10). The Pauline letters offer us no additional information on this point.

The concluding book of the New Teatament fittingly concerns itself with the future Kingdom and we find in chapter 20 the only New Testament passage which mentions the millennium, with the possible exception of 2 Pet. 3:8. The thousand years, during which the devil is bound in a pit and Christ reigns with His saints, takes place apparently on the earth (cf. 20:9; also 5:10).

Revelation 21 begins with the statement: "Then I saw a new heaven and a new earth: for the first heaven and the first earth had passed away, and the sea was no more. And I saw the holy city, new Jerusalem, coming down out of heaven from God, prepared as a bride adorned for her husband; and I heard a great voice from the throne saying, Behold, the dwelling of God is with men. He will dwell with them, and they shall be his people, and God himself will be with them; he will wipe away every tear from their eyes, and death shall be no more, neither shall there be mourning nor crying nor pain any more, for the former things have passed away" (21:1-4, RSV). Chapter 21 seems to be a further extension of the domain beyond the earth. However, no scholar can afford to be dogmatic at this point because of the limited number of references to the character of the future Kingdom. Several undeniable facts concerning the Kingdom to come can be noted:

---

25. Cf. G. L. Ladd, *"The Kingdom of God in Apocryphal Literature,"* *Bibliotheca Sacra,* CIX (1952).

1. Since the future Kingdom is related to the return of Christ, its establishment will be attended by catastrophic and supernatural events (Mark 13:24-27; 1 Thess. 4:15-17).

2. Judgment will fall upon the present order (2 Thess. 1:5-12; 2 Pet. 3:4-10; Rev. 19:11-16).

3. All antagonists will be subdued and become submissive to God. (Phil. 2:9-10; 1 Cor. 15:20-23).

4. A total renewal of the cosmic order, both morally and materially, will take place (Rev. 21:5-8; 22:1-5).

5. The hopes of the redeemed will be realized fully (Rev. 21:3-4).

SUMMARY

The phrase "the kingdom of God" pretty well summarizes the message of the entire Bible. Jesus initiated His ministry by going to the people in the surrounding towns of Galilee and preaching the good news of the Kingdom.

The Greek word *basileia* denotes both "realm" and "sovereignty." The phrase "kingdom of God" likewise has a dual thrust, referring at one instance to the realization of the power of God in redemption now and at another instance to future fulfillment of God's purpose in the establishment of an imperishable and eternal order. The history of interpretation of the kingdom of God shows that scholars have tended to vacillate between the "here and now" and the "there and then" character of the Kingdom. A survey of Christ's teachings demonstrates clearly that an intimacy exists between the Kingdom and the Church. The Church in its ideal or invisible dimension is identical to the Kingdom. All of the redemptive purposes of God will be fulfilled in the establishment of the future Kingdom.

CHAPTER 22

The Second Coming of Christ

"We believe that the Lord Jesus will come again."[1]

For many years interest in the second coming of Christ was confined quite largely to advocates of conservative Christianity and to certain somewhat heterodox groups. For perhaps a decade after 1954, when the Second Assembly of the World Council of Churches met to consider this theme, the attention of the entire Christian world was once more focused upon this important segment of Christian theology. A flood of literature, produced by many of the finest minds of Christendom, poured from the presses.[2]

During the intervening years a resurgent theological liberalism, strengthened by an existential theology, has robbed the Church of a virile faith in a real *parousia*.[3] The task of proclaiming this biblical message is now largely in the hands of evangelical, orthodox Christians.[4]

---

1. *Manual,* Church of the Nazarene, 1976, p. 30.

2. Some of the leading titles were: Emil Brunner, *Eternal Hope,* trans. Harold Knight (Philadelphia: Westminster Press, 1954); J. E. Fison, *The Christian Hope* (London: Longmans, Green and Co., 1954); T. A. Kantonen, *The Christian Hope* (Philadelphia: Muhlenberg Press, 1954); and J. A. T. Robinson, *Jesus and His Coming* (New York: Abingdon Press, 1958).

3. A New Testament word generally translated *coming* and used extensively for the *second* coming of Christ. See the discussion that follows.

4. Some of the newer titles include G. C. Berkouwer, *The Return of Christ* (Grand Rapids: Wm. B. Eerdmans Publishing Co., 1972); Leon Morris, *The Revelation of St. John* (London: The Tyndale Press, 1969); and A. L. Moore, *The Parousia in the New Testament* (Leiden: E. J. Brill, 1966).

Thus it has come to pass that in one of the most critical hours in world history Christendom has once again been confronted with the biblical message of the coming of the Day of the Lord, the end time, including the second coming of Christ, the resurrection and judgment, and the final consummation of all things. The current interest in these matters is surely providential. A new age has dawned, the atomic and space age, but man is frightened. A world that should be full of promise and hope is troubled by the threat of global war with atomic weapons. Many responsible persons fear that if such a war were to come it would mean the end of life on this planet. Biblical passages that once seemed to be only fantasy now become very plausible pictures of how this world may come to a fiery, explosive end. Man has attained amazing scientific and technological success, but at the same time has lagged far behind in his moral and spiritual progress.

The time has literally come when the hearts of men are "failing them for fear, and for looking after those things which are coming on the earth: for the powers of heaven shall be shaken" (Luke 21:26). Does the Christian faith have a message for times like these? It does, and it is one of hope rather than gloom. "Looking for that blessed hope, and the glorious appearing of the great God and our Saviour Jesus Christ" (Titus 2:13). It is imperative that the Christian doctrine of last things be recovered from the hands of the dispensationalists and the heterodox and restored to the position of significance the Scriptures give it.

It will be the concern of this chapter, first of all, to discover the biblical basis for the Christian doctrine of the second coming of Christ and then to seek ways of understanding its meaning for us today. Thus we shall look first at the *fact* of the biblical evidence and then seek *clues* to help us understand this solid evidence.

I. THE FACT OF THE BIBLICAL EVIDENCE

As we have noted earlier, in our time a new appreciation for the Bible as the Word of God has brought with it a renewed study of biblical theology, the faith of the Hebrew and Christian men who "spake as they were moved by the Holy Ghost" (2 Pet. 1:21). A careful study of the Bible yields the unmistakable conclusion that a central theme is the coming of the kingdom of God, that is to say, the rule or government of God over the affairs of men. It is the purpose of God that His will shall be done on earth, for only thus can man become his best. Even though man has spurned the will of God, the kingdom of God will yet prevail among men. The Christian teaching on eschatology is an integral part of this theme.

A. Anticipation in the Old Testament

A strain of eschatology runs through much of the Old Testament, particularly in the prophets, stressing "that day" or "the day of the Lord" (Cf. Isa. 24:21; 52:6; Joel 3:14; Amos 5:18; *et al.*) This expression is usually associated with a time of judgment because of the disobedience of Israel. However, a promise of God's coming in mercy and blessing also appears from time to time. "Thus says the Lord: I will return to Zion, and will dwell in the midst of Jerusalem, and Jerusalem shall be called the faithful city, and the mountain of the Lord of hosts, the holy mountain" (Zech. 8:3, RSV). The coming of the day of the Lord is certain, and it will mean both judgment and hope.

Another significant Old Testament message is the coming of the Messiah. He is sometimes thought of as a King who will be the Heir of promises made to Judah and David; sometimes He is described as the "servant" or the Lord's "anointed." As H. Roux has said:

> His coming is accompanied by warning signs of judgment and of vengeance which he comes to exact (Isa. 40:10), or of paradisal peace which he brings with him (Isa. 9:6 and 11:6 f.), or else of universal reconciliation among the peoples (Isa. 2:2-4). . . . Finally, the Messianic hope is linked with the coming of a heavenly personage "like a son of man", "coming on the clouds of heaven" and to whom God Himself grants the eternal kingship and dominion which belong to him (cf. Dan. 2:44; 7:13-14 and Ps. 24).[5]

During the period between the Testaments, when the political hopes of Israel were both renewed and crushed, the eschatological teaching of the Hebrew people included a portrayal of a Messiah who would realize for them their highest national dreams. Incidentally, this is one of the reasons why the Jews did not accept Jesus as the Christ, or Messiah. They fully expected a political leader with supernatural powers to destroy their enemies and bring in a period of unprecedented prosperity and abundance. When Jesus said, "My kingdom is not of this world" (John 18:36), the Jews were disappointed.

Beginning in the intertestamental period, Israel began to produce a certain type of literature, known as apocalyptic, that set forth her hopes in dramatic symbols such as we find in Daniel and the

---

5. "Advent," *Companion to the Bible,* Von Allmen, ed., p. 14.

Book of Revelation. Apocalyptic imagery was often used in a time of tribulation to portray the hope of the faithful that God would intervene in a wicked world to put down His enemies and establish His rule. The strange, even weird, creatures, dreams, and catastrophic happenings were intended to confuse hostile unbelievers, but bring hope and courage to believers. From all of this it is evident that the Old Testament closes with an attitude of waiting and expectancy, of unfulfilled promise. Thus it was that "when the fulness of the time was come, God sent forth his Son" (Gal. 4:4).

It should become increasingly clear, as we look at the mounting biblical evidence, that the Christian belief in the second coming of Christ and its accompanying events is deeply rooted in the Bible. When one sees that the roots of Christian eschatology are to be found far back in the Old Testament, the evidence becomes even more compelling. Many elements in the Christian doctrine of the end have come directly from the Old Testament: the day of the Lord as a time of both mercy and judgment; the coming of the Messiah, who is seen to be a King, a Servant, a Judge, a Son of Man; the kingdom of God, that cannot be thwarted. As we begin to think about the "last things," we see striking anticipations of it in the Old Testament.

B. Disclosure in the New Testament

If we find anticipations of Christian eschatology in the Old Testament, we find a more complete disclosure or unveiling of it in the New Testament. For those who hold the Bible to be the Word of God, any teaching deeply embedded therein is of serious importance. However, the biblical doctrine of the second coming of Christ has suffered both distortion and neglect—the former at the hands of some of its friends, the latter from its enemies. Dispensationalists who placard great charts, purporting to map in detail the future, have usually spoken with such dogmatism and appalling ignorance of accepted biblical interpretation as to alienate many earnest Christians from the study of this subject altogether. Theological liberals, on the other hand, have long considered the subject a dead issue of an earlier and less enlightened day. The following is a typical comment from the latter group: "Many are obliged to doubt that a 'second' coming—whether conceived naively or in sophisticated terms—is essential to the Christian hope of Christ's final triumph."[6] Both

---

6. Georgia Harkness, "Progress in Eschatology," *Christian Century*, Jan. 14, 1953, p. 45; cited by Kantonen. *Christian Hope*, p. 72.

groups have thus tended to rob the Church of a wholesome understanding of a doctrine so rooted in the Christian Scriptures as to be
ineradicable.

A careful study of the biblical evidence, together with a history
of its recent interpretation, can scarcely fail to leave one with the
feeling that the Church must not allow the teaching on the Second
Advent to be distorted by the "ignorant and unstable" (2 Pet. 3:16,
RSV) or discarded by theological liberalism. Let us now turn to the
New Testament evidence.

It will be of considerable value for the student to read, in their
context, the scriptures to be cited herein. Only thus can one come to
see the significance of this doctrine for the biblical writers and to feel
the accumulative effect of the weight of evidence. It is for these reasons that extensive references will be made.

Several different terms are used in the New Testament to refer
to the second coming of our Lord. Chief among these is the term
parousia. G. Abbott-Smith gives two meanings for the word: "1. usually in classics *a being present, presence:* 1 Cor. 16:17; 2 Cor. 10:10 . . . 2. *a
coming, arrival, advent . . . :* 2 Cor. 7:6, 7; Phil. 1:26; 2 Thess. 2:9; in late
writers . . . as technical term for the visit of a king; hence, in the N.T.,
specifically of the *Advent,* or *Parousia* of Christ."[7] It should be added
that the references just cited show the general usage of the term; the
instances where it refers to the Second Coming now follow.

The following list includes all the instances where the term
parousia is used with reference to the coming of Christ: Matt. 24:3, 27,
37, 39; 1 Cor. 15:23; 1 Thess. 2:19; 3:13; 4:15; 5:23; 2 Thess. 2:1, 8;
Jas. 5:7-8; 2 Pet. 1:16; 3:4, 12; 1 John 2:28.

Let us look at one each of these from the Gospels and the Pauline
Epistles, and two from the General Epistles. As indicated above, the
student will profit from a study of *all* the references. In each case
throughout this present study the translation of the term under discussion will be italicized.

Matt. 24:27: "For as the lightning cometh out of the east, and
shineth even unto the west; so shall also the *coming* of the Son of man
be."

1 Thess. 4:15: "For this we declare to you by the word of the
Lord, that we who are alive, who are left until the *coming* of the Lord,
shall not precede those who have fallen asleep" (RSV).

---

7. *Manual of the Greek Lexicon,* p. 347.

Jas. 5:7-8: "Be patient, therefore, brethren, unto the *coming* of the Lord. Behold, the husbandman waiteth for the precious fruit of the earth, and hath long patience for it, until he receive the early and latter rain. Be ye also patient; stablish your hearts: for the *coming* of the Lord draweth nigh."

2 Pet. 3:12: "Waiting for and hastening the *coming* of the day of God, because of which the heavens will be kindled and dissolved, and the elements will melt with fire!" (RSV)

Another New Testament term employed to describe the second coming of Christ is the word *apokalupsis.* G. Abbott-Smith defines it thus: *"an uncovering,* laying bare . . . Metaph., *a revealing, revelation:* a disclosure of divine truth, or a manifestation from God."[8] Instances in the New Testament where this term refers to the coming of Christ include: 1 Cor. 1:7; 2 Thess. 1:7; 1 Pet. 1:7, 13; 4:13. The verb form *apokalupto* occurs also in Luke 17:30.

Let us take one of the references from the writing of the apostle Peter, who knew our Lord so well: "That the trial of your faith, being much more precious than of gold that perisheth, though it be tried with fire, might be found unto praise and honour and glory at the *appearing* of Jesus Christ. . . . Wherefore gird up the loins of your mind, be sober, and hope to the end for the grace that is to be brought unto you at the *revelation* of Jesus Christ" (1 Pet. 1:7, 13).

A third important New Testament term for the second coming of Christ is *epiphaneia,* defined by G. Abbott-Smith as *"a manifestation, appearance."*[9] Instances where the word is so used include: 2 Thess. 2:8; 1 Tim. 6:14; 2 Tim. 4:1, 8; Titus 2:13. The first of these is of special interest: "And then the lawless one will be revealed, and the Lord Jesus will slay him with the breath of his mouth and destroy him by his *appearing* and his coming" (RSV).

One more New Testament word may be noted in this connection; this is the verb *phaneroo,* meaning *"to make visible, clear, manifest, or known."*[10] This word is found in the following places: Col. 3:4; 1 Pet. 5:4; 1 John 2:28; 3:2. We may profitably quote two of these usages:

Col. 3:4: "When Christ, who is our life, shall *appear,* then shall ye also appear with him in glory."

1 John 3:2: "Beloved, now are we the sons of God, and it doth not yet appear what we shall be: but we know that, when he shall

8. *Ibid.,* p. 50.
9. *Ibid.,* p. 176.
10. *Ibid.,* p. 465.

appear, we shall be like him; for we shall see him as he is." As an interesting sidelight on this reference, it may be noted that in 1 John 3:5, 8 the same term is used for the Lord's first coming, indicating that John must have thought the second coming of Christ would be as real as His first.

An examination of the foregoing terminology in context will give some idea of how widespread was the belief in the second coming of Christ on the part of those who wrote the New Testament. It will also indicate the various shades of meaning attached to the event. The teaching on the Second Coming is not confined to the references just listed, however, for there are many others of a miscellaneous nature. The following should be read carefully, with the context: Matt. 24:29-35; 25:31; Mark 13:24-26; Luke 9:26; 17:24; 21:27; John 14:3; Acts 1:9-11; 3:20-21; Phil. 1:6; 3:20-21; Heb. 9:28; Jude 14-15; Rev. 1:7; 22:20.

Perhaps none of these sets forth more cogently the expectation of the first Christians than Acts 1:9-11: "And when he had spoken these things, while they beheld, he was taken up; and a cloud received him out of their sight. And while they looked stedfastly toward heaven as he went up, behold, two men stood by them in white apparel; which also said, Ye men of Galilee, why stand ye gazing up into heaven? this same Jesus, which is taken up from you into heaven, shall so come in like manner as ye have seen him go into heaven."

Notwithstanding the force of all these passages of scripture, perhaps none carry a greater impact than the words of our Lord in Matt. 26:64. Seeking grounds for condemning Him, the high priest demanded of Jesus whether He was the Christ, the Son of God. Jesus replied: "You have said so. But I tell you, hereafter you will see the Son of man seated on the right hand of Power, and coming on the clouds of heaven" (RSV. See the parallel references in Mark 14:62 and Luke 22:69.)

Thus far it has been our purpose to compile as fairly and fully as possible the *facts* concerning the biblical teaching on the Day of the Lord and the second coming of Christ. The references have been listed, not because the proof-text method is thought to be superior, but because each may become an entering wedge to larger areas of truth. It should go without saying that there are difficulties to be faced, but one can hardly ask about the meaning of a fact until he has become acquainted with that fact. Some of these problems will be considered in the next section, when clues will be offered for the understanding of the biblical evidence. To conclude this section, we may summarize the teaching on the second coming of Christ as seen in the scripture under review.

There can be little doubt as to the nature of what the Early Church expected. As early as A.D. 50, when Paul wrote to the infant church in Thessalonica, it was the clear understanding of Christians that Jesus Christ would "return from heaven to earth in manifest and final glory."[11] Some have argued that Jesus never really taught this,[12] even though within 20 years of His death and resurrection the disciples were preaching a real Second Coming. Others have said that Paul slowly changed his mind, while still others have urged that the whole matter should be taken seriously but not literally.[13] Nonetheless, the fact remains that, if we are to trust the message of the Gospels and have faith in the apostolic writings as communicating to us the word of God, we should be happy to confess that "for its final consummation the Christian hope points to an event at the end of history, the *parousia*, the second coming of the Lord Jesus in divine majesty and judgment."[14]

II. CLUES TO UNDERSTANDING THE BIBLICAL EVIDENCE

Having assembled the biblical evidence for belief in the second coming of Christ, we are ready to assess its meaning and face candidly some of the questions and problems the evidence seems to call forth. By way of preview, the issues may be grouped in some such fashion as this:

1. The question of *imminency*. What can it mean, after 20 centuries, to say, "The coming of the Lord draweth nigh" (Jas. 5:8)? In this connection, conservatives should face frankly the sayings of Jesus that *seem* to teach that He expected His own return very shortly, perhaps within the first generation of Christians. The words of Jesus in Mark 13:30 require some explanation: "Verily I say unto you, that this generation shall not pass, till all these things be done." (See Matt. 24:34 and Luke 21:32 for parallel passages.) It was through a wrestling with this problem as seen in Matt. 10:23 that Albert

---

11. Robinson, *Jesus and His Coming,* p. 18.
12. *Ibid.;* this is the thesis of Robinson's book.
13. See Niebuhr, *Nature and Destiny of Man,* 2:287-98.
14. Kantonen, *Christian Hope,* p. 71.

Schweitzer compelled the Christian world to take seriously again the apocalyptic utterances of Jesus.[15]

2. The problem of *the order of events* at the time of the end. Is it possible or wise to diagram, as many have, a certain pattern for the close of the age? What about the millennium? What occurrences, if any, are clearly indicated by the Scriptures as taking place at the time of the Second Advent?

3. The need for interpreting *the end time as described in apocalyptic writings* such as Daniel and Revelation. Is it possible to take the Second Coming *seriously* without taking it *literally*, as some allege?

4. The issue of *the practical effect* of eschatological or so-called "prophetic" teaching. What is the place of hope in the Christian understanding of life? Is pessimism a necessary result of a belief in the Second Coming, particularly with respect to the present world order?

It would be quite beyond the intention and scope of this chapter to attempt a final answer to all these questions. One has only to consult in a cursory fashion the literature in this field to see how many differences of honest conviction exist among earnest Christians. That such problems do exist is not in question, however, and the serious student of the Bible must face up to them. Some clues are offered here that, it is hoped, will lead to a better understanding of "that blessed hope."

A. The Meaning of Imminence

Our first clue may be found in learning what it means to say that the return of the Lord is imminent. The term *imminence* has been defined as "the condition or quality of being about to happen . . . that which impends."[16] The New Testament is filled with a sense of the imminent return of the Lord. If there were scoffers at the time 2 Pet. 3:3-4 was written, it is small wonder that the 20th century has skeptics too. In what sense can the coming of the Lord be said to be impending or imminent?

For one thing, there is some indication that the time of the return is not a fixed date, but a flexible one subject to postponement. This thought is not offered as a flat assertion but as an observation on the views of some scholars. If the gospel must "be preached in all the

---

15. See Albert Schweitzer, *The Quest of the Historical Jesus* (New York: The Macmillan Co., 1922).

16. *The Winston Dictionary, College Edition,* p. 483.

world" (Matt. 24:14) before the end, may this not suggest a variable time because of the freedom of man? Also, does 2 Pet. 3:9 imply that the delay in the return of the Lord is due not at all to the slackness of the divine promises but to the long-suffering of the Lord, who is "not willing that any should perish, but that all should come to repentance"? One cannot say with dogmatism, but it may be a valid interpretation.

It may be said more confidently, however, that it was the habit of prophets and apocalyptists to announce "... as near those results of which the speaker is certain."[17] In the life, death, and resurrection of Jesus Christ, the kingdom of God *has* come to men. Jesus began His preaching in Galilee saying, "The time is fulfilled, and the kingdom of God is at hand: repent ye, and believe the gospel" (Mark 1:15). In another place Jesus admonished His disciples that while they were in the world they would have tribulation. "But be of good cheer," He said, "*I have overcome the world*" (John 16:33). When Jesus lived a sinless life, He vanquished temptation; when He died on the Cross and rose from the tomb, He conquered death and sin; when He ascended to the Father and poured out the Holy Spirit upon believers, He gave men an earnest, or foretaste, of the life to come. The meaning of life and human existence thus has been revealed in Jesus Christ: "He that hath seen me hath seen the Father" (John 14:9). Every obstacle to the fulfillment of human possibilities has been conquered in our Lord Jesus Christ. "The kingdom of the world *has* become the kingdom [sovereignty, royal power, dominion] of our Lord and of his Christ, and he shall reign for ever and ever" (Rev. 11:15, RSV). It is true, of course, that "we do not yet see everything in subjection to him" (Heb. 2:8, RSV); but heaven, as it were, has established a beachhead on earth, and it is only a matter of time until complete victory comes. The final outcome of the struggle has never been in doubt, for the Son of God has already revealed His power.

Evangelicals, equally devout, differ as to the interpretation of the "signs" of the Lord's coming "and of the end of the world" (Matt. 24:3). Some interpreters feel that such passages as Matt. 24:3-14 and 2 Tim. 3:1-5 offer believers clear-cut facts as to the approach of the *parousia.* Others are impressed by the warning of Jesus in Acts 1:7, "It is not for you to know the times or dates the Father has set by his

17. H. A. A. Kennedy, *Vital Forces of the Early Church,* p. 89, quoted by Shaw, *Christian Doctrine,* p. 366.

own authority" (NIV), and urge caution as to the interpretation of details. The real danger is that belief in the imminent return of the Lord will be undercut by speculation on such "signs."[18]

With respect to the *apparent* assertions of Jesus that His return would come before that generation passed, two things at least must be remembered. Jesus openly confessed that He did not know the time of the end: "But of that day and hour knoweth no man, no, not the angels of heaven, but my Father only" (Matt. 24:36). This statement follows only 14 words after one of the references in question. Thus it is difficult to believe that Jesus actually predicted His return within a generation. It must also be recalled that in His eschatological addresses Jesus spoke not only of His final coming in glory but also of the impending destruction of Jerusalem. In some cases it is difficult to determine which of these events a particular passage may refer to. Unless one is ready to espouse the position that Jesus actually was mistaken and spoke out of ignorance (and some do just this), we should look for an explanation of the sort just offered.

It is remarkable that Millar Burrows, whose position theologically could be fairly described as liberal, has written thus on the subject of imminence:

> However interpreted, the eschatological expectation cannot be regarded as merely a "mythological" expression of God's eternal sovereignty. It at least embodies three inescapable facts: (1) for every individual the end of the world is coming and may come at any moment; (b) for every people and civilization there will come a sure doom if it fails to obey God's laws; and (c) the end of physical existence on earth must come eventually, and no hopes dependent upon the continuance of this world-order can be permanent.[19]

We may close this section by recalling the sobering words of the influential preacher of 17th-century England, John Donne, "What if this present were the world's last night?"[20] High above Alpine valleys tower mountains bearing great masses of snow. It is said that almost any disturbance, such as a gunshot, a shout, or vibration, will set in motion a massive, destructive avalanche. This onslaught of

---

18. This is the fatal flaw in *The Late Great Planet Earth*, by Hal Lindsey (Grand Rapids: Zondervan Publishing Company, 1970). Repeatedly the author posits events which, in his view, *must* take place before the Lord's return (pp. 54-55, e.g.) and thus effectively eliminates the conviction that the *parousia* could occur at any time.

19. *Outline of Biblical Theology*, p. 218.

20. Quoted by C. S. Lewis, "The Christian Hope—Its Meaning for Today," *Religion in Life*, Vol. XXI, No. 1 (Winter, 1951-52), p. 29.

nature may occur at any time; it is impending. It is likewise with the second coming of Christ.

This is our *first clue:* The coming of the Lord is imminent, not in the sense that it *must* take place at a designated time, but that it is impending; it *may* occur at any moment.

B. The Problem of the Order of Events

A second clue is to be found in discovering whether the Scriptures provide us with a detailed map of the end time. Is it possible or wise to diagram a sequence of events for the close of the age? Not a few have attempted this, with the result that a plethora of schemes have appeared.

It is quite natural for the human mind to inquire into the unknown and to seek to resolve mysteries of every sort. The disciples themselves sought specific information as to the minutiae of the future. "Tell us," they inquired of Jesus, "when shall these things be? and what shall be the sign of thy coming, and of the end of the world?" (Matt. 24:3) It must be granted that Jesus offered them some general answers to their questions, but no blueprints. Even after the Resurrection, His followers were still seeking particular information on the end: "Lord, wilt thou at this time restore again the kingdom to Israel?" (Acts 1:6)

The answer Jesus gave them should be sufficient to discourage all attempts to chart the future: "And he said unto them, It is not for you to know the times or the seasons, which the Father hath put in his own power" (Acts 1:7). It would seem that when this rebuke has been heard and compared with the passage where Jesus himself professed no knowledge of when the end would occur (Matt. 24:36), no one would have the temerity to set dates or plan in detail and with dogmatism the "times or the seasons" set by the Father's authority.

Nonetheless, this is precisely what has been done. One William Miller, for example, in 1843 dated the Second Coming to the day and minute, with the result that the theology of Seventh-day Adventism has labored under a strange distortion of the intercessory ministry of Christ since that time.[21] Moreover, closer to our own day, the influence of dispensationalism, pioneered by J. N. Darby and widely

---

21. See James E. Bear, "The Bible and Modern Religions: I. The Seventh-day Adventists," *Interpretation,* Vol. X, No. 1 (January, 1956), pp. 45-71.

disseminated by C. I. Scofield through his *Reference Bible,* has been enormous.

It is odd that these men, who as Calvinists have so ardently opposed the doctrine of entire sanctification, should have had such influence in the holiness movement. This is not the place to discuss at length the various facets of their teaching, but it may be said that any interpretation which places much of the Bible outside the use of Christians ought to be suspect from the outset. The whole system of dispensationalism rests upon a reading into the Bible *(eisegesis)* the ideas of men, rather than *a leading out* of the Word *(exegesis)* of the truths of revelation.[22]

In view of the considerable differences among devout Christians on such questions as millennialism (*pre-, post-,* or *nil-*), the great tribulation (an issue that actually divides *pre*millennialists into two camps), the rapture, and the revelation, the several resurrections of certain "prophetic" schools, the Articles of Faith of the Church of the Nazarene simply affirm an unqualified belief in the second coming of Christ, the resurrection of the dead, the future judgment of all men, and the eternal destiny of both the believers and the impenitent.[23]

It is both wise and scriptural to affirm what is reasonably beyond doubt, but refrain from making assertions about matters no man *can* know. The following is an interesting summary of what Jesus taught on this aspect of our study: "His teaching on the subject quite clearly consisted of three propositions. (1) That he will certainly return; (2) That we cannot possibly find out when; (3) And that therefore we must always be ready for him."[24]

This is our *second clue:* The Scriptures clearly indicate certain general facts concerning the end time, namely, that the Lord will return again, and the righteous and the wicked will be raised from the dead to face the final judgment and their eternal destinies. However, the Bible does not provide us with a detailed chart of all events; this is among the times and seasons the Father has fixed by His own authority.

---

22. For a careful study of this issue, see John Wick Bowman, "The Bible and Modern Religions: II. Dispensationalism," *Interpretation,* Vol. X, No. 2 (April, 1956), pp. 170-87.

23. For a more detailed, yet balanced, account of the "Order of Events in the Lord's Day," see Wiley, *Christian Theology,* 3:306-19.

24. Lewis, "Christian Hope—Meaning for Today," p. 28.

C. The Language of Apocalyptic

The third clue to a better understanding of the Second Coming is to be found in the nature of apocalyptic writings. We have already seen the meaning of the term from which the expression comes: *apokalupsis*, "an uncovering," "laying bare," or "a revealing." Apocalypses profess to uncover or reveal the future. Thus the last book in the New Testament, called Revelation, is an apocalypse.

As stated above, the production of this *genre* of literature was extensive among the Hebrews just before and after the time of Christ. Because the books were often written in a time of persecution, the writers employed dramatic symbols that were at once meaningful to believers and confusing to the persecutors. Revelation is only one of many such books written during that period. In fact, parts of the Old Testament contain apocalyptic elements, even though they come from an earlier period.

Many of the difficulties that have arisen over our present subject have come through a failure to recognize that the apocalyptic writers were trying to convey great facts and truths by means of picture and symbol. That these books use symbolic language does not mean that they deal with fantasy as opposed to fact. Rather, it means that facts and truths are presented in a *pictorial* rather than an abstract or prosaic fashion. Thus, readers must interpret such books with caution and charity.

Revelation may be taken as an example. Conservative scholars, as well as others, are pretty well agreed that this book must have brought a message of hope and courage to those who read it first. It cannot have been intended exclusively for those who live at the time of the end. If that were the case, who could know for whom it was written? Furthermore, the various symbols—beasts, dragons, eagles, and the like—must not be pressed too far to support a preconceived eschatological framework. The meaning of all these pictures must have been clear to the first readers, but not all of them are clear to us.

Nevertheless, the symbolic language of Revelation does mean something. John was more than a poet painting pictures of the ultimate triumph of God over the forces of evil. He wrote to Christians under his care who were faced with the possibility of enforced emperor worship. For them to say, "Caesar is Lord," was altogether incompatible with the Christian confession, "Christ is the Lord"; such a practice would have meant the destruction of the Church. But it was also given to John to see the logical issue of these forces of Christ and Antichrist in the sweep of human history. Thus, using the experience of the early Christians, he painted a picture not only of their crisis but also of the crisis that confronts Christians in every age, and one that will appear at the time of the Second Coming. A British scholar, G. R. Beasley-Murray, has written:

> As the Church was then faced with a devastating persecution by Rome, so will the Church of the last days find itself violently opposed by the prevailing world power. The outcome of that great struggle will be the advent of Christ in glory, and with Him the establishment of the kingdom of God in power.[25]

If it is a mistake to interpret apocalyptic literature, including Revelation, too woodenly, it is also a grave error to dismiss it all as "mythological" fancy. Many theologians, outside conservative circles, are coming to a new appreciation of the New Testament figures for the end. Emil Brunner, for example, argues that it is better to remain loyal to the language of the New Testament than to attempt any alteration, as some, including Rudolf Bultmann, have urged.[26]

This, then, is our *third clue:* The language of apocalyptic is a pictorial but meaningful presentation of the eschatological elements in the Christian faith.

D. The Joyfulness of the Christian Hope

A fourth and final clue to a better understanding of the biblical data concerning the end is to be seen in the attitude Christians should have toward it. The day of the Lord, whether in the Old or New Testament, is often thought of as a time of gloom and doom. *It is* that, to be sure, for those who oppose the kingdom of God, but for the Christian it is a time of great hope and unspeakable joy. The child of God lives by hope as well as by faith and love.

Hope is a necessary ingredient of human existence, but the natural man is without hope as he is without God (Eph. 2:12). Man lives from day to day by his little hopes, but when it comes to the great hopes of the soul, such as meaning and purpose for the whole of life, he falls into despair. H. G. Wells once wrote that man is "like a convoy lost in the darkness on an unknown rocky coast, with quarreling

---

25. Donald Guthrie, ed., *The New Bible Commentary,* Revised, p. 1280. Therein see the general article, "The Apocryphal and Apocalyptic Literature," by G. R. Beasley-Murray and F. F. Bruce, as well as the commentary on Revelation for excellent treatment of this area of biblical thought.

26. Brunner, *Eternal Hope,* p. 139.

pirates in the chartroom and savages clambering up the sides of the ship to plunder and do evil as the whim may take them."[27]

It is the Christian's understanding of history that ultimately the kingdom of God will prevail among men. In the humdrum of everyday life we need the undergirding of this assurance, not only for richness of religious living, but for strength in the struggle against opposing eschatologies. The materialistic atheism of Marxist Leninism, seen savagely alive in the Soviet Union and Communist China, has a breathtaking faith in a future under its control. Communists unquestionably believe that history is on their side. They aim at dominating and rebuilding the world according to their philosophy and morals.

At the same time, and certainly with *none* of the brutality of communism, Jewish Messianism shames a Christian Church that looks backward to the events of biblical history without ever looking forward to that "blessed hope, and the glorious appearing of the great God . . ." It has been said that "a Christian faith without expectation of Parousia is like a ladder which leads nowhere but ends in the void."[28]

Jesus Christ is indeed the Hope of the world. He is the Hope of individuals. To believe on the Lord Jesus Christ means eternal life here and hereafter. Beyond the grave lies the resurrection from the dead and an everlasting life with ineffable possibilities. He is also the only Hope for society. Mystery veils a full insight into this assertion, but the Bible is far from pessimistic about the future. The Old Testament prophets, for example, saw a day when "the earth shall be full of the knowledge of the Lord, as the waters cover the sea" (Isa. 11:9), a time when men "shall beat their swords into plowshares, and their spears into pruninghooks: nation shall not lift up sword against nation, neither shall they learn war any more" (Mic. 4:3). The Apocalypse intimates something of this hope when it speaks of the heavenly fruit tree whose leaves were "for the healing of the nations" (Rev. 22:2).

When will these things come to pass? No man can answer that question. Another question, however, *How* will these things come to pass? can be answered only by the power of God through Christ. Will some measure of these promises be fulfilled *before* the coming of

---

27. See Scott McCormick, "The Bible as Record and Medium," *Interpretation,* Vol. XII, No. 3 (July, 1958), p. 299.

28. Brunner, *Eternal Hope,* p. 139.

the Lord? Will there be a Messianic reign on earth bringing in these conditions? Or can they be understood only as descriptive of "a new heaven and a new earth" (Rev. 21:1)? No one can say for sure. Jesus taught that the wheat and tares will grow together until the harvest at the end of the world (Matt. 13:30). One wonders, however, if the Church has forgotten that the *wheat* as well as the tares will grow until the end. Not a few first-rate theologians are convinced that no real progress will be made in history toward the kingdom of God, but all are sure that, in the end, history will be fulfilled rather than negated. The end of time will mean not only *finis*, but *telos* as well; i.e., the sign at the end of the world's highway will not be "Dead-end Street" but "Destination Reached." Christians are the salt of the earth and the light of the world. The only hope for our social order lies in the application of the healing, savoring salt and the shining abroad of the gospel light.

Jesus Christ is the Hope of the entire cosmos. A universe that is plagued by natural as well as moral evil will one day be cleansed and renewed: "For the creation waits with eager longing for the revealing of the sons of God; for the creation was subjected to futility, not of its own will but by the will of him who subjected it in hope; because the creation itself will be set free from its bondage to decay and obtain the glorious liberty of the children of God" (Rom. 8:19-21, RSV).

It is of interest that this biblical truth of the renewal of the entire cosmos through Christ, the *Logos*, has gripped the imagination of leading contemporary theologians. Nels F. S. Ferré, for example, writes that because the history of nature preceded the history of man as preparation, it will probably not come to an end with him, but will be transformed or created into a new earth to correspond with man's new eternal state.[29] Likewise, the continental theologian Paul Althaus believes that the whole cosmos will be redeemed. The form of this we cannot imagine, but we may see in nature "as it is now, a parable and a prelude of the coming world of glory."[30] Jesus Christ is the Hope of individual men, the social order, and the entire cosmos.

Does all this mean that those who believe in the Second Coming are necessarily pessimistic and likely to be fruitless "quietists"? It

---

29. *Christian Understanding of God*, p. 219.

30. "Eschatology," Halverson and Cohen, *Handbook of Christian Theology*, p. 106.

must be admitted that this has sometimes been the case, but such an attitude is a betrayal of the Christian's true spirit. Can one who prays, "Thy kingdom come," be true to his petition and fail to do all in his power to bring the Kingdom in? The implication of Mark 13:34-36 is significant, coming as it does at the close of Christ's teaching on His return: "Watch ye therefore: . . . lest coming suddenly he find you sleeping." This is surely aimed at indolence as well as indifference.

Our *final clue*, then: There is joyfulness in the Christian hope of the return of the Lord; our prayer: "Thy kingdom come. Thy will be done, as in heaven, so in earth" (Luke 11:2), will someday be fully answered. "He which testifieth these things saith, Surely I come quickly. Amen. Even so, come, Lord Jesus" (Rev. 22:20).

SUMMARY

Let us try now to summarize the argument of this chapter. Providentially, it would seem, our time has experienced a revival of interest in the doctrine of the second coming of Christ. This is true not merely of fringe groups but of the Christian Church as a whole. An intelligent study of the subject by dedicated minds is earnestly desired.

When we turn to the Bible, for us verily the Word of God, we find there a concern for eschatology greater than for cosmogony—more is said about the end of all things than the beginning. In the Old Testament the theme of the coming day of the Lord is prominent, while in the New Testament the return of Christ in glory is a major doctrine. Evidence for the latter is plentiful in both the Gospels and the Epistles, not to mention the Apocalypse. What does it all mean?

The biblical evidence is taken here to mean that, just as Jesus Christ came once to be the Savior of all men, so He will return to this earth as Redeemer and Judge to establish the kingdom of God with power. No man can know when this event will occur, but it is impending. None can say precisely what the calendar of events during the end time will be, but the resurrection from the dead, the judgment, and the coming of the new heaven and earth are associated with the Parousia.

We must be cautious and charitable in interpreting the apocalyptic books of the Bible, but we may be sure their pictorial language symbolizes real events yet to take place. Finally, the Second Coming is bound up with the Christian hope for our personal existence, the social order, and the entire cosmos. This is a glorious hope of the children of God.

When someone asserts that the doctrine of the return of Christ should be taken seriously but not literally, we reply that unless, with proper reserve as to details, the Second Coming is taken literally it is difficult if not impossible to take it seriously. Conservatives are grateful for the renewed appreciation for the Parousia on the part of Christians generally, but believe it is necessary to affirm ". . . that the Second Advent will be a sudden and glorious appearing of our Lord, bursting in upon the ordinary course of the world as an unexpected, cataclysmic event."[31] Remember, "What if this present were the world's last night?"

> We believe that the Lord Jesus Christ will come again; that we who are alive at His coming shall not precede them that are asleep in Christ Jesus; but that, if we are abiding in Him, we shall be caught up with the risen saints to meet the Lord in the air, so that we shall ever be with the Lord.[32]

"Wherefore comfort one another with these words" (1 Thess. 4:18).

The nature of the life beyond the Parousia will be the next study to be undertaken in exploring the Christian faith.

31. Wiley, *Christian Theology,* 3:259.
32. *Manual,* Church of the Nazarene, 1976, p. 30.

CHAPTER 23

The Future Life

Christianity contrasts sharply with many religions in the emphasis it places on the future life. Paul wrote: "If in this life only we have hope in Christ, we are of all men most miserable" (1 Cor. 15:19). None could read Paul and think that he depreciates the importance of Christ for this present life. There is no trace of "religion as the opiate of the masses" in the New Testament. Renunciation of life in this world is not original to Christianity, but is an import from paganism. Social betterment and the full realization of God's kingdom are the steady aims of all New Testament faith.

When all this is said, it must still be realized that the Christian hope has a trans-temporal dimension without which it would not be Christian. If it is a mistake to emphasize the future life at the expense of constructive living in the present, it is equally wrong to stress the values of the present at the cost of a vital sense of the future.

We have already observed the eschatological orientation of the New Testament writers. The biblical view of history is not cyclical, an unceasing repetition, but linear. History proceeds toward a conclusion. The temporal process is not final. Death and all it represents will be swallowed up in victory (1 Cor. 15:54). Time will be no more (Rev. 10:6), and "the kingdoms of this world . . . [shall] become the kingdoms of our Lord, and of his Christ; and he shall reign for ever and ever" (Rev. 11:15). As Herman N. Ridderbos has written:

> In this conception of God and of the kingdom of God lies the nature and the strength of the biblical belief in immortal life and the eternal world to come. This faith is not built upon human imagination. It is no mere projection of a perfect future in an imperfect world, for the biblical belief is not under the delusion of human dignity. It does not underrate the power of sin and death,

neither does it borrow its strength from spiritual dreams. It is belief in the future only because and in so far as it is belief in God and in his Kingdom.[1]

In our consideration of the future life, we shall view four important topics: (1) The Resurrection; (2) The Judgment; (3) The Final State of the Impenitent; and (4) "The Glory Which Shall be Revealed."

I. THE RESURRECTION

Two great opposing views of the immortal state are to be noted. The first is the philosophical belief in the immortality of the soul, which had its rise in the speculation of Greek thinkers as early as Socrates and Plato, four centuries before Christ. The other is the biblical view of the resurrection, which has its early intimations in the Old Testament and comes to full flower in the New Testament.

The opposition of these two points of view is illustrated in two of the Ingersoll Lectures on Immortality delivered at Harvard University. The first, by Harry Emerson Fosdick in 1926-27, was a revival of Plato's arguments in the *Phaedo* for the immortality of the human spirit. The other, by Oscar Cullmann in 1954-55, was in direct contrast. It was based on the fact that, while Socrates and the Emperor Julian died confident of the worth of the human soul and thus its survival after death, Stephen and Paul died with eyes fixed on Jesus, who was crucified for their sins and had risen again for their justification.

William C. Robinson incisively contrasts these points of view in the statement:

> For Socrates, death is the friend of the soul; for Paul, death is its last enemy. To the former, the body is the soul's prison; to the latter, it is the temple of the Holy Spirit. For the one, man's eternal state begins at death; for the other, it begins at the parousia. Christ invaded the domains of death despite its terrors, and by dying he conquered it and all the enemies of God. His resurrection body and his Spirit in the hearts of believers are the firstfruits of the final resurrection at his coming. Between death and this second advent, believers are in special proximity to Christ but are not in their final state. Every item of hope, the easing of death, the assurance of going to be with Christ, the resurrection of our

---

1. "Final Triumph: Eternal Kingdom," *Christianity Today,* Vol. II, No. 19 (June 23, 1958), pp. 18, 24.

434 / Exploring Our Christian Faith

bodies comes not out of the worth of the soul, but from Christ, his death for us, his resurrection as our representative.[2]

Since the eternal state is a resurrected state, it is of great importance that we note the essential outlines of the biblical view. Nowhere has our Greek heritage of thought so colored our understanding of scripture as at this point.

A. Old Testament Intimations of Future Life

In the Old Testament, death is viewed through two lenses. On one side it is seen as a natural phenomenon, the end of all men. On the other side it is regarded as "something at variance with the innermost essence of human personality, a judgment; and whenever this personality has reached its pure and perfect ideal, it must at the same time be conceived of as raised above death."[3] As Hermann Schultz noted, even in the oldest portions of the Scriptures, death is never seen as actually the complete end of existence.[4] A. B. Davidson summarizes the Old Testament position in these words:

> The life and immortality brought to light in the gospel are being reached from many sides, in fragments, and many times only by the arm of faith reached out and striving to grasp them as brilliant rainbow forms. In the Old Testament, truth has not yet attained its unity. But everywhere in it the ground of hope or assurance is the spiritual fellowship already enjoyed with God. Our Lord's argument, "God is not the God of the dead, but of the living," is the expression of the whole spirit of the Old Testament on this great subject.[5]

Examples of the Old Testament faith may be found in Ps. 49:15:

> But God will redeem my soul from the power of Sheol;
> For He will receive me. Selah (NASB).

Ps. 73:24-26 is a strong statement of faith:

> With Thy counsel Thou wilt guide me,
> And afterward receive me to glory.
> Whom have I in heaven but Thee?
> And besides Thee, I desire nothing on earth.
> My flesh and my heart may fail;
> But God is the strength of my heart and my portion forever (NASB).

---

2. Review of *Immortality of the Soul, or Resurrection of the Dead?* by Oscar Cullmann, in *Christianity Today*, Vol. II, No. 20 (July 7, 1958), p. 36.

3. Hermann Schultz, *Old Testament Theology*, translated by J. A. Paterson, 2 vols. (Edinburgh: T. and T. Clark, 1909), 2:313.

4. *Ibid.*, p. 321.   5. *Theology of the Old Testament*, p. 532.

Isa. 26:19 would be meaningless apart from the assumption of a resurrection of the dead: "Thy dead men shall live, together with my dead body shall they arise. Awake and sing, ye that dwell in dust: for thy dew is as the dew of herbs, and the earth shall cast out the dead." Strikingly clear is Dan. 12:2-3: "And many of them that sleep in the dust of the earth shall awake, some to everlasting life, and some to shame and everlasting contempt. And they that are wise shall shine as the brightness of the firmament; and they that turn many to righteousness as the stars for ever and ever." Job goes through his great trial with the confidence of vindication before men, and while he fully expects his sufferings to end in death, he cherishes the assurance that his Vindicator, his Redeemer, will stand upon the earth and that he will see Him (Job 19:23-27).[6]

B. The Light on Life and Resurrection

Paul says of our Savior Jesus Christ that He "hath abolished death, and hath brought life and immortality to light through the gospel" (2 Tim. 1:10). In the New Testament, then, we find expression on a far higher level of what was intimated in the Old Testament. The testimony of Jesus himself is unambiguous: "Marvel not at this: for the hour is coming, in the which all that are in the graves shall hear his voice, and shall come forth; they that have done good, unto the resurrection of life; and they that have done evil, unto the resurrection of damnation" (John 5:28-29); "I am the resurrection, and the life: he that believeth in me, though he were dead, yet shall he live: and whosoever liveth and believeth in me shall never die" (11:25-26).

Christ's resurrection is said to be the pattern for the resurrection of believers: "Who will change our lowly body to be like his glorious body" (Phil. 3:21, RSV); "But if the Spirit of him that raised up Jesus from the dead dwell in you, he that raised up Christ from the dead shall also quicken your mortal bodies by his Spirit that dwelleth in you" (Rom. 8:11); "For if we believe that Jesus died and rose again, even so them also which sleep in Jesus will God bring with him" (1 Thess. 4:14); and, "For since by man came death, by man came also the resurrection of the dead. For as in Adam all die, even so in Christ shall all be made alive" (1 Cor. 15:21-22).

C. "With What Body Do They Come?" (1 Cor. 15:35)

There is much we would like to know about the resurrection which

---

6. Cf. *ibid.,* pp. 466-95.

is not revealed in Scripture. It is clear, however, that it is the body which is the subject of the resurrection, and that there is a real and important identity between the body which is buried and the body which is raised. That this is not necessarily a material identity, most theologians will admit. H. Orton Wiley gives meaningful analogy at this point:

> In the inorganic realm, identity depends upon substance and form. If a stone be pulverized and scattered abroad, the substance remains but the form is destroyed, and, therefore, the identity of the object. If water be frozen or heated, the form is changed into ice or steam, but it is still water. If, however, the water be separated into its constituent elements, oxygen and hydrogen, it is no longer water. In the organic world of living substance, identity is something higher. The acorn grows into the oak, and the infant into the man, but here the principle of identity does not appear to lie in either the substance or the form, for both are constantly undergoing change. That there is a continuity between the seed and the plant, the infant and the man, cannot be doubted. So also, although it cannot be explained, it is perfectly rational to assert a continuity between our present and our future bodies, even though we admit that we do not know in what this identity consists.[7]

Paul answers the question which is the heading of this section: "But some man will say, How are the dead raised up? and with what body do they come? Thou fool, that which thou sowest is not quickened, except it die: and that which thou sowest, thou sowest not that body that shall be, but bare grain, it may chance of wheat, or of some other grain: but God giveth it a body as it hath pleased him, and to every seed his own body" (1 Cor. 15:35-38). The material atoms and molecules in the seed never come up in the plant, but each seed expresses one individual life and no other.

Paul uses a series of contrasts to relate the body which is buried with the body which is raised (vv. 42-44). (1) It is sown in corruption; it is raised in incorruptibility, free from everything that tends toward dissolution and death, disease, pain, and suffering. (2) It is sown in dishonor, as having been an instrument of sin; it is raised in glory, as in the overwhelming brightness of the Transfiguration (Mark 9:2-8). (3) It is sown in weakness, the result of its mortal limitations; it is raised in power beyond our capacity to imagine. (4) It is sown a creature subject to or dependent on nature, a natural body; it is raised a spiritual body, perfectly adapted to the conditions of the future state.

---

7. *Christian Theology,* 3:326.

The entire fifteenth chapter of 1 Corinthians, the *classicus locus* on the resurrection of the believer, will repay careful study.

D. The General Resurrection

Before leaving the biblical teaching concerning the resurrection, it is important to note two further facts: (1) the resurrection includes all men, unbelievers as well as believers; and (2) there is clear indication that the righteous and unbelievers do not rise at the same time; there is "a resurrection of the righteous."

1. All are to be raised. John in prophetic vision "saw the dead, small and great, stand before God; . . . And the sea gave up the dead which were in it; and death and the grave [marg.] delivered up the dead which were in them" (Rev. 20:12-13). The pronoun is used in its widest extent when Jesus says, "When they shall rise from the dead, they neither marry, nor are given in marriage" (Mark 12:25), and He immediately adds, "And as touching the dead, that they rise: have ye not read in the book of Moses, how in the bush God spake unto him, saying, I am the God of Abraham, and the God of Isaac, and the God of Jacob?" (v. 26)

2. There is a sharp distinction between the resurrections of righteous and wicked. This is indicated in some of the references which speak of the general resurrection: as Dan. 12:2, "some to everlasting life" and "some to shame and everlasting contempt"; and John 5:29, "the resurrection of life" and "the resurrection of damnation." A frequent New Testament expression in regard both to the resurrection of Jesus and to that of believers is "resurrection out from the dead."[8] John speaks of the first resurrection as a resurrection of particular blessedness (Rev. 20:5-6); and Paul prizes resurrection "out from the dead" as worthy of particular aspiration (Phil. 3:11-14).

II. THE JUDGMENT

The judgment is the final tribunal before which the works and motives of men will ultimately be tried. The fact of a divine judgment upon human life is one of the strongest and most consistent affirmations of Scripture. In the Old Testament the term is often used in relation to the inflictions of temporal punishment or death upon those outside of the covenant, or who had broken covenant. Thus

---

8. Cf., e.g., Matt. 17:9; Luke 20:35-36. See also Wiley, *Christian Theology,* 3:334-36.

Abraham affirmed of God's dealings with Lot in Sodom: "Shall not the Judge of all the earth do right?" (Gen. 18:25) The righteous are judged when they are vindicated before their enemies (Ps. 7:11). Yet even in the Old Testament, a day of the Lord is foreseen in which all shall be judged (Dan. 7:9-10). Even the writer of Ecclesiastes, who describes his intellectual pilgrimage from skepticism of life to a faith in the divine, finally realizes that "God shall bring every work into judgment, with every secret thing, whether it be good, or whether it be evil" (12:14).

In the New Testament, indication is given of what theologians call a "particular" or "provisional" judgment. That is, men judge themselves at death, and by nature go to their own place (Acts 1:25). Paul affirmed a present particular judgment in his address to the synagogue at Antioch in Pisidia: "It was necessary that the word of God should first have been spoken to you: but seeing ye put it from you, and judge yourselves unworthy of everlasting life, lo, we turn to the Gentiles" (Acts 13:46). In harmony with this is Paul's confidence that to be "absent from the body" was "to be present with the Lord" (2 Cor. 5:8), and the word of Jesus to the dying thief, "To day shalt thou be with me in paradise" (Luke 23:43). Similar is the teaching of Christ in reference to the rich man who was tormented and Lazarus who was at peace soon or immediately after death (Luke 16:19-31).

This is never allowed to obscure the fact, however, that there is a final judgment in which all men shall stand before the throne of God. It is spoken of as a "day of judgment," which need not be understood as indicating duration, but rather an appointed time: "It shall be more tolerable for Tyre and Sidon at the day of judgment, than for you" (Matt. 11:22, 24); "The men of Nineveh shall rise in judgment with this generation, and shall condemn it" (Matt. 12:41); "He hath appointed a day, in the which he will judge the world in righteousness by that man whom he hath ordained" (Acts 17:31); "In the day when God shall judge the secrets of men by Jesus Christ according to my gospel" (Rom. 2:16); "Behold, the Lord cometh with ten thousands of his saints, to execute judgment upon all" (Jude 14-15); "I saw a great white throne, and him that sat on it, from whose face the earth and the heaven fled away; and there was found no place for them. And I saw the dead, small and great, stand before God; and the books were opened: and another book was opened, which is the book of life: and the dead were judged out of those things which were written in the books, according to their works. And the sea gave up the dead which were in it; and death and hell delivered up the dead which were in them: and they were judged every man according to their works" (Rev. 20:11-13).

A. Christ Is the Judge

It is Jesus Christ, God the Son, through whom the Father will judge mankind. This has been indicated in several of the references in the last paragraph. It is definitely stated in John 5:22-23: "For the Father judgeth no man, but hath committed all judgment unto the Son: that all men should honour the Son, even as they honour the Father." As Christ, the Divine-human Person, alone is able to be a Mediator between God and man, so He alone is most properly qualified to judge the humanity to which He is so intimately related. Absolute justice is assured when we "all appear before the judgment seat of Christ; that every one may receive the things done in his body, according to that he hath done, whether it be good or bad" (2 Cor. 5:10).

Paul relates the exaltation of Christ to His judgment: "Wherefore God also hath highly exalted him, and given him a name which is above every name: that at the name of Jesus every knee should bow, of things in heaven, and things in earth, and things under the earth; and that every tongue should confess that Jesus Christ is Lord, to the glory of God the Father" (Phil. 2:9-11).

B. The Nature of the Judgment

The judgment will be concerned with men's works, thoughts, purposes, and motives. Its standard will be the amount of light given to each individual. As H. Orton Wiley has said, "The measure of revealed truth granted to men will be the standard by which they are judged in the last day. To this also, we may add the words of our Lord —*For unto whomsoever much is given, of him shall be much required* (Luke 12:48)."[9] For those who have heard the gospel the ultimate question will be, "What did you do with Jesus which is called Christ?"

Not the discovery but the manifestation of character is the purpose of the final judgment. It is essential to the divine government that sin be punished and the works which flow from the righteousness of faith be rewarded. As Dr. Wiley again comments:

> Men are saved by faith, but they are rewarded according to their works, and these works spring out of the true nature of faith. As we are justified now by faith without works in the sense of

---

9. *Christian Theology*, 3:347.

merit, but by a faith that is always evidenced in works; so will it be in the final judgment, when the righteousness which is by faith will be vindicated by the works which flow from it.[10]

III. THE FINAL STATE OF THE IMPENITENT

At few points does the biblical faith cut more sharply across the sentiments of the age than at the point of its teaching concerning the eternal state of those who die in rebellion against God. The New Testament has but one good thing to say about hell (Greek, *gehenna*), and that is that no one need be lost there. Any who are finally lost will be lost in spite of all that Christ and the gospel can do to prevent that end.

Roger Nicole has said:

> Admittedly, the doctrine of hell is the darkest subject on the pages of Scripture, but it provides the necessary background to an understanding of the true gravity of sin, of the magnitude of the human soul, of the depth of Christ's redeeming work, of the power of divine grace which plucks man out of the abyss like firebrands, of the urgency of the Gospel call, and of the supreme importance of the ministry of preaching and of missions. It is an integral and vital element of our Christian faith.[11]

A. Alternatives to the Biblical Doctrine

Efforts to escape the awful implications of the scriptural teaching generally take two directions. One is universalism, the doctrine that ultimately all shall be saved and live in eternal blessedness. The other is the doctrine of conditional immortality, that only those who accept Christ will live forever, all others either ceasing to exist at death or else being annihilated at the conclusion of a period of punishment.

1. Both of these views run counter to the teachings of the Bible, and universalism in particular betrays some serious ethical faults. If all are finally saved without regard to their actions in this life, ultimate moral distinctions between right and wrong, good and evil, are either completely obliterated or seriously blurred. As C. S. Lewis has incisively said in the preface to *The Great Divorce* with reference to all attempts to wed heaven and hell:

---

10. *Ibid.,* p. 341.

11. "The Punishment of the Wicked," *Christianity Today,* Vol. II, No. 18 (June 9, 1958), p. 15.

The attempt is based on the belief that reality never presents us with an absolutely unavoidable "either-or"; that, granted skill and patience and (above all) time enough, some way of embracing both alternatives can always be found; that mere development or adjustment or refinement will somehow turn evil into good without our being called on for a final and total rejection of anything we should like to retain. This belief I take to be a disastrous error. You cannot take all luggage with you on all journeys; on one journey even your right hand and your right eye may be among the things you have to leave behind.[12]

The Bible makes it inescapably clear that life on this earth has consequences which are unchangeable. There is sin which is "unpardonable" (Matt. 12:32), a "sin unto death" for which no prayer avails (1 John 5:16). There is a point beyond which repentance may not be known (Heb. 6:4-6; 12:14-17). There is a gulf which is impassable (Luke 16:26). It would be better for some never to have been born (Matt. 26:24). Jesus came to bring life, and "he that believeth on the Son hath everlasting life: and he that believeth not the Son shall not see life; but the wrath of God abideth on him" (John 3:36). Although questioned on textual grounds, Mark 16:16 still represents the universal conviction of the Apostolic Church: "He that believeth and is baptized shall be saved; but he that believeth not shall be damned."

2. As to the view that immortality is conditional, and that only the saved shall live forever, we encounter a paradoxical situation. For the very same scriptural language which declares the eternity of life for those who are finally saved also declares the eternity of punishment and separation from God for those who are finally lost. It has been argued, for example, that *aionios,* which is commonly and correctly translated "everlasting" or "eternal," means only "of the ages," and does not necessarily mean "without end." However, while this term is used 7 times of the future punishment of the wicked, it is used some 51 times of the future happiness of the redeemed. If the future punishment of the impenitent is limited in time or terminated by annihilation, then there is no valid biblical basis for arguing for the eternity of the heavenly estate.

---

12. (New York: The Macmillan Co., 1946), p. v. Attention may be directed to the viewpoint represented by Nels F. S. Ferré (*Evil and the Christian Faith* [New York: Harper and Brothers, 1947], pp. 117-22; *Christian Understanding of God,* pp. 229-30; *et passim*) to the effect that hell is the ultimate in the severity of God, and will finally bring about repentance and self-surrender on the part of those who die in sin. It need scarcely be pointed out, on biblical grounds, how slim such a hope really is.

B. The Nature of the Lost Estate

When we turn to the Scriptures and observe the manner in which they describe the estate of the finally lost, we are impressed with the awful majesty and sober portrayal we find there. Completely absent is the type of imagination which pictures the lost as being tormented by the devil and his demons armed with pitchforks. As Nicole further states, such ideas are probably due to the influence of Moslem teaching or uninspired Jewish thought: "In fact, both the variety and the restraint in expression suggest that there is depth of sadness in the misery of the lost which our minds are unable to plumb in this life."[13]

Three words in the original are translated "hell" in the King James Version of the New Testament. These words are *hades, tartarus,* and *gehenna*. H. Orton Wiley holds that *hades* and *tartarus* are properly considered to be the intermediate state of wicked men and fallen angels respectively. *Gehenna* is the term used to describe the place reserved after the judgment for the unrepentant.[14] It is derived from the name of the Valley of Hinnom, the deep gulch south of Jerusalem where in Old Testament times the wicked kings Ahaz and Manasseh sacrificed their sons in the vicious worship of the false god Moloch (cf. 2 Chron. 28:3; 33:6). Josiah, in his effort to stamp out idolatry, turned it into a place for the burning of refuse and the disposal of unclean corpses (2 Kings 23:10), and it was the place into which the bodies of those slain in the destruction of Jerusalem were thrown (Isa. 66:24; Jer. 7:32). It thus became associated in the prophetic writings with the place of judgment and doom (cf. Jer. 7:31; 19:6; Isa. 31:9). In the New Testament, *gehenna* means eternal punishment, no longer identified with the Valley of Hinnom as such.

It is startling to note that of the 12 times in the New Testament the term *gehenna,* or the hell of final punishment, is used, 11 of those times it was used in the gospel reports of Jesus' own teaching (the exception is Jas. 3:6). Paul does not use the term, but speaks instead of "wrath" (Rom. 2:5; 5:9); "indignation and wrath, tribulation and anguish" (Rom. 2:8-9); "destruction" or "perdition" (Rom. 9:22; Phil. 3:19); reprobation (1 Cor. 9:27); and "corruption" (Gal. 6:8).

Other terms which are the equivalent of *gehenna* in the Scriptures are numerous and awe-inspiring. They include eternal and unquenchable fire (Matt. 18:8-9; 25:41; Mark 9:44-48); the furnace of

---

13. "Punishment of the Wicked," p. 14.
14. *Christian Theology,* 3:363-64.

fire (Matt. 13:42); the lake of fire, and of fire and brimstone (Rev. 14:10; 19:20; 20:10; 20:14); the fire and the worm (Mark 9:48; Isa. 66:24); the pit (Rev. 20:3); a place prepared for the devil and his angels (Matt. 25:41); torment (Luke 16:23, 28; Rev. 14:10-11); the second death (Rev. 20:14; 21:8); chains of darkness (2 Pet. 2:4, 17; Jude 6); banishment from God (Matt. 25:41); outer darkness (Matt. 8:12; 22:13; 25:30); and eternal punishment (Matt. 25:46). As F. Baudraz has well stated:

> In contrast to Jewish apocalyptic the N.T. takes no pleasure in describing the torments of Gehenna. Jesus Christ came not for an immediate final judgment, which would restrict Him to pronouncing a decisive sentence, but to give His life as a ransom to snatch men back from perdition (Mark 10:45; John 3:16; Rom. 6:23); those who believe in Him have passed from death to life, from perdition to the Kingdom of God (John 5:24; Col. 1:12-14).
>
> But the coming of Jesus Christ can also have the opposite effect: those who do not believe in Him, who reject His words, condemn themselves (John 12:47 f.). Jesus Christ confronts every man with a life or death decision; each must decide for himself what his eternal portion is to be. Left to themselves men go straight to Gehenna; only the intervention, the work of Jesus Christ, accepted in faith, can give them a different destiny.[15]

IV. "THE GLORY WHICH SHALL BE REVEALED"

The glories of heaven are almost as difficult to comprehend as the terrors of hell. A wise providence has drawn a veil over much of the future state. Enough is given us to assure us of its reality, and to caution us to live our lives *sub species aeternitatis,* under the form of eternity. But curiosity still asks many questions revelation does not answer. As has been said, the consummation of all things at the final judgment is the "vanishing point to which all the rays of revelation converge."[16]

A. Heaven as a Place

Some scholars tend to write heaven off as a state of being in which all reality seems to dissolve in a haze. Nothing could be farther from the biblical conception. Here the state of blessedness is consistently described in terms denoting place as well as condition. Best remembered is Christ's statement: "In my Father's house are many man-

---

15. "Gehenna," Von Allmen, ed., *Companion to the Bible,* p. 136.
16. Wiley, *Christian Theology,* 3:355.

sions: if it were not so, I would have told you. I go to prepare a place for you. And if I go and prepare a place for you, I will come again, and receive you unto myself; that where I am, there ye may be also" (John 14:2-3). Striking also is John's vision of "the holy city, new Jerusalem, coming down from God out of heaven, prepared as a bride adorned for her husband" (Rev. 21:2). The apostle also heard a voice say, "Behold, the tabernacle of God is with men, and he will dwell with them, and they shall be his people, and God himself shall be with them, and be their God" (v. 3).

Emanuel V. Gerhart in his *Institutes of the Christian Religion* has pointed out the fact that our present spatial categories cannot be used in considering this heavenly place. For heaven is represented, not as part of the created order, with its spatial and temporal forms, but as the self-produced and uncreated *oikia* or dwelling of God. Since it is not part of the created universe, it is not to be located in the spatial order in which that universe subsists. "Heaven is the form of existence which differs essentially from the present economy of mankind or of the cosmos, as the Creator differs from His creation."[17]

B. The Nature of Heaven's Blessedness

The blessedness of heaven is described in both negative and positive terms. It is marked by the absence of sin, unrighteousness, and all that would defile: "There shall in no wise enter into it any thing that defileth, neither whatsoever worketh abomination, or maketh a lie" (Rev. 21:27). The consequences of sin will also be banished: "And God shall wipe away all tears from their eyes; and there shall be no more death, neither sorrow, nor crying, neither shall there be any more pain: for the former things are passed away" (Rev. 21:4). Isaiah describes the end of the way of holiness in similar terms: "And the ransomed of the Lord shall return, and come to Zion with songs and everlasting joy upon their heads: they shall obtain joy and gladness, and sorrow and sighing shall flee away" (Isa. 35:10; cf. v. 8).

In positive terms, heaven is described as the perfect fulfillment of every holy desire in communion with God and the Lamb: "The throne of God and of the Lamb shall be in it; and his servants shall serve him: and they shall see his face; and his name shall be in their foreheads. And there shall be no night there; and they need no candle, neither light of the sun; for the Lord God giveth them light: and

---

17. 2:889; quoted, *ibid.*, 3:378.

they shall reign for ever and ever" (Rev. 22:3-5). As Wiley says in an eloquent passage:

> For those who are weary, it is everlasting rest; for the sorrowing, it is a place where God shall wipe away all tears; for the suffering, there shall be no more pain; for the mistakes and blunders of a sincere but imperfect service, the throne of God shall be there, and His servants shall serve Him—every deed being performed in His presence and under His approving smile; for those who are perplexed and bewildered by the uncertainties and disappointments of this life, it is promised that there shall be no night there; for the Lord God giveth them light, and they shall reign with Him forever and ever.[18]

Unblemished fellowship with the redeemed will be an important feature of the blessedness of the heavenly state. Jesus spoke of those who shall come from "the east and west, and shall sit down with Abraham, and Isaac, and Jacob, in the kingdom of heaven" (Matt. 8:11). Paul looks forward to his future joy in the presence of his Thessalonian converts in the day of Christ: "For what is our hope, or joy, or crown of rejoicing? Are not even ye in the presence of our Lord Jesus Christ at his coming?" (1 Thess. 2:19)

The eternal state is a place of rest, but should not on that account be thought of as a place of inactivity. The joys of ever-new visions of divine grace and glory, the abiding satisfaction of new insights into exhaustless treasuries of truth, and the possibilities of service unhindered by the shortcomings of sin-marred brains and bodies will doubtless be features of the heavenly world.

All that is involved in the redemption of the creation (Rom. 8:19-23) and the "new heavens and a new earth, wherein dwelleth righteousness" (2 Pet. 3:13) we may not now be able to understand. We must note, however, that the scriptures speak of a complete restoration of "all things" (Acts 3:21). The biblical record comes to full circle. It starts with creation as it comes from the hand of God, and ends with the new creation described in Revelation 21 and 22. It opens in a garden with the tree of life, and closes in a city with the tree of life whose leaves are "for the healing of the nations" (Rev. 22:2). It begins with the fact of sin and the curse coming therefrom, and ends with the banishment of evil and evildoers (Rev. 21:8) and the assurance, "There shall be no more curse" (Rev. 22:3).

---

18. *Ibid.*, p. 381.

SUMMARY

The present chapter has dealt with a final phase of biblical eschatology, the resurrection, the final judgment, and the eternal states which perpetuate eternally the moral dichotomy of sin and righteousness begun in this world. The Bible not only provides an interpretation of history, but a view of human destiny which is unending. To bring all who can be persuaded to obey the gospel of God to that place of eternal happiness is the ultimate end and purpose of our Christian faith.

We turn in a final section to consider some aspects of Christian living in these times "between the ages."

PART V

Christian Living in Today's World

CHAPTER 24

The Maturing Personal Christian Life

We close our survey of the Christian faith with five chapters given to subjects relating to Christian living in today's world.

The life of man is never static. It is either growing and developing or it is regressing. It is moving toward a goal or moving away from it. We have noted the meaning of "crisis" in Christian experience. We must now give more attention to what might be called "process" in the Christian life, the development of a mature character.

It is not to be thought that growth proceeds smoothly and at the same rate in the spiritual life, any more than in the physical and psychological development of the person. In the growth of a child there are periods of very rapid growth, followed by periods of slower growth, which one psychologist calls "accelerations and decelerations."[1] Similarly, in the spiritual life there are periods of acquisition followed by periods of consolidation.

The New Testament consistently emphasizes the importance of growth and maturity. Of Jesus himself it is said that He "increased in wisdom and stature, and in favour with God and man" (Luke 2:52). Paul places great stress on the importance of maturity in such a passage as Eph. 4:11-16, where the purpose of the ministry is declared to be not only the perfecting of the saints, but bringing them to the measure of the stature of the fulness of Christ, no longer children in the faith, but growing up into Christ. Peter likewise urges his readers

---

1. Louis P. Thorpe, *Child Psychology and Development* (New York: Ronald Press Co., 1955), p. 269.

to "grow in grace, and in the knowledge of our Lord and Saviour Jesus Christ" (2 Pet. 3:18).

Maturation, however, is not entirely an automatic and unfailing process. For it to proceed as it should, attention must be given to the conditions of maximum growth. As L. T. Corlett has noted:

> The possibilities of development in a life perfected in love are almost unlimited. But the child of God should remember that progress in grace can be made only by continual choices for good, by a daily self-discipline and determination to adorn the doctrine of God our Saviour in all things. The Christian must keep his will continually submissive to the will of God. His choices must be centered more firmly in the pleasures of the Almighty and the affections so enraptured in the qualities and characteristics of the divine Lover that nothing of self and sense will have any drawing power. Greater faith must be exercised in the guidance of the Spirit and firmer reliance be placed in His wisdom. To mature in love man must direct his paths continually in following the footsteps of the Master.[2]

In this connection it is important to stress again the fact that entire sanctification plays a vital part in Christian maturation. Mention has already been made (in Chapter 17) of the processes of growth which follow the crisis experience of heart cleansing. Here it should strongly be said that maximum growth in the grace of God demands the purging of the heart from inner sin and the fullness of the Spirit. Without such cleansing and fullness the believer will fail of the greatest possible development in the spiritual life. It is no accident that the graces which mark the maturing of Christian character—"love, joy, peace, longsuffering, gentleness, goodness, faith, meekness, [and] temperance"—are known as *the fruit of the Spirit* (Gal. 5:22-23).

In addition, it must be observed that each person matures according to an individual pattern. While general principles of growth may be stated, these will be found effective in different degrees in different persons.

We turn now to factors affecting Christian maturation.

I. Maturing Through Overcoming Temptation

Temptation is a solicitation to evil, to the perversion of good, or a suggestion to choose self in the place of God. This is illustrated in the biblical account of the Fall as recorded in Genesis 3. The serpent's

---

2. *Holiness, the Harmonizing Experience* (Kansas City: Beacon Hill Press of Kansas City, 1951), p. 87.

suggestion was, "God doth know that in the day ye eat thereof, then your eyes shall be opened, and ye shall be as gods, knowing good and evil" (v. 5). Looking at the fruit, "the woman saw that the tree was good for food, and that it was pleasant to the eyes, and a tree to be desired to make one wise" (v. 6). Temptation came through natural desires of taste, for beauty, and the thirst for knowledge. As Orval J. Nease has said:

> The enemy approaches at the place of natural appetite, capacity, and instinct. It is no sin to be hungry. God put within us the call for food, that physical life might be sustained. One may, however, pervert that normal appetite for food so that the appetite for food overshadows every other normal function of life. The whole man serves the appetite. He becomes a gormandizer, a glutton, with an inordinate demand for food. The appetite as originally given was of God and intended to serve the physical well-being of the individual. Perverted, it becomes a dominating master which enslaves every other physical capacity.[3]

James indicates that this is the way in which all men are tempted: "But every man is tempted, when he is drawn away of his own lust, and enticed. Then when lust hath conceived, it bringeth forth sin: and sin, when it is finished, bringeth forth death" (Jas. 1:14-15). Man is tempted to use his natural desires in a wrong way or for a wrong goal. Unless there is desire, there is no temptation. But desire is not sin. Sin enters when desire has conceived or united with one's will or when one has given willing consent to the desire.

L. T. Corlett summarizes the nature of temptation:

> Temptation is always accompanied by a desire to follow the suggestion. First in the process the attention is drawn either to a mental contemplation or to an object outside of man. If that attention is centered on either one, a legitimate desire is aroused for that object. The suggestion is made from the tempter that it would be advantageous to enjoy the situation. The next step is the suggestion of how to obtain this end. Then the will is attacked, and the individual must make a decision as to whether or not the suggestion for satisfaction in an illegitimate manner will be carried out. The desire will at times be very strong and it may last for a period of time, but the guilt and condemnation do not come to an individual because of the desire. Temptation has not become sin simply because desire has been awakened. Temptation becomes sin only when the will decides in favor of the suggestion of the tempter. At times the battle is intense, and the child of God is

---

3. *Heroes of Temptation* (Kansas City: Beacon Hill Press of Kansas City, 1950), p. 13.

perplexed because of the intensity of the desire and the length of the conflict; but, as long as the will is held steady in alignment with the will of God and against the suggestion to evil, the individual has not sinned.[4]

There are some kinds of temptation which even the most advanced Christian must face. Olin Curtis states that such a person may have struggles coming from three sources:

First, spiritual discouragement. A saint in this world, in situations where Christ is not triumphant, can have a sort of discouragement which actually grows out of his supreme love for his Lord; and there is very great peril in such a mood. Second, spiritual pride. There is no experience so lofty in this life to a moral person as entirely to protect him from spiritual pride. In studying the temptations of our Saviour you see the whole method of its approach. A regenerate man is not half so likely to have this temptation as is the saint who is filled with love. Third, spiritual ambition. A holy man may have an ambition to be a great leader in the church, or a great preacher or a great evangelist; and his ambition may have been created by his love for Jesus Christ; and yet there may come such a turn in his affairs that he must choose between his ambition and his Master. That is, his ambition is so interesting to the man now that it stands over against the very love which created it.[5]

To these temptations, Corlett would add: (1) self-centeredness under the guise of religion; (2) sitting on the judgment seat and adopting the "holier than thou" attitude; (3) the attitude of self-pity.[6]

Suggestions for overcoming temptation may be found in the example of Jesus, who was tempted in all points as we are, yet without sin (Heb. 4:14-16). These temptations struck at the heart of Christ's highest purposes (cf. Matt. 4:1-11). It was His purpose to live for others. He was tempted to satisfy His own desires, but He refused to do so. He refused to bow to any other thing or person except to God. God alone is worthy to be praised. The kingdoms of the world are not worth the price of one's soul (Mark 8:36).

The adversary also tempted Jesus to do the spectacular and use a quicker method of winning the admiration of people. But Jesus knew that favor quickly gained could be quickly lost. Against each one of these offers Jesus quoted scripture. O. J. Nease insists that we, too, should use this method in overcoming temptation:

---

4. *Holiness in Practical Living* (Kansas City: Beacon Hill Press of Kansas City, 1948), p. 56.

5. *Christian Faith*, p. 393.

6. *Holiness in Practical Living*, pp. 60-61.

As Christian warriors, we should familiarize ourselves with the use of the "sword of the Spirit, which is the word of God." We should know God's Word! In it is to be found the pointed "Thus saith the Lord" that makes hell stand back. These are the promises of divine utterance that bring strength and courage to the tempted soul.[7]

God has promised that all temptations will be common ones and that He will not forsake a person in the hour of temptation and will provide a way through: "There hath no temptation taken you but such as is common to man: but God is faithful, who will not suffer you to be tempted above that ye are able; but will with the temptation also make a way to escape, that ye may be able to bear it" (1 Cor. 10:13). Corlett assures us that:

> The Spirit of God is an active partner in victorious Christian living, and regardless of how dark the hour, how strenuous the temptation, or how fierce the conflict, he will not forsake. He will stand by and guide to victory.[8]

II. MATURING THROUGH INFIRMITIES AND TROUBLE

In an earlier chapter we noted that infirmities must not be confused with sin. Here we observe that infirmities may be turned into steppingstones for Christian growth. To change the figure, infirmities may serve as the string on a kite. The string holds the kite to the earth, but the wind can carry the kite as high as the string will allow. However, if the string is broken or cut, the kite is not "liberated," but falls to the earth. Infirmities remind us that we are still earthbound creatures, but that God's grace is sufficient as the wind to carry the soul to heights of spiritual blessing.

Christianity is not promise of immunity from life, but of adequacy for life. The Christian must learn the creative use of trouble if he is to grow up into Christ (Eph. 4:15). A recent writer has pointed out the supreme example of this in the Cross:

> . . . Christ did not just submit to this dread event of the Crucifixion with what we miscall "resignation." He took hold of the situation. Given those circumstances which evil had produced, it was also God's will that Jesus should not just die like a trapped animal, but that he should so react to evil, positively and creatively, as to wrest good out of evil circumstances; and that is why the Cross is not just a symbol of capital punishment similar to the

---

7. *Heroes of Temptation,* p. 19.
8. *Holiness in Practical Living,* p. 64.

hangman's rope, but is a symbol of the triumphant use of evil in the cause of the Holy purpose of God. In other words, by doing the circumstantial will of God we open up the way to God's ultimate triumph with no loss of anything of value to ourselves.[9]

The relationship between God and a person who suffers is the relationship between a father and a son, or a teacher and a pupil. Both discipline with a purpose, and such discipline does not go without its reward. It bears fruit unto holiness and unto perfection (cf. Heb. 12:10-11). One may not be able to understand, and often the cry wrung from the heart is the plaintive "Why?" which finds no answer. But faith can trust where it cannot comprehend, and rest in the will of One too good to be unkind and too wise to make a mistake. As has wisely been said:

> You see, even Jesus did not say, "I have explained the world." What he did say was, "I have overcome the world." And if we can only trust where we cannot see, walking in the light we have—which is often very much like hanging on in the dark—if we do faithfully that which we see to be the will of God in the circumstances which evil thrusts upon us, we can rest our minds in the assurance that circumstances which God allows, reacted to in faith and trust and courage, can never defeat purposes which God ultimately wills. So doing, we shall wrest from life something big and splendid. We shall find peace in our own hearts. We shall achieve integration in our own minds. We shall be able to serve our fellows with courage and joy. And then one day—for this has been promised us—we shall look up into His face and understand. Now we see in a mirror, darkly, but then face to face. Frankly, hard though it be to say so, it is a lack of faith not to be able to bear the thought of anything which God allows.[10]

III. MATURING THROUGH THE INTEGRATION OF PERSONALITY

It isn't long before the person who is consciously trying to mature is confronted with the need for bringing all parts of his life into an integrated whole. It has been said, "Maturity is the integration of personality, the balance of all of the components of human exis-

---

9. Leslie D. Weatherhead, *The Will of God* (New York: Abingdon-Cokesbury Press, 1944), pp. 22-23.

10. *Ibid.,* p. 31.

tence."[11] Integration refers to the coordinated working of the total organism toward the attainment of some end goal or purpose.[12]

Paul suggests that this integration is to be found in the sanctifying power of God. "And the very God of peace sanctify you wholly; and I pray God your whole spirit and soul and body be preserved blameless unto the coming of our Lord Jesus Christ. Faithful is he that calleth you, who also will do it" (1 Thess. 5:23-24). This ideal in Christ serves as the outside integrating force.

The effectiveness of entire sanctification in promoting a real integration of personality is to be found also in the removal of the major source of inner discord, what we have seen to be identified as "the carnal mind." It is James in the New Testament who warns against the instability of the "double minded" (1:8), and who exhorts not only sinners to cleanse their hands, but the double-minded to purify their hearts (4:8). The tensions and stresses produced by the inner struggle of the "mind of the Spirit" and "the mind of the flesh" result in a major limitation to the spiritual life (Gal. 5:17).

At this point it is important to distinguish again between the carnal and the human in the Christian life. Although Paul could testify: "The law of the Spirit of life in Christ Jesus hath made me free from the law of sin and death" (Rom. 8:2), he also could say, "I keep under my body, and bring it into subjection: lest that by any means, when I have preached to others, I myself should be a castaway" (1 Cor. 9:27). Here we have the destruction of the carnal, but the direction of the human. The integration which is here in view is the long process of bringing every element of a redeemed and sanctified human being into "captivity . . . to the obedience of Christ" (2 Cor. 10:5).

> *Now rest, my long divided heart;*
> *Fixed on this blissful center, rest;*
> *Nor ever from my Lord depart,*
> *With Him of ev'ry good possessed.*

Important in integration is balancing the forces of personality. Young identifies balance as "the process of restoring equilibrium to the organism through the development of additional substitutive or

---

11. Howard H. Hamlin, *From Here to Maturity* (Kansas City: Beacon Hill Press of Kansas City, 1955), p. 26.

12. Kimball Young, *Personality and the Problems of Adjustment* (New York: F. S. Crofts and Co., 1940), p. 785.

ambivalent activities."[13] The body, mind, and spirit must be in proper balance with each other in order to integrate properly. One spends many hours giving attention to the needs of the body, but he must balance this bodily care by focusing his attention upon the things of the spirit and the things of the mind. Jesus took time to rest and sleep, and He took time to pray and meditate. Every part of His life was in perfect balance, and His personality represents the truly integrated person.

IV. Maturing Through Spiritual Disciplines

According to Peter there are some steps to maturity the individual Christian may take: "And beside this, giving all diligence, add to your faith virtue; and to virtue knowledge; and to knowledge temperance; and to temperance patience; and to patience godliness; and to godliness brotherly kindness; and to brotherly kindness charity" (2 Pet. 1:5-7). The aid of the Holy Spirit is available, but the primary responsibility rests upon the individual involved. There are limitless possibilities open to the individual who makes conscious effort toward improvement.

One must have faith in order to begin growth toward maturity. This is the basis of all spiritual graces and disciplines.

By virtue is meant moral power, or as in the Phillips translation, "goodness of life." Inward faith must first work out in holiness of life; and the graces that adorn such a life: cleanliness, naturalness, love, courage, humility, and courtesy.

Knowledge must be added to virtue. The sanctified must not be content to dwell in ignorance. Our modern culture places demands upon the maturing Christian, and he must study in order to be an effective witness for Christ. Yet the sanctified realizes his limitations and knows that God expects no service beyond one's reasonable best. He is careful not to make extravagant claims to greater revelations and knowledge than that which is given or acquired. A mature attitude does not impart talent, but it gives power to improve talent. Dr. Howard Hamlin gives these as marks of maturity.

> The immature mind wanders peripherally; the mature mind bores directly to the center. The immature mind becomes completely inundated by minutiae; the mature mind climbs on top of the heap and surveys the whole. The immature mind is exempli-

---

13. *Loc. cit.*

fied by the army private who condemns the entire army and its "high brass" because his foxhole is wet; the mature mind is represented by the soldier who realizes that his is a microcosmal existence with little general application. . . .

. . . If we are epistles "known and read of all men," then our ethics must keep pace with our testimony. If our ethics are to be unimpeachable, then we must learn to think in terms of basic moral issues. We must live "centrally," not "peripherally."[14]

We see that one cannot live centrally and deal in basic values and ideals without conscious effort. Peter recommends five other qualities to be added to faith, and these are discussed in conjunction with other aspects of the maturing Christian life in this chapter. All are examples of the fact that conscious effort toward maturity is of great importance.[15]

V. MARKS OF A MATURING CHRISTIAN

Maturity, like humility, is largely unconscious and therefore hard to define. Some have attempted to determine the marks of a maturing Christian. Rev. J. A. Wood suggests 12 in his book *Perfect Love:*

(1) An increasing comfort and delight in the Holy Scriptures. (2) An increasing interest in prayer, and an increasing spirit of prayer. (3) An increasing desire for the holiness of others. (4) A more heart-searching sense of the value of time. (5) Less desire to hear, see, and know for mere curiosity. (6) A growing inclination against magnifying the faults and weaknesses of others, when obliged to speak of their characters. (7) A greater readiness to speak freely to those who do not enjoy religion, and to backward professors of religion. (8) More disposition to glory in reproach for Christ's sake, and suffer, if need be, for Him. (9) An increasing tenderness of conscience, and being more scrupulously conscientious. (10) Less affected by changes of place and circumstances. (11) A sweeter enjoyment of the Holy Sabbath, and the services of the sanctuary. (12) An increasing love for the searching means of grace.[16]

Johnson cites five major tasks for maturity to accomplish:

(1) Self-knowledge. . . . Religious self-knowledge corrects both conceit and inferiority in the devotion to a larger cause. It seeks the optimal pattern of life—to learn what is best and then pro-

---

14. *From Here to Maturity,* pp. 13, 21.

15. T. M. Anderson, *After Holiness, What?* (Kansas City: Nazarene Publishing House, 1929) discusses these in detail.

16. Pp. 311-12.

ceed without hesitation to do it. . . . (2) Controlled desire. . . . lives for a purpose, and by that purpose he controls his unruly impulses. . . . (3) Maximum efficiency; (4) Wisdom of experience—a true sense of values; (5) Seasoned faith.[17]

Some of these may be listed and elaborated:

A. Greater Desire to Study the Scriptures

The Bereans searched the Scriptures daily to find the truth which Paul preached unto them (Acts 17:11). Such searching of the Scriptures becomes an important part of the growing Christian's life. It becomes his soul food. It is no wonder that Paul admonished Timothy: "Study to shew thyself approved unto God, a workman that needeth not to be ashamed, rightly dividing the word of truth" (2 Tim. 2:15).

B. A Constant Attitude of Prayerfulness

Those who become like Christ want to imitate His constant dependence upon God. Frequent talks with God mean close contact with the source of strength.

C. An Interest in the Salvation of Others

Those who are growing are working in the interest of sharing their salvation with others. Each action and attitude becomes important in conveying the proper witness to others.

D. Desire to Glorify God

The maturing Christian wants to use every moment for the benefit and glory of God. Time becomes valuable and he has no desire to waste it. Whatever he does, he wants to do for the glory of God (Col. 3:17).

E. Careful Speech

The growing Christian is also careful in his choice of words. The tongue is an unruly member and the Christian must learn to bridle it (Jas. 3:1-13). He is careful to season his speech with grace (Col. 4:6).

F. Desire to Be Natural

There should come a naturalness about one's actions as he matures.

---

17. Paul E. Johnson, *Psychology of Religion* (New York: Abingdon-Cokesbury Press, 1945), p. 83.

He has no desire to deceive, but he desires to be himself. There is no cause to put on a cloak of righteousness or to act an age which he is not. Quite often some are admonished to act their age, but the maturing Christian can act his age. Life is not filled with pretense, but it is lived in honesty and becomes a life without a strain.

G. Charity with the Faults and Failures of Others

He believes the best about others until he is proved wrong.

H. Maturing Interests

There is an increasing interest in the higher things of life. Paul testifies: "When I became a man, I put away childish things" (1 Cor. 13:11*b*).

I. Realism in Limiting Desires

In addition, there is a growing contentment with whatever state or circumstance in which one may find himself and a willingness to suffer for the sake of Christ.

J. Recognition of the Spiritual

The means of grace become more important. He desires to attend every available means of grace and gives increasing attention to holy matters. He also desires to join some existing organization for the promotion of the spiritual way of life and cooperates for the fulfillment of God's will on earth.

K. Pressing Toward a Goal

This is also one which has already been discussed. No maturing Christian can ever be satisfied in remaining static. The Christian must not glory in his accomplishments, but he must press toward the highest goal. This is Paul's advice in Phil. 3:4-14.

L. Creativity

Most of all, life becomes sacred to the maturing Christian and he wants to invest his life in some worthwhile activity. In creativity we become most like God. Kunkel explains:

> We should learn to co-operate with the creative will of God, which means we should develop our own creativity. God has created us as creative beings and therefore given us freedom to err; we have erred for thousands of years, we are deeply deviated, we shall err again; but we must take the risk, bear the conse-

quences, pay the price; otherwise we can never find the way out. And we can take the terrible responsibility for our future errors only if we can find, gradually or suddenly, the trust in God's creativity which time and again restores us as His children.[18]

This is the goal of every growing Christian—to become like God. To attain this, we must walk as Jesus walked (1 John 2:6). Abraham was commanded to walk before God and be perfect (Gen. 17:1). Jesus becomes our ideal and perfect Example. If this is one's aim, then he must have the mind of Christ (cf. Phil. 2:5-11).

As we walk in the footsteps of Christ, we become like Him. As one practices the presence of God, he takes on the characteristics of such a Presence. John indicates that it is possible to be like Jesus when He appears: "Behold, what manner of love the Father hath bestowed upon us, that we should be called the sons of God: therefore the world knoweth us not, because it knew him not. Beloved, now are we the sons of God, and it doth not yet appear what we shall be: but we know that, when he shall appear, we shall be like him; for we shall see him as he is" (1 John 3:1-2).

It is no wonder that someone has said, "It is great to be saved; and it is even greater to be sanctified; but the greatest thrill in life is to walk and talk with Jesus day by day."

SUMMARY

We have very briefly outlined some of the aspects of that growth in grace and in the knowledge of our Lord Jesus Christ which is the proper goal of every Christian. Overcoming temptation, the creative use of infirmities and trouble, the integration of personality around the ideal of Christlikeness, and the spiritual disciplines listed in 1 Peter 1 are a few of the factors involved. The marks of growing maturity likewise provide some goals and suggestions which may be found of value. We look next at the outgoing character of the Christian life in our task of exploring our Christian faith.

---

18. Fritz Kunkel, *In Search of Maturity* (New York: Charles Scribner's Sons, 1946), p. 239.

CHAPTER 25

The Outreach of
the Holy Life

The outreach of the holy life begins in a realization of the Christian meaning of life. As one fulfills this purpose, his life reaches out in witness to others and in the use of all of its resources for the glory of God. But life reveals its meaning only to those who diligently search for it. Anyone who does some serious thinking concerning life soon realizes that there must be some purpose or design behind it.

I. The Biblical View of Life

For the Christian, life has one great meaning: it is a sacred trust given to him by God, and as a trust, must glorify the Creator. Lewis T. Corlett says: "A life of holiness is one in which God's will, plan, and purpose are kept as the ideal and criterion of life—a life in which the believer consciously follows the guidance of the Spirit of God in all things."[1]

The fulfillment of this purpose for life is found in the new life in Christ. God had promised to put His laws into the heart of man (Jer. 31:31-34), and the New Testament writers testify that this is done through Christ. "But this man, after he had offered one sacrifice for sins for ever, sat down on the right hand of God; from henceforth expecting till his enemies be made his footstool. For by one offering he hath perfected for ever them that are sanctified. Wherefore the

---

1. *Holiness in Practical Living*, p. 73.

Holy Ghost also is a witness to us: for after that he had said before, This is the covenant that I will make with them after those days, saith the Lord, I will put my laws into their hearts, and in their minds will I write them; and their sins and iniquities will I remember no more" (Heb. 10:12-17).

This inward writing of the gospel on the heart must then be turned outward to the world. Howard Grimes insists that this is the very essence of the gospel:

> . . . the Christian's outreach, be it through evangelism, missions, social service, or Christian action, must come out of his central commitment and not be conceived in legalistic-humanitarian terms, as the so-called "social gospel" of the early twentieth century tended to be. The Christian's concern is not primarily humanitarian, though he is the most humanitarian of persons. His impetus comes not from a "feeling" of kindness toward all mankind; his is a more fundamental motive, his response to almighty God.[2]

Hence this new life in Christ finds its greatest manifestation in the witness of good works. Paul told Titus that this should be an outstanding characteristic of the peculiar people who are redeemed by Christ: "For the grace of God that bringeth salvation hath appeared to all men, teaching us that, denying ungodliness and worldly lusts, we should live soberly, righteously, and godly, in this present world; looking for that blessed hope, and the glorious appearing of the great God and our Saviour Jesus Christ; who gave himself for us, that he might redeem us from all iniquity, and purify unto himself a peculiar people, zealous of good works" (Titus 2:11-14).

In following this admonition to be a peculiar people zealous of good works, we become involved in the great creative act which keeps us in close harmony with God. The purpose of God is to enhance and to build up, while the purpose of the adversary is to destroy and to tear down. In God's permissive will in the present economy, man can tip the scales in either direction. He can help God by becoming a part of the creative action to build up or he can assist the devil in destroying this temporal order. But it is God's purpose that man will, through the help of Christ's redemptive power, fulfill His original plan to have creatures and a creation which will fully express Him in all of His glory.

James indicates that doing good works is one half of pure religion. "Pure religion and undefiled before God and the Father is this, To visit the fatherless and widows in their affliction, and to keep himself unspotted from the world" (Jas. 1:27).

The religion of Jesus makes it possible for man to join hands with God in fulfilling a purpose on earth. God loved and gave His Son that man might be made whole and be able, in return, to love and give in a measure as God does. "For we are his workmanship, created in Christ Jesus unto good works, which God hath before ordained that we should walk in them" (Eph. 2:10). The same thought was expressed by John. To be a Christian means to produce good fruits or works (John 15:1-8).

Corlett shows that holiness and Christian service are distinct parts of God's plan for man's life and he says, "He expects a life of useful service by each one of his children."[3]

II. Obedience and Power

A. The Command to Go

The holy life reaches out because Christ has commanded the Christian to go as a witness to redeeming grace. This is expressed in the Great Commission: "And Jesus came and spake unto them, saying, All power is given unto me in heaven and in earth. Go ye therefore, and teach all nations, baptizing them in the name of the Father, and of the Son, and of the Holy Ghost: teaching them to observe all things whatsoever I have commanded you: and, lo, I am with you alway, even unto the end of the world. Amen" (Matt. 28:18-20).

In a previous chapter we have discussed this command as being the mission of the Church. Thus the individual finds his purpose and meaning in life through Christ as he joins with other Christians in carrying out this command. It is a specific command, not just to good works, but to do certain things: (1) to go; (2) to make disciples; (3) to baptize; and (4) to teach. The Great Commission is a command given to all disciples. Special tasks are given to chosen men, but the commission is given to all of Christ's followers.

Paul put the commission on an individual basis as he expressed his debt in sharing the gospel: "I am debtor both to the Greeks, and to the Barbarians; both to the wise, and to the unwise. So, as much as in me is, I am ready to preach the gospel to you that are at Rome also. For I am not ashamed of the gospel of Christ: for it is the power of God unto salvation to every one that believeth; to the Jew first, and also to the Greek" (Rom. 1:14-16). In the light of such a debt and in the light of the commission of Christ, Phineas F. Bresee, one of the founders of the Church of the Nazarene, said, "We are debtors to give the gospel to every man in the same measure as we have received it."

In order to pay this debt and to carry out this mission, the individual must be trained. C. E. Matthews says this Great Commission puts responsibility upon the Church to train the individual:

> First, soul-winners are made. No Christian is a natural born soul-winner. He must be developed in the art of winning others to Christ. Who is responsible for this development? The answer is the church. It must ever accept the responsibility of making disciples and teaching [developing] them.[4]

As the Church develops these witnesses to carry out the Great Commission, they begin to see that the whole world is their parish. The commission calls the Church to go and teach all nations. Someone has said that no man has a right to hear the gospel twice until every man has heard it once.

But the commission is not given without a promise of divine help. Christ promised to be with those who go, and to make all power available to them. It is no wonder Jesus told His disciples that they would do greater work than He had done (John 14:12).

In addition to these promises, Christ also promised power to witness through the Holy Spirit.

B. The Power of the Holy Spirit

Jesus commanded His followers to tarry in the city of Jerusalem until they were endued with power from on high (Luke 24:49), and He promised that the Holy Spirit would come upon them and make them witnesses: "But ye shall receive power, after that the Holy Ghost is come upon you: and ye shall be witnesses unto me both in Jerusalem, and in all Judaea, and in Samaria, and unto the uttermost part of the earth" (Acts 1:8).

The disciples obeyed the command of Christ and tarried. When the Day of Pentecost came, they were filled with the Holy Spirit and became tireless witnesses (Acts 2).

Witnessing for Christ is a channel of outreach in the holy life

---

4. *Every Christian's Job* (Nashville: Broadman Press, 1955), p. 1.

through the power of the Holy Spirit. This is true not only of the Early Church, but of Christians through the centuries. Wherever Christ has been preached and a great religious revival has come, it has been due to an emphasis upon and the use of the power of the Holy Spirit.

III. THE NEED OF MAN

The objective basis for Christian witnessing is the fact that man is in need and in God is his help. Christ and His followers stand between the two to bring them together. This places a great incentive before the Christian as well as a great responsibility upon him. Matthews observes:

> There is no doubt that an overwhelming number of believers are convinced that human agency is involved in the salvation of lost souls, but it is a tragic fact that a large percentage of them live and die without ever putting their belief into practice. A great burden and a tremendous responsibility would be lifted from the shoulders of Christian people if no human being were responsible for the salvation of his fellowmen. On the other hand, if human agency be involved in the salvation of lost souls, it constitutes the most serious responsibility known to the human race.[5]

To meet the need of man by pointing him to the Savior is a task for all Christians, and it does not go without its reward. "Brethren, if any of you do err from the truth, and one convert him; let him know, that he which converteth the sinner from the error of his way, shall save a soul from death, and shall hide a multitude of sins" (Jas. 5:19-20). "The fruit of the righteous is a tree of life; and he that winneth souls is wise" (Prov. 11:30). "And they that be wise shall shine as the brightness of the firmament; and they that turn many to righteousness as the stars for ever and ever" (Dan. 12:3). These promises represent some of the incentive to go and tell the good news. Matthews observes:

> Surely God would not bestow these priceless rewards for something man is not expected to do. The great loving and seeking heart of God trying to rescue souls from death is a rewarder of all who help him. Every inducement possible, according to his infinite wisdom, is offered for the rescue of the perishing.[6]

---

5. *Ibid.*, pp. 21-22.

6. *Ibid.*, p. 28.

IV. METHODS

A. The Evangelism of Christ

Jesus is the master Witness, and His methods serve as an ideal example to follow. He knew men, and He knew God. He talked to crowds, and He dealt with individuals. He was able to take ordinary events and circumstances and turn them into occasions for witnessing. His purpose was to bring life to men everywhere.

Visitation was a method used by Jesus. He visited in the homes of people, and He visited people by the wayside. He was seen in the homes of the Pharisees, and in the homes of the publicans and sinners. He was in the homes of Levi and Zacchaeus and in the home of His friends, Mary and Martha. He witnessed on these occasions. Even festive events might serve as an occasion for witnessing as He changed the water into wine at the marriage in Cana of Galilee (John 2:1-11).

Every contact with a person along the wayside proved to be an opportunity to witness. He used His thirst as an occasion to portray a message to the Samaritan woman at the well (John 4:1-42). "Jesus answered and said unto her, If thou knewest the gift of God, and who it is that saith to thee, Give me to drink; thou wouldest have asked of him, and he would have given thee living water" (John 4:10).

B. The Work of the Early Church

The Early Church had a tremendous momentum from the power of the Holy Spirit. Peter became the spokesman and preached to the crowds, and thousands responded to his invitation. The disciples visited in various places, in the synagogues and homes, and preached in the marketplaces. They tried to preach and teach in every house: "Daily in the temple, and in every house, they ceased not to teach and preach Jesus Christ" (Acts 5:42). They were not content to wait for the crowds; they went into homes, and they witnessed to individuals. Philip serves as a typical example as he dealt with the Ethiopian eunuch (Acts 8:26-39).

Visitation was also a method of the Early Church, and John T. Sisemore points out that not only were individuals won through this method, but churches at Antioch, Philippi, and Rome were established by visitation.[7] He also estimates that the church at Jerusalem

---

7. *The Ministry of Visitation* (Nashville: Broadman Press, 1955), pp. 10-16.

grew rapidly and increased through this method until it reached a number between 20,000 and 100,000.

> Just how did the Jerusalem church reach so many people? They were not reached because of a beautiful cathedral, marvelous music, or a magnetic pastor. Their pastor was a plain man; they had no outstanding music program. They did not even have a building in which to worship, since the first church building was erected during the reign of Alexander Severus, A.D. 222-235.
>
> The Jerusalem church is the outstanding example of what a good visitation program can accomplish. If it could build a membership counted in the multiplied thousands, without a building or equipment, just what could be done by a church with all the marvelous provisions of the present time?[8]

Paul practiced various methods of evangelism, and the classic missionary impetus comes from his call to go into Macedonia (Acts 16:6-10). The Macedonian call still rings in the ears of the Christian Church, and this incident has often been quoted in church circles to show the need of people in the remote places of the earth. The Church has responded as Paul responded.

C. The Church Today Is a Result of Witnessing

The Early Church carried out its mission to witness to the uttermost part of the earth. As a result of its labors, the Christian evangel went to all parts of the earth, spreading most quickly throughout the Roman Empire. The march of the gospel through the centuries was northward and westward. Through the efforts of the English-speaking nations, the good news has spread to America, to the islands of the sea, and to the continents of the world. The missionary societies of the last two centuries have been very influential in carrying out the command of Christ.

We have heard the gospel today because someone dared to go in obedience to the command of Christ. As David H. C. Read puts it, "We have all derived our knowledge of the Faith directly from the church."[9]

D. Mass Evangelism

Moses preached to the Israelites, and crowds have heard the Word ever since. Jesus is famous for His Sermon on the Mount, which was preached to the multitude (Matt. 5:1). Peter is remembered for his

---

8. *Ibid.*, p. 17.

9. *The Christian Faith* (London: English Universities Press, Ltd., 1955), p. 135.

sermon on the Day of Pentecost, when he saw 3,000 believe (Acts 2:41). Paul is known for his sermon on Mars' Hill (Acts 17:16-34).

Revivalism, as we know it today, takes its impetus from the work of the Wesleys, Whitefield, Jonathan Edwards, Charles G. Finney, Dwight L. Moody, and Billy Sunday. These have had a tremendous influence upon life in America and England, and the influence of Billy Graham, today's most prominent proponent of mass evangelism, is being felt around the world.

It would be absurd for one to say that mass evangelism has not fallen into some disrepute. Criticisms have come from America and England, and one writer's objections serve as an example. Montague Goodman says:

> First, and most important, it is derogatory to the dignity of the gospel. The gospel is the noblest, grandest, most majestic and profoundest message that ever fell upon the ears of men and to present it in an atmosphere of lighthearted gaiety cannot but detract from these qualities in the minds of the hearers. . . .
>
> The second objection is, that there is a more effective and at the same time, a more Scriptural mode of presentation. It is a striking reflection that neither our Lord himself nor any of the Apostles is represented as seeking to organize great crowds for the purpose of preaching to them.[10]

While Goodman does admit that God has used these mass meetings for His glory,[11] he seems to forget that Jesus was moved with compassion when He saw the multitudes and utilized their interest and curiosity to unfold the way of life to them.

However, in spite of objections to its use, revivalism is still an effective means for the promotion of the cause of Christ. William Warren Sweet concludes that revivalism has put an emphasis upon several aspects of vital religion which are essential to our way of life.[12] Timothy L. Smith has shown that revivalism and the quest for Christian perfection paved the way for the social reforms of this century.[13] Thus we may conclude that mass evangelism is still effective and important.

E. Personal Evangelism

Personal soul winning, too, has been used through the years and has

---

10. "Evangelists and Evangelism," *The Church,* J. B. Watson, ed., pp. 144-45.

11. *Ibid.,* p. 145.

12. *Revivalism in America* (New York: Charles Scribner's Sons, 1944), p. 178.

13. *Revivalism and Social Reform* (New York: Abingdon Press, 1957), p. 8.

just recently received new emphasis. It is preeminently a New Testament method being used effectively in our modern world. Modern psychology and recognition of individual differences have contributed to the success of this method.

Personal evangelism utilizes the influence of one individual upon another. Each soul is dealt with individually and personally. His questions are answered, and his need pointed out, and the power of personal persuasion employed. A New Testament example is that of Andrew: "One of the two which heard John speak, and followed him, was Andrew, Simon Peter's brother. He first findeth his own brother Simon, and saith unto him, We have found the Messias, which is, being interpreted, the Christ. And he brought him to Jesus" (John 1:40-42*a*).

F. Visitation Evangelism

As has already been pointed out, visitation has been used by the Early Church and by the Church through the years. Sisemore points out its primary importance from the very beginnings of religious work.[14]

This method utilizes door-to-door campaigns, literature distribution, and organized calling nights. Such a method may be seen in the parable of the sower. The sower sowed the seed everywhere (Mark 4). The method should carry some of the dignity of the message, but there must be some "holy recklessness" in our effort to get the gospel to every creature. The Psalmist promises success in such endeavors: "He that goeth forth and weepeth, bearing precious seed, shall doubtless come again with rejoicing, bringing his sheaves with him" (Ps. 126:6).

V. WITNESSING TO WIN

A. Why?

We have already mentioned the reason the Christian must witness. Christ has commanded, and men are in need. The Christian must share the good news, and the power has been promised. A sense of oughtness must stir every heart as Paul's when he said, "Yea, woe is unto me, if I preach not the gospel!" (1 Cor. 9:16). Matthews quotes a famous Baptist preacher and soul winner, Lee R. Scarborough, as

---

14. *Ministry of Visitation,* pp. 5-17.

saying: "To refuse to witness a saving gospel to a lost world day by day is nothing short of high treason, spiritual rebellion, and inexcusable disobedience to his holy commands."[15]

B. What?

The message has always been the same, that Jesus is the Christ, the Son of God. Philip witnessed to Nathanael and told him to come and see for himself (John 1:45-46). Peter and John said they could not do anything else except witness about those things which they had seen and heard, and so they were bold to speak in the name of Jesus (Acts 4:20). Philip preached Christ (Acts 8:5). John continued the idea in his First Epistle: "That which was from the beginning, which we have heard, which we have seen with our eyes, which we have looked upon, and our hands have handled, of the Word of life; . . . that which we have seen and heard declare we unto you, that ye also may have fellowship with us" (1 John 1:1-3).

Millar Burrows elaborates on the content of the message:

> As to the content of missionary and evangelistic preaching if theological orthodoxy and unanimity are not made primary, we may say that the Christian purpose in life, the Christian spirit, commitment to Christian ends is the most urgent, desperate need of the world now as always. The Church must preach for conviction of sin, to convince the world that living for unChristian, sub-Christian, and anti-Christian ends is sin, and the wages of sin is death. Materialism, secularism, nationalism, imperialism, militarism, and all other unChristian "isms" are lanes in the broad highway that leads to destruction. And when conviction of sin and a hunger and thirst for righteousness have been aroused, the gospel of God's free gift of salvation and the way of salvation must be proclaimed in terms all men can understand, with emphasis on the commitment of heart and will rather than intellectual assent.[16]

C. When?

Every opportunity which comes our way should be the time to witness. Jesus stated that the fields are white unto harvest: "Therefore said he unto them, The harvest truly is great, but the labourers are few: pray ye therefore the Lord of the harvest, that he would send forth labourers into his harvest" (Luke 10:2). The writer of the Book of Hebrews indicates the time is now: "But exhort one another daily,

---

15. *Every Christian's Job*, p. 26.
16. *Outline of Biblical Theology*, p. 284.

while it is called To day; lest any of you be hardened through the deceitfulness of sin" (Heb. 3:13). Paul also states that today is the day of salvation (2 Cor. 6:2).

When the appropriateness of time is mentioned, many critics have turned to the time of the altar call or invitation and have said that this is not the moment for personal work. Matthews answers this criticism:

> There is no doubt that this practice can be and has been hurtful in the matter of winning the lost to Christ. If those who engage in personal work in the church at the time of the invitation do so in a professional manner, going promiscuously from one person to another without regard to impressions from the Holy Spirit, they likely will offend some of the unsaved. It is, however, the writer's opinion, based upon experience, observation, and personal testimony, that the invitation period following a warmhearted gospel sermon affords the most fruitful of all opportunities for personal soul-winning. He has never been in a church in which personal work was carried on in the congregation that he did not find a warm-hearted and friendly people and a wholesome spiritual atmosphere. We learn from the example of Jesus that he seized upon every opportunity to win the lost, without regard to place or time.[17]

D. How?

Jesus sent the 70 two by two (Luke 10:1). These came back to report with joy (Luke 10:17). This would imply a possibiliy of organized effort, and record keeping. The Lord encourages diligence in seeking the lost, and one should search until he finds them. This is seen in His stories concerning the lost coin, the lost sheep, and the lost son (Luke 15).

Paul implies the use of personal influence. He became an example of all of the believers in Thessalonica (1 Thess. 1:7). He also emphasized the importance of all good methods in winning men to Christ. Empathy, self-identification, with the lost is useful in saving some. "For though I be free from all men, yet have I made myself servant unto all, that I might gain the more. And unto the Jews I became as a Jew, that I might gain the Jews; to them that are under the law, as under the law, that I might gain them that are under the law; to them that are without law, as without law, (being not without law to God, but under the law to Christ,) that I might gain them that are without law. To the weak became I as weak, that I might

---

17. *Every Christian's Job,* p. 61.

gain the weak: I am made all things to all men, that I might by all means save some. And this I do for the gospel's sake, that I might be partaker thereof with you" (1 Cor. 9:19-23). Goodman elaborates here:

> So the would-be successful evangelist must be prepared to adapt his methods to varying needs to become not only all things to all men but particular things to particular men that he may by particular means save some of them. But whatever means, let us remember that the urgency remains that the churches' motto must be today more than ever it was, "Evangelize or Perish."[18]

It is therefore possible for men to be won through an approach from many angles appealing to the various sides of personality. Some may be attracted through an appeal to the mind. Others may be approached through physical activities, as in boys' and girls' club work and scouting. Through the area of social activities and fellowship some have been attracted to the fellowship of Christ. These are all in addition to the methods which were discussed earlier in this chapter.

Paul's idea has led some churches to use times of sorrow and death, times of graduation, marriage, times of joy, and times of crisis as the occasion for a visit or call in a home, and souls have been won to Christ.

Everyone, then, has a part in witnessing to win others. Each one has something which is useful in the task. God only asks, "What is that in thine hand?" (Exod. 4:2) He uses the abilities and talents one has for a witness to himself.

VI. THE SPECIAL CALL TO SERVICE

God expects all of His followers to witness, but He has chosen some for full-time service. He chose Aaron to be the first high priest, and a long line of called priests and ministers have followed. Jesus called 12 men to be His apostles. He said, "Ye have not chosen me, but I have chosen you, and ordained you, that ye should go and bring forth fruit, and that your fruit should remain: that whatsoever ye shall ask of the Father in my name, he may give it you" (John 15:16).

After Paul was struck blind, God directed Ananias to go to him and indicated that He had chosen Paul for a special task. "But the Lord said unto him, Go thy way: for he is a chosen vessel unto me, to

---

18. "Evangelists and Evangelism," *The Church*, J. B. Watson, ed., p. 151.

bear my name before the Gentiles, and kings, and the children of Israel: for I will shew him how great things he must suffer for my name's sake" (Acts 9:15-16).

The setting apart of those specially called is one of God's methods for men to hear the gospel: "For whosoever shall call upon the name of the Lord shall be saved. How then shall they call on him in whom they have not believed? and how shall they believe in him of whom they have not heard? and how shall they hear without a preacher? And how shall they preach, except they be sent? as it is written, How beautiful are the feet of them that preach the gospel of peace, and bring glad tiding of good things!" (Rom. 10:13-15)

There are various ways in which men are called to special service. We have many biblical examples. God called Moses while he was tending sheep (Exodus 3). He called Samuel in the night (1 Samuel 3). Isaiah volunteered for service after he caught a vision of a holy God and after he heard the challenge of a needy people (Isaiah 6). Jeremiah was called, but he felt that he was still too young and could not obey. But God encouraged him, and he became a great witness in his day (Jeremiah 1). Amos heard his call while he was following sheep. He had seen the wickedness and idolatry in the land, and could only cry out against it (Amos 7:14-15).

Jesus called His apostles from various walks of life, fishermen, tax collectors, and others. Each responded and forsook all to give his life for the cause of Christ.

A sample of called ministers today would reveal a variety of methods used in calling them into this special service. But one can be sure: it is a definite call; it is a personal call; it is a call to service which can be rendered according to the ability of the called; it is a real challenge; and to refuse it is to go against God's will. G. C. D. Howley gives three suggestions as to how one can know his gift from God and fulfill it:

> Firstly, a strong inward desire to labour along certain lines; secondly, an ability manifesting itself to serve in that particular manner; and thirdly, some measure of blessing in engaging in such work—these three things, when together, would suggest the call of God towards some specific service.[19]

There is also an obligation upon the church to provide the kind of atmosphere in which gifted people may realize these calls to special service. Howley continues:

---

19. "The Christian Ministry," *The Church*, J. B. Watson, ed., p. 117.

In a healthy Christian assembly scope will be found for the development of the gifts of the Spirit, so that there will arise from the midst of the church those qualified of God to meet the needs of the saints. And ample, encouragement is given for seeking the increase of gift, as when we notice, no less than three times in the section devoted to this subject in the letter to Corinth, an exhortation summed up in these words: "desire earnestly the greater gifts" (1 Cor. 12). . . .

The touch of God's hand, an inward consciousness of spiritual vocation, with the fellowship of one's brethren in Christ, all these prepare the man of God for his life service; and the man or woman with such an experience will so labour, whatever his or her ministry, that Christ will be magnified and His people built up in holy things.[20]

VII. THE WITNESS OF POSSESSIONS

There should be no question but that God is the Owner of heaven and earth (Gen. 14:19). The Psalmist says, "The earth is the Lord's, and the fulness thereof; the world, and they that dwell therein. For he hath founded it upon the seas, and established it upon the floods" (Ps. 24:1-2). Everything man has, God has given. It is God who gives power to get wealth (Deut. 8:18).

In order that we might remember that God is the Owner, He has ordained adoration, praise, worship, and the offering of gifts. Lewis Corlett writes:

God desires that each one of His children should learn the true meaning of stewardship. A steward is one who handles or supervises the use of the wealth or possessions of another, generally greater and richer than the steward himself. God is the Creator and rightful Owner of all material wealth in the universe. He allows man to gather some about him for his use in this world; yet He does not intend that man should allow his affections to go out to these things in such a way that the person forgets his Maker.[21]

A. The Tithe

The basic biblical provision in stewardship is the paying of tithes, or a tenth of the increase one receives. The first mention of the tithe is found in Abraham's payment to Melchizedek of a tithe of the booty taken in the liberation of Lot (Gen. 14:20). Jacob also vowed that he

---

20. *Ibid.*, pp. 117-18.
21. *Holiness in Practical Living*, pp. 72-73.

would pay the Lord a tenth of all his increase (Gen. 28:22). With such a background, the tithe became a part of the law, and God commanded that it be regarded as holy and that it should be brought to the priests (Lev. 27:30).

Tithing became the touchstone of stewardship and blessing in the Old Testament economy. A man was considered a thief if he did not pay his tithe to God. "Will a man rob God? Yet ye have robbed me. But ye say, Wherein have we robbed thee? In tithes and offerings. Ye are cursed with a curse: for ye have robbed me, even this whole nation. Bring ye all the tithes into the storehouse, that there may be meat in mine house, and prove me now herewith, saith the Lord of hosts, if I will not open you the windows of heaven, and pour you out a blessing, that there shall not be room enough to receive it" (Mal. 3:8-10).

B. The New Testament Standard

There are some who argue that tithing belongs only to the Old Testament period and need not be practiced by Christians. But one cannot rest in such an idea. The principle of the tithe has never been rescinded. Surely love under grace should give as much as duty under law.

One of our Lord's constantly reiterated themes was the danger of covetousness and of heaping up treasures on earth. He required His followers to forsake all (Matt. 19:27, 29). He told the rich young ruler to sell everything and give to the poor and follow Him (Matt. 19:21). The early Christians gave all they had to the Church. "And all that believed were together, and had all things common; and sold their possessions and goods, and parted them to all men, as every man had need" (Acts 2:44-45).

Paul encouraged the Corinthians to give systematically (1 Cor. 16:1-2). He asked them to consider the generosity of God as He gave His Son, and exhorted them to be just as liberal (2 Cor. 8:1-9). Paul also accents the grace of generosity by saying that one tends to receive in the measure that he gives (2 Cor. 9:6-8).

In these words there is expressed the true Christian spirit. God has been generous in His love and giving, and challenges every Christian to give in the same measure as he has received. This means life, money, material goods. The outreach of the holy life demands complete consecration and dedication to use all of one's possessions for the glory of God. This could mean more than tithing, as Corlett observes: "While tithing is good, to help a correct attitude toward material things and to assure a person that God must be kept first, the Christian should give offerings over and above the tithe."[22]

To gain wealth is never a sufficient reason to live. Jesus indicated this in the story of the rich man who tore down old barns in order to build larger ones in which to store his grain: "But God said unto him, Thou fool, this night thy soul shall be required of thee: then whose shall those things be, which thou hast provided? So is he that layeth up treasure for himself, and is not rich toward God" (Luke 12:20-21). Jesus also emphasized the idea that the true treasure is to be found in heaven as a result of our stewardship here upon earth (Matt. 6:19-21). Anyone who follows Christ must be willing to lay up treasures in heaven by giving to the good of humanity and the glory of God (Matt. 19:23-30).

SUMMARY

In this chapter we have tried to show the outreach of the Christian life and the stewardship of life and possessions as it relates to the fulfillment of the will and plan of God for humanity. This will find its fullest expression in the new life in Christ. Being redeemed in Christ means that one will show forth the mighty works of Christ and that one will bring forth the fruits of righteousness and good works.

This outreach of the holy life obeys the command of Christ to go into all the world and utilizes the power of the Holy Spirit and every available means and worthy method to point men to Christ. All Christians must be witnesses, and yet some are called to be special servants. God demands a stewardship of time and life, but He also demands a stewardship of material possessions. The measure of our gift is found here: Freely we have received; freely we must give!

We turn next to the consideration of Christian values in relation to the full ethical life of the child of God.

---

22. *Ibid.*, p. 74.

CHAPTER 26

Christian Values

Values are the ideals we live by and accept as the guides to our actions. Values refer to those aspects of human existence that are considered to be of primary importance in the meaningful and satisfactory fulfilling of one's life. The field of values is larger than ethics, which has to do primarily with conduct. Values lie behind our choices. Values are what we strive for, appreciate, steer by.

Values refer to the ideals of life as well as to a pattern of activities. For example: The ideal of home is a value, but so is the activity associated with members of the family. Value as an ideal becomes the guide for the development and continuation of the activities associated with that ideal. Values refer to those experiences, whether individual or in association with others, which are considered to be of special worth. They are that without which life would not be worth living. Values which are held or prized for their own inherent worth are called intrinsic. Values which serve as means to other, more basic values are instrumental.[1]

Not all races, societies, communities, or even individuals agree on what the basic values for living are, but each person or group does have values. *It is an empirical fact that people live by values.* In some types of philosophy, values are accorded little or no status, largely because they are difficult to define and cannot always be reduced to a set of operations. But what people value does determine how they live and what they strive for.

The technical term for the theory of values is axiology. The word

---

1. On the distinction between these and many other kinds of values, see Walter G. Everett, *Moral Values* (New York: Henry Holt and Co., 1918), Chapter VII.

comes from *axios,* "worthy," and *logos,* "word." Axiology is reasoning about values.

I. SIGNIFICANCE OF VALUES FOR CHRISTIAN LIVING

Why should a discussion of values be included in a work on the Christian faith? There are at least four reasons:

First, concern with values is a bridge which leads from the more technical aspect of systematic theology to the area of life where the demands of existence make themsleves felt in the human person. Values tie theology in with experience, giving to theology a practical side as a balance to its theoretical concern.

Second, a consideration of values helps to arouse interest among the people who think that theology is only for the scholars trained in making precise intellectual and terminological distinctions. Systematic theology often is highly technical and perhaps necessarily so; but even for those who have been theologically initiated, there is the feeling that theology has been too much a debate between a few theological giants.

Third, values are necessary to give content to religious feeling. Theology is the intellectual side of religion. If religion without theology is formless, then theology without religious values is empty. Values are the existential aspects of doctrine.

Fourth, values reflect the adequacy or inadequacy of doctrinal formulations. "Ye shall know them by their fruits" (Matt. 7:16). Doctrines, no matter how beautifully arranged, which do not effectively transform life are in themselves of little worth. Theology must never be separated from ethics.

In brief, the question, "What are Christian values?" is equivalent to asking, "What is the Christian dimension of life?"

II. THE BIBLICAL BASIS FOR VALUES

The Bible provides an adequate basis for a doctrine of Christian axiology both in its positive precepts and in its wealth of example.

In the Old Testament the so-called "wisdom literature," particularly Proverbs, is rich in its concentrated maxims of wisdom and advice. A proverb is a highly condensed statement or aphorism which reflects a wide area of experience. Proverbs might be called a value book. It sets forth ideals in a great variety of categories, primarily in the area of practical living and interpersonal relationships. It extols the worth of wisdom, wealth, industry, self-discipline, education, and suggests guidance in many social, civil, and personal life-situations. Its constant underlying motif is to teach discrimination among values, and its guiding axiom is the fear of the Lord.

In the New Testament, the Sermon on the Mount and much of the practical advice of Paul deal with matters pertaining to problems of personal experience. The New Testament, along with the grandeur of its religious insights, does not neglect the matter of practical living. To live is to choose. One cannot escape the necessity of selecting his values. The New Testament is the Christian's basic guide to value choices. It sets forth the norm for both Christian character and conduct.

In the context of value terminology, the ideal of personal worth is set forth by Jesus when He presents the person as the special object of the Father's concern. The Father cares for the sparrows, "not one of them is forgotten"; but persons "are of more value than many sparrows" (Luke 12:4-7; cf. also Matt. 6:25-26). The word which Jesus uses for value is *diaphero,* which means literally "to bear through." It also means "to bring to an end" or "to bring to perfection." A person, according to Jesus, is a "value bearer" capable of being brought to fulfillment. Personality and values thus are integral to each other. The essence of personality is the ability to bear values. Values are possible only for persons. This is the basic value axiom. The axiom is amply illustrated by Jesus' personal concern with individuals and His estimate of comparative worth when He teaches that it is of no profit if a man gain the world and lose his soul (Mark 8:36).

The ideal of Christian conduct and character is set forth by Paul in a beautiful value passage in Eph. 4:1-3: "I therefore, the prisoner of the Lord, beseech you that ye walk worthy of the vocation wherewith ye are called, with all lowliness and meekness, with longsuffering, forbearing one another in love; endeavouring to keep the unity of the Spirit in the bond of peace." The word which is translated "worthy" is *axios.*

Some form of the word is used many times in the New Testament, usually rendered as "worthy" or "counted worthy" or "worthily." Among the many passages, the following are particularly strong in their import for Christian value theory. In 2 Thess. 1:11, Paul prays, as in the passage above, that God would count his readers worthy of their calling. He repeats essentially the same message in Col. 1:10 and 1 Thess. 2:12. The people of Rome were admonished by Paul to receive Phoebe in a manner as becometh, or is worthy of, saints (Rom. 16:2). Paul encourages the Philippians to let their conversation or manner of life be worthy of the gospel of Christ (Phil. 1:27). John the Baptist urged his listeners to bring forth fruit worthy of repentance (Luke 3:8).

A basis for a standard of values is suggested by the New Testament use of *axios*. In the parable of the prodigal son as told by Jesus the prodigal laments that he is not worthy to be called a son (Luke 15:19, 21). In another place Jesus says that any person who lets family relationships interfere with his love for Christ is not worthy of Him. Neither is anyone worthy of Christ who refuses to bear his cross and follow Him (Matt. 10:37-38). All these passages imply a *kind* of character or action which *is* worthy of God or of one who is a follower of God. In other words, one might say there is a quality which could be described as having God-worth. Values, according to the New Testament, are those therefore which possess the quality of God-worth. A simple word to express this concept can be constructed from *theos*, "God," and *axios*, "worthy." *Theoaxia* is the quality of God-worthiness, the Christian criterion of all value claims. True or genuine values are those values which possess *theoaxia*. The word "genuine," as defined in the *Oxford English Dictionary*, means something "really proceeding from its reputed source." Reduced to a simple summarizing statement, a genuine value is one which is God-worthy.

The Christian is interested in the true, the genuine human values as implied in the Scriptures, and proved by the individual and collective experience of the race. History is the testing ground of all values, Christian and non-Christian. While it is true that genuine values do not constitute the only motivational forces in history, nevertheless history has a way of "pushing up" those values which have special meaning and significance for mankind. History is the arena for moral action, whether good or bad. All value-claims, all ideals, all opinions, theories, utopias, are tested in the life of the race, and judgment is rendered by the passage of time and the demands of existence. History is the laboratory of ideals.

It is the Christian claim that the values for living as set forth in the Bible are the values which, after being tried in the fire of existence, provide the most stable basis for individual fulfillment and for social relations. In other words, the genuine values, i.e., those possessing God-worth, constitute the only adequate basis for the Christian life. This is not meant to imply that only Christians can appreciate genuine values. The majority of men accept God's gifts without

Christian Values / 481

acknowledgment. Most human values are common to both the religiously devout and the secular; but Christian faith transforms all values—not only adding a new dimension to them but setting them in a wider perspective. A Christian is a person who sees life from the widest possible perspective. Values for the committed Christian become transmuted by virtue of their wider coherence.

III. Some Fundamental Human Values

The following discussion of some specific values is not arranged according to any scale of importance. The attempt to establish a definite hierarchy is probably a fruitless task, not only as indicated by the great variety of opinion among value theorists, but because of the complementary and reciprocal nature of the values themselves.[2] At first glance it might appear that, say, health values are inferior to vocational ideals, but despite a few hardy souls who have been able to rise above their health limitations, there is no doubt that vocational ideals are limited by pain or bodily deformity. Many vocations are impossible without a sound body. Insofar as there is any pattern to the list, it begins with those that are more closely personal and proceeds to those that are more inclusive. The aesthetic, which is treated last, is probably an element in all values. The values chosen for consideration are not meant to be exhaustive in either selection or treatment. The purpose is to show briefly the Christian dimension of some of the basic values of human living. Throughout the discussion the moral, ethical, and character values are already assumed.

A. Bodily Values

These values relate primarily to bodily health and care. A sound, clean, healthy, disciplined body qualifies as a genuine value. In a hierarchy of values it would be very difficult, as suggested above, to establish its level of significance. It is a good example of how values interpenetrate and mutually determine each other. In many cases the status of one's physical health largely influences one's ability to achieve the fullness of other values.

The Bible is strong in its indication that the body is to be neither despised nor neglected. The human body is presented as God's own

---

2. For a sample hierarchy or scale, see Edgar Sheffield Brightman's *Introduction to Philosophy* (New York: Holt, Rinehart and Winston, Inc., 1925), p. 148; 3rd edition, p. 192.

handiwork, into which He breathed the breath of life. Without implying the anthropomorphic notion that the image of God refers to the human physical likeness, it is undoubtedly the Hebrew view that the human personality was a unity.[3] It was the whole being of man, body and soul, which constituted his personality, and which, in its totality, was made in the likeness of God.

The body therefore was important in the eyes of the Hebrews. Physical health was desirable, as in the case of Hezekiah and Job. Perfection of body had special significance for the Levites, especially to the sons of Aaron, who would serve in the sanctuary (Lev. 21: 17-23).

In the New Testament the great concern of Jesus for the healing of the sick, the blind, the deformed, shows His estimate of the worth of bodily health. In James the healing of the sick is set forth as one of the functions of the Church. In his teaching Paul clearly shows the close interrelation of a wholesome physical organism with cleanness of spirit. In 1 Corinthians 6 he teaches that it is against the dignity of the body to use it for fornication. "Know ye not that your bodies are the members of Christ? shall I then take the members of Christ, and make them the members of an harlot? God forbid" (v. 15). Paul climaxes his argument for the sanctity of the body by reminding his readers that the body not only belongs to God by right of redemption, but it is the veritable temple of the Holy Spirit (vv. 19-20).

There is no case to be made from the teaching of Paul for the abject humiliation of the physical organism, as practiced by the ascetics in the Church.[4] Paul's emphasis is on discipline, wholesomeness, cleanness. Paul brings his body into subjection (1 Cor. 9:27), for it is Christian to be master of one's body and not mastered by it. Self-control is part of the fruit of the Spirit. But Paul would readily reject the notion that a deliberately abused, effeminate, emaciated body is honoring to God. He forcefully warns the Colossians against the ascetic practices which had crept into the church, including the neglect of the body. These practices had a show of wisdom, he admits, but they are actually not to be held in honor (Col. 2:18-23).

B. Recreational Values

Recreation as a genuine value grows out of the basic human need for

---

3. Baab, *Theology of the Old Testament*, p. 221.

4. George Barker Stevens, *The Theology of the New Testament* (New York: Charles Scribner's Sons, 1936), pp. 347 ff.

change and release from physical and mental tension. Proper recreation is the kind that re-creates. Some may find it in various artistic hobbies such as painting, weaving. Others find it in the pleasures associated with the outdoors, such as fishing, hiking, boating. To others, the best form of recreation is reading, writing, listening to music. Whatever the form of recreation, its value lies in its ability to relax the mind and body.

There is a "law of diminishing returns" which operates in regard to recreation. At the point where it lessens one's enthusiasm for his major task, or where it enervates rather than invigorates, it ceases to qualify as a genuine value.[5] It is not possible to say what constitutes proper recreation for every individual. Specific rules are inadequate. The principles and norms of Christian living must constitute the criteria. Discriminating good sense in the light of other Christian values is the best guide to wholesome recreation.

C. Familial Values

One of the glories of the Christian faith is the home. Next to the grace of God itself, the Christian home is the most important influence in the life of a person. The Bible, human experience, and the findings of sociology, all unite in saying that the home is the foundation of our social structure.

No other value can qualify so readily as a genuine value. The very first family unit was directly organized by God and received His special blessing. Father, mother, and child constitute the most beautiful social synthesis in human existence.

The value of the home is shown by the following characteristics:

First, it is in the home that the child discovers the meaning of love. Through the creative wonder of being loved, the child responds with love for his parents and family. He soon learns that love is the cord which binds together his whole family world, through joy or sorrow, health or pain. Love "is the bond of perfectness" (Col. 3:14), and it covers "the multitude of sins" (1 Pet. 4:8). By loving and being loved at home, the child is ready to respond to the love of others beyond his own environment and, above all, to the love of his Heavenly Father.

---

5. The well-known advice of Mrs. Susanna Wesley to her son John comes to mind. See John Whitehead, *The Life of the Rev. John Wesley, M. A.* (New York: The United States Book Company, n.d.), p. 222.

Second, in the Christian home the child first hears about God. The honoring of God by prayer, and the giving of thanks, become the natural pattern in the life of the child. His tenderest years and earliest memories are permeated with the feeling of God's care and concern. There is no more potent factor in value building than this early religious training. Better late than never, but parents who do not begin the religious training of their children until they are of school age have lost the most formative years of a young child's life. The damage is probably irreparable.

Third, it is in the home that children first learn the meaning of cooperation and democracy. The child soon discovers that there are others in the house and that he cannot always have his own way when he want it. He learns to acknowledge the rights of others and to sacrifice his own desires for the general welfare of the whole. The happy home is one where each has his rightful place, but where all work together to make the family a well-knit unit. A family that works, plays, eats, and worships together is a masterpiece of Christian social structure.

Fourth, in the home the child first learns the meaning of authority. Respect for parents is the first step in teaching respect for God. Training, discipline, correction are among the basic ingredients for the development of respect. Home as a genuine value is impossible without them.

Fifth, the home is the key to the continuity of the values which constitute the moral fabric of our social structure. The Hebrews provided for the perpetuation of their religious structure through the device of family participation in major religous rituals. The children, in turn, had to teach the rituals and laws to their children, thus assuring perpetuity (Exod. 12:14, 26-27; Deut. 6:6-7; 31:12-13). The remarkable vitality and unity of the Hebrew religion after these thousands of years testify to the wisdom of their family-centered religious training.

In our present American society the best guarantee of the growth and perpetuation of loyalty, democracy, respect for God and country, education, church, and home itself, is that these values be honored and taught in the home.

D. Educational Values

Education is the process of discipline through training and study in the acquisition of skills and knowledge. It also implies a certain level of attainment in such skill or knowledge. For instance, a young person in college is in the disciplinary process of education, but after rigorous training and learning he may be said to *have* an education. Of course, education, regardless of achievement, should continue to be a process until one dies.

Two major reasons justify the selection of education as a genuine Christian value:

First, the presence of normal capacities in the human personality is an implied divine command. Each person is obligated to develop his normal capacities to the greatest extent of their usefulness. Education, whether under official auspices or private instigation, is the fulfilling of the intellectual capacities which God has given. Of course not every person will have the same ability, and the development of the intellect or skills must be related to other values and responsibilities. Education is probably not the highest value per se, but like seasoning in food, it is one of those disciplines that bring out the flavor in the other values.

Second, education when seen in a religious perspective is, in a very real sense, the understanding of God's creation. Nature is one of the divine textbooks through which we learn how God acts. "The heavens declare the glory of God: and the firmanent sheweth his handywork" (Ps. 19:1). The study of physics may at first glance seem far removed from religion. But it depends upon one's total view of the universe whether physics is secular or religious. As a means to the understanding of God's laws and methods of operation, the sciences are almost sacramental. This was the thought of Paul when he said that "the invisible things of him from the creation of the world are clearly seen, being understood by the things that are made, even his eternal power and Godhead" (Rom. 1:20).

Besides the two broad reasons for education, i.e., the development of oneself and the understanding of the world, other indications of the axiological status of education come to mind. They are inseparably intrinsic and functional. First, education gives deep personal satisfaction. It is sheer joy to learn about the wonder of human personality and to discover through literature, history, and art the tremendous powers and expressions of human creativity. Appreciation of one's world is predicated upon knowledge. The ability to appreciate truth as truth is a demanding but profoundly satisfying experience. Again, knowledge of ourselves and the world broadens the perspective in which one must relate his facts. Different interpretations of the same set of facts may be due to lack of perspective on one or all sides of the problem. On the other hand, knowledge enables one to view a problem or fact in a more coherent and tolerant manner. Lack of knowledge is one of the basic ingredients in prejudice and fanaticism. Finally, education is a key to responsible citizenship. Without the knowledge of one's heritage—political, cultural, religious—no one, least of all a Christian, can take a significant place in the planning and development of his community or state.

E. Vocational Values

These represent the values associated with one's regular occupation or employment, whether it be manual labor or a profession. Vocation as a value applies whether one is a bricklayer or a lawyer. Whatever the type of employment by which a person earns his living, work is, and should be, more than a mere matter of trading labor and time for money. In our society, if a man is to take his place as a citizen, have a home, raise a family, he must consider the remunerative aspect of his work. But there is something very pathetic, if not tragic, in the picture of a man in a job or profession where his labor is purely instrumental. The tragedy is deeper if the man, by force of circumstances, has to work under conditions which create an aversion to his daily task. Under such conditions, where work is debased to common drudgery, it is difficult to find any Christian dimension. Such work is certainly not an intrinsic value.

Work becomes a genuine, or Christian, value when it provides opportunity for creativity.[6] The need to create is rooted deep in the nature of man. Made in the image of his Creator, man expresses the natural likeness when he is creative. In many persons, the urge to create amounts almost to a frenzy. The great artists are the best examples of this tremendous creative urge; for instance, Mozart in music, Van Gogh in painting. These are extreme types, but in every normal person there are the desire and the *need* for creative expression.

For most people, the medium for "making a contribution" is their vocations, because here is where they exert most of their energy and spend at least half or more of their waking time. For one whose calling is some aspect of Christian work, there is particular joy in being a laborer together with God in helping to build His kingdom; but every honest profession may also qualify as contributory to the

---

6. Dorothy Sayers has some valuable insights on the Christian meaning of work in *The Mind of the Maker* (London: Methuen and Co., Ltd., 1941), pp. 177-84.

increase of the thoroughly Christian values of law and order, beauty, health, education, in our society. Labor, as seen from the divine perspective, is not a secular enterprise. "Six days shalt thou labour" is as much a command of the Lord as "remember the sabbath day." Both parts of the commandment have their ground in God. To call one secular and the other religious is to make a false cleavage in one's obligation to God.

One great contribution of the Reformation was the view that work is essentially a religious enterprise, demanding honesty, loyalty, and thrift.[7] These are old-fashioned virtues in the modern world; but a rebirth of the sense of divine vocation, whether tilling the soil or running a business, would go far to restore the worker to the dignity which he should possess as a creature not only made in the image of God but also His co-worker. Certainly work is not a curse upon man. It is true that the presence of evil has made it more difficult to extract one's livelihood from nature. Man eats bread by the sweat of his face. But work did not begin with the sin of Adam and Eve. Before any sin is recorded, God told man to "replenish the earth, and subdue it" (Gen. 1:28). He put man in the Garden with the order "to dress it and to keep it" (Gen. 2:15). Eden is not the absence of physical exertion. In fact it appears that God deliberately left an unfinished task in order that Adam and Eve might have immediate opportunity to express themselves creatively as literal co-workers with God.

Work becomes a genuine value, (1) when it provides opportunity for creativity, (2) when it is a source of joy *in itself* apart from its means as an economic end, and (3) when it is of such a nature that it upholds the dignity of man as a person made in the image of God. Without these elements, work is reduced to its lowest status as a mere instrumental value.

F. Aesthetic Values

The writer of Ecclesiastes said that God "hath made every thing beautiful in his time" (Eccles. 3:11). Aesthetics is the philosophy of the beautiful, together with its standards and its psychological implications.[8] It is a tremendously large field, in both subject matter and

---

7. Some would even trace the rise of modern capitalism to the Reformation impulse of thrift and good management. See, e.g., Tawney, *Religion and the Rise of Capitalism,* "Mentor," No. 22.

8. For an introduction to the field of aesthetics, see DeWitt H. Parker, *The Principles of Aesthetics* (New York: Appleton-Century-Crofts, Inc., 1920).

significance. Its primary data come from the arts, but it includes all areas of beauty. If God is the basic source of beauty, then aesthetics is a genuine value. Where it fits into a hierarchy of values is impossible to say. It is much easier and more nearly correct to think of it, not as one value among others, but as a dimension or quality of all values. Some of the characteristics of beauty are unity, harmony, proportion, balance, symmetry. Every value, whether moral, intellectual, or recreational, is more nearly the value it ought to be when it possesses harmony and proportion. It is ever a question whether there can be a genuine value without beauty. Morality without beauty is fearful. Truth without beauty is cold. Beauty gives to truth and morality the infectious quality without which they are unattractive and forbidding.

Religion and aesthetics come most fruitfully together in art.[9] Each has brought vitality and richness to the other. The saying that "religion is the mother of the arts" finds constant support, not only in the archaeological evidence that the oldest artifacts are religious in character, but in the continued productivity of religion as a source. Probably the greatest single impulse ever given to artistic vision and expression, in the West at least, was the birth of Christianity. Omit from art Bible themes and Christian motifs and the great art of the Western world is totally impoverished. On the other hand, not only has art brought to Christianity warmth and richness, but it has become a positive ally in seeking to set forth ideals, arouse moral endeavor, and find solutions to the problems of evil and ugliness. When the Puritans deliberately smashed the stained-glass windows of the great English churches, they were acting under the grossly misguided notion that Christianity and beauty are incompatible. Paradoxically, the Puritan desire for sheer simplicity has produced one of the most appealing of architectural forms in the beautiful, white New England churches.

In the Bible, the aesthetic and the holy are united in the religion and ceremonies of the Hebrews.[10] The ceremonial and dietary practices of the Hebrews were demonstrations in symbol of the inseparability of holiness and beauty. Religion for them, from the con-

---

9. For a significant discussion with special reference to a great work of art, see F. David Martin, "The Beautiful as Symbolic of the Holy," *Christian Scholar*, June, 1958, 125-33.

10. The concept of the aesthetic as the key to the Hebrew ceremonial and dietary practices is suggested by Davidson, *Theology of the Old Testament*, pp. 157 ff.

gregational worship associated with the highly colored Tabernacle to the most minute personal regulation, was a continuous exercise in aesthetic discrimination. The Levitical code is aesthetic from beginning to end. The garments of the high priest and the dietary laws illustrate the aesthetico-holy relationship. In Exodus 28, God gives the specifications for the garments of the priests. Holiness and beauty are associated in the very first command given to Moses regarding Aaron's attire: "And thou shalt make holy garments for Aaron thy brother for glory and for beauty" (Exod. 28:2). The remaining description of Aaron's garments throughout the chapter is an aesthetic masterpiece.

The division of animals and other living creatures into clean and unclean is certainly not an arbitrary classification. Actually some of the creatures listed as "unclean" are not necessarily "dirty." But the lists of forbidden animals and birds have one thing in common: they are aesthetically revolting. It seems possible that aesthetic aversion is the edibility criterion which in turn becomes the basis for classification into the holy and unholy. This interpretation seems clear from the passage in Lev. 11:43-47.

Beauty and holiness are united in the admonition to "worship the Lord in the beauty of holiness" (Ps. 29:2). David expresses the desire to "behold the beauty of the Lord, and to inquire in his temple" (Ps. 27:4). In the New Testament, among the things that Paul urges his readers to think upon are "whatsoever things are lovely" (Phil. 4:8). The word for lovely is *prosphiles*, "pleasing, acceptable." Moffatt translates the phrase "whatever is attractive."

The aesthetic is the attractive quality which should permeate all other values. Beauty is a value with God-worth. The Christian attitude toward beauty is by no means a mere matter of sophisticated appreciation of art, music, or drama. A person might be a thorough Christian and never know the difference between Bach and Brahms. But it by no means follows that the ignorance is a virtue, or that the knowledge is somehow incompatible with Christian faith. Art, whether visual, auditory, or plastic, is one of God's great gifts to man. A great human artist in his creative role is demonstrating his natural likeness to God. In the appreciation of beauty one is demonstrating his ability to respond to the aesthetic nature of God. Art is both an expression of the creative beauty in the soul and a pathway to the soul.

At the end of the *Phaedrus*, Socrates prays: "Give me beauty in the inward soul; and may the outward and inward man be at one."

The heart cry of Moses, "the man of God," is, "Let the beauty of the Lord our God be upon us" (Ps. 90:17). In the answer to that prayer is fulfilled the ultimate meaning and end of aesthetics as a Christian value.

SUMMARY

In brief summary, Christian axiology deals with the values which constitute the ideals and content of Christian living. The standard of values is found in the Scriptures as implied in the concept of worth. A genuine value is one which has God-worth. While most values are common to all people, the Christian faith transforms all human values. The ideal of the Christian faith and the ideal human values should be in harmony.

CHAPTER 27

Personal Christian Ethics

Judged by its roots as well as by its fruits, personal Christian ethics is older than the New Testament itself. Springing from an immediate relationship between Jesus and His followers, the stream of Christian moral life was well on its way before the earliest of the New Testament writings began. Its novelty, which is equivalent to a totally new way of life, stems from the spirituality of its virtues, the inclusiveness of its standards, the dependability of its dynamic, and the ultimate nature of its ideals. It provides a completely new look into the world of personal morality. It describes a type of moral character unknown to naturalistic or speculative ethics.

But Christian ethics involved more than a break with the intellectuality of the day. It marked a distinct departure from its religious emphasis as well. Its certainties replaced the guesswork of the Greek schools; its spirit of love transcended the rigidities of the Jewish law. An excellent summary of this point has been given by R. A. Tsanoff in *The Moral Ideals of Our Civilization:*

> The Christian gospel produced a spiritual reorientation of ancient ways and ideals. For the rigidity of law it substituted the life of the spirit; it scorned the cautious wisdom of the sage to bless the trusting faith of a child; from the beauty of flesh it turned to the beauty of holiness; it regarded man as the prodigal son and a lost sheep, lost but for the grace of the Divine Shepherd. This life and this world were to it but the threshold and doormat to the mansions of the hereafter. The startling gospel gripped the downtrodden Jew and stirred to fresh spiritual life the world of classical antiquity. Christianity offered salvation and peace to the

heavy laden; it guaranteed the certainties of faith to the disenchanted pagan intellect.[1]

I. The Forerunners of Christian Ethics

This does not mean, however, that the two systems, speculative and revealed ethics, exist in isolation from each other. Their compartments are neither watertight nor windowless. To say that the Christian ethic is different from the non-Christian is not to say that it is entirely or "wholly" other. The same human factors—reason, emotion, conscience, and volition—function in both. But in natural ethics these elements are the last word while in Christian ethics they are only the first. The finality in Epicurean ethics, for instance, was feeling; in Platonic, intelligence; in Aristotelian, will; in Kantian, conscience. But while in such systems these components, either singly or jointly, constituted the whole cloth of moral raiment, in the Christian system they comprise but the warp of that raiment, needing to be shot through and through with the cross-threads of revealed truth, spiritual purposes, and divine love.

We are brought therefore to this distinction, that while natural ethics implies an attainment, supernatural or religious ethics requires both an attainment and an obtainment. The former, or moral character on the human level, crowns both the educational and the sociological task of mankind; being the best that man can do, it is the highest for which one can hope. But moral character raised to the Christian level crowns the primary task of both the Church and her Lord; it is the highest achievement that God and man can effect.

The distinction here noted springs from that added area of consciousness which we know as Christian experience. This in turn issues from a vital contact of the human with the divine, described by some as "encounter," or an "I-Thou" relationship between God and man. Expressed in scriptural and more familiar terms, this experience is identified as "the washing of regeneration and renewing by the Holy Spirit" (Titus 3:5, NASB). Christian personal ethics as a science therefore can be nothing less than the systematic investigation of the character and conduct of the truly regenerate individual who is constantly renewed, indwelt, empowered, and guided by the Holy Spirit. In Christian ethics we must look, not to reason, but to revelation, for our sources; not to the schools, but to the Scriptures,

---

1. (New York: E. P. Dutton and Co., Inc., 1942), p. 35.

for our principles; and to the Church, not to the world, for our examples.

Christian ethics presupposes the moral nature as written in the constitution of man. Hebrew and Christian writers alike have found in conscience the most dependable clue to the once perfect but now fallen and distorted *Imago Dei*—the image of God in man. And upon this natural capacity for making ethical or qualitative judgments rest the theoretical structures of all the great ethical systems of the past. And since many of these had arisen—and even fallen—before the Christian era began, the source from which they sprang was necessarily in operation before the Christian ethic began. Historically as well as psychologically, the natural in ethics has been prior to the spiritual.

But this antecedence in time does not imply a logical precedence of naturalistic ethics to the Christian system. Primitive reflection on moral problems was really not a systematic ethics at all. No system of principles was worked out. Assumptions such as naturalistic ethics makes—for instance, that man is an animal, right is relative, nature is ultimate or God nonexistent—came as a much later development.

But simple and unsystematic as early ethics may have been, it was not even necessarily naturalistic in its naivete. Earliest Greek and Roman thought, to say nothing of Egyptian and Babylonian, was essentially "theological," with "gods many, and lords many" (1 Cor. 8:5) supplying the motif. More significantly than this, the Hebrew ethic had functioned effectively for more than 500 years before "naturalism" really began, whether the elementary naturalism of the Cyrenaics or the more systematic brand of the Epicureans and the Stoics. And Jewish ethics, both of Moses and of the prophets, was persistently nonnaturalistics. For the Hebrews, man was more than an animal; he was a rational self, a soul created in, though fallen from, the moral likeness of God. Nature, too, was not a self-sufficient system, in either origin or operation, but rather the immediate handiwork of God and sustained by His perpetual care. And as for God himself, He was the eternal, self-sufficient One, whose will, expressive of His nature, was determinative in the whole field of moral activity.

This really gives us two antecedents to the Christian ethic, a natural and a supernatural point of view. The one assumes that moral values can be justified on natural grounds, without recourse to any supernatural sanctions; the other asserts that true value is ultimately from God and can be fully known only in harmony with the Divine. The former makes the present world the terminus of value, while the latter projects the moral life with its rewards or punishments into the life to come. What Christian ethics does with both these viewpoints, correcting and enriching the one and illuminating and fulfilling the other, will be seen in the further exposition of the Christian system.

II. THE NATURE OF CONSCIENCE

Conscience as a phase of human intelligence must be distinguished both by *what* it knows and by *how* it knows. This uniqueness is discoverable in its basic etymology as well as in its cutomary usages. Derived immediately from the Latin *conscientia*, it combines the preposition *con*, "together," with the noun *scientia*, "science" or "knowledge." Stemming ultimately from the Greek term *suneidesis*, it involves the preposition *sun*, "along with," and the noun *eidesis*, "knowledge" or "intelligence." As this noun in turn is rooted in the verb *eido*, "to see," "to behold," it was used to express knowledge as based upon sight or immediate perception. The manner of its knowing is thus instinctive or intuitive, and not discursive or deductive.

More significant than this, however, is the content of its knowledge, or what the conscience knows. It is concerned, not with facts, as historical events, but with acts as moral performances. It "sees" these acts in a new light, beholds them in a different perspective. Through its eyes they have a new meaning; in its appraisal they possess a new quality. And it is precisely this quality which, in a moral universe, makes men's actions significantly different.

A. Interpretations of Conscience

The "together" aspect of moral knowledge needs yet to be noted. It is knowledge "along with another," whoever that other may be. In the history of its uses, three interpretations are possible: first, it is knowledge "along with" another form of knowledge or state of consciousness; second, it is knowledge "along with" another knower or group of knowers or persons; third, it is knowledge "along with" the Supreme Knower, or God.

Aligning it with another form of consciousness, the first of these indicates that conscience is a specialized awareness of consciousness itself. It thus identifies the person as good or bad, true or false, pure or unholy. In so doing it uses no uncertain language. Its voice is as unmistakable as its dictates are imperative. As a sort of second person speaking to the first person, it carries on a dialectical process within the same individual. Raising questions, challenging motives, and passing judgments, it speaks for a higher tribunal than human juries, and intimates a justice after death "according to the deeds done in the body."

In the second instance of "knowing together with," we see conscience, not so much in its personal as in its social setting. It is now viewed both as something less than the "voice of God" and something more than the voice of the individual. It is the voice of society itself. Here the empirical theory of its origin takes over, and attributes the sum total of its inspirations, inhibitions, and prohibitions to the accumulated moral heritage of the race. According to this view all moral sentiments are products of racial or individual experience. Supplementing and enforcing the inheritance from the past is the complex of social attitudes and customs in the present. Accordingly man builds up a conscience which is really a reflection of the social consciousness in matters of right and wrong. And this is but to say that in his conscience he has knowledge "along with" society as a whole.

In the third way of interpreting conscience as "knowing together with another," the human is blended with the divine. Conscience is neither the intuition of the individual nor the echo of the social consciousness, but "the voice of God." Early in the history of the Church, Chrysostom (345-407) identified "Conscience and Nature as two books in which the human mind can read of God previous to supernatural revelation." Cardinal Newman of the Roman Catholic faith stated: "Conscience is the aboriginal vicar of Christ, a prophet in its informations, a monarch in its preemptoriness, a priest in its blessings and anathemas." This view, with varying modifications, has generally characterized the teaching of theological ethics. Speaking of this point of view, Tsanoff in his *Ethics* states:

> The earliest answer to these questions is that of theological tradition. It regards conscience as the voice of God in our souls, a divinely implanted conviction of right and wrong. If we obey this voice of God we do right; if we disobey, we sin. God has made the inherent rightness of his law evident to our better judgment. Were it not for the corruption of our will by sin, we should never have any uncertainty regarding the voice of conscience or any hesitation about obeying its behests.[2]

---

2. Revised Edition (New York: Harper and Brothers, 1955), p. 165.

B. The Unity Underlying These Views

The solution of the problem involved in these divergent views seems at first to be impossible. No two of them can be reconciled either with one another or with the third. And since they are three in number, one can neither apply the principle of either/or nor the Aristotelian solution of finding the golden mean between two extremes.

A second look, however, will show that their number simplifies the problem rather than complicates it, since it points to the complexity of the content of our moral intelligence. This, in turn, shows the resemblance between it and our knowledge in general, which is also seen in the use of the word *scientia,* common to both.

Just how, then, is our common store of knowledge built up? By no simple means, since some of it comes from reason, some from experience, some from authorities, and some from intuition or immediate insight. Its sources are many; but once it becomes knowledge, its validity is the same and its services equally valuable.

The case with moral intelligence is identical. Its sources are varied and its content is composite. Experience, reason, intuition, authority, and revelation all contribute their quota to that fund of ethical insights or guiding principles by which we must fashion character and work out our moral destiny. This makes conscience a growing concern, keeping step with both our own psychological development, the enlarging experience of the race, and the specific revelations of God. The conscience which is a valid guide for us all works "together with" our own clear personal convictions of the right, "together with" the moral intuitions of humanity at large, and preeminently "together with" God in the varied disclosures of His will.

C. Conscience and the Christian Life

This brings us to the point which is most determinative in the personal ethics of the Christian. It is the relation of the will of God to our own individual conduct, the sources of our knowledge of that will, and the means by which it becomes effective in our lives. As to sources, three general forms of revelation have always been recognized by the Christian Church: the Holy Scriptures, the Incarnate Word, and the Holy Spirit. Supplemented continuously by these three fountains of truth, the Christian's conscience will be corrected where in error, regulated where too slow or too fast, enlightened where still uninformed, and sensitized where too apathetic or indifferent.

III. The Scriptures and Conscience

Since man's first duty is to know his duty, his obligation to "search the scriptures" is unavoidable. As ignorance of the law excuses no man before a human court, so ignorance of the will of God, when made accessible in His word, exonerates no man before a divine tribunal.

But how do the Scriptures view conscience itself? Significantly the New Testament alone makes use of the term, while its correlative, the "heart," or "the reins" (KJV), was commonly used in the Old. At any rate, the term *suneidesis* occurs some 32 times in the New Testament and most frequently of all in the Epistles of Paul.

According to the New Testament as a whole, it is interesting to note that conscience does actually perform the function of a kind of "second person" within the individual. Acting in this role it "convicts" (John 8:9), approves (Acts 23:1), "bears witness" (Rom. 2:15), "accuses" (1 Cor. 8:7), reacts to "wounds" (1 Cor. 8:12), offers testimony which rejoices the heart (2 Cor. 1:12), coincides with the voice of the Holy Spirit (Rom. 9:1), and makes bold to answer before God (1 Pet. 3:21). Whether as legislator, judge, or executor, conscience is thus accorded a regal position, second only in authority to that of the Moral Ruler himself.

But the Scriptures do more than describe conscience; they prescribe for it by relating it to themselves. This they do by presenting the divine will in both the Old and New Testaments. This has been called by Carl F. H. Henry, the "biblical particularization of moral life" where found in the Old Testament, and "biblical particularization of will of God" as found in the New.

Assuming, as he rightfully does, that only in Scripture can "the content of the moral life" be finally determined, Henry points out that the law as given to Moses at Sinai contains the heart of Old Testament ethics. He states clearly:

> The Ten Words enunciated on Sinai contain the essential principles of a righteousness that truly mirrors the pure character of a holy God. Their explicit definition of man's religious and moral duty unveiled with one bold stroke the holy nature and purpose of the living God and amorality of permanent universal obligation. They stand apart from all temporal injunctions in the scriptural revelation; they are valid for all men in all places and at all times.[3]

---

3. *Personal Christian Ethics* (Grand Rapids: Wm. B. Eerdmans Publishing Co., 1957), p. 269.

At the same time he recognizes the principle of progression in that revelation as well as "the distinction between interminable and limited obligation" in the content of the Mosaic legislation. The different insights given to the patriarchs, to Moses, to the psalmists, and to the prophets indicate its progressive character, while the priestly ordinances and ceremonial formulas indicated the temporary or transient. For the devoted Israelite, even these, however, were matters of tremendous import to conscience, for they were connected at once with the will of God for His people in their particular situation.

In the New Testament the divine will is "particularized" notably in the Sermon on the Mount and in the Epistles. In this "Sermon," Jesus did not break with the law, but rather amplified it by "unveiling its inner requirements."[4] Henry then proceeds to show the relation of the commandments to New Testament principles, making it plain always that Jesus came not "to destroy, but to fulfil." A few of his self-explanatory statements may be quoted:

1. Jesus gives the inner meaning of the commandments. Hence if the Sermon is irrelevant as commandment, so is the Old Testament law.

2. Jesus understood the law to be the will of God in propositional form. He so interpreted it in the Sermon.

3. What he criticizes is not the Law itself, but contemporary formulations of the Law.

4. The Sermon has for its intention the same as the Torah did: that it be fulfilled.

5. The Sermon is the final and deepest statement of the Law.

6. The Sermon presents Christ in the role of moral legislator.

7. The Sermon is a guide in the immediate "one-and-one" neighbor relationships of life.

8. The Sermon remains an "ethical directory" for Christians. It is the ultimate formula of ethics for which ideal human nature was fashioned by creation and is destined in eternity. Fallen nature is justified in Christ in conformity to it, and redeemed nature approximates it by the power of the indwelling Spirit of God.[5]

This "moral Gospel of Jesus," as Tsanoff calls it, is consequently the consummation of Old Testament righteousness and the beginning of New Testament grace. As such it is central and supreme for both personal and social ethics and the enlightenment of Christian conscience.

---

4. *Ibid.,* p. 307.

5. *Ibid.,* pp. 299, 306, 308, 316, 320, 325-26.

IV. THE INCLUSIVENESS OF CHRISTIAN ETHICS

In the history of natural ethics, each system or school which has appeared has taken its cue from some one central aim, standard, or purpose in life. Thus we have such types of ethics as the following. (1) Happiness Ethics, the view which makes well-being and happiness the ultimate end of duty; (2) Perfection Ethics, which teaches that virtue consists in seeking personal excellence, full self-realization, and a certain perfection of character and conduct; (3) Motivity Ethics, the theories that make the regulation of one's motives by conscience, reason, or love the all-comprehensive requirement of the law; (4) Authority Ethics, the view that obedience to the will of a superior enforced by law or habit is the foundation of morality; (5) Duty Ethics, the theory that the aim of true morality is to realize the right by the performance of one's duty.[6]

In answering or attempting to answer the age-old question, What is the supreme end of man's mortal life? each of these theories has left some points along the route to the *summum bonum,* man's highest good. Each has thus contributed some note of truth to the whole of ethical thought. The pleasure-loving Cyrenaics with their self-indulgent slogan, "Eat, drink, and be merry, for tomorrow we die," were not completely wrong. They at least called attention to the brevity of life, and as for being "merry" when we eat, cheerfulness at mealtime is always morally finer and dietetically better than eating with a grouch. The early Christians ate "their meat with gladness and singleness of heart" (Acts 2:46).

The Cynics with their victory over Cyrenaic sensuality; the Epicureans with their refined pleasure theory; Socrates, Plato, and Aristotle with their personal perfection goals and their unforgettable quartet of philosophic virtues—Wisdom, Justice, Courage, and Temperance; the Stoics with their universal law, or reason; Utilitarianism with its aim of "the greatest good to the greatest number"—these and all the other great ethical quests of history have certain underlying principles to which the Christian, as a man, will find himself related.

Some systems, it will be seen, come much closer to Christian ethics than do others. They are more inclusive in their goals and more noble in their ideals. Reinterpreted in the light of Christian principles and invested with the Christian spirit, they may offer valuable insights for the development of personal Christian charac-

---

6. Hervin U. Roop, *Christian Ethics* (New York: Fleming H. Revell, 1926), p. 157.

ter. We have chosen three such ethical standards for the values they may offer in understanding the Christian way of life: happiness (in the higher sense of personal well-being), duty, and perfection.

A. The Christian's Right to Happiness

That we start the race of life as "little egoists" is self-evident. William James described a baby as "the completest egoist." But that we should end that race as "selfish brutes" is an outrage to all ethical sense. Consequently both natural and Christian ethics aim to modify man's selfish desires, redistribute his interests, and encourage the principle of sharing or giving along with getting. Nor is he considered by either to be normal ethically until he realizes that "both his own interests and the interests of his neighbor are natural and seemingly legitimate objects of regard."[7]

Meanwhile the desire for happiness, or personal well-being, is as justifiable as it is natural and universal. To banish all interest in the good things of life would lead, not to self-renunciation, but to self-elimination. It would necessarily banish all sense of value, and to rob a man of his values leaves him, not "a little lower than the angels," but a little lower than the beasts of the field. Christian ethics assumes that sense of values and seeks to raise it to its noblest expression.

Accordingly, biblical ethics operates on the principle that man has a right to be happy. He was not created to be miserable; neither has he been redeemed to be wretched. Generally speaking, his misery has been brought on either by his neighbors or by himself. "So God created man in his own image, in the image of God created he him" (Gen. 1:27) seems to leave little room for "melancholia," "frustration," or "inferiority complexes" in the original pair. "And God blessed them, and said unto them, Be fruitful, and multiply, and replenish the earth, and subdue it" (Gen. 1:28) is a description scarcely indicative of economic worry, introverted personality, or matrimonial maladjustment in the experience of our unfallen ancestors. And as if to stamp the principle of enjoyment as valid throughout the universe, the record concludes, "And God saw every thing that he had made, and, behold, it was very good" (Gen. 1:31). Rejoicing in the work of His hands, the Creator himself set the example for us by taking delight in the good.

The chief weakness of Happiness Ethics is that it seeks enjoy-

---

7. *Ibid.*, p. 169.

ment at too low a level. Hedonism, as it has been called, comes from a Greek term meaning physical or sensual pleasure. Hence the early Cyrenaics with their "crass egoism" often stooped to voluptuous living as man's greatest good in life. The Epicureans, with their more refined egoism, gave more importance to the pleasures of the mind, and physical pleasures as sanctioned by reason. For them as for John Stuart Mill later on, a "dissatisfied Socrates was better than a satisfied pig." Utilitarianism, the final and finest expression of the Hedonistic principle, socialized its satisfactions and made "the greatest good to the greatest number" the index of the *summum bonum.*

The Christian ethic includes all of the valid enjoyments of these partial systems, and more. It sees man as more than an animal, more than a mind, and more than a social being. It views him as an immortal spirit as well, made in the likeness of God, made for the glory of God, and made for the enjoyment of God. "Thou hast made us for Thyself," said St. Augustine, "and our hearts are restless till they rest in Thee."[8] "Happy is that people, that is in such a case:" adds the Psalmist, "yea, happy is that people, whose God is the Lord" (Ps. 144:15). The Christian, therefore, finds his highest enjoyment in spiritual blessings from above, and not in material or even social benefits from below. Seeking first "the kingdom of God, and his righteousness" (Matt. 6:33), the Christian finds a happiness beyond happiness, guaranteed to him by the word "blessed," found in each beatitude of the Kingdom for which he lives (Matt. 5:1-11).

B. The Christian's Debt to Duty

Historically considered, the Duty Ethics owes more to Immanuel Kant (1724-1807) than to any other thinker, ancient or modern. For him the standard is the entire moral law, to every part of which we must conform. We are ethical only as we are right, and we are right only as we do our duty.

Involved in this duty are three basic principles: (1) the principle of universality—"Act as if the maxim from which you act were through your will to become a universal law"; (2) the principle of humanity as an end in itself—"Act so as to use humanity, whether in your own person or in the person of another, always as an end, never as merely a means"; (3) the principle of good will—"Nothing can possibly be called good without qualification except a Good Will." A fourth principle of "autonomy" should be added, by which

---

8. *Confessions,* Book 1.

he means that "the moral laws to which man is subject are laws he imposes on himself."[9]

Influential in its history as it is lofty in its principles, this system has much in it to enlist and challenge Christian thought. Personal Christian ethics certainly considers persons as ends, not instruments: "Thou shalt love thy neighbour as thyself" (Matt. 22:39). It is certainly universal in its golden rule: "Whatsoever ye would that men should do to you, do ye even so to them" (Matt. 7:12). And as to his benevolent attitude, "With good will doing service," (Eph. 6:7) would seem to be the Christian's norm.

But Kantian ethics at best is self-determining in its content and self-imposed in its requirements. Man is not governed from without, but from within. As Titus states it further, "In obeying the sense of duty within himself, Man is not obeying an outside legislator; he is obeying a law imposed by his own reason."[10] Here Christian ethics and Kant part company. Christian ethics sees man as morally bound to principles beyond his own formulation. These derive their sanction or validity, not because they are founded in human will, but because they are grounded in a transcendent revelation and inhere in the express will of God for man. Thus while Kant "stands in awe at the starry heavens above and the moral law within," the Christian stands also "in awe of thy word" (Ps. 119:161), seeking to "serve God acceptably with reverence and godly fear" (Heb. 12:28).

C. The Christian's Call to Perfection

Personal wholeness, or completeness of being, was the quest of natural ethics centuries before Christianity began. The same Greek mind that contemplated the Good, the Beautiful, and the True considered also the goal of full self-realization as the highest attainment in personal morality. Socrates (469-399 B.C.) maintained that man is imperfect and evil because he is ignorant. The cure for both ills therefore lies in his slogan: "Knowledge is Virtue," and this, when achieved, brings personal wholeness. Plato (427-347 B.C.) finds the most perfect life in the contemplation of eternal Ideas, the patterns or concepts belonging to the world of true Being, after which our phenomenal world was fashioned. Aristotle (384-322 B.C.) in his Nicomachean Ethics joins the active with the contemplative life as man's highest

---

9. Harold H. Titus, *Ethics for Today* (New York: American Book Co., 1947), p. 145.

10. *Ibid.*

good and the path to personal perfection. This enlists the "moral virtues" (Courage, Temperance, and Justice) with the "intellectual" (Philosophic Wisdom, Intuitive Reason, Practical Wisdom, Science, and Art) in a total enterprise of self-unfoldment, the enabling of one to function as a man.

But as in the case of happiness and duty, so perfection received a new meaning when used by Christianity. To all that it had previously meant there were now added: (1) a perfection of motive, (2) a perfection of conscience, (3) and a perfection of love—on all three of which the Greeks had been strangely silent. In clearing the conscience from guilt and condemnation for sin (Heb. 9:9, 14), in implanting the one supreme motive of gratitude for redeeming love (1 John 4:19), and in perfecting God's love within our hearts (1 John 4:12), Christianity has both identified and met a need in the heart of man which naturalistic perfectionism has persistently ignored.

Identifying the content of that moral and spiritual perfection to which the Christian is called is the following statement of H. Orton Wiley:

> When Jesus in His Sermon on the Mount enjoined upon His disciples the principles of perfection, saying, *Be ye therefore perfect, even as your Father which is in heaven is perfect* (Matt. 5:48), He could have referred to nothing short of that freedom from inner contradictions which constitutes a holy being . . . The perfection He enjoins upon His disciples is not the absolute perfection of the Divine Being, but that in human personality which corresponds to the divine nature. It is the deliverance of the soul from the inner contradictions brought about by sin, or inherited depravity, and its restoration to purity of heart and simplicity of purpose. . . . Perfection in this sense is intensely ethical, in that it includes both inner holiness and outward righteousness.[11]

D. The Situational Ethic of "Love"

A further observation should be made concerning the function of "love" in the new morality or situation ethics propounded by Joseph Fletcher among others. To the casual observer, Fletcher seems to be saying that love is the be-all and end-all of ethical theory—its source, substance, and consequence. Key chapters in his 1966 *Situation Ethics* are titled as follows: "Love Only Is Always Good" (iii), "Love Is the

---

11. *Christian Theology,* 1:309.

Only Norm" (ii), "Love Justifies Its Means" (vii), "Love Decides There and Then" (viii), and "Love and Justice Are the Same" (v).[12]

It seems clear, however, that this is an oversimplification of both the problem and its solution. That love is the highest good was asserted by Christianity 1,900 years before situation ethics was conceived. But in its Christian setting, love did not detract from but rather added to and enriched all the other classical virtues: wisdom, justice, courage, and temperance.

This is but to say that love must be given its own position or "situation" among the other virtues which form the warp and woof of moral character. This is precisely what Christian ethics does. Said the New Testament writer who spoke most discerningly and eloquently of love (1 Corinthians 13), "Now the end of the commandment [law] is love out of a pure heart, and a good conscience, and a faith unfeigned" (1 Tim. 1:5). Its true locus is, therefore, a purified spiritual nature, a conscience void of offence before God and man, and a faith which "overcomes the world" (1 John 5:4). It is at this point that the lines are drawn most clearly between scriptural love and the "love" of situation ethics. In other words, love itself demands a psychological setting which is the responsible functioning of will, choice, and purpose within a prior context of divine law and civil order. If love prescribes the motive for our conduct, it is law which prescribes the purpose of our love.

Fletcher properly objects to pietism, moralism, and legalism in Christian ethics. A biblical ethic, however, advances piety without pietism, morality without moralism, and lawfulness without legalism. It stands for neither love without law which would be sentimentalism, nor for law without love which would be legalism (John 14:15, 21, 23-24; 15:10; 1 John 5:3).

V. The Dynamic of Christian Ethics

Personal Christian ethics is peculiarly an ethic backed by spiritual power. Its forces spring from more-than-human sources. The individual bent on building Christian character is not left to his own devices, but is offered an enduement of "power from on high" (Luke 24:49). And this enduement as seen at Pentecost was effected by the "baptism with the Holy Ghost" (Acts 1:5, 8).

---

12. (Philadelphia: The Westminster Press, 1966), pp. 57-145. See also Harvey Cox, ed., *The Situation Ethics Debate* (Philadelphia: The Westminster Press, 1968).

This supplementation of human resources by the divine was contingent upon an antecedent relation to Christ. It was promised, not to men generally, but to Christ's followers specifically (John 14:16-17). It presupposed a type of moral character already made clean through Christ's word (John 15:3), and not of the world even as He was not of the world in its origin (John 17:16). United to Christ by faith and obedience, the disciples already shared His life as the branches share the life of the vine (John 15:1-5).

But even so, the Christian character of the disciples was not fully established. They were unsteady, vacillating, and unsure. They needed the stabilizing power of the Divine Spirit, "a power not of themselves which worked for righteousness." As to this ethical importance of the Spirit, both in the individual and the Church, Dr. Henry has well observed:

> It is apparent both from the teaching of Jesus before the events of Pentecost and from the apostles who passed through them that the New Testament inaugurates at once a new advance of the Kingdom of God and the new ethical era of the Holy Spirit. Jesus spoke of an impending signal gift or impartation of the Holy Spirit in conjunction with his own glorification (Jn. 7:38). Then he added that he would send the Comforter to "abide forever" with his followers, and to do so not merely by dwelling "with" but by dwelling "in" them (Jn. 14:16). His own presence would abide in his followers in and through that relationship (Jn. 14:18). In the post-resurrection appearances he instructed the apostles to remain in Jerusalem until they had received "the promise of the Father," or the gift of the Holy Spirit (Acts 1:4).[13]

The ethical dynamic of the individual and the Church is thus clearly identified as the Holy Spirit. Consistent with this, Wesleyan theology attributes the perfection of Christian character to that "sanctification of the Spirit and belief of the truth" (2 Thess. 2:13) which always presupposes the same Spirit as the one indispensable dynamic of the moral life.

VI. THE FINALITY OF CHRISTIAN ETHICS

The fourth arresting antithesis between speculative and Christian ethics is the finality of its ideals. These must be distinguished from its norms or standards. Norms are prescriptions, ideals are inspirations; norms are determinate, ideals are limitless; norms are characterized

---

13. *Personal Christian Ethics*, p. 447.

by their fixity, ideals are identified by their dynamic character; norms are to be kept, ideals are to be attained.

All the great ideal systems of ethics or philosophy have been marked by "the mind's involuntary protest against the present." To them the actual was only a fragment of the possible, and the real but a passing shadow of the ideal. And in the sense of final fulfillment in the present order, this is true of Christianity as well.

But in the certification of those ideals there is a difference. Some are warranted and some are not. Some deserve to live and others deserve to die. Consequently one view challenges the credentials of another view, only to be counter-challenged in return. System rises against system, such as Naturalism against Idealism, and often there is trouble in the same family.

But in the history of the world's thought the ideals of Christian ethics stand supreme. This is because they are more than a system of human thought. They are the expression of a Life which embodied all the divine ideals for man. And these ideals are ultimate; above them or beyond them the thinking of man cannot go.

Jesus did something unique in the history of ethics: He enunciated a perfect system and authenticated it with His life. Other leaders have invariably failed either to live as well as they preached or preach as well as they lived. But Jesus did both. "The magnificent feature of Jesus Christ," writes Carl Henry, "is that he not only proclaimed a superlative ethic, but he lived it out to the full. His pure walk is the wonder of our world of mixed motives and deeds. Alongside him even the best of men must confess unholiness. Here the moral life is unveiled with no discordant note, with nothing that is less than ethically superlative."[14]

The "ethics of Jesus" was therefore more than a "body of teaching" to be recovered after loss by a more critical reexamination of the documents. It was an organic unity, a perfect blend of spirit, teaching, and doing, a complete way of life which can be recovered only by discovering the One who lived it.

Indicative of this new way of life are several commanding principles, or emphases, which interpenetrate both His teaching and the teaching of the entire New Testament. They constitute the focal centers around which personal Christian ethics revolves. Beach and Niebuhr call them "ethical motifs," habits of life that show forth in

---

14. *Ibid.,* p. 399.

the man who would call himself a Christian.[15] These authors distinguish four:

1. The principle of a practical faith—"single-minded belief in the true God."

2. The principle of an "un-self-centered love, unqualified concern for the well-being of the neighbor."

3. The principle of humility—"the fruit of *agape,* or love."

4. The principle of personal purity: "Blessed are the pure in heart: for they shall see God" (Matt. 5:8).

In addition to these a fifth should be added, namely, the principle of autonomy, or inwardness of control. This is stressed by Roop in his *Christian Ethics* as follows: "The whole aim of Jesus is to reach the autonomous moral center of men." The cultivation of this inner moral mastery of life is the goal of His teaching. The ethical life must unfold from within. We can understand personality only from within. "The Kingdom of Heaven is within men—it must root and grow from within, not from without."[16]

SUMMARY

In the light of these principles one can recognize the broad outlines of his responsibility to both God, his fellowman, and himself. In his obedient faith toward God he will demonstrate his faithfulness to God and thus meet all the requirements of "theistic ethics," however particularized these may be. In his love for mankind as well as for himself, as the property of God, he will endeavor to fulfill every claim of "social" and "individual" ethics whether in the family, the school, the church, or the state. In his purity of heart and life he will endeavor to be an example for others, and thus glorify his "Father which is in heaven." And in mastering the principle of autonomy, establishing a kingdom of order and peace within, conquering the whole inner world of man's life, with all of its unbelief, ignorance, prejudice, bitterness, waywardness, and sin, he will have solved, in terms of personal Christian ethics, the most crucial problem of our day. We turn next to the area of social ethics in exploring our Christian faith.

---

15. Waldo Beach and Reinhold Niebuhr, editors, *Christian Ethics* (New York: Ronald Press Co., 1955), p. 52.

16. Pp. 248-57.

CHAPTER 28

Christian
Social Ethics

In Christian social ethics a new dimension has been opened up in the field of practical or applied theology. It is the dimension of "breadth" as contrasted with the dimension of "depth," emphasized in the writings of Paul Tillich. Around these two concepts with their theological implications revolves much of the religious and ethical thought of the past half century. Referring to the latter, Tillich speaks of "depth" as "the lost dimension in religion," entailing the disappearance of any "infinite concern" over life and its meanings. "This," he states, "is the decisive element in the predicament of Western man in our period."[1] Concerning the former, the proponents of the "social gospel" have alerted the Church to its loss of concern for society at large and its censurable indifference to the affairs of the world in general. The recovery of the "horizontal" rather than the "vertical" dimension in religion has been therefore the absorbing quest of social religion during the contemporary period.

I. CHRISTIAN SOCIAL CONCERN

The causes back of the revival of the social gospel were the extreme individualism of the Protestant movement and the indifference of the churches to deplorable social conditions. Added to the age-old evils of society, new problems had been created by the industrial revolution of the 19th century. These arose from its large-scale pro-

---

1. "The Lost Dimension in Religion," *Saturday Evening Post* (June 14, 1958).

duction, the concentration of wealth, rapid urbanization, intolerable factory conditions, and the division of society into the capitalistic and working classes. With these realistic evils, theoretical Christianity seemed powerless to cope. In consequence of this, a new interpretation of religion with specific social applications was demanded by aggressive groups within the Church.

Based upon the messages of the prophets and the social teachings of Jesus, these new versions of Christianity were expected both to purge society of its growing evils and also pave the way for the establishment of the kingdom of God on earth. Springing up in various sections of Christendom, the social gospel movement eventually became widely diversified with varying theological, denominational, social, and political emphases. Spreading so widely, it spread too thinly and thus gained "breadth" at the sacrifice of "depth."

In viewing the moral responsibility of the Christian, we find that it involves a three-dimensional field: himself, his society, and his God. This triune context of his mortal existence impinges upon the individual from within, from without, and from above. These three areas—the personal, the social, and the divine—indicate the ultimate boundaries of that moral and spiritual world within which we "live, and move, and have our being." The Pauline outlook that we should "live soberly, righteously, and godly, in this present world" (Titus 2:12) blends these three into a unified program for each Christian life.

If the moral life is to consist of this integrated whole, the principles which govern it in any one of these three areas must be consistent with those which obtain in both the other areas. That is, our obligations to God must not conflict with our obligations either to ourselves or to society, while the latter in turn must not contravene the former. True duties therefore will be seen not to conflict but to cooperate with each other; and all genuine values, whether personal, social, or spiritual, will be mutually conserved. An ethical program such as this, so comprehensive in its scope and at the same time so coherent in its structure, is the unique contribution of Christianity to the individual, and through him to the world. The broad outlines of that program are seen in the injunction of the Master: "Seek ye first the kingdom of God, and his righteousness, and all these things shall be added unto you" (Matt. 6:33), while its spirit and substance are indicated in the two great commandments of the law: "Thou shalt love the Lord thy God with all thy heart . . . and thy neighbour as thyself" (Luke 10:27).

Clearly and in logical order the three centers of our moral responsibility are here indicated—"God," our "neighbour," and ourselves. In relation to these, Christian social ethics emphasizes (1) the need of a socialized conscience, (2) the practice of certain supreme social virtues, and (3) the establishment of the kingdom of God on earth as the fulfillment of the ultimate social ideal. These three points form the outline of the remainder of this chapter.

II. A SOCIALIZED CONSCIENCE

That conscience functions as an arbiter of duty both Godward and manward is evident both from Scripture and human experience. Said the apostle to the Gentiles, "And herein do I exercise myself, to have always a conscience void of offence toward God, and toward men" (Acts 24:16). Our interpersonal relationships and attitudes are its province, as well as our relationship toward God. In our study of personal Christian ethics we discovered that conscience needs to be sensitized by the Divine Spirit and enlightened by the Scriptures to become a safe guide in spiritual matters. To be dependable as a guide in the social sphere, conscience needs a corresponding enlightenment and enlargement in respect to group responsibilities. This growing sensitivity of the moral nature to the rights and duties of mankind we shall designate as a "socialized conscience."

A. A Socialized Conscience as Seen in Sociology

Apart from Christianity itself, sociology has made the greatest contribution toward the regeneration of the social conscience. From the days of Auguste Comte (1798-1847), the founder of sociology, to the present time the emphasis has been shifting from individualism to the interests of the "associated life of humanity." Significant writers in this field have been Herbert Spencer, Emile Durkheim, Gabriel Tarde, Lester F. Ward, Franklin Giddings, C. H. Cooley, E. A. Ross, Emory S. Bogardus, W. I. Thomas, and Florian Znaniecki. In their thinking as well as in that of a multitude of other workers in the field the center of impact has been that "socialization tends toward moralization."

As defined by Bogardus, "Socialization is the process whereby individuals unconsciously and consciously learn to act, feel, and think dependably together . . . in behalf of human welfare outside their own." Based in the original social nature of all persons, socialization is best promoted by cultivating the "sympathetic emotions," "social imagination," and social intelligence or the "cognitive recognition of common problems." By sympathetic insight and understanding the chasm between isolated individuals is bridged. By social imagination a person is enabled "to slip into the skins of other persons," and consequently feel with something of the sensitivity of that skin, whatever its texture or color may be. By social intelligence we come to see the interrelatedness of all human problems and the consequent need of sharing with one another in their solution. The consciousness of kindred interests thus developed, resulting in that "cooperative activity" which "habitually responds to the welfare of other persons without expectation of reward," marks the socialization of the individual at the highest level. And the resultant personality is more than psychical; it is moral, combining "honesty, reliability, balance, chastity, and courage of convictions."[2]

But groups as well as individuals need to be socialized. Simultaneously with the development of the group consciousness ought to be the development of the group "conscience." If this were so, group morals might keep pace with group morale and partisan prejudices be replaced by human loyalties. Meanwhile group conflicts, whether racial, political, religious, sectional, or industrial, would disappear in the solvent of universal love. This would mark the highest level of group moralization and the full attainment of moral maturity. Such maturity, therefore, whether of the individual or the group, is the ideal goal toward which the socialization of conscience consistently moves.

B. A Socialized Conscience in Social Gospel Thought

At the same time the study of sociology was gaining momentum, a new movement arose in England at the close of the Industrial Revolution of the 18th century, "this most wonderful of all changes." Men like Frederick Maurice, Charles Kingsley, and John Ruskin sought a cure for the evils resulting from the sudden industrialization of society in a new type of political theory called "Christian Socialism." It was felt by them that a God of love would overlook no human need, and therefore Christianity as the supreme revelation of that love should provide a "balm in Gilead," not only for the individual sinner, but for the slaving, starving, despairing multitudes as well. Hence the Church was summoned to a new examination of the rec-

---

2. Emory S. Bogardus, *Fundamentals of Social Psychology* (New York: The Century Co., 1924), pp. 229-31; 234-35.

ord, a serious re-searching of the Scriptures to see if they did not indeed contain an "emancipation proclamation" in reality for the poor, the brokenhearted, the imprisoned, and the bruised (Luke 4:18).

Later the reverberations of the movement in England and on the Continent were picked up in America. One of the strong contributing factors to these newer emphases was the impact of mid-century revivalism, as Timothy L. Smith has so clearly shown in *Revivalism and Social Reform* (1957). The result was the development of what came to be known as the social gospel. New patterns of thought and programs of "social action" were formulated which were reforming and progressive in nature. Sponsored chiefly by the Congregational, Presbyterian, Episcopal, Baptist, and Methodist churches, the movement was at first geographically strongest in the Northeast and Midwest, but later spread throughout the continent.

The upshot was that a new flood of hortatory and expository literature was speedily released upon the Christian world which emphasized the social teachings of both the Old and New Testaments, but found its specific anchoring in the ethics of Jesus and the teachings of Paul. Pioneered by such works as *Jesus Christ and the Social Question,* by Peabody; *Christianity and Social Problems,* by Lyman Abbott; *How the Other Half Lives,* by Jacob Riis; and *In His Steps,* by Charles M. Sheldon, it was later given its official charter in the writings of Walter Rauschenbusch. Outstanding productions from his pen were: *Christianizing the Social Order* (1912), *Social Principles of Jesus* (1916), and *A Theology for the Social Gospel* (1917). Many other and later writers of equal intellectual stature could be mentioned including Shailer Matthews, Charles A. Ellwood, John Bennett, and the Niebuhr brothers, Reinhold and Richard.

For the innumerable shades of difference in interpretation and points of emphasis in the social philosophy thus represented, it would be necessary to examine the individual writings of each representative. But since all agree as to the need of the churches for a more truly socialized conscience, an excerpt from a joint report such as that issued by the Malvern Conference held in England in 1941 would be sufficient to point up representative points of emphasis. The report, in part, reads:

> It is not enough to say that if we change the individual we will of necessity change the social order. This is a half truth. For the social order is not made up entirely of individuals now living. It is made up of inherited attitudes which have come down from

generation to generation through customs, laws, institutions, and these exist in large measure independently of individuals now living. Change those individuals and you do not necessarily change the social order unless you organize those changed individuals into collective action in a wide-scale frontal attack upon those corporate evils.[3]

Special stumbling blocks to a Christian life, as Lorwin points out further, are (1) "the supremacy of the economic motive," which subordinates property rights to personal interest; (2) the "acquisitive temper," which carries on production for profits rather than for the satisfaction of the consumer; (3) the lack of recognition of the rights of labor as being "in principle equal to those of capital in the control of industry"; and (4) "the struggle for a so-called favorable balance" in international trade.

But while the Malvern Conference report addressed itself to the collective responsibility of Christian groups, other leaders in the movement addressed themselves to the individuals within the groups. Preeminent among these is Walter Rauschenbusch, the acknowledged spokesman for the social gospel point of view. Taking the New Testament specifically as His Guidebook, he found in the teaching and example of Jesus the norm for our attitudes and conduct, not only in the economic sphere, but in the total area of our social life. In *The Social Principles of Jesus* (1916), he attempted to sharpen up the individual Christian conscience by such "axiomatic social convictions of Jesus" as these: "Human Life and Personality Are Sacred" (Mark 10:13-16); "Men Belong Together," highlighting human solidarity (Matt. 22:35-40); and "The Strong Must Stand Up for the Weak," showing that Jesus himself took sides with the oppressed (Luke 6:20-26).

As Rauschenbusch views the whole moral battlefield, "the social ideal of Jesus," which is the kingdom of God, stands arrayed against stubborn social forces, and is assured of victory only in terms of "Conquest by Conflict." The new "values of the Kingdom" which imply that "the right social order is the highest good for all" give rise to the new "tasks of the Kingdom," which assume that "the right social order is the supreme task for each." Meanwhile "as the Kingdom comes ethical standards must advance" to meet the "new age of the Kingdom"; leadership must be trained to seek "its satisfaction by

---

3. Lewis L. Lorwin, *Postwar Plans of the United Nations* (New York: The Twentieth Century Fund, 1943), p. 118.

serving Humanity"; "private property must serve social welfare"; and "religion must become socially efficient" by squaring itself with "social realities." Finally, in its constant contact with evil, "the Kingdom of God" will have to fight for its advance. "Evil is socialized, institutionalized, and militant," he states. "The Kingdom of God and its higher laws can displace it only in conflict."[4] Symbolical of the suffering occasioned by this collision emerges "the cross as a social principle," proving that "social redemption is wrought by vicarious suffering" alone. According to Rauschenbusch, the Christian conscience as thus enlightened and sensitized is confronted with an ultimatum: "The Social Principles of Jesus Demand Personal Allegiance and Social Action."[5] In identifying His followers as "the salt of the earth" and "the light of the world" (Matt. 5:13-14), Jesus speaks with "the consciousness of an historic mission to the whole of humanity."

That the social gospel movement was deficient in its view of human nature and the need for personal regeneration would now be rather generally conceded.[6] An overly optimistic view of the divine worth, dignity, intelligence, and natural good will of man led to the view of sin as primarily horizontal; that is, selfishness in the face of the needs and interests of others, rather than revolt of the will against God.[7] Recent evaluations of human nature and its spiritual needs have been more sober, and much more inclined to recognize the deep-seated disorder of man's moral nature theologically described as "original sin."[8]

III. THE SUPREME SOCIAL VIRTUES

In the history of ethics, both secular and sacred, certain virtues stand out like stars of the first magnitude in the moral firmament. With the Greeks these were wisdom, justice, courage, and temperance. With the Hebrews they were justice, mercy, and humility, (Mic. 6:8); and with the early Christians they were faith, hope, and love (1 Corin-

---

4. (New York: The Association Press, 1916), p. 175.

5. *Ibid.*, p. 184.

6. Cf. the excellent summary treatment by Waldo Beach and John C. Bennett in *Protestant Thought in the Twentieth Century,* Arnold Nash (New York: The Macmillan Co., 1951), pp. 125-38.

7. *Ibid.*, p. 129.

8. *Ibid.*, pp. 132-33.

thians 13). As seen in the development of recent social thought, a new trinity of virtues emerges consisting of love, service, and self-sacrifice. In these is the social gospel fulfilled.

A. The Cardinal Virtue of Love

Strictly speaking, love as social good will has never been absent from any great ethical system. Whether interpreted by Plato as *Eros,* by Paul as *Agape,* or by Augustine as *Caritas,* the principle of "good will toward men" always has been regarded as the moral cement which holds society together. "Love binds together; hate and anger cut apart," states Rauschenbusch. "Therefore the chief effort of the Christian spirit must be to reestablish fellowship wherever men have been sundered by ill-will."[9] Hence in the outlook of Christian social ethics, which envisions the solidarity of mankind, love must always be considered the cardinal Christian virtue.

This follows too from the content of love as well as from its scope or intent. For the Christian, love is more than a transient human attachment based on affinities of sex, race, or temperament. It is a divine principle implanted in the human soul by God himself. Paul speaks of it as the "love of God . . . shed abroad in our hearts by the Holy Ghost which is given unto us" (Rom. 5:5). Bishop Nygren in his *Agape and Eros* shows most clearly that in the thinking of the apostles this love, *Agape,* was equated with the nature of God himself. He states in part: "We think here primarily of the great text, 'God is Agape' (1 John 4:8, 16), but also of the no less important 'God so loved the world that He gave His only begotten Son, that whosoever believeth in Him should not perish, but have eternal life.' (John 3:16)."[10] Rauschenbusch follows through on this "Christian intensification of love" by citing 1 John 4:7-9, 11-12, as further "evidence of the emphasis put on love as a distinctive doctrine of the new religion."[11]

Viewed in its outflow from the heart of God to the heart of man, this "heavenly *Agape*" marks the ultimate objective of the Christian atonement (1 John 4:11-12). Viewed in its outflow from the individual life to the life of mankind, it signalizes the fulfillment of the moral law (Rom. 13:10, 1 Tim. 1:5). It is with the issues of love, then,

---

9. *Social Principles of Jesus,* p. 19.

10. P. 158.

11. *Social Principles of Jesus,* p. 20.

as it is channeled out through the needy areas of society, that Christian social ethics is primarily concerned.

Of particular importance to social ethics is (1) the outflow of *agape* to one's neighbor as "disinterested love," and (2) its work in the world at large in "creating and conserving community" life. These functions of love are particularly specified and developed by Professor Paul Ramsey in his *Basic Christian Ethics* (1950). Identifying the first as "love for neighbor for his own sake," he shows that this is not incompatible with loving one's self at the same time. True "neighbor love" is, in fact, an "inverted self love" according to the second commandment (Luke 10:27), and is consequently an equal regard for persons as ends in themselves. It is, however, a certain "leap" by which Christian love accepts as "duty" the rights or needs of one's neighbor. As Luther puts it: "A Christian man lives not in himself but in Christ and his neighbor. He lives in Christ through faith in his neighbor through love; by faith he is caught up beyond himself into God, by love he sinks down beneath himself into his neighbor."[12]

Negatively, by working no ill to his neighbor (Rom. 13:10) love will steer clear of all violations of brotherly love such as malicious anger, revenge, ill will, lying, and slander, whether religious or political. Positively, by seeking not his own, but his neighbor's good (1 Cor. 10:24, ARV), it will safeguard the rights and privileges of others, whether they be the right to life, liberty, property, or the pursuit of happiness.

The second phase of socialized love has to do with the reconstruction of the broken relationships of society. Scattered individuals, separated by either geographical or social distance, are to be reunited with one another in cooperative, harmonious groups. These groups in turn are to cooperate with each other for their own self-fulfillment and for the enrichment of the world. This is the work of love in "creating community."

As Ramsey points out, two types of solution besides Christian love have been suggested for bridging the gulf separating man from man. One is "self-centered" and the other "value-centered." The "greatest happiness for the greatest number" could conceivably anticipate the most votes from the greatest number. Hence utilitarianism itself might be a generous cloak for a selfish purpose. "Public virtues" can be "private vices." Hiring the handicapped because "it's good

---

12. Cf. *Basic Christian Ethics* (New York: Charles Scribner's Sons, 1950), p. 101.

business," dealing fairly because "honesty is the best policy," or driving carefully "because the life you save may be your own" suggest policies sprinkled a bit too generously with the salt of self-interest to be unqualifiedly virtuous.[13]

Christian love on the other hand goes so far as to practice disinterested benevolence. It lends, "hoping for nothing again" (Luke 6:35), and banquets "the poor, the maimed, the lame, the blind," who cannot recompense in return (Luke 14:13). This is the "tie that binds our hearts in Christian love." It creates homes, unites parents, stabilizes families, founds churches, builds peace-loving governments, evangelizes the heathen, and pours itself out for the life of the world. The one true builder of "the beloved community," it would gather together in one not only the "outcasts of Israel" (Ps. 147:2) but the scattered and plundered of all the nations of the earth.

B. The Cooperative Virtue of Service

This may be called the eventuating virtue since love fulfills itself in service. "By love serve one another," (Gal. 5:13) was a permanent injunction, issued for the life span of the Church. The spiritual graces which adorned the Thessalonian church—their "work of faith, labour of love, and patience of hope" (1 Thess. 1:3)—were meant to adorn the Church in all succeeding ages. "Let us not love in word, neither in tongue; but in deed and in truth," (1 John 3:18) was an exhortation meant to be as valid today as it was in the first century of the Christian era.

The "service motive" rightfully deserves to replace the "competitive motive," according to all social gospel thinkers. Certainly the two must at least be held in balanced equilibrium if we are to love our neighbor as ourselves. Rivalries as such, either in getting or in spending, tend to overstrain one's personal integrity as well as deteriorate the sense of "community." One congressman stated that he had to spend all his salary "in keeping up with his fool neighbors." A more wholesome form of activity might have been to join with his neighbors in ridding the community of its evils of gangsterism, immorality, and political duplicity. Cooperation in socially constructive purposes is always better than imitation for personal ends.

Service demands both leadership and "followership." Only those who have learned to follow are qualified fully to lead. Begin-

---

13. Cf. Wiley, *Christian Theology,* 3:168-79.

ning on the top rung of the social ladder is often the prelude to a fall. Even Jesus, the Leader of all, said, "I am among you as he that serveth" (Luke 22:27). His example gives the cue to all His followers: leadership is for service and not for self-aggrandizement. Ambition may thus "realize its satisfaction in serving humanity."

The payment of this debt of service which one owes to society imposes a twofold claim upon the individual. First, it demands that he shall develop to the utmost his latent powers and potentialities. Second, it requires that he shall seek that field in which he can most fully meet the demands of his own nature, his generation, and his God (cf. Acts 13:36).

In the development of one's inherent capacities certain psychical factors are indispensable. Four of these, as Bogardus points out, are:

(1) Mental energy and its focalization. Mental endurance at an intellectual task is more fruitful in developing leadership than physical endurance in a corporal task.

(2) Confidence in one's ability. One may believe that he can measure up to the occasion without exploiting himself. Between overconfidence, which invites disaster, and under-confidence, which stifles abilities, one has slim grounds for moral preference.

(3) Painstaking forethought. Only long-range planning can prevent short-range failures. Jesus recommended the foresight of calculation rather the hindsight of lamentation (Luke 14:28-32).

(4) Mental flexibility. The dependable leader is one who is "old enough to have assimilated the work of his predecessors, but not so old as to have lost the ardor and flexibility of youth." Mental flexibility, like spiritual vitality, is not predetermined by physical age.[14]

It may here be noted that the above factors do double service. They promote the self-realization of the individual on the one hand, and enable him to pay his obligation to society on the other. The consistency of the ethical system is hereby indicated. Christian personal ethics and Christian social ethics here unite and henceforth move harmoniously together.

The second requirement that the individual find his lifework is equally important. In Christ's commission to His followers—not to the "Twelve" only, but to all—they found their abiding sense of mission to the world (Acts 1:8). Accordingly the Protestant reformers

---

14. *Fundamentals of Social Psychology,* pp. 411-15.

constantly emphasized the "Christocentric vocation" for each individual Christian. This involved love in all his activities, and specific loyalty to the "same calling wherein he was called" (1 Cor. 7:20). Commenting on this point, Ramsey makes the following observation:

> The Reformation doctrine of vocation requires that Christian love penetrate everything a man does, absolutely everything without the slightest exception. This means that he has every possible stimulus for carrying on the philosophical quest for determining the universal needs of human beings, for ascending the scale of values as far as possible, for finding out the highest good, for becoming as enlightened and effective in the attainment of these ends as his capacity allows.[15]

Roop in his discussion of "the Christian and his life work" emphasizes the nature and importance of Christian vocation:

> God wants man to do that which will call into play the greatest number of his strongest powers. He wants his vocation to be his self-expression in its entirety, not a mere mockery of his possibilities. It is a sin against self and against the Creator to botch one's whole life by refusing to work to the program which is outlined in his very constitution, and through laziness, indifference or greed, to substitute an inferior one.[16]

Renouncing a life of ease, and espousing a program of constant self-discipline through work, the individual Christian strives to convert every ability into serviceability, and thus return to His Master His own with increase (Matt. 25:27). In thus fulfilling the vocation of Christian manhood, he pays his debt to society, squares accounts with himself, and discharges the reasonable claims of his stewardship to his Creator and Lord.

C. The Consummatory Virtue of Self-sacrifice

The crowning virtue of the Christian life involves more than the giving of service; it demands the sacrifice of self. Service is rendered by the unselfish application of one's time, talents, strength, and substance to the procurement of another's good. Sacrifice in its supreme manifestation is indicated when a man lays down his life "for his friends" (John 15:13).

The necessity for this, at times, is seen in the fact that we are in a world of conflict. There are satanic forces at work in the world as well as spiritual graces. Commenting on the parable of the wheat and

---

15. *Basic Christian Ethics,* p. 189.
16. *Christian Ethics,* p. 294.

the tares (Matt. 13:24-30), Rauschenbusch flatly states: "Here we encounter the devil. There is more in sin than our own frailty and stupidity, and the bad influence of other individuals. There is a permanent force of organized evil which vitiates every higher movement and sows tares among the grain over night."[17] Caught in the coils of an "immoral society," as Niebuhr puts it, "moral man" will always be involved in struggle. Much more so will Christian man, who would be spiritual as well as moral. Hereby is precipitated "the irrepressible conflict" which so often demands one's soul, one's life, one's all.

It was so of the Founder of Christianity, and His followers were assured it would be so with them. States Rauschenbusch further:

> Into a world controlled by sin was launched the life of Christ. The more completely he embodied the divine character and will, the more certain and intense would be the conflict between him and the powers dominating the old order. He accepted the fight, not only for himself but for his followers. But when the fight is for the Kingdom of God, those who dodge, lose; and those who lose, win.[18]

With Christ then as our Guide and His kingdom as our goal, our greatest loss may be our greatest gain. The symbol of the supreme sacrifice, which is His cross, may become the symbol of life's supreme success.

IV. THE ULTIMATE SOCIAL IDEAL

From time immemorial men have dreamed dreams and seen visions of an ideal social order in which love would be law, purity the practice, justice the standard, goodness the rule, and the abundant life the joyous possession of all. Plato envisioned it in his *Republic,* Augustine in his *City of God,* More in his *Utopia,* Bacon in his *New Atlantis,* and Campanella in his *City of the Sun.* The prophets of Israel foresaw it as a "Holy Commonwealth" under the rule of their Messiah, and Jesus authoritatively announced it as the "kingdom of God" on earth (Luke 11:2).

A. Human Ideals

In all these political utopias, apart from the biblical view of the kingdom of God, certain common elements of lasting social value appear.

---

17. *Social Principles of Jesus,* p. 155.
18. *Ibid.,* p. 156.

Those which have been common to the greater majority and tend to have the greatest validity have been pointed out by Jerome Davis in his work, *Contemporary Social Movements.* Included are the following:

(1) Where government is outlined, the attempt is made to make it function for the common good of all.

(2) The ideals of equality, social solidarity, common interests, and mutual helpfulness are stressed.

(3) Science is devoted to the bettering of life for the common good.

(4) Industry is reorganized to meet human need more effectively and to conserve human values. All are usually required to serve society. Its toil is reduced to a minimum, thus permitting a higher cultural life.

(5) Acquisition as a motive is subordinated to creative production.

(6) Cooperation supplants competition in the social order.

(7) An all-round moral and cultural life is stressed as more important than mere material welfare.

(8) The infinite worth of each personality is usually recognized.

(9) The utopias radiate optimism and faith in the possibility of their achievement.

(10) Freedom of speech, of press, and assembly are declared necessary and criticism is welcome.[19]

While at some points these utopias were too idealistic to be practical, they at least were significant pointers, turning man's attention toward the social whole and away from the individual as the center of true value. This new criterion of human values, later embraced by the sciences of sociology and politics, has now become embedded in the constitutions of all the major governments of the world.

Concerning this cosmopolitan viewpoint, or gain in world values, sociology has something to say in its own right. Emory S. Bogardus has indicated this as clearly as any writer in the field. He states in part:

(1) The world is being characterized by an expansion of the individual's sense of social and ethical reponsibility.

(2) Human civilization is slowly moving toward a world political institution superior in strength to the most powerful nations today, and yet jealously guarding the needs of individual nations, both large and small.

(3) Democratic world leaders alone are certain of permanent social esteem.

(4) Leaders wholly filled by the dynamic of genuine Christian love

---

19. (New York: The Century Co., 1930), pp. 50-51.

are needed in order that the most spiritual world values may
be realized in all lands.[20]

B. The Divine Realization

This final emphasis of sociology—"the most spiritual world values"—
is the beginning emphasis of Christianity. "Seek ye first the kingdom
of God, and his righteousness," was Christ's introductory admonition.
He takes up where politics and sociology both fail. They reveal the
social needs; He reveals the supply. They diagnose the disease; He
provides the cure. This cure, as He states it and as His Church has
always believed it, lies in the establishment of the kingdom of God
upon the earth.

For the New Testament Christian the kingdom of God is envisioned as both immanent and imminent, present and future, contemporary and contingent. In each of these contrasting aspects it
involves both a crisis and a process. The entrance into the Kingdom
in the present involves the "crisis experience" of regeneration, known
in Scripture also as the "new birth" (Titus 3:5; John 3:3, 5-7). This
inward experience starts the process of individual transformation
which looks toward the complete sanctification of the personality
(1 Thess. 5:23), and the consequent conformity of one's spiritual,
intellectual, and physical life with the principles of the Kingdom.
Meanwhile the projection of the spiritual principles of the Kingdom
into family, church, or state may be viewed as the Kingdom in "process" in our contemporary group life.

As seen in its futuristic aspect, the kingdom of God is likewise
introduced by a crisis. This crisis is the personal and visible return of
Jesus Christ to the earth on which He lived, for which He died, and
over which He alone is entitled to rule. This climactic event, dis-
believed by the world (2 Pet. 3:4), and unexpected even by the Church
(Matt. 25:5), will be both sudden and unmistakable (Rev. 1:7) in its
arrival. The arrival of "that one, far-off divine event, toward which
the whole creation moves" will be indicated by the advent of the
King himself.

The investigation of the processes of His government as King of
Kings and Lord of Lords must, however, be left to its proper place in
the field of Christian theology. Its thrilling significance to the individual Christian must also be passed by, for it is written, "Eye hath not

---

20. Cf. *Fundamentals of Social Psychology,* pp. 467-69.

seen, nor ear heard, neither have entered into the heart of man, the things which God hath prepared for them that love him" (1 Cor. 2:9).

C. When the Kingdom Comes

In the first place it will be a "kingdom beyond caste." This description, coined by Liston Pope of Yale University, indicates that the Kingdom in view will solve finally the problems of the "classes and the masses," remove racial prejudice, eliminate social strain, and, by blending all the peoples of the world into a family of cooperative races, remove any further problems of racial integration. Both in the teaching of Jesus—"There shall be one fold, and one shepherd" (John 10:16), and in the insight of Paul—"There is neither Greek nor Jew, . . . Barbarian, Scythian, bond nor free" (Col. 3:11), we are able "to discern the lineaments of a kingdom beyond caste, already foreshadowed but yet to come."[21]

Second, it will be a Kingdom beyond war. Wars have been the agonizing curse of mankind since the beginning of human sin. Increasing in scope and destructiveness through 6,000 years of history, they have culminated in two global conflicts in our own generation. Ever present is the threat of a third and possibly final holocaust.

Over against this ominous outlook stands the "sure word of prophecy" for an eventual Kingdom of peace under the Prince of Peace. "And he shall judge among many people, and rebuke strong nations afar off; and they shall beat their swords into plowshares, and their spears into pruninghooks: nation shall not lift up sword against nation, neither shall they learn war any more" (Mic. 4:3).

Third, it will be a Kingdom beyond want. The struggle for existence against poverty has been even more universal than the struggle for existence against military might. Wars have arisen and run their course, but hunger, undernourishment, and starvation never cease. In the kingdom of Christ on earth, the poor will eventually come into their own. For "he shall judge the poor of the people, he shall save the children of the needy, and shall break in pieces the oppressor" (Ps. 72:4). "The meek also shall increase their joy in the Lord, and the poor among men shall rejoice in the Holy One of Israel" (Isa. 29:19).

Economic want, however, with all its tensions and industrial disputes between "the haves and the have-nots," is only one phase of

---

21. *The Kingdom Beyond Caste* (New York: Friendship Press, 1957), xvii.

human need. There are intellectual, social, and spiritual hungers as urgent in their demands as the craving for food. And since "man shall not live by bread alone," those Kingdom-blessings yet in store shall include all the other elements of the abundant life (John 10:10). Accordingly there is knowledge for the intellect, and that in its divinest dimension: "For the earth shall be filled with the knowledge of the glory of the Lord, as the waters cover the sea" (Hab. 2:14). For the thirsty "there shall be showers of blessing" (Ezek. 34:26), and "times of refreshing . . . from the presence of the Lord" (Acts 3:19). For the longing heart there shall be "peace . . . like a river" (Isa. 66:12), and for the eye there awaits a view of "the king in his beauty: [and] . . . the land that is very far off" (Isa. 33:17).

These values, at best, are but typical. They can only intimate the nature, never the boundaries or final meanings, of that Kingdom which God has prepared for them that love Him. Pointers only that they are, they can at least assure us that the ideal of Christian ethics will one day be the real. Thus, undergirding the "hope [that] springs eternal in the human breast," we may fix our eyes more steadily on the day when the King shall say: "Come, ye blessed of my Father, inherit the kingdom prepared for you from the foundation of the world" (Matt. 25:34).

SUMMARY

In this final chapter we have considered the importance of Christian social ethics in relation to social conscience, the supreme social virtues, and the ultimate social ideal of the kingdom of God. As with all who share our Christian faith we pray each day, "Thy kingdom come" (Matt. 6:10).

Bibliography

ABBOTT-SMITH, G. *A Manual of the Greek Lexicon of the New Testament.* 3rd ed. Edinburgh: T. and T. Clark, 1937.

ANDERSON, GERALD H. *The Theology of the Christian Mission.* Nashville: Abingdon Press, 1961.

ANDERSON, J. N. D. (ed.). *The World's Religions.* Chicago: The Inter-Varsity Christian Fellowship, 1950.

ANDERSON, T. M. *After Holiness, What?* Kansas City, Mo.: Nazarene Publishing House, 1929.

ANONYMOUS. *More than Words.* Greenwich, Conn.: The Seabury Press, 1955.

ARCHER, JOHN CLARK. *Faiths Men Live By.* New York: Thomas Nelson and Sons, 1934.

ARMINIUS, JAMES. *The Writings of Arminius.* James Nichols and W. R. Bagnall, editors. Grand Rapids: Baker Book House, reprint 1956.

AULEN, GUSTAF. *Christus Victor.* Translated by A. G. Hebert. New York: The Macmillan Co., 1931.

BAAB, OTTO J. *Theology of the Old Testament.* New York: Abingdon-Cokesbury Press, 1949.

BAILLIE, DONALD M. *The Theology of the Sacraments.* New York: Charles Scribner's Sons, 1957.

BAILLIE, JOHN. *The Idea of Revelation in Recent Thought.* New York: Columbia University Press, 1956.

————, et al. *Science and Faith Today.* London: Lutterworth Press, 1953.

BAINTON, ROLAND H. *Here I Stand: A Life of Martin Luther.* New York: Abingdon-Cokesbury Press, 1950.

BAKER, ARCHIBALD G. *A Short History of Christianity.* Chicago: The University Press, 1974.

BAKER, ROBERT A. *A Summary of Christian History.* Nashville: Broadman Press, 1959.

BANGS, CARL. *Arminius: A Study in the Dutch Reformation.* Nashville: Abingdon Press, 1971.

BARCLAY, WILLIAM. *The Mind of Jesus.* New York: Harper and Brothers, 1961.

BARRY, F. R. *To Recover Confidence.* Naperville, Ill.: SCM Book Club, 1974.

BARTH, KARL. *The Doctrine of the Word of God. Prolegomena to Church Dogmatics,* Vol. I, Part I. Translated by G. T. Thompson. New York: Charles Scribner's Sons, 1936.

BARTON, GEORGE A. *The Religions of the World.* 4th ed. Chicago: The University of Chicago Press, 1937.

BAXTER, BATSELL B. *I Believe Because . . . :* A Study of the Evidence Supporting Christian Faith. Grand Rapids: Baker Book House Company, 1971.

BEACH, WALDO, and NIEBUHR, REINHOLD (eds.). *Christian Ethics.* New York: Ronald Press Co., 1955.

Beacon Bible Commentary, 10 vols. Albert F. Harper, general editor. Kansas City, Mo.: Beacon Hill Press of Kansas City, 1964-69.

BEAVAN, ALBERT W. *The Local Church.* New York: Abingdon-Cokesbury Press, 1937.

BERGER, PETER. *Rumor of Angels:* Modern Society and the Rediscovery of the Supernatural. Garden City, N.Y.: Doubleday and Company, Inc., 1969.

BERKHOF, LOUIS. *The Kingdom of God.* Grand Rapids: Wm. B. Eerdmans Publishing Co., 1951.

———. *Vicarious Atonement Through Christ.* Grand Rapids: Wm. B. Eerdmans Publishing Co., 1936.

BERKOUWER, G. C. *Faith and Sanctification.* Grand Rapids: Wm. B. Eerdmans Publishing Co., 1952.

———. *The Person of Christ.* Grand Rapids: Wm. B. Eerdmans Publishing Co., 1954.

———. *Man: The Image of God.* Grand Rapids: Wm. B. Eerdmans Publishing Co., 1962.

———. *The Return of Christ.* Grand Rpiads: Wm. B. Eerdmans Publishing Co., 1972.

BLANEY, HARVEY J. S. *Speaking in Unknown Tongues: The Pauline Position.* Kansas City: Beacon Hill Press of Kansas City, 1973.

BOGARDUS, EMORY S. *Fundamentals of Social Psychology.* New York: The Century Co., 1924.

BOWNE, BORDEN PARKER. *Metaphysics.* Boston: Boston University Press, revised edition, 1898; copyright, 1943.

———. *The Atonement.* Boston: Houghton Mifflin Co., 1909.

———. *Theory of Thought and Knowledge.* New York: American Book Co., 1897.

BRIGHT, JOHN. *The Kingdom of God.* New York: Abingdon-Cokesbury Press, 1953.

BRIGHTMAN, EDGAR SHEFFIELD. *Person and Reality.* New York: Ronald Press Company, 1958.

———. *A Philosophy of Religion.* New York: Prentice-Hall, Inc., 1940.

———. *An Introduction to Philosophy.* New York: Holt, Rinehart and Winston, Inc., 1925.

BROCKETT, HENRY E. *Scriptural Freedom from Sin.* Kansas City: Beacon Hill Press, 1941.

BROMILEY, GEOFFREY W. "Barth's Doctrine of the Bible." *Christianity Today,* 1:6, December 24, 1956.

BROWN, CHARLES EWING. *The Meaning of Salvation.* Anderson, Ind.: The Warner Press, 1944.

———. *The Meaning of Sanctification.* Anderson, Ind.: The Warner Press, 1945.

BROWN, WILLIAM ADAMS. *Christian Theology in Outline.* New York: Charles Scribner's Sons, 1906.

BRUNNER, EMIL. *The Christian Doctrine of God: Dogmatics:* Vol. I. Philadelphia: Westminster Press, 1950.

————. *Eternal Hope.* Translated by Harold Knight. Philadelphia: Westminster Press, 1954.

————. *The Scandal of Christianity.* Philadelphia: Westminster Press, 1951.

BULTMANN, RUDOLF. *Theology of the New Testament.* New York: Charles Scribner's Sons, 2 vols., 1951, 1955.

————. *Kerygma and Myth.* Edited by H. W. Bartsch. London: S.P.C.K., 1953.

BURROWS, MILLAR. *An Outline of Biblical Theology.* Philadelphia: Westminster Press, 1946.

BURTNER, ROBERT W.; and CHILES, ROBERT E. *A Compend of Wesley's Theology.* New York: Abingdon Press, 1954.

CALVIN, JOHN. *Institutes of the Christian Religion.* Translated by Henry Beveridge. 2 vols. Grand Rapids: Wm. B. Eerdmans Publishing Co., 1953.

CANNON, WILLIAM. *The Theology of John Wesley.* New York: Abingdon-Cokesbury Press, 1946.

CHAFER, LEWIS SPERRY. *Systematic Theology.* 8 vols. Dallas, Tex.: Dallas Seminary Press, 1947.

CHAMBERS, WHITTAKER. *Witness.* New York: Random House, 1942.

CHERBONNIER, EDMUND LAB. *Hardness of Heart.* Garden City, N.Y.: Doubleday and Co., Inc., 1955.

CLARK, ELMER T. *The Small Sects in America.* New York: Abingdon-Cokesbury Press, 1949.

CLARKE, WILLIAM NEWTON. *An Outline of Christian Theology.* New York: Charles Scribner's Sons, 1898.

CONNICK, C. MILO. *Jesus: The Man, the Mission, and the Message.* Englewood Cliffs, N.J.: Prentice-Hall, Inc., 1974.

COOK, THOMAS C. *New Testament Holiness.* London: Epworth Press, 13th printing, 1952.

CORLETT, LEWIS T. *Holiness in Practical Living.* Kansas City: Beacon Hill Press, 1948.

————. *Holiness, the Harmonizing Experience.* Kansas City: Beacon Hill Press, 1951.

COWAN, HENRY. *Landmarks of Church History to the Reformation.* New edition, revised and enlarged. New York: Fleming H. Revell, n.d.

COX, HARVEY, editor. *The Situation Ethics Debate.* Philadelphia: The Westminster Press, 1968.

COX, LEO G. *John Wesley's Concept of Perfection.* Kansas City: Beacon Hill Press of Kansas City, 1964.

CURTIS, OLIN A. *The Christian Faith.* New York: Methodist Book Concern, 1903. Grand Rapids: Kregel Book Store, reprint, 1956.

DAVIDSON, A. B. *The Theology of the Old Testament.* Edinburgh: T. and T. Clark, 1904.

DAVIDSON, FRANCIS (ed.). *The New Bible Commentary.* Grand Rapids: Wm. B. Eerdmans Publishing Co., 1956.

DAVIES, D. R. *Secular Illusion or Christian Realism.* London: Latimer House, 1942.

DAVIS, JEROME. *Contemporary Social Movements.* New York: The Century Co., 1930.

DEWEY, JOHN. *Democracy and Education.* New York: The Macmillan Co., 1939.

DEWOLF, L. HAROLD. *A Theology of the Living Church.* New York: Harper and Brothers, 1953.

DODD, C. H. *According to the Scripture.* New York: Charles Scribner's Sons, 1953.

———. *The Epistle of Paul to the Romans:* "Moffatt New Testament Commentary." New York: Charles Scribner's Sons, 1932.

EASTON, W. BURTON, JR. *Basic Christian Beliefs.* Philadelphia: Westminster Press, 1957.

EDMAN, VICTOR RAY. *They Found the Secret.* Grand Rapids: Zondervan Publishing House, 1960.

EICHRODT, WALTHER. *Man in the Old Testament.* Chicago: Henry Regnery Co., 1951.

ELLWOOD, ROBERT S., JR. *Many Peoples, Many Faiths.* Englewood Cliffs, N.J.: Prentice-Hall, Inc., 1976.

ELLYSON, E. P. *Ye Must.* Marshalltown, Ia.: Christian Messenger Publishing Co., 1904.

EVERETT, WALTER G. *Moral Values.* New York: Henry Holt and Co., 1918.

FERM, VERGILIUS. *Living Schools of Religion.* Ames, Ia.: Littlefield, Adams and Co., 1956 (originally published as *Religion in the Twentieth Century.* New York: The Philosophical Library, 1948).

FERRÉ, NELS F. S. *The Christian Understanding of God.* New York: Harper and Brothers, 1951.

———. *Evil and the Christian Faith.* New York: Harper and Brothers, 1947.

FILSON, FLOYD V. *The New Testament Against Its Environment.* Chicago: Henry Regnery Co., 1950.

———. *One Lord, One Faith.* Philadelphia: Westminster Press, 1943.

———. *Jesus Christ the Risen Lord.* Nashville: Abingdon Press, 1941.

FISHER, GEORGE PARK. *History of Christian Doctrine.* New York: Charles Scribner's Sons, 1911.

FISON, J. E. *The Christian Hope.* London: Longmans, Green and Co., 1954.

FLETCHER, JOSEPH. *Situation Ethics: The New Morality.* Philadelphia: The Westminster Press, 1966.

FLEW, R. N. *Jesus and His Church.* London: The Epworth Press, 1943.

FLEWELLING, RALPH TYLER. *Personalism and the Problems of Philosophy.* New York: The Methodist Book Concern, 1915.

FOREMAN, KENNETH J. "What Is the Bible?" *The Layman's Bible Commentary,* Balmer H. Kelley, editor. Richmond, Va.: John Knox Press, 1959.

FORSYTH, PETER TAYLOR. *Positive Preaching and the Modern Mind.* New York: George H. Doran Co., 1907.

FULLER, R. H. *The Mission and Achievement of Jesus.* London: SCM Press, 1953.

GELIN, ALBERT. *The Key Concepts of the Old Testament.* New York: Sheed and Ward, 1955.

GODET, FREDERICK C. *Commentary on the Epistle to the Romans.* Translated by A. Cusin, revised by T. W. Chambers. Grand Rapids: Zondervan Publishing House, reprint, 1956.

GONZALEZ, JUSTO L. *A History of Christian Thought.* 3 vols. Nashville: Abingdon Press, 1970.

GRANT, FREDERICK C. *Introduction to New Testament Thought.* New York: Abingdon-Cokesbury Press, 1950.

GREATHOUSE, WILLIAM M. *The Fullness of the Spirit.* Kansas City: Nazarene Publishing House, 1958.

GREEN, THOMAS SHELDON. *A Greek-English Lexicon to the New Testament.* New York: The Macmillan Co., 1890.

GRIFFITH, LEONARD. *Barriers to Christian Belief.* New York: Harper and Row, Publishers, 1962.

GRIMES, HOWARD. *The Church Redemptive.* New York: Abingdon Press, 1958.

HALVERSON, MARVIN, and ARTHUR A. COHEN (eds.). *A Handbook of Christian Theology.* New York: Meridian Books, Inc., 1958.

HAMILTON, FLOYD E. *The Basis of Christian Faith.* Third Revised Edition. New York: Harper and Brothers, 1946.

HAMLIN, HOWARD H. *From Here to Maturity.* Kansas City, Mo.: Beacon Hill Press, 1955.

HARKNESS, GEORGIA. *Does God Care?* Waco, Tex.: Word Books, Publisher, 1960.

HARRINGTON, JOHN B. *Essentials in Christian Faith.* New York: Harper and Brothers, 1958.

HASTINGS JAMES (ed.). *Prayer.* "Great Christian Doctrines" Series. New York: Charles Scribner's Sons, 1915.

HAZELTON, ROGER. *Renewing the Mind.* New York: The Macmillan Co., 1949.

HEADINGLY LECTURES. *The Doctrine of the Holy Spirit.* London: The Epworth Press, 1937.

HEDLEY, GEORGE. *The Christian Heritage in America.* New York: The Macmillan Co., 1946.

HEINISCH, PAUL. *Theology of the Old Testament.* Collegeville, Minn.: The Liturgical Press, 1950.

HENRY, CARL F. H. *Christian Personal Ethics.* Grand Rapids: Wm. B. Eerdmans Publishing Co., 1957.

———. *God, Revelation and Authority.* Vol. I, "God Who Speaks and Shows." Waco, Tex.: Word Books, Publisher, 1976.

HILLERBRAND, HANS J., editor. *The Protestant Reformation.* New York: Harper and Row, Publishers, 1968.

HILLS, A. M. *Fundamental Christian Theology.* 2 vols. Pasadena, Calif.: Pasadena College, 1931. Abridged edition, C. J. Kinne, 1932.

HOCKING, WILLIAM ERNEST. *The Meaning of God in Human Experience.* New Haven: Yale University Press, 1912.

HODGE, A. A. *The Atonement.* Grand Rapids: Wm. B. Eerdmans Publishing Co., 1953.

HODGE, CHARLES. *Systematic Theology.* 3 vols. New York: Charles Scribner's Sons, 1893.

HODGES, J. W. *Christ's Kingdom and Coming.* Grand Rapids: Wm. B. Eerdmans Publishing Co., 1957.

HORDERN, WILLIAM. *A Layman's Guide to Protestant Theology.* New York: The Macmillan Co., 1955.

HOWARD, RICHARD E. *Newness of Life.* Kansas City: Beacon Hill Press of Kansas City, 1975.

HUNTER, ARCHIBALD M. *Introducing New Testament Theology.* Philadelphia: Westminster Press, 1957.

———. *The Message of the New Testament.* Philadelphia: Westminster Press, 1944.

HUTCHISON, JOHN A. *Paths of Faith.* Second edition. New York: McGraw Hill Book Company, 1975.

HUXTABLE, JOHN. *The Bible Says.* Naperville, Ill.: SCM Book Club, 1962.

ISBELL, CHARLES D. "Glossolalia and Propheteialalia: A Study of 1 Corinthians 14." *Wesleyan Theological Journal,* Vol. 10 (spring, 1975).

JACOB, EDMOND. *Theology of the Old Testament.* New York: Harper and Brothers, 1958.

JEANS, SIR JAMES. *This Mysterious Universe.* New and Revised Edition. New York: The Macmillan Co., 1937.

JESSOP, T. E., *et al. The Christian Understanding of Man.* London: George Allen and Unwin Ltd., 1938.

JOHNSON, PAUL E. *Psychology of Religion.* New York: Abingdon-Cokesbury Press, 1945.

JONES, E. STANLEY. *Christ and Human Suffering.* New York: Abingdon Press, 1933.

———. *Victory Through Surrender.* New York: Abingdon Press, 1966.

JURJI, EDWARD J. (ed.). *The Great Religions of the Modern World.* Princeton, N.J.: Princeton University Press, 1946.

KANTONEN, T. A. *The Christian Hope.* Philadelphia: Muhlenberg Press, 1954.

KENNEDY, GERALD. *God's Good News.* New York: Harper and Brothers, 1955.

KEPLER, THOMAS S. (ed.). *The Fellowship of the Saints.* New York: Abingdon-Cokesbury Press, 1948.

KILDAHL, JOHN P. *The Psychology of Speaking in Tongues.* New York: Harper and Row, 1972.

KITAGAWA, JOSEPH M. *Religions of the East.* Enlarged edition. Philadelphia: The Westminster Press, 1960.

KUITERT, H. M. *Do You Understand What You Read?* On Understanding and Interpreting the Bible. Translated by Lewis B. Smedes. Grand Rapids: Wm. B. Eerdmans Publishing Co., 1970.

KUNG, HANS. *On Being a Christian*. Edward Quinn, translator. Garden City, N.Y.: Doubleday & Co., Inc., 1976.

KUNKEL, FRITZ. *In Search of Maturity*. New York: Charles Scribner's Sons, 1946.

LADD, GEORGE L. *Crucial Questions About the Kingdom of God*. Grand Rapids: Wm. B. Eerdmans Publishing Co., 1952.

————. *I Believe in the Resurrection of Jesus*. Grand Rapids: Wm. B. Eerdmans Publishing Co., 1975.

LATOURETTE, KENNETH SCOTT. *A History of Christianity*. New York: Harper and Brothers, 1953.

LAWSON, JOHN. *The Biblical Theology of Saint Irenaeus*. London: Epworth Press, 1948.

LEIGHTON, J. A. *Man and the Cosmos*. New York: D. Appleton and Co., 1922.

LEWIS, C. S. *The Case for Christianity*. New York: The Macmillan Co., 1944.

————. *The Great Divorce*. New York: The Macmillan Co., 1946.

————. *Miracles*. New York: The Macmillan Co., 1947.

LEWIS, EDWIN. *The Creator and the Adversary*. New York: Abingdon-Cokesbury Press, 1948.

————. *A Manual of Christian Beliefs*. New York: Charles Scribner's Sons, 1927.

LINDSEY, HAL. *The Late Great Planet Earth*. With Carole C. Carlson. Grand Rapids: Zondervan Publishing House, 1970.

LINK, HENRY C. *The Return to Religion*. New York: The Macmillan Co., 1937.

LOETSCHER, LEFFERTS A. (ed.). *Twentieth Century Encyclopedia of Religious Knowledge*. Grand Rapids: Baker Book House, 1955.

LORWIN, LEWIS L. *Postward Plans of the United Nations*. New York: The Twentieth Century Fund, 1943.

LOWRY, CHARLES W. *The Trinity and Christian Devotion*. New York: Harper and Brothers, 1946.

MARSTON, LESLIE R. *From Chaos to Character*. Winona Lake, Ind.: Light and Life Press, 1944.

MATTHEWS, C. E. *Every Christian's Job*. Nashville: Broadman Press, 1955.

McKIBBEN, FRANK M. *Christian Education Through the Church*. New York: Abingdon-Cokesbury Press, 1947.

METZ, DONALD S. *Studies in Biblical Holiness*. Kansas City: Beacon Hill Press of Kansas City, 1971.

MILLER, H. V. *The Sin Problem*. Kansas City: Nazarene Publishing House, 1947.

————. *When He Is Come*. Kansas City: Nazarene Publishing House, 1941.

MILLER, M. S. and J. L. (eds.). *Harper's Bible Dictionary*. New York: Harper and Brothers, 1952.

MINEAR, PAUL S. *The Eyes of Faith*. Philadelphia: Westminster Press, 1946.

MITCHELL, T. CRICHTON. *Mr. Wesley*. Kansas City: Beacon Hill Press, 1957.

MOORE, A. L. *The Parousia in the New Testament*. Leiden: E. J. Brill, 1966.

MORRIS, LEON. *The Apostolic Preaching of the Cross*. London: Tyndale Press, 1955.

————. *The Epistles of Paul to the Thessalonians.* "The Tyndale New Testament Commentaries." Grand Rapids: Wm. B. Eerdmans Publishing Co., 1957.

————. *The Revelation of St. John.* London: The Tyndale Press, 1969.

MORRIS, THOMAS V. *Francis Schaeffer's Apologetics: A Critique.* Chicago: Moody Press, 1976.

MORRISON, A. CRESSY. *Man Does Not Stand Alone.* New York: Fleming H. Revell, 1944.

MOULE, H. C. G. *Veni Creator.* London: Hodder and Stoughton, 1895.

NASH, ARNOLD S. (ed.). *Protestant Thought in the Twentieth Century.* New York: The Macmillan Co., 1951.

NEASE, ORVAL J. *Heroes of Temptation.* Kansas City: Beacon Hill Press, 1950.

NEVE, J. L. *A History of Christian Thought.* 2 vols. Philadelphia: Muhlenberg Press, 1946.

NIEBUHR, REINHOLD. *Beyond Tragedy.* New York: Charles Scribner's Sons, 1948.

————. *The Nature and Destiny of Man.* 2 vols. New York: Charles Scribner's Sons, 1943.

NILES, DANIEL T. *The Preacher's Task and the Stone of Stumbling.* New York: Harper and Brothers, 1958.

NYGREN, ANDERS. *Agape and Eros.* Translated by Philip S. Watson. Philadelphia: Westminster Press, 1953.

OCKENGA, HAROLD J. *Faith in a Troubled World.* Wenham, Mass.: Gordon College Press, 1972.

OEHLER, GUSTAV. *Theology of the Old Testament.* Grand Rapids: Zondervan Publishing House, reprint, 1950.

One Volume New Testament Commentary. Grand Rapids: Baker Book House, 1957.

ORR, JAMES (ed.). *The International Standard Bible Encyclopedia.* Grand Rapids: Wm. B. Eerdmans Publishing Co., 1939.

OTTO, RUDOLF. *The Idea of the Holy.* J. W. Harvey, translator. London: Oxford University Press, 1957.

PARKER, DEWITT H. *The Principles of Aesthetics.* New York: Appleton-Century-Crofts, Inc., 1920.

PEIRCE, CHARLES S. *Essays in the Philosophy of Science.* Edited by Vincent Tomas. "The American Heritage Series." New York: The Liberal Arts Press, 1957.

PETERS, JOHN. *Christian Perfection and American Methodism.* New York: Abingdon Press, 1956.

POLLARD, WILLIAM G. *Science and Faith: Twin Mysteries.* New York: Thomas Nelson, Inc., 1970.

POPE, LISTON. *The Kingdom Beyond Caste.* New York: Friendship Press, 1957.

POPE, WILLIAM B. *A Compendium of Christian Theology.* 3 vols. New York: Phillips and Hunt, 1881.

PURKISER, W. T. *Conflicting Concepts of Holiness*. Kansas City: Beacon Hill Press, 1953.

————; TAYLOR, RICHARD S.; and TAYLOR, WILLARD H. *God, Man, and Salvation:* A Biblical Theology. Kansas City: Beacon Hill Press of Kansas City, 1977.

————. *The Gifts of the Spirit*. Kansas City: Beacon Hill Press of Kansas City, 1975.

RAMM, BERNARD. *The God Who Makes a Difference:* A Christian Appeal to Reason. Waco, Tex.: Word Books, Publisher, 1972.

RAMSEY, PAUL. *Basic Christian Ethics*. New York: Charles Scribner's Sons, 1950.

RAUSCHENBUSCH, WALTER. *The Social Principles of Jesus*. New York: Association Press, 1916.

READ, DAVID H. C. *The Christian Faith*. London: English Universities Press, Ltd., 1955.

REES, PAUL S. *Stir Up the Gift*. Grand Rapids: Zondervan Publishing House, 1952.

REID, J. K. S. *The Authority of Scripture*. London: Methuen and Co., Ltd., 1957.

————. *Christian Apologetics*. Grand Rapids: Wm. B. Eerdmans Publishing Co., 1970.

RICHARDSON, ALAN (ed.). *Theological Word Book of the Bible*. London: SCM Press, 1950. New York: The Macmillan Co., 1955.

RICHARDSON, CYRIL C. *The Church Through the Centuries*. New York: Charles Scribner's Sons, 1938.

RIDDERBOS, HERMAN. *Paul: An Outline of His Theology*. John Richard DeWitt, translator. Grand Rapids: Wm. B. Eerdmans Publishing Co., 1975.

ROBINSON, J. A. T. *Jesus and His Coming*. New York: Abingdon Press, 1958.

ROGERS, A. K. *A Student's History of Philosophy*. 3rd ed. New York: The Macmillan Co., 1932.

ROOP, HERVIN U. *Christian Ethics*. New York: Fleming H. Revell, 1926.

ROUSSEAU, JEAN JACQUES. *The Social Contract*. New York: E. P. Dutton and Co., n.d.

ROWLEY, HAROLD H. *The Faith of Israel*. Philadelphia: Westminster Press, 1956.

————. *The Unity of the Bible*. Philadelphia: Westminster Press, 1953.

SAMARIN, WILLIAM J. *Tongues of Men and Angels. The Religious Language of Pentecostalism*. New York: The Macmillan Co., 1972.

SANDAY, WILLIAM, and HEADLAM, ARTHUR C. *A Critical and Exegetical Commentary on the Epistle to the Romans*. New York: Charles Scribner's Sons, 1896.

SANGSTER, W. E. *The Path to Perfection*. New York: Abingdon-Cokesbury Press, 1943.

————. *The Pure in Heart*. A Study in Christian Sanctity. New York: Abingdon Press, 1954.

SAYERS, DOROTHY. *The Mind of the Maker.* London: Methuen and Co., Ltd., 1941.

SCHROEDER, FREDERICK W. *Preaching the Word with Authority.* Philadelphia: Westminster Press, 1954.

SCHULTZ, HERMANN. *Old Testament Theology.* Translated by J. A. Paterson. 2 vols. Edinburgh: T. and T. Clark, 1909.

SCHWEITZER, ALBERT. *The Quest of the Historical Jesus.* New York: The Macmillan Co., 1922.

SCOTT, E. F. *The Kingdom and the Messiah.* Edinburgh: T. and T. Clark, 1911.

———. *The Kingdom of God in the New Testament.* New York: The Macmillan Co., 1931.

SHAW, JOHN M. *Christian Doctrine: A One-Volume Outline of Christian Beliefs.* New York: Philosophical Library, 1954.

SHELDON, H. C. *System of Christian Doctrine.* Revised Edition. New York: Methodist Book Concern, 1903.

SHELTON, O. L. *The Church Functioning Effectively.* St. Louis: Christian Board of Publication, 1946.

SINGER, KURT, compiler. "Nine Scientists Look at Religion." *Reader's Digest,* Jan., 1963.

SISEMORE, JOHN T. *The Ministry of Visitation.* Nashville: Broadman Press, 1955.

SMITH, C. RYDER. *The Bible Doctrine of Man.* London: Epworth Press, 1951.

———. *The Bible Doctrine of Sin.* London: Epworth Press, 1953.

SMITH, DAVID. *The Days of His Flesh.* New York: George H. Doran Co., n.d.

SMITH, TIMOTHY L. *Revivalism and Social Reform.* New York: Abingdon Press, 1957.

SNAITH, NORMAN H. *The Distinctive Ideas of the Old Testament.* Philadelphia: Westminster Press, 1946.

———. *Hymns of the Temple.* London: SCM Press, Ltd., 1951.

SOLZHENITSYN, ALEXANDER. *The First Circle.* Thomas P. Witney, translator. New York: Harper and Row, Pub., 1968.

SPERRY, WILLARD L. *Religion in America.* New York: The Macmillan Co., 1947.

SPROXTON, VERNON. *Teilhard de Chardin.* Naperville, Ill.: SCM Book Club, 1971.

STAUFFER, ETHELBERT. *New Testament Theology.* Translated from the German by John Marsh. New York: The Macmillan Co., 1955.

STEELE, DANIEL. *The Gospel of the Comforter.* Chicago: The Christian Witness Company, 1917. Kansas City: Beacon Hill Press, abridged reprint, 1960.

STEVENS, GEORGE BARKER. *The Theology of the New Testament.* New York: Charles Scribner's Sons, 1936.

STEWART, JAMES S. *A Faith to Proclaim.* New York: Charles Scribner's Sons, 1953.

———. *The Life and Teaching of Jesus Christ.* New York: Abingdon Press, n.d.

———. *A Man in Christ.* New York: Harper and Brothers, n.d.

STRONG, A. H. *Systematic Theology.* Philadelphia: Griffith and Roland Press, 1907.

SWEET, WILLIAM WARREN. *Revivalism in America.* New York: Charles Scribner's Sons, 1944.

SYNAN, VINSON. *The Holiness-Pentecostal Movement in the United States.* Grand Rapids: Wm. B. Eerdmans Publishing Co., 1971.

TASKER, R. V. G. *The Old Testament in the New Testament.* Philadelphia: Westminster Press, 1947.

TAYLOR, RICHARD S. *A Right Conception of Sin.* Kansas City: Beacon Hill Press, 1945.

———. *Life in the Spirit.* Kansas City: Beacon Hill Press of Kansas City, 1966.

TEMPLE, WILLIAM. *Foundations.* London: Macmillan and Co., Ltd., 1912.

———. *Nature, Man, and God.* London: Macmillan and Co., Ltd., 1934.

THELEN, MARY F. *Man as Sinner.* New York: King's Crown Press, 1946.

THORPE, LOUIS P. *Child Psychology and Development.* Second edition. New York: Ronald Press Co., 1955.

TILLETT, WILBUR F. *Personal Salvation.* Nashville: Cokesbury Press, 1930.

TILLICH, PAUL. *Systematic Theology.* Vol. II. Chicago: University of Chicago Press, 1957.

TITUS, HAROLD H. *Ethics for Today.* New York: American Book Co., 1947.

TORRANCE, T. F. In *Christianity Today,* Vol. XX, No. 25 (September 24, 1976).

TORREY, REUBEN A. *The Person and Work of the Holy Spirit.* New York: Fleming H. Revell Co., 1910.

TRUEBLOOD, D. ELTON. *The Logic of Belief.* New York: Harper and Brothers, 1942.

———. *Philosophy of Religion.* New York: Harper and Brothers, 1957.

———. *The Trustworthiness of Religious Experience.* London: George Allen and Unwin, Ltd., 1939.

TSANOFF, R. A. *The Moral Ideals of Our Civilization.* New York: E. P. Dutton and Co., Inc., 1942.

———. *Ethics.* Revised Edition. New York: Harper and Brothers, 1955.

TURNER, GEORGE ALLEN. *The More Excellent Way.* Winona Lake, Ind.: Light and Life Press, 1952.

———. *The Vision Which Transforms: Is Christian Perfection Scriptural?* Kansas City: Beacon Hill Press of Kansas City, 1964.

TURRETIN, FRANCIS. *The Atonement.* New York: Board of Publication of the Reformed Protestant Dutch Church, 1859.

UNDERHILL, EVELYN. *Worship.* New York: Harper and Brothers, 1937.

VINE, W. E. *Expository Dictionary of New Testament Words.* 4 vols. London: Oliphants, Ltd., 1939-41.

VON ALLMEN, J.-J. (ed.). *A Companion to the Bible.* New York: The Oxford Press, 1958.

VOS, GEERHARDUS. *The Teaching of Jesus Concerning the Kingdom of God and His Church.* New York: American Tract Society, 1903.

————. *Biblical Theology.* Grand Rapids: Wm. B. Eerdmans Publishing Co., 1954.

WAKEFIELD, SAMUEL. *Systematic Theology.* New York: Nelson and Phillips, 1859.

WALVOORD, JOHN F. (ed.). *Inspiration and Interpretation.* Grand Rapids: Wm. B. Eerdmans Publishing Co., 1957.

WATSON, GEORGE D. *Spiritual Feasts.* Cincinnati: Revivalist Office, 1904.

WATSON, J. B. (ed.). *The Church.* London: Pickering and Inglis, Ltd., 1949.

WEATHERHEAD, LESLIE D. *The Will of God.* New York: Abingdon-Cokesbury Press, 1944.

WESLEY, JOHN. *Explanatory Notes upon the New Testament.* London: The Epworth Press, reprint, 1950.

————. *The Plain Account of Christian Perfection.* Boston: The Christian Witness Co., n.d.

————. *Sermons.* 2 vols. New York: Lane and Scott, 1852.

————. *Works.* 14 vols. Kansas City: Nazarene Publishing House, reprint, 1958.

WHALE, J. S. *Christian Doctrine.* New York: The Macmillan Co., 1945.

WHITE, R. E. O. *A Guide to Preaching.* Grand Rapids: Wm. B. Eerdmans Publishing Co., 1973.

WHITE, STEPHEN S. *Essential Christian Beliefs.* Kansas City: Beacon Hill Press, n.d.

WHITEHEAD, JOHN. *The Life of the Rev. John Wesley, M.A.* New York: The United States Book Company, n.d.

WILEY, H. ORTON. *Christian Theology.* 3 vols. Kansas City: Beacon Hill Press, 1940.

————; and CULBERTSON, PAUL T. *Introduction to Christian Theology.* Kansas City: Nazarene Publishing House, 1945.

WILLIAMS, R. T. *Temptation: A Neglected Theme.* Kansas City: Nazarene Publishing House, 1920.

WOOD, J. A. *Perfect Love.* Chicago: Christian Witness Co., 1905.

————. *Purity and Maturity.* Chicago: S. K. J. Chesbro, 1903.

WRIGHT, G. ERNEST; and FULLER, REGINALD H. *The Book of the Acts of God.* New York: Doubleday and Co., Inc., 1957.

WYNKOOP, MILDRED BANGS. *A Theology of Love.* Kansas City: Beacon Hill Press of Kansas City, 1972.

YOUNG, KIMBALL. *Personality and the Problems of Adjustment.* New York: F. S. Crofts and Co., 1940.

ZENOS, ANDREW C. *Compendium of Church History.* Philadelphia: Presbyterian Board of Publication, 1896.

ZWEMER, SAMUEL M. *The Moslem Doctrine of God.* New York: Young People's Missionary Movement, 1905.

INDEX OF SUBJECTS

INDEX OF AUTHORS AND NAMES